Bravo ASL! Curriculum

Instructor's Guide

Jenna Cassell

Published by Sign Enhancers, Inc.
All Rights Reserved. Copyright ©1996 by Sign Enhancers, Inc.
With the exception of the Appendix section of this Instructor's Guide, this book may not be reproduced in whole or in part, by any means, without written permission from Sign Enhancers, Inc.
Copies and/or transparencies of appendices are authorized for classroom use only.

ISBN 1-882872-98-3

Sign Enhancers, Inc., 1535 State Street, Salem, OR 97301
US: 1-800-767-4461 (V/TDD) International: 503-370-9721 (V/TDD) Fax: 503-370-6457
E-mail: SignEn@AOL.Com or Sign@teleport.com
Web Site: http://www.teleport.com/~sign

To Mima Bravo. Your gentle hands, loving heart, and courageous spirit were always keenly focused on opening the world to Deaf people through Sign Language. My wish is that this curriculum earn its name by continuing the work you so loved.

                              in memorium
                              June, 1996

The Beginning ASL VideoCourse (affectionately known as "the Bravo family tapes") is the recipient of the following awards: Silver Telly Award (1993), Parents' Choice Honor (1994), Kid's First Honor (1995) and an International CINDY Award (1996).

Acknowledgments

Work is love made visible. Kahlil Gibran

The textbook you now hold in your hands – along with the 17 companion videotapes and Student Workbook – demonstrates the truth of the above quote. I extend special thanks to several people who helped make this course a reality:

Mark Azure, a talented Deaf artist who meticulously hand-drew each ASL sign illustration and expertly fine-tuned each detail on a computer. Mark demonstrates his love for and pride in his language with every stroke of his pen.

Len Roberson, Ph.D. candidate, Gallaudet University Education Department, contributing author to this Instructor's Guide with creative, effective, and varied instructional activities that reinforce the content of the VideoCourse. We thank him for his efforts and for providing tried-and-true instructional techniques for high school and college ASL students.

Karla Holland and **Dian Cox**, the tireless editorial team whose diligence transformed these 924 pages into publishable form. There are no words to thank them for their hours of meticulous work.

Pam Piesker and **Dan Meireis**, at L. Grafix, who provided more than three gigabytes(!) of graphics and design and layout assistance.

Billy Seago, **Nathie Marbury**, and **Lou Fant** for their unending support and willingness to share their articulate language skills on video. They made an ASL party of producing hundreds of beautiful linguistic samples!

Lynn Jacobowitz, Assistant Professor, Department of ASL, Linguistics and Interpretation, Gallaudet University; **Samuel Holcomb**, Sign Communication Specialist, NTID; and **Nathie Marbury**, Director of the Educational Division, Sign Enhancers, Inc., for reviewing content and design. Their unique expertise in the field of ASL instruction, combined with a Deaf perspective, was extremely valuable.

Lisa Hariton, Curriculum Specialist, whose astute comments helped us pinpoint age-appropriate activities for middle and high school curriculum, and **Bonnie Massaud**, who checked the finest details in content and copy.

Major thanks to a wonderful **video production team** including **Billy Seago**, Co-Director and Model Instructor, who consistently treats viewers to a fun way to learn, and to **Jer Loudenbeck, Jen Reece, Scott Pfaff, Anna Musick, and Lady Cassell**, whose portrayal of the Bravo family touches many hearts and moves many hands. Many thanks to children signers **Kyle E. Gilstrap** (age 7), **Marissa Fae Protus** (age 4), **Dianna Rodriquez** (age 16), **Julia Baird** (age 11), **Aaron E. Yankus** (age 12), as well as **Jacqueline Collier** and **Lori Engichy** for their contributions to the Activities and Assessment Videos.

Scott Griffith, Aurion Productions, for his award-winning videography. Special thanks for the calm and competent help from **Carl F. Garner**, **Ronda Wymore-O'Neall**, and **Karla Holland**, Production Assistants during some action-packed video shoots, and **Virgil Sipes**, superb on-line editor.

My extreme gratitude to the **Sign Enhancers staff**, who pulled together during an intense and demanding production period. I am honored to work with each of you and thank you with my whole heart for your support and contributions as we fulfill our mission to enhance the quality of life for Deaf people through education and access.

Loving thanks go to my family, **Fran**, **Chuck**, **Lisa**, **Jesse**, and **Max** for a life-time of love and support.

Last, and most importantly, I want to thank **Jack R. Cassell** for being the most marvelous partner in the biggest project of all… life.

Bravo ASL! Table of Contents

Curriculum Overview: .... Page x

Lesson One: Page   Page   Page
1.1 Begin Class 1-1
1.2 Pretest 1-2
1.3 Lesson Objectives 1-4
1.4 Lesson Focus 1-5
1.5 Bravo Family Visit 1-6
1.6 Learning New Signs 1-8
1.7 Intro to New Vocabulary 1-10
1.8 Point and Sign 1-11
1.9 Bravo Family Visit 1-14
1.10 Comprehension Quiz 1-15

1.11 Point and Sign 1-16
1.12 Learning New Signs 1-18
1.13 Intro to New Vocabulary ... 1-20
1.14 Point and Sign 1-21
1.15 Bravo Family Visit 1-24
1.16 Comprehension Quiz 1-25
1.17 Cultural Notes 1-26
1.18 Hey, You... 1-27
1.19 Grammatical Notes 1-29
1.20 What Kind of Question? 1-30

1.21 Pass the Question 1-32
1.22 Culture/Grammar Quiz 1-34
1.23 Review Session 1-35
1.24 Practice Sentences 1-38
1.25 What's the Sentence About? 1-39
1.26 It's Just a Drill! 1-40
1.27 Practice Story 1-41
1.28 Comprehension Quiz 1-43
1.29 Homework Assignment 1-44
1.30 Post-test 1-45

Lesson Two:
2.1 Begin Class 2-1
2.2 Homework Review 2-2
2.3 Pretest 2-3
2.4 Lesson Objectives 2-4
2.5 Lesson Focus 2-5
2.6 Learning New Signs 2-6
2.7 Intro to New Vocabulary 2-8
2.8 Point and Sign 2-9

2.9 Bravo Family Visit 2-12
2.10 Comprehension Quiz 2-13
2.11 Point and Sign 2-14
2.12 Cultural Notes 2-16
2.13 Cultural Adventure 2-17
2.14 Grammatical Notes 2-20
2.15 Modify Me! 2-21
2.16 Cultural/Grammar Quiz 2-22

2.17 Review Session 2-24
2.18 Practice Sentences 2-26
2.19 What's the Sentence About? 2-27
2.20 It's Just a Drill! 2-29
2.21 Practice Story 2-30
2.22 Comprehension Quiz 2-31
2.23 Homework Assignment 2-32
2.24 Post-test 2-33

Lesson Three:
3.1 Begin Class 3-1
3.2 Homework Review 3-2
3.3 Pretest 3-3
3.4 Lesson Objectives 3-4
3.5 Lesson Focus 3-5
3.6 Learning New Signs 3-6
3.7 Intro to New Vocabulary 3-8
3.8 Matchmaker 3-9
3.9 Bravo Family Visit 3-11

3.10 Comprehension Quiz 3-12
3.11 Learning New Signs 3-13
3.12 Intro to New Vocabulary 3-15
3.13 Put it There, Pal! 3-16
3.14 Bravo Family Visit 3-18
3.15 Comprehension Quiz 3-19
3.16 Cultural Notes 3-20
3.17 Home Improvement 3-21
3.18 Grammatical Notes 3-23

3.19 To Be, or NOT to Be... 3-24
3.20 Review Session 3-26
3.21 Practice Sentences 3-28
3.22 Now, Where Did I Put?... 3-29
3.23 You Want Me to Do What? 3-31
3.24 Practice Story 3-32
3.25 Comprehension Quiz 3-33
3.26 Homework Assignment 3-34
3.27 Post-test 3-35

Lesson Four:
4.1 Begin Class 4-1
4.2 Homework Review 4-2
4.3 Pretest 4-3
4.4 Lesson Objectives 4-4
4.5 Lesson Focus 4-5
4.6 Learning New Signs 4-7
4.7 Intro to New Vocabulary 4-9

4.8 Review Session 4-12
4.9 Con-SIGN-tration 4-14
4.10 Don't Forget to Buy the... ... 4-16
4.11 Practice Sentences 4-18
4.12 What's the Sentence About? 4-19
4.13 Cultural Notes 4-20
4.14 The Food Store Cashier 4-22

4.15 Simple as One, Two, Three! 4-23
4.16 Grammatical Notes 4-24
4.17 Topic Search 4-25
4.18 Practice Story 4-27
4.19 Comprehension Quiz 4-28
4.20 Homework Assignment 4-29
4.21 Post-test 4-30

Lesson Five:

		Page			Page			Page
5.1	Begin Class	5-1	5.13	Lesson 2 Review: Sentences	5-14	5.25	Lesson 4 Review: Sentences	5-29
5.2	Homework Review	5-2	5.14	Lesson 2 Review: Dialogue	5-15	5.26	Lesson 4 Review: Dialogue	5-30
5.3	Lesson Objectives	5-3	5.15	Dynamic-Duo Dialogue	5-17	5.27	Dynamic-Duo Dialogue	5-31
5.4	Lesson Introduction	5-4	5.16	Bravo Family Revisited	5-18	5.28	Bravo Family Revisited	5-32
5.5	Crossword Puzzle	5-5	5.17	Matchmaker	5-19	5.29	Pictures in the Air	5-33
5.6	Lesson 1 Review: Vocabulary	5-7	5.18	Lesson 3 Review: Vocabulary	5-21	5.30	Lessons 1-4 Review: Culture	5-34
5.7	Lesson 1 Review: Sentences	5-8	5.19	Lesson 3 Review: Sentences	5-22	5.31	Number Story: The Bug	5-35
5.8	Lesson 1 Review: Dialogue	5-9	5.20	Lesson 3 Review: Dialogue	5-23	5.32	Lessons 1-4 Review: Grammar	5-36
5.9	Dynamic-Duo Dialogue	5-10	5.21	Dynamic-Duo Dialogue	5-24	5.33	Lessons 1-4 Review: Story	5-38
5.10	Bravo Family Revisited	5-11	5.22	Bravo Family Revisited	5-25	5.34	Homework Assignment	5-39
5.11	It's Your Turn to Set the Table!	5-12	5.23	Point and Sign	5-26	5.35	Post-test	5-40
5.12	Lesson 2 Review: Vocabulary	5-13	5.24	Lesson 4 Review: Vocabulary	5-28			

Lesson Six:

6.1	Begin Class	6-1	6.11	Color Time Again!	6-15	6.21	Access to Culture	6-30
6.2	Homework Review	6-2	6.12	Learning Fingerspelling	6-17	6.22	Grammatical Notes	6-33
6.3	Pretest	6-3	6.13	Intro to Fingerspelling	6-18	6.23	What Sign am I Thinking...?	6-34
6.4	Lesson Objectives	6-4	6.14	Practice Fingerspelling	6-19	6.24	Practice Sentences	6-35
6.5	Lesson Focus	6-5	6.15	SIGN-O	6-20	6.25	Practice Story	6-36
6.6	Bravo Family Visit	6-7	6.16	Fingerspelling Usage	6-22	6.26	Comprehension Quiz	6-37
6.7	Read My Lips	6-9	6.17	Fingercises	6-23	6.27	Homework Assignment	6-38
6.8	Learning New Signs	6-11	6.18	ABC Story	6-26	6.28	Post-test	6-39
6.9	Intro to New Vocabulary	6-13	6.19	Simple as A,B,C!	6-28			
6.10	Bravo Family Visit	6-14	6.20	Cultural Notes	6-29			

Lesson Seven:

7.1	Begin Class	7-1	7.11	Intro to New Vocabulary	7-13	7.21	Cultural Notes	7-27
7.2	Homework Review	7-2	7.12	Point and Sign	7-14	7.22	Culture/Grammar Quiz	7-28
7.3	Pretest	7-3	7.13	Crossword Puzzle	7-16	7.23	Practice Sentences	7-30
7.4	Lesson Objectives	7-4	7.14	Bravo Family Visit	7-18	7.24	Receptivity Race	7-31
7.5	Lesson Focus	7-5	7.15	Comprehension Quiz	7-19	7.25	Practice Story	7-32
7.6	Learning New Signs	7-6	7.16	Grammatical Notes	7-20	7.26	Comprehension Quiz	7-33
7.7	Intro to New Vocabulary	7-8	7.17	It's Your Move	7-22	7.27	Homework Assignment	7-34
7.8	Bravo Family Visit	7-9	7.18	Bravo Family Visit	7-23	7.28	Post-test	7-35
7.9	Comprehension Quiz	7-10	7.19	Review Session	7-24			
7.10	Learning New Signs	7-11	7.20	Signs and Origins	7-26			

Lesson Eight:

8.1	Begin Class	8-1	8.11	Fish, Go You!	8-14	8.21	Grammatical Notes	8-28
8.2	Homework Review	8-2	8.12	Bravo Family Visit	8-15	8.22	What Do You Mean?	8-30
8.3	Pretest	8-3	8.13	Comprehension Quiz	8-17	8.23	Practice Sentences	8-31
8.4	Lesson Objectives	8-4	8.14	Learning New Signs	8-18	8.24	Sign-A-Problem	8-32
8.5	Lesson Focus	8-5	8.15	Intro to New Vocabulary	8-20	8.25	Practice Story	8-33
8.6	Bravo Family Visit	8-7	8.16	Bravo Family Visit	8-21	8.26	Comprehension Quiz	8-34
8.7	Learning New Signs	8-8	8.17	Comprehension Quiz	8-22	8.27	Homework Assignment	8-35
8.8	Practice Session Numbers	8-10	8.18	Review Session	8-23	8.28	Post-test	8-36
8.9	Learning New Signs	8-11	8.19	Cultural Notes	8-25			
8.10	Intro to New Vocabulary	8-13	8.20	Special Guests	8-27			

Lesson Nine:

		Page			Page			Page
9.1	Begin Class	9-1	9.12	Crossing Comm. Barrier	9-14	9.23	Grammatical Notes	9-28
9.2	Homework Review	9-2	9.13	Learning New Signs	9-15	9.24	Is the Price Right?	9-29
9.3	Pretest	9-3	9.14	Intro to New Vocabulary	9-17	9.25	Dollar-to-Dollar	9-31
9.4	Lesson Objectives	9-4	9.15	Bravo Family Visit	9-18	9.26	Review Session	9-32
9.5	Lesson Focus	9-5	9.16	Comprehension Quiz	9-19	9.27	Practice Sentences	9-34
9.6	Bravo Family Visit	9-6	9.17	Learning New Signs	9-20	9.28	Practice Story	9-36
9.7	Learning New Signs	9-7	9.18	Intro to New Vocabulary	9-22	9.29	Comprehension Quiz	9-37
9.8	Intro to New Vocabulary	9-9	9.19	Tic-Tac-Dough	9-23	9.30	Silent Games Revisited	9-38
9.9	Bravo Family Visit	9-10	9.20	Bravo Family Visit	9-25	9.31	Homework Assignment	9-39
9.10	Comprehension Quiz	9-12	9.21	Comprehension Quiz	9-26	9.32	Post-test	9-40
9.11	Communication Strat.	9-13	9.22	Cultural Notes	9-27			

Lesson Ten:

10.1	Begin Class	10-1	10.14	Lesson 7: Sentences	10-16	10.27	Lesson 9: Dialogue	10-30
10.2	Homework Review	10-2	10.15	Lesson 7: Dialogue	10-17	10.28	Dynamic-Duo Dialogue	10-31
10.3	Lesson Objectives	10-3	10.16	Dynamic-Duo-Dialogue	10-18	10.29	Bravo Family Revisited	10-32
10.4	Lesson Introduction	10-4	10.17	Bravo Family Revisited	10-19	10.30	Pictures in the Air	10-33
10.5	Color Commands	10-5	10.18	Matchmaker	10-20	10.31	Cultural Notes Review	10-34
10.6	Lesson 6: Vocabulary	10-6	10.19	Lesson 8: Vocabulary	10-21	10.32	Grammatical Review	10-35
10.7	Lesson 6: Sentences	10-7	10.20	Lesson 8: Sentences	10-22	10.33	Lessons 6-9: Dialogues	10-36
10.8	Fingerspelling Practice	10-8	10.21	Lesson 8: Dialogue	10-23	10.34	Dynamic-Duo Dialogue	10-38
10.9	Flying Fingers	10-10	10.22	Dynamic-Duo-Dialogue	10-24	10.34	Lessons 6-9: Story	10-39
10.10	Lesson 6: Dialogue	10-11	10.23	Bravo Family Revisited	10-25	10.36	Create-A-Story	10-40
10.11	Bravo Family Revisited	10-12	10.24	Point and Sign	10-26	10.37	Post-test	10-41
10.12	Crossword Puzzle	10-13	10.25	Lesson 9: Vocabulary	10-28			
10.13	Lesson 7: Vocabulary	10-15	10.26	Lesson 9: Sentences	10-29			

Lesson Eleven:

11.1	Begin Class	11-1	11.10	Comprehension Quiz	11-14	11.19	Review Session	11-26
11.2	Homework Review	11-2	11.11	Learning New Signs	11-15	11.20	Practice Sentences	11-28
11.3	Pretest	11-3	11.12	Intro to New Vocabulary	11-17	11.21	Practice Story	11-29
11.4	Lesson Objectives	11-4	11.13	Bravo Family Visit	11-18	11.22	Comprehension Quiz	11-31
11.5	Lesson Focus	11-5	11.14	Grammatical Notes	11-19	11.23	Use of Space Exercise	11-32
11.6	Learning New Signs	11-7	11.15	Up, Up, and Away	11-20	11.24	A Healthy Visit to Doc	11-33
11.7	Intro to New Vocabulary	11-9	11.16	Bravo Family Visit	11-22	11.25	Post-test	11-34
11.8	Spot the Sport	11-10	11.17	Cultural Notes	11-23			
11.9	Bravo Family Visit	11-12	11.18	It's an Emergency	11-24			

Lesson Twelve:

12.1	Begin Class	12-1	12.12	Bravo Family Visit	12-15	12.23	Cultural Notes	12-31
12.2	Homework Review	12-2	12.13	Bravo Family Visit	12-17	12.24	Bravo Family Visit	12-32
12.3	Pretest	12-3	12.14	Grammatical Notes	12-18	12.25	Review Session	12-33
12.4	Lesson Objectives	12-4	12.15	What Kind of Face...?	12-20	12.26	Signs and Origins	12-35
12.5	Lesson Focus	12-5	12.16	Bravo Family Visit	12-21	12.27	Practice Sentences	12-36
12.6	Bravo Family Visit	12-6	12.17	Learning New Signs	12-23	12.28	Practice Story	12-37
12.7	Learning New Signs	12-8	12.18	Intro to New Vocabulary	12-25	12.29	Comprehension Quiz	12-39
12.8	Intro to New Vocabulary	12-10	12.19	Diagnosis Dialogue	12-26	12.30	Help! We Need Help...!	12-40
12.9	Point and Sign	12-11	12.20	Bravo Family Visit	12-27	12.31	Accessibility Analysis	12-41
12.10	Bravo Family Visit	12-12	12.21	Comprehension Quiz	12-28	12.32	Post-test	12-42
12.11	Cultural Quiz	12-14	12.22	Bravo Family Visit	12-29			

Lesson Thirteen:

		Page
13.1	Begin Class	13-1
13.2	Homework Review	13-2
13.3	Pretest	13-3
13.4	Lesson Objectives	13-4
13.5	Help Wanted	13-5
13.6	Learning New Signs	13-7
13.7	Intro to New Vocabulary	13-9
13.8	Bravo Family Visit	13-10
13.9	Comprehension Quiz	13-11
13.10	Learning New Signs	13-12
13.11	Intro to New Vocabulary	13-14
13.12	Bravo Family Visit	13-15
13.13	Comprehension Quiz	13-17
13.14	Learning New Signs	13-18
13.15	Intro to New Vocabulary	13-20
13.16	Point and Sign	13-21
13.17	Bravo Family Visit	13-22
13.18	Comprehension Quiz	13-24
13.19	Learning New Signs	13-26
13.20	Intro to New Vocabulary	13-27
13.21	Bravo Family Visit	13-28
13.22	Comprehension Quiz	13-29
13.23	Review Session	13-30
13.24	Practice Sentences	13-34
13.25	Create-A-Sentence	13-35
13.26	Cultural Notes	13-36
13.27	Grammatical Notes	13-37
13.28	Name the Number	13-38
13.29	Practice Story	13-40
13.30	Comprehension Quiz	13-41
13.31	Homework Assignment	12-42
13.32	Post-test	12-43

Lesson Fourteen:

		Page
14.1	Begin Class	14-1
14.2	Homework Review	14-2
14.3	Pretest	14-3
14.4	Lesson Objectives	14-4
14.5	Lesson Focus	14-5
14.6	Learning New Signs	14-7
14.7	Intro to New Vocabulary	14-9
14.8	Point and Sign	14-10
14.9	Bravo Family Visit	14-12
14.10	Comprehension Quiz	14-14
14.11	Learning New Signs	14-15
14.12	Intro to New Vocabulary	14-17
14.13	Bravo Family Visit	14-18
14.14	Cultural Notes	14-19
14.15	Panel Discussion	14-21
14.16	Bravo Family Visit	14-22
14.17	Comprehension Quiz	14-24
14.18	Review Session	14-26
14.19	Wacky Wardrobe Stories	14-28
14.20	Grammatical Notes	14-30
14.21	Classy Classifiers	14-31
14.22	Practice Sentences	14-33
14.23	You're Going to Wear...?	14-34
14.24	Practice Story	14-35
14.25	Comprehension Quiz	14-37
14.26	Homework Assignment	14-38
14.27	Post-test	14-39

Lesson Fifteen:

		Page
15.1	Begin Class	15-1
15.2	Homework Review	15-2
15.3	Lesson Objectives	15-3
15.4	Lesson Introduction	15-4
15.5	Sports Stories	15-5
15.6	Lesson 11: Vocabulary	15-6
15.7	Lesson 11: Sentences	15-7
15.8	Lesson 11: Dialogue	15-8
15.9	Dynamic-Duo Dialogue	15-9
15.10	Bravo Family Revisited	15-10
15.11	Medical Drama	15-11
15.12	Lesson 12: Vocabulary	15-12
15.13	Lesson 12: Sentences	15-13
15.14	Lesson 12: Dialogue	15-14
15.15	Dynamic-Duo Dialogue	15-15
15.16	Bravo Family Revisited	15-16
15.17	Matchmaker	15-18
15.18	Lesson 13: Vocabulary	15-19
15.19	Lesson 13: Sentences	15-20
15.20	Lesson 13: Dialogue	15-21
15.21	Dynamic-Duo Dialogue	15-22
15.22	Bravo Family Revisited	15-23
15.23	Point and Sign	15-24
15.24	Lesson 14: Vocabulary	15-25
15.25	Lesson 14: Sentences	15-27
15.26	Bravo Family Revisited	15-28
15.27	Pictures in the Air	15-29
15.28	Grammatical Review	15-30
15.29	Cultural Notes Review	15-31
15.30	Lessons 11-14: Story	15-33
15.31	Congratulations	15-34
15.32	Post-test	15-36

Overview

About this *Bravo ASL! Curriculum*

The goal of this *Bravo ASL!* course is to provide a carefully designed, high-quality, standardized course for offering American Sign Language to middle school, high school, college, and community education programs throughout the United States and Canada. *Bravo ASL!* provides a comprehensive, easy-to-follow guide to instructors while offering students fun and effective ways to develop fluency with ASL. This curriculum includes all the instructional components necessary for offering American Sign Language for academic credit.

To the Instructor

This curriculum was designed as a comprehensive beginning-level ASL course for use by novice or seasoned ASL instructors – Deaf or hearing – teaching Deaf and/or hearing students.

The Instructor's Guide is intentionally complete and easy-to-follow. It contains all of the information necessary for conducting this course, including instructions for class activities, lectures, exercises, and the use of video segments. However, this course and this Instructor's Guide have also been designed to be very flexible teaching tools. *The Bravo ASL! Curriculum* may be modified to meet individual instructional needs, used in conjunction with other ASL materials, or used to supplement existing curricula.

Bravo ASL! as a stand-alone course includes objectives, step-by-step experiential activities, media support, and assessment tools. *Bravo ASL!* curriculum goals include:

- Supporting academic programs and ASL instructors in providing high-quality ASL coursework.
- Creating a positive, fun, and effective learning environment.
- Providing a comprehensive instructional plan in order to standardize ASL course work and assessment in academic settings.
- Providing an eclectic approach to ASL as a second language in order to maximize language learning outcomes for students with varying learning styles and linguistic abilities.

Learning Objectives

Upon completion of the course, students will be able to:

1. Identify and accurately produce approximately 500 ASL vocabulary items.
2. Provide an explanation of the cultural aspects of ASL as presented in the course.
3. Identify and apply the grammatical features of ASL presented in the course.
4. Demonstrate a beginning conversational level of comprehension when receiving ASL.
5. Demonstrate a beginning conversational level of expressive fluency when using ASL.

Curriculum Components

1. Instructor's Guide
2. Student Workbook
3. The Beginning ASL VideoCourse (15 lessons)
4. Activities Videotape (73 minutes)
5. Assessment Videotape (35 minutes)

1. Instructor's Guide

Containing more than 900 pages of support for ASL instructors, this Guide includes:

Objectives: Specific learning outcomes for each lesson with regard to vocabulary, culture, grammar, comprehension, and expressive skills.

Lesson Focus: An activity allowing students to experience a need for the content of each lesson.

Language Learning Instruction: An opportunity for the instructor to expose students to new signs using ASL and visual aids. Overhead transparency masters provided in the Appendix.

Introduction to New Vocabulary: Billy Seago demonstrates accurate production of each new ASL vocabulary item, modeling each sign twice. Additional learner support is provided by captioned and audible glosses.

Sign Illustration Section: Illustrations of each ASL vocabulary item, organized by lesson with an alphabetical index for easy access, serve as references for instructor and students.

Video Learning Experiences: Activities designed to assist learners in maximizing the benefits of the video segments of *The Beginning ASL VideoCourse*. Step-by-step instructions in both the Instructor's Guide and Student Workbooks.

Experiential Activities/Materials: Experiential activities to reinforce VideoCourse content, with simple instructions (all supplemental material masters in the Appendix).

Quizzes: Quizzes to check student progress on a regular basis regarding cultural and grammatical information and comprehension skills.

Homework Assignments: Out-of-class practice activities designed to reinforce the content of each lesson and help students develop skills.

Assessment Tools: Pretests to measure student knowledge level prior to the lesson and post-tests to measure student progress in the areas of comprehension, culture and grammar, and expressive skills. Step-by-step instructions and an assessment video are integral to the course assessment program.

2. Student Workbook

Workbooks serve as student tools for practice and for recording progress throughout the course. Components of the Student Workbook include:

Lesson Objectives: Clearly stated objectives inform students of expected learning outcomes for each lesson.

Activity Goals and Instructions: Stated goals and the instructions for each activity demystify the instructional plan and encourage partnership between instructor and student for accomplishing desired learning outcomes.

Visual Aids and Worksheets: Pictures, worksheets, puzzles, and a variety of written stimuli increase students' participation in each lesson's activities.

Content Outlines: To reinforce the cultural and grammatical content presented in each video lesson.

Quizzes: Tools for assessing students' ASL comprehension and assimilation of cultural and grammatical information.

Thought/Discussion Questions: To encourage students to maximize the benefits derived from Experiential activities.

Homework Assignments: Opportunities for students to integrate the skills and knowledge they've gained in your classroom into extended learning experiences.

Sign Illustration Section: Illustrations of each ASL vocabulary item, organized according to lesson number and indexed alphabetically, for instructor and students to refer to as needed.

3. The Beginning ASL VideoCourse

The fifteen videotaped lessons of Sign Enhancers' *The Beginning ASL VideoCourse* unfold around the daily life events of the Bravo family – two Deaf children, a Deaf father, and a hearing mother. Deaf Instructor Billy Seago guides student viewers as the Bravos apply each lesson's vocabulary in situational life experiences.

Each lesson teaches conversational vocabulary as used in specific settings. For example, ASL signs representing foods are presented as the Bravos shop at the food store.

The VideoCourse includes the following in each lesson:

Introduction to New Vocabulary: A vocabulary of approximately 500 signed items is introduced throughout the *Bravo ASL!* course.

Bravo Family Interaction: New vocabulary is applied within the context of a scenario featuring the Bravo family. These segments are not voiced or captioned in order to develop and reinforce comprehension skills.

Cultural Notes: Cultural Notes expose students to the cultural aspects of ASL.

Grammatical Notes: Grammatical Notes introduce students to the grammatical aspects of ASL.

Review Session: Retention of new vocabulary is reinforced by a review session in which Instructor Billy Seago presents signs with explanations and visual cues.

Practice Session: Sentences: Opportunities for students to practice ASL comprehension skills during practice sentence sessions.

Practice Session: Story: Comprehension skills are reinforced by means of an ASL signed story using vocabulary introduced in the current lesson.

4. Activities Video

This 73-minute video provides language stimuli for many experiential activities described in the Instructor's Guides and Student Workbooks.

This video exposes students to a variety of signing styles (multi-cultural and age-variant signers) while reinforcing the material presented in the VideoCourse. Featured models on this video include ASL instructors Billy Seago, Nathie Marbury, and Lou Fant, in addition to five Deaf signers ranging in age from four to sixteen.

5. Assessment Video

This 35-minute video provides examples and signed stimuli for the standardized assessment strategies outlined in the Instructor's Guide, allowing assessment consistency from class to class. This video exposes students to a variety of signing styles.

Curriculum Philosophy

In analyzing the attrition rates of students in beginning ASL classes throughout the US, it became apparent that programs relying on one instructional method fail to satisfy the varied needs of students taking ASL as a second language. As Rod Ellis states in *Understanding Second Language Acquisition* (1986, Oxford University Press), "No two learners acquire a second language in the same way."

That perception – along with the desire to promote ASL and to satisfy a need for curriculum options – has been the driving force behind the creation of this *Bravo! ASL Curriculum*.

Eclectic in nature, this course incorporates many experiential activities for maximum interaction and successful second language acquisition among students with a variety of learning styles. Course objectives are accomplished through video presentation, group activities, role-playing, individual and group practice, lecture, review, discussion, and assigned work outside the classroom.

The varied activities and learning strategies in this course promote second language success among students who learn in a variety of ways. For example, some students are *visual learners*. This course provides the option to use ASL and visual aids exclusively to introduce new signs (*Language Learning Instruction*), based on the Direct Experience Method developed by William Newell, Sam Holcomb, Barbara Ray Holcomb, Donna Pocobello and colleagues at the National Technical Institute for the Deaf in Rochester, N.Y.

Many students learn best by "doing" (*psychomotor* or *tactile assimilation*). Experiential activities in this course involve students on a tactile level through role-playing, games, and class activities.

Bravo ASL! presents vocabulary in functional groupings within the context of everyday situations to appeal to learners who must connect content with function in order to best assimilate a new language and to make the new language immediately applicable. Examples of functional units include the vocabulary for morning routines; breakfast and dining; household-related objects and activities; food shopping; banking and money; school-related objects and activities; etc. As the Bravo family members go about their lives, the viewing students acquire higher levels of language skills. Cultural and grammatical aspects of ASL are incorporated in a practical way.

Adult learners experience less frustration and greater second language learning success when strategies build upon the knowledge and language fluency they already possess. Several of the strategies used within this course provide modeling, with the added support of audible and/or captioned glosses in order to carry the student further into a new language.

Various proven instructional strategies, including cooperative work groups, partnerships, and independent study, allow teachers options to select methods that best suit a particular group of students, their own teaching style, and the programmatic structure of the class.

Instructor Preparation

The Beginning ASL VideoCourse includes 15 video lessons varying in length from 30 to 65 minutes and up to 35 activities per video lesson in the accompanying Instructor's Guide. Based on your needs you may follow the lesson plan as provided or customize this course.

This curriculum has been intentionally designed to provide more ASL-skill-enhancing activities and more options for teaching those activities than the typical language program could feasibly make use of during scheduled class time. Also, we have chosen not to dictate the allowable amount of time per activity for this course. For these reasons, it is important that instructors follow these recommendations during preparation:

1. Read this guide and review the companion media.
2. Assess how this curriculum fits into your current or proposed course offering.
3. Make activity selections and lesson plans according to the number of total class hours available.
4. Consider which of your personal experiences, skills, or other resources you wish to include.
5. Make sure you have copies of the materials you will need. (Refer to Materials Needed at the beginning of each lesson and find the masters for overheads, hand outs, and written test materials in the Appendix.)
6. Check A/V equipment before class to be sure it is functional.

We recommend that you respond to student needs when determining the amount of time spent in any particular learning strategy. For example, if your students are benefiting from role-play, we do not recommend interrupting this learning experience in order to adhere to a schedule.

Prerequisites

This course has been designed for beginning ASL students. There are no specific prerequisite skills or knowledge levels for students taking this course. Instructors must determine if any programmatic prerequisites are necessary.

Class Size/Set-up

Because this is a visual language class, it is recommended that the class size be restricted to groups small enough (10–15 students) for easy visual access to all activities. Class size may be determined based on individual program needs.

For maximum visibility, a U-shaped classroom arrangement is recommended. Movable chairs are conducive to role-playing and other activities.

Videotaping Suggestions

When videotaping students' work, avoid backlit situations, which will produce a silhouette effect. Ask students to wear clothing that contrasts with their own skin tones. If possible, videotape students in front of an uncluttered background that contrasts with students' clothing.

For best results, use a tripod to steady your videocamera. Frame students as tightly as possible in the viewfinder, while including the entire signing space – for most people, from just below the belt to two inches above the head. Advise students of limitations to their range of motion while signing on camera.

If your videocamera has an auto-focus feature, it is recommended that you turn this feature off, as it will cause the camera to refocus in response to the movements of the signs. It is recommended that you manually focus prior to each student's performance.

Videotapes may be retained by the instructor for written feedback, viewed one-on-one with each student, or (if each student has provided her/his own blank videotape) sent home with students for out-of-class critiquing. Students may also view videotapes in a lab setting.

One of the most valuable strategies for using videotape as an educational tool is viewing the tapes in class and providing constructive criticism, however, this may be intimidating to some students.

Sign Transcription Symbols

ASL is *not a written language*, nor is there a word-for-sign correlation between ASL and English. For these reasons, this curriculum uses glosses (symbols) to identify the meaning of signs and signed sentences.

These glosses are not intended to be the only appropriate English translation, nor are they exact interpretations of signs. The glosses included in this curriculum are cues primarily for the instructor to use in linking meaning with the sign or signed discourse.

The only transcription symbols intended for students include: "t" (indicating the topic), "q" (indicating a yes/no question), and "wh" (indicating a wh-question).

The symbols and glosses listed on the following page are used to link meaning between the written references and the actual signs.

Gloss	Samples	Description
CAPITALS	DOG MOTHER BED	If a word is capitalized, it means it is a gloss for the concept represented by a sign
- (hyphen)	GO-TO BRUSH-TEETH WAKE-UP	One sign is used for the meaning of glosses connected with a hyphen
/ (slash)	BATHROOM/TOILET PAST/BEFORE MOTHER/MOM	A slash is used to show more than one commonly used gloss for a sign
+ (plus)	EAT+MORNING MOTHER+FATHER BED+ROOM	Two signs connected with a plus indicate a compound sign
W-O-R-D	D-A-N C-O B-A-R-B	Hyphens between letters in a gloss means the word is fingerspelled
(GLOSS)	_____q DEAF (YOU)	The gloss in parenthesis, may not actually be needed if the appropriate non-manual behavior is demonstrated.

Non-manual Grammatical Markers

t	__t__ __q__ BOOK, YOUR	The gloss directly below the "t" is the topic of the signed sentence.
wh-q	__t__ __wh-q__ MOM, WHERE	A "wh-q" indicates a WH question. This is a question including: what, where, when, which, how or why.
q	_____q HEARING (YOU)	A "q" indicates a question in which the response is YES or NO.
rh-q	_____rh-q GO WHERE, HOME	An "rh-q" indicates a rhetorical question.

Note: In recognition and respect of the culture of Deaf people, the word Deaf is capitalized throughout all written materials associated with this course.

Lesson 1
MEET THE BRAVO FAMILY

Materials Needed

Equipment: VCR and TV monitor
Overhead projector and screen
Chalk/dry erase board
Optional: video camera for activity 1.30

Materials: Instructor's Guide
Student Workbook: one per student
Overhead transparencies for activities 1.1, 1.2, 1.3, 1.6, 1.8, 1.10, 1.12, 1.14, 1.16, 1.20, 1.22, 1.25 and 1.28 (See Appendix for masters)
Optional: blank videotape (or have students bring their own) for activity 1.30
Post-test: Appendix 1.30

Videotapes: The Beginning ASL VideoCourse Lesson One
Activities Video for activities 1.20 and 1.25
Assessment Video for Post-test 1.30

1.1 Begin Class

Welcome and Introductions

Goal: To welcome students by introducing yourself and the course.

Instructions:
1. **Show** the overhead transparency (Appendix 1.1).

2. **Use** overhead to introduce yourself and the course. For example, **point** to the teacher and **sign** HE, TEACHER, then **point** to yourself and **sign** ME, TEACHER. **Write** your name on the board.

   Point to the students in the overhead and **sign** STUDENTS. **Point** to your students and **sign** STUDENTS. You may **invite** students to write their names on the board or on an attendance sheet.

Lesson One: *Meet the Bravo Family*

Write the name of the course and course number (if applicable) on the board. **Add** any other information you would like by miming, signing and using the overhead/board.

3. Optional: **Explain** that the format of the class is based on interactive "hands-on" activities. The goal of the course is to provide a safe, positive learning environment in which students can learn not only about ASL, but also about the people who use it.

4. **Hand out** any necessary paperwork that is conducive to your specific program requirements (i.e., syllabus, roll, drop/add cards, etc.).

Overhead Master:
Appendix 1.1

1.2 Pretest

What Do You Know?

Pretest Goal: To identify students' current level of knowledge pertaining to the lesson content.

Pretest Instructions:
1. **Ask** students to read and answer the questions in the lesson pretest in their workbooks (activity 1.2).

2. **Show** overhead (Appendix 1.2) and **ask** individual students to indicate the correct answers on the overhead while class members correct their own work.

3. **Inform** students that the contents of the pretest will be taught throughout the lesson.

Lesson One: *Meet the Bravo Family*

Student Workbook:
Activity 1.2

Overhead Master:
Appendix 1.2

1.2 Pretest

What Do You Know?

Pretest Goal: To see how much you already know about what will be taught in this lesson.

Pretest Instructions: Read each question and circle the best answer.

1. Deaf people actually have their own culture.
   A. True
   B. False

2. American Sign Language is not a real language, it is a shortened form of English.
   A. True
   B. False

3. In ASL, a statement can become a question by simply raising the eyebrows and tilting the head slightly.
   A. True
   B. False

4. The sign for LOVE looks like you are hugging someone.
   A. True
   B. False

5. If you want to get a Deaf person's attention, it would be appropriate to flash the lights.
   A. True
   B. False

6. If you want to get a Deaf person's attention, it would be appropriate to throw a light object at him/her.
   A. True
   B. False

7. ASL grammar is the same as English grammar except that ASL is visual.
   A. True
   B. False

Instructor Tip: *The answers to written activities, quizzes, and tests are identified throughout this Instructor's Guide in **bold** type. These answers are **not** provided in the Student Workbook or on the overhead masters.*

Instructor's Guide: Lesson One
Bravo ASL! Curriculum

Lesson One: *Meet the Bravo Family*

1.3 Lesson Objectives

Planning for Success

Goal: To identify the learning outcomes associated with successful completion of this lesson.

Instructions:
1. **Ask** students to read the objectives in their workbooks (activity 1.3).

2. **Show** overhead (Appendix 1.3) and **read** through the objectives with the class.

Student Workbook: Activity 1.3

Overhead Master: Appendix 1.3

1.3 Lesson Objectives

Planning for Success

Goal: To see what you will learn by the end of this lesson.

Instructions: Read the objectives below.

Upon completing this VideoCourse lesson, you will be able to...

1. Identify the four members of the Bravo family (including their names, name signs, who is Deaf, who is hearing and the children's ages).

2. Recognize and accurately produce the ASL vocabulary introduced in this lesson.

3. Identify Deaf people as a cultural group with their own language, customs and values.

4. Describe culturally appropriate ways to get a Deaf person's attention.

5. Describe culturally appropriate ways to wake a Deaf person.

6. Identify ASL as a distinct language with its own grammatical rules.

7. Recognize and identify yes/no and wh-question types.

8. Accurately produce yes/no and wh-question types including the non-manual grammatical markers associated with each.

1.4 Lesson Focus

Meet the Fam

Activity Goal: To develop a need for the ASL vocabulary introduced in this lesson.

Activity Instructions:

1. **Ask** students to read *Meet the Fam* in their workbooks (activity 1.4).

2. **Divide** the class into small groups of four or five students.

3. **Explain** that students are **not** to use their voices for this activity. **Encourage** students to use signs they may know, gestures, mime, drawing, etc.

4. **Ask** students to take turns introducing themselves and giving a description of their families to each other. **Inform** students they should include information about each of their family members, identifying if there is a mother, father, daughter, son, etc.

   Note: For students who do not wish to discuss their family situations, give the option of describing a fictitious family.

5. **Circulate** among the groups to **observe** their progress.

6. When students have completed this activity, you may **choose**:

   Option A: **Bring** the whole class together and **lead** a discussion using the following Thought/Discussion Questions:

   1) What are some signs related to family introductions that would have been useful to know during this activity?

   2) How did it feel to be limited in your ability to communicate?

   3) What are some ways that Deaf people could introduce their families to people who don't sign?

   OR

   Option B: **Ask** students to complete the Thought/Discussion Questions in their workbooks in class or for homework. **Collect** for grading or to provide students with written feedback.

7. **Inform** students that they will learn several of the signs they needed to perform this activity by the end of the lesson.

Lesson One: *Meet the Bravo Family*

Student Workbook: Activity 1.4

1.4 Lesson Focus

Meet The Fam

Activity Goal: To introduce yourself and your family to classmates without using your voice.

Activity Instructions: Take turns introducing yourself to your classmates. Share information about your family, such as if there is a mother, father, daughter, son, etc.

Remember, do not use your voice! You may use signs, gestures, fingerspelling, mime (acting things out), pointing, etc. Be creative, and have fun!

PS: Don't worry, after this lesson, you will have the sign vocabulary you need to introduce your family.

Thought/Discussion Questions

1. What are some signs related to family introductions that would have been useful to know during this activity?

2. How did it feel to be limited in your ability to communicate?

3. What are some ways that Deaf people could introduce their families to people who don't sign?

1.5 Video Learning Experience

Bravo Family Visit

Meet the Bravo Family

Viewing Goal: To assist students in recognizing the members of the Bravo family.

Viewing Instructions:
1. **Ask** students to read *Meet the Bravo Family* in their workbooks (activity 1.5).

2. **Play** the video segment entitled *Meet the Bravo Family* (segment 1.5). Billy introduces each of the family members by giving their names, name signs, family role identification, whether they are Deaf or hearing, and the age of each child. Because the presentation of this segment is beyond the linguistic ability of beginning students, please **turn on** the audio and/or captions to optimize its educational value.

3. **Instruct** students to watch how Billy produces the signs and the accompanying facial/body expressions.

4. After viewing the segment, **instruct** students to fill in the Bravo family tree as explained in their workbooks.

Lesson One: *Meet the Bravo Family*

Video Segment Content: The following is a translation of the content presented in this video segment.
(4 Minutes)

The family's name is Bravo. This is the father. His name is Dennis. His name sign is this... He is Deaf. He is the father. (Dad repeats introduction using ASL.)

This is the mother. Her name is Jennifer. Her name sign is this... Jennifer is hearing. She is the mother. (Mom repeats introduction using ASL.)

This is the daughter. Her name is Anna. Her name sign is this... Anna is Deaf. She is twelve years old. She is the daughter. (Anna repeats introduction using ASL.)

This is the son. His name is Scott. His name sign is this... Scott is Deaf. He is ten years old. He is the son. (Scott repeats introduction using ASL.)

As you watch this family's natural interaction, you will learn about Deaf people, their world, how they live, and their language... American Sign Language, commonly abbreviated as ASL. As you observe the family, watch for the signs I will show you now.

Student Workbook: Activity 1.5

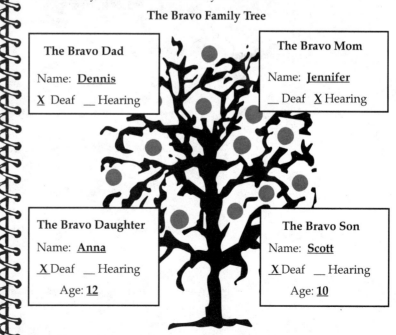

1.5 Video Learning Experience

Meet the Bravo Family

Viewing Goal: To identify the members of the Bravo family including their names, who is Deaf and who is hearing, and the children's ages.

Viewing Instructions: After viewing the introduction of Billy and the Bravo family, fill in the Bravo family tree below.

The Bravo Family Tree

The Bravo Dad
Name: **Dennis**
X Deaf __ Hearing

The Bravo Mom
Name: **Jennifer**
__ Deaf **X** Hearing

The Bravo Daughter
Name: **Anna**
X Deaf __ Hearing
Age: **12**

The Bravo Son
Name: **Scott**
X Deaf __ Hearing
Age: **10**

Lesson One: *Meet the Bravo Family*

1.6 Language Learning Instruction

Learning New Signs

Goal: To use ASL and visual aids to introduce this lesson's vocabulary.

Instructions:
1. **Ask** students to read *Learning New Signs* in their workbooks (activity 1.6).

2. **Show** overhead (Appendix 1.6) and **use** it to **introduce** the corresponding vocabulary. For example, **point** to a mother in the picture and **sign**, SHE, MOTHER, then **point** to a baby in the picture and **sign**, SHE, BABY.

3. After introducing several signs in this manner, **reinforce** retention and **check** students' comprehension by **using** these signs to **ask** students questions.

   For example, **point** to the baby in the picture and **sign**, SHE, MOTHER? **Ask** students to respond appropriately, such as NO, SHE BABY.

   Note: When asking these questions be sure to:
   A) **Use** only signs that have already been taught or that could be figured out from the overhead or the context of the question to avoid confusion.
   B) **Model** grammatically correct ASL.
   C) **Model** appropriate non-manual grammatical markers.
   D) **Model** appropriate facial/body expression.

4. **Continue** steps 2-3 above (point, label, and use the new signs) until all the ASL vocabulary items have been introduced.

Instructor Tip:

This curriculum provides two methods for introducing new vocabulary. The Language Learning Instruction activities are provided for instructors who wish to use the Direct Experience Method to introduce vocabulary. For more information about this method, see the Curriculum Overview.

The Video Learning Experiences entitled "Introduction to New Vocabulary" (see activity 1.7) provides a method whereby each sign is supported with an English gloss and a voiced translation.

You may choose to use either or both techniques depending on the learning needs and styles of your particular students. Both of these options are presented throughout the curriculum.

Lesson One: *Meet the Bravo Family*

Overhead Content: Use the pictures in the overhead (Appendix 1.6) to introduce the signs representing the following concepts:

1.	MOM/MOTHER	13.	DEAF
2.	CHILDREN	14.	HEARING
3.	BABY	15.	WHICH
4.	GOOD	16.	WANT
5.	MORNING	17.	TOILET/BATHROOM
6.	COFFEE	18.	BRUSH-TEETH
7.	HUNGRY	19.	TIME
8.	YES	20.	WAKE-UP
9.	NO	21.	SCHOOL
10.	THANK-YOU	22.	BREAKFAST
11.	WHERE	23.	PAST/BEFORE
12.	LOVE	24.	GO

Note: Some pictures can be used to represent several concepts. For verbs and more abstract concepts, you may need to supplement these pictures with mime, gestures, using actual objects, and acting out the concepts in class.

Overhead Master: Appendix 1.6

Lesson One: *Meet the Bravo Family*

Student Workbook: Activity 1.6

1.6 Language Learning Instruction

Learning New Signs

Goal: To help you learn new ASL vocabulary.

Instructions: Your instructor will teach you new signs! Watch closely to learn what these signs mean and how they are produced.

In the space below, record any notes to help you remember the signs.

Notes: _____
_____
_____
_____

1.7 Video Learning Experience

Introduction to New Vocabulary

Viewing Goal: To provide a signed demonstration of the accurate production of the new ASL vocabulary.

Viewing Instructions:
1. **Ask** students to read *Introduction to New Vocabulary* in their workbooks (activity 1.7).

2. **Play** the video segment entitled *Introduction to New Vocabulary* (segment 1.7). Billy introduces and signs each new vocabulary item twice. (If you wish to keep this a strictly visual presentation, **turn off** audio.)

3. **Instruct** students to watch how Billy produces the signs as well as the accompanying facial/body expressions.

4. **Ask** students to copy the signs and the facial/body expressions as Billy repeats each one.

Instructor Tip: *Illustrations of all ASL vocabulary items are included in the Sign Illustration Section in the back of this Guide and the Student Workbook.*

Lesson One: *Meet the Bravo Family*

Video Segment Content: See the following Student Workbook excerpt for the content
(4 Minutes) of this video segment.

Student Workbook:
Activity 1.7

> 1.7 Video Learning Experience
>
> *Introduction to New Vocabulary*
>
> **Viewing Goal:** To help you learn new ASL vocabulary.
>
> **Viewing Instructions:** Watch how Billy produces each sign. Be sure to notice the facial/body expressions. Copy the signs as Billy repeats each one.
>
> Signs representing the following concepts are introduced in this video segment:
>
> 1. MOM/MOTHER
> 2. CHILDREN
> 3. BABY
> 4. GOOD
> 5. MORNING
> 6. COFFEE
> 7. HUNGRY
> 8. YES
> 9. NO
> 10. THANK-YOU
> 11. WHERE
> 12. LOVE
> 13. DEAF
> 14. HEARING
> 15. WHICH
> 16. WANT
> 17. TOILET/BATHROOM
> 18. BRUSH-TEETH
> 19. TIME
> 20. WAKE-UP
> 21. SCHOOL
> 22. BREAKFAST
> 23. PAST/BEFORE
> 24. GO
>
> **Note**: Illustrations of each ASL sign can be found in the Sign Illustration Section at the back of this Student Workbook.

1.8
Experiential Activity

Point and Sign

Activity Goal: To assist students in recognizing the new ASL vocabulary in the context of signed communication.

Activity Instructions:
1. **Ask** students to read *Point and Sign* in their workbooks (activity 1.8).

2. **Show** overhead (Appendix 1.8) containing the activity pictures.

3. **Point** to the various people in the pictures as indicated and sign the questions to the students. You may want to **create** additional questions.

Lesson One: *Meet the Bravo Family*

4. **Instruct** students to respond appropriately to the following questions by signing either YES or NO. Depending on your students' skill level, you might also **ask** them to respond using complete sentences.

   A. **Point** to a mother on the overhead and use ASL to **ask**:
      1. $\overline{\text{SHE FATHER}}^q$
      2. $\overline{\text{SHE MOTHER}}^q$
      3. $\overline{\text{SHE SON}}^q$

   B. **Point** to a father on the overhead and use ASL to **ask**:
      1. $\overline{\text{HE FATHER}}^q$
      2. $\overline{\text{HE MOTHER}}^q$
      3. $\overline{\text{HE DAUGHTER}}^q$

   C. **Point** to a daughter on the overhead and use ASL to **ask**:
      1. $\overline{\text{SHE FATHER}}^q$
      2. $\overline{\text{SHE SON}}^q$
      3. $\overline{\text{SHE MOTHER}}^q$
      4. $\overline{\text{SHE DAUGHTER}}^q$

   D. **Point** to a son on the overhead and use ASL to **ask**:
      1. $\overline{\text{HE FATHER}}^q$
      2. $\overline{\text{HE SON}}^q$
      3. $\overline{\text{HE MOTHER}}^q$
      4. $\overline{\text{HE DAUGHTER}}^q$

   E. **Use** ASL to **ask** various students:
      1. $\overline{\text{HUNGRY YOU}}^q$
      2. $\overline{\text{COFFEE,}}^t \overline{\text{WANT (YOU)}}^q$
      3. $\overline{\text{MOTHER,}}^t \overline{\text{LOVE (YOU)}}^q$
      4. $\overline{\text{DEAF YOU}}^q$
      5. $\overline{\text{HEARING YOU}}^q$
      6. $\overline{\text{BREAKFAST,}}^t \overline{\text{WANT}}^q$
      7. $\overline{\text{DAUGHTER YOU}}^q$

Lesson One: *Meet the Bravo Family*

Overhead Master:
Appendix 1.8

Student Workbook:
Activity 1.8

1.8 Experiential Activity

Point and Sign

Activity Goal: To help you recognize the new ASL vocabulary within the context of signed communication.

Activity Instructions: Your instructor will point to some pictures and ask you questions using ASL. Watch carefully and follow your instructor's directions in responding to these questions.

Lesson One: *Meet the Bravo Family*

1.9 Video Learning Experience

Bravo Family Visit

Viewing Goal: To improve ASL comprehension skills by watching a Bravo family interaction.

Viewing Instructions:
1. **Ask** students to read *Bravo Family Visit* in their workbooks (activity 1.9).
2. **Play** the video segment of the Bravo family (segment 1.9). The Bravos will use the new ASL vocabulary within the context of their daily morning routine.
3. **Instruct** students to watch for comprehension and write a summary of the main points.
4. **Replay** any portion of this video segment that students experienced difficulty understanding.

**Video Segment Content:
(3 Minutes)**

The following is a summary of the Bravo family interaction:

Dad is sitting in the kitchen. Mom enters, kisses Dad, and says "Good Morning." Dad asks her if she wants any coffee. She says no, but that she is very hungry.

Noticing the time, Mom asks Dad where the children are. He indicates that they are still sleeping. Mom goes upstairs to wake them.

Mom goes into Anna's room first. Mom gently wakes Anna with a kiss and tells her it's time to get up and get ready for school.

Anna taps Mom to get her attention and asks her to sit on the bed for awhile. Mom sits on the bed with Anna. Anna then asks Mom, "A long time ago, when I was a baby... did you want a hearing or Deaf baby?"

Mom responds, "Did I want a Deaf or a hearing baby?... I wanted you! I love you!" Anna responds that she loves Mom too, and they hug.

Mom asks Anna if she would have preferred a Deaf or a hearing mother. Anna pauses to consider the question and responds, "I wanted you!"

Mom lets Anna know it is now time to brush her teeth and get dressed and ready for school. Anna gets out of bed and goes to the bathroom to brush her teeth.

Lesson One: *Meet the Bravo Family*

Student Workbook: Activity 1.9

1.9 Video Learning Experience

Bravo Family Visit

Viewing Goal: To improve your ASL comprehension skills by watching a Bravo family interaction.

Viewing Instructions: Watch the signed interaction and write a summary of the main points (in your own words) to help you remember.

Summary: _____
_____
_____
_____

1.10 Comprehension Quiz

What Did You Understand?

Quiz Goal: To assess students' comprehension of the signed interaction.

Quiz Instructions:
1. **Instruct** students to complete the quiz in their workbooks (activity 1.10).

2. **Collect** for grading or **show** overhead (Appendix 1.10) and **ask** individual students to indicate the correct answers on the overhead while class members correct their own work.

3. **Ask** students to indicate which item(s) from the quiz they found difficult. **Review** by **modeling** or **replaying** that segment of the videotape.

Lesson One: *Meet the Bravo Family*

Student Workbook: Activity 1.10

Overhead Master: Appendix 1.10

1.10 Comprehension Quiz

What Did You Understand?

Quiz Goal: To see how much of the Bravo family interaction you understood.

Quiz Instructions: Read and answer each question below.

1. Dad offers Mom coffee. Does she want any?
   A. Yes
   B. No

2. Mom asks Dad where the children are. What does he tell her?
   A. "At school."
   B. "Eating breakfast."
   C. "Sleeping upstairs."
   D. "Playing with the dog."

3. "What does Anna ask Mom?"
   A. "A long time ago, did you want a hearing or Deaf baby?"
   B. "A long time ago, did you have a hearing baby?"
   C. "Did you want all your babies to be Deaf?"
   D. "Did you want all your babies to be hearing?"

4. How does Mom answer this question?
   A. "I want you to shower."
   B. "I wanted a hearing child."
   C. "I wanted a Deaf child."
   D. "I wanted you."

5. When Mom asks Anna if she wanted a Deaf or hearing mom, Anna said she would have preferred a Deaf mom, but she loves her mom anyway.
   A. True
   B. False

1.11 Experiential Activity

Point and Sign

Activity Goal: To assist students in recognizing and producing the new ASL vocabulary.

Activity Instructions:
1. **Instruct** students to read *Point and Sign* in their workbooks (activity 1.11).

2. **Divide** the class into pairs.

3. **Select** and **model** the variation of the *Point and Sign* activity you would like your students to perform. You may **choose** to have students perform all three variations.

Instructor's Guide: Lesson One
Bravo ASL! Curriculum

Lesson One: *Meet the Bravo Family*

4. **Inform** students that this activity is to be done without using their voices.

   Variation A:

   1) **Ask** each pair of students to take turns pointing to an object or action in the picture and producing the sign or signs that best match its meaning.

   2) **Instruct** the partner to provide feedback on the correct choice and production of the signs.

   Variation B:

   1) **Ask** each pair of students to take turns having one student point to an object or action in the picture.

   2) **Instruct** the partner to produce the sign or signs that best match its meaning.

   Variation C:

   1) **Ask** each pair of students to take turns having one student produce a sign or signs that corresponds to one of the objects or actions in the picture.

   2) **Instruct** the partner to point to the object or action in the picture that best matches the meaning of the sign or signs presented by her/his partner.

5. **Circulate** among the pairs to **observe** student performance. **Encourage** students to use the following vocabulary: MOTHER, FATHER, BABY, LOVE, DEAF, HEARING, HUNGRY, CHILDREN, WHICH, YES, NO, GOOD, WHERE and BATHROOM.

6. **Model** the signs as needed.

Student Workbook: Activity 1.11

1.11 Experiential Activity

Point and Sign

Activity Goal: To help you recognize and produce the new ASL vocabulary.

Activity Instructions: Using the pictures below, follow your teacher's instructions and practice using your new sign vocabulary such as: MOTHER, FATHER, BABY, LOVE, DEAF, HEARING, HUNGRY, CHILDREN, WHICH, YES, NO, GOOD, WHERE and BATHROOM.

Instructor's Guide: Lesson One
Bravo ASL! Curriculum

©1996 Sign Enhancers, Inc.
ALL RIGHTS RESERVED.

Lesson One: *Meet the Bravo Family*

1.12 Language Learning Instruction

Learning New Signs

Viewing Goal: To use ASL and visual aids to introduce this lesson's vocabulary.

Viewing Instructions:
1. **Ask** students to read *Learning New Signs* in their workbooks (activity 1.12).

2. **Show** the overhead (Appendix 1.12) and **use** it to **introduce** the corresponding vocabulary.

   For example, **point** to a dog in the picture and **sign**, IT, DOG, then **point** to the spider in the picture and **sign**, IT, SPIDER.

3. After introducing several signs in this manner, **reinforce** retention and **check** students' comprehension by **using** these signs to **ask** students questions.

   For example, **point** to the spider in the picture and **sign** IT, DOG? **Ask** students to respond appropriately, such as NO, IT SPIDER.

   Note: When asking these questions be sure to:
   A) **Use** only signs that have already been taught or that could be figured out from the overhead or the context of the question to avoid confusion.
   B) **Model** grammatically correct ASL.
   C) **Model** appropriate non-manual grammatical markers.
   D) **Model** appropriate facial/body expression.

4. **Continue** steps 2-3 above (point, label, and use the new signs) until all the ASL vocabulary items have been introduced.

Overhead Content: Use the pictures in the overhead (Appendix 1.12) to introduce the signs representing the following concepts:

1. DOG
2. FOOL-YOU
3. SHOWER
4. KITCHEN (COOK+ROOM)
5. SON (BOY + BABY)
6. DAUGHTER (GIRL+BABY)
7. SCARED/AFRAID
8. BED
9. SPIDER
10. ALMOST
11. GET-DRESSED

Lesson One: *Meet the Bravo Family*

Note: Some pictures can be used to represent several concepts. For verbs and more abstract concepts, you may need to supplement these pictures with mime, gestures, using actual objects, and acting out the concepts in class.

Overhead Master: Appendix 1.12

Lesson One: *Meet the Bravo Family*

Student Workbook:
Activity 1.12

1.12 Language Learning Instruction

Learning New Signs

Goal: To help you learn new ASL vocabulary.

Instructions: Your instructor will teach you new signs! Watch closely to learn what these signs mean and how they are produced.

In the space below, record any notes to help you remember the signs.

Notes: _____
_____
_____
_____

Note: Remember, you can find illustrations of each sign in the Sign Illustration Section at the end of this workbook.

1.13 Video Learning Experience

Introduction to New Vocabulary

Viewing Goal: To provide a signed demonstration of the accurate production of the new ASL vocabulary.

Viewing Instructions:
1. **Ask** students to read *Introduction to New Vocabulary* in their workbooks (activity 1.13).

2. **Play** the video segment entitled *Introduction to New Vocabulary* (segment 1.13). Billy introduces and signs each new vocabulary item twice. (If you wish to keep this a strictly visual presentation, **turn off** audio.)

3. **Instruct** students to watch how Billy produces the signs and the accompanying facial/body expressions.

4. **Ask** students to copy the signs and the facial/body expressions as Billy repeats each one.

Lesson One: *Meet the Bravo Family*

Video Segment Content: See the following Student Workbook excerpt for the content
(2 Minutes) of this video segment.

Student Workbook: Activity 1.13

1.13 Video Learning Experience

Introduction to New Vocabulary

Viewing Goal: To help you learn new ASL vocabulary.

Viewing Instructions: Watch how Billy produces each sign. Be sure to notice the facial/body expressions. Copy the signs as Billy repeats each one.

Signs representing the following concepts are introduced in this video segment:

1. DOG
2. FOOL-YOU
3. SHOWER
4. KITCHEN (COOK+ROOM)
5. SON (BOY+BABY)
6. DAUGHTER (GIRL+BABY)
7. SCARED/AFRAID
8. BED
9. SPIDER
10. ALMOST
11. GET-DRESSED

1.14 Experiential Activity

Point and Sign

Activity Goal: To assist students in recognizing the new ASL vocabulary in the context of signed communication.

Activity Instructions:

1. **Ask** students to read *Point and Sign* in their workbooks (activity 1.14).

2. **Show** overhead (Appendix 1.14) containing the activity pictures.

3. **Point** to the various people/animals/objects in the pictures as indicated and **sign** the questions to the students. You may want to **create** additional questions.

4. **Instruct** students to respond appropriately to the following questions by signing either YES or NO. Depending on your students' skill level, you might **ask** them to respond using complete sentences.

Instructor's Guide: Lesson One
Bravo ASL! Curriculum

©1996 Sign Enhancers, Inc.
ALL RIGHTS RESERVED.

Lesson One: *Meet the Bravo Family*

A. **Point** to one of the dogs on the overhead and **ask**:
   1. $\overline{\text{IT SPIDER}}^{q}$
   2. $\overline{\text{IT DOG}}^{q}$
   3. $\overline{\text{IT BABY}}^{q}$

B. **Point** to the spider on the overhead and **ask**:
   1. $\overline{\text{IT SPIDER}}^{q}$
   2. $\overline{\text{IT DOG}}^{q}$
   3. $\overline{\text{IT GET-DRESSED}}^{q}$

C. **Point** to the girl brushing her teeth and **ask**:
   1. $\overline{\text{SHE SHOWER}}^{q}$
   2. $\overline{\text{SHE GET-DRESSED}}^{q}$
   3. $\overline{\text{SHE BRUSH-TEETH}}^{q}$

D. **Point** to the baby in the shower and **ask**:
   1. $\overline{\text{HE MOTHER}}^{q}$
   2. $\overline{\text{HE BABY}}^{q}$
   3. $\overline{\text{HE GET-DRESSED}}^{q}$
   4. $\overline{\text{HE SHOWER}}^{q}$

E. **Point** to the woman in the bed and ask:
   1. $\overline{\text{SHE WAKE-UP}}^{q}$
   2. $\overline{\text{SPIDER, SHE LOVE}}^{q}$
   3. $\overline{\text{SHE FATHER}}^{q}$

F. **Ask** various students in your class:
   1. $\overline{\text{DOG,}}^{t}$ $\overline{\text{YOU SCARED}}^{q}$
   2. $\overline{\text{DOG,}}^{t}$ $\overline{\text{YOU LOVE}}^{q}$
   3. $\overline{\text{YOU DOG}}^{q}$
   4. $\overline{\text{YOU SHOWER}}^{q}$
   5. $\overline{\text{TIME YOU WAKE-UP}}^{wh\text{-}q}$

Lesson One: *Meet the Bravo Family*

Overhead Master:
Appendix 1.14

Student Workbook:
Activity 1.14

1.14 Experiential Activity

Point and Sign

Activity Goal: To help you recognize the new ASL vocabulary within the context of signed communication.

Activity Instructions: Your instructor will point to some pictures and ask you questions using ASL. Watch carefully and follow your instructor's directions in responding to these questions.

Instructor's Guide: Lesson One
Bravo ASL! Curriculum

©1996 Sign Enhancers, Inc.
ALL RIGHTS RESERVED.

Lesson One: *Meet the Bravo Family*

1.15 Video Learning Experience

Bravo Family Visit

Viewing Goal: To improve ASL comprehension skills by watching a Bravo family interaction.

Viewing Instructions:
1. **Ask** students to read *Bravo Family Visit* in their workbooks (activity 1.15).
2. **Play** the video segment of the Bravo family (segment 1.15). The Bravos will use the new ASL vocabulary within the context of their daily morning routine.
3. **Instruct** students to watch for comprehension and write a summary of the main points.
4. **Replay** any portion of this video segment that students experienced difficulty understanding.

Video Segment Content: (2 Minutes)

The following is a summary of the Bravo family interaction:

Mom goes into Scott's bedroom to wake him up. She enters, sits on the bed and gently taps the lump under the blanket. Instead of Scott, the family dog appears! Mom wonders where Scott could be.

Scott, from the top bunk bed, lowers his hand like a "spider" and makes the "spider" crawl in her hair. She pulls him down and tickles him.

He asks, "Did I fool you?" Mom says, "Yes! I almost sent the dog to school!"

Scott asks if he scared Mom. She answers, "You scared me good! I'm scared of spiders!"

Mom reminds Scott that it is time to wake up and get showered, get dressed, get ready for school and come down to the kitchen for breakfast. Scott indicates that he is very hungry!

Lesson One: *Meet the Bravo Family*

Student Workbook: Activity 1.15

1.15 Video Learning Experience

Bravo Family Visit

Viewing Goal: To improve ASL comprehension skills by watching a Bravo family interaction.

Viewing Instructions: Watch the signed interaction and write a summary of the main points (in your own words) to help you remember.

Summary: _____
_____
_____
_____

1.16 Comprehension Quiz

What Did You Understand?

Quiz Goal: To assess students' comprehension of the signed interaction.

Quiz Instructions:
1. **Instruct** students to complete the quiz in their workbooks (activity 1.16).

2. **Collect** for grading or **show** overhead (Appendix 1.16) and **ask** individual students to indicate the correct answers on the overhead while class members correct their own work.

3. **Ask** students to indicate which item(s) from the quiz they found difficult. **Review** by **modeling** signs or **replaying** that segment of the videotape.

Lesson One: *Meet the Bravo Family*

Student Workbook:
Activity 1.16

Overhead Master:
Appendix 1.16

1.16 Comprehension Quiz

What Did You Understand?

Quiz Goal: To see how much of the Bravo family interaction you understood.

Quiz Instructions: Read and answer each question below.

1. When Mom went into Scott's room, what did she find in his bed?
   A. There was a spider on Scott's head.
   B. A spider was in the dog's mouth.
   C. The dog was in the bed with Scott.
   D. The dog was in bed instead of Scott.

2. Did Scott fool Mom?
   A. Yes, she almost sent the dog to school.
   B. No, she knew the spider was there the whole time.
   C. No, she knew the dog was there the whole time.
   D. Yes, she thought the spider was the dog.

3. How does Mom feel about spiders?
   A. She eats them for breakfast.
   B. She is scared of them.
   C. She likes them better than dogs.
   D. She didn't want to talk about it because it was time for breakfast.

4. Scott wanted to go straight to school since he was not very hungry.
   A. True
   B. False

1.17 Video Learning Experience

Cultural Notes

Viewing Goal: To assist students in learning about the cultural aspects of ASL.

Viewing Instructions:

1. **Ask** students to read *Cultural Notes* in their workbooks (activity 1.17).

2. **Play** the video segment entitled *Cultural Notes* (segment 1.17). Because the presentation of this segment is beyond the linguistic ability of beginning students, please **turn on** the audio and/or captions to optimize its educational value.

3. **Instruct** students to view the segment.

4. At completion of the video segment, **review** the content presented, and **answer** any questions students may have.

Instructor's Guide: Lesson One
Bravo ASL! Curriculum

Lesson One: *Meet the Bravo Family*

Video Segment Content: See the following Student Workbook excerpt for the content
(3 Minutes) of this video segment.

Student Workbook:
Activity 1.17

1.17 Video Learning Experience

Cultural Notes

Viewing Goal: To learn about the cultural aspects of ASL.

Viewing Instructions: View the *Cultural Notes* segment carefully for the following:

I. Deaf people have their own distinct culture:
   A. Deaf Culture is equal to that of other cultures such as American, French, or English cultures.
   B. Just like all cultures, Deaf culture includes a set of shared customs and values.
   C. As in any language instruction, cultural information must be included when learning ASL.

II. Culturally appropriate ways to get a Deaf person's attention include:
   A. A gentle tap on the shoulder.
   B. Waving one's hand toward the Deaf person.
   C. Calling out in a low tone.
   D. Stomping a foot that causes a vibration.

III. To wake a Deaf person it would be appropriate to use:
   A. A brief flashing of the light.
   B. A gentle tap.

1.18
Experiential Activity

Hey, You...

Activity Goal: To apply the culturally appropriate attention-getting techniques presented in this lesson.

Activity Instructions:
1. **Divide** the class into small groups of four or five students.
2. **Ask** students to read *Hey You...* in their workbooks (activity 1.18).
3. **Ask** students to take turns being the Deaf person in each of the suggested situations. **Encourage** each student to explore ways of getting the "Deaf" person's attention.

Instructor's Guide: Lesson One
Bravo ASL! Curriculum

©1996 Sign Enhancers, Inc.
ALL RIGHTS RESERVED.

Lesson One: *Meet the Bravo Family*

Instructor Tip: *Several activities throughout the course ask students to role-play being a Deaf person. It is suggested that you strongly discourage students from "acting Deaf" outside of the classroom. You might explain that these activities are intended to enhance sensitivity regarding how Deaf people feel, yet it is inappropriate to act Deaf once outside the learning environment.*

4. When students have completed the activity **ask** each group to demonstrate for the class the attention-getting techniques that were deemed most effective.

5. To close this activity, you may **choose**:

    Option A: **Lead** a class discussion using the following Thought/Discussion Questions:

    1) How did it feel to be the Deaf person? Were there any attempts at getting your attention you felt were rude or not effective?

    2) When you were trying to get the Deaf person's attention, what worked the best?

    3) Did you try any new techniques not described by the video? What were the results?

    OR

    Option B: **Ask** students to complete the above Thought/Discussion Questions in their workbooks in class or for homework. **Collect** for grading or to provide students with written feedback.

Student Workbook: Activity 1.18

1.18 Experiential Activity

Hey, You...

Activity Goal: To apply culturally appropriate ways of getting a Deaf person's attention.

Activity Instructions: Your instructor will divide the class into small groups. Within your group, take turns role-playing a Deaf person in each of the situations below while the other group members try to get his/her attention.

You want to get your Deaf friend's attention but s/he is...

1. Looking in the other direction.
2. Standing in line, two people ahead of you.
3. Chatting in ASL with some other Deaf friends.
4. Sitting down, reading a book.
5. Working on a computer.
6. Sleeping.

Lesson One: *Meet the Bravo Family*

> **Thought/Discussion Questions**
>
> 1. How did it feel to be the Deaf person? Were there any attempts to get your attention you felt were rude or not effective?
>
> 2. When you were trying to get the Deaf person's attention, what worked the best?
>
> 3. Did you try any new techniques not described by the video? What were the results?
>
> **Note:** Remember that although it is helpful to role-play within the educational setting, it is not appropriate to "act Deaf" outside the learning environment.

1.19 Video Learning Experience

Grammatical Notes

Viewing Goal: To assist students in learning about the grammatical aspects of ASL.

Viewing Instructions:
1. **Ask** students to read *Grammatical Notes* in their workbooks (activity 1.19).

2. **Play** the video segment entitled *Grammatical Notes* (segment 1.19). Because the presentation of this segment is beyond the linguistic ability of beginning students, please **turn on** the audio and/or captions to optimize its educational value.

3. **Instruct** students to view the segment.

4. At completion of segment, **review** the content presented and **answer** any questions students may have.

Lesson One: *Meet the Bravo Family*

Video Segment Content: See the following Student Workbook excerpt for the content
(3 Minutes) of this video segment.

Student Workbook:
Activity 1.19

1.19 Video Learning Experience

Grammatical Notes

Viewing Goal: To learn about the grammatical aspects of ASL.

Viewing Instructions: View the *Grammatical Notes* segment carefully for the following:

I. ASL grammar and English grammar are different.

II. There are many ways of asking questions in ASL. This lesson focuses on two:

A. The yes/no question format elicits a YES or NO response. The non-manual grammatical markers associated with a yes/no question are:
1. The eyebrows are raised.
2. The head is slightly tilted.
3. The eyes make direct contact.
4. The last sign is held, waiting for a response.

B. The wh-question format asks who, what, where, when, how, which, why, etc. The non-manual grammatical markers associated with a wh-question are:
1. The eyebrows are furrowed (down).
2. The head is slightly tilted.
3. The last sign is held, waiting for a response.

Note: As you can see above, the term "non-manual grammatical marker" refers to physical movements (other than the actual signs) including eyebrow raise/furrow, eye gaze, head tilt, mouth movements, and others. These markers provide important grammatical information such as question types.

1.20
Experiential
Activity

What Kind of Question is That?!

Activities Video

Activity Goal: To apply the grammatical information by identifying ASL question types.

Activity Instructions: 1. **Ask** students to read *What Kind of Question is That?!* in their workbooks (activity 1.20).

Lesson One: *Meet the Bravo Family*

2. **Play** the question samples on the Activities Video (segment 1.20) while students indicate the question type of each by circling either "yes/no" or "wh" in their workbooks.

3. **Remind** students of the non-manual grammatical markers for each type of question (as presented in the *Grammatical Notes*).

4. **Show** overhead (Appendix 1.20) and **ask** individual students to indicate the correct answers on the overhead while class members correct their own work.

Video Segment Content: (3 1/2 Minutes)

ASL glosses and English translations:

Question Types:

1. $\overline{\text{MOTHER,}}^{t} \overline{\text{YOU LOVE}}^{q}$
   Do you love your mother?   yes/no

2. $\overline{\text{CHILDREN,}}^{t} \overline{\text{HAVE}}^{q}$
   Do you have children?   yes/no

3. $\overline{\text{DEAF YOU}}^{q}$
   Are you Deaf?   yes/no

4. $\overline{\text{BATHROOM,}}^{t} \overline{\text{WHERE}}^{wh-q}$
   Where is the bathroom?   wh

5. $\overline{\text{WAKE-UP, WHEN}}^{wh-q}$
   When did you wake up?   wh

6. $\overline{\text{COFFEE,}}^{t} \overline{\text{WANT}}^{q}$
   Do you want coffee?   yes/no

7. $\overline{\text{SCHOOL,}}^{t} \overline{\text{WHERE}}^{wh-q}$
   Where is the school?   wh

8. $\overline{\text{DEAF,}}^{t} \overline{\text{WHO}}^{wh-q}$
   Who is Deaf?   wh

9. $\overline{\text{YOU DEAF, HEARING, WHICH}}^{wh-q}$
   Are you Deaf or Hearing... which?   wh

10. $\overline{\text{GOOD MORNING, HUNGRY}}^{q}$
    Good morning, are you hungry?   yes/no

Lesson One: *Meet the Bravo Family*

Student Workbook:
Activity 1.20

Overhead Master:
Appendix 1.20

1.20 Experiential Activity

What Kind of Question is That?!

Activity Goal: To apply the grammatical information you learned.

Activity Instructions: You will see several signed questions. Watch each sample closely and decide whether the question is a yes/no-question or a wh-question.

Don't worry if you do not understand the meaning of the question, just watch the non-manual grammatical markers to determine your answer.

Circle your answer:

1.	**yes/no**	wh	6.	**yes/no**	wh
2.	**yes/no**	wh	7.	yes/no	**wh**
3.	**yes/no**	wh	8.	yes/no	**wh**
4.	yes/no	**wh**	9.	yes/no	**wh**
5.	yes/no	**wh**	10.	**yes/no**	wh

1.21 Experiential Activity

Pass the Question

Activity Goal: To recognize and produce the non-manual grammatical markers associated with ASL question types.

Activity Instructions:

1. **Ask** students to read *Pass the Question* in their workbooks (activity 1.21).

2. **Divide** the class into teams of about five students each (all teams should have the same number of students). **Ask** each team to line up, single file (one student behind the other), facing the back of the room.

3. **Ask** the students at the back of each line (closest to you) to turn and face you while the rest of the students remain facing toward the back of the room.

4. **Show** the students facing you one of the questions listed under instruction number eight. **Demonstrate** the appropriate non-manual markers with the sign(s) as indicated.

5. **Ask** these students to pass the question (including the non-manual markers) to the next person in line.

6. **Continue** the activity until the question is passed to the last student. If this student can produce the correct question with the non-manual markers, s/he runs to the board and writes either yes/no or wh.

7. **Reward** the first team to correctly produce the question/non-manual markers and write the correct response on the board. **Tell** students to shift positions.

8. **Continue** this activity with the questions listed below. **Create** additional questions as needed.

Questions:	Non-manual markers:
<u> wh-q </u> WHAT	(brow furrowed, head tilted)
<u> q </u> DEAF YOU	(brow raised, head tilted)
<u> q </u> BREAKFAST WANT	(brow raised, head tilted)
<u> wh-q </u> SPIDER WHERE	(brow furrowed and head tilted with expression of fear)
<u> wh-q </u> HUNGRY WHO	(brow furrowed, head tilted)
<u> q </u> DOG HAVE	(brow raised, head tilted)

Student Workbook: Activity 1.21

1.21 Experiential Activity

Pass the Question

Activity Goal: To recognize and produce the non-manual grammatical markers for ASL question types within the context of a game.

Activity Instructions: This game is similar to "The Rumor Game." Your instructor will divide your class into teams. Each team will line up, single file, facing away from the teacher.

Your instructor will show the first student in each line a signed question. That student will watch carefully, tap the next student in line and repeat the question (including the non-manual grammatical markers). Each team will continue to pass the question until the last student in the line sees it.

The last student in each line must sign the question. If correct, this student goes to the board and writes whether it is a yes/no or a wh-question. If not correct, the team begins again with the first student passing the question to the second person in line, and so on.

The first team to demonstrate the correct question (including the non-manual markers) and write the correct question type on the board wins.

Good luck and have fun!

Lesson One: *Meet the Bravo Family*

1.22 Cultural and Grammatical Quiz

What Did You Learn?

Quiz Goal: To assess students' mastery of this lesson's cultural and grammatical information.

Quiz Instructions:
1. **Ask** students to complete the quiz in their workbooks (activity 1.22).
2. **Collect** the written quiz for grading or **show** the overhead (Appendix 1.22) and **ask** individual students to indicate the correct answers on the overhead while class members correct their own work.

Student Workbook: Activity 1.22

Overhead Master: Appendix 1.22

1.22 Cultural and Grammatical Quiz

What Did You Learn?

Quiz Goal: To see how much of this lesson's cultural and grammatical information you learned.

Quiz Instructions: Read and answer each question below.

1. Deaf people do not have their own culture because they belong to the American culture.
   A. True
   B. False

2. Cultural information must be included within any language learning experience.
   A. True
   B. False

3. The French, German and American people have distinct cultures, but Deaf people only belong to a community.
   A. True
   B. False

4. All cultures, including that of Deaf people, include customs and values.
   A. True
   B. False

5. Culturally appropriate ways for getting a Deaf person's attention include (check all that apply):
   _X_ **A gentle tap on the shoulder**
   _X_ **Wave one's hand toward the Deaf person**
   _X_ **Call out in a low tone**
   _X_ **Stomp a foot causing a vibration**
   ___ Gently spray water at the Deaf person

Instructor's Guide: Lesson One
Bravo ASL! Curriculum

©1996 Sign Enhancers, Inc.
ALL RIGHTS RESERVED.

Lesson One: *Meet the Bravo Family*

> 6. Culturally appropriate ways for waking a Deaf person include (check all that apply):
>   - **X** **A light flashed briefly**
>   - **X** **A gentle tap**
>   - ___ Gently spray water at the Deaf person
>
> 7. The non-manual markers associated with a yes/no question are (check all that apply):
>   - **X** **Eyebrows raised**   **X** **Slight head tilt**
>   - ___ Eyebrows furrowed   ___ Lean back
>   - **X** **Direct eye contact**   **X** **Last sign held for response**
>
> 8. The non-manual markers associated with a wh-question are (check all that apply):
>   - ___ Eyebrows raised   **X** **Slight head tilt**
>   - **X** **Eyebrows furrowed**   ___ Lean back
>   - ___ Direct eye contact   **X** **Last sign held for response**
>
> 9. A yes/no question can be responded to with a "yes" or "no" answer.
>   - **A. True**
>   - B. False
>
> 10. A wh-question can ask (check all that apply):
>   - **X** **Which?**   **X** **How?**
>   - **X** **When?**   **X** **Why?**

1.23 Video Learning Experience

Review Session

Viewing Goal: To reinforce recognition and production of the signs introduced in this lesson.

Viewing Instructions:

1. **Ask** students to read *Review Session* in their workbooks (activity 1.23).

2. **Play** the video segment entitled *Review Session* (segment 1.23). Billy compares the symbolic nature of ASL to the use of symbols in other languages. He then reviews all the ASL vocabulary and provides visual cues and origin information. Because the presentation of this segment is beyond the linguistic ability of beginning students, please **turn on** the audio and/or captions to optimize its educational value.

3. **Ask** students to pay careful attention to the signed vocabulary items and take note of visual hints offered by Billy that might help them remember.

Lesson One: *Meet the Bravo Family*

4. **Suggest** that students copy the signs to reinforce retention of sign production.

Video Segment Content: See the following Student Workbook excerpt for the content
(11 Minutes) of this video segment.

Student Workbook:
Activity 1.23

1.23 Video Learning Experience

Review Session

Viewing Goal: To help you remember how to produce the signs introduced in this lesson.

Viewing Instructions: Watch this video segment carefully to see how each sign is made, and take note of any hints given that might help you remember. You may want to copy the signs as you watch Billy.

The following are the vocabulary and explanations offered in this video segment:

MORNING	One arm becomes the horizon. The other hand is the sun rising.
GOOD	This sign is a symbol representing the concept GOOD.
COFFEE	This sign comes from the old hand-operated coffee grinder.
NO	N-O, this was originally spelled out. This has since evolved into a sign.
THANK-YOU	This sign is like blowing a kiss.
HUNGRY	This sign shows there's no food in your stomach. You're empty.
CHILDREN	This sign is as if you are patting children on the head.
WHERE	This is a symbol representing the concept WHERE.
TIME	This sign refers to a watch on the wrist.
WAKE-UP	You're sleeping and when you wake up, your eyes open.
NOW	The space in front of the body represents the future. The space behind the body is the past. Directly in front and close to the body is NOW.
PAST	Remember the space behind the body represents the PAST.
OK	This sign is spelled out... O-K.
MOTHER	In ASL, feminine signs tend to occur on or near the chin.
GIRL	This sign comes from the bonnets worn long ago and represents the strap tied under the chin.
FATHER	ASL tends to place masculine signs on or near the forehead.
BOY	This sign comes from the brim of a baseball cap.
BABY	This looks like holding a BABY.
DAUGHTER	A compound sign combining the signs for GIRL and BABY.
SON	Another compound sign using the signs BOY and BABY.

Lesson One: *Meet the Bravo Family*

YES	This sign represents the head nodding YES.
WHAT	This is a symbol representing the concept of WHAT.
HEARING	This sign really means people who can talk. But, I want to make it clear that this doesn't mean Deaf people cannot talk. It means that Deaf people cannot hear themselves talk.
DEAF	This means that the ears and the mouth are closed. Again, this does not mean Deaf people can't talk, because most (physiologically) can.
WANT	There are things out there that you want, so you pull them to you.
WHICH	On one side is YES, on the other side is NO... WHICH will it be?
LOVE	This sign shows holding the one you love close to your heart.
BRUSH-TEETH	This looks like brushing your teeth.
GET-DRESSED	This sign shows the activity of putting clothes on.
SCHOOL	When teachers want a class's attention, they clap their hands.
READY	This sign shows your body poised and ready to go, using the "R" handshapes.
BATHROOM/ TOILET	This is the symbol for BATHROOM. The "T" represents the "T" in TOILET.
GO	You're in one place and you want to go to another place. This sign represents that movement.
DOG	When you want a dog's attention, you whistle or slap your thighs.
MY/MINE	These signs show possession: MINE, OURS, HIS, and HERS.
FOOL-YOU	The index finger on one hand represents a person and the other hand is hitting (fooling) that person.
ALMOST	One hand slides up the other hand, not all the way to the top, but ALMOST.
SHOWER	This sign represents the water spraying down on you.
BREAKFAST	This is a compound sign combining FOOD and MORNING.
KITCHEN	This is another compound sign combining the signs for COOK and ROOM.

Lesson One: *Meet the Bravo Family*

1.24 Video Learning Experience

Practice Session: Sentences

Viewing Goal: To improve comprehension skills by watching sentences presented in ASL.

Viewing Instructions:
1. **Ask** students to read *Practice Session: Sentences* in their workbooks (activity 1.24).

2. **Play** the video segment entitled *Practice Session: Sentences* (segment 1.24). Each sentence is signed twice and an English translation is provided.

3. **Remind** students to watch the face of each signer to see the facial/body expressions and non-manual grammatical markers as well as the signs.

Video Segment Content: (1 1/2 Minutes)

The following are English translations of the practice sentences:

1. Are you Deaf?
2. Yes, I am Deaf.
3. I'm not a Deaf person, I'm a hearing person.
4. Good morning! Do you want some coffee?
5. I love you.
6. It's time to wake up now.

Student Workbook: Activity 1.24

1.24 Video Learning Experience

Practice Session: Sentences

Viewing Goal: To improve your comprehension skills by watching sentences presented in ASL.

Viewing Instructions: Watch the signed sentences for comprehension. Remember to watch the face of each signer to see the facial/body expressions and the non-manual grammatical markers as well as the signs.

It is recommended that you copy each signed sentence when it is repeated.

In the space below, record any questions or notes you have regarding the sentences.

Notes: _____
_____
_____
_____

1.25 Experiential Activity

What's the Sentence About?

Activities Video

Activity Goal: To improve comprehension skills using sentences presented in ASL.

Activity Instructions:
1. **Ask** students to read *What's the Sentence About?* in their workbooks (activity 1.25).

2. **Show** students the *What's the Sentence About?* segment of the Activities Video (segment 1.25). Each sample will be signed twice.

3. **Instruct** students to view the sentences carefully and select the answer which best describes what the sentence is about. **Ask** students to record the answers in their workbooks.

4. Upon completing this activity, **show** overhead (Appendix 1.25) and **review** the answers. **Model** any items the students found to be difficult. You may want to **show** the video again, **working** with the students as they review their answers.

Video Segment Content: The following are the samples presented in this segment
(1 1/2 Minutes) of the Activities Video (segment 1.25):

1. GOOD MORNING
2. MOM, WHERE (t, wh-q)
3. BATHROOM, WHERE (t, wh-q)
4. TIME BRUSH-TEETH
5. SCHOOL, GO WHICH (t, wh-q)

Lesson One: *Meet the Bravo Family*

Student Workbook: Activity 1.25

Overhead Master: Appendix 1.25

1.25 Experiential Activity

What's the Sentence About?

Activity Goal: To improve your comprehension skills using sentences presented in ASL.

Activity Instructions: You will see five signed sentences. Each sentence will be signed twice. Determine what each sentence is about and circle the correct answer below:

1. A. Going to school
   B. A morning greeting
   C. Taking a shower

2. A. Looking for Dad
   B. Looking for Daughter
   C. Looking for Mom

3. **A. Needing a bathroom**
   B. Needing a drink
   C. Needing a shower

4. A. Time to eat
   B. Time to brush your teeth
   C. Time to have coffee

5. **A. Asking about school**
   B. Asking about work
   C. Asking about breakfast

1.26 Experiential Activity

It's Just a Drill!

Activity Goal: To apply the grammatical aspects and the ASL vocabulary introduced in this lesson by doing practice drills.

Activity Instructions:
1. **Ask** students to read *It's Just a Drill!* in their workbooks (activity 1.26).

2. **Divide** the class into pairs.

3. **Ask** pairs to practice signing the drills.

4. **Observe** student performance and **model** necessary corrections.

Lesson One: *Meet the Bravo Family*

Student Workbook: Activity 1.26

1.26 Experiential Activity

It's Just a Drill!

Activity Goal: To improve your expressive skills by doing practice drills.

Activity Instructions: With a partner, practice the following drills together. Remember to include the non-manual question markers to identify the type of question you are asking.

```
                        ____q
COFFEE,                 WANT
SHOWER,
GO SCHOOL,

                        ____wh-q
MOTHER,                 WHERE
FATHER,
SON,
DAUGHTER,

                        ____q
HUNGRY,                 YOU
MOTHER,
GO SCHOOL,
READY,

                        ____q
BATHROOM,               YOU GO
SCHOOL,
KITCHEN,

                        ____q
BRUSH-TEETH,            YOU
HEARING,
DEAF,
WAKE-UP,
```

Note: A "q" means this is a yes/no question. A "wh-q" means it is a wh-question type. To review how to produce these question types, see the *Grammatical Notes* (activity 1.19).

1.27 Video Learning Experience

Practice Session: Story

Viewing Goal: To improve comprehension skills by watching a story presented in ASL.

Viewing Instructions:
1. **Ask** students to read *Practice Session: Story* in their workbooks (activity 1.27).

2. **Show** the video segment entitled *Practice Session: Story* (segment 1.27). Billy signs a story using the vocabulary introduced in this lesson. **Turn off** audio and captions.

Lesson One: *Meet the Bravo Family*

Video Segment Content:
(2 1/2 Minutes)

3. **Instruct** students to watch the signed story and write a summary of the main points.

The following is an English translation of the story:

It was morning. The children woke up and went to the kitchen. They were hungry.

The mother was there. The dog was there, eating.

The mother looked at the children and said, "Both of you go upstairs to the bathroom, brush your teeth, shower, and get dressed. Then you can come back to the kitchen and we'll have breakfast."

The son said, "Okay!"

But the daughter said, "I'm hungry! I want to eat now! The dog is eating now! I want to eat now!"

The mother said, "Okay, you can have the dog's food. Help yourself!"

The daughter said, "No, thank you! I'll go upstairs to the bathroom, brush my teeth, take a shower and get dressed, and then come back to the kitchen to eat breakfast. Okay?"

The mother smiled and said, "Okay. Good girl. I love you."

Student Workbook:
Activity 1.27

1.27 Video Learning Experience

Practice Session: Story

Viewing Goal: To improve your comprehension skills by watching a story presented in ASL.

Viewing Instructions: Watch the signed story for comprehension. In the space below, write a summary of the main points from the story.

Summary: _____
_____
_____
_____

Lesson One: *Meet the Bravo Family*

1.28 Comprehension Quiz

What Did You Understand?

Quiz Goal: To assess students' comprehension of the signed story.

Quiz Instructions:
1. **Instruct** students to complete the quiz in their workbooks (activity 1.28).

2. **Collect** for grading or **show** overhead (Appendix 1.28) and **ask** individual students to indicate the correct answers on the overhead while class members correct their own work.

3. **Ask** students to indicate which item(s) from the quiz they found difficult. **Review** by **modeling** or **replaying** that segment of the videotape.

Student Workbook: Activity 1.28

Overhead Master: Appendix 1.28

1.28 Comprehension Quiz

What Did You Understand?

Quiz Goal: To see how much of the signed story you understood.

Quiz Instructions: Read and answer each question below.

1. When did this story take place?
   In the morning.

2. Where did the story take place?
   In the kitchen.

3. Who was there?
   The mother, daughter, son and the dog.

4. What did the children want?
   They were hungry and wanted breakfast.

5. What did Mom want the children to do?
   Brush their teeth, shower, get dressed, and then come back to the kitchen for breakfast.

6. How did the son respond?
   The son said, "Okay!"

7. How did the daughter respond?
   The daughter said, "I'm hungry! I want to eat now! The dog is eating! I want to eat!"

8. What did the mother suggest?
   "Okay, you can have the dog's food. Help yourself!"

9. Did the daughter want to do that?
   No.

10. What did the daughter decide to do?
    She decided to do as her mother asked (get ready, then eat).

Instructor's Guide: Lesson One
Bravo ASL! Curriculum

©1996 Sign Enhancers, Inc.
ALL RIGHTS RESERVED.

Lesson One: *Meet the Bravo Family*

1.29 Homework Assignment

Meet My Family

Homework Goal: To provide students with the opportunity to improve ASL expressive skills.

Homework Instructions:
1. **Ask** students to read *Meet My Family* in their workbooks (activity 1.29).
2. **Request** that students bring in pictures of their own families or a family pictured in a magazine. (You may want to **bring** a picture of your family or a family pictured in a magazine to **model** the activity for students.)
3. **Ask** students to be prepared to "introduce" each person in the picture by pointing and using the new sign vocabulary.

Instructor Tip: *An opportunity for students to perform this assignment has been scheduled in the next lesson (Homework Review 2.2).*

Student Workbook: Activity 1.29

1.29 Homework Assignment

Meet My Family

Homework Goal: To help you improve your ASL expressive skills.

Homework Instructions: For the next class session, bring in a picture(s) of your own family, or one pictured in a magazine. Be prepared to "introduce" each person in the picture(s) by pointing and using the new ASL vocabulary.

Lesson One: *Meet the Bravo Family*

1.30 Post-test

What Do You Know Now?

Assessment Video

Post-test Goal: To assess students' mastery of the lesson objectives.

Post-test Instructions:

1. **Ask** students to read the Post-test Introduction in their workbooks (activity 1.30).

2. **Copy** and **distribute** the Lesson One Post-test (Appendix 1.30).

3. **Play** the Assessment Video (segment 1.30) and allow students to complete Section One (comprehension portion) of the test.

4. **Instruct** students to complete Section Two (culture and grammar portion) of the test individually and hand in their papers when they are finished.

5. **Assign** Section Three (expressive portion) of the test and **schedule** a time when students are to perform. If possible, it is strongly recommended that you **videotape** this portion of the Post-test.

6. **Determine** grading options based upon programmatic requirements. A recommended guideline for measuring successful mastery of objectives is 80% accuracy.

Video Segment Content:
(2 Minutes)

The following are English translations of the comprehension sentences:

1. I am Deaf.
2. The daughter needs to go to the bathroom.
3. Mother wants coffee.
4. The children go to school.
5. The son loves the dog.

Lesson One: *Meet the Bravo Family*

Student Workbook:
Activity 1.30

1.30 Post-test Introduction

What Do You Know Now?

Post-test Goal: To assess your mastery of the lesson objectives.

Post-test Introduction: This test has three sections:

Section One: The Comprehension section tests your ability to understand ASL.

Section Two: The Culture and Grammar section tests your knowledge of the material presented in the *Cultural* and *Grammatical Notes*.

Section Three: The Expressive portion tests your ability to use ASL.

Simply follow the instructions for each section. **Good luck!**

Post-test Master:
Appendix 1.30

1.30 Post-test

Section One: Comprehension

Instructions: You will see five signed sentences. Watch carefully and answer each question below.

1. The signer is _____.
   A. Hearing
   B. Deaf
   C. A father

2. The daughter needs to go to _____.
   A. The bathroom
   B. The kitchen
   C. School

3. Who wants coffee?
   A. Father
   B. Mother
   C. The son

4. Where do the children go?
   A. To the bathroom
   B. To the kitchen
   C. To school

5. Who loves the dog?
   A. The father
   B. The daughter
   C. The son

Post-test Master:
Appendix 1.30

1.30 Post-test

Section Two: Culture and Grammar

Instructions: Read each statement carefully and determine if it is True or False (circle your answer).

6. Deaf culture has its own language, customs, and values.
   A. True
   B. False

7. A gentle tap on the shoulder is an appropriate technique for getting a Deaf person's attention.
   A. True
   B. False

8. The non-manual markers associated with yes/no questions include raised eyebrows and the head slightly tilted.
   A. True
   B. False

9. The non-manual markers associated with wh-questions include raised eyebrows and the head slightly tilted.
   A. True
   B. False

10. ASL grammar is the same as English grammar except that ASL is visual.
    A. True
    B. False

Lesson One: *Meet the Bravo Family*

Post-test Master:
Appendix 1.30

1.30 Post-test

Section Three: Expressive Portion

Instructions: Describe your family's morning routine, using at least seven signs learned in Lesson One. Also include three questions: two yes/no questions and one wh-question. Be sure to use appropriate non-manual markers.

Your instructor will schedule a specific time for you to perform this section of the post-test. You may prepare and practice prior to your scheduled time. Use the space below to prepare for your expressive performance.

Include at least seven signs from Lesson One.

11. _____
12. _____
13. _____
14. _____
15. _____
16. _____
17. _____

Include two yes/no questions:

18. _____
19. _____

Include one wh-question:

20. _____

*Congratulations!
You have completed
Lesson One!*

Lesson 2
BREAKFAST WITH THE BRAVO FAMILY

Materials Needed

Equipment: VCR and TV monitor
Overhead projector and screen
Chalk/dry erase board
Optional: video camera for activity 2.24

Materials: Instructor's Guide
Student Workbook: one per student
Overhead transparencies for activities 2.3, 2.4, 2.6, 2.8, 2.10, 2.16, 2.19 2.20, and 2.22 (see Appendix for masters)
Handouts 2.13A and 2.13B (see Appendix for masters)
Optional: blank videotape (or have students bring their own) for activity 2.24
Post-test: Appendix 2.24

Videotapes: The Beginning ASL VideoCourse Lesson Two
Activities Video for activity 2.19
Assessment Video for Post-test 2.24

2.1 Begin Class
Housekeeping

Goal: To prepare students for this lesson.

Instructions: 1. Welcome students to Lesson Two of the VideoCourse.

2. Perform any necessary tasks (such as taking attendance) that may be required by your specific program.

Instructor's Guide: Lesson Two
Bravo ASL! Curriculum

©1996 Sign Enhancers, Inc.
ALL RIGHTS RESERVED.

Lesson Two: *Breakfast With the Bravo Family*

2.2 Homework Review

Meet My Family

Activity Goal: To provide feedback on previously assigned homework and to reinforce materials learned in Lesson One.

Activity Instructions:

1. **Ask** students to read *Meet My Family* in their workbooks (activity 2.2), and take out the family picture they brought to class (*Homework Assignment 1.29*).

2. **Divide** the class into small groups of four or five students.

3. **Begin** this activity by using ASL to **introduce** your own family (or one pictured in a magazine) to the class. This will reinforce previously learned information as the students see you **model** the signs for family members.

4. **Instruct** students to take turns using ASL to introduce each of the family members in the pictures they brought.

5. **Circulate** among the groups to **observe** their progress.

6. At completion of the group work, **ask** for two or three volunteers to introduce their family members to the entire class. **Praise** them for their willingness to share their new skills with the class.

Student Workbook: Activity 2.2

2.2 Homework Review

Meet My Family

Activity Goal: To show what you did for homework.

Activity Instructions: Take out the picture(s) of your own family or a family pictured in a magazine. Using ASL, introduce each person in the picture(s) by pointing and using the ASL vocabulary.

2.3 Pretest
What Do You Know?

Pretest Goal: To identify students' current level of knowledge pertaining to the lesson content.

Pretest Instructions:
1. **Ask** students to complete the pretest in their workbooks (activity 2.3).

2. **Show** overhead (Appendix 2.3) and **ask** individual students to indicate the correct answers on the overhead while class members correct their own work.

3. **Inform** students that the contents of the pretest will be taught throughout the lesson.

Student Workbook: Activity 2.3

Overhead Master: Appendix 2.3

2.3 Pretest

What Do You Know?

Pretest Goal: To see how much you already know about what will be taught in this lesson.

Pretest Instructions: Read each question and circle the best answer.

1. Deaf people should be viewed with pity.
   A. True
   B. False

2. Families with Deaf members can be closely connected.
   A. True
   B. False

3. Like English, adjectives in ASL are usually placed before the noun.
   A. True
   B. False

4. Signs can be modified by changing the movement of the sign.
   A. True
   B. False

5. Adjectives can be modified simply by changing facial expressions.
   A. True
   B. False

Lesson Two: *Breakfast With the Bravo Family*

2.4 Lesson Objectives

Planning for Success

Goal: To identify the learning outcomes associated with successful completion of this lesson.

Instructions:
1. **Ask** students to read the objectives in their workbooks (activity 2.4).
2. **Show** overhead (Appendix 2.4) and **read** through the objectives with the class.

Student Workbook: Activity 2.4

Overhead Master: Appendix 2.4

> 2.4 Lesson Objectives
>
> *Planning for Success*
>
> **Goal:** To see what you will learn by the end of this lesson.
>
> **Instructions:** Read the objectives below.
>
> Upon completing this VideoCourse lesson, you will be able to...
>
> 1. Recognize and accurately produce the ASL vocabulary introduced in this and the previous lesson.
> 2. Describe two distinct perspectives generally held regarding members of the Deaf community.
> 3. Use noun/adjective combinations appropriately in ASL.
> 4. Demonstrate how signs can be modified in ASL.

Lesson Two: *Breakfast With the Bravo Family*

2.5 Lesson Focus

That's NOT What I Ordered!

Activity Goal: To develop a need for the ASL vocabulary introduced in this lesson.

Activity Instructions:

1. **Ask** students to read *That's NOT What I Ordered!* in their workbooks (activity 2.5).

2. **Divide** the class into small groups of four or five.

3. **Indicate** that students are to role-play going out to breakfast. **Assign** them the task of placing food orders with a "server" without using their voices.

4. **Ask** the students to begin the activity. **Tell** each group to select one student to be the "server" (who will record all breakfast orders) while the other members in the group will be "diners." **Instruct** students to take turns ordering their favorite breakfast without using their voices. **Encourage** students to use mime, gestures, and any signs they know.

5. **Circulate** among the groups to **observe** their progress. **Assist** by **modeling** (with a student volunteer in the role of the server) several appropriate ways to order a meal with the use of mime and gestures.

6. When students have completed this activity, you may **choose**:

   Option A: **Bring** the whole class together and **lead** a discussion using the following Thought/Discussion Questions:

   1) What are some signs related to ordering breakfast that would have been useful to know during this activity?

   2) How did it feel to be limited in your ability to communicate?

   3) When Deaf people go out to a restaurant, what are some communication techniques they could use?

   OR

   Option B: **Ask** students to complete the Thought/Discussion Questions in their workbooks in class or for homework. **Collect** for grading or to provide students with written feedback.

Lesson Two: *Breakfast With the Bravo Family*

7. **Inform** students that they will learn several of the signs they needed to perform this activity by the end of this lesson.

Student Workbook: Activity 2.5

2.5 Lesson Focus

That's NOT What I Ordered!

Activity Goal: To practice communicating about breakfast without using your voice.

Activity Instructions: Your instructor will divide the class into small groups. Each group will role-play going out to breakfast. Select one student to be the "server" while the other members are the "diners."

When ordering breakfast, all participants should use mime, gestures, or signs. The diners are not to write or use their voices.

The server should write down the order as s/he understood it. After all the orders in the group have been taken, see if the order taken was what you wanted. Enjoy your breakfast!

Thought/Discussion Questions

1. What are some signs related to ordering breakfast that would have been useful to know during this activity?

2. How did it feel to be limited in your ability to communicate?

3. When Deaf people go out to a restaurant, what are some communication techniques they could use?

2.6 Language Learning Activity

Learning New Signs

Goal: To use ASL and visual aids to introduce this lesson's vocabulary.

Instructions:

1. **Ask** students to read *Learning New Signs* in their workbooks (activity 2.6).

2. **Show** the overhead (Appendix 2.6). **Introduce** the vocabulary by **pointing** to items presented in the pictures while **demonstrating** the signs.

3. **Reinforce** retention and **check** students' comprehension by **using** these signs to **ask** students questions.

Note: For a step-by-step review of this method, see Lesson One (activities 1.6 and 1.12).

Lesson Two: *Breakfast With the Bravo Family*

4. **Continue** this process until all the ASL vocabulary items have been introduced.

Overhead Content: Use the pictures in the overhead (Appendix 2.6) to introduce the signs representing the following concepts:

1. COOK	11. GIVE	21. NAPKIN
2. EAT	12. TELL	22. WORK
3. EGG	13. WAITER	23. DO-WHAT
4. TOAST	14. GONE	24. WASH
5. CEREAL	15. SET+TABLE	25. HELP
6. ORANGE+JUICE	16. PLATE	26. MY-TURN
7. BANANA	17. GLASS	27. YOUR-TURN
8. MILK	18. FORK	28. YESTERDAY
9. ONE: (1)	19. KNIFE	
10. TWO: (2)	20. SPOON	

Note: Some pictures can be used to represent several concepts. For verbs and more abstract concepts, you may need to supplement these pictures with mime, gestures, using actual objects, and acting out the concepts in class.

Overhead Master: Appendix 2.6

Lesson Two: *Breakfast With the Bravo Family*

Student Workbook:
Activity 2.6

2.6 Language Learning Instruction

Learning New Signs

Goal: To help you learn new ASL vocabulary.

Instructions: Your instructor will teach you new signs! Watch closely to learn what these signs mean and how they are produced.

In the space below, record any notes to help you remember the signs.

Notes: _____
_____
_____
_____

2.7 Video Learning Experience

Introduction to New Vocabulary

Viewing Goal: To provide a signed demonstration of the accurate production of the new ASL vocabulary.

Viewing Instructions:
1. **Ask** students to read *Introduction to New Vocabulary* in their workbooks (activity 2.7).

2. **Play** the video segment entitled *Introduction to New Vocabulary* (segment 2.7). It begins with the Bravo family at the breakfast table with Billy giving a brief introduction. Billy then introduces and signs each new vocabulary item twice. (If you wish to keep this activity a strictly visual presentation, **turn off** audio.)

3. **Instruct** students to watch how Billy produces the signs as well as the accompanying facial/body expressions.

4. **Ask** students to copy the signs and the facial/body expressions as Billy repeats each one.

Video Segment Summary: The following is a summary of Billy's introduction:
(6 Minutes)

Billy joins the Bravo family as they prepare for breakfast. He says he is hungry and invites you to join them. The dad comes in and greets the family. He has been cooking all morning, and asks if everyone is hungry. Anna and Scott are both hungry, especially Scott after his busy morning. Billy then introduces the new vocabulary.

Lesson Two: *Breakfast With the Bravo Family*

See the following Student Workbook excerpt for the remaining content.

Student Workbook: Activity 2.7

2.7 Video Learning Experience

Introduction to New Vocabulary

Viewing Goal: To help you learn the new ASL vocabulary.

Viewing Instructions: Watch how Billy produces each sign. Be sure to notice the facial/body expressions. Copy the signs as Billy repeats each one.

Signs representing the following concepts are introduced in this video segment:

1. COOK	11. GIVE	21. NAPKIN
2. EAT	12. TELL	22. WORK
3. EGG	13. WAITER	23. DO-WHAT
4. TOAST	14. GONE	24. WASH
5. CEREAL	15. SET+TABLE	25. HELP
6. ORANGE+JUICE	16. PLATE	26. MY-TURN
7. BANANA	17. GLASS	27. YOUR-TURN
8. MILK	18. FORK	28. YESTERDAY
9. ONE	19. KNIFE	
10. TWO	20. SPOON	

2.8 Experiential Activity

Point and Sign

Activity Goal: To assist students in recognizing the new ASL vocabulary in the context of signed communication.

Activity Instructions:

1. **Ask** students to read *Point and Sign* in their workbooks (activity 2.8).

2. **Show** overhead (Appendix 2.8) containing the activity pictures.

3. **Point** to various items on the picture and sign questions A-F to the students. You may want to **create** additional questions.

4. **Instruct** students to respond appropriately to the questions by signing either YES or NO. Depending on your students' skill level, you might **ask** them to respond using complete sentences.

Lesson Two: *Breakfast With the Bravo Family*

A. **Point** to the milk on the overhead and use ASL to **ask**:
   1. $\overline{\text{IT MILK}}^{q}$
   2. $\overline{\text{IT COFFEE}}^{q}$
   3. $\overline{\text{IT ORANGE+JUICE}}^{q}$

B. **Point** to the banana on the overhead and use ASL to **ask**:
   1. $\overline{\text{IT TOAST}}^{q}$
   2. $\overline{\text{IT BANANA}}^{q}$
   3. $\overline{\text{IT CEREAL}}^{q}$

C. **Point** to the orange juice on the overhead and use ASL to **ask**:
   1. $\overline{\text{IT MILK}}^{q}$
   2. $\overline{\text{IT EGG}}^{q}$
   3. $\overline{\text{IT ORANGE+JUICE}}^{q}$

D. **Point** to the eggs on the overhead and use ASL to **ask**:
   1. $\overline{\text{IT BANANA}}^{q}$
   2. $\overline{\text{IT EGGS}}^{q}$
   3. $\overline{\text{IT MILK}}^{q}$

E. **Point** to the coffee on the overhead and use ASL to **ask**:
   1. $\overline{\text{IT BANANA}}^{q}$
   2. $\overline{\text{IT ORANGE+JUICE}}^{q}$
   3. $\overline{\text{IT MILK}}^{q}$

F. **Use** ASL to **ask** various students in your class:
   1. $\overline{\text{YOU HUNGRY}}^{q}$
   2. $\overline{\text{COFFEE}}^{t}$, $\overline{\text{YOU WANT}}^{q}$
   3. $\overline{\text{ORANGE+JUICE}}^{t}$, $\overline{\text{YOU LOVE}}^{q}$
   4. $\overline{\text{BANANA}}^{t}$, $\overline{\text{EAT WANT}}^{q}$
   5. $\overline{\text{EGG}}^{t}$, $\overline{\text{WANT}}^{q}$

Lesson Two: *Breakfast With the Bravo Family*

Overhead Master:
Appendix 2.8

Student Workbook:
Activity 2.8

2.8 Experiential Activity

Point and Sign

Activity Goal: To help you recognize the new ASL vocabulary within the context of signed communication.

Activity Instructions: Your instructor will point to some pictures and ask you questions using ASL. Watch carefully and follow your instructor's directions in responding to these questions.

Lesson Two: *Breakfast With the Bravo Family*

2.9 Video Learning Experience

Bravo Family Visit

Viewing Goal: To improve ASL comprehension skills by watching a Bravo family interaction.

Viewing Instructions:
1. **Ask** students to read *Bravo Family Visit* in their workbooks (activity 2.9).
2. **Play** the video segment of the Bravo family visit (segment 2.9). The Bravos will use the new ASL vocabulary within the context of having breakfast.
3. **Instruct** students to watch for comprehension and write a summary of the main points.
4. **Replay** any portion of this video segment that students experienced difficulty understanding.

Video Segment Content: (5 Minutes)

The following is a summary of the Bravo family interaction:

Dad is asking the family what they would like for breakfast. He offers them eggs, toast, orange juice, cereal, milk, and bananas. Mom wants a banana.

Dad asks Scott what he would like to have. Scott explains that he wants two eggs, two pieces of toast, a large bowl of cereal with a banana in it, a large glass of milk, and a large glass of orange juice.

Dad acts like a waiter and serves breakfast (signing each item as he serves it to Scott).

Mom explains to Scott that Dad has been cooking and giving Scott all this food. Mom asks what Scott should say to him in return. Instead of saying "thank you," Scott looks around his plate and asks his dad, "Hey, where's the banana?!" Dad laughs and brings Scott a banana. Scott thanks Dad and gives him a tip.

Anna gets her dad's attention and places her order with the "waiter." She requests one egg, one piece of toast, and some orange juice "if it's not all gone!" Dad signs each item as he serves it and Anna thanks him. When Dad puts his hand out for a tip, Anna gives him a "high five" instead!

Lesson Two: *Breakfast With the Bravo Family*

Mom explains to the kids that Dad cooked and that she set the plates, forks, spoons, knives, and cups on the table. Then she asks, since she and Dad have finished their share of the work, what are the children going to do?

Anna tells her that they will work at eating their food! Mom asks who will wash the dishes? Scott licks his fork and explains that he's finished washing his dishes. He complains that now it's Anna's turn.

Anna complains that she washed the dishes yesterday. Scott gives in and says he will finish eating, wash the dishes, and hurry off to school.

Student Workbook:
Activity 2.9

2.9 Video Learning Experience

Bravo Family Visit

Viewing Goal: To improve your ASL comprehension skills by watching a Bravo family interaction.

Viewing Instructions: Watch the signed interaction and write a summary of the main points.

Summary: _____
_____
_____
_____

2.10 Comprehension Quiz

What Did You Understand?

Quiz Goal: To assess students' comprehension of the signed interaction.

Quiz Instructions:
1. **Instruct** students to complete the quiz in their workbooks (activity 2.10).

2. **Collect** for grading or **show** overhead (Appendix 2.10) and **ask** individual students to indicate the correct answers on the overhead while class members correct their own work.

3. **Ask** students to indicate which item(s) from the quiz they found difficult. **Review** by **modeling** or **replaying** that segment of the videotape.

Instructor's Guide: Lesson Two
Bravo ASL! Curriculum

©1996 Sign Enhancers, Inc.
ALL RIGHTS RESERVED.

Lesson Two: *Breakfast With the Bravo Family*

Student Workbook:
Activity 2.10

Overhead Master:
Appendix 2.10

2.10 Comprehension Quiz

What Did You Understand?

Quiz Goal: To see how much of the Bravo family interaction you understood.

Quiz Instructions: Read and answer each question below.

1. Mom wants a(n) _____ for breakfast.
   A. Orange
   B. Banana
   C. Piece of toast
   D. Bowl of cereal

2. Scott orders _____ egg(s).
   A. One
   B. Two
   C. Three
   D. Four

3. Scott also orders a _____ glass of orange juice.
   A. Small
   B. Large

4. Anna orders _____ to drink.
   A. Milk
   B. Water
   C. Orange juice
   D. Coffee

5. Who will be washing the dishes after breakfast?
   A. Mom
   B. Dad
   C. Anna
   D. Scott

2.11 Experiential Activity

Point and Sign

Activity Goal: To assist students in recognizing and producing the new ASL vocabulary.

Activity Instructions:
1. **Ask** students to read *Point and Sign* in their workbooks (activity 2.11).

2. **Divide** the class into pairs and **instruct** students to look at the picture in their workbooks.

3. **Select** and **model** the variation of the *Point and Sign* activity you would like your students to perform. You may **choose** to have students to perform all three variations.

Variation A:

1) **Ask** each pair of students to take turns pointing to an object or action in the picture and producing the sign or signs that best match its meaning.

2) **Instruct** the partner to provide feedback on the correct choice and production of the signs.

Variation B:

1) **Ask** each pair of students to take turns having one student point to an object or action in the picture.

2) **Instruct** the partner to produce the sign or signs that best match its meaning.

Variation C:

1) **Ask** each pair of students to take turns having one student produce a sign or signs that correspond to one of the objects or actions in the picture.

2) **Instruct** the partner to point to the object or action in the picture that best matches the meaning of the sign or signs presented by her/his partner.

4. **Inform** students that this activity is to be done using ASL.

5. **Circulate** among the pairs to **observe** student performance. **Encourage** students to use vocabulary such as: MILK, FATHER, SON, DAUGHTER, BANANA, ORANGE, COFFEE, PLATE, GLASS, EAT, COOK, WASH, SET+TABLE, etc.

6. **Model** the signs as needed.

Student Workbook: Activity 2.11

2.11 Experiential Activity

Point and Sign

Activity Goal: To help you recognize and produce the new ASL vocabulary.

Activity Instructions: Using the picture below, follow your teacher's instructions and practice using your new ASL vocabulary such as: MILK, FATHER, SON, DAUGHTER, BANANA, ORANGE, COFFEE, PLATE, GLASS, EAT, COOK, WASH, SET+TABLE, etc.

Lesson Two: *Breakfast With the Bravo Family*

2.12 Video Learning Experience

Cultural Notes

Viewing Goal: To assist students in learning about the cultural aspects of ASL.

Viewing Instructions:
1. **Ask** students to read *Cultural Notes* in their workbooks (activity 2.12).
2. **Play** the video segment entitled *Cultural Notes* (segment 2.12). Because the presentation of this segment is beyond the linguistic ability of beginning students, please **turn on** the audio and/or captions to optimize its educational value.
3. **Instruct** students to view the segment.
4. At completion of segment, **review** the content presented and **answer** any questions students may have.

Video Segment Content: See the following Student Workbook excerpt for the content
(4 Minutes) of this video segment.

Student Workbook:
Activity 2.12

2.12 Video Learning Experience

Cultural Notes

Viewing Goal: To learn about the cultural aspects of ASL.

Viewing Instructions: View the *Cultural Notes* segment carefully for the following:

I. Families with Deaf members can be very closely connected.
   A. The Bravo family is an example of how families with Deaf members can be warm and fun-loving.
   B. The Bravos demonstrate how wit and cleverness can be used for enhancing the enjoyment of life.

II. There are two common ways of looking at Deaf people:
   A. The handicapped perspective:
      1. This perspective views Deaf people with pity.
      2. This perspective emphasizes what Deaf people can't do...
         a. Can't hear.
         b. Can't talk.
         c. Can't laugh.
         d. Can't live a normal, full life.
      3. This perspective perceives being Deaf as a problem that needs to be fixed.

Instructor's Guide: Lesson Two
Bravo ASL! Curriculum

> B. The cultural perspective:
>   1. This perspective views Deaf people as belonging to a culture equal to all the other cultures of the world.
>   2. This perspective views Deaf people in a positive light, focusing on the potential of Deaf people...
>   a. Deaf people can have full lives.
>   b. They can laugh.
>   c. They have sorrows.
>   d. They have good times and bad.
>
> III. Deaf people are equal to all other peoples.
>
> IV. All people and all cultures should be respected.
>
> V. The Deaf culture exists all around us, making it readily accessible to people wishing to enhance their cultural awareness.

2.13 Experiential Activity

A Cultural Adventure

Activity Goal: To experience a minority/majority culture shift by becoming a visitor within a new culture.

Activity Instructions:

1. **Ask** students to read *A Cultural Adventure** in their workbooks (activity 2.13).

2. **Divide** the class into two groups (preferably each group in a different room). **Inform** students they are to perform this activity without using their voices.

3. **Give** each group a copy of handout 2.13A or 2.13B that explains the rules of the particular "cultural group" to which they have been assigned.

4. **Allow** students 8-10 minutes to learn the rules of their culture. You may want to select one student in each group to be the "cultural leader." **Encourage** students to practice their cultural rituals for a few minutes.

5. **Ask** each group to send two members to the other culture for a three- to four-minute visit (after which the visitors return home to their own culture).

Lesson Two: *Breakfast With the Bravo Family*

6. When all the visits are complete, you may **choose**:

    Option A: **Lead** a discussion with the whole class. **Ask** cultural groups to sit at opposite sides of the room. **Ask** each of the two groups the following Thought/Discussion Questions:

    1) How would you describe the other culture?
        A. What customs did you observe?
        B. What do you think was important to the members of this cultural group?

    2) What was it like for you when you went to visit the other culture?
        A. How did you feel about the other culture?
        B. Did you feel welcome and comfortable?
        C. How did you communicate? Did you learn the language?
        D. What were you able to learn about their culture?

    3) Do you think this is similar to how Deaf people feel in an environment that is dominated by the hearing culture and its values? Give some examples...

    OR

    Option B: **Instruct** students to respond to these Thought/Discussion Questions in the space provided in their workbooks in class or for homework. **Collect** for grading or to provide written feedback.

    Note: This activity is a modification of *BAFA BAFA: A Cross-Cultural Simulation Game* developed by Garry Shirtz (published by Simile II, Del Mar, CA).

Lesson Two: *Breakfast With the Bravo Family*

Student Handout Master:
Appendix 2.13A

2.13 Experiential Activity
Student Handout 2.13A

Grokker Culture: Orientation Training

You are now a proud member of the Grokker Culture!

Ours is a beautiful culture. We value loving connections with others above all else! We therefore choose only to communicate when physically touching one another. It is considered very rude and anti-loving to communicate unless you are touching the other person either shoulder-to-shoulder, foot-to-foot, or arm-to-arm.

The activity we most value is gathering in a loving group, shoulder-to-shoulder. We lovingly invite everyone to get "connected." Anyone NOT connected in a group is always invited. To invite someone to join in a group, we scratch our noses. To answer "Yes, I want to join!" we stomp our feet on the floor. To answer "No, I'd rather not join!" we nod our heads up and down.

The language we use is ASL. We mostly spend our time appreciating each other shoulder-to-shoulder, but when we do communicate, it is usually to discuss our favorite topic... FOOD! A very common greeting would include a question about what a person ate for breakfast.

We will visit another culture today - the Artifs. We know little about who they are or what they value. We must ask to "join" with others, Grokkers and Artifs alike, by nose scratching.

Good luck! May the loving connection be with you!

Student Handout Master:
Appendix 2.13B

2.13 Experiential Activity
Student Handout 2.13B

Artif Culture: Orientation Training

You are a proud member of the Artif Culture!

Ours is a very intelligent and practical culture based on the productive goals of trade.

Ours is a mathematical and scientific world. We communicate in numerical values. For example, "3" means "yes" and "2" means "no" in our culture. We simply hold up the correct number of fingers to show the numbers.

Our goal is to trade and gather as many pens and pencils of like colors as we can from all people we meet. In our language, "1" means "pen" and "4" means "pencil."

We ask for a pen or pencil by holding up one or four fingers and then holding up fingers for the number of pens/pencils we want (1, 2, 3, etc.). To indicate desired color, we point to something with that color. For example, to ask for five red pens you would hold up one finger (pen), then five fingers, and then point to something red. Because we always keep our trading goals in mind, we are a people of few words!

We will visit another culture today - the Grokkers. We know little about who they are or what they value. We must trade with others - Grokkers and Artifs alike - in order to collect pens and pencils.

Good luck! May the numbers be with you!

Lesson Two: *Breakfast With the Bravo Family*

Student Workbook:
Activity 2.13

2.13 Experiential Activity

A Cultural Adventure!

Activity Goal: To provide you with a new cultural experience!

Activity Instructions: Your class will be divided into two cultures: The Grokkers and the Artifs.

Each culture will live in a different room. When you join your group, you will receive a cultural orientation.

You will also have the opportunity to visit the other culture! Enjoy the experience!

Thought/Discussion Questions

1. How would you describe the other culture?
   A. What customs did you observe?
   B. What do you think was important to the members of this cultural group?

2. What was it like for you when you went to visit the other culture?
   A. How did you feel about the other culture?
   B. Did you feel welcome and comfortable?
   C. How did you communicate? Did you learn the language?
   D. What were you able to learn about their culture?

3. Do you think this is similar to how Deaf people feel in an environment that is dominated by the hearing culture and its values? Give some examples.

2.14 Video Learning Experience

Grammatical Notes

Viewing Goal: To assist students in learning about the grammatical aspects of ASL.

Viewing Instructions:
1. **Ask** students to read *Grammatical Notes* in their workbooks (activity 2.14).

2. **Play** the video segment entitled *Grammatical Notes* (segment 2.14). Because the presentation of this segment is beyond the linguistic ability of beginning students, please **turn on** the audio and/or captions to optimize its educational value.

3. **Instruct** students to view the segment.

4. At the completion of the segment, **review** the content presented, and **answer** any questions students may have.

Lesson Two: *Breakfast With the Bravo Family*

Video Segment Content: See the following Student Workbook excerpt for the content
(5 Minutes) of this video segment.

Student Workbook:
Activity 2.14

2.14 Video Learning Experience

Grammatical Notes

Viewing Goal: To learn about the grammatical aspects of ASL.

Viewing Instructions: View the *Grammatical Notes* segment carefully for the following:

I. Adjectives:
   A. The English language tends to place the adjective before the noun.
   B. ASL tends to put the adjective after the noun.

II. Adjectives can be modified by:
   A. Changing the movement of the sign.
   B. Using facial expressions.
   C. Using body language.

III. Signs can be modified by:
   A. Inflection.
   B. Repetition.
   C. Placement or location.

2.15 Experiential Activity

Modify Me!

Activity Goal: To apply the grammatical information by modifying meaning through inflection, repetition, and location.

Activity Instructions:

1. **Ask** students to read *Modify Me!* in their workbooks (activity 2.15).

2. **Divide** the class into groups of four or five students.

3. **Instruct** students to take turns producing the signs listed in their workbooks, applying the modifications indicated.

4. **Circulate** among the groups to **observe** student performance.

5. **Correct** production errors by **modeling** the accurate production of the signs.

6. When the group work is completed, **ask** various students to select one of the signs listed in the activity and demonstrate one of the suggested modifications. **Instruct** the other students to determine which item the student is demonstrating.

Instructor's Guide: Lesson Two
Bravo ASL! Curriculum

Lesson Two: *Breakfast With the Bravo Family*

7. **Continue** the activity until accurate production of all modifications has been demonstrated.

Student Workbook: Activity 2.15

2.15 Experiential Activity

Modify Me!

Activity Goal: To use the grammatical information by modifying the meaning of various signs.

Activity Instructions: Practice producing the list of signs below. Modify the production of each as indicated. Use inflection, repetition, and changing the location as discussed in the *Grammatical Notes* segment.

Note: Remember to use the appropriate facial/body expressions!

Sign	Modify the sign to show...			
WORK	a short time	a long time	really hard	very easy
COOK	a short time	a long time	boring	fun
EAT	quickly	slowly	a long time	a lot of food
GIVE	a lot to you	a little to me	to everyone	over and over
TELL	many people	one person	a secret	over and over
HELP	many people	me quickly	struggling	over and over
WANT	desperately	excitedly	many things	begging
GO	many places	same place	happily	sadly

2.16 Cultural and Grammatical Quiz

What Did You Learn?

Quiz Goal: To assess students' mastery of the cultural and grammatical information.

Quiz Instructions:
1. **Ask** students to complete the quiz in their workbooks (activity 2.16).

2. **Collect** written quiz for grading or **show** overhead (Appendix 2.16) and **ask** individual students to indicate the correct answers on the overhead while class members correct their own work.

2.16 Culture and Grammar Quiz

What Did You Learn?

Quiz Goal: To see how much of this lesson's cultural and grammatical information you learned.

Quiz Instructions: Read and answer each question below.

1. Families with Deaf members can be closely connected.
   A. True
   B. False

2. The handicapped perspective views Deaf people in a positive manner.
   A. True
   B. False

3. The culture of Deaf people is equal to all other cultures.
   A. True
   B. False

4. The cultural perspective views Deaf people as having full lives.
   A. True
   B. False

5. Adjective placement in ASL follows the same rules as adjective placement in English.
   A. True
   B. False

6. In ASL, adjectives tend to be placed _____.
   A. Before the noun
   B. At the end of the sentence
   C. After the noun
   D. At the beginning of the sentence

7. Adjectives are modified in the following ways (check all that apply):
   X Changing the movement of the sign
   X Changing facial expression
   X Changing body language
   __ Changing dominant/non-dominant hands

8. Signs can be modified by (check all that apply):
   X Inflection
   X Repetition
   __ Slight head tilt
   X Changing location/placement

Student Workbook:
Activity 2.16

Overhead Master:
Appendix 2.16

Lesson Two: *Breakfast With the Bravo Family*

2.17 Video Learning Experience

Review Session

Viewing Goal: To reinforce recognition and production of the signs introduced in this lesson.

Viewing Instructions:

1. **Ask** students to read *Review Session* in their workbooks (activity 2.17).

2. **Play** the video segment entitled *Review Session* (segment 2.17). Billy compares the symbolic nature of ASL to the use of symbols in other languages. He then reviews all the ASL vocabulary and provides visual cues and origin information. Because the presentation of this segment is beyond the linguistic ability of beginning students, please **turn on** the audio and/or captions to optimize its educational value.

3. **Ask** students to pay careful attention to the signed vocabulary items and take note of visual hints offered by Billy that might help them remember.

4. **Suggest** that students copy the signs to reinforce retention of sign production.

Video Segment Content: See the following Student Workbook excerpt for the content
(8 1/2 Minutes) of this video segment.

Student Workbook: Activity 2.17

2.17 Video Learning Experience

Review Session

Viewing Goal: To help you remember how to produce the signs introduced in this lesson.

Viewing Instructions: Watch this video segment carefully to see how each sign is made, and take note of any hints given that might help you remember. You may want to copy the signs as you watch Billy.

The following are the vocabulary and explanations offered in this video segment:

EAT	Where does the food go? In your mouth.
EGG	This sign reflects breaking an eggshell.
TOAST	This sign reflects the bread being cooked on both sides.
CEREAL	This is a symbol representing CEREAL.

Lesson Two: *Breakfast With the Bravo Family*

ORANGE+JUICE	The first part of the sign means ORANGE. When referring to the juice we add "J."
BANANA	This sign looks like peeling a banana.
MILK	This sign looks like milking a cow.
BOWL	This sign follows the shape of the BOWL.
COOK	This sign looks like cooking eggs or pancakes. You need to flip them over.
GIVE	Someone has something and gives it to another person.
TELL	This sign shows the direction of information as it is passed from one person to another.
WAITER	The first part of this compound sign means SERVE. The last part represents the PERSON who serves.
GONE	Something is no longer there.
FOOD	Well, what do you eat?
TABLE	This sign follows the physical shape of a table.
SET+TABLE	This is an action sign showing the activity of putting things on the table.
PLATE	This sign shows the shape of a plate.
GLASS	This sign shows the shape of a glass.
FORK	This sign shows the shape and use of a fork.
KNIFE	Knives are sharp. Thus, the sign KNIFE.
SPOON	This sign shows how you use a spoon.
NAPKIN	Well, how does one use a napkin?
WORK	This sign comes from the old sign for WORK and has since evolved into the present sign.
DO-WHAT	This sign started out as a fingerspelled word D-O and has evolved into a sign.
WASH	You have a plate, you take a cloth, and you scrub.
WHO	This is the symbol for the concept WHO.
HELP	Long ago this sign looked like helping someone up by the arm. It now uses a smaller movement.
MY-TURN	This sign means you are finished, now, it's my turn.
YOUR-TURN	This sign means I'm finished, now you do it.
YESTERDAY	This sign means one day in the past.
ZOOM	This shows how things become smaller as they go into the distance.

Instructor's Guide: Lesson Two
Bravo ASL! Curriculum

Lesson Two: *Breakfast With the Bravo Family*

2.18 Video Learning Experience

Practice Session: Sentences

Viewing Goal: To improve comprehension skills by watching sentences presented in ASL.

Viewing Instructions:
1. **Ask** students to read *Practice Session: Sentences* in their workbooks (activity 2.18).
2. **Play** the video segment entitled *Practice Session: Sentences* (segment 2.18).
3. **Inform** students that each sentence is signed twice and an English translation is provided.
4. **Remind** students to watch the face of each signer to see the facial/body expressions and non-manual grammatical markers as well as the signs.

Video Segment Content: The following are English translations of the practice
(2 Minutes) sentences:

1. Good morning!
2. I've cooked breakfast. Are you hungry?
3. It's your turn to set the table.
4. Yesterday, the children went to school.
5. I'm hungry. I want to eat now.
6. Do you want a banana?
7. The waiter told me the food was all gone.

Lesson Two: *Breakfast With the Bravo Family*

Student Workbook: Activity 2.18

2.18 Video Learning Experience

Practice Session: Sentences

Viewing Goal: To improve your comprehension skills by watching sentences presented in ASL.

Viewing Instructions: Watch the signed sentences for comprehension. Remember to watch the face of each signer to see the facial/body expressions and the non-manual grammatical markers as well as the signs.

It is recommended that you copy each signed sentence when it is repeated.

In the space below, record any questions or notes you have regarding the sentences.

Notes: _____
_____
_____
_____

2.19 Experiential Activity

What's the Sentence About?

Activities Video

Activity Goal: To improve comprehension skills using sentences presented in ASL.

Activity Instructions:

1. **Ask** students to read *What's the Sentence About?* in their workbooks (activity 2.19).

2. **Show** students the *What's the Sentence About?* segment of the Activities Video (segment 2.19). Each sample will be signed twice.

3. **Instruct** students to view each sentence carefully and select the answer which best describes what the sentence is about. **Ask** students to record each answer in their workbooks.

4. Upon completing this activity, **show** overhead (Appendix 2.19) and **review** the answers. **Model** any items the students found to be difficult. You may want to **show** the video again, **working** with the students as they review their answers.

Lesson Two: *Breakfast With the Bravo Family*

Video Segment Content:
(1 1/2 Minutes)

The following are the samples presented in this segment of the Activities Video (segment 2.19).

1. $\underline{t}$ $\underline{wh\text{-}q}$
   BANANA, WANT WHO

2. $\underline{t}$
   PLATE, ME WASH

3. $\underline{t}$
   EGG, LOVE ME

4. $\underline{t}$
   FOOD, GONE

5. $\underline{t}$ $\underline{wh\text{-}q}$
   SPOON, WHERE

Student Workbook:
Activity 2.19

Overhead Master:
Appendix 2.19

2.19 Experiential Activity

What's the Sentence About?

Activity Goal: To improve your comprehension skills using sentences presented in ASL.

Activity Instructions: You will see five signed sentences. Each sentence will be signed twice. Determine what each sentence is about, and circle the correct answer below:

1. A. Asking who wants milk
   B. Asking who wants to cook
   C. Asking who wants a banana

2. A. Cooking
   B. Washing the plate
   C. Washing the glass

3. **A. A food the signer loves**
   B. A person the signer loves
   C. A person who loves the signer

4. A. There is no time left
   B. There are no spoons left
   C. There is no food left

5. A. Looking for food
   B. Looking for a napkin
   C. Looking for a spoon

Lesson Two: *Breakfast With the Bravo Family*

2.20 Experiential Activity

It's Just a Drill!

Activity Goal: To apply the grammatical aspects and the ASL vocabulary introduced in this lesson by doing practice drills.

Activity Instructions:
1. **Ask** students to read *It's Just a Drill!* in their workbooks (activity 2.20).
2. **Divide** the class into pairs.
3. **Ask** students to practice signing the drills with partners.
4. **Observe** student performance and **model** necessary corrections.

Student Workbook: Activity 2.20

2.20 Experiential Activity

It's Just A Drill!

Activity Goal: To improve your expressive skills by doing practice drills.

Activity Instructions: Find a partner and practice the following drills together. Remember to include non-manual question markers to show questions.

```
                            ____q
EGG,                        WANT
FOOD,
BANANA,
MILK,
                            ____wh-q
PLATE,                      WHO WASH
FORK,
SPOON,
BOWL,
GLASS,

TOAST,                      GIVE-ME
NAPKIN,
KNIFE,
FOOD,

ORANGE+JUICE,               GONE
NAPKIN,
TOAST,
BOWL,

WASH PLATE,                 YOUR-TURN
SET+TABLE,
HELP BABY,
WORK,
```

Instructor's Guide: Lesson Two
Bravo ASL! Curriculum

Lesson Two: *Breakfast With the Bravo Family*

2.21 Video Learning Experience

Practice Session: Story

Viewing Goal: To improve comprehension skills by watching a story presented in ASL.

Viewing Instructions:
1. **Ask** students to read *Practice Session: Story* in their workbooks (activity 2.21).
2. **Show** the video segment entitled *Practice Session: Story* (segment 2.21). Billy signs a story using the vocabulary introduced in this lesson.
3. **Turn off** audio and captions.
4. **Instruct** students to watch the signed story and write a summary of the main points.

Video Segment Content: (2 Minutes)

The following is an English translation of the story:

Once there was a family. There was a mom, a dad, a son and a daughter. The mom was hearing. The dad, the son, and the daughter were Deaf. They also had a dog.

Now, one morning at breakfast, Anna, whose name sign is this ("A" on chest), didn't want to eat. The mother had cooked and cooked. She gave Anna an egg and some toast. But Anna didn't want it. So what did Anna do? She snuck the food under the table and the dog happily ate it all. Later on, when Anna was in school, she was hungry!

Student Workbook: Activity 2.21

2.21 Video Learning Experience

Practice Session: Story

Viewing Goal: To improve your comprehension skills by watching a story presented in ASL.

Viewing Instructions: Watch the signed story for comprehension. In the space below, write a summary to help you remember the story.

Summary: _____
_____
_____
_____

Lesson Two: *Breakfast With the Bravo Family*

2.22 Comprehension Quiz

What Did You Understand?

Quiz Goal: To assess students' comprehension of the signed story.

Quiz Instructions:
1. **Instruct** students to complete the quiz in their workbooks (activity 2.22).

2. **Collect** for grading or **show** overhead (Appendix 2.22) and **ask** individual students to indicate the correct answers on the overhead while class members correct their own work.

3. **Ask** students to indicate which item(s) from the quiz they found difficult. **Review** by **modeling** or **replaying** that segment of the videotape.

Student Workbook: Activity 2.22

Overhead Master: Appendix 2.22

2.22 Comprehension Quiz

What Did You Understand?

Quiz Goal: To see how much of the signed story you understood.

Quiz Instructions: Read and answer each question below.

1. The family in the story consisted of...
   A. A mom, dad and a son
   B. A mom and a daughter
   C. A dad, son and a daughter
   D. A mom, dad, son, and a daughter

2. _____ family member(s) were Deaf.
   A. One
   B. Two
   C. Three
   D. Five

3. The family had a _____ for a pet.
   A. Spider
   B. Cow
   C. Dog
   D. Chicken

4. In the story, who cooked breakfast?
   A. Dad
   B. Mom
   C. Anna
   D. Mom and Anna

Instructor's Guide: Lesson Two
Bravo ASL! Curriculum

©1996 Sign Enhancers, Inc.
ALL RIGHTS RESERVED.

Lesson Two: *Breakfast With the Bravo Family*

5. Why didn't Anna eat?
   A. She doesn't like Dad's cooking.
   B. The dog had taken a bite out of her food.
   C. She wasn't hungry yet.
   D. She was late for school.

6. What did Anna do with her breakfast food?

   She snuck the food under the table for the dog to eat.

7. Later on, what happened to Anna at school?

   She became hungry!

2.23 Homework Assignment

Did You Hear The One About Breakfast?

Homework Goal: To provide students with the opportunity to improve ASL expressive skills.

Homework Instructions:
1. **Ask** students to read *Did You Hear The One About Breakfast?* in their workbooks (activity 2.23).

2. **Ask** students to create a story about their family having breakfast. **Inform** students that the story should include:

   A) At least eight of the vocabulary items introduced in this lesson, and

   B) At least three adjectives or modified signs as demonstrated in the *Grammatical Notes* segment.

Instructor Tip: *An opportunity for students to perform this assignment has been scheduled in the next lesson (Homework Review 3.2). If possible, it is recommended that you arrange to videotape each student's performance of this activity.*

Lesson Two: *Breakfast With the Bravo Family*

Student Workbook:
Activity 2.23

2.23 Homework Assignment

Did You Hear The One About Breakfast?

Homework Goal: To help you improve your ASL expressive skills.

Homework Instructions: Create a story about your family having breakfast. The story must include at least eight of the ASL vocabulary introduced in this lesson. Also use at least three adjectives or signs modified in ways demonstrated in the *Grammatical Notes* section.

2.24 Post-test

What Do You Know Now?

Assessment Video

Post-test Goal: To assess students' mastery of the lesson objectives.

Post-test Instructions:
1. **Ask** students to read the Post-test Introduction in their workbooks (activity 2.24).

2. **Copy** and **distribute** the Lesson Two Post-test (Appendix 2.24).

3. **Play** the Assessment Video (segment 2.24) and allow students to complete Section One (comprehension portion) of the test.

4. **Instruct** students to complete Section Two (culture and grammar portion) of the test individually and hand in their papers when they are finished.

5. **Assign** Section Three (expressive portion) of the test and **schedule** a time when students are to perform. If possible, it is strongly recommended that you **videotape** this portion of the Post-test.

6. **Determine** grading options based upon programmatic requirements. A recommended guideline for measuring successful mastery of objectives is 80% accuracy.

Lesson Two: *Breakfast With the Bravo Family*

**Video Segment Content:
(2 Minutes)**

The following is an English translation of the comprehension story:

It was time for breakfast. The father had already set the table and the mother was cooking the eggs. The son helped pour the orange juice. The daughter fed the dog.

Everyone sat at the table and ate their breakfast. Father had three eggs, two pieces of toast, a banana, and a cup of coffee. Mother had one egg, a piece of toast, and some orange juice.

The son doesn't like eggs, so he had cereal, toast, and orange juice. The daughter had two eggs, one piece of toast, and some orange juice.

After breakfast, the father and daughter washed the dishes. Then Mom and Dad went to work and the children went to school.

Student Workbook:
Activity 2.24

2.24 Post-test Introduction

What Do You Know Now?

Post-test Goal: To assess your mastery of the lesson objectives.

Post-test Introduction: This test has three sections:

Section One: The Comprehension section tests your ability to understand ASL.

Section Two: The Culture and Grammar section tests your knowledge of the material presented in the *Cultural* and *Grammatical Notes*.

Section Three: The Expressive portion tests your ability to use ASL.

Simply follow the instructions for each section. **Good luck!**

Post-test Master:
Appendix 2.24

2.24 Post-test

Section One: Comprehension

Instructions: You will see a signed story. Watch carefully and answer each question below.

1. _____ was cooking breakfast for the family.
   A. The father
   B. The mother
   C. The son
   D. The daughter

2. _____ set the table for breakfast.
   A. Father
   B. Mother
   C. The son
   D. The daughter

3. Who poured the orange juice for breakfast?
   A. Father
   B. Mother
   C. The son
   D. The daughter

4. The daughter gave food to her _____.
   A. Brother
   B. Mother
   C. Sister
   D. Dog

5. What did Father eat for breakfast?
   A. Two eggs, two pieces of toast, an apple, and coffee
   B. Two eggs, two pieces of toast, an apple, and orange juice
   C. Three eggs, two pieces of toast, a banana, and coffee
   D. One egg, two pieces of toast, a banana, and coffee

Lesson Two: *Breakfast With the Bravo Family*

Post-test Master:
Appendix 2.24

2.24 Post-test

Section Two: Culture and Grammar

Instructions: Read and answer each question.

6. In the *Cultural Notes* section, two perspectives commonly held about Deaf people are described as...
   A. Disabled and handicapped
   B. Cultural and subcultural
   C. Monocultural and bicultural
   D. Handicapped and cultural

7. The cultural perspective perceives being Deaf as a problem that needs to be fixed.
   A. True
   B. False

8. According to our *Cultural Notes*, which is **NOT** true:

   A. The Deaf culture is made up of people who share a common language and enjoy loving support of one another.
   B. All cultures deserve equal respect.
   C. To learn ASL correctly, one must fly halfway around the world to experience the true culture.
   D. A non-signing, hearing person entering a room filled with Deaf people might experience a "communication handicap."

9. The way you can modify the meaning of a sign is by:
   A. Repeating the sign to indicate "for a long time."
   B. By changing the movement of the sign to show intensity.
   C. By using your facial expression and body language.
   D. All of the above are correct ways of modifying the meaning of a sign.

10. ASL often places the noun first, followed by the adjective.
    A. True
    B. False

Post-test Master:
Appendix 2.24

2.24 Post-test

Section Three: Expressive Portion

Instructions: Create a story about your favorite breakfast, using at least eight signs learned in Lesson Two. Also, use at least two adjectives or signs you modify as demonstrated in the *Grammatical Notes*.

Your instructor will schedule a specific time for you to perform this section of the Post-test. You may prepare and practice prior to your scheduled time.

Include at least eight signs from Lesson Two:

11. _____
12. _____
13. _____
14. _____
15. _____
16. _____
17. _____
18. _____

Include at least two adjectives or sign modifications:

19. _____
20. _____

Congratulations!
You have completed
Lesson Two!

Lesson 3
Where's The TV Remote?

Materials Needed:

Equipment: VCR and TV monitor
Overhead projector and screen
Optional: video camera for activities 3.2 and 3.27

Materials: Instructor's Guide
Student Workbook: one per student
Overhead transparencies for activities 3.3, 3.4, 3.6, 3.8, 3.10, 3.11, 3.13, 3.15, 3.17, 3.19, 3.22 and 3.25 (see Appendix for masters)
Optional: blank videotape (or have students bring their own) for activities 3.2 and 3.27
Post-test: Appendix 3.27

Videotapes: The Beginning ASL VideoCourse Lesson Three
Activities Video for activities 3.13, 3.19, 3.22
Assessment Video for Post-test 3.27

3.1 Begin Class
Housekeeping

Goal: To prepare students for this lesson.

Instructions:
1. **Welcome** students to Lesson Three of the VideoCourse.

2. **Perform** any necessary tasks (such as taking attendance) that may be required by your specific program.

Lesson Three: *Where's The TV Remote?*

3.2 Homework Review

Did You Hear the One About Breakfast?

Activity Goal: To provide feedback on previously assigned homework and to reinforce materials learned in earlier lessons.

Activity Instructions:

1. **Ask** students to read *Did You Hear the One About Breakfast?* in their workbooks (activity 3.2).

2. **Divide** the class into pairs.

3. **Instruct** students to take turns signing the story they were asked to prepare (*Homework Assignment 2.23*) while their partners practice comprehension.

4. **Encourage** each partner to use ASL to ask questions about the story to indicate accurate comprehension. **Allow** students to help each other with sign production.

5. **Circulate** to **observe** student progress.

6. When students have finished practicing, **ask** for volunteers to demonstrate their stories for the class. If possible, **videotape** each student's performance of this activity.

7. **Close** this activity by **modeling** any signs or grammatical features the students may have had trouble producing.

Student Workbook: Activity 3.2

3.2 Homework Review

Did You Hear the One About Breakfast?

Activity Goal: To show what you did for homework.

Activity Instructions: Find a partner and take turns signing the story you were assigned in Lesson Two.

Remember to include at least eight of the ASL vocabulary introduced in Lesson Two and at least three adjectives or sign modifications.

When your partner is signing, pay close attention and practice your ASL comprehension skills! Use ASL to ask questions about your partner's story.

Lesson Three: *Where's The TV Remote?*

3.3 Pretest
What Do You Know?

Pretest Goal: To identify students' current level of knowledge pertaining to the lesson content.

Pretest Instructions:
1. **Ask** students to read and answer the questions in the pretest in their workbooks (activity 3.3).

2. **Show** overhead (Appendix 3.3) and **ask** individual students to indicate the correct answers on the overhead while class members correct their own work.

3. **Inform** students that the contents of the pretest will be taught throughout the lesson.

Student Workbook: Activity 3.3

Overhead Master: Appendix 3.3

3.3 Pretest

What Do You Know?

Pretest Goal: To see how much you already know about what will be taught in this lesson.

Pretest Instructions: Read each question and circle the best answers.

1. What do Deaf people use in order to communicate on the telephone? (Circle all that apply.)
   A. Caption decoder
   B. TTY
   C. Specially trained hearing dogs
   D. TTY/TDD relay service

2. What does "GA" mean?
   A. Good Attempt
   B. Great Aunt
   C. Go Ahead
   D. Get Advice

3. What does "SK" mean?
   A. Spatial Kinetics
   B. Serial Kinetics
   C. Stop Kidding
   D. Stop Key

4. What are some ways that Deaf people gain access to the sounds in their homes? (Circle that all apply.)
   A. Flashing lights
   B. Caption decoders
   C. Specially trained hearing dogs
   D. TTY/TDD

5. In ASL, a simple side-to-side headshake can turn a positive statement into a negative.
   A. True
   B. False

6. In ASL, negation is always indicated at the beginning of the sentence for clarity.
   A. True
   B. False

Instructor's Guide: Lesson Three
Bravo ASL! Curriculum

Lesson Three: *Where's The TV Remote?*

3.4 Lesson Objectives

Planning for Success

Goal: To identify the learning outcomes associated with successful completion of this lesson.

Instructions:
1. **Ask** students to read the objectives in their workbooks (activity 3.4).
2. **Show** overhead (Appendix 3.4) and **read** through the objectives with the class.

Student Workbook: Activity 3.4

Overhead Master: Appendix 3.4

3.4 Lesson Objectives

Planning for Success

Goal: To see what you will learn by the end of this lesson.

Instructions: Read the objectives below.

Upon completing this VideoCourse lesson, you will be able to...

1. Recognize and accurately produce the ASL vocabulary introduced in this and all previous lessons.
2. Name and describe several ways in which Deaf people make the sounds in their homes visible to gain more access and independence.
3. Explain the use of "GA" and "SK" within a TTY/TDD phone conversation.
4. Recognize how negation is demonstrated in ASL.
5. Recognize the "use of space" features of ASL addressed in this lesson.

Instructor's Guide: Lesson Three
Bravo ASL! Curriculum

3.5 Lesson Focus

Which Way Did It Go?

Activity Goal: To develop a need for the ASL vocabulary introduced in this lesson.

Activity Instructions:

1. **Ask** students to read *Which Way Did It Go?* in their workbooks (activity 3.5).

2. **Ask** for a volunteer to be the first "seeker."

3. **Show** the class an item from the room (such as an eraser, small book, or pencil).

4. **Ask** the seeker to leave the room while the remaining students hide the object.

5. **Invite** the seeker back into the room. **Instruct** students to give the seeker clues with the use of mime and gestures only (no pointing, looking towards the object, or using voices).

6. After the seeker locates the object, **ask** him/her to select the next seeker.

7. If the students need assistance, **model** the use of gestures.

8. At the completion of the activity, you may **choose**:

    Option A: **Lead** a discussion using the following Thought/Discussion Questions:

    1) What are some signs related to giving directions that would have been useful to know during this activity?

    2) How did it feel to be limited in your ability to communicate?

    3) What are some techniques that Deaf people could use in giving directions to people who do not sign?

    OR

    Option B: **Ask** students to complete the above Thought/Discussion Questions in their workbooks in class or for homework. **Collect** for grading or to provide students with written feedback.

9. **Inform** students that they will learn the signs needed to describe the location of objects by the end of this lesson.

Lesson Three: *Where's The TV Remote?*

Student Workbook:
Activity 3.5

3.5 Lesson Focus

Which Way Did it Go?

Activity Goal: To practice giving directions without using your voice.

Activity Instructions: One student will be the "seeker" and leave the room while an item is hidden somewhere in the classroom. Your job is to give the seeker clues - using mime and gestures - to help the seeker find the item.

To add to the fun, do not use your voice, point, or look in the direction of the object. Once the object is found, a new seeker will be selected. Good luck!

Thought/Discussion Questions

1. What are some signs related to giving directions that would have been useful to know during this activity?

2. How did it feel to be limited in your ability to communicate?

3. What are some techniques that Deaf people could use in giving directions to people who do not sign?

3.6 Language Learning Instruction

Learning New Signs

Goal: To use ASL and visual aids to introduce this lesson's vocabulary.

Instructions:
1. **Ask** students to read *Learning New Signs* in their workbooks (activity 3.6).

2. **Show** the overhead (Appendix 3.6). **Introduce** the vocabulary by **pointing** to items presented in the pictures while **demonstrating** the signs.

3. **Reinforce** retention and **check** students' comprehension by **using** these signs to **ask** students questions.

   Note: For a step-by-step review of this method, see Lesson One (activities 1.6 and 1.12).

4. **Continue** this process until all the ASL vocabulary items have been introduced.

Instructor's Guide: Lesson Three
Bravo ASL! Curriculum

Overhead Content: Use the pictures in the overhead (Appendix 3.6) to introduce the signs representing the following concepts:

1. REMOTE-CONTROL
2. CHAIR
3. COUCH
4. LIVING+ROOM
5. T-V
6. ON
7. UNDER
8. BEHIND
9. IN
10. BED+ROOM
11. BED
12. DRESSER
13. UPSTAIRS

Note: Some pictures can be used to represent several concepts. For verbs and more abstract concepts, you may need to supplement these pictures with mime, gestures, using actual objects, and acting out the concepts in class.

Overhead Master: Appendix 3.6

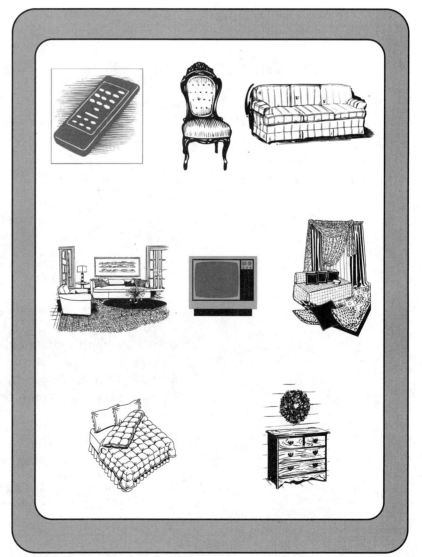

Lesson Three: *Where's The TV Remote?*

Student Workbook:
Activity 3.6

3.6 Language Learning Instruction

Learning New Signs

Goal: To help you learn new ASL vocabulary.

Instructions: Your instructor will teach you new signs! Watch closely to learn what these signs mean and how they are produced.

In the space below, record any notes to help you remember the signs.

Notes: _____
_____
_____
_____

3.7 Video Learning Experience

Introduction to New Vocabulary

Viewing Goal: To provide a signed demonstration of the accurate production of the new ASL vocabulary.

Viewing Instructions:
1. **Ask** students to read *Introduction to New Vocabulary* in their workbooks (activity 3.7).

2. **Play** the segment from the beginning of the Lesson Three videotape (segment 3.7). It begins with an introduction by Billy of the family situation. The family then determines that the TV remote control is lost. Because Billy's introduction is beyond the linguistic ability of beginning students, please **turn on** audio and/or captions to optimize its educational value.

3. **Instruct** students to watch how Billy produces the signs as well as the accompanying facial/body expressions.

4. **Ask** students to copy the signs and the facial/body expressions as Billy repeats each one.

Lesson Three: *Where's The TV Remote?*

Video Segment Content:
(3 1/2 Minutes)

The following is a summary of Billy's introduction:

Billy joins the Bravo family on a Saturday morning. They are getting ready to watch a TV program with closed captioning. They can't find the remote control, and Mom tells everyone that they need to look for it. Billy then introduces the vocabulary.

See the following Student Workbook excerpt for the remainder of the segment content.

Student Workbook:
Activity 3.7

3.7 Video Learning Experience

Introduction to New Vocabulary

Viewing Goal: To help you learn the new ASL vocabulary.

Viewing Instructions: Watch how Billy produces each sign. Be sure to notice the facial/body expressions. Copy the signs as Billy repeats each one.

Signs representing the following concepts are introduced in this video segment:

1. REMOTE-CONTROL
2. CHAIR
3. COUCH
4. LIVING+ROOM
5. T-V
6. ON
7. UNDER
8. BEHIND
9. IN
10. BED+ROOM
11. BED
12. DRESSER
13. UPSTAIRS

3.8 Experiential Activity

Matchmaker

Activity Goal: To assist students in recognizing the new ASL vocabulary.

Activity Instructions:
1. **Ask** students to read *Matchmaker* in their workbooks (activity 3.8).

2. **Instruct** students to draw a line from the sign illustration to the picture that best matches its meaning.

3. **Show** overhead (Appendix 3.8) and **ask** individual students to indicate correct answers on the overhead while class members correct their own work.

Lesson Three: *Where's The TV Remote?*

3.8 Experiential Activity

Matchmaker

Activity Goal: To help you recognize the new ASL vocabulary.

Activity Instructions: Look at the illustrations of your new ASL vocabulary below. Draw a line from the illustration of the sign to the picture that best matches its meaning.

Student Workbook:
Activity 3.8

Overhead Master:
Appendix 3.8

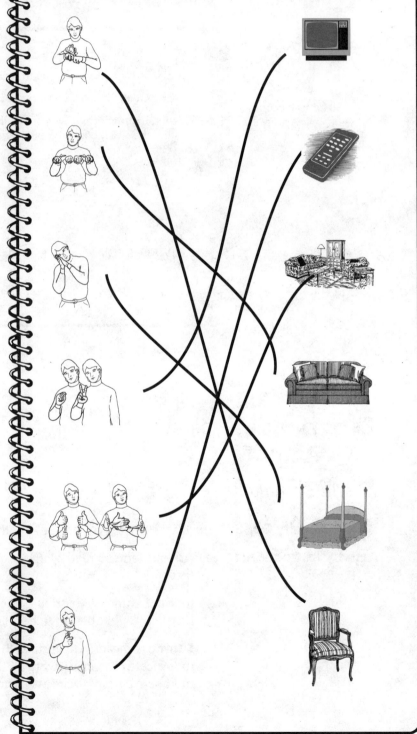

Instructor's Guide: Lesson Three
Bravo ASL! Curriculum
©1996 Sign Enhancers, Inc.
ALL RIGHTS RESERVED.

Lesson Three: *Where's The TV Remote?*

3.9 Video Learning Experience

Bravo Family Visit

Viewing Goal: To improve ASL comprehension skills by watching a Bravo family interaction.

Viewing Instructions:
1. **Ask** students to read *Bravo Family Visit* in their workbooks (activity 3.9).

2. **Play** the video segment of the Bravo family (segment 3.9). They will use the new ASL vocabulary within the context of searching for their TV remote control.

3. **Instruct** students to watch for comprehension and write a summary of the main points.

4. **Replay** any portion of this video segment that students experienced difficulty understanding.

Video Segment Content: (4 Minutes)

The following is a summary of the Bravo family interaction:

Mom asks Scott to search the living room to try to find the remote control. She asks him to search under the couch, behind the couch, on the TV, under the chair and behind the chair. Scott says okay and Mom leaves.

Scott decides that first he will check under the couch but the remote control is not there. It's not behind the couch either. Next, he checks under the chair and it's not there, nor is it behind the chair. Scott checks on top of the TV, but still doesn't find the remote.

Mom asks Anna to search her bedroom for the remote control. Mom asks her to check on, under, and in her bed. She then asks Anna to check on her dresser.

Anna goes to her room and checks on her bed and doesn't find the remote control. She doesn't find it when she looks in her bed. Next, Anna searches under her bed and doesn't find it. Finally, she searches on her dresser but doesn't find it there, either.

Lesson Three: *Where's The TV Remote?*

Student Workbook:
Activity 3.9

3.9 Video Learning Experience

Bravo Family Visit

Viewing Goal: To improve your ASL comprehension by watching a Bravo family interaction.

Viewing Instructions: Watch the signed interaction and write a summary of the main points.

Summary: _____
_____
_____
_____

3.10 Comprehension Quiz

What Did You Understand?

Quiz Goal: To assess students' comprehension of the signed interaction.

Quiz Instructions:
1. **Instruct** students to complete the quiz in their workbooks (activity 3.10).

2. **Collect** for grading or **show** overhead (Appendix 3.10) and **ask** individual students to indicate correct answers on the overhead while class members correct their own work.

3. **Ask** students to indicate which item(s) from the quiz they found difficult. **Review** by **modeling** or **replaying** that segment of the videotape.

Lesson Three: *Where's The TV Remote?*

Student Workbook:
Activity 3.10

Overhead Master:
Appendix 3.10

3.10 Comprehension Quiz

What Did You Understand?

Quiz Goal: To see how much of the Bravo family interaction you understood.

Quiz Instructions: Read each question and circle the best answer.

1. Where does Mom ask Scott to look for the TV remote control?
   A. Next to the couch.
   B. Under the couch.
   C. In the bed.
   D. All of the above.

2. Where does Anna look for the remote control?
   A. In the closet.
   B. In the dresser.
   C. Behind the door.
   D. In the bed.

3. Where does Anna find the remote control?
   A. Under the bed.
   B. Inside the bed.
   C. On the dresser.
   D. She doesn't find it.

4. Where does Scott find the remote?
   A. Under the couch.
   B. Behind the chair.
   C. In the kitchen.
   D. He doesn't find it.

3.11 Language Learning Instruction

Learning New Signs

Goal: To use ASL and visual aids to introduce this lesson's vocabulary.

Instructions:
1. **Ask** students to read *Learning New Signs* in their workbooks (activity 3.11).

2. **Show** the overhead (Appendix 3.11). **Introduce** the vocabulary by **pointing** to items presented in the pictures while **demonstrating** the signs.

3. **Reinforce** retention and **check** students' comprehension by **using** these signs to **ask** students questions.

Lesson Three: *Where's The TV Remote?*

> Note: For a step-by-step review of this method, see Lesson One (activities 1.6 and 1.12).
>
> 4. **Continue** this process until all the ASL vocabulary items have been introduced.

Overhead Content: Use the pictures in the overhead (Appendix 3.11) to introduce the signs representing the following concepts:

1. OVEN
2. REFRIGERATOR
3. SINK
4. TTY/TDD
5. TELEPHONE
6. LIGHT
7. FLASHING-LIGHT
8. BATH

Note: Some pictures can be used to represent several concepts. For verbs and more abstract concepts, you may need to supplement these pictures with mime, gestures, using actual objects, and acting out the concepts in class.

Overhead Master: Appendix 3.11

Instructor's Guide: Lesson Three
Bravo ASL! Curriculum

Lesson Three: *Where's The TV Remote?*

Student Workbook:
Activity 3.11

3.11 Language Learning Instruction

Learning New Signs

Goal: To help you learn new ASL vocabulary.

Instructions: Your instructor will teach you new signs! Watch closely to learn what these signs mean and how they are produced.

In the space below, record any notes to help you remember the signs.

Notes: _____
_____
_____
_____

3.12 Video Learning Experience

Introduction to New Vocabulary

Viewing Goal: To provide a signed demonstration of the accurate production of the new ASL vocabulary.

Viewing Instructions:
1. **Ask** students to read *Introduction to New Vocabulary* in their workbooks (activity 3.12).

2. **Play** the video segment entitled *Introduction to New Vocabulary* (segment 3.12). Billy introduces and signs each new vocabulary item twice. (If you wish to keep this a strictly visual presentation, **turn off** audio.)

3. **Instruct** students to watch how Billy produces the signs and the accompanying facial/body expressions.

4. **Ask** students to copy the signs and the facial/body expressions as Billy repeats each one.

Instructor's Guide: Lesson Three
Bravo ASL! Curriculum

Lesson Three: *Where's The TV Remote?*

Video Segment Content: See the following Student Workbook excerpt for the content
(1 1/2 Minutes) of this video segment.

Student Workbook:
Activity 3.12

3.12 Video Learning Experience

Introduction to New Vocabulary

Viewing Goal: To help you learn new ASL vocabulary.

Viewing Instructions: Watch how Billy produces each sign. Be sure to notice the facial/body expressions. Copy the signs as Billy repeats each one.

Signs representing the following concepts are introduced in this video segment:

1. OVEN
2. REFRIGERATOR
3. SINK
4. TTY/TDD
5. TELEPHONE
6. LIGHT
7. FLASHING-LIGHT
8. BATH

3.13 Experiential Activity

Put it There, Pal!

Activities Video

Activity Goal: To assist students in recognizing the new ASL vocabulary and ASL grammatical feature of "use of space."

Activity Instructions:
1. **Ask** students to read *Put it There, Pal!* in their workbooks (activity 3.13).

2. **Show** students the *Put it There, Pal!* segment of the Activities Video (segment 3.13). Each sample will be signed twice.

3. **Ask** students to put an "X" in each location indicated by the signed samples on the videotape.

4. **Show** overhead (Appendix 3.13) and **ask** individual students to indicate correct answers on the overhead while class members correct their own work.

Lesson Three: *Where's The TV Remote?*

Video Segment Content: The signers on the video will instruct students to place the
(3 Minutes) "X"...

1. Under the chair
2. Behind the couch
3. On the television
4. On the remote control
5. Inside the bed
6. Under the bed
7. Behind the dresser
8. In the sink

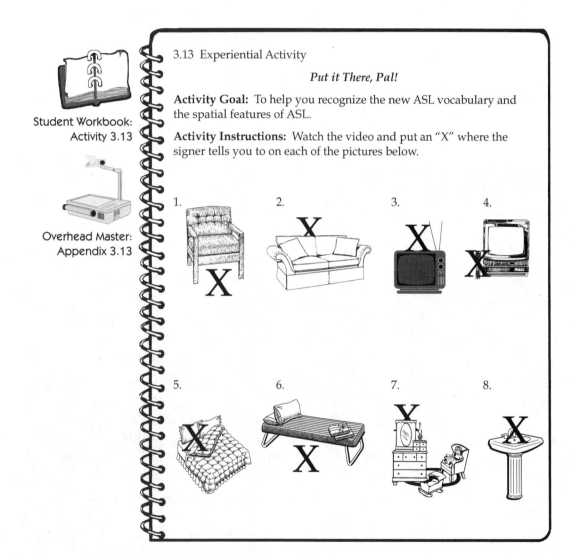

Student Workbook:
Activity 3.13

Overhead Master:
Appendix 3.13

3.13 Experiential Activity

Put it There, Pal!

Activity Goal: To help you recognize the new ASL vocabulary and the spatial features of ASL.

Activity Instructions: Watch the video and put an "X" where the signer tells you to on each of the pictures below.

Instructor's Guide: Lesson Three
Bravo ASL! Curriculum

©1996 Sign Enhancers, Inc.
ALL RIGHTS RESERVED.

Lesson Three: *Where's The TV Remote?*

3.14 Video Learning Experience

Bravo Family Visit

Viewing Goal: To improve ASL comprehension skills by watching a Bravo family interaction.

Viewing Instructions:

1. **Ask** students to read *Bravo Family Visit* in their workbooks (activity 3.14).

2. **Play** the video segment of the Bravo family (segment 3.14). They will use the new ASL vocabulary within the context of their continued search for the TV remote control.

3. **Instruct** students to watch for comprehension and write a summary of the main points.

4. **Replay** any portion of this video segment that students experienced difficulty understanding.

Video Segment Content: (4 Minutes)

The following is a summary of the Bravo family interaction:

Mom asks Dad if he has found the remote and he says "no." She suggests he check the bathroom. He finds that an odd place to look for the remote control. Mom explains that maybe one of the children carried it into the bathroom and left it there. Dad playfully salutes her and heads off to the bathroom.

Mom decides to search the kitchen. She looks inside the refrigerator. The remote control is not there. Then she checks in the sink. It's not in the sink. She decides to search in the oven but still doesn't find the remote.

The phone rings (light flashes) and Mom answers it. It is a TTY user on the phone so she places the receiver on the TTY. The call is for Anna. Anna comes down and tells Mom that she saw the light flash and was wondering if the call was for her. Mom tells her it is, and Anna sits down for her TTY conversation.

Mom walks into the bathroom and finds Dad standing in the tub. She comments that he has been searching for a long time in the bathroom and asks if he is planning on taking a bath. He says "no," that he is searching for the remote.

He suggests that they check the toilet and they do. They do not find the remote there. They are very perplexed as to where the remote could be and decide to go back to the living room.

On her way to the living room, Mom tells Anna she needs to end her TTY conversation and Anna says okay and does so.

Instructor's Guide: Lesson Three
Bravo ASL! Curriculum
©1996 Sign Enhancers, Inc.
ALL RIGHTS RESERVED.

Lesson Three: *Where's The TV Remote?*

The Bravo family still has not found the remote. Dad plops down on the couch and the TV switches on. He looks surprised, looks under the cushion he is sitting on, and finds the remote!

Mom, Dad, and Anna all look accusingly at Scott. He explains that he was not told to look there, so it is not his fault!!

Student Workbook: Activity 3.14

3.14 Video Learning Experience

Bravo Family Visit

Viewing Goal: To improve your ASL comprehension skills by watching a Bravo family interaction.

Viewing Instructions: Watch the signed interaction and write a summary of the main points.

Summary: _____
_____
_____
_____

3.15 Comprehension Quiz

What Did You Understand?

Quiz Goal: To assess students' comprehension of the signed interaction.

Quiz Instructions:
1. **Instruct** students to complete the quiz in their workbooks (activity 3.15).

2. **Collect** for grading or **show** overhead (Appendix 3.15) and **ask** individual students to indicate correct answers on the overhead while class members correct their own work.

3. **Ask** students to indicate which item(s) from the quiz they found difficult. **Review** by **modeling** or **replaying** that segment of the videotape.

Instructor's Guide: Lesson Three
Bravo ASL! Curriculum

©1996 Sign Enhancers, Inc.
ALL RIGHTS RESERVED.

Lesson Three: *Where's The TV Remote?*

Student Workbook:
Activity 3.15

Overhead Master:
Appendix 3.15

3.15 Comprehension Quiz

What Did You Understand?

Quiz Goal: To see how much of the Bravo family interaction you understood.

Quiz Instructions: Read and answer each question below.

1. Why did Mom think the TV remote control might be in the bathroom?
   Maybe one of the children carried it in and left it there.

2. What did it mean when the light flashed?
   The telephone was ringing.

3. When Anna came into the room after the light flashed, what did she ask Mom?
   "I saw the light flash, is the phone for me?"

4. When Mom found Dad in the bathroom, what was he doing?
   Looking for the remote in the tub.

5. Anna is still on the phone when Mom passes her. What does Mom tell her?
   A. "Say hello to your friend for me."
   B. "Let me talk to your friend's mother."
   C. "Time to take the dog for a walk."
   D. "Time to end your phone conversation."

6. Where did the Bravo family find the remote control?
   Under the couch cushion in the living room.

7. What did Scott say when the family looked at him accusingly?
   A. "It's not my fault, you didn't tell me to look there!"
   B. "I fooled you! I hid it there!"
   C. "I didn't want to watch TV anyway!"
   D. "Anna told me to put it there!"

3.16 Video Learning Experience

Cultural Notes

Viewing Goal: To assist students in learning about the cultural aspects of ASL.

Viewing Instructions:
1. **Ask** students to read *Cultural Notes* in their workbooks (activity 3.16).

2. **Play** the video segment entitled *Cultural Notes* (segment 3.16). Because the presentation of this segment is beyond the linguistic ability of beginning students, please **turn on** the audio and/or captions to optimize its educational value.

Lesson Three: *Where's The TV Remote?*

3. **Instruct** students to view the segment.

4. At completion of the video segment, **review** the content presented, and **answer** any questions students may have.

Video Segment Content: See the following Student Workbook excerpt for the content
(4 Minutes) of this video segment.

Student Workbook:
Activity 3.16

3.16 Video Learning Experience

Cultural Notes

Viewing Goal: To learn about the cultural aspects of ASL.

Viewing Instructions: View the *Cultural Notes* segment carefully for the following:

The sounds in Deaf people's homes are made accessible with:

A. Flashing lights that identify audible signals such as:
   1. Doorbell
   2. Fire alarm
   3. Baby crying
   4. Alarm clock
   5. Telephone ringing

B. Hearing dogs that are specially trained to alert Deaf people to environmental sounds.

C. Caption decoders that make the audio from the TV accessible.

D. TTYs (also known as TDDs) that make phone conversation visible.
   1. "GA" is used for turn taking (Go Ahead).
   2. "SK" is used to end a conversation (Stop Key).

E. TDD relay services that make telephone communication with hearing people accessible.

3.17 Experiential Activity

Home Improvement

Activity Goal: To apply the cultural information presented in this lesson regarding accessibility for Deaf people.

Activity Instructions:
1. **Ask** students to read *Home Improvement* in their workbooks (activity 3.17).

2. **Inform** students they are to review the situations described in their workbooks and determine what modifications

Lesson Three: *Where's The TV Remote?*

could be made to ensure accessibility for Deaf people within each situation. **Encourage** students to consider several options for each situation.

3. **Ask** students to record their answers in the space allotted in their workbooks.

4. **Show** overhead (Appendix 3.17) and **ask** individual students to indicate correct answers on the overhead while class members correct their own work.

6. When the students have completed this activity, you may **choose**:

   Option A: **Lead** the class in a discussion using the following Thought/Discussion Questions:

   1) What would be the cost of some of your recommendations for access?

   2) Who should pay these costs?

   3) Think about how it would be if you were Deaf... how would you gain access to educational opportunities, emergency medical care, movies and theater, social events, etc.?

   4) If you were Deaf, what adjustments would you make in your own home?

   OR

   Option B: **Ask** students to complete the above Thought/Discussion Questions in their workbooks in class or for homework. **Collect** for grading or to provide students with written feedback.

Student Workbook:
Activity 3.17

Overhead Master:
Appendix 3.17

3.17 Experiential Activity

Home Improvement

Activity Goal: To apply the cultural information you have learned about accessibility for Deaf people.

Activity Instructions: Read each situation below and consider what steps could be taken to ensure accessibility within each. For each situation, decide what visual modifications could be applied. Write your ideas and suggestions below.

Situation 1: A Deaf woman wants to start a business taking care of infants/children in her home.
_____
_____

Situation 2: A Deaf man needs to make a telephone call to his Deaf friend.
_____
_____

Lesson Three: *Where's The TV Remote?*

Situation 3: Your Deaf sister isn't waking up in time for school.

Situation 4: A Deaf girl needs to make a telephone call to her hearing friend.

Situation 5: A Deaf person is expecting a visit from a friend.

Situation 6: A Deaf college student needs to remain up-to-date with current world events.

Thought/Discussion Questions

1. What would be the cost of some of your recommendations for access?

2. Who should pay these costs?

3. Think about how it would be if you were Deaf... how would you gain access to educational opportunities, emergency medical care, movies and theater, social events, etc.?

4. If you were Deaf, what adjustments would you make in your own home?

3.18 Video Learning Experience

Grammatical Notes

Viewing Goal: To assist students in learning about the grammatical aspects of ASL.

Viewing Instructions:
1. **Ask** students to read *Grammatical Notes* in their workbooks (activity 3.18).

2. **Play** the video segment entitled *Grammatical Notes* (segment 3.18). Because the presentation of this segment is beyond the linguistic ability of beginning students, please **turn on** the audio and/or captions to optimize its educational value.

3. **Instruct** students to view the segment.

4. At completion of the segment, **review** the content presented, and **answer** any questions students may have.

Lesson Three: *Where's The TV Remote?*

Video Segment Content: See the following Student Workbook excerpt for the content
(1 1/2 Minutes) of this video segment.

Student Workbook:
Activity 3.18

3.18 Video Learning Experience

Grammatical Notes

Viewing Goal: To learn about the grammatical aspects of ASL.

Viewing Instructions: View the *Grammatical Notes* segment carefully for the following:

How negation is demonstrated in ASL:

A. ASL tends to place the sign indicating a negative at the end of the signed sentence.

B. A negative headshake accompanies the sign indicating negation.

3.19 Experiential Activity

To Be, or NOT To Be...

Activities Video

Activity Goal: To apply the grammatical information by distinguishing between affirmative and negative sentences.

Activity Instructions:
1. **Ask** students to read *To Be, or NOT To Be...* in their workbooks (activity 3.19).

2. **Show** students the segment entitled *To Be, or NOT To Be...* of the Activities Video (segment 3.19).

3. **Ask** students to watch each sentence and indicate whether it is affirmative or negative by circling the answers in their workbooks. Each sentence is presented twice.

4. **Show** overhead (Appendix 3.19) and **review** the answers. **Model** any sentences that seemed difficult for the students.

5. **Show** the sentences a second time and **ask** students to copy the sentences, including the non-manual signals that demonstrate negation and affirmation.

Instructor's Guide: Lesson Three
Bravo ASL! Curriculum

Lesson Three: *Where's The TV Remote?*

**Video Segment Content:
(3 1/2 Minutes)**

The following are ASL glosses of the sentences presented in this segment of the Activities Video:

1. ME DEAF
2. $\overline{\text{FATHER DEAF}}^{\text{rh-q}}$, NOT
3. $\overline{\text{BANANA WANT}}^{\text{rh-q}}$, NO
4. $\overline{\text{MOTHER}}^{\text{t}}$, ME LOVE
5. $\overline{\text{DOG, MINE}}^{\text{rh-q}}$, NOT
6. $\overline{\text{CHILDREN}}^{\text{t}}$, SCHOOL GO
7. $\overline{\text{SPOON, HAVE}}^{\text{rh-q}}$, NONE
8. $\overline{\text{PLATE, WASH}}^{\text{nod}}$, HELP-YOU
9. $\overline{\text{MOTHER}}^{\text{t}}$, TELL-ME, NOT
10. $\overline{\text{TV REMOTE}}^{\text{t}}$ $\overline{\text{COUCH, UNDER}}^{\text{rh-q}}$, NOT

Student Workbook:
Activity 3.19

Overhead Master:
Appendix 3.19

3.19 Experiential Activity

To Be, or NOT To Be

Activity Goal: To practice identifying whether an ASL sentence is affirmative (positive) or negative.

Activity Instructions: You will see ten sentences signed in ASL. The sentences are either affirmative or negative. After viewing each sentence, circle the appropriate response below.

1. **AFFIRMATIVE**   NEGATIVE
2. AFFIRMATIVE   **NEGATIVE**
3. AFFIRMATIVE   **NEGATIVE**
4. **AFFIRMATIVE**   NEGATIVE
5. AFFIRMATIVE   **NEGATIVE**
6. **AFFIRMATIVE**   NEGATIVE
7. AFFIRMATIVE   **NEGATIVE**
8. **AFFIRMATIVE**   NEGATIVE
9. AFFIRMATIVE   **NEGATIVE**
10. AFFIRMATIVE   **NEGATIVE**

Lesson Three: *Where's The TV Remote?*

3.20 Video Learning Experience

Review Session

Viewing Goal: To reinforce recognition and production of the signs introduced in this lesson.

Viewing Instructions:
1. **Ask** students to read *Review Session* in their workbooks (activity 3.20).

2. **Play** the video segment entitled *Review Session* (segment 3.20). Billy reviews all the ASL vocabulary and provides visual cues and origin information. Because the presentation of this segment is beyond the linguistic ability of beginning students, please **turn on** the audio and/or captions to optimize its educational value.

3. **Ask** students to pay careful attention to the signed vocabulary items and take note of visual hints offered by Billy that might help them remember.

4. **Suggest** students copy the signs to reinforce retention of sign production.

Video Segment Content: See the following Student Workbook excerpt for the content
(4 1/2 Minutes) of this video segment.

Student Workbook: Activity 3.20

3.20 Video Learning Experience

Review Session

Viewing Goal: To help you remember how to produce the signs introduced in this lesson.

Viewing Instructions: Watch this video segment carefully to see how each sign is made, and take note of any hints given to help you remember. You may want to copy the signs as you watch Billy.

The following are the vocabulary and explanations offered in this video segment:

CHAIR	This sign shows that a chair is something you sit on.
COUCH	This looks like several chairs next to each other... showing that several people can sit on it at the same time.
TV	This is fingerspelled T-V.
REMOTE-CONTROL	This sign shows both the shape and function of a remote control.

Lesson Three: *Where's The TV Remote?*

ON	The left hand becomes the surface of a thing. The right hand shows that something is ON it.
UNDER	The left hand is an object, the right hand shows the location of another thing UNDER it.
BEHIND	One thing is located BEHIND another.
IN	This sign shows the location of IN/INSIDE.
OVEN	This sign reflects the activity of putting something in an oven.
REFRIGERATOR	This compound sign shows how you OPEN it and indicates that it is COLD.
SINK	This sign indicates the basic shape and how you use a sink.
BED+ROOM	This is a compound sign using the signs BED and ROOM.
TOILET/BATHROOM	This is a symbol for BATHROOM. The "T" represents the letter in the word TOILET.
BED	This sign represents someone's head on the pillow.
DRESSER	This sign is based on the shape and function of a dresser.
BATH	You take a washcloth and soap and you scrub away.
PHONE	This is a sign indicating a phone's shape and use.
TTY	This is a device the phone is placed on. One types the conversation so it becomes visible.
LIGHT	The hand becomes the light bulb and the fingers represent the LIGHT.
FLASHING-LIGHT	The hand is the bulb, and the fingers show the light going on and off.

Lesson Three: *Where's The TV Remote?*

3.21 Video Learning Experience

Practice Session: Sentences

Viewing Goal: To improve comprehension skills by watching sentences presented in ASL.

Viewing Instructions:
1. **Ask** students to read *Practice Session: Sentences* in their workbooks (activity 3.21).
2. **Play** the video segment entitled *Practice Session: Sentences* (segment 3.21).
3. **Inform** students that each sentence is signed twice and an English translation is provided.
4. **Remind** students to watch the face of each signer to see the facial/body expressions and non-manual grammatical markers as well as the signs.

Video Segment Content: (1 1/2 Minutes)

The following are English translations of the practice sentences:

1. Where is the TV remote control?
2. The food is in the kitchen in the oven.
3. I sit on the couch in the living room.
4. The light flashes when the telephone rings.
5. I shower in the bathroom.

Student Workbook: Activity 3.21

3.21 Video Learning Experience

Practice Session: Sentences

Viewing Goal: To improve your ASL comprehension skills by watching signed sentences.

Viewing Instructions: Watch the signed sentences for comprehension. Remember to watch the face of each signer to see the facial/body expressions and the non-manual grammatical markers as well as the signs. It is recommended that you copy each signed sentence when it is repeated.

In the space below, record any questions or notes you have regarding the sentences.

Notes: _____
_____
_____
_____

3.22 Experiential Activity

Now, Where Did I Put That...?

Activities Video

Activity Goal: To improve students' ASL comprehension skills with the spatial features of ASL..

Activity Instructions:
1. **Ask** students to read *Now, Where Did I Put That...?* in their workbooks (activity 3.22).

2. **Show** students the segment entitled *Now, Where Did I Put That...?* on the Activities Video (segment 3.22). Each sample will be signed twice.

3. **Instruct** students to view the signed directions carefully, and place the number of the object in the appropriate location in the "house" illustrated in their workbooks.

4. Upon completing this activity, **show** overhead (Appendix 3.22) and **review** the answers. **Model** any items the students found to be difficult. You may want to **show** the video again, as students review their answers.

Video Segment Content: The following are the signed directions presented in the
(4 1/2 Minutes) Activities Video.

              rh-q
1. GLASS WHERE, TV ON
                             rh-q
2. REMOTE-CONTROL WHERE, COFFEE TABLE, THERE
              rh-q
3. COFFEE WHERE, COOK+ROOM CHAIR, ON
              rh-q
4. BANANA WHERE, SHOWER, IN
          rh-q
5. EGG WHERE, TOILET IN
          rh-q
6. DOG WHERE, BED IN
            rh-q
7. SPIDER WHERE, BED UNDER
              rh-q
8. TELEPHONE WHERE, COOK+ROOM, TABLE, ON
          rh-q
9. TTY WHERE, LIGHT BEHIND
           rh-q
10. MILK WHERE, COUCH, UNDER

Lesson Three: *Where's The TV Remote?*

Student Workbook:
Activity 3.22

Overhead Master:
Appendix 3.22

3.22 Experiential Activity

Now, Where Did I Put That...?

Activity Goal: To improve your comprehension skills with the spatial features of ASL.

Activity Instructions: You will see signed directions that tell you where in the house (see picture below) the ten items belong. Place the number corresponding to the item in the correct location in the house. If, for example, in item #1 the signer informs you, "the glass is on the table," you would write "1" on the table in the picture.

1. GLASS
2. REMOTE-CONTROL
3. COFFEE
4. BANANA
5. EGG
6. DOG
7. SPIDER
8. TELEPHONE
9. TTY
10. MILK

3.23 Experiential Activity

You Want Me to Do What?

Activity Goal: To improve comprehension and the application of the spatial features of ASL.

Activity Instructions:

1. **Ask** students to read *You Want Me to Do What?* in their workbooks (activity 3.23).

2. **Point** to a student and **give** a command to be followed. Be sure to **incorporate** the spatial features of ASL. These commands may include...

   A. CHAIR (point), LOOK-UNDER

   B. DESK (point), GO-BEHIND

   C. BATHROOM, YOU-GO

   D. BOOK (point), TABLE, YOU-PUT-UNDER

   E. BOOK-SHELF (point) GO, BOOK, YOU-GIVE-ME

   F. HELP-ME (mime moving your desk)

3. After you have given several commands to various students, **instruct** students to pair up and practice giving each other commands to follow.

Student Workbook: Activity 3.23

3.23 Experiential Activity

You Want Me to Do What?

Activity Goal: To improve your comprehension and your ability to recognize the spatial features of ASL.

Activity Instructions: Pay close attention as your instructor signs commands for the students to follow. When you are selected, complete the task signed to you in ASL.

Practice giving and receiving commands with a classmate.

Lesson Three: *Where's The TV Remote?*

3.24 Video Learning Experience

Practice Session: Story

Viewing Goal: To improve ASL comprehension skills by watching a signed story.

Viewing Instructions:
1. **Ask** students to read *Practice Session: Story* in their workbooks (activity 3.24).

2. **Show** the video segment entitled *Practice Session: Story* (segment 3.24). Billy signs a story using the vocabulary introduced in this lesson. **Turn off** audio and captions.

3. **Instruct** students to watch the story for comprehension and write a summary of the main points.

Video Segment Content:
(1 1/2 Minutes)

The following is an English translation of the story:

A family has a house. It has two bedrooms, a kitchen, living room, and a bathroom.

If you want to go to bed, go to the bedroom. If you want food, go to the kitchen. If a light is flashing, go to the phone. If you need to go to the bathroom, then go to the bathroom! If you want to watch the TV, go to the living room.

Ohhh... but where's the remote control? You'll have to look for it!

Student Workbook:
Activity 3.24

3.24 Video Learning Experience

Practice Session: Story

Viewing Goal: To improve your ASL comprehension by watching a story presented in ASL.

Viewing Instructions: Watch the signed story for comprehension. In the space below, write a summary of the main points from the story.

Summary: _____
_____
_____
_____

Instructor's Guide: Lesson Three
Bravo ASL! Curriculum

Lesson Three: *Where's The TV Remote?*

3.25 Comprehension Quiz

What Did You Understand?

Quiz Goal: To assess students' comprehension of the signed story.

Quiz Instructions:
1. **Instruct** students to complete the quiz in their workbooks (activity 3.25).

2. **Collect** for grading or **show** overhead (Appendix 3.25) and **ask** individual students to indicate correct answers on the overhead while class members correct their own work.

3. **Ask** students to indicate which item(s) from the quiz they found difficult. **Review** by **modeling** or **replaying** that segment of the videotape.

Student Workbook: Activity 3.25

Overhead Master: Appendix 3.25

3.25 Comprehension Quiz

What Did You Understand?

Quiz Goal: To see how much of the signed story you understood.

Quiz Instructions: Read each question below and choose the best answer.

1. How many bedrooms does the house in the story have?
   A. One
   B. Two
   C. Three
   D. Four

2. The house in the story was unusual because it did not have a kitchen.
   A. True
   B. False

3. According to the story, where should you go if you are hungry?
   A. Since there is no kitchen, to a restaurant
   B. To a neighbor's house
   C. To the kitchen
   D. To a friend's house

4. According to this story, if a light is flashing, where should you go?
   A. To the bathroom
   B. To the bedroom
   C. To the front door
   D. To the phone

5. In this story, if you want to watch TV, where should you go?
   A. The bedroom
   B. The TV room
   C. The living room
   D. A hardware store to buy a new remote control

Instructor's Guide: Lesson Three
Bravo ASL! Curriculum

©1996 Sign Enhancers, Inc.
ALL RIGHTS RESERVED.

Lesson Three: *Where's The TV Remote?*

3.26 Homework Assignment

Read Any Good TV Lately?

Homework Goal: To provide students with the opportunity to have firsthand experience with access issues.

Homework Instructions:

1. **Ask** students to read *Read Any Good TV Lately?* in their workbooks (activity 3.26). Students are to watch an entire television program or movie without sound.

2. **Encourage** them to use closed captions to access the programs. If their televisions do not have built-in decoders, they should go to a friend's home or to the library.

3. **Inform** students they should try to watch their favorite program or movie if it is captioned.

4. **Ask** students to write a one- to three-page paper reporting their experiences including:

   A. Was it easy to find a decoder to access closed captions?

   B. Was the program you wanted to watch accessible with captions?

   C. What was it like to view the program with captions instead of sound?

   D. Were you able to read the captions and view all the action?

Instructor Tip: *An opportunity for students to share the results of this assignment has been scheduled in the next lesson (Homework Review 4.2).*

Instructor's Guide: Lesson Three
Bravo ASL! Curriculum

Lesson Three: *Where's The TV Remote?*

Student Workbook:
Activity 3.26

3.26 Homework Assignment

Read Any Good TV Lately?

Homework Goal: To give you an opportunity to experience access to television through captions.

Homework Instructions: Find a television that has a built-in caption decoder or visit a friend who has one. Watch your favorite television program or movie *without the sound* by reading the captions.

Write a one- to three-page paper describing your experience including:

   A. Was it easy to find a decoder to access closed captions?
   B. Was the program you wanted to watch accessible with captions?
   C. What was it like to view the program with captions instead of sound?
   D. Were you able to read the captions and view all the action?

3.27 Post-test

What Do You Know Now?

Assessment Video

Post-test Goal: To assess students' mastery of the lesson objectives.

Post-test Instructions:

1. **Ask** students to read the Post-test Introduction in their workbooks (activity 3.27).

2. **Copy** and **distribute** the Lesson Three Post-test (Appendix 3.27).

3. **Play** the Assessment Video (segment 3.27) and allow students to complete Section One (comprehension portion) of the test.

4. **Instruct** students to complete Section Two (culture and grammar portion) of the test individually and hand in their papers when they are finished.

5. **Assign** Section Three (expressive portion) of the test and **schedule** a time when students are to perform. If possible, it is strongly recommended that you **videotape** this portion of the Post-test.

6. **Determine** grading options based upon programmatic requirements. A recommended guideline for measuring successful mastery of objectives is 80% accuracy.

Lesson Three: *Where's The TV Remote?*

**Video Segment Content:
(2 Minutes)**

The following is an English translation of the comprehension story:

Dad is watching TV and begins to smell something funny. He goes to the kitchen to see if the smell is coming from there, but he can't find it. He looks in the sink and in the refrigerator, but doesn't find it. He goes into the bathroom and looks in the toilet, but still can't find what smells so bad. He goes back to the living room, sits on the couch to watch TV again, and notices something on top of the TV. It is an old smelly banana!

Student Workbook:
Activity 3.27

3.27 Post-test Introduction

What Do You Know Now?

Post-test Goal: To assess your mastery of the lesson objectives.

Post-test Introduction: This test has three sections:

Section One: The Comprehension section tests your ability to understand ASL.

Section Two: The Culture and Grammar section tests your knowledge of the material presented in the *Cultural* and *Grammatical Notes*.

Section Three: The Expressive portion tests your ability to use ASL.

Simply follow the instructions for each section. **Good luck!**

**Post-test Master:
Appendix 3.27**

3.27 Post-test

Section One: Comprehension

Instructions: You will see a signed story. Watch carefully and answer each question below.

1. When Dad is watching TV, what is the problem?
   A. He can't find the TV remote.
   B. He is tired and can't find his bed.
   C. He hears someone crying, but can't find them.
   D. He smells something funny, but can't find what it is.

2. Where is the first place he looks?
   A. Bathroom
   B. Kitchen
   C. Garage
   D. Living Room

3. Does he find what he is looking for in the bathroom?
   A. Yes
   B. No

4. When he went into the kitchen, where did he look?
   A. On top of the refrigerator and in the sink
   B. Inside the sink, in the refrigerator and in the oven
   C. Inside the refrigerator and in the sink
   D. On and under the table

5. Where did Dad find what he was looking for?
   A. In the kitchen
   B. In the bathroom
   C. Under the couch
   D. On the TV

6. What was it that Dad found?
   A. An eggplant
   B. An apple
   C. A melon
   D. A banana

Lesson Three: *Where's The TV Remote?*

Post-test Master: Appendix 3.27

3.27 Post-test

Section Two: Culture and Grammar

Instructions: Read each statement carefully and determine if it is True or False (circle your answer).

7. A caption decoder can be used by a Deaf person to communicate on the telephone.
   A. True
   B. False

8. With simple modifications, a Deaf person is able to know when someone is at the door.
   A. True
   B. False

9. According to the video, a TTY can be used to wake a Deaf person.
   A. True
   B. False

10. In ASL, negatives usually appear at the end of a sentence.
    A. True
    B. False

11. When using a TTY, GA means "go ahead."
    A. True
    B. False

12. A TDD helps make the audio on a television visible.
    A. True
    B. False

13. A relay service can assist a hearing person who does not have a TDD to call a Deaf person.
    A. True
    B. False

14. It is very important to use a negative headshake when signing a negative statement in ASL.
    A. True
    B. False

15. When using ASL to express a sentence meaning, "I am not Deaf," it would be appropriate to sign DEAF first and then the sign NOT.
    A. True
    B. False

Post-test Master:
Appendix 3.27

3.27 Post-test

Section Three: Expressive Portion

Instructions: Create a story about losing something and searching for it in your house, using at least four signs learned in this lesson. Also sign at least one sentence in which you apply negation as taught in this lesson.

Your instructor will schedule a time for you to perform this section of the Post-test. You may prepare and practice prior to your scheduled time.

Include at least four signs from Lesson Three.

16. _____

17. _____

18. _____

19. _____

Include negation:

20. _____

Congratulations!
You have completed
Lesson Three!

Lesson 4
Let's Go Food Shopping

Materials Needed:

Equipment: VCR and TV monitor
Overhead projector and screen
Chalk/dry erase board
Optional: video camera for activities 4.15 and 4.21

Materials: Instructor's Guide
Student Workbook: one per student
Overhead transparencies for activities 4.3, 4.4, 4.6, 4.10, 4.12, 4.17 and 4.19 (see Appendix for masters)
Con-Sign-Tration Cards (Appendix 4.9)
Optional: blank videotape (or have students bring their own) for activities 4.15 and 4.21)
Post-test: Appendix 4.21

Videotapes: The Beginning ASL VideoCourse Lesson Four
Activities Video for activities 4.10, 4.12, and 4.17
Assessment Video for Post-test 4.21

4.1 Begin Class
Housekeeping

Goal: To prepare students for this lesson.

Instructions:
1. **Welcome** students to Lesson Four of the VideoCourse.
2. **Perform** any necessary tasks (such as taking attendance) that may be required by your specific program.

Lesson Four: *Let's Go Food Shopping*

4.2 Homework Review

Read Any Good TV Lately?

Activity Goal: To provide students with the opportunity to share the results of their experience with access issues (*Homework Assignment 3.26*).

Activity Instructions:

1. **Ask** students to read *Read Any Good TV Lately?* in their workbooks (activity 4.2).

2. You may **choose**:

    Option A: **Ask** for volunteers or **select** several students to share the main points from their papers including:

    1) Was it easy to find a decoder to access closed captions?

    2) Was the program you wanted to watch accessible with captions?

    3) What was it like to view the program with captions instead of sound?

    4) Were you able to read the captions and view all the action?

    OR

    Option B: **Collect** the homework papers for grading or to provide students with written feedback.

Student Workbook: Activity 4.2

> 4.2 Homework Review
>
> *Read Any Good TV Lately?*
>
> **Activity Goal:** To share the results of your homework assignment.
>
> **Activity Instructions:** Be prepared to share the main points from your paper regarding watching television with captions including:
>
> A. Was it easy to find a decoder to access closed captions?
>
> B. Was the program you wanted to watch accessible with captions?
>
> C. What was it like to view the program with captions instead of sound?
>
> D. Were you able to read the captions and view all the action?

Instructor's Guide: Lesson Four
Bravo ASL! Curriculum

Lesson Four: *Let's Go Food Shopping*

4.3 Pretest
What Do You Know?

Pretest Goal: To identify students' current level of knowledge pertaining to the lesson content.

Pretest Instructions:
1. **Ask** students to read and answer the questions in the pretest in their workbooks (activity 4.3).

2. **Show** overhead (Appendix 4.3) and **ask** individual students to indicate the correct answers on the overhead while class members correct their own work.

3. **Inform** students that the contents of the pretest will be taught throughout the lesson.

Student Workbook: Activity 4.3

Overhead Master: Appendix 4.3

4.3 Pretest

What Do You Know?

Pretest Goal: To see how much you already know about what will be taught in this lesson.

Pretest Instructions: Read each question and circle the best answer.

1. ASL is often creative and imaginative.
   A. True
   B. False

2. ASL can make a "play on signs" like English can make a "play on words."
   A. True
   B. False

3. ASL and English have the same word order.
   A. True
   B. False

4. In ASL, the topic of a sentence is often signed first.
   A. True
   B. False

5. ASL has rules of grammar just like spoken languages.
   A. True
   B. False

6. A Number Story is always limited to two minutes.
   A. True
   B. False

Instructor's Guide: Lesson Four
Bravo ASL! Curriculum

©1996 Sign Enhancers, Inc.
All Rights Reserved

Lesson Four: *Let's Go Food Shopping*

4.4 Lesson Objectives
Planning for Success

Goal: To identify the learning outcomes associated with successful completion of this lesson.

Instructions:
1. **Ask** students to read the objectives in their workbooks (activity 4.4).
2. **Show** overhead (Appendix 4.4) and **read** through the objectives with the class.

Student Workbook: Activity 4.4

Overhead Master: Appendix 4.4

> 4.4 Lesson Objectives
>
> *Planning For Success*
>
> **Goal:** To see what you will learn by the end of this lesson.
>
> **Instructions:** Read the objectives below.
>
> Upon completing this VideoCourse lesson, you will be able to...
>
> 1. Recognize and accurately produce the ASL vocabulary introduced in this and all previous lessons.
> 2. Describe a Number Story as a form of Deaf folklore and contribute to the creation of an original Number Story.
> 3. Name and describe several ways in which Deaf people share the folklore of Deaf culture.
> 4. Recognize and apply topic/comment grammatical structure.

Lesson Four: *Let's Go Food Shopping*

4.5 Lesson Focus

Where's The Beef?

Activity Goal: To develop a need for the ASL vocabulary introduced in this lesson.

Activity Instructions:

1. **Ask** students to read *Where's the Beef?* in their workbooks (activity 4.5).

2. **Divide** the class into small groups of four or five students.

3. **Explain** that students are not to use their voices for this activity. **Encourage** students to use signs they know, as well as gestures, mime, pointing, etc.

4. **Ask** one student in each group to take on the role of a "grocer" and the remaining students to be shoppers who need to find the location of the food items listed in the Student Workbooks.

5. **Tell** students to switch roles after the grocer guesses the correct food item.

6. **Circulate** among the groups to **observe** their progress.

7. When students have completed this activity, you may **choose**:

   Option A: **Bring** the whole class together and **lead** a discussion using the following Thought/Discussion Questions:

   1) What are some signs related to food that would have been useful to know during this activity?

   2) How did it feel to be limited in your ability to communicate?

   3) What are some ways that Deaf people could ask for the location of items in a food store?

   OR

   Option B: **Ask** students to complete the above Thought/Discussion Questions in their workbooks in class or for homework. **Collect** for grading or to provide students with written feedback.

8. **Inform** students that they will learn the signs related to food needed to perform this activity by the end of this lesson.

Instructor's Guide: Lesson Four
Bravo ASL! Curriculum

Lesson Four: *Let's Go Food Shopping*

Student Workbook:
Activity 4.5

4.5 Lesson Focus

Where's The Beef?

Activity Goal: To experience a situational role-play related to food shopping.

Activity Instructions: Imagine that you are in a grocery store. The store is owned by a Deaf family and the language used in the store is ASL. You need help to find certain items.

Role-play this situation in your group and think of how you might request the location of the following twelve items using gestures and mime.

Use the space provided below to list your ideas. Be creative! Although you may not know the signs for the items, try to overcome the communication barrier by using natural gestures/body movements to "act out" each item.

You need the following food items:

1. Soda	4. Popcorn	7. Chicken	10. Eggs
2. Milk	5. Lobster	8. Dog food	11. Eggplant
3. Soup	6. Bananas	9. Fish	12. Hamburger

Communication ideas:

1. _____ 7. _____
2. _____ 8. _____
3. _____ 9. _____
4. _____ 10. _____
5. _____ 11. _____
6. _____ 12. _____

In this lesson, you will learn the signs for the above food items and more. Next time you need something from this grocery store, you will be ready!

Thought/Discussion Questions

1. What are some signs related to food that would have been useful to know during this activity?

2. How did it feel to be limited in your ability to communicate?

3. What are some ways that Deaf people could ask for the location of items in a food store?

Lesson Four: *Let's Go Food Shopping*

4.6 Language Learning Instruction

Learning New Signs

Goal: To use ASL and visual aids to introduce this lesson's vocabulary.

Instructions:
1. **Ask** students to read *Learning New Signs* in their workbooks (activity 4.6).

2. **Show** the overhead (Appendix 4.6). **Introduce** the vocabulary by **pointing** to items presented in the picture while **demonstrating** the signs.

3. **Reinforce** retention and **check** students' comprehension by **using** these signs to **ask** students questions.

   Note: For a step-by-step review of this method, see Lesson One (activities 1.6 and 1.12).

4. **Continue** this process until all the ASL vocabulary items have been introduced.

Overhead Content: Use the pictures in the overhead (Appendix 4.6) to introduce the signs representing the following concepts:

1. SODA/ POP	14. CHEESE	27. CANDY
2. ALL-GONE	15. HOT-DOG	28. COOKIES
3. FOOD	16. HAMBURGER	29. ICE-CREAM
4. SHOPPING	17. TURKEY	30. #1
5. BANANA	18. FISH	31. #2
6. MELON	19. CHICKEN	32. #3
7. PLANT	20. BREAD	33. #4
8. EGG+PLANT	21. POPCORN	34. #5
9. LETTUCE	22. KETCHUP	35. #6
10. ONION	23. SOUP	36. #7
11. CARROT	24. TOMATO	37. #8
12. COW	25. DOG+FOOD	38. #9
13. MILK	26. LOBSTER	39. #10

Note: Some pictures can be used to represent several concepts. For verbs and more abstract concepts, you may need to supplement these pictures with mime, gestures, using actual objects, and acting out the concepts in class.

Lesson Four: *Let's Go Food Shopping*

Overhead Master:
Appendix 4.6

Instructor's Guide: Lesson Four
Bravo ASL! Curriculum

Lesson Four: *Let's Go Food Shopping*

Student Workbook:
Activity 4.6

4.6 Language Learning Instruction

Learning New Signs

Goal: To help you learn new ASL vocabulary.

Instructions: Your instructor will teach you new signs! Watch closely to learn what these signs mean and how they are produced.

In the space below, record any notes to help you remember the signs.

Notes: _____
_____
_____
_____

4.7 Video Learning Experience

Introduction to New Vocabulary

Let's Go Food Shopping

Instructor Tip: This lesson's "Let's Go Food Shopping" introduces the new ASL vocabulary within the context of the family trip to the grocery store. This is a different format than that of previous lessons, and it is recommended that you prepare students to watch for the new signs.

Viewing Goal: To introduce this lesson's ASL vocabulary within the context of a trip to the grocery store.

Viewing Instructions:
1. **Ask** students to read *Let's Go Food Shopping* in their workbooks (activity 4.7).

2. **Play** the segment from the beginning of the Lesson Four videotape (segment 4.7). It begins with an introduction by Billy of the family situation, and continues with the family deciding to go food shopping. **Continue** to play tape as new vocabulary is presented within the context of the family food shopping trip. Because Billy's introduction is beyond the linguistic ability of beginning students, please **turn on** the audio and/or captions to optimize its educational value.

Instructor's Guide: Lesson Four
Bravo ASL! Curriculum

Lesson Four: *Let's Go Food Shopping*

3. **Instruct** students to watch how the ASL signs related to food are produced.

4. **Replay** any portion of this video segment that students experienced difficulty understanding.

5. **Inform** students that these signs will be shown again in the *Review Session* following this segment.

Video Segment Content: (16 Minutes)

The following is a summary of the Bravo family interaction:

Introduction Scenario: Dad decides that he wants a soda. Mom informs him that they don't have any soda; she needs to go grocery shopping because they are out of food.

Dad asks if he can go grocery shopping with her. She says no, that he takes a long time to shop and she can do it faster alone. Dad disagrees; he says that if he and the children join Mom the shopping will be faster. Mom explains that it only takes her a half hour to shop and it takes Dad hours and hours. She adds that if the children join in, it would take even longer.

Dad tells her that she is wrong. If he, Scott, and Anna join her, the shopping will only take fifteen minutes. Mom shows him her long shopping list and explains that she must buy everything on the list. Dad is shocked at the long list, but not discouraged.

Dad calls to the children by stomping his foot on the floor and waving, and asks them if they want to help Mom with the grocery shopping. The children excitedly answer yes and beg Mom to let them go. Mom gives in and they head for the store.

Food Shopping Scenario: The Bravo family arrives at the grocery store and they start joking with each other. Mom hands the list to Dad and he begins ripping it in two. They all look at him as if he is crazy, but he rips it into four parts and hands one to each person. He reminds them to hurry, tells them each to get a cart, get everything on their list, and meet at the front of the store when they are finished. They all agree and head off.

Anna is confused by one of the items on her list and asks Mom where a "plant with eggs" can be found. Mom looks at Anna's list and shows Anna an eggplant.

Billy: Hmm... Dad is smart. His plan was to take the shopping list, divide it up, and give each family member a part of it. He thinks it will be faster. Do you agree? Well, we'll see.

Anna is getting an eggplant. She thought this was a plant with eggs! The sign is conceptually inaccurate of course, but many people use this sign (demonstrated on video) for eggplant: EGG +PLANT.

Lesson Four: *Let's Go Food Shopping*

Now, let's watch as the family continues to shop, focusing on the ASL signs related to food.

Note: Anna, Dad and Scott show the ASL signs used to represent each item as they shop.

Billy: Why is the sign for milk made this way (demonstrated on video)? Can you guess? Yeah. You guessed it. Hmm... Which kind of cow gives chocolate milk? Ah, well, maybe it's a brown cow! Ha Ha!

Wow, you are learning a lot of new signs related to food! But wait, we have more. Are you ready?

The family continues shopping and showing the signs for the items.

Near the popcorn, Scott sees the candy. Mom comes up behind him and redirects him to the ketchup. He points to the candy with a questioning look and she says, "You are right, that is candy. But we are not buying candy." She then points him back to the ketchup and reminds him to get a large bottle for the family.

Anna asks Dad if she can get ice cream and he says okay.

Mom comes up and thanks the family for all their help with the grocery shopping.

Student Workbook: Activity 4.7

4.7 Video Learning Experience

Introduction to New Vocabulary

Viewing Goal: To help you learn the new ASL vocabulary.

Viewing Instructions: As the family shops, they will show you new signs. Watch how each sign is produced. Be sure to notice the facial/body expressions.

During the food shopping trip, signs representing the following concepts are introduced:

1. SODA/ POP
2. ALL-GONE
3. FOOD
4. SHOPPING
5. BANANA
6. MELON
7. PLANT
8. EGG+PLANT
9. LETTUCE
10. ONION
11. CARROT
12. COW
13. MILK
14. CHEESE
15. HOT-DOG
16. HAMBURGER
17. TURKEY
18. FISH
19. CHICKEN
20. BREAD
21. POPCORN
22. KETCHUP
23. SOUP
24. TOMATO
25. DOG+FOOD
26. LOBSTER
27. CANDY
28. COOKIES
29. ICE-CREAM
30. # 1
31. # 2
32. # 3
33. # 4
34. # 5
35. # 6
36. # 7
37. # 8
38. # 9
39. # 10

Lesson Four: *Let's Go Food Shopping*

4.8 Video Learning Experience

Review Session

Viewing Goal: To reinforce recognition and production of the signs introduced in this lesson.

Viewing Instructions:
1. **Ask** students to read *Review Session* in their workbooks (activity 4.8).

2. **Play** the video segment entitled *Review Session* (segment 4.8). Billy reviews all the ASL vocabulary and provides visual cues and origin information. Because the presentation of this segment is beyond the linguistic ability of beginning students, please **turn on** the audio and/or captions to optimize its educational value.

3. **Ask** students to pay careful attention to the signed vocabulary items and to take note of the visual hints offered by Billy that might help them remember.

4. **Suggest** that students copy the signs to reinforce retention of sign production.

Video Segment Content: See the following Student Workbook excerpt for the content
(8 Minutes) of this video segment.

Student Workbook: Activity 4.8

> 4.8 Video Learning Experience
>
> *Review Session*
>
> **Viewing Goal:** To help you remember how to produce the signs introduced in this lesson.
>
> **Viewing Instructions:** Watch this video segment carefully to see how each sign is made, and take note of any hints given to help you remember. You may want to copy the signs as you watch Billy.
>
> The following are the vocabulary and explanations offered in this video segment:
>
> SODA/POP — This sign looks like opening a soda can.
>
> ALL-GONE — The left hand represents a pile of things. The right hand shows the depletion of those things.
>
> FOOD — Where does the food go? In the mouth.
>
> SHOPPING — The sign BUY is like taking money out of your hand and giving it to someone. When you repeat the sign several times (to buy many things), you are... SHOPPING.

Lesson Four: *Let's Go Food Shopping*

BANANA	This sign looks like peeling a banana.
MELON	How do you test a melon to see if it's good? You thump it.
PLANT	This sign looks like something growing up out of the ground.
EGG+PLANT	This is a compound sign using EGG and PLANT. This vegetable is shaped similar to an egg.
LETTUCE	The head becomes the plant itself and the right hand represents a leaf.
ONION	When you're eating or chopping an onion, your eyes water.
CARROT	The index finger shows the shape of the carrot. The right hand represents the action of peeling the carrot.
COW	This clearly represents an animal with horns.
MILK	This sign looks like milking a cow.
CHEESE	To make cheese, milk is processed and becomes solid. This sign represents the compressed liquid becoming CHEESE.
HOT-DOG	This sign represents how the hot dogs are made.
HAMBURGER	This shows how a person makes a hamburger patty.
TURKEY:	This describes what a turkey looks like, specifically its wattle.
FISH	The hand becomes a fish swimming.
CHICKEN	This sign looks like a chicken's beak.
BREAD	You have a loaf of bread, and you slice it.
POPCORN	When cooked, popcorn kernels explode and pop up.
KETCHUP	Most people hit the bottle to get the ketchup out.
SOUP	The left hand represents the bowl. The right hand represents the spoon.
TOMATO	The first part of the sign means RED. The left hand becomes the tomato, while the right hand slices it.
DOG+FOOD	This is a compound sign using the signs for DOG and FOOD.
LOBSTER	This sign clearly depicts a lobster's claws.
CANDY	This sign shows the candy in the mouth.
COOKIES	This looks like a cookie cutter when making cookies.
ICE-CREAM	This sign shows the way a person licks an ice cream cone.

Instructor's Guide: Lesson Four
Bravo ASL! Curriculum

Lesson Four: *Let's Go Food Shopping*

4.9 Experiential Activity

Con-SIGN-tration

Activity Goal: To assist students in recognizing and producing the new ASL vocabulary.

Activity Instructions:

1. **Prepare** the Con-SIGN-tration cards to be used in this activity by making two copies of the master (Appendix 4.9) and cutting the cards on the dotted lines.

2. **Attach** the cards to a board (a chalkboard, dry erase board, poster board, etc.) with strips of magnets, tape, or Velcro. Be certain the pictures are facing the board so students can't see the pictures.

3. **Ask** students to read *Con-SIGN-tration* in their workbooks (activity 4.9).

4. **Divide** the class into two teams seated across from each other.

5. **Instruct** one student from the first team to go to the board and select a Con-SIGN-tration card. The student must sign the ASL vocabulary that best represents the picture selected. If this sign is produced correctly, the student selects a second picture from the board. If the pictures match, and the student signs it correctly, that team gets a point. Another student from that same team gets to take another turn. If there is no match, or the signs are not made correctly, the other team gets a turn.

6. **Continue** playing the game until all the cards have been matched.

7. **Model** correct production of signs as needed.

Lesson Four: *Let's Go Food Shopping*

Con-SIGN-tration Cards Master:
Appendix 4.9

Student Workbook:
Activity 4.9

4.9 Experiential Activity

Con-SIGN-tration

Activity Goal: To help you recognize and produce the new ASL vocabulary.

Activity Instructions: Your class will be divided into two teams and will play a game called "Con-SIGN-tration."

One person will go to the board and select a Con-SIGN-tration card. This student must sign the vocabulary item that best represents the picture to the class. If the sign is correct and produced accurately, s/he selects a second card. If the pictures match, his/her team gets a point and another student from the same team gets a turn.

If there is no match, or the signs are not produced correctly, the other team gets a turn.

Have fun and remember to con-SIGN-trate!

Instructor's Guide: Lesson Four
Bravo ASL! Curriculum

©1996 Sign Enhancers, Inc.
All Rights Reserved.

Lesson Four: *Let's Go Food Shopping*

4.10 Experiential Activity

Don't Forget to Buy the...!

Activities Video

Activity Goal: To assist students in recognizing the new ASL vocabulary.

Activity Instructions:
1. **Ask** students to read *Don't Forget to Buy the...!* in their workbooks (activity 4.10).

2. **Show** students the *Don't Forget to Buy the...!* segment of the Activities Video (segment 4.10).

3. **Ask** students to circle the food items each signer indicates s/he needs from the grocery store.

4. **Show** overhead (Appendix 4.10) and **ask** individual students to indicate correct answers on the overhead while class members correct their own work.

Video Segment Content: (2 Minutes)

The following are the shopping lists requested by the signers on this segment of the Activities Video (segment 4.10):

Friend #1: Hot dogs, bread and eggs
Friend #2: Cookies, milk and candy
Friend #3: Carrots, lettuce and onion

Student Workbook:
Activity 4.10

Overhead Master:
Appendix 4.10

4.10 Experiential Activity

Don't Forget to Buy the...!

Activity Goal: To help you recognize the new ASL vocabulary.

Activity Instructions: You are going food shopping for three of your friends. Watch the video carefully as each one tells you what s/he wants you to buy at the grocery store. Circle the pictures of each of the items they sign so you don't forget!

Friend #1 wants you to buy...

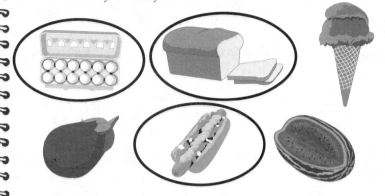

Friend #2 wants you to buy...

Friend #3 wants you to buy...

Lesson Four: *Let's Go Food Shopping*

4.11 Video Learning Experience

Practice Session: Sentences

Viewing Goal: To improve comprehension skills by watching sentences presented in ASL.

Viewing Instructions:
1. **Ask** students to read *Practice Session: Sentences* in their workbooks (activity 4.11).

2. **Play** the video segment entitled *Practice Session: Sentences* (segment 4.11). Each sentence is signed twice and an English translation is provided.

3. **Remind** students to watch the face of each signer to see the facial/body expressions and non-manual grammatical signals as well as the signs.

Video Segment Content:
(1 1/2 Minutes)

The following are English translations of the practice sentences:

1. I'm buying carrots, lettuce, and onions.
2. Cooking onions makes me cry.
3. I like to watch TV and eat popcorn.
4. When cooking soup, put carrots in.
5. The food I like is ice cream.
6. I cook hot dogs and hamburgers.

Student Workbook: Activity 4.11

4.11 Video Learning Experience

Practice Session: Sentences

Viewing Goal: To improve your comprehension skills by watching sentences presented in ASL.

Viewing Instructions: Watch the signed sentences for comprehension. Remember to watch the face of each signer to see the facial/body expressions and the non-manual grammatical signals as well as the signs.

It is recommended that you copy each signed sentence when it is repeated.

In the space below, record any questions or notes you have regarding the sentences.

Notes: _____
_____
_____
_____

Instructor's Guide: Lesson Four
Bravo ASL! Curriculum

©1996 Sign Enhancers, Inc.
All Rights Reserved.

4.12 Experiential Activity

What's the Sentence About?

Activities Video

Activity Goal: To improve comprehension skills using sentences presented in ASL.

Activity Instructions:

1. **Ask** students to read *What's the Sentence About?* in their workbooks (activity 4.12).

2. **Show** students the *What's the Sentence About?* segment of the Activities Video (segment 4.12). Each sample will be signed twice.

3. **Instruct** students to view each sentence carefully and select the answer which best describes what the sentence is about. **Ask** students to record each answer in their workbooks.

4. Upon completing this activity, **show** overhead (Appendix 4.12) and **review** the answers. **Model** any items the students found to be difficult. You may want to **show** the video again, **working** with the students as they review their answers.

Video Segment Content:
(2 Minutes)

The following are the samples presented in this segment of the Activities Video (segment 4.12):

      _____t_____
1. POPCORN, WANT ME

      _____t_____
2. CARROTS, BUY YOU

     _____t____
3. ONION, COOK ME

   _t_
4. TV, WATCH ME

5. HUNGRY NOW ME

Lesson Four: *Let's Go Food Shopping*

Student Workbook:
Activity 4.12

Overhead Master:
Appendix 4.12

4.12 Experiential Activity

What's the Sentence About?

Activity Goal: To improve your comprehension skills using sentences presented in ASL.

Activity Instructions: You will see five signed sentences. Each sentence will be signed twice. Determine what each sentence is about, and circle the correct answer below:

1. A. Watching fireworks
   B. Wanting lobster
   C. Wanting popcorn

2. **A. Buying carrots**
   B. Buying onions
   C. Eating cheese

3. A. Making soup
   B. Cooking onions
   C. Eating onions

4. **A. Watching TV**
   B. Watching me
   C. Eating TV dinners

5. A. Being good
   B. Being tired
   C. Being hungry

4.13 Video Learning Experience

Cultural Notes

Viewing Goal: To assist students in learning about the cultural aspects of ASL.

Viewing Instructions:
1. **Ask** students to read *Cultural Notes* in their workbooks (activity 4.13).

2. **Play** the video segment entitled *Cultural Notes* (segment 4.13). Because the presentation of this segment is beyond the linguistic ability of beginning students, please **turn on** audio and/or captions to optimize its educational value.

3. **Instruct** students to view the segment.

4. At completion of the video segment, **review** the content presented and **answer** any questions students may have.

Lesson Four: *Let's Go Food Shopping*

Video Segment Content: (5 Minutes) See the following Student Workbook excerpt for the content of this video segment.

Student Workbook: Activity 4.13

4.13 Video Learning Experience

Cultural Notes

Viewing Goal: To learn about the cultural aspects of ASL.

Viewing Instructions: View the *Cultural Notes* segment carefully for the following:

ASL storytelling is often creative and imaginative.
1. One example of this is the creation of Number Stories that use only the handshapes of numbers to tell the story.
2. Billy demonstrates a story using only the handshapes for numbers 1-10. The story is entitled "The Grocery Store Cashier." Billy explains the components of the story as:

Handshape:	What each handshape means:
1	A person working (a grocery store cashier)
2	The green bow tie worn by the cashier
3	The items being purchased
4	The clerk ringing up the prices on the register
5	A physical characteristic of the cashier (her hair)
6	The big bow in her hair
7	The cashier broke a fingernail
8	The cashier using a nail file
9	Her eyes turning to notice something
10	Many people waiting in line

Note: Following the explanation, Billy performs the whole story (see activity 4.14).

Lesson Four: *Let's Go Food Shopping*

4.14 Video Learning Experience

The Food Store Cashier

Viewing Goal: To provide students with the opportunity to see a Number Story performed.

Viewing Instructions:
1. **Ask** students to read *The Food Store Cashier* in their workbooks (activity 4.14).
2. **Play** the video segment entitled *The Food Store Cashier* (segment 4.14).
3. **Instruct** students to watch the Number Story performance.
4. **Play** the segment again. **Invite** students to copy the signs and facial/body expressions.

Video Segment Content: See activity 4.13 for the content of the Number Story.
(2 Minutes)

Billy explains that there are other examples of ASL creative sign-play in the Bravo family interaction at the food store. Two examples are: Anna wagging her index finger at Scott and Scott turning it into the sign for BANANA and Anna signing MELON on Scott's head, meaning he is a "melon-head."

Student Workbook: Activity 4.14

> 4.14 Video Learning Experience
>
> *The Food Store Cashier*
>
> **Viewing Goal:** To see an example of a Number Story performed.
>
> **Viewing Instructions:** Watch Billy perform the Number Story. Notice the handshapes he uses in the story.
>
> In the space below, record any questions or notes regarding the performance.
>
> Notes: _____
> _____
> _____

Lesson Four: *Let's Go Food Shopping*

4.15 Experiential Activity

Simple as One, Two, Three!

Activity Goal: To enhance students' appreciation of Deaf folklore by contributing to the production of an original Number Story.

Activity Instructions:

1. **Ask** students to read *Simple as One, Two, Three!* in their workbooks (activity 4.15).

2. **Inform** students that the class will work together to create a Number Story similar to the one demonstrated by Billy in the *Cultural Notes* segment.

3. **Ask** one student to volunteer to go to the board to write the numbers 1-10 and record what concept each letter will represent in the story.

4. **Lead** the class in creating their own Number Story. **Assist** as necessary, **encouraging** students to come up with the ideas themselves.

5. When the story is complete, **divide** the class into small groups and **ask** them to practice signing the story to each other.

6. **Circulate** among the students and **observe** their progress.

7. When all students have finished practicing the story, **ask** for volunteers to sign the Number Story to the class. If possible, **videotape** each student's performance of this activity.

8. **Close** the activity by **encouraging** the students to share the Number Story with someone outside of class and explain to others how creative and fun ASL can be.

Lesson Four: *Let's Go Food Shopping*

Student Workbook:
Activity 4.15

4.15 Experiential Activity

Simple as One, Two, Three!

Activity Goal: To create a Number Story.

Activity Instructions: You and your classmates will create a Number Story similar to the one demonstrated by Billy. Be creative, but remember to only use the handshapes of the numbers 1-10!

Don't worry; if you get stuck, your teacher will help you! When the story is complete, you will be given a chance to practice signing the story.

Use the lines below to record notes about what each number represents to help you remember the story.

Handshape: What each handshape means:
1
2
3
4
5
6
7
8
9
10

4.16 Video Learning Experience

Grammatical Notes

Viewing Goals: To assist students in learning about the grammatical aspects of ASL.

Viewing Instructions:
1. **Ask** students to read *Grammatical Notes* in their workbooks (activity 4.16).

2. **Play** the video segment entitled *Grammatical Notes* (segment 4.16). Because the presentation of this segment is beyond the linguistic ability of beginning students, please **turn on** audio and/or captions to optimize its educational value.

3. **Instruct** students to view the segment.

4. At completion of segment, **review** the content presented and **answer** any questions students may have.

Lesson Four: *Let's Go Food Shopping*

Video Segment Content:
(2 Minutes)

See the following Student Workbook excerpt for the content of this video segment.

Student Workbook:
Activity 4.16

> 4.16 Video Learning Experience
>
> *Grammatical Notes*
>
> **Viewing Goal:** To learn about the grammatical aspects of ASL.
>
> **Viewing Instructions:** View the *Grammatical Notes* segment carefully for the following:
>
> I. ASL Grammatical Structure:
>   A. ASL sentence structure is different from English.
>   B. ASL has many grammatical rules.
>   C. A commonly used structure is that of "topic/comment" structure.
>
> II. Topic/Comment Structure:
>   A. In ASL, the topic of the sentence (what the sentence is about) is signed first.
>   B. The comment (what you want to say about the topic) is signed after the topic. Here are some examples:
>   1. In English, we say "three carrots." In ASL, first the topic is established, CARROT, then the comment follows, THREE.
>   2. ONION, (the topic) FOUR (the comment) is demonstrated by Anna at the food store.
>   C. Some of the ways the topic of a sentence is identified:
>   1. Eyebrows raised
>   2. The last sign of the topic is held longer
>   3. There is a slight head-tilt
>
> **Note:** Watch for these topic markers to help you recognize the topics of sentences structured this way.

4.17 Experiential Activity

Topic Search

Activities Video

Activity Goal: To apply the grammatical information by identifying the topic within signed sentences.

Activity Instructions:
1. **Ask** students to read *Topic Search* in their workbooks (activity 4.16).

2. **Show** students the *Topic Search* segment of the Activities Video (segment 4.17). Each sentence will be signed twice.

Instructor's Guide: Lesson Four
Bravo ASL! Curriculum

©1996 Sign Enhancers, Inc.
All Rights Reserved.

Lesson Four: *Let's Go Food Shopping*

3. **Instruct** students to view the sentences carefully and determine the topic in each. **Ask** students to record the answers in their workbooks.

4. Upon completing this activity, **show** overhead (Appendix 4.17) and **review** the answers. **Model** any items the students found to be difficult. You may want to show the video again, **working** with the students as they review their answers.

Video Segment Content:
(1 1/2 Minutes)

The following are ASL glosses of the sentences:

1. $\overline{\text{MOTHER}}^{\,t}$, ME LOVE

2. $\overline{\text{HOT-DOG}}^{\,t}$, FOUR

3. $\overline{\text{POPCORN}}^{\,t}$, ME LOVE

4. $\overline{\text{MILK}}^{\,t}$, WANT

5. $\overline{\text{CHILDREN}}^{\,t}$, HUNGRY

Student Workbook:
Activity 4.17

Overhead Master:
Appendix 4.17

4.17 Experiential Activity

Topic Search

Activity Goal: To identify the topic within sentences presented in ASL.

Activity Instructions: You will see five sentences signed in ASL. For each sentence, circle the topic.

1. I love **mother**.

2. There are four **hotdogs**.

3. I love **popcorn**.

4. I want some **milk**.

5. **The children** are hungry.

Lesson Four: *Let's Go Food Shopping*

4.18 Video Learning Experience

Practice Session: Story

Viewing Goal: To improve comprehension skills by watching a story presented in ASL.

Viewing Instructions:
1. **Ask** students to read *Practice Session: Story* in their workbooks (activity 4.18).

2. **Show** the video segment entitled *Practice Session: Story* (segment 4.18). Billy signs a story using the vocabulary introduced in this lesson. **Turn off** audio and closed captions.

3. **Instruct** students to watch the story for comprehension and write a summary of the main points.

Video Segment Content: (1 1/2 Minutes)

The following is an English translation of the story:

A family went grocery shopping. Mom wanted to go shopping, and Dad wanted to help. The children wanted to help, too. Mom didn't want their help, but she accepted, and the whole family went to the market.

They needed to buy carrots, lettuce, bread, milk, soup, hot dogs, cookies and cheese.

Scott likes to go shopping. He buys ice cream, candy and cookies.

The whole family likes to go shopping.

Student Workbook: Activity 4.18

4.18 Video Learning Experience

Practice Session: Story

Viewing Goal: To improve your comprehension skills by watching a story presented in ASL.

Viewing Instructions: Watch the signed story for comprehension. In the space below, write a summary to help you remember the story.

Summary: _____
_____
_____
_____

Lesson Four: *Let's Go Food Shopping*

4.19 Comprehension Quiz

What Did You Understand?

Quiz Goal: To assess students' comprehension of the signed story.

Quiz Instructions:
1. **Instruct** students to complete the quiz in their workbooks (activity 4.19).

2. **Collect** for grading or **show** overhead (Appendix 4.19) and **ask** individual students to indicate the correct answers on the overhead while class members correct their own work.

3. **Ask** students to indicate which item(s) from the quiz they found difficult. **Review** by **modeling** or **replaying** that segment of the videotape.

Student Workbook: Activity 4.19

Overhead Master: Appendix 4.19

4.19 Comprehension Quiz

What Did You Understand?

Quiz Goal: To see how much of the signed story you understood.

Quiz Instructions: Read and answer each question below.

1. What did the family in the story do?
   A. Go grocery shopping
   B. Go to the movies
   C. Cook breakfast
   D. Clean the house

2. _____ wanted to go alone, but everyone wanted to help.
   A. Scott
   B. Mom
   C. Dad
   D. Anna

3. Scott likes to go food shopping.
   A. True
   B. False

4. Name at least three things the family bought.
   Carrots, lettuce, bread, milk, soup, hot dogs, cookies, and cheese.

5. What did Scott buy?
   Ice cream, cookies, and candy.

Instructor's Guide: Lesson Four
Bravo ASL! Curriculum

Lesson Four: *Let's Go Food Shopping*

4.20 Homework Assignment

A Food Shopping Adventure

Homework Goal: To provide students with the opportunity to improve ASL expressive skills.

Homework Instructions:

1. **Ask** students to read *A Food Shopping Adventure* in their workbooks (activity 4.20).

2. **Tell** students to create a short story about their family going food shopping, using at least ten of the vocabulary items introduced in this lesson.

3. **Ask** students to be sure to include at least two sentences using topic/comment structure as demonstrated during the *Grammatical Notes* segment.

Instructor Tip: *An opportunity for students to perform this assignment has been scheduled in the next lesson (Homework Review 5.2). If possible, it is recommended that you arrange to videotape each student's performance of this activity.*

Student Workbook: Activity 4.20

> 4.20 Homework Assignment
>
> *A Food Shopping Adventure*
>
> **Homework Goal:** To improve your ASL expressive skills.
>
> **Homework Instructions:** Create a signed story about your family going food shopping. Use at least ten of the vocabulary items introduced in this lesson. Be sure to also include at least two sentences using topic/comment structure as taught in the *Grammatical Notes*.
>
> Be prepared to sign your story to the class.

Instructor's Guide: Lesson Four
Bravo ASL! Curriculum

©1996 Sign Enhancers, Inc.
All Rights Reserved.

Lesson Four: *Let's Go Food Shopping*

4.21 Post-test
What Do You Know Now?

Assessment Video

Post-test Goal: To assess students' mastery of the lesson objectives.

Post-test Instructions:

1. **Ask** students to read the Post test Introduction in their workbooks (activity 4.21).

2. **Copy** and **distribute** the Lesson Four Post-test (Appendix 4.21).

3. **Play** the Assessment Video (segment 4.21) and allow students to complete Section One (comprehension portion) of the test.

4. **Instruct** students to complete Section Two (culture and grammar portion) of the test individually and hand in their papers when they are finished.

5. **Assign** Section Three (expressive portion) of the test and **schedule** a time when students are to perform. If possible, it is strongly recommended that you **videotape** this portion of the Post-test.

6. **Determine** grading options based upon programmatic requirements. A recommended guideline for measuring successful mastering of objectives is 80% accuracy.

Video Segment Content:
(2 Minutes)

The following is an English translation of the comprehension story:

The family was hungry. Dad wanted to cook dinner. Dad and the children went shopping to buy food. They needed to buy milk, bread, chicken, and carrots. The daughter wanted to buy cookies. The son wanted to buy popcorn. Dad told them no because it was time to go home.

Once they got home, Dad carried the bag of groceries into the kitchen. He took the bread out of the bag and noticed cookies under it. Then, he took the chicken out of the bag and was surprised at what was under the chicken. He pulled out some popcorn. The children just smiled.

Lesson Four: *Let's Go Food Shopping*

Student Workbook:
Activity 4.21

4.21 Post-test Introduction

What Do You Know Now?

Post-test Goal: To assess your mastery of the lesson objectives.

Post-test Introduction: This test has three sections.

Section One: The Comprehension section tests your ability to understand ASL.

Section Two: The Culture and Grammar section tests your knowledge of the material presented in the *Cultural* and *Grammatical Notes*.

Section Three: The Expressive portion tests your ability to use ASL.

Simply follow the instructions for each section. **Good luck!**

Post-test Master:
Appendix 4.21

4.21 Post-test

Section One: Comprehension

Instructions: You will see a signed story. Watch carefully and answer each question below.

1. _____ wanted to cook dinner for the family.
   A. Father
   B. Mother
   C. Son
   D. Daughter

2. Who went shopping?
   A. Father
   B. Mother
   C. Father and the children
   D. Mother and the children

3. What did the father find under the bread?
   A. Soda
   B. Ice cream
   C. Cookies
   D. Candy

4. What did the father find under the chicken?
   A. Ice cream
   B. Soda
   C. Candy
   D. Popcorn

5. What did Dad buy for dinner?
   A. Hot dogs
   B. Turkey
   C. Chicken
   D. Hamburgers

Lesson Four: *Let's Go Food Shopping*

Post-test Master:
Appendix 4.21

4.21 Post-test

Section Two: Culture and Grammar

Instructions: Read and answer each of the questions below.

6. The sentence structure for ASL is always the same as the sentence structure for English.
   A. True
   B. False

7. Because ASL is a visual language, it doesn't have any grammatical rules.
   A. True
   B. False

8. When signing a sentence, ASL tends to put the _____ first.
   A. Adjective
   B. Negative
   C. Topic
   D. Comment

9. A Number Story is:
   A. A story in which the number of signs is limited.
   B. A story comprised of handshapes of the alphabet.
   C. A story comprised of handshapes of numbers.
   D. A form of French folklore.

10. Because ASL has strict grammatical rules, you can't make a "play on signs" like English can make a "play on words."
    A. True
    B. False

Post-test Master:
Appendix 4.21

4.21 Post-test

Section Three: Expressive Portion

Instructions: Create five sentences about food that you will sign using topic/comment structure. Use any of the ASL vocabulary you have learned from Lessons One through Four. You can write the topic and comment of your sentences in the space below to help you prepare.

Your instructor will schedule a time for you to perform this section of the Post-test. You may prepare and practice prior to your scheduled time.

Topic	Comment
11. _____	_____
12. _____	_____
13. _____	_____
14. _____	_____
15. _____	_____

Congratulations!
You have completed
Lesson Four!

Lesson 5
REVIEW & PRACTICE SESSION

Materials Needed:

Equipment: VCR and TV monitor
Overhead projector and screen
Optional: video camera for activities 5.2, 5.9, 5.15, 5.21, 5.27, 5.29 and 5.35

Materials: Instructor's Guide
Student Workbook: one per student
Overhead transparencies for activities 5.3, 5.5 and 5.17 (see Appendix for masters)
Optional: blank videotape (or have students bring their own) for activities 5.2, 5.9, 5.15, 5.21, 5.27, 5.29 and 5.35
Post-test: Appendix 5.35

Videotapes: The Beginning ASL VideoCourse Lesson Five
Activities Video for activity 5.5
Assessment Video for Post-test 5.35

5.1 Begin Class
Housekeeping

Goal: To prepare students for this lesson.

Instructions: 1. **Welcome** students to Lesson Five of the VideoCourse.

2. **Perform** any necessary tasks (such as taking attendance) that may be required by your specific program.

Lesson Five: *Review & Practice Session*

5.2 Homework Review

A Food Shopping Adventure

Activity Goal: To provide feedback on previously assigned homework and to reinforce materials learned in earlier lessons.

Activity Instructions:

1. **Ask** students to read *A Food Shopping Adventure* in their workbooks (activity 5.2).

2. **Divide** the class into pairs.

3. **Instruct** students to take turns practicing the stories they were asked to prepare (*Homework Assignment 4.20*) while their partners practice comprehension.

4. **Remind** students to use at least ten of the ASL vocabulary items introduced in Lesson Four and at least two sentences using topic/comment structure.

5. When students have finished practicing, **ask** individual students to demonstrate their stories for the class. **Encourage** partners to use ASL to ask the storytellers questions about their stories. If possible, **videotape** each student's performance of this activity.

6. **Close** this activity by **modeling** any signs or grammatical features the students may have had trouble producing.

Student Workbook: Activity 5.2

> 5.2 Homework Review
>
> *A Food Shopping Adventure*
>
> **Activity Goal:** To show the results of your homework assignment.
>
> **Activity Instructions:** Find a partner and take turns signing the story, *A Food Shopping Adventure*, that was assigned in Lesson Four. Remember to use at least ten of the ASL vocabulary items introduced in Lesson Four and at least two sentences using topic/comment structure.
>
> When your partner is signing, pay close attention and practice your ASL comprehension skills! Use ASL to ask questions about your partner's story.
>
> Be prepared to sign your story to the class.

Instructor's Guide: Lesson Five
Bravo ASL! Curriculum

©1996 Sign Enhancers, Inc.
ALL RIGHTS RESERVED.

Lesson Five: *Review & Practice Session*

5.3 Lesson Objectives

Planning for Success

Goal: To identify the learning outcomes associated with successful completion of this lesson.

Instructions:
1. **Ask** students to read the objectives in their workbooks (activity 5.3).
2. **Show** the overhead (Appendix 5.3) and **read** through the objectives with the class.

Student Workbook: Activity 5.3

Overhead Master: Appendix 5.3

> 5.3 Lesson Objectives
>
> *Planning for Success*
>
> **Goal:** To see what you will learn by the end of this lesson.
>
> **Instructions:** Read the objectives below.
>
> Upon completing this VideoCourse lesson, you will be able to...
>
> 1. Recognize and accurately produce the ASL vocabulary introduced in Lessons One, Two, Three, and Four.
>
> 2. Demonstrate knowledge of the cultural information presented in Lessons One, Two, Three, and Four.
>
> 3. Recognize and apply the grammatical features presented in Lessons One, Two, Three, and Four.
>
> 4. Accurately use the ASL vocabulary and grammatical features presented in Lessons One, Two, Three, and Four in sentences, dialogues, and stories.

Lesson Five: *Review & Practice Session*

5.4 Video Learning Experience

Lesson Introduction

Viewing Goal: To assist students in understanding the format of this review lesson.

Viewing Instructions:
1. **Ask** students to read *Lesson Introduction* in their workbooks (activity 5.4).

2. **Play** the video segment in which Billy introduces the format of this review lesson (segment 5.4). Because this presentation is beyond the linguistic ability of beginning students, please **turn on** the audio and/or captions to optimize its educational value.

3. **Instruct** students to watch this segment to learn what to expect in this lesson.

Video Segment Content: (2 Minutes)

The following is an English translation of Billy's introduction:

Hi! Welcome to the Sign Enhancers, Inc. review tape!

Wow! You have learned a lot since you first started! There was a lot included in those first four videotapes! In this videotape, we are going to review the material together to help you. The more you practice, the more fluent you'll become!

We are going to take examples from each of the videotapes in the following areas:

The first is vocabulary. We'll review those signs we've already learned.

Second, we'll watch the Bravo Family, reviewing what they did and what happened to them. Seeing the signs again will help you remember them.

Third, we will have a person sign ASL sentences. Oh, now - don't get nervous! It will be clear and easy to understand.

Fourth, we'll have a dialogue between two people. Let me tell you, this will be something new and fun for you. This will be good practice. We'll see if you understand!

Fifth, we'll have a review of the *Grammatical Notes*. Those four videotapes discussed many different rules. It will be hard to condense it all! I will extract certain aspects of the information to see what you remember. We'll do the same thing for the

Lesson Five: *Review & Practice Session*

Cultural Notes. We'll quiz you on what you remember and see if you can guess the right answers.

And finally, we will have a practice story. You'll practice understanding the story and also signing it yourself! I promise that this tape will be fun!

Student Workbook:
Activity 5.4

5.4 Video Learning Experience

Lesson Introduction

Viewing Goal: To help you prepare for this review session.

Viewing Instructions: Watch carefully as Billy explains what you can expect from this *Review & Practice Session*.

Pay attention to what he is signing, but also notice *how* he expresses these ideas. Perhaps you will learn a few more signs! Watch how Billy uses facial/body expression, non-manual grammatical markers, and use of space.

In the space below, write any notes or questions you may have.

Notes: _____
_____
_____
_____

5.5 Experiential Activity

Crossword Puzzle

Activities Video

Activity Goal: To reinforce students' comprehension of the vocabulary from Lesson One.

Activity Instructions:

1. **Ask** students to look at the crossword puzzle in their workbooks (activity 5.5).

2. **Inform** students that they will see several of the Lesson One vocabulary items signed with references to their location on the puzzle (for example, 1 Across, 2 Down). **Ask** students to write the English word that best represents each sign and fits in the appropriate boxes of the puzzle. **Inform** the students that each item will be presented twice.

3. **Play** the Activities Video (segment 5.5).

4. When the activity is finished, **show** overhead (Appendix 5.5) and **ask** individual students to indicate correct answers on the overhead while class members correct their work.

Instructor's Guide: Lesson Five
Bravo ASL! Curriculum

©1996 Sign Enhancers, Inc.
ALL RIGHTS RESERVED.

Lesson Five: *Review & Practice Session*

Video Segment Content:
(5 Minutes)

The following is the content of this segment of the Activities Video (segment 5.5).

Across	Down
3. DAUGHTER	1. TIME
7. BREAKFAST	2. SHOWER
9. AFRAID	3. DOG
10. DRESSER	4. FATHER
11. COFFEE	5. WANT
12. GO	6. EAT
13. MOTHER	7. BATHROOM
	8. SPIDER

Student Workbook:
Activity 5.5

Overhead Master:
Appendix 5.5

5.5 Experiential Activity

Crossword Puzzle

Activity Goal: To help you remember the ASL vocabulary learned in Lesson One.

Activity Instructions: You will see several ASL vocabulary items from Lesson One signed on the video, as well as each answer's location on the puzzle, for example: 1 Across - MOTHER.

Decide what English word describes what is being signed and fits in the puzzle. Write it in the correct boxes. Each sign will be presented twice.

Lesson Five: *Review & Practice Session*

5.6 Video Learning Experience

Lesson One Review: Vocabulary

Viewing Goal: To reinforce comprehension skills of the ASL vocabulary introduced in Lesson One.

Viewing Instructions:
1. **Ask** students to read *Lesson One Review: Vocabulary* in their workbooks (activity 5.6).

2. **Play** the video segment entitled *Lesson One Review: Vocabulary* (segment 5.6). Billy reviews and signs each ASL vocabulary item twice.

    Note: **Use** this review as needed. **Place** in a lab setting for individual viewing or **increase** the level of difficulty by **turning off** audio and **covering** glosses on the monitor.

3. **Instruct** students to copy the signs as they watch the vocabulary review. **Encourage** students to raise their hands if they have difficulty remembering a particular sign.

Video Segment Content: (5 1/2 Minutes) See the following Student Workbook excerpt for the content of this video segment.

Student Workbook: Activity 5.6

5.6 Video Learning Experience

Lesson One Review: Vocabulary

Viewing Goal: To help you review the ASL vocabulary from Lesson One.

Viewing Instructions: Watch the Lesson One vocabulary review while you copy the signs. Raise your hand if there is a sign you do not remember, and your instructor will help you.

Signs representing the following concepts are reviewed in this video segment:

1. MOM/MOTHER
2. CHILDREN
3. BABY
4. GOOD
5. MORNING
6. COFFEE
7. HUNGRY
8. YES
9. NO
10. THANK-YOU
11. WHERE
12. LOVE
13. DEAF
14. HEARING
15. WHICH
16. WANT
17. TOILET/BATHROOM
18. BRUSH-TEETH
19. TIME
20. WAKE-UP
21. SCHOOL
22. BREAKFAST
23. PAST/BEFORE
24. GO
25. DOG
26. FOOL-YOU
27. SHOWER
28. KITCHEN
29. SON
30. DAUGHTER
31. SCARED/AFRAID
32. BED
33. SPIDER
34. ALMOST
35. GET-DRESSED

Lesson Five: *Review & Practice Session*

5.7 Video Learning Experience

Lesson One Review: Sentences

Viewing Goal: To improve students' comprehension skills by watching sentences presented in ASL.

Viewing Instructions:
1. **Ask** students to read *Lesson One Review: Sentences* in their workbooks (activity 5.7).

2. **Play** the video segment entitled *Lesson One Review: Sentences* (segment 5.7). Each sentence is signed twice and an English translation is provided.

3. **Remind** students to watch the face of each signer to see the facial/body expressions and non-manual grammatical markers as well as the signs.

Video Segment Content: (2 Minutes)

The following are English translations of the practice sentences:

1. Do you want to learn Sign Language?
2. Have you showered and brushed your teeth?
3. Good morning. Are the children awake?
4. Where is the baby?
5. Dad is scared of the spider!
6. Are you a girl or a boy?
7. Coffee? Yes, thank you.
8. I love my mother!

Student Workbook: Activity 5.7

5.7 Video Learning Experience

Lesson One Review: Sentences

Viewing Goal: To improve your comprehension skills by watching sentences presented in ASL.

Viewing Instructions: Watch the signed sentences for comprehension. Remember to watch the face of each signer to see the facial/body expressions, non-manual grammatical markers, and the signs.

It is recommended that you copy each signed sentence when it is repeated.

Notes: _____
_____
_____
_____

Instructor's Guide: Lesson Five
Bravo ASL! Curriculum

©1996 Sign Enhancers, Inc.
ALL RIGHTS RESERVED.

Lesson Five: *Review & Practice Session*

5.8 Video Learning Experience

Lesson One Review: Practice Dialogue

Viewing Goal: To improve comprehension skills by watching a dialogue presented in ASL.

Viewing Instructions:
1. **Ask** students to read *Lesson One Review: Practice Dialogue* in their workbooks (activity 5.8).
2. **Show** the video segment entitled *Lesson One Review: Practice Dialogue* (segment 5.8).
3. **Instruct** students to watch the dialogue for comprehension and take notes or write a summary in the space provided.

Video Segment Content: **The following is a summary of the dialogue presented in this segment:**
(1/2 Minute)

Dad says good morning to Anna and asks if she is hungry. Anna replies yes, she wants some coffee. Dad is surprised that she would want coffee. She laughs and tells him she fooled him. She really wants breakfast.

He laughs and says that he was fooled.

Student Workbook: Activity 5.8

> 5.8 Video Learning Experience
>
> *Lesson One Review: Practice Dialogue*
>
> **Viewing Goal:** To improve your comprehension skills by watching a dialogue presented in ASL.
>
> **Viewing Instructions:** Watch the signed dialogue for comprehension and take notes or write a summary in the space provided.
>
> Notes/Summary: _____
> _____
> _____
> _____

Instructor's Guide: Lesson Five
Bravo ASL! Curriculum

©1996 Sign Enhancers, Inc.
ALL RIGHTS RESERVED.

Lesson Five: *Review & Practice Session*

5.9 Experiential Activity

Dynamic-Duo Dialogue

Activity Goal: To improve students' expressive and receptive ASL skills.

Activity Instructions:
1. **Ask** students to read the *Dynamic-Duo Dialogue* in their workbooks (activity 5.9).

2. **Divide** the class into pairs.

3. **Instruct** pairs of students to create dialogues using the vocabulary from Lesson One. Each student should take a minimum of three turns.

4. After students have practiced, **ask** for volunteers to share their dialogues with the class. If possible, **videotape** each student's performance of this activity.

5. **Correct** production by **modeling** as needed.

Student Workbook: Activity 5.9

5.9 Experiential Activity

Dynamic-Duo Dialogue

Activity Goal: To improve your expressive and receptive ASL skills.

Activity Instructions: Work with a partner to create a dialogue using the Lesson One vocabulary (see the Sign Illustration Section for Lesson One vocabulary). Use ASL (no voices needed!) and be sure each person takes at least three turns signing.

Be prepared to share your dialogue with the class!

In the space below, record any ideas or notes you have regarding the dialogue.

Notes: _____
_____
_____
_____

Lesson Five: *Review & Practice Session*

5.10 Video Learning Experience

Bravo Family Revisited

Viewing Goal: To reinforce ASL expressive and receptive skills by reviewing a Bravo family interaction from Lesson One.

Viewing Instructions:

1. **Ask** students to read *Bravo Family Revisited* in their workbooks (activity 5.10).

2. **Play** the video segment of the Bravo family (segment 5.10). The Bravos use the ASL vocabulary within the context of their morning routine.

3. **Instruct** students to watch for review and take note of any portion they experienced difficulty understanding.

4. When the video segment is over, **divide** the class into small groups of four or five.

5. **Instruct** groups to re-enact the scene shown on the video. **Tell** students their version need not be identical, but they should use ASL and recreate the scene as closely as possible. Everyone in the group should actively participate.

6. When the group work is complete, **ask** each group to demonstrate their "Bravo Family Re-enactment" for the class.

Video Segment Content:
(2 1/2 Minutes)

The following is a summary of the Bravo family interaction:

Dad is sitting in the kitchen. Mom enters. Dad asks her if she wants any coffee. She says no, but that she is very hungry.

Noticing the time, Mom asks Dad where the children are. He indicates that they are still sleeping. Mom goes upstairs.

Mom goes into Anna's room first. Mom gently wakes Anna with a kiss and tells her it is time to get up and get ready for school.

Anna taps Mom to get her attention and asks her to sit on the bed for awhile. Mom sits on the bed with Anna. Anna then asks Mom, "A long time ago, when I was a baby... did you want a hearing or Deaf baby?"

Mom responds, "Did I want a Deaf or a hearing baby?... I wanted you! I love you!" Anna responds that she loves Mom too, and they hug.

Instructor's Guide: Lesson Five
Bravo ASL! Curriculum

©1996 Sign Enhancers, Inc.
ALL RIGHTS RESERVED.

Lesson Five: *Review & Practice Session*

Mom asks Anna if she would have preferred a Deaf or a hearing mother. Anna pauses to consider the question and responds, "I wanted you!"

Mom lets Anna know it is time to brush her teeth and get dressed and ready for school. Anna gets out of bed and goes to the bathroom to brush her teeth.

Student Workbook: Activity 5.10

5.10 Video Learning Experience

Bravo Family Revisited

Viewing Goal: To reinforce your ASL receptive and expressive skills by reviewing a Bravo family interaction from Lesson One.

Viewing Instructions: Watch the *Bravo Family Revisited* for review. Be prepared to re-enact this scene (using ASL) with your classmates!

Notes/Summary: _____
_____
_____
_____

5.11 Experiential Activity

It's Your Turn to Set the Table!

Activity Goal: To reinforce students' skills with ASL vocabulary from Lesson Two.

Activity Instructions:
1. **Ask** students to read *It's Your Turn to Set the Table!* in their workbooks (activity 5.11).

2. **Divide** the class into pairs.

3. **Instruct** students to take turns using ASL to describe setting the table for breakfast. **Encourage** students to use as many of the ASL signs introduced in Lesson Two as possible.

4. **Circulate** among pairs to **observe** student performance, **modeling** corrections as needed.

Lesson Five: *Review & Practice Session*

Student Workbook:
Activity 5.11

5.11 Experiential Activity

It's Your Turn to Set the Table!

Activity Goal: To help you remember the ASL vocabulary learned in Lesson Two.

Activity Instructions: With a partner, take turns using ASL to describe setting the table for breakfast. Use as many of the Lesson Two signs as possible. (See the Illustration Section for Lesson Two vocabulary.)

5.12 Video Learning Experience

Lesson Two Review: Vocabulary

Viewing Goal: To reinforce comprehension skills of the ASL vocabulary introduced in Lesson Two.

Viewing Instructions:
1. **Ask** students to read *Lesson Two Review: Vocabulary* in their workbooks (activity 5.12).

2. **Play** the video segment entitled *Lesson Two Review: Vocabulary* (segment 5.12). Billy reviews and signs each ASL vocabulary item twice.

   Note: **Use** this review as needed. **Place** in a lab setting for individual viewing or **increase** the level of difficulty by **turning off** audio and **covering** glosses on the monitor.

3. **Instruct** students to copy the signs as they watch the vocabulary review. **Encourage** students to raise their hands if they have difficulty remembering a particular sign.

Lesson Five: *Review & Practice Session*

Video Segment Content: See the following Student Workbook excerpt for the content
(4 Minutes) of this video segment.

Student Workbook:
Activity 5.12

5.12 Video Learning Experience

Lesson Two Review: Vocabulary

Viewing Goal: To help you review the ASL vocabulary from Lesson Two.

Viewing Instructions: Watch the Lesson Two vocabulary review while you copy the signs. Raise your hand if there is a sign you do not remember, and your instructor will help you.

Signs representing the following concepts are reviewed in this video segment:

1. COOK	11. GIVE	21. NAPKIN
2. EAT	12. TELL	22. WORK
3. EGG	13. WAITER	23. DO-WHAT
4. TOAST	14. GONE	24. WASH
5. CEREAL	15. SET+TABLE	25. HELP
6. ORANGE+JUICE	16. PLATE	26. MY-TURN
7. BANANA	17. GLASS	27. YOUR-TURN
8. MILK	18. FORK	28. YESTERDAY
9. ONE	19. KNIFE	
10. TWO	20. SPOON	

5.13 Video Learning Experience

Lesson Two Review: Sentences

Viewing Goal: To improve students' comprehension skills by watching sentences presented in ASL.

Viewing Instructions:
1. **Ask** students to read *Lesson Two Review: Sentences* in their workbooks (activity 5.13).

2. **Play** the video segment entitled *Lesson Two Review: Sentences* (segment 5.13). Each sentence is signed twice and an English translation is provided.

3. **Remind** students to watch the face of each signer to see the facial/body expressions and non-manual grammatical markers as well as the signs.

Instructor's Guide: Lesson Five
Bravo ASL! Curriculum

©1996 Sign Enhancers, Inc.
ALL RIGHTS RESERVED.

Lesson Five: *Review & Practice Session*

Video Segment Content: The following are English translations of the practice
(2 1/2 Minutes) sentences:

1. Where is my bowl?
2. I want to eat toast and eggs.
3. It is your turn to set the table.
4. Yesterday, I went to school.
5. Could you give me the plate, fork, and glass?
6. Waiter, I want a banana.
7. The orange juice is all gone. Give me the milk.
8. What is done in the kitchen? Cooking and washing dishes.

Student Workbook:
Activity 5.13

5.13 Video Learning Experience

Lesson Two Review: Sentences

Viewing Goal: To improve your comprehension skills by watching sentences presented in ASL.

Viewing Instructions: Watch the signed sentences for comprehension. Remember to watch the face of each signer to see the facial/body expressions and the non-manual grammatical markers as well as the signs.

It is recommended that you copy each signed sentence when it is repeated.

In the space below, record any questions or notes you have regarding the sentences.

Notes: _____
_____
_____
_____

5.14 Video Learning Experience

Lesson Two Review:
Practice Dialogue

Viewing Goal: To improve comprehension skills by watching a dialogue presented in ASL.

Viewing Instructions:
1. **Ask** students to read *Lesson Two Review: Practice Dialogue* in their workbooks (activity 5.14).

2. **Show** the video segment entitled *Lesson Two Review: Practice Dialogue* (segment 5.14).

Lesson Five: *Review & Practice Session*

3. **Instruct** students to watch the dialogue for comprehension and answer the comprehension questions in their workbooks.

4. **Review** answers while the students correct their work.

Video Segment Content: (1 Minute)

The following is a summary of the dialogue presented in this segment:

Mom asks Scott to help her get the spider out of the shower. Scott tells her that he loves spiders and she says that they scare her.

Scott says he will help and asks Mom for a fork. She is confused and asks him what he's going to do with the fork... eat the spider? He tells her he's going to fling the spider out of the tub with the fork.

Mom asks Scott for a glass. He asks her what she's going to do with the glass... drink the spider? She says, "No, I'm going to have a glass of milk!"

Student Workbook: Activity 5.14

5.14 Video Learning Experience

Lesson Two Review: Practice Dialogue

Viewing Goal: To improve your comprehension skills by watching a dialogue presented in ASL.

Viewing Instructions: Watch the signed dialogue for comprehension and answer the questions below.

1. Where is the spider?
   In the shower/tub.

2. How does Scott feel about spiders?
   He loves spiders.

3. How does Mom feel about spiders?
   She is scared of them.

4. What does Scott want to do with a fork?
   A. Eat the spider.
   B. Eat breakfast.
   C. Fling the spider.
   D. Kill the spider.

5. What does Mom want to do with the glass?
   A. Drink the spider.
   B. Capture the spider.
   C. Drink water.
   D. Drink milk.

5.15 Experiential Activity

Dynamic-Duo Dialogue

Activity Goal: To improve students' expressive and receptive ASL skills.

Activity Instructions:
1. **Ask** students to read *Dynamic-Duo Dialogue* in their workbooks (activity 5.15).

2. **Divide** the class into pairs.

3. **Instruct** pairs of students to create dialogues using the vocabulary from Lesson Two. Each student should take a minimum of three turns.

4. After students have practiced, **ask** for volunteers to share their dialogues with the class. If possible, **videotape** students' performance of this activity.

5. **Correct** production by **modeling** as needed.

Student Workbook: Activity 5.15

> 5.15 Experiential Activity
>
> *Dynamic-Duo Dialogue*
>
> **Activity Goal:** To improve your expressive and receptive ASL skills.
>
> **Activity Instructions:** Work with a partner to create a dialogue using the Lesson Two vocabulary (see the Sign Illustration Section for Lesson Two vocabulary). Use ASL (no voices needed!) and be sure each person takes at least three turns signing.
>
> Be prepared to share your dialogue with the class!
>
> In the space below, record any ideas or notes you have regarding the dialogue.
>
> Notes: _____
> _____
> _____
> _____

Lesson Five: *Review & Practice Session*

5.16 Video Learning Experience

Bravo Family Revisited

Viewing Goal: To reinforce ASL expressive and receptive skills by reviewing a Bravo family interaction from Lesson Two.

Viewing Instructions:
1. **Ask** students to read *Bravo Family Revisited* in their workbooks (activity 5.16).

2. **Play** the video segment of the Bravo family (segment 5.16). They will use the ASL vocabulary during their family breakfast.

3. **Instruct** students to watch for review and take note of any portion they experienced difficulty understanding.

4. When the video segment is over, **divide** the class into small groups of four or five.

5. **Instruct** groups to re-enact the scene shown on the video. **Tell** students their version need not be identical, but they should use ASL and recreate the scene as closely as possible. Everyone in the group should actively participate.

6. When the group work is complete, **ask** each group to demonstrate their "Bravo Family Re-enactment" for the class.

Video Segment Content: (2 Minutes)

The following is a summary of the Bravo family interaction:

The family is sitting at the table having breakfast. Dad is serving Scott eggs, toast, cereal, orange juice, and milk.

Mom explains to Scott that Dad has been cooking and giving Scott all this food. Mom asks what Scott should say to him in return. Instead of saying "thank you," Scott looks around his plate and asks his dad, "Hey, where's the banana?!"

Dad laughs and brings Scott a banana. Scott thanks Dad and gives him a tip.

Anna gets her dad's attention and places her order with the "waiter." She requests one egg, one piece of toast, and some orange juice "if its not all gone!" Dad signs each item as he serves it and Anna thanks him. When Dad puts his hand out for a tip, Anna gives him a "high five" instead!

Lesson Five: *Review & Practice Session*

Student Workbook: Activity 5.16

5.16 Video Learning Experience

Bravo Family Revisited

Viewing Goal: To reinforce your ASL receptive and expressive skills by reviewing a Bravo family interaction from Lesson Two.

Viewing Instructions: Watch the *Bravo Family Revisited* for review. Be prepared to re-enact this scene (using ASL) with your classmates!

Notes/Summary: _____
_____
_____
_____

5.17 Experiential Activity

Matchmaker

Activity Goal: To reinforce students' comprehension of Lesson Three vocabulary.

Activity Instructions:
1. **Ask** students to read *Matchmaker* in their workbooks (activity 5.17).

2. **Instruct** students to draw a line from each sign illustration to the picture that best matches its meaning.

3. **Show** the overhead (Appendix 5.17) and **ask** individual students to indicate the correct answers on the overhead while class members correct their own work.

Lesson Five: *Review & Practice Session*

Student Workbook:
Activity 5.17

Overhead Master:
Appendix 5.17

5.17 Experiential Activity

Matchmaker

Activity Goal: To help you remember some of the ASL vocabulary learned in Lesson Three.

Activity Instructions: Look at the illustrations of the Lesson Three vocabulary below. Draw a line from the illustration of the sign to the picture that best matches its meaning.

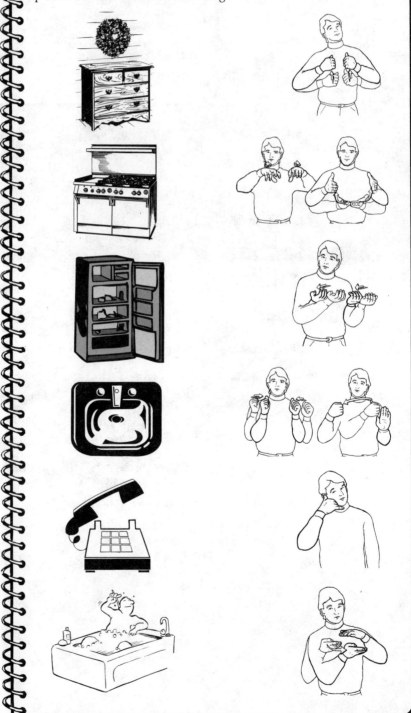

Instructor's Guide: Lesson Five
Bravo ASL! Curriculum

©1996 Sign Enhancers, Inc.
ALL RIGHTS RESERVED.

Lesson Five: *Review & Practice Session*

5.18 Video Learning Experience

Lesson Three Review: Vocabulary

Viewing Goal: To reinforce comprehension skills of the ASL vocabulary introduced in Lesson Three.

Viewing Instructions:
1. **Ask** students to read *Lesson Three Review: Vocabulary* in their workbooks (activity 5.18).

2. **Play** the video segment entitled *Lesson Three Review: Vocabulary* (segment 5.18). Billy reviews and signs each ASL vocabulary item twice.

   Note: **Use** this review as needed. **Place** in a lab setting for individual viewing or **increase** the level of difficulty by **turning off** audio and **covering** glosses on the monitor.

3. **Instruct** students to copy the signs as they watch the vocabulary review. **Encourage** students to raise their hands if they have difficulty remembering a particular sign.

Video Segment Content: See the following Student Workbook excerpt for the contents
(3 1/2 Minutes) of this video segment.

Student Workbook: Activity 5.18

5.18 Video Learning Experience

Lesson Three Review: Vocabulary

Viewing Goal: To help you review the ASL vocabulary from Lesson Three.

Viewing Instructions: Watch the Lesson Three vocabulary review while you copy the signs. Raise your hand if there is a sign you do not remember, and your instructor will help you.

Signs representing the following concepts are reviewed in this video segment:

1. REMOTE-CONTROL
2. CHAIR
3. COUCH
4. LIVING+ROOM
5. TV
6. ON
7. UNDER
8. BEHIND
9. IN
10. BED+ROOM
11. BED
12. DRESSER
13. UPSTAIRS
14. OVEN
15. REFRIGERATOR
16. SINK
17. TTY/TDD
18. TELEPHONE
19. LIGHT
20. FLASHING-LIGHT
21. BATH

Instructor's Guide: Lesson Five
Bravo ASL! Curriculum

Lesson Five: *Review & Practice Session*

5.19 Video Learning Experience

Lesson Three Review: Sentences

Viewing Goal: To improve students' comprehension skills by watching sentences presented in ASL.

Viewing Instructions:
1. **Ask** students to read *Lesson Three Review: Sentences* in their workbooks (activity 5.19).
2. **Play** the video segment entitled *Lesson Three Review: Sentences* (segment 5.19). Each sentence is signed twice and an English translation is provided.
3. **Remind** students to watch the face of each signer to see the facial/body expressions and non-manual grammatical markers as well as the signs.

Video Segment Content: (1 1/2 Minutes)

The following are English translations of the practice sentences:

1. I am going to the bathroom NOW!
2. There is no food in the oven.
3. Where are the eggs? In the refrigerator.
4. The father loves his children.
5. When a light flashes, it is the telephone/TTY.

Student Workbook: Activity 5.19

5.19 Video Learning Experience

Lesson Three Review: Sentences

Viewing Goal: To improve your comprehension skills by watching sentences presented in ASL.

Viewing Instructions: Watch the signed sentences for comprehension. Remember to watch the face of each signer to see the facial/body expressions and the non-manual grammatical markers as well as the signs.

It is recommended that you copy each signed sentence when it is repeated.

In the space below, record any questions or notes you have regarding the sentences.

Notes: _____
_____
_____

Lesson Five: *Review & Practice Session*

5.20 Video Learning Experience

Lesson Three Review: Practice Dialogue

Viewing Goal: To improve students' comprehension skills by watching a dialogue presented in ASL.

Viewing Instructions:
1. **Ask** students to read *Lesson Three Review: Practice Dialogue* in their workbooks (activity 5.20).
2. **Show** the video segment entitled *Lesson Three Review: Practice Dialogue* (segment 5.20).
3. **Instruct** students to watch the dialogue for comprehension and write a summary in the space provided.

Video Segment Content: (1/2 Minutes)

The following is a summary of the dialogue presented in this segment:

Anna is telling Scott to brush his teeth. He explains that he can't use the bathroom because Dad is in the shower.

Anna says that they have to leave for school.

Scott tells her he will brush his teeth in the kitchen sink.

She tells him that he can't use the kitchen sink because it is full of dishes.

He replies that in that case, he won't brush his teeth at all!

Student Workbook: Activity 5.20

> 5.20 Video Learning Experience
>
> *Lesson Three Review: Practice Dialogue*
>
> **Viewing Goal:** To improve your comprehension skills by watching a dialogue presented in ASL.
>
> **Viewing Instructions:** Watch the signed dialogue for comprehension and write a summary in the space provided.
>
> Summary: _____
> _____
> _____
> _____

Instructor's Guide: Lesson Five
Bravo ASL! Curriculum

©1996 Sign Enhancers, Inc.
ALL RIGHTS RESERVED.

Lesson Five: *Review & Practice Session*

5.21 Experiential Activity

Dynamic-Duo Dialogue

Activity Goal: To improve students' expressive and receptive ASL skills.

Activity Instructions:

1. **Ask** students to read *Dynamic-Duo Dialogue* in their workbooks (activity 5.21).

2. **Divide** the class into pairs.

3. **Instruct** pairs of students to create dialogues using the vocabulary from Lesson Three. Each student should take a minimum of four turns.

4. After students have practiced, **ask** for volunteers to share their dialogues with the class. If possible, **videotape** each dialogue.

5. **Correct** production by **modeling** as needed.

Student Workbook: Activity 5.21

5.21 Experiential Activity

Dynamic-Duo Dialogue

Activity Goal: To improve your expressive and receptive ASL skills.

Activity Instructions: Work with a partner to create a dialogue using the Lesson Three vocabulary (see the Sign Illustration Section for Lesson Three vocabulary). Use ASL (no voices needed!) and be sure each person takes at least four turns.

Be prepared to share your dialogue with the class!

In the space below, record any ideas or notes you have regarding the dialogue.

Notes: _____
_____
_____
_____

5.22 Video Learning Experience

Bravo Family Revisited

Viewing Goal: To reinforce ASL expressive and receptive skills by watching a Bravo family interaction from Lesson Three.

Viewing Instructions:
1. **Ask** students to read *Bravo Family Revisited* in their workbooks (activity 5.22).

2. **Play** the video segment of the Bravo family (segment 5.22). The Bravos use the ASL vocabulary as they look for the TV remote control.

3. **Instruct** students to watch for review and take notes of the main points.

4. When the video segment is over, **divide** the class into pairs.

5. **Instruct** pairs to use ASL to create a summary of the Bravo visit.

6. When they have finished, **ask** pairs to demonstrate their signed summaries for the class.

Video Segment Content: (2 Minutes)

The following is a summary of the Bravo family interaction:

Mom is looking in the refrigerator. The remote control is not there. Then she checks in the sink. It's not in the sink. She decides to search in the oven but still doesn't find the remote.

The phone rings (light flashes) and Mom answers it. It is a TTY user on the phone so she places the receiver on the TTY. Anna comes down and tells Mom that she saw the flashing light and was wondering if the call was for her. Mom tells her it is, and Anna sits down for her TTY conversation.

Mom walks into the bathroom and finds Dad standing in the tub. She comments that he has been searching for a long time in the bathroom and asks if he is planning on taking a bath. He says no, that he is searching for the remote.

He suggests that they check the toilet and they do. They do not find the remote there. They are perplexed as to where the remote could be and decide to go back to the living room.

Lesson Five: *Review & Practice Session*

Student Workbook:
Activity 5.22

5.22 Video Learning Experience

Bravo Family Revisited

Viewing Goal: To reinforce your ASL expressive and receptive skills by reviewing a Bravo family interaction from Lesson Three.

Viewing Instructions: Watch the *Bravo Family Revisited* for review. Be prepared to use ASL to summarize what happened in this video segment!

Summary: _____
_____
_____
_____

5.23 Experiential Activity

Point and Sign

Activity Goal: To reinforce comprehension and expressive skills with Lesson Four vocabulary.

Activity Instructions:
1. **Divide** the class into pairs.

2. **Instruct** students to read *Point and Sign* in their workbooks (activity 5.23).

3. **Instruct** students to look at the pictures and take turns pointing to items while their partners sign sentences using the sign(s) that best match the meaning of each picture.

4. **Inform** students that this activity is to be done entirely in ASL (no voice).

5. **Circulate** among the pairs to **observe** student performance, **assisting** as needed.

Lesson Five: *Review & Practice Session*

Student Workbook:
Activity 5.23

5.23 Experiential Activity

Point and Sign

Activity Goal: To improve your skills with the ASL vocabulary learned in Lesson Four.

Activity Instructions: Using the pictures below, follow your teacher's instructions to practice your signing skills.

Lesson Five: *Review & Practice Session*

5.24 Video Learning Experience

Lesson Four Review: Vocabulary

Viewing Goal: To reinforce comprehension skills of the ASL vocabulary introduced in Lesson Four.

Viewing Instructions:
1. **Ask** students to read *Lesson Four Review: Vocabulary* in their workbooks (activity 5.24).

2. **Play** the video segment entitled *Lesson Four Review: Vocabulary* (segment 5.24). Billy reviews all the ASL vocabulary. Because this presentation is beyond the linguistic ability of beginning students, please **turn on** the audio and/or captions to optimize its educational value.

   Note: **Use** this review as needed. **You may also place** in a lab setting for individual viewing.

3. **Instruct** students to copy the signs as they watch the vocabulary review. **Encourage** students to raise their hands if they have difficulty remembering a particular sign.

Video Segment Content: (8 Minutes) See the following Student Workbook excerpt for the content of this video segment.

Student Workbook: Activity 5.24

5.24 Video Learning Experience

Lesson Four Review: Vocabulary

Viewing Goal: To help you review the ASL vocabulary from Lesson Four.

Viewing Instructions: Watch the Lesson Four vocabulary review.

Signs representing the following concepts are reviewed in this video segment:

1. SODA-POP	14. CHEESE	27. CANDY
2. ALL-GONE	15. HOT-DOG	28. COOKIES
3. FOOD	16. HAMBURGER	29. ICE-CREAM
4. SHOPPING	17. TURKEY	30. ONE
5. BANANA	18. FISH	31. TWO
6. MELON	19. CHICKEN	32. THREE
7. PLANT	20. BREAD	33. FOUR
8. EGG+PLANT	21. POPCORN	34. FIVE
9. LETTUCE	22. CATSUP/KETCHUP	35. SIX
10. ONION	23. SOUP	36. SEVEN
11. CARROT	24. TOMATO	37. EIGHT
12. COW	25. DOG+FOOD	38. NINE
13. MILK	26. LOBSTER	39. TEN

Instructor's Guide: Lesson Five
Bravo ASL! Curriculum

©1996 Sign Enhancers, Inc.
ALL RIGHTS RESERVED.

5.25 Video Learning Experience

Lesson Four Review: Sentences

Viewing Goal: To improve students' comprehension skills by watching sentences presented in ASL.

Viewing Instructions:

1. **Ask** students to read *Lesson Four Review: Sentences* in their workbooks (activity 5.25).

2. **Play** the video segment entitled *Lesson Four Review: Sentences* (segment 5.25). Each sentence is signed twice and an English translation is provided.

3. **Remind** students to watch the face of each signer to see the facial/body expressions and non-manual grammatical markers as well as the signs.

Video Segment Content: (2 Minutes)

The following are English translations of the practice sentences:

1. The food is all gone, so I am going food shopping.
2. The children are hungry and want hamburgers.
3. The dog does not want dog food. The dog wants popcorn!
4. I want ice cream. Give me the bowl and spoon.
5. Which do you want, milk or soda pop?
6. When cooking soup, put in onions, carrots, and chicken.

Student Workbook: Activity 5.25

5.25 Video Learning Experience

Lesson Four Review: Sentences

Viewing Goal: To improve your comprehension skills by watching sentences presented in ASL.

Viewing Instructions: Watch the signed sentences for comprehension. Remember to watch the face of each signer to see the facial/body expressions and the non-manual grammatical markers as well as the signs.

It is recommended that you copy each signed sentence when it is repeated.

In the space below, record any questions or notes you have regarding the sentences.

Notes: _____
_____
_____
_____

Lesson Five: *Review & Practice Session*

5.26 Video Learning Experience

Lesson Four Review: Practice Dialogue

Viewing Goal: To improve students' comprehension skills by watching a dialogue presented in ASL.

Viewing Instructions:
1. **Ask** students to read *Lesson Four Review: Practice Dialogue* in their workbooks (activity 5.26).

2. **Show** the video segment entitled *Lesson Four Review: Practice Dialogue* (segment 5.26).

3. **Instruct** students to watch the dialogue for comprehension and write a summary in the space provided.

Video Segment Content: (1 Minute)

The following is a summary of the dialogue presented in this segment:

Mom asks Dad if he will help her with the food shopping. He says yes, but is curious about what she plans to buy. She tells him onions, tomatoes, carrots, and eggplant. Dad says that they should get hamburgers, hot dogs, ice cream, candy, cookies, and soda.

Mom says no, because she wants good food. Dad asks her if she will cook hamburgers and hot dogs. She tells him if he wants them, he will have to cook them himself. She is willing to cook chicken, turkey, fish, and eggplant. She asks him which one he would like. Because she will do the cooking, he decides on eggplant.

Student Workbook: Activity 5.26

5.26 Video Learning Experience

Lesson Four Review: Practice Dialogue

Viewing Goal: To improve your comprehension skills by watching a dialogue presented in ASL.

Viewing Instructions: Watch the signed dialogue for comprehension and write a summary in the space provided.

Summary: _____
_____
_____
_____

5.27 Experiential Activity

Dynamic-Duo Dialogue

Activity Goal: To improve students' expressive and receptive ASL skills.

Activity Instructions:

1. **Ask** students to read *Dynamic-Duo Dialogue* in their workbooks (activity 5.27).

2. **Divide** the class into pairs.

3. **Instruct** pairs of students to create dialogues using the vocabulary from Lesson Four. Each student should take a minimum of four turns.

4. After students have practiced, **ask** for volunteers to share their dialogues with the class. If possible, **videotape** each dialogue.

5. **Correct** production by **modeling** as needed.

Student Workbook: Activity 5.27

5.27 Experiential Activity

Dynamic-Duo Dialogue

Activity Goal: To improve your expressive and receptive ASL skills.

Activity Instructions: Work with a partner to create a dialogue using Lesson Four vocabulary (see the Sign Illustration Section for Lesson Four vocabulary). Use ASL (no voices needed!) and be sure each person takes at least four turns.

Be prepared to share your dialogue with the class!

In the space below, record any ideas or notes you have regarding the dialogue.

Notes: _____
_____
_____
_____

Lesson Five: *Review & Practice Session*

5.28 Video Learning Experience

Bravo Family Revisited

Viewing Goal: To reinforce ASL comprehension skills by reviewing a Bravo family interaction from Lesson Four.

Viewing Instructions:

1. **Ask** students to read *Bravo Family Revisited* in their workbooks (activity 5.28).

2. **Play** the video segment of the Bravo family (segment 5.28). The Bravos will use the ASL vocabulary within the context of grocery shopping.

3. **Instruct** students to watch for review and write a summary of the main points.

4. **Replay** any portion of this video segment that students experienced difficulty understanding.

Video Segment Content: (1 1/2 Minutes)

The following is a summary of the Bravo family interaction:

Dad is at the grocery store picking out turkey. He then requests a big fish.

Dad sees Scott goofing around at the lobster tank and sends him off to get groceries. Then Dad plays at the lobster tank.

Student Workbook: Activity 5.28

> 5.28 Video Learning Experience
>
> *Bravo Family Revisited*
>
> **Viewing Goal:** To reinforce your ASL comprehension skills by watching a Bravo family interaction from Lesson Four.
>
> **Viewing Instructions:** Watch the *Bravo Family Revisited* for review. In the space below, take notes or write a summary of the main points.
>
> Notes/Summary: _____
> _____
> _____
> _____

Lesson Five: *Review & Practice Session*

5.29 Experiential Activity

Pictures in the Air

Activity Goal: To improve students' expressive and comprehension skills

Activity Instructions:

1. **Ask** students to read *Pictures in the Air* in their workbooks (activity 5.29).

2. **Divide** the class into four groups.

3. **Assign** each group one of the pictures provided in the Student Workbook. **Tell** each group to create a short skit about their picture using ASL (no voice).

4. **Instruct** students to begin the activity by planning and practicing their skits with their groups. **Remind** students that they are not to use their voices during this activity.

5. **Circulate** among the groups to **observe** student performance, **assisting** as needed.

6. **Ask** each group to perform their skit for the class. If possible, it is recommended that you **videotape** each group's performance of this activity.

Student Workbook:
Activity 5.29

5.29 Experiential Activity

Pictures in the Air

Activity Goal: To improve your expressive and comprehension skills.

Activity Instructions: Your instructor will divide the class into four groups and assign each group one of the pictures below.

Based on your picture, work with your group to create a skit using ASL. Your group will have time to prepare and practice your skit and then show it to the whole class.

A.    B.

C.   D.

Instructor's Guide: Lesson Five
Bravo ASL! Curriculum

©1996 Sign Enhancers, Inc.
ALL RIGHTS RESERVED.

Lesson Five: *Review & Practice Session*

5.30 Video Learning Experience

Lessons One Thru Four Review: Cultural Notes

Viewing Goal: To assist students in reviewing the cultural aspects of ASL presented in Lessons One, Two, Three, and Four.

Viewing Instructions:

1. **Ask** students to read *Lessons One Thru Four Review: Cultural Notes* in their workbooks (activity 5.30).

2. **Instruct** students to complete the questions in their workbooks before viewing the segment.

3. **Play** the video segment entitled *Lessons One Thru Four Review: Cultural Notes* (segment 5.30) while students correct their work. Because the presentation of this segment is beyond the linguistic ability of beginning students, please **turn on** the audio and/or captions to optimize its educational value.

4. At completion of the segment, **answer** any questions students may have.

Video Segment Content: (3 Minutes) See the following Student Workbook excerpt for the content of this video segment.

Student Workbook: Activity 5.30

5.30 Video Learning Experience

Lessons One Thru Four Review: Cultural Notes
A Cultural Challenge

Viewing Goal: To help you review the cultural aspects of ASL presented in Lessons One, Two, Three, and Four.

Viewing Instructions: Answer the questions below to see how well you remember these cultural aspects of ASL. When you are finished, watch the video. Billy will provide the answers so you can correct your work.

1. What three things do all cultures of the world have in common?
   A. A common language
   B. Shared customs
   C. Cultural values

2. Name three culturally-appropriate ways to get a Deaf person's attention.
   A. Waving your hand
   B. Gently tapping a person's shoulder
   C. Stomping on the floor
   D. Flashing a light

3. Name two commonly held perspectives of Deaf people.
   A. **The perspective of Deaf people as handicapped**
   B. **The perspective of Deaf people as members of a culture**

4. Name three ways a Deaf person's home might be altered to become visually oriented.
   A. **With flashing lights**
   B. **TTY/TDD for using the phone**
   C. **Captions for the TV**

5.31 Video Learning Experience

Cultural Notes

Number Story: The Bug

Viewing Goal: To enjoy a part of Deaf folklore by watching and practicing a Number Story.

Viewing Instructions:
1. **Ask** students to read *Number Story: The Bug* in their workbooks (activity 5.31).

2. **Play** the video segment entitled *Number Story: The Bug* (segment 5.31). Because the presentation of this segment is beyond the linguistic ability of beginning students, please **turn on** the audio and/or captions to optimize its educational value.

3. **Play** the story again. This time, **turn off** audio and captions.

4. **Divide** the class into pairs. Following the viewing of the Number Story, **instruct** students to practice signing the story with their partners. **Encourage** students to help each other in the production of the story.

Video Segment Content: The following is a summary of the Number Story:
(1 Minute)

Billy: In the four videotapes that we have seen, we've discussed Deaf folklore, traditions, and different forms of expression. One way is through Number Stories. I think it was in

Lesson Five: *Review & Practice Session*

Lesson Three that I showed you one. Do you want to see another one? Have I got a nice surprise for you, because my friend has a Number Story to show you. He will perform it now. It's called *The Bug*.

Handshape:	What the handshape represents:
ONE	I'm looking
TWO	I see it
THREE	It's a bug
FOUR	It's a spider
FIVE	I'm scared
SIX	The spider jumps
SEVEN	His hair's on end
EIGHT	I hate it
NINE	I don't like it
TEN	Squish the spider

Student Workbook: Activity 5.31

5.31 Experiential Activity

Number Story: The Bug

Viewing Goal: To enjoy a part of Deaf folklore by watching and practicing a signed Number Story.

Viewing Instructions: You will see a Number Story performed. Watch the story carefully, taking note of how each number is used.

When you have finished viewing *The Bug*, practice signing it with your partner. Help each other sign the story the way it was done on the video. Remember, facial expression is an important part of the story!

5.32 Video Learning Experience

Lessons One Thru Four Review: Grammatical Notes

Viewing Goal: To review the grammatical aspects of ASL presented in Lessons One through Four.

Viewing Instructions: 1. **Ask** students to read *Lessons One Thru Four Review: Grammatical Notes* in their workbooks (activity 5.32).

Lesson Five: *Review & Practice Session*

2. **Play** the video segment entitled *Lessons One Thru Four Review: Grammatical Notes* (segment 5.32). Because the presentation of this segment is beyond the linguistic ability of beginning students, please **turn on** the audio and/or captions to optimize its educational value.

3. **Tell** students that Billy will present several questions related to yes/no or wh-questions. Be prepared to **stop** the video after each question so students can identify the question types and record the answers in their workbooks. (The answers come up quickly, so be ready with the pause button!)

4. **Continue** to play the video. Billy reviews topic/comment structure.

5. **Tell** students that Billy will present several sentences using topic/comment structure and they will be asked to identify the topic and comment within each. Be prepared to **stop** the video after each sentence is presented so students can record the answers in their workbooks.

Video Segment Content: See the following Student Workbook excerpt for the content
(4 Minutes) of this video segment.

Student Workbook:
Activity 5.32

5.32 Video Learning Experience

Lessons One Thru Four Review: Grammatical Notes
A Grammatical Challenge

Viewing Goal: To help you apply the grammatical aspects of ASL presented in Lessons One through Four.

Viewing Instructions: Watch Billy review the grammatical information taught in Lessons One through Four.

1. You will see three questions signed. Decide if these questions are all yes/no or wh-questions. Circle your answer.
   yes/no-questions   wh-questions

2. What are the non-manual markers that identify a wh-question?
   A. Eyebrows furrowed (down)
   B. Head tilted

3. Billy will show you three examples. You decide which are yes/no and which are wh-questions.
   1. Yes/no
   2. Wh
   3. Yes/no

4. Now you will see three sentences using topic/comment structure. Write the topic and comment for each sentence.

<u>Topic</u>	<u>Comment</u>
1. My Mother	I love (her)
2. Spider	Dad scared (of it)
3. Bathroom	I go (there) now(!)

Instructor's Guide: Lesson Five
Bravo ASL! Curriculum

Lesson Five: *Review & Practice Session*

5.33 Video Learning Experience

Lessons One Thru Four Review: Practice Story

Viewing Goal: To improve ASL comprehension skills by watching a signed story.

Viewing Instructions:
1. **Ask** students to read *Lessons One Thru Four Review: Practice Story* in their workbooks (activity 5.33).

2. **Show** the video segment entitled *Lessons One Thru Four Review: Practice Story* (segment 5.33). Billy signs a story using the vocabulary from Lessons One, Two, Three, and Four. **Turn off** audio and captions.

3. **Instruct** students to watch the story for comprehension and write a summary of the main points.

Video Segment Content: **The following is an English translation of the story:**
(2 Minutes)

A long time ago, when I was a little boy, I really wanted a dog. I asked my parents, "Can I have a dog? Say yes!"

My mom said, "Who's going to feed the dog?"

I said, "I will. I will, every morning!"

My Dad said, "Who's going to give the dog a bath?"

I said, "I will. I'll give the dog a bath!"

My mom said, "Who's going to help the dog learn to come, to sit, and where to go to the bathroom?"

I said, "I will. I'll help the dog learn!"

My Dad said, "Where is the dog going to sleep?"

I said, "Oh! Right next to my bed!"

My parents said, "Yes!" I could have a dog!

Now, who feeds the dog every morning? I do. Who helps the dog learn? I do. Who takes the dog to go to the bathroom? I do. Who gives the dog a bath? I do. Who loves the dog? I do!

Lesson Five: *Review & Practice Session*

Student Workbook:
Activity 5.33

5.33 Video Learning Experience

Lessons One Thru Four Review: Practice Story

Viewing Goal: To improve your ASL comprehension skills by watching a story presented in ASL.

Viewing Instructions: Watch the signed story for comprehension and write a summary of the main points.

Summary: _____
_____
_____
_____

5.34 Homework Assignment

Create-A-Story

Homework Goal: To improve students' expressive and receptive ASL skills.

Homework Instructions:

1. **Ask** students to read *Create-A-Story* in their workbooks (activity 5.34).

2. **Instruct** students to create a story using a topic they choose from the list provided in their workbooks. These topics are included in the following excerpt from the Student Workbook.

3. **Tell** students to be prepared to perform their stories to the class.

Instructor Tip: *An opportunity for students to perform this assignment is scheduled in the next lesson (Homework Review 6.2). It is recommended that you arrange to videotape each student's performance of this activity.*

Student Workbook:
Activity 5.34

5.34 Homework Assignment

Create-A-Story

Homework Goal: To improve your expressive ASL skills.

Homework Instructions: Create a story using one of the topics below. Be prepared to demonstrate your ASL story to the class!

A. You won't believe what happened when I woke up!

B. A funny thing happened at the food store!

C. You think your family is weird...

D. The breakfast of champions!

E. I found my dog in the most amazing place!

Lesson Five: *Review & Practice Session*

5.35 Post-test

What Do You Know Now?

Assessment Video

Post-test Goal: To assess students' mastery of the lesson objectives.

Post-test Instructions:

1. **Ask** students to read the Post-test Introduction in their workbooks (activity 5.35).

2. **Copy** and **distribute** the Lesson Five Post-test (Appendix 5.35).

3. **Play** the Assessment Video (segment 5.35) and allow students to complete Section One (comprehension portion) of the test.

4. **Instruct** students to complete Section Two (culture and grammar portion) of the test individually and hand in their papers when they are finished.

5. **Assign** Section Three (expressive portion) of the test and **schedule** a time when students are to perform. If possible, it is strongly recommended that you **videotape** this portion of the Post-test.

6. **Determine** grading options based upon programmatic requirements. A recommended guideline for measuring successful mastery of objectives is 80% accuracy.

Video Segment Content:
(2 Minutes)

The following is an English translation of the comprehension story:

There was a Deaf girl who was helping her mother set the table. She put the plates, glasses, forks, spoons, and knives on the table. She also put milk, orange juice, and melon on the table. She was putting down bowls for cereal when a spider crawled onto a plate. She was scared and went to the kitchen to tell her mother.

Her mom came to the table and asked where the spider was. The girl pointed, but the spider was gone. The mother went back to the kitchen.

The little girl put napkins on the table and the spider crawled onto a glass. The girl ran to the kitchen and told her mom. Her mother came to the table again, but no spider!

"Are you trying to fool me?" asked her mom.

"No," said the little girl, "the spider is trying to fool me!"

Lesson Five: *Review & Practice Session*

Student Workbook:
Activity 5.35

5.35 Post-test Introduction

What Do You Know Now?

Post-test Goal: To assess your mastery of the lesson objectives.

Post-test Introduction: This test has three sections:

Section One: The Comprehension section tests your ability to understand ASL.

Section Two: The Culture and Grammar section tests your knowledge of the material presented in the *Cultural* and *Grammatical Notes*.

Section Three: The Expressive portion tests your ability to use ASL.

Simply follow the instructions for each section. **Good luck!**

Post-test Master:
Appendix 5.35

5.35 Post-test

Section One: Comprehension

Instructions: You will see a signed story. Watch carefully and answer each question below.

1. What was the little girl doing?
   A. Looking for bugs
   B. Helping her mom cook in the kitchen
   C. Setting the table
   D. Trying to fool her mother

2. Name three things the girl put on the table:
   Plates; glasses; forks; knives; spoons; orange juice; melon; napkins; and milk

3. How does the girl feel about the spider?
   A. She likes it.
   B. She's afraid of it.
   C. She wants to capture it.
   D. She wants to give it to her mother.

4. When she first sees the spider, where is it?
   A. On a fork
   B. On a spoon
   C. On a knife
   D. On a plate

5. What does she do when she sees the spider?
   A. Hits it with napkin
   B. Takes it outside
   C. Takes it to her mother
   D. Tells her mother about it

6. What happens when Mom comes to the table?
   A. She takes the spider outside.
   B. She gets mad at the spider.
   C. She can't find the spider.
   D. She fools the daughter about the spider.

Instructor's Guide: Lesson Five
Bravo ASL! Curriculum

©1996 Sign Enhancers, Inc.
ALL RIGHTS RESERVED.

Lesson Five: *Review & Practice Session*

Post-test Master: Appendix 5.35

5.35 Post-test

Section Two: Culture and Grammar

Instructions: Read each statement carefully and determine if it is true or false (circle your answer).

7. Since Deaf people are part of American culture, they don't have their own culture.
   A. True
   B. False

8. The non-manual markers associated with yes/no questions include a furrowed (down) brow.
   A. True
   B. False

9. ASL often places the noun first, followed by the adjective.
   A. True
   B. False

10. In ASL, negatives usually appear at the end of a sentence.
    A. True
    B. False

11. When using a TTY, GA means "go ask."
    A. True
    B. False

12. A TDD helps make the audio on a television visible.
    A. True
    B. False

13. A relay service can assist a hearing person who does not have a TDD to call a Deaf person.
    A. True
    B. False

14. Since ASL is a visual language, it doesn't have any grammatical rules.
    A. True
    B. False

15. A Number Story is an example of Deaf folklore.
    A. True
    B. False

Lesson Five: *Review & Practice Session*

Post-test Master:
Appendix 5.35

5.35 Post-test

Section Three: Expressive Portion

Instructions: Create a story about one of the following topics:

1. Breakfast in My House
2. The Day Dad Broke the Chair
3. Food Shopping With My Family
4. My Morning Routine

Be sure to include:
    One sentence that is a yes/no question.
    One sentence with topic/comment structure.
    One sentence that asks a wh-question.
    One sentence that includes negation.
    Appropriate facial expression and non-manual markers.

Your instructor will schedule a time for you to perform this section of the Post-test. You may prepare and practice prior to your scheduled time.

16. ____ One sentence that is a yes/no question
17. ____ One sentence with topic/comment structure
18. ____ One sentence that asks a wh-question
19. ____ One sentence that includes negation
20. ____ Appropriate facial expression and non-manual markers.

Congratulations!
You have completed
Lesson Five!

Instructor's Guide: Lesson Five
Bravo ASL! Curriculum

©1996 Sign Enhancers, Inc.
ALL RIGHTS RESERVED.

Lesson 6
READ ANY GOOD FINGERS LATELY?

Materials Needed:

Equipment: VCR and TV monitor
Overhead projector and screen
Chalk/dry erase board
Optional: video camera for activities 6.2, 6.19, and 6.28

Materials: Instructor's Guide
Student Workbook: one per student
Overhead transparencies for activities 6.3, 6.4, 6.5, 6.7, 6.8, 6.11, 6.16, 6.17A, 6.17B, 6.17C, 6.26 (see Appendix for masters)
Colored crayons, pens, or markers for each student or group of students (or request that students bring their own) for activities 6.5, 6.11, 6.15, and 6.26
Optional: blank videotape (or have students bring their own) for activities 6.2, 6.19, and 6.28
Post-test: Appendix 6.28

Videotapes: The Beginning ASL VideoCourse Lesson Six
Activities Video for activities 6.5, 6.7, 6.21
Assessment Video for Post-test 6.28

6.1 Begin Class
Housekeeping

Goal: To prepare students for this lesson.

Instructions:
1. **Welcome** students to Lesson Six of the VideoCourse.

2. **Perform** any necessary tasks (such as taking attendance) that may be required by your specific program.

Lesson Six: *Read Any Good Fingers Lately?*

6.2 Homework Review

Create-A-Story

Activity Goal: To provide feedback on previously assigned homework and to reinforce materials learned in earlier lessons.

Activity Instructions:

1. **Ask** students to read *Create-A-Story* in their workbooks (activity 6.2).

2. **Divide** the class into groups of four or five students.

3. **Instruct** students in each group to take turns demonstrating the stories they practiced (*Homework Assignment 5.34*).

4. **Circulate** among the groups to **observe** their progress.

5. When students have finished demonstrating their stories, **ask** for volunteers to perform their stories for the class. If possible, **videotape** each student's performance of this activity.

6. **Close** this activity by **modeling** any signs or grammatical features the students may have had trouble producing.

Student Workbook: Activity 6.2

> 6.2 Homework Review
>
> *Create-A-Story*
>
> **Activity Goal:** To show the results of your homework assignment.
>
> **Activity Instructions:** In small groups, take turns demonstrating the story you practiced for your homework assignment. You may use the sign illustrations in your workbooks for reference.
>
> Remember you were to choose one of the following topics:
>
> A. You won't believe what happened when I woke up!
> B. A funny thing happened at the food store!
> C. You think your family is weird...
> D. The breakfast of champions!
> E. I found my dog in the most amazing place!
>
> Be creative! Ask each other questions in ASL about the topic of the story.

Instructor's Guide: Lesson Six
Bravo ASL! Curriculum

Lesson Six: *Read Any Good Fingers Lately?*

6.3 Pretest

What Do You Know?

Pretest Goal: To identify students' current level of knowledge pertaining to the lesson content.

Pretest Instructions:

1. **Ask** students to read and answer the questions in the pretest in their workbooks (activity 6.3).

2. **Show** the overhead (Appendix 6.3) and **ask** individual students to indicate the correct answers on the overhead while class members correct their own work.

3. **Inform** students that the contents of the pretest will be taught throughout the lesson.

Student Workbook: Activity 6.3

Overhead Master: Appendix 6.3

6.3 Pretest

What Do You Know?

Pretest Goal: To see how much you already know about what will be taught in this lesson.

Pretest Instructions: Read each question and circle the best answer.

1. Since Deaf people have complete mobility (they can walk), "access" is never a problem.
   A. True
   B. False

2. If you do not sign when a Deaf person is present, that person is likely to feel excluded.
   A. True
   B. False

3. When there are Deaf children in a family, it is especially important for the entire family to sign at all times.
   A. True
   B. False

4. Every sign has four parts. These parts are called:
   A. Hand-parts
   B. Sign-parts
   C. Parameters
   D. Paragrammars

5. Every sign is made of what four parts?
   A. Slow, medium, intermediate, and fast movements
   B. Fingers, waving, flipping, and flashing movements
   C. Circular, perpendicular, horizontal, and vertical movements
   D. Handshape, movement, location, and palm orientation

6. A sign produced accurately, but with the wrong movement, can change the meaning completely.
   A. True
   B. False

Instructor's Guide: Lesson Six
Bravo ASL! Curriculum

Lesson Six: *Read Any Good Fingers Lately?*

> 7. The manual alphabet is also referred to as "fingerspelling."
>   **A. True**
>   B. False
>
> 8. There are two sets of manual alphabets, one for capital letters and one for lower case letters.
>   A. True
>   **B. False**
>
> 9. Fingerspelling is used for proper names that don't have established signs.
>   **A. True**
>   B. False
>
> 10. If you are with a hearing friend and you see a Deaf person enter the room, you should start to sign even if your hearing friend doesn't understand Sign Language.
>   A. True
>   B. False

6.4 Lesson Objectives

Planning for Success

Goal: To identify the learning outcomes associated with successful completion of this lesson.

Instructions:
1. **Ask** students to read the objectives in their workbooks (activity 6.4).

2. **Show** overhead (Appendix 6.4) and **read** through the objectives with the class.

Student Workbook: Activity 6.4

Overhead Master: Appendix 6.4

> 6.4 Lesson Objectives
>
> *Planning for Success*
>
> **Goal:** To see what you will learn by the end of this lesson.
>
> **Instructions:** Read the objectives below.
>
> Upon completing this VideoCourse lesson, you will be able to...
>
> 1. Recognize and accurately produce the ASL vocabulary introduced in this and all previous lessons.
>
> 2. Explain the importance of equal access and inclusion of Deaf people in all communication events.
>
> 3. Define and demonstrate the four parameters of sign production.
>
> 4. Correctly identify and accurately produce all 26 handshapes that represent the letters of the American manual alphabet.
>
> 5. Understand when and how fingerspelling is used within the context of signed communication.

Lesson Six: *Read Any Good Fingers Lately?*

6.5 Lesson Focus

Color Time

Activities Video

Activity Goal: To develop a need for the ASL vocabulary introduced in this lesson.

Activity Instructions:
1. **Ask** students to read *Color Time* in their workbooks (activity 6.5).
2. **Distribute** crayons, colored pens, or markers to the students (or **ask** the students to take out their own).
3. **Play** the Activities Video (segment 6.5). This segment will show signed directions as to what color the students are to color each of the pictures provided in their workbooks. **Ask** students to color the pictures as indicated. If they do not know the signs for colors, **encourage** them to guess.
4. **Show** overhead (Appendix 6.5) and **ask** individual students to indicate the correct answers on the overhead while class members correct their own work.
5. **Inform** students that the signs related to colors will be taught in this lesson and they will be given the opportunity to do this activity again.

Video Segment Content: Signed directions include:
(4 Minutes)

Item	Color
1. ONION	SILVER
2. KNIFE	ORANGE
3. BABY	TAN
4. COFFEE	YELLOW
5. CHAIR	PURPLE
6. COUCH	WHITE
7. TELEVISION	RED
8. BED	PINK
9. DRESSER	GREEN
10. BANANA	BLACK
11. CARROT	BLUE
12. COW	GOLD
13. ICE-CREAM	BROWN

Lesson Six: *Read Any Good Fingers Lately?*

**Student Workbook:
Activity 6.5**

**Overhead Master:
Appendix 6.5**

(This overhead will be used
again in activity 6.11)

6.5 Lesson Focus

Color Time

Activity Goal: To experience an activity with "colorful" signs!

Activity Instructions: Watch the signed instructions to see what colors to use for the objects in the pictures below. If you do not understand the signs, try to guess which colors to use.

Instructor's Guide: Lesson Six
Bravo ASL! Curriculum

©1996 Sign Enhancers, Inc.
ALL RIGHTS RESERVED.

6.6 Video Learning Experience

Bravo Family Visit

Viewing Goal: To become sensitized to issues dealing with inclusion and exclusion.

Viewing Instructions:

1. **Ask** students to read *Bravo Family Visit* in their workbooks (activity 6.6).

2. **Play** the video segment of the Bravo family (segment 6.6). The Bravos meet a hearing school teacher and help her understand the concept of inclusion. Because this segment includes an interaction with a hearing person, **turn on** audio and/or captions to optimize its educational value.

3. **Instruct** students to watch the segment to learn information about inclusion and write a summary of the main points.

4. At completion of the video segment, you may **choose**:

    Option A: **Lead** a discussion using the following Thought/Discussion Questions:

    1) Have you ever been in a situation where you didn't know the language being spoken? If so, how did you feel?

    2) What are some situations in which Deaf people might still be excluded from full access? (How might access be improved for TV programs, movies, radio programming, airport communication, restaurants, paging systems, religious ceremonies, etc.?)

    3) What are things you could do to help increase access for Deaf people?

    OR

    Option B: **Ask** students to answer the Thought/Discussion Questions in their workbooks in class or for homework. **Collect** for grading or to provide written feedback.

Lesson Six: *Read Any Good Fingers Lately?*

Video Segment Content:
(3 1/2 Minutes)

The following is a summary of the Bravo family interaction:

The family has finished food shopping. Outside the store, they are approached by a woman who asks Mom if she can hear. Mom explains (by signing and speaking at the same time) that she is a hearing person.

The woman tells her that she is an art teacher and currently has a Deaf student in her class. She also tells Mom that it is unnecessary to sign because she is hearing. Mom explains that she is signing so that her Deaf family has access to the conversation.

Dad asks Mom not to interpret and begins signing to the woman. The woman is confused and asks Mom to interpret for her. Dad tells Mom it is okay for her to voice interpret as he signs.

He tells the woman that when a person doesn't understand what is being said, the result is a feeling of being confused and lost. He explains it is important to have equal communication for everyone.

The woman says that she understands. She then asks the family to teach her the signs for different colors. Anna and Scott say they will teach her.

Student Workbook:
Activity 6.6

6.6 Video Learning Experience

Bravo Family Visit

Viewing Goal: To get information about inclusion from watching a Bravo family interaction.

Viewing Instructions: Watch the Bravo family as they meet a school teacher at the food store. In the space below, write a summary of the main points.

Summary: _____
_____
_____
_____

Thought/Discussion Questions

1. Have you ever been in a situation where you didn't understand the language being spoken? If so, how did you feel?

2. What are some situations in which Deaf people might still be excluded from full access? (How might access be improved for TV programs, movies, radio programming, airport communication, restaurants, paging systems, religious ceremonies, etc.?)

3. What are things you could do to help increase access for Deaf people?

Lesson Six: *Read Any Good Fingers Lately?*

6.7 Experiential Activity

Read My Lips

Activities Video

Activity Goal: To provide students with firsthand experience with access issues.

Activity Instructions:

1. **Ask** students to read *Read My Lips* in their workbooks (activity 6.7).

2. **Inform** students that you will be showing them a video segment. **Tell** them to watch carefully, as there will be a quiz following the segment.

3. **Play** the activities video (segment 6.7A). There are no captions or voice-overs provided.

4. **Instruct** students to complete the *Read My Lips* quiz in their workbooks.

5. **Show** overhead (Appendix 6.7) and **ask** individual students to indicate correct answers on the overhead while class members correct their own work. If students to not know the answers, **proceed** to the next portion of this activity **without** giving the correct answers.

6. **Play** next video segment (segment 6.7B). Open captions are provided without audio.

7. **Ask** students to take the *Read My Lips* quiz again.

8. When students have completed the quiz, you may **choose**:

   Option A: **Lead** a discussion about the students' experience in this activity, using the following Thought/Discussion Questions:

   1) How did you do on the quiz when the program was not accessible?

   2) How would you do in school if you had to depend on lipreading?

   3) What are some adjectives to describe how you felt while viewing the tape?

   4) How would you deal with a lifetime of these kinds of experiences?

Instructor's Guide: Lesson Six
Bravo ASL! Curriculum

©1996 Sign Enhancers, Inc.
ALL RIGHTS RESERVED.

Lesson Six: *Read Any Good Fingers Lately?*

5) What was it like depending on the captions?

6) What did you learn from this experience?

OR

Option B: **Ask** students to complete the above Thought/Discussion Questions in their workbooks in class or for homework. **Collect** for grading or to provide students with written feedback.

Video Segment Content: (2 Minutes)

The following is a transcript of the information presented in this segment:

Today's topic is speech-reading, more commonly known as lipreading. We call it speech-reading because a person receives informational cues from more than just the lips. For example, a lot of information is received from the person's facial expressions.

Some people are much better speech-readers than others, although research shows that the ability to speech-read is not linked to intelligence.

In fact, speech-reading is a very challenging communication tool. Only 15 to 25% of the English language is actually visible on the lips.

Student Workbook: Activity 6.7

Overhead Master: Appendix 6.7

6.7 Experiential Activity

Read My Lips

Activity Goal: To show you a lecture to help you learn.

Activity Instructions: Watch the video very carefully. There will be a quiz immediately following this segment.

Quiz:

1. What was the main topic of this talk?
   Speech-reading

2. The term speech-reading is also called **lipreading**.

3. The ability to lip-read is directly linked to a how smart a person is.
   A. True
   B. **False**

4. A person who lip-reads also gets a lot of information from **facial expressions**.

5. According to the speaker, what percentage of the English language can be seen on the lips?
   15% to 25%

Instructor's Guide: Lesson Six
Bravo ASL! Curriculum

Lesson Six: *Read Any Good Fingers Lately?*

Thought/Discussion Questions

1. How did you do on the quiz when the program was not accessible?
2. How would you do in school if you had to depend on lipreading?
3. What are some adjectives to describe how you felt while viewing the tape?
4. How would you deal with a lifetime of these kinds of experiences?
5. How did you feel about using the captions for access to this program?
6. What did you learn from this experience?

6.8 Language Learning Instruction

Learning New Signs

Goal: To use ASL and visual aids to introduce this lesson's vocabulary.

Instructions:

1. **Ask** students to read *Learning New Signs* in their workbooks (activity 6.8).

2. **Show** the overhead (Appendix 6.8). **Introduce** the vocabulary by **pointing** to items presented in the pictures while **demonstrating** the signs.

3. **Reinforce** retention and **check** students' comprehension by **using** these signs to **ask** students questions.

   Note: For a step-by-step review of this method, see Lesson One (activities 1.6 and 1.12).

4. **Continue** this process until all the ASL vocabulary items have been introduced.

Lesson Six: *Read Any Good Fingers Lately?*

Overhead Content: Use the pictures in the overhead (Appendix 6.8) to introduce the signs representing the following concepts:

1. RED
2. ORANGE
3. BLUE
4. GREEN
5. YELLOW
6. PURPLE
7. WHITE
8. BROWN
9. SILVER
10. GOLD
11. PINK
12. BLACK
13. TAN

Note: For the pictures provided on this overhead, introduce the color of each object. You can use colored transparency markers to reinforce instruction.

Overhead Master: Appendix 6.8

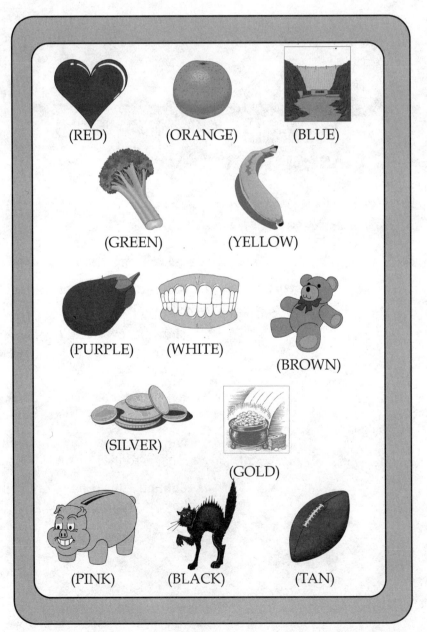

Lesson Six: *Read Any Good Fingers Lately?*

Student Workbook: Activity 6.8

6.8 Language Learning Instruction

Learning New Signs

Goal: To help you learn new ASL vocabulary.

Instructions: Your instructor will teach you new signs! Watch closely to learn what these signs mean and how they are produced.

In the space below, record any notes to help you remember the signs.

Notes _____
_____
_____
_____

6.9 Video Learning Experience

Introduction to New Vocabulary

Viewing Goal: To provide a signed demonstration of the accurate production of the new ASL vocabulary.

Viewing Instructions:
1. **Ask** students to read *Introduction to New Vocabulary* in their workbooks (activity 6.9).

2. **Play** the video segment entitled *Introduction to New Vocabulary* (segment 6.9). Billy introduces and signs each new vocabulary item twice. (If you wish to keep this a strictly visual presentation, **turn off** audio.)

3. **Instruct** students to watch how Billy produces the signs as well as the accompanying facial/body expressions.

4. **Ask** students to copy the signs and the facial/body expressions as Billy repeats each one.

Instructor's Guide: Lesson Six
Bravo ASL! Curriculum

©1996 Sign Enhancers, Inc.
ALL RIGHTS RESERVED.

Lesson Six: *Read Any Good Fingers Lately?*

Video Segment Content: See the following Student Workbook excerpt for the content
(2 Minutes) of this video segment.

Student Workbook:
Activity 6.9

6.9 Video Learning Experience

Introduction to New Vocabulary

Viewing Goal: To help you learn new ASL vocabulary.

Viewing Instructions: Watch how Billy produces each sign. Be sure to notice the facial/body expressions. Copy the signs as Billy repeats each one.

Signs representing the following concepts are introduced:

1. ORANGE
2. BLUE
3. GREEN
4. RED
5. YELLOW
6. PURPLE
7. WHITE
8. BROWN
9. SILVER
10. GOLD
11. PINK
12. BLACK
13. TAN

6.10 Video Learning Experience

Bravo Family Visit

Viewing Goal: To improve ASL comprehension skills by watching a Bravo family interaction.

Viewing Instructions:
1. **Ask** students to read *Bravo Family Visit* in their workbooks (activity 6.10).

2. **Play** the video segment of the Bravo family (segment 6.10). The Bravos will use the new ASL vocabulary within the context of teaching the school teacher the signs for colors.

3. **Instruct** students to watch for comprehension and write a summary of the main points.

4. **Replay** any portion of this video segment that students experienced difficulty understanding.

Video Segment Content: The following is a summary of the Bravo family interaction:
(3 Minutes)

The children take the art teacher through the vegetable department of the grocery store teaching her the signs: ORANGE, GREEN, BLUE, PURPLE, YELLOW, WHITE, RED, BROWN, SILVER, and GOLD. Then the kids tell her they have to leave.

Lesson Six: *Read Any Good Fingers Lately?*

Student Workbook:
Activity 6.10

6.10 Video Learning Experience

Bravo Family Visit

Viewing Goal: To improve your ASL comprehension skills by watching a Bravo family interaction.

Viewing Instructions: Watch the signed interaction and write a summary of the main points.

Summary: _____
_____
_____
_____

6.11 Experiential Activity

Color Time Again!

Activities Video

Activity Goal: To assist students in recognizing new ASL vocabulary.

Activity Instructions:

1. **Ask** students to read *Color Time Again!* in their workbooks (activity 6.11).

2. **Distribute** colored crayons, pens, or markers to the students (or **ask** the students to take out their own.)

3. **Play** the Activities Video (segment 6.11) and **ask** students to color the pictures as indicated.

4. **Show** overhead (Appendix 6.5) and **ask** individual students to indicate correct answers on the overhead while class members correct their own work.

5. **Ask** students to compare their performance with that of the *Lesson Focus* (activity 6.5).

Lesson Six: *Read Any Good Fingers Lately?*

Video Segment Content: (4 Minutes) The content of this segment is identical to that presented in activity 6.5.

Student Workbook: Activity 6.11

Overhead Master: Appendix 6.5

6.11 Experiential Activity

Color Time Again!

Activity Goal: To assist you in recognizing new vocabulary.

Activity Instructions: Look at the pictures below. Use colored pens or crayons to color the objects in the picture following the signed directions.

(SILVER) (ORANGE)

(TAN) (YELLOW)

(PURPLE) (WHITE) (RED)

(PINK) (GREEN) (BLACK)

(BLUE) (GOLD) (BROWN)

Instructor's Guide: Lesson Six
Bravo ASL! Curriculum

©1996 Sign Enhancers, Inc.
ALL RIGHTS RESERVED.

6.12 Language Learning Instruction

Learning Fingerspelling

Goal: To use ASL and visual aids to introduce fingerspelling.

Instructions:
1. **Ask** students to read *Learning Fingerspelling* in their workbooks (activity 6.12).

2. **Request** that one student write his/her name on the board.

3. **Fingerspell** the student's name (as written on the board) and **sign,** NICE-MEET-YOU. **Shake** the student's hand.

4. **Repeat** steps 2 and 3 above for several students (if you have a small enough class, do this with all the students).

5. **Reinforce** retention and **check** students' comprehension by **fingerspelling** students' names to ask questions. For example:

$$\overline{\text{E-L-L-E-N, WHO}}^{\text{wh-q}}$$

$$\overline{\text{T-O-M, YOU}}^{\text{q}}$$

$$\overline{\text{S-A-R-A-H, HER}}^{\text{q}}$$

$$\overline{\text{L-I-S-A, ME}}^{\text{q}}$$

Instructor Tip: *When introducing and practicing fingerspelling with this method, it is recommended that you fingerspell fluently and at a conversational pace.*

Student Workbook: Activity 6.12

6.12 Language Learning Instruction

Learning Fingerspelling

Goal: To help you learn to recognize fingerspelling.

Instructions: Your instructor will show you how to fingerspell names. Watch carefully to learn how to recognize your name and your classmates' names!

In the space below, record any notes to help you remember.

Notes: _____

_____

_____

Lesson Six: *Read Any Good Fingers Lately?*

6.13 Video Learning Experience

Introduction to Fingerspelling

Viewing Goal: To assist students in recognizing and producing the manual alphabet.

Viewing Instructions:
1. **Ask** students to read *Introduction to Fingerspelling* in their workbooks (activity 6.13).

2. **Play** the video (segment 6.13). Billy signs each letter of the manual alphabet and then explains how each letter is produced.

3. **Instruct** students to watch the video carefully to see how Billy produces each fingerspelled letter.

Video Segment Content: (5 Minutes) The American manual alphabet is introduced in this segment. Illustrations of each of the fingerspelled letters introduced are included with the Sign Illustrations at the end of this Instructor's Guide and the Student Workbook.

Student Workbook: Activity 6.13

6.13 Video Learning Experience

Introduction to Fingerspelling

Viewing Goal: To help you learn each letter of the manual alphabet (fingerspelling).

Viewing Instructions: Watch the video carefully to see how Billy produces each fingerspelled letter.

Fingerspelled letters representing each letter of the alphabet are introduced in this video segment.

A B C D E F G H I J K L M N O P Q R S T U V W X Y Z

Hint: This great practice sentence contains every letter in the alphabet! See if you can fingerspell the whole sentence...

"The quick brown fox jumped over the lazy dogs."

Instructor's Guide: Lesson Six
Bravo ASL! Curriculum

©1996 Sign Enhancers, Inc.
ALL RIGHTS RESERVED.

Lesson Six: *Read Any Good Fingers Lately?*

6.14 Video Learning Experience

Practice Session: Fingerspelling

Viewing Goal: To reinforce learning and assist students in correctly producing each letter of the manual alphabet.

Viewing Instructions:

1. **Ask** students to read *Practice Session: Fingerspelling* in their workbooks (activity 6.14).

2. **Play** the video (segment 6.14). Billy signs each letter of the manual alphabet, showing both the signer's and the recipient's perspectives.

3. **Instruct** students to practice producing each letter with Billy.

4. **Observe** the students while they practice the manual alphabet and take note of any production errors. When this segment of the video is finished, **model** any letters you saw produced incorrectly.

Video Segment Content: (2 Minutes) Fingerspelled letters representing the entire English alphabet are reviewed in this segment.

Student Workbook: Activity 6.14

6.14 Video Learning Experience

Practice Session: Fingerspelling

Viewing Goal: To produce each of the fingerspelled letters correctly.

Viewing Instructions: Watch how Billy produces each fingerspelled letter. The video will show you how each letter should look from both your perspective as well as the person to whom you are fingerspelling. Copy the handshapes as Billy signs each one.

Lesson Six: *Read Any Good Fingers Lately?*

6.15 Experiential Activity

SIGN-O

Activity Goal: To assist students in recognizing the new vocabulary including colors and the manual alphabet.

Activity Instructions:

1. **Ask** students to read *SIGN-O* in their workbooks (activity 6.15) and locate the *SIGN-O* cards provided there.

2. **Distribute** colored crayons, pens, or markers to the students (or **ask** them to take out their own).

3. **Instruct** the students (without voice) to color the five shapes located on their *SIGN-O* card. **Use** the color scheme below. You could **draw** each shape in the air and follow it with the sign for the corresponding color.

Shape (**Draw** in air)	Color (**Sign** to class)
Square	RED
Circle	BLUE
Triangle	GREEN
Diamond	ORANGE
Rectangle	BROWN

5. **Ask** students to *randomly* write the letters of the alphabet in the 24 squares on the card. **Suggest** that the students use a pencil so they can change the placement of the letters for future games.

6. **Begin** the game by randomly signing to the students various color-letter combinations (i.e. RED-A, ORANGE-F, GREEN-S, etc.) while students mark the appropriate squares with coins, chips, paper scraps, or a pencil. **Continue** with the game until a student completes a row (in any direction).

7. It is suggested that you **write down** the letter combinations in order to verify the winning card.

Student Workbook: Activity 6.15

6.15 Experiential Activity

SIGN-O

Activity Goal: To practice comprehension of colors and finger-spelling.

Activity Instructions: The class will play SIGN-O (just like the game BINGO). Use the SIGN-O card below.

Follow your instructor's signed directions and use markers or crayons to color the shapes on the top of the card.

Write the letters of the alphabet in random order (not in alphabetical order) in the blank squares on the card.

Your instructor will sign a color and then a letter. For example, BLUE - F. If this color/letter combination is on your card, place a coin, chip, scrap of paper or an "X" with a pencil (so you can use the card again) on the appropriate square.

When you have an entire row marked, you should stand up and fingerspell S-I-G-N-O. Good luck and have fun!

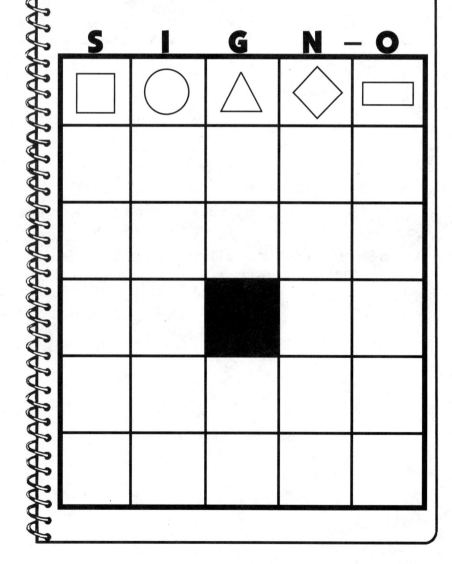

Lesson Six: *Read Any Good Fingers Lately?*

6.16 Video Learning Experience

Practice Session: Fingerspelling Usage

Viewing Goal: To learn the appropriate usage for fingerspelling and begin practicing production of fingerspelled words.

Viewing Instructions:
1. **Ask** students to read *Practice Session: Fingerspelling Usage* in their workbooks (activity 6.16).

2. **Play** the video segment entitled *Practice Session: Fingerspelling Usage* (segment 6.16A).

3. **Ask** students to view the instructional information for understanding. An outline of the information Billy presents about when to fingerspell and the rules regarding fingerspelling are included in the Student Workbook.

4. You may want to **stop** the tape and **show** overhead (Appendix 6.16) to **review** the information presented, answering any questions students may have.

5. **Proceed** with the practice session of this video segment (segment 6.16B).

6. **Ask** students to practice reading the fingerspelled words and copy Billy as he fingerspells each word.

Video Segment Content: Billy fingerspells and invites students to fingerspell along...
(4 Minutes)

1. C-A-T
2. B-A-T
3. F-A-T
4. M-A-T
5. B-O-Y
6. T-O-Y
7. C-O-Y
8. S-I-L-L-Y
9. B-I-L-L-Y

Lesson Six: *Read Any Good Fingers Lately?*

Student Workbook:
Activity 6.16

Overhead Master:
Appendix 6.16

6.16 Video Learning Experience

Practice Session: Fingerspelling Usage

Viewing Goal: To learn when to use fingerspelling and practice forming words.

Viewing Instructions: There are specific times when you should fingerspell words. There are also specific rules for fingerspelling. The following is an outline of what Billy teaches about the use of fingerspelling. Please review the information below.

I. When is fingerspelling used?

  A. For a person's name.
  B. For the name of a place.
  C. For things for which there is no established sign.

II. Rules regarding fingerspelling:

  A. Fingerspell smoothly (go from one letter to the next without extra movements).
  B. Keep the movement going (avoid stopping after each letter).
  C. Keep hand steady (do not bounce your hand with each letter).
  D. When you are reading fingerspelling, sound the word out the way you do when you are reading a book (do not say each letter as it is signed).
  E. When fingerspelling, look at the person to whom you are signing (rather than looking at your hand).

6.17 Experiential Activity

Fingercises

Activity Goal: To assist students in developing expressive and receptive fingerspelling skills.

Activity Instructions: Three *Fingercises* activities are provided below. **Select** one or all for students to perform.

Fingercise #1:

1. **Ask** students to read *Fingercise #1* in their workbooks (activity 6.17A).

2. **Instruct** students to fill in the boxes with the appropriate letters to show students the importance of watching for the fingerspelled word's shape when reading fingerspelling, instead of trying to see each individual letter.

3. **Show** overhead (Appendix 6.17A) and **ask** individual students to indicate correct answers on the overhead while class members correct their own work.

Instructor's Guide: Lesson Six
Bravo ASL! Curriculum

©1996 Sign Enhancers, Inc.
ALL RIGHTS RESERVED.

Lesson Six: *Read Any Good Fingers Lately?*

Student Workbook: Activity 6.17A

Overhead Master: Appendix 6.17A

6.17A Experiential Activity

Fingercise #1

Activity Goal: To learn how to read fingerspelling by watching for the shape of words that are fingerspelled instead of trying to see each individual letter.

Activity Instructions: Fill in the blank boxes below with the correct letters. Think about the shape of the whole word as well as the category to which the word belongs.

Names:	Animals:	Fruits:
Bob	cat	apple
Kelly	dog	pear
Joe	horse	melon
Debbie	monkey	grape

Fingercise #2:

1. **Ask** students to read the *Fingercise #2* in their workbooks (activity 6.17B).

2. **Instruct** students to fill in the blanks in the sentences to simulate the experience of missing information when reading fingerspelling. Students will need to apply closure skills to fill in the missing parts (an important skill for both fingerspelling and receiving signed communication).

3. **Show** overhead (Appendix 6.17B) and **ask** individual students to indicate the correct answers on the overhead while class members correct their own work.

Lesson Six: *Read Any Good Fingers Lately?*

Student Workbook:
Activity 6.17B

Overhead Master:
Appendix 6.17B

6.17B Experiential Activity

Fingercise #2

Activity Goal: To improve receptive fingerspelling skills.

Activity Instructions: Fill in the blanks below with the correct letters. This activity will help you see that you can miss several letters in a fingerspelled word and still be able to figure out what is being fingerspelled.

I w _ n _   to   g _   _ o   th _   s _ _ _ _.
(I want to go to the store)

Wh _   a _ e   y _ _   l _ _ k _ _ g   at   _ e?
(Why are you looking at me?)

D _   y _ _   l _ v _   S _ _ _   L _ _ _ _ _ _ e?
(Do you love American Sign Language?)

H _ _   o _ _   ar _   y _ _?
(How old are you?)

F _ ng _ _ _ _ _ l _ _ _ g   c _ _   be f _ _!!
(Fingerspelling can be fun!)

Fingercise #3:

1. **Ask** students to read *Fingercise #3* in their workbooks (activity 6.17C).

2. **Model** introducing yourself to a student. For example,

         __t__   __t__ __wh-q__
   MY NAME, P-A-T-T-Y   YOUR NAME, WHAT

                 __t__
   Fingerspell each name back, T-O-M, NICE MEET YOU

3. **Instruct** students to find partners and introduce themselves using fingerspelling as demonstrated. **Tell** students to continue introducing themselves to several students for additional practice.

4. **Observe** and **model** any necessary corrections.

Lesson Six: *Read Any Good Fingers Lately?*

Student Workbook:
Activity 6.17C

6.17C Experiential Activity

Fingercise #3

Activity Goal: To practice the use of expressive and receptive fingerspelling within the context of signed communication.

Activity Instructions: Your teacher will show you how to introduce yourself to another person using signs and fingerspelling.

Find a partner and introduce yourself the way you saw your teacher do it. When you have both finished your introductions, switch partners and practice again. Continue with different students until your teacher tells you to stop.

6.18 Video Learning Experience

ABC Story

Viewing Goal: To assist students in learning about ABC Stories as a part of Deaf folklore.

Viewing Instructions:
1. **Ask** students to read *ABC Story* in their workbooks (activity 6.18).
2. **Play** the video segment entitled *ABC Story* (segment 6.18).
3. **Instruct** students to view the segment (it is recommended that you **turn on** the audio and/or captions the first time.)
4. **Play** the segment again, and **turn off** the audio and/or captions. **Invite** students to copy the signs and facial/body expressions.

Lesson Six: *Read Any Good Fingers Lately?*

Video Segment Content: The following is a translation of the ABC Story.
(2 Minutes)

"A" I'm sleeping.
"B" I open my eyes.
"C" My hair's a mess.
"D" My toothbrush.
"E" The toothpaste.
"F" Ugh! There's something on my brush.
"G" I brush my teeth.
"H" How's my tongue look?
"I" What's on my tooth?
"J" Pick it out!
"K" How do my eyes look?
"L" How are the bags under my eyes?
"M" Pick up a tissue…
"N" Blow my nose.
"O" Two spots of color on my cheeks.
"P" Make them pink.
"Q" My hair curls back.
"R" It's hanging down.
"S" I take the brush.
"T" I have to go to the bathroom.
"U" I sit…
"V" I stand up.
"W" It needs to be flushed.
"X" I flush it.
"Y" Whew, something smells bad…
"Z" I'll spray the air.

Student Workbook:
Activity 6.18

6.18 Video Learning Experience

ABC Story

Viewing Goal: To learn about ABC Stories as a part of Deaf folklore.

Viewing Instructions: Watch as Billy introduces an original ABC Story. Notice how the handshapes used in the story follow the manual alphabet. Be sure to notice how Billy uses the handshapes with facial/body expression to create the story! You may want to copy Billy as he signs the story!

Notes/Summary: _____
_____
_____
_____

Lesson Six: *Read Any Good Fingers Lately?*

6.19 Experiential Activity

Simple as A, B, C!

Activity Goal: To teach students to appreciate Deaf folklore by participating in the creation of an original ABC Story.

Activity Instructions:

1. **Ask** students to read *Simple as A, B, C!* in their workbooks (activity 6.19).

2. **Inform** students that the class will work together to create an ABC Story similar to the one Billy demonstrated.

3. **Ask** for one student to volunteer to go to the board to write the alphabet and record what concept each letter will represent in the story.

4. **Lead** the class in creating its own ABC Story. **Assist** as necessary, **encouraging** students to come up with the ideas themselves.

5. When the story is complete, **divide** the class into small groups and **ask** students to practice signing the story to each other.

6. **Circulate** among the students and **observe** their progress.

7. When all students have finished practicing the story, **ask** for volunteers to sign the ABC Story to the class. If possible, **videotape** each student's performance of this activity.

8. **Close** the activity by **encouraging** the students to share the ABC Story with someone outside of class and explain to others how creative and fun ASL can be.

Lesson Six: *Read Any Good Fingers Lately?*

Student Workbook: Activity 6.19

6.19 Experiential Activity

Simple as A, B, C!

Activity Goal: To participate in creating an ABC Story.

Activity Instructions: You and your classmates will create an ABC Story similar to the one Billy showed you on the video.

Be creative, but remember to only use the handshapes of the alphabet!

Don't worry. If you get stuck, your teacher will help you. When the story is complete, you will be given a chance to practice signing the story.

Use the lines below to record notes about what each letter represents to help you remember the story.

A _____	J _____	S _____
B _____	K _____	T _____
C _____	L _____	U _____
D _____	M _____	V _____
E _____	N _____	W _____
F _____	O _____	X _____
G _____	P _____	Y _____
H _____	Q _____	Z _____
I _____	R _____	

6.20 Video Learning Experience

Cultural Notes

Viewing Goal: To assist students in learning about the cultural aspects of ASL.

Viewing Instructions:

1. **Ask** students to read *Cultural Notes* in their workbooks (activity 6.20).

2. **Play** the video segment entitled *Cultural Notes* (segment 6.20). Because the presentation of this segment is beyond the linguistic ability of beginning students, please **turn on** the audio and/or captions to optimize its educational value.

3. **Instruct** students to view the segment.

4. At completion of the segment, **review** the content presented and **answer** any questions students may have.

Instructor's Guide: Lesson Six
Bravo ASL! Curriculum

©1996 Sign Enhancers, Inc.
ALL RIGHTS RESERVED.

Lesson Six: *Read Any Good Fingers Lately?*

Video Segment Content: See the following Student Workbook excerpt for the content
(2 Minutes) of this video segment.

Student Workbook:
Activity 6.20

6.20 Video Learning Experience

Cultural Notes

Viewing Goal: To learn about the cultural aspects of ASL.

Viewing Instructions: View the *Cultural Notes* segment carefully for the following:

Inclusion and accessibility:

A. Example given: The art teacher who met the Bravo family at the food store learned about the importance of using Sign Language when Deaf people (such as the members of the Bravo family) are present so that they may feel included.

B. Viewers are encouraged to sign whenever there is a Deaf person present.

C. Billy shared the importance of signing at all times when there are Deaf children in a family. This provides the children with an opportunity to participate and to know they are important and valued members of the family.

6.21
Experiential Activity

Access to Another Culture!

Activities Video

Activity Goal: To allow students to apply the cultural information presented in this lesson regarding access to communication.

Activity Instructions: 1. **Ask** students to read *Access to Another Culture!* in
(6.21 A) their workbooks (activity 6.21).

2. **Inform** students that you will show a video segment presenting a speaker from another country. **Do not tell** students that this speaker is using a language other than English. **Instruct** the students to take notes on the main points of the speaker's lecture, in which she compares life in her country to living in the United States.

3. **Play** the Activities Video segment entitled *Access to Another Culture!* (segment 6.21A).

Instructor's Guide: Lesson Six ©1996 Sign Enhancers, Inc.
Bravo ASL! Curriculum ALL RIGHTS RESERVED.

Lesson Six: *Read Any Good Fingers Lately?*

4. **Allow** the class to experience the frustration and confusion of not having access to the information. (The next video segment will present the interpreted version of the speaker's lecture.)

5. **Ask** the class to share their notes about the speaker's topic.

6. You may **choose**:

   Option A: **Discuss** the experience, **allowing** students to share their feelings about the situation. **Help** the students relate this activity to what Deaf people experience when they are not included or given access. **Use** the following Thought/Discussion Questions:

   1) Were you interested in what this person was saying?
   2) Could you figure out some of the information?
   3) What are some adjectives to describe how you felt during this experience?
   4) Do you think this is similar to how Deaf people might feel sometimes?
   5) How could this information be made accessible to you?
   6) Would you like to view this segment again, with captions or an interpreter?

   OR

   Option B: **Ask** students to complete the above Thought/Discussion Questions in their workbooks in class or for homework.

Activity Instructions: (6.21 B)

7. **Play** the interpreted segment of video entitled *Access to Another Culture: Interpreted Version* (segment 6.21B).

8. When the segment is over, you may **choose**:

   Option A: **Lead** a discussion using the following Thought/Discussion Questions:

   1) How did the interpreter and/or captions change this experience for you?
   2) What are some adjectives to describe how you felt while you were viewing the interpreted/captioned version?
   3) Do you think this is similar to how Deaf people feel when they are using interpreters/captions?
   4) Do you think society provides adequate access to Deaf people?

   OR

   Option B: **Ask** students to complete the Thought/Discussion Questions in their workbooks in class or for homework. **Collect** for grading or to provide students with written feedback.

Lesson Six: *Read Any Good Fingers Lately?*

Note: To further reinforce the issue of access through interpreters, you may **choose** to **lead** this discussion using ASL and the services of a professional interpreter, thereby giving students a firsthand experience depending on an interpreter.

**Video Segment Content:
(2 Minutes)**

Segment 6.21 A presents a non-interpreted lecture in a foreign language; segment 6.21B presents an interpreted/captioned version of the same lecture.

Hi, my name is Jacquelline Collier. I'm from Pohnpei. I like my island, because I like to visit my aunt to see if she is okay. I like my island because our food is different. We eat banana, tapioca, tara, and yams.

When I came to America, it was different from my island because the weather is different. In Pohnpei, my island, we never get cold. In America the weather is different, because sometimes it gets cold and other times it is hot.

When I came here, I liked it because it is different from my island. I came here to go to school and help my family.

Student Workbook:
Activity 6.21A

6.21A Experiential Activity

Access to Another Culture!

Activity Goal: To learn cultural information from a person who comes from a different country.

Activity Instructions: Watch the video of a speaker from another country and use the space below to take notes:

___

Thought/Discussion Questions:

1. Were you interested in what this person was saying?

2. Could you figure out some of the information?

3. What are some adjectives to describe how you felt during this experience?

4. Do you think this is similar to how Deaf people might feel sometimes?

5. How could this information be made accessible to you?

6. Would you like to view this segment again, with captions or an interpreter?

Lesson Six: *Read Any Good Fingers Lately?*

6.21B Experiential Activity

Access to Another Culture!

Activity Goal: To gain access to the speaker from another country with the use of an interpreter or captions.

Activity Instructions: You will view the speaker from another country again. This time, you will have access to the information through an interpreter and/or captions. Use the space below to take notes:

_____
_____
_____
_____

Thought/Discussion Questions:

1. How did the interpreter and/or captions change this experience for you?

2. What are some adjectives to describe how you felt while you were viewing the interpreted/captioned version?

3. Do you think this is similar to how Deaf people feel when they are using interpreters?

4. Do you think society provides adequate access for Deaf people?

6.22 Video Learning Experience

Grammatical Notes

Viewing Goal: To assist students in learning about the grammatical aspects of ASL.

Viewing Instructions:
1. **Ask** students to read *Grammatical Notes* in their workbooks (activity 6.22).

2. **Play** the video segment entitled *Grammatical Notes* (segment 6.22). Because the presentation of this segment is beyond the linguistic ability of beginning students, please **turn on** the audio and/or captions to optimize its educational value.

3. **Instruct** students to view the segment.

4. At completion of segment, **review** the content presented and **answer** any questions students may have.

Lesson Six: *Read Any Good Fingers Lately?*

Video Segment Content: See the following Student Workbook excerpt for the content
(2 1/2 Minutes) of this video segment.

Student Workbook:
Activity 6.22

6.22 Video Learning Experience

Grammatical Notes

Viewing Goal: To learn some of the grammatical aspects of ASL.

Viewing Instructions: View the *Grammatical Notes* segment carefully for the following:

I. The four parts - or parameters - of every sign include:
   A. Handshape
   B. Movement
   C. Location/Position
   D. Palm orientation

II. Example: The four parameters of the sign YELLOW are:
   A. The handshape is a "Y."
   B. The movement demonstrated shows a side-to-side, wrist twisting movement.
   C. The position/location demonstrated is at the front of body on the dominant hand side.
   D. Palm orientation is facing to the side opposite the dominant hand.

III. Billy's recommendation: As you view the video, observe each of the four parameters for all the new vocabulary to ensure accurate production.

6.23 Experiential Activity

What Sign Am I Thinking Of?

Activity Goal: To allow students the opportunity to practice identifying the four parameters of given signs.

Activity Instructions:
1. **Ask** students to read *What Sign Am I Thinking Of?* in their workbooks (activity 6.23).

2. **Model** describing the parameters of several signs, while the class tries to determine what sign you are describing. For example, the sign YES can be described this way...

   A. Handshape - an "S" handshape on dominant hand.
   B. Location - in front of signer on dominant hand side.
   C. Movement - up and down, bending at the wrist.
   D. Palm orientation - palm faces down and rotates to face forward.

Lesson Six: *Read Any Good Fingers Lately?*

3. **Divide** the class into pairs.

4. **Ask** student "A" of each pair to select a vocabulary item from this or any previous lesson and describe each of the four parameters of that sign to their partner. **Instruct** student "B" to attend carefully to the parameters and begin to produce the sign until they can guess and correctly produce the sign.

4. **Tell** students that when "B" correctly produces the sign, partners should switch roles, with "B" selecting and describing the four parameters of a sign to "A" until "A" can correctly produce the sign.

5. **Repeat** the activity for several minutes to give students practice with the four parameters.

Student Workbook: Activity 6.23

6.23 Experiential Activity

What Sign Am I Thinking Of?

Activity Goal: To have the opportunity to practice using the four parameters of sign production.

Activity Instructions: Your teacher will divide the class into pairs. Student "A" will go first. "A" will select a vocabulary item from this or any previous lesson and describe each of the four parameters of that sign to student "B."

"B" should follow the parameters being described and begin to produce the sign until "B" can guess and correctly produce the sign that "A" described.

Switch roles and repeat this exercise several times.

6.24 Video Learning Experience

Practice Session: Sentences

Viewing Goal: To improve comprehension skills by watching sentences presented in ASL.

Viewing Instructions:

1. **Ask** students to read *Practice Session: Sentences* in their workbooks (activity 6.24).

2. **Play** the video segment entitled *Practice Session: Sentences* (segment 6.24). Each sentence is signed twice and an English translation is provided.

Instructor's Guide: Lesson Six
Bravo ASL! Curriculum

Lesson Six: *Read Any Good Fingers Lately?*

3. **Remind** students to watch the face of each signer to see the facial/body expressions and non-manual grammatical markers as well as the signs.

Video Segment Content: The following are English translations of the practice
(1 Minute) sentences.

1. The colors I like are pink and red.

2. The colors I like are blue and green.

3. I don't want the brown banana. I want the yellow banana.

4. The color of milk is white.

Student Workbook: Activity 6.24

6.24 Video Learning Experience

Practice Session: Sentences

Viewing Goal: To improve your comprehension skills by watching sentences presented in ASL.

Viewing Instructions: Watch the signed sentences for comprehension. Remember to watch the face of each signer to see the facial/body expressions and the non-manual grammatical markers as well as the signs.

It is recommended that you copy each signed sentence when it is repeated.

In the space below, record any questions or notes you have regarding the sentences.

Notes: _____
_____
_____
_____

6.25 Video Learning Experience

Practice Session: Story

Viewing Goal: To improve comprehension skills by watching a story presented in ASL.

Viewing Instructions:
1. **Ask** students to read *Practice Session: Story* in their workbooks (activity 6.25).

2. **Show** the video segment entitled *Practice Session: Story* (segment 6.25). Billy signs a story using the vocabulary introduced in this lesson. **Turn off** audio and closed captions.

Lesson Six: *Read Any Good Fingers Lately?*

3. **Instruct** students to watch for comprehension and write a summary of the main points.

Video Segment Content:
(1 1/2 Minutes)

The following is an English translation of the story:

I need to go grocery shopping.

When I woke up this morning, I went to the kitchen. I opened the refrigerator to get some milk, but the milk was not white. Ugh! So I reached for the bread. It was green! Eeew! My onion was black. Yuck! And the cheese... was brown. So I closed the refrigerator door.

I need to go food shopping!

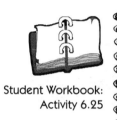

Student Workbook: Activity 6.25

6.25 Video Learning Experience

Practice Session: Story

Viewing Goal: To improve your comprehension by watching a story presented in ASL.

Viewing Instructions: Watch the signed story for comprehension. In the space below, write a summary of the main points to help you remember the story.

Summary: _____
_____
_____
_____

6.26 Comprehension Quiz

What Did You Understand?

Practice Session: Story

Quiz Goal: To assess students' comprehension of the signed story.

Quiz Instructions:
1. **Instruct** students to turn to the quiz in their workbooks (activity 6.25). **Distribute** colored crayons, markers, or pens (or **ask** students to take out their own).

2. **Replay** the practice story (segment 6.25) and **ask** students to color the pictures provided based on the information Billy gives in the story.

Instructor's Guide: Lesson Six
Bravo ASL! Curriculum

©1996 Sign Enhancers, Inc.
ALL RIGHTS RESERVED.

Lesson Six: *Read Any Good Fingers Lately?*

3. **Collect** for grading or **show** overhead (Appendix 6.26) and **ask** individual students to indicate correct answers on the overhead while class members correct their own work.

Video Segment Content: For a translation of the story, see previous Video Learning
(1 1/2 Minutes) Experience (Instructor's Guide 6.25).

Student Workbook:
Activity 6.26

Overhead Master:
Appendix 6.26

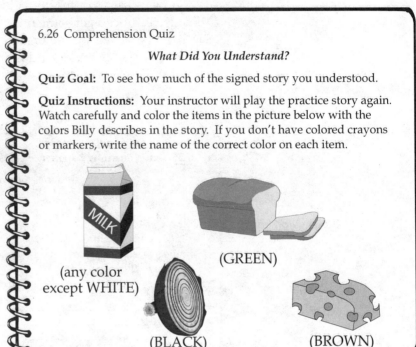

6.26 Comprehension Quiz

What Did You Understand?

Quiz Goal: To see how much of the signed story you understood.

Quiz Instructions: Your instructor will play the practice story again. Watch carefully and color the items in the picture below with the colors Billy describes in the story. If you don't have colored crayons or markers, write the name of the correct color on each item.

(any color except WHITE)
(GREEN)
(BLACK)
(BROWN)

6.27 Homework Assignment

Come Home With Me!

Homework Goal: To provide students with the opportunity to improve ASL expressive skills.

Homework Instructions:
1. **Ask** students to read *Come Home With Me!* in their workbooks (activity 6.27).

2. **Instruct** students to create a short story about their home. In the story, they should include who lives in their home (fingerspelling all the names) and describe all the rooms (color and contents).

Lesson Six: *Read Any Good Fingers Lately?*

Instructor Tip: An opportunity for students to perform this assignment has been scheduled in the next lesson (Homework Review 7.2). If possible, it is recommended that you arrange to videotape each student's performance of this activity.

Student Workbook: Activity 6.27

6.27 Homework Assignment

Come Home With Me!

Homework Goal: To practice using the new vocabulary and fingerspelling in a story.

Homework Instructions: Create a short story about your home. Be sure to include who lives there (fingerspell all the names) and describe all the rooms, including room color and contents.

6.28 Post-test

What Do You Know Now?

Assessment Video

Post-test Goal: To assess students' mastery of the lesson objectives.

Post-test Instructions:
1. **Ask** students to read the Post-test Introduction in their workbooks (activity 6.28).

2. **Copy** and **distribute** the Lesson Six Post-test (Appendix 6.28).

3. **Play** the Assessment Video (segment 6.28) and allow students to complete Section One (comprehension portion) of the test.

4. **Instruct** students to complete Section Two (culture and grammar portion) of the test individually and hand in their papers when they are finished.

5. **Assign** Section Three (expressive portion) of the test and **schedule** when students are to perform. It is strongly recommended that you **videotape** this portion of the Post-test.

Lesson Six: *Read Any Good Fingers Lately?*

6. **Determine** grading options based upon programmatic requirements. A recommended guideline for measuring successful mastery of objectives is 80% accuracy.

Video Segment Content: (1 1/2 Minutes)

The following is an English translation of the comprehension story:

Hi! My name is Jan. My mother's name is Pam. My father's name is Ben. My son's name is Sam.

The colors in my house are great! My bedroom is purple. My son's bedroom is red! My kitchen is orange! Do you like the colors of my house?

Student Workbook: Activity 6.28

> 6.28 Post-test Introduction
>
> *What Do You Know Now?*
>
> **Post-test Goal:** To assess your mastery of the lesson objectives.
>
> **Post-test Introduction:** This test has three sections:
>
> Section One: The Comprehension section tests your ability to understand ASL.
>
> Section Two: The Culture and Grammar section tests your knowledge of the material presented in the *Cultural* and *Grammatical Notes*.
>
> Section Three: The Expressive portion tests your ability to use ASL.
>
> Simply follow the instructions for each section. **Good luck!**

Post-test Master:
Appendix 6.28

6.28 Post-test

Section One: Comprehension

Instructions: You will see a short signed story. Watch carefully and answer each question below.

1. My mother's name is _____.
   A. Kay
   B. Pam
   C. Patty
   D. Kim

2. My father's name is _____.
   A. Ben
   B. Dan
   C. Bob
   D. Dave

3. The color of my bedroom is _____.
   A. Yellow
   B. Blue
   C. Purple
   D. Green

4. The color of my son's room is _____.
   A. Brown
   B. Silver
   C. Pink
   D. Red

5. My son's name is _____.
   A. Zack
   B. Bob
   C. Sam
   D. Steven

Post-test Master: Appendix 6.28

6.28 Post-test

Section Two: Culture and Grammar

Instructions: Read each statement carefully and circle the best answer.

6. There are two sets of manual alphabets, one for spelling the names of people and one for spelling the names of places.
   A. True
   B. False

7. When there are Deaf children in a family it is especially important for the entire family to sign at all times.
   A. True
   B. False

8. Every sign has four parts. These parts are called:
   A. Hand-parts
   B. Sign-parts
   C. Parameters
   D. Paragrammars

9. Every sign is made of four things: handshape, movement, location, and...
   A. Palm orientation
   B. Fingerspelling
   C. Two hands
   D. Fast movements

10. A sign can be produced accurately, but if the handshape is wrong, the meaning can be changed completely.
    A. True
    B. False

Post-test Master:
Appendix 6.28

6.28 Post-test

Section Three: Expressive Portion

Instructions: Describe a friend's house and the people who live there, using at least five signs learned in Lesson Six. Also include at least three fingerspelled names.

Your instructor will schedule a time for you to perform this section of the Post-test. You may prepare and practice prior to your scheduled time. Use the space below to prepare for your expressive performance.

Include at least five signs from Lesson Six.

11. _____
12. _____
13. _____
14. _____
15. _____

Include three fingerspelled names:

16. _____
17. _____
18. _____

Congratulations!
You have completed
Lesson Six!

Lesson 7
A School 'Daze'

Materials Needed:

Equipment: VCR and TV monitor
Overhead projector and screen
Chalk/dry erase board
Optional: video camera for activities 7.2 and 7.28

Materials: Instructor's Guide
Student Workbook: one per student
Overhead transparencies for activities 7.3, 7.4, 7.6, 7.9, 7.10, 7.13, 7.15, 7.22, and 7.26 (see Appendix for masters)
Optional: blank videotape (or have students bring their own) for activities 7.2 and 7.28
Post-test: Appendix 7.28

Videotapes: The Beginning ASL VideoCourse Lesson Seven
Activities Video for activity 7.13
Assessment Video for Post-test 7.28

7.1 Begin Class
Housekeeping

Goal: To prepare students for this lesson.

Instructions:
1. **Welcome** students to Lesson Seven of the VideoCourse.

2. **Perform** any necessary tasks (such as taking attendance) that may be required by your specific program.

Lesson Seven: *A School 'Daze'*

7.2 Homework Review

Come Home With Me!

Activity Goal: To provide feedback on previously assigned homework and to reinforce materials learned in earlier lessons.

Activity Instructions:

1. **Ask** students to read *Come Home With Me!* in their workbooks (activity 7.2).

2. **Divide** the class into groups of three or four students.

3. **Instruct** students in each group to take turns signing the story about their home (*Homework Assignment 6.27*). **Remind** students that their stories should include the fingerspelled names of all who live there as well as a description of the rooms (including the color of the rooms and furniture).

4. **Circulate** among the groups to **observe** their progress.

5. When students have finished demonstrating their stories, **ask** for volunteers to perform their stories for the class. If possible, **videotape** each student's performance of this activity.

6. **Close** this activity by **modeling** any signs or grammatical features the students may have had trouble producing.

Student Workbook: Activity 7.2

7.2 Homework Review

Come Home With Me!

Activity Goal: To show the results of your homework assignment.

Activity Instructions: In your small group, take turns signing the story about your home that you practiced for your homework assignment.

Remember to include the fingerspelled names of all the people who live in your home and a description of the rooms (including room color and contents).

Be creative! Ask questions about each other's homes using ASL.

Lesson Seven: *A School 'Daze'*

7.3 Pretest
What Do You Know?

Pretest Goal: To identify students' current level of knowledge pertaining to the lesson content.

Pretest Instructions:
1. **Ask** students to read and answer the questions in the pretest in their workbooks (activity 7.3).
2. **Show** overhead (Appendix 7.3) and **ask** individual students to indicate the correct answers on the overhead while class members correct their own work.
3. **Inform** students that the contents of the pretest will be taught throughout the lesson.

Student Workbook: Activity 7.3

Overhead Master: Appendix 7.3

7.3 Pretest

What Do You Know?

Pretest Goal: To see how much you already know about what will be taught in this lesson.

Pretest Instructions: Read each question and circle the best answer.

1. All Deaf children attend schools for the Deaf.
   A. True
   B. False

2. In order for a Deaf child to attend a school for the Deaf, s/he must live away from home.
   A. True
   B. False

3. The self-esteem and self-identity of a Deaf child is an important factor when making educational decisions.
   A. True
   B. False

4. In ASL, the movement of a sign often gives vital information.
   A. True
   B. False

5. In ASL, the meaning of a sign can be changed by simply changing the movement of the sign.
   A. True
   B. False

Lesson Seven: *A School 'Daze'*

7.4 Lesson Objectives

Planning for Success

Goal: To identify the learning outcomes associated with successful completion of this lesson.

Instructions:
1. **Ask** students to read the objectives in their workbooks (activity 7.4)
2. **Show** overhead (Appendix 7.4) and **read** through the objectives with the class.

Student Workbook: Activity 7.4

Overhead Master: Appendix 7.4

7.4 Lesson Objectives

Planning For Success

Goal: To see what you will learn by the end of this lesson.

Instructions: Read the objectives below.

Upon completing this VideoCourse lesson, you will be able to...

1. Recognize and accurately produce the ASL vocabulary introduced in this and all previous lessons.
2. Explain what directional verbs are and how they are used.
3. Demonstrate at least three verbs that are directional.
4. Explain the importance of schools for the Deaf.
5. Explain the importance of fostering strong self-esteem and self-identity in Deaf children.
6. Identify some of the basic educational options available to Deaf children.
7. Identify the criteria that must be considered when choosing the best educational option for each Deaf child.

Lesson Seven: *A School 'Daze'*

7.5 Lesson Focus
Charades Race

Activity Goal: To develop a need for the ASL vocabulary introduced in this lesson.

Activity Instructions:

1. **Ask** students to read *Charades Race* in their workbooks (activity 7.5).

2. **Divide** the class into two teams.

3. **Explain** the game as follows: Each team will send one person to the front of the classroom. These two players will face the teams while you stand behind them and **write** a word from the list below on the board (so the two players **cannot** see it). Once the other students have seen the word, **erase** the word from the board. **Instruct** the students on both teams to use gestures and mime to help their player guess the word. The first team player to guess the word and write it on the board receives a point.

4. **Tell** students that they are not to use their voices or written words.

   Word List:

School	Teacher	Book	Read
Sit	Tired	Flower	Each
Learn	Student	Study	Play
Pencil	Paper	Sorry	Give

5. **Inform** students that they will learn the signs for these and other school-related concepts throughout this lesson.

Student Workbook: Activity 7.5

7.5 Lesson Focus

Charades Race

Activity Goal: To play a game that will help you improve your skills.

Activity Instructions: Your instructor will divide your class into two teams. Each team will send one person to the front of the classroom. These two players will face their teams while your instructor stands behind them and writes a word on the board.

Use gestures and mime to help your team player guess the word. The team that gets their player to write the correct word on the board first receives a point. Remember, you are not allowed to use your voice or written words.

Have fun and good luck!

Lesson Seven: *A School 'Daze'*

7.6 Language Learning Instruction
Learning New Signs

Goal: To use ASL and visual aids to introduce this lesson's vocabulary.

Instructions:

1. **Ask** students to read *Learning New Signs* in their workbooks (activity 7.6).

2. **Show** the overhead (Appendix 7.6). **Introduce** the vocabulary by **pointing** to items presented in the pictures while **demonstrating** the signs.

3. **Reinforce** retention and **check** students' comprehension by **using** these signs to **ask** students questions.

   Note: For a step-by-step review of this method, see Lesson One (activities 1.6 and 1.12).

4. **Continue** this process until all the ASL vocabulary items have been introduced.

Overhead Content: Use the pictures in the overhead (Appendix 7.6) to introduce the signs representing the following concepts:

1. SCHOOL
2. TEACHER
3. BOOK
4. READ
5. SIT
6. TIRED
7. SORRY
8. FLOWER
9. PICK+FLOWER
10. HERE
11. THERE
12. GROW-UP

Note: Some pictures can be used to represent several concepts. For verbs and more abstract concepts, you may need to supplement these pictures with mime, gestures, using actual objects, and acting out the concepts in class.

Lesson Seven: *A School 'Daze'*

Overhead Master:
Appendix 7.6

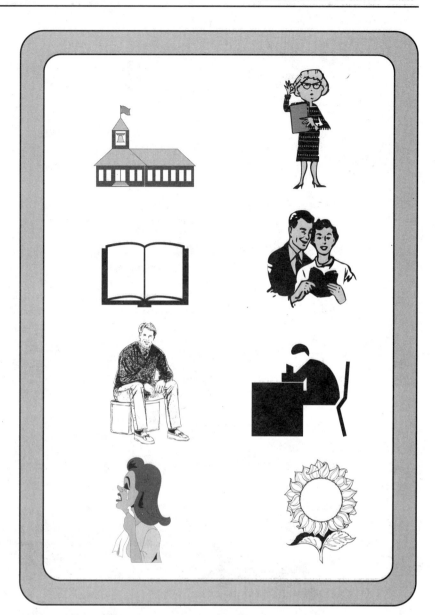

Student Workbook:
Activity 7.6

7.6 Language Learning Instruction

Learning New Signs

Goal: To help you learn new ASL vocabulary.

Instructions: Your instructor will teach you new signs! Watch closely to learn what these signs mean and how they are produced.

In the space below, record any notes to help you remember the signs.

Notes: _____
_____
_____
_____

Instructor's Guide: Lesson Seven
Bravo ASL! Curriculum

©1996 Sign Enhancers, Inc.
ALL RIGHTS RESERVED.

Lesson Seven: *A School 'Daze'*

7.7 Video Learning Experience

Introduction to New Vocabulary

Viewing Goal: To provide a signed demonstration of the accurate production of the new ASL vocabulary.

Viewing Instructions:

1. **Ask** students to read *Introduction to New Vocabulary* in their workbooks (activity 7.7).

2. **Play** the video segment entitled *Introduction to New Vocabulary* (segment 7.7). Billy introduces and signs each new vocabulary item twice. (If you wish to keep this a strictly visual presentation, **turn off** audio.)

3. **Instruct** students to watch how Billy produces the signs as well as the accompanying facial/body expressions.

4. **Ask** students to copy the signs and the facial/body expressions as Billy repeats each one.

Video Segment Content: See the following Student Workbook excerpt for the content
(2 1/2 Minutes) of this video segment.

Student Workbook: Activity 7.7

> 7.7 Video Learning Experience
>
> *Introduction to New Vocabulary*
>
> **Viewing Goal:** To help you learn new ASL vocabulary.
>
> **Viewing Instructions:** Watch how Billy produces each sign. Be sure to notice the facial/body expressions. Copy the signs as Billy repeats each one.
>
> Signs representing the following concepts are introduced in this segment:
>
> 1. SCHOOL
> 2. TEACHER
> 3. BOOK
> 4. READ
> 5. SIT
> 6. TIRED
> 7. SORRY
> 8. FLOWER
> 9. PICK+FLOWER
> 10. HERE
> 11. THERE
> 12. GROW-UP

Lesson Seven: *A School 'Daze'*

7.8 Video Learning Experience

Bravo Family Visit

Viewing Goal: To improve ASL comprehension skills by watching a Bravo family interaction.

Viewing Instructions:
1. **Ask** students to read *Bravo Family Visit* in their workbooks (activity 7.8).

2. **Play** the video segment of the Bravo family (segment 7.8). The Bravos will use the new vocabulary within the context of going to school.

3. **Instruct** students to watch for comprehension and write a summary of the main points.

4. **Replay** any portion of this video segment that students experienced difficulty understanding.

Video Segment Content: (4 Minutes)

The following is a summary of the Bravo family interaction:

The family is walking down a path. Dad asks the kids if they are ready for school. Scott says "Yes," and Anna says "No." Anna throws a wrapper on the ground and her parents stop her and tell her, "No!"

Anna sees a flower and starts to pick it. The groundskeeper walks up and tells her not to pick the flower.

Anna goes into the library and finds a book she wants to borrow but the librarian tells her it is only for teachers, not students.

Anna then walks into the classroom and sits down. The teacher tells her she cannot sit in that chair, she must sit in another chair.

Anna is tired of people telling her "No" all the time. She decides that when she is an adult and in charge, she will tell children "Yes" instead of "No." Anna puts her head down and falls asleep.

Billy: Ahh, it seems that Anna is having a bad day. She's having a hard time. It's no fun being told "No" all the time. Anna probably feels that all adults are mean. But we can't let that stop us from continuing to learn Sign Language. I'm not one of those mean adults. I'm soft-hearted. Now, watch Anna and I'll meet you in just a minute.

Lesson Seven: *A School 'Daze'*

(Anna wakes up dressed as the teacher. She sits down to read the book the librarian forbade her to read while waiting for the students to arrive.)

Student Workbook: Activity 7.8

7.8 Video Learning Experience

Bravo Family Visit

Viewing Goal: To improve your ASL comprehension skills by watching a Bravo family interaction.

Viewing Instructions: Watch the signed interaction and write a summary of the main points.

Summary: _____
_____
_____
_____

7.9 Comprehension Quiz

What Did You Understand?

Quiz Goal: To assess students' comprehension of the signed interaction.

Quiz Instructions:

1. **Instruct** students to complete the quiz in their workbooks (activity 7.9).

2. **Collect** for grading or **show** overhead (Appendix 7.9) and **ask** individual students to indicate the correct answers on the overhead while class members correct their own work.

3. **Ask** students to indicate which item(s) from the quiz they found difficult. **Review** by **modeling** or **replaying** that segment of the videotape.

Lesson Seven: *A School 'Daze'*

Student Workbook:
Activity 7.9

Overhead Master:
Appendix 7.9

7.9 Comprehension Quiz

What Did You Understand?

Quiz Goal: To see how much of the Bravo family interaction you understood.

Quiz Instructions: Read and answer each question below.

1. Scott and Anna are both ready to go to school.
   A. True
   B. False

2. The gardener invites Anna to pick a beautiful flower at her school.
   A. True
   B. False

3. The book Anna wants is only for _____.
   A. Students
   B. Mothers
   C. Teachers
   D. Children

4. Once in class, Anna is told by the teacher that she is in the wrong chair.
   A. True
   B. False

5. Anna decides to leave school for the day so nobody will tell her "No!"
   A. True
   B. False

7.10 Language Learning Instruction

Learning New Signs

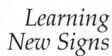

Goal: To use ASL and visual aids to introduce this lesson's vocabulary.

Instructions:
1. **Ask** students to read *Learning New Signs* in their workbooks (activity 7.10).

2. **Show** the overhead (Appendix 7.10). **Introduce** the vocabulary by **pointing** to items presented in the pictures while **demonstrating** the signs.

3. **Reinforce** retention and **check** students' comprehension by **using** these signs to **ask** students questions.

Note: For a step-by-step review of this method, see Lesson One (activities 1.6 and 1.12).

Lesson Seven: *A School 'Daze'*

4. **Continue** this process until all the ASL vocabulary items have been introduced.

Overhead Content: Use the pictures in the overhead (Appendix 7.10) to introduce the signs representing the following concepts:

1. TEACH
2. LEARN
3. STUDENT
4. STUDY
5. GIVE
6. PLAY
7. WHAT-WRONG
8. NOT
9. WHO
10. PENCIL
11. PAPER
12. GOOD
13. NEED
14. PLEASE
15. HAVE
16. WANT
17. LATE
18. FINISH

Note: Some pictures can be used to represent several concepts. For verbs and more abstract concepts, you may need to supplement these pictures with mime, gestures, using actual objects, and acting out the concepts in class.

Overhead Master: Appendix 7.10

Lesson Seven: *A School 'Daze'*

**Student Workbook:
Activity 7.10**

7.10 Language Learning Instruction

Learning New Signs

Goal: To help you learn new ASL vocabulary.

Instructions: Your instructor will teach you new signs! Watch closely to learn what these signs mean and how they are produced.

In the space below, record any notes to help you remember the signs.

Notes: _____
_____
_____
_____

7.11 Video Learning Experience

Introduction to New Vocabulary

Viewing Goal: To provide a signed demonstration of the accurate production of the new ASL vocabulary.

Viewing Instructions:
1. **Ask** students to read *Introduction to New Vocabulary* in their workbooks (activity 7.11).

2. **Play** the video segment entitled *Introduction to New Vocabulary* (segment 7.11). Billy introduces and signs each new vocabulary item twice. (If you wish to keep this activity a strictly visual presentation, **turn off** audio.)

3. **Instruct** students to watch how Billy produces the signs and the accompanying facial/body expressions.

4. **Ask** students to copy the signs and the facial/body expressions as Billy repeats each one.

Lesson Seven: *A School 'Daze'*

Video Segment Content: See the following Student Workbook excerpt for the content
(2 Minutes) of this video segment.

Student Workbook:
Activity 7.11

> 7.11 Video Learning Experience
>
> *Introduction to New Vocabulary*
>
> **Viewing Goal:** To help you learn new ASL vocabulary.
>
> **Viewing Instructions:** Watch how Billy produces each sign. Be sure to notice the facial/body expressions. Copy the signs as Billy repeats each one.
>
> Signs representing the following concepts are introduced in this video segment:
>
> 1. TEACH
> 2. LEARN
> 3. STUDENT
> 4. STUDY
> 5. GIVE
> 6. PLAY
> 7. WHAT-WRONG
> 8. NOT
> 9. WHO
> 10. PENCIL
> 11. PAPER
> 12. GOOD
> 13. NEED
> 14. PLEASE
> 15. HAVE
> 16. WANT
> 17. LATE
> 18. FINISH

7.12 Experiential Activity

Point and Sign

Activity Goal: To improve students' ASL receptive and expressive skills.

Activity Instructions:

1. **Ask** students to read *Point and Sign* in their workbooks (activity 7.12).

2. **Divide** the class into pairs.

3. **Instruct** students to look at the activity pictures.

4. **Select** and **model** the variation of the *Point and Sign* activity you would like your students to perform:

Variation A:

1) **Ask** each pair of students to take turns pointing to an object or action in the picture and producing the sign or signs that best match its meaning.

2) **Instruct** the partner to provide feedback on the correct choice and production of the signs.

Lesson Seven: *A School 'Daze'*

Variation B:

1) **Ask** each pair of students to take turns having one student point to an object or action in the picture.

2) **Instruct** the partner to produce a sign, signs, or a sentence that best describes the picture.

Variation C:

1) **Ask** each pair of students to take turns having one student produce a sign, signs, or a sentence that corresponds to one of the objects or actions in the picture.

2) **Instruct** the partner to point to the object or action in the picture that best matches the meaning of the sign, signs, or sentence presented by her/his partner.

5. **Inform** students that they are not to use their voices.

6. **Circulate** among the pairs to **observe** student performance.

7. **Correct** production errors by **modeling** as necessary.

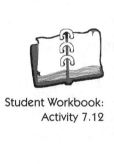

Student Workbook:
Activity 7.12

7.12 Experiential Activity

Point and Sign

Activity Goal: To improve your ASL receptive and expressive skills.

Activity Instructions: Using the pictures below, follow your teacher's instructions and practice using your new ASL vocabulary.

Lesson Seven: *A School 'Daze'*

7.13 Experiential Activity

Crossword Puzzle

Activities Video

Activity Goal: To assist students in recognizing the new ASL vocabulary.

Activity Instructions:
1. **Ask** students to look at the crossword puzzle in their workbooks (activity 7.13).

2. **Inform** students that they will see several of their new ASL vocabulary items signed with a reference to their location on the puzzle (for example: 1 Across, 2 Down, etc.). **Ask** students to decide what English word best represents each sign and write the word in the appropriate boxes of the puzzle. **Inform** the students that each sign will be presented twice.

3. **Play** Activities Video (segment 7.13).

4. When the activity is finished, **show** overhead (Appendix 7.13) and **ask** individual students to indicate the correct answers on the overhead while class members correct their own work.

Video Segment Content: The following is the content of this video segment:
(5 1/2 Minutes)

Down:
2. HERE
3. PLEASE
5. TIRED
6. TEACHER
7. FLOWER
8. GOOD
9. STUDY
11. PLAY
13. NOT

Across:
1. FINISH
3. PAPER
4. STUDENT
8. GIVE
10. WHO
12. LATE
14. READ
15. SORRY

Lesson Seven: *A School 'Daze'*

Student Workbook:
Activiy 7.13

Overhead Master:
Appendix 7.13

7.13 Experiential Activity

Crossword Puzzle

Activity Goal: To help you recognize the ASL vocabulary learned in this lesson.

Activity Instructions: You will see several of your new ASL vocabulary items signed with a reference as to where you should write them on the puzzle. For example, the signer might tell you, "One Across - SCHOOL."

Write the English word that fits in the puzzle and describes what is being signed in the correct boxes. Each item will be presented twice.

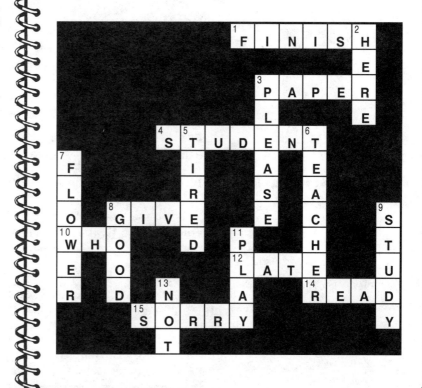

Instructor's Guide: Lesson Seven
Bravo ASL! Curriculum

©1996 Sign Enhancers, Inc.
ALL RIGHTS RESERVED.

Lesson Seven: *A School 'Daze'*

7.14 Video Learning Experience

Bravo Family Visit

Viewing Goal: To improve ASL comprehension skills by watching a Bravo family interaction.

Viewing Instructions:
1. **Ask** students to read *Bravo Family Visit* in their workbooks (activity 7.14).
2. **Play** the video segment of the Bravo family (segment 7.14). The Bravos will use the new ASL vocabulary within the context of being in school.
3. **Instruct** students to watch for comprehension and write a summary of the main points.
4. **Replay** any portion of this video segment that students experienced difficulty understanding.

Video Segment Content: (4 Minutes)

The following is a summary of the Bravo family interaction:

Anna is dressed as the teacher and the students begin arriving. The first student walks in yawning and Anna asks her what is wrong. The student explains that she is tired but had to come to school.

More students arrive. One student (the gardener from the previous scene) brings Anna the flower she had wanted to pick.

One student (her teacher from a previous scene) walks in late and Anna asks her why she is late. Is it because she doesn't like reading, writing, and learning? The student says no, that she wants to learn and study, that she likes school and she apologizes for being late.

Anna tells the students to get out a pencil and paper. One student doesn't have a pencil, another doesn't have paper.

Two of the students (Mom and Dad) begin arguing over a book. Anna stops them and asks who the book belongs to. Finally the owner is found and he loans the book to the other student to read.

Lesson Seven: *A School 'Daze'*

Student Workbook: Activity 7.14

7.14 Video Learning Experience

Bravo Family Visit

Viewing Goal: To improve your ASL comprehension skills by watching a Bravo family interaction.

Viewing Instructions: Watch the signed interaction and write a summary of the main points.

Summary: _____
_____
_____
_____

7.15 Comprehension Quiz

What Did You Understand?

Quiz Goal: To assess students' comprehension of the signed interaction.

Quiz Instructions:
1. **Instruct** students to complete the quiz in their workbooks (activity 7.15).

2. **Collect** for grading or **show** overhead (Appendix 7.15) and **ask** individual students to indicate the correct answers on the overhead while class members correct their own work.

3. **Ask** students to indicate which item(s) from the quiz they found difficult. **Review** by **modeling** or **replaying** that segment of the videotape.

Lesson Seven: *A School 'Daze'*

Student Workbook:
Activity 7.15

Overhead Master:
Appendix 7.15

7.15 Comprehension Quiz

What Did You Understand?

Quiz Goal: To see how much of the Bravo family interaction you understood.

Quiz Instructions: Read and answer each question below.

1. The first student in Anna's class comes in feeling _____.
   A. Sick
   B. Tired
   C. Happy
   D. Hungry

2. The student who was late doesn't like school.
   A. True
   B. False

3. The student who was late told Anna that she was _____.
   A. Tired
   B. Sorry
   C. Good
   D. Playing

4. Anna asks her students to get their _____ ready.
   A. Books
   B. Flowers
   C. Paper and pencils
   D. Paper and crayons

5. Two students argue over a book. This book belongs to _____.
   A. Mom
   B. Dad
   C. The teacher
   D. The library

7.16 Video Learning Experience

Grammatical Notes

Viewing Goals: To assist students in learning about the grammatical aspects of ASL.

Viewing Instructions:
1. **Ask** students to read *Grammatical Notes* in their workbooks (activity 7.16).

2. **Play** the video segment entitled *Grammatical Notes* (segment 7.16). Because the presentation of this segment is beyond the linguistic ability of beginning students, please **turn on** the audio and/or captions to optimize its educational value.

Lesson Seven: *A School 'Daze'*

3. **Instruct** students to view the segment.

4. At completion of segment, **review** the content presented and **answer** any questions students may have.

Video Segment Content: See the following Student Workbook excerpt for the content
(4 Minutes) of this video segment.

Student Workbook:
Activity 7.16

7.16 Video Learning Experience

Grammatical Notes

Viewing Goal: To learn about the grammatical aspects of ASL.

Viewing Instructions: View the *Grammatical Notes* segment carefully for the following:

Some verbs in ASL are called "directional verbs."

A. The movement of directional verbs gives important information about who is doing or receiving an action. For example, HELP-ME can become HELP-YOU or HELP-HIM/HER simply by changing the direction of the sign's movement.

B. Example from the video: The kids fighting over the book...
GIVE-ME
GIVE-HIM, NOT
GIVE-ME, ME-GIVE-HER

C. You can change the meaning of WRITE:
WRITE-PAPER
WRITE-BOARD
WRITE-BACK+FORTH

D. Other examples:
JOIN
WATCH

Lesson Seven: *A School 'Daze'*

7.17 Experiential Activity

It's Your Move

Activity Goal: To apply the grammatical information by modifying meaning through the use of directionality.

Activity Instructions:

1. **Ask** students to read *It's Your Move* in their workbooks (activity 7.17).

2. **Divide** the class into pairs.

3. **Instruct** students to practice using directionality as described in their workbooks, changing the meaning of signs by changing the direction of the sign's movement within the context of sentences.

4. **Circulate** among the pairs to **observe** student performance.

5. **Correct** production errors by **modeling** the accurate production of the signs.

6. **Ask** individual students to demonstrate one of the signs with at least two different movements for the class.

Student Workbook: Activity 7.17

7.17 Experiential Activity

It's Your Move

Activity Goal: To practice using directional verbs.

Activity Instructions: You have just learned about different meanings that a sign might have, depending on the directionality of the sign. HELP, for example, can be signed in one direction for "I'll help you," and in a different direction for "You help me."

With a partner, practice signing different sentences using some of the examples in this video lesson. Remember that you need to change the movement/directionality in order to change the meaning.

Create sentences using the following directional verbs:

| HELP | GIVE | READ |
| WRITE | WATCH | TEACH |

Lesson Seven: *A School 'Daze'*

7.18 Video Learning Experience

Bravo Family Visit

Viewing Goal: To improve comprehension skills by watching a Bravo family interaction.

Viewing Instructions:
1. **Ask** students to read *Bravo Family Visit* in their workbooks (activity 7.18).
2. **Play** the video segment of the Bravo family (segment 7.18). The new ASL vocabulary will be used within the context of Anna's dream at school.
3. **Instruct** students to watch for comprehension and write a summary of the main points.
4. **Replay** any portion of this video segment that students experienced difficulty understanding.

Video Segment Content: (1 1/2 Minutes)

The following is a summary of the signed interaction:

The whole class is misbehaving. They are throwing paper at Anna. She tells each of them to sit down. She tells them not to look up, not to look down, not to look at each other, and not to play around. She tells them "No" a lot.

The students all begin copying her and mocking her by signing, "No, no, no."

Billy enters and says that Anna is not having an easy time of it. He hopes the viewers are having an easy time and says he can help by reviewing all the signs they learned.

Student Workbook: Activity 7.18

7.18 Video Learning Experience

Bravo Family Visit

Viewing Goal: To improve your ASL comprehension skills by watching a Bravo family interaction.

Viewing Instructions: Watch the signed interaction and write a summary of the main points to help you remember the interaction.

Summary: _____
_____
_____
_____

Instructor's Guide: Lesson Seven
Bravo ASL! Curriculum

©1996 Sign Enhancers, Inc.
ALL RIGHTS RESERVED.

Lesson Seven: *A School 'Daze'*

7.19 Video Learning Experience

Review Session

Viewing Goal: To reinforce recognition and production of the signs introduced in this lesson.

Viewing Instructions:

1. **Ask** students to read *Review Session* in their workbooks (activity 7.19).

2. **Play** the video segment entitled *Review Session* (segment 7.19). **Play** Anna's Dream, followed by Billy reviewing the ASL vocabulary items. Because the presentation of this segment is beyond the linguistic ability of beginning students, please **turn on** the audio and/or captions to optimize its educational value.

3. **Ask** students to pay careful attention to the signed vocabulary items and take note of visual hints offered by Billy that might help them remember.

4. **Suggest** that students copy the signs to reinforce retention of sign production.

Video Segment Content: See the following Student Workbook excerpt for the content
(7 1/2 Minutes) of this video segment.

Student Workbook: Activity 7.19

7.19 Video Learning Experience

Review Session

Viewing Goal: To help you remember how to produce the signs introduced in this lesson.

Viewing Instructions: Watch this video segment carefully to see how each sign is made, and note any hints that might help you remember. You may want to copy the signs as you watch Billy.

Following are the vocabulary items and explanations offered in this video segment:

TEACH   The information from one person's head is given to another person.

TEACHER   This sign indicates a person who teaches.

LEARN   You take the information from a book and put it in your mind.

STUDENT   This is similar to the sign for TEACHER, as it indicates a person who is learning.

Lesson Seven: *A School 'Daze'*

SCHOOL	When a teacher wants to get the students' attention, s/he claps her/his hands.
BOOK	This sign indicates how a person opens a book.
READ	The index and middle fingers are the "eyes." The flat hand is a book. The "eyes" move along, reading the book.
STUDY	This follows the same idea as READ but now there are more fingers indicating eyes staring at the page or reading the page again and again.
SORRY	Someone's feelings (over the heart) have been hurt. Your face must reflect that you are SORRY.
FLOWER	The sign for FLOWER is placed around the nose because most flowers smell good.
PICK+FLOWER	This is an action sign that looks like picking a flower.
GIVE-TO-ME	This is another example of a directional verb. Perhaps something has been picked and given to me. Now, I can change the direction of the sign to show... ME-GIVE-HIM, HE-GIVE-ME, HE-GIVE-HER, etc.
PLAY	This sign represents the attitude of being relaxed and playful.
WHAT-WRONG	The sign for WRONG is used. But when we soften it, repeat the movement, and give a questioning look it becomes, WHAT-WRONG.
WHO	The old sign for WHO was this (shown on tape), but it has evolved into the present sign WHO.
PENCIL	Long ago, you had to moisten the lead to soften it so that you could write with it. That is the origin of the sign PENCIL.
PAPER	Paper was once manufactured in a very large machine which flattened it out and rolled it up.
WRITE	Remember the description of the sign for PENCIL? Well, this sign shows the action of WRITING.
NEED/MUST	This sign reflects the position of the body of a person who is saying you have to, you MUST.
HAVE	This shows that there is something you hold in your possession (toward your body).
WANT	There is something out there that I want, so I pull it to me.
DON'T-WANT	If I don't want something, I push it away.
LATE	When I'm late, I run to get there on time.
FINISH	It's like a rodeo. In steer roping, they lasso the steer, tie its legs, and raise their hands to say, FINISH!
PLEASE	This sign is made over the heart.
GROW-UP	This sign shows the top of the head raising as the child grows taller.
SIT	This sign follows the action of a person sitting down.
TIRED	The body droops when a person is TIRED.

Lesson Seven: *A School 'Daze'*

7.20 Experiential Activity

Signs and Origins

Activity Goal: To assist students in remembering how to produce a sign by applying the visual cues and origin information introduced in the review segment.

Activity Instructions:
1. **Ask** students to read *Signs and Origins* in their workbooks (activity 7.20).
2. **Divide** the class into pairs.
3. **Encourage** students to use ASL to discuss and record their answers.
4. **Review** the origins with the class.

Instructor Tip: *It is recommended that this be done as a no-voice activity. Tell your students that they may sign and fingerspell or use gestures to communicate, but they may not use their voices. This will reinforce all of the ASL vocabulary and conversational principles learned to date.*

Student Workbook: Activity 7.20

7.20 Experiential Activity

Signs and Origins

Activity Goal: To help you remember how to produce some of the new ASL vocabulary.

Activity Instructions: With a partner, use ASL to discuss the hints Billy gave you about each of the signs listed below (from the video review session). These hints will help you remember how to make each sign. You may take notes in the space below to help you remember.

Sign	Origin/visual hint
1. SCHOOL	_____
2. TEACHER	_____
3. BOOK	_____
4. FLOWER	_____
5. GROW-UP	_____
6. LEARN	_____
7. GIVE	_____
8. PAPER	_____
9. TIRED	_____
10. STUDY	_____

Lesson Seven: *A School 'Daze'*

7.21 Video Learning Experience

Cultural Notes

Viewing Goal: To assist students in learning about the cultural aspects of ASL.

Viewing Instructions:
1. **Ask** students to read *Cultural Notes* in their workbooks (activity 7.21).

2. **Play** the video segment entitled *Cultural Notes* (segment 7.21). Because the presentation of this segment is beyond the linguistic ability of beginning students, please **turn on** the audio and/or captions to optimize its educational value.

3. **Instruct** students to view the segment.

4. At completion of the video segment, **review** the content presented and **answer** any questions students may have.

Video Segment Content: (5 Minutes) See the following Student Workbook excerpt for the content of this video segment.

Student Workbook: Activity 7.21

> 7.21 Video Learning Experience
>
> *Cultural Notes*
>
> **Viewing Goal:** To help you learn about the cultural aspects of ASL.
>
> **Viewing Instructions:** View the *Cultural Notes* segment carefully for the following:
>
> I. The topic of this segment is Deaf Education:
>   A. The potential success of Deaf students (academic and personal) is dependent on teaching methods, the school the child attends, and the way the child learns.
>   B. School-age children learn many things:
>   1. Education is not limited to reading, writing, and arithmetic.
>   2. It is important for children to have the opportunity for self-discovery (finding out who they are, what they can do, and how they feel about themselves).
>   C. How can self-esteem and positive self-identity be addressed?
>   1. Historically, discussions regarding Deaf education often overlooked critical issues regarding self-esteem.
>   2. These issues impact how children relate to the world, set goals, and make decisions about their futures.
>   D. Schools must be accessible!
>   1. Focus on what the child **can** do.
>   2. Encourage capabilities.
>   3. Provide exciting possibilities for each child.

Instructor's Guide: Lesson Seven
Bravo ASL! Curriculum

II. Educational options for Deaf children:
   A. Schools for the Deaf options:
      1. Residential school where students live at the school.
      2. Day school where students live at home and commute.
      Note: Deaf adults serve as role models in both options.
   B. Mainstream program (with the use of interpreters):
      1. A self-contained classroom typically has all Deaf students.
      2. Deaf students are placed in classrooms with hearing students.
III. Making an educational decision:
   A. An appropriate placement must consider the child's:
      1. Skills
      2. Capabilities
      3. Motivation
      4. Personal interests
   B. Overall well-being must be a factor, including:
      1. Mental and spiritual needs.
      2. Opportunity for growth, learning, building self-pride, resources for learning about Deaf culture and ASL, and encouragement of self-discovery.

7.22 Cultural and Grammatical Quiz

What Did You Learn?

Quiz Goal: To assess students' mastery of this lesson's cultural and grammatical information.

Quiz Instructions:
1. **Ask** students to complete the quiz in their workbooks.
2. **Collect** written quiz for grading or **show** overhead (Appendix 7.22) and **ask** individual students to indicate the correct answers on the overhead while class members correct their own work.

Lesson Seven: *A School 'Daze'*

Student Workbook: Activity 7.22

Overhead Master: Appendix 7.22

7.22 Cultural and Grammatical Quiz

What Did You Learn?

Quiz Goal: To see how much of this lesson's cultural and grammatical information you learned.

Quiz Instructions: Read and answer each question.

1. Self-esteem and self-identity are important factors in choosing a school for a Deaf child.
   A. **True**
   B. False

2. In order to get an education, Deaf children must live away from their families.
   A. True
   B. **False**

3. Having Deaf adult role models is one benefit of residential schools for the Deaf.
   A. **True**
   B. False

4. How can movement change an ASL sign? (Select all that apply.)
   A. **Gives additional information**
   B. **Changes the meaning of the sign**
   C. Changes the facial expression
   D. Changes who is doing the signing

5. Give two examples of ASL signs that are considered directional verbs.
   GIVE, HELP, WRITE, JOIN, WATCH

6. If a Deaf student were to attend your school, what modifications (changes) would be needed so that student would gain full access to all educational activities? (Check all that apply.)
   A. **Interpreters for classes**
   B. **Lights flashing for bells**
   C. **TTY for phone calls**
   D. **TV decoders for captioned videotapes**

Lesson Seven: *A School 'Daze'*

7.23 Video Learning Experience

Practice Session: Sentences

Viewing Goal: To improve comprehension skills by watching sentences presented in ASL.

Viewing Instructions:
1. **Ask** students to read *Practice Session: Sentences* in their workbooks (activity 7.23).
2. **Play** the video segment entitled *Practice Session: Sentences* (segment 7.23).
3. **Inform** students that each sentence is signed twice and an English translation is provided.
4. **Remind** students to watch the face of each signer to see the facial/body expressions and non-manual grammatical markers as well as the signs.

Video Segment Content: The following are English translations of the practice sentences:
(2 Minutes)

1. The girl is tired.
2. The Deaf boy and the hearing girl write notes back and forth.
3. Do you want a pencil and paper for writing?
4. Whose book is this? Yours or mine?
5. I am not a teacher. I am a student.
6. Do you like to read books?

Student Workbook: Activity 7.23

7.23 Video Learning Experience

Practice Session: Sentences

Viewing Goal: To improve your comprehension skills by watching sentences presented in ASL.

Viewing Instructions: Watch the signed sentences for comprehension. Remember to watch the face of each signer to see the facial/body expressions and the non-manual grammatical markers as well as the signs. It is recommended that you copy each signed sentence when it is repeated.

In the space below, record any questions or notes you have regarding the sentences.

Notes: _____
_____
_____
_____

Instructor's Guide: Lesson Seven
Bravo ASL! Curriculum

©1996 Sign Enhancers, Inc.
ALL RIGHTS RESERVED.

7.24 Experiential Activity

Receptivity Race!

Activity Goal: To improve expressive and receptive ASL skills.

Activity Instructions:

1. **Ask** students to read *Receptivity Race!* in their workbooks (activity 7.24).

2. **Divide** the class into two teams. **Ask** one player from each team to come to the front of the room.

3. **Show** the two players one of the topics from the recommended topic list. You can **write** each topic on a piece of paper. **Make sure** none of the other students can see the topic.

4. **Tell** both players to show their team signs that relate to the topic. The first team to guess the correct topic earns a point.

5. **Continue** the game until all the topics have been used. You may want to **create** additional topics.

Recommended topics:

Food	Letters of the alphabet
Furniture	Breakfast foods
School	Rooms in the house
Colors	Family members

Student Workbook: Activity 7.24

7.24 Experiential Activity

Receptivity Race

Activity Goal: To improve your receptive and expressive ASL skills.

Activity Instructions: Your class will be divided into two teams. One player from each team will go to the front of the room. Your teacher will show each player a topic. The player is to sign several examples related to each topic to his/her team.

Watch closely and try to guess the topic! The team to guess the topic first wins a point. Take turns going to the front of the class to help your team win!

Good luck!

Lesson Seven: *A School 'Daze'*

7.25 Video Learning Experience

Practice Session: Story

Viewing Goal: To improve comprehension skills by watching a story presented in ASL.

Viewing Instructions:

1. **Ask** students to read *Practice Session: Story* in their workbooks (activity 7.25).

2. **Show** the video segment entitled *Practice Session: Story* (segment 7.25). Billy signs a story using the vocabulary introduced in this lesson. **Turn off** audio and captions.

3. **Instruct** students to watch this signed story and write a summary of the main points.

Video Segment Content: (2 Minutes)

The following is an English translation of the story:

A hearing girl, whose name is Alice, went to school. There was a Deaf boy named Bob, whose name sign was this (shown on tape). The teacher at the school was hearing and did not use Sign Language. The students there were hearing too, and they didn't use Sign Language. Bob is the only Deaf student.

Bob likes Alice and sits next to her, and the two of them pass notes back and forth. Bob taught Alice signs, and Alice enjoyed learning. Yesterday, Bob was teaching Alice the sign for flower. When he had finished teaching the sign, he gave Alice a flower.

You are like Alice, learning signs, and I am like Bob, teaching them. Now I have something special for you. There... (a flower) do you like it? Oh, good.

Student Workbook: Activity 7.25

7.25 Video Learning Experience

Practice Session: Story

Viewing Goal: To improve your comprehension skills by watching a story presented in ASL.

Viewing Instructions: Watch the signed story for comprehension. In the space below, write a summary to help you remember the story.

Summary: _____
_____
_____
_____

Lesson Seven: *A School 'Daze'*

7.26 Comprehension Quiz

What Did You Understand?

Quiz Goal: To assess students' comprehension of the signed story.

Quiz Instructions:
1. **Instruct** students to complete the quiz in their workbooks (activity 7.26).

2. **Collect** for grading or **show** overhead (Appendix 7.26) and **ask** individual students to indicate the correct answers on the overhead while class members correct their own work.

3. **Ask** students to indicate which item(s) from the quiz they found difficult. **Review** by **modeling** or **replaying** that segment of the videotape.

Student Workbook: Activity 7.26

Overhead Master: Appendix 7.26

7.26 Comprehension Quiz

What Did You Understand?

Quiz Goal: To see how much of the signed story you understood.

Quiz Instructions: Read and answer each question below.

1. The teacher in the story signed fluently.
   A. True
   B. False

2. The other children in the class were also Deaf.
   A. True
   B. False

3. How many members of the boy's family were Deaf?
   A. 1
   B. 2
   C. 3
   D. 5

4. The boy taught his family _____.
   A. Math
   B. Sign Language
   C. Baseball plays
   D. English

5. The boy was happy.
   A. True
   B. False

Instructor's Guide: Lesson Seven
Bravo ASL! Curriculum

©1996 Sign Enhancers, Inc.
ALL RIGHTS RESERVED.

Lesson Seven: *A School 'Daze'*

7.27 Homework Assignment

A Funny Thing Happened At School

Activity Goal: To assist students in recognizing and producing new ASL vocabulary.

Activity Instructions:

1. **Ask** students to read *A Funny Thing Happened At School* in their workbooks (activiy 7.27).

2. **Instruct** students to prepare a short story about a day at school. **Ask** students to use at least six new signs from this lesson and at least three directional verbs as described in this lesson's grammatical information.

3. **Inform** students to be prepared to sign these stories in class.

Instructor Tip:

An opportunity for students to perform this assignment has been scheduled in the next lesson (Homework Review 8.2). If possible, it is recommended that you arrange to videotape each student's performance of this activity.

Student Workbook: Activity 7.27

7.27 Homework Assignment

A Funny Thing Happened At School

Activity Goal: To improve your expressive skills.

Activity Instructions: Prepare a signed story about a day at school. Use at least six of your new vocabulary signs and at least three directional verbs (as taught in the *Grammatical Notes* segment).

Be prepared to sign your story for the class.

Lesson Seven: *A School 'Daze'*

7.28 Post-test

What Do You Know Now?

Assessment Video

Post-test Goal: To assess students' mastery of the lesson objectives.

Post-test Instructions:

1. **Ask** students to read the Post-test Introduction in their workbooks (activity 7.28).

2. **Copy** and **distribute** the Lesson Seven Post-test (Appendix 7.28).

3. **Play** the Assessment Video (segment 7.28) and **allow** students to complete Section One (comprehension portion) of the test.

4. **Instruct** students to complete Section Two (culture and grammar portion) of the test individually and hand in their papers when they are finished.

5. **Assign** Section Three (expressive portion) of the test and **schedule** a time when students are to perform. It is strongly recommended that you **videotape** this portion of the Post-test.

6. **Determine** grading options based upon programmatic requirements. A recommended guideline for measuring successful mastery of objectives is 80% accuracy.

Video Segment Content:
(3 Minutes)

The following are English translations of the descriptions for Section One.

1. The teacher writes on the board.
2. The baby is sleeping.
3. The teacher helps the boy learn.
4. Where is the pencil?
5. I read the book.
6. The children are playing.
7. Where is the book?
8. Where is the school?
9. The student raises his hand.

Lesson Seven: *A School 'Daze'*

Student Workbook:
Activity 7.28

7.28 Post-test Introduction

What Do You Know Now?

Post-test Goal: To assess your mastery of the lesson objectives.

Post-test Introduction: This test has three sections.

Section One: The Comprehension section tests your ability to understand ASL.

Section Two: Culture and Grammar section tests your knowledge of the material presented in the *Cultural* and *Grammatical Notes*.

Section Three: Expressive portion tests your ability to use ASL.

Simply follow the instructions for each section. **Good luck!**

Post-test Master:
Appendix 7.28

7.28 Post-test

Section One: Comprehension

Instructions: You will be presented with nine descriptions signed in ASL. Each sample will be numbered.

Below, you will find nine pictures. Choose the picture that best matches the signed description and write the correct number by each picture.

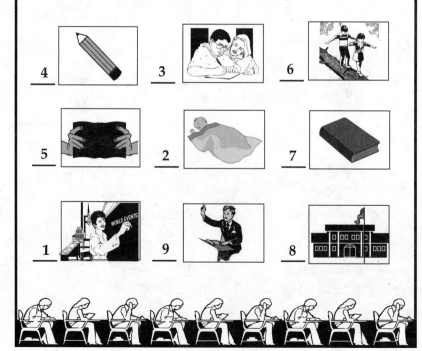

Post-test Master:
Appendix 7.28

7.28 Post-test

Section Two: Culture and Grammar

Instructions: Read each statement carefully and choose the best answer.

6. Deaf children should have the following options for education (select all that apply):
   A. School for the Deaf (residential)
   B. School for the Deaf (day school)
   C. Mainstreamed classroom (with interpreter)
   D. Mainstreamed classroom (without interpreter)

7. Self-esteem and self-identity should always be considered when educational placement decisions are made concerning Deaf children.
   A. True
   B. False

8. Schools for the Deaf can be residential or day programs.
   A. True
   B. False

9. Changing the movement or direction of a sign does not change its meaning.
   A. True
   B. False

10. Which of the following are examples of directional verbs? (Circle all that apply):
    A. GIVE
    B. HELP
    C. FOOD
    D. WATCH

Lesson Seven: *A School 'Daze'*

Post-test Master: Appendix 7.28

7.28 Post-test

Section Three: Expressive Portion

Instructions: Describe a room in your school, using at least seven signs learned in Lesson Seven. Include at least three directional verbs.

Your instructor will schedule a time for you to perform this section of the Post-test. You may prepare and practice prior to your scheduled time. Use the space below to prepare for your expressive performance.

Include at least seven signs from Lesson Seven.
11. _____
12. _____
13. _____
14. _____
15. _____
16. _____
17. _____

Include three directional verbs:
18. _____
19. _____
20. _____

Congratulations! You have completed Lesson Seven!

Lesson 8
A School 'Daze' - The Sequel

Materials Needed

Equipment: VCR and TV monitor
Overhead projector and screen
Chalk/dry erase board
Optional: video camera for activities 8.2 and 8.28

Materials: Instructor's Guide
Student Workbook: one per student
Overhead transparencies for activities 8.3, 8.4, 8.7, 8.9, 8.13, 8.14, 8.17, 8.22, and 8.26 (see Appendix for masters)
Playing cards (one deck for each group of four or five students) for activity 8.11
Optional: blank videotape (or have students bring their own) for activities 8.2 and 8.28
Post-test: Appendix 8.28

Videotapes: The Beginning ASL VideoCourse Lesson Eight
Activities Video for activity 8.5
Assessment Video for Post-test 8.28

8.1 Begin Class
Housekeeping

Goal: To prepare students for this lesson.

Instructions:
1. **Welcome** students to Lesson Eight of the VideoCourse.

2. **Perform** any necessary tasks (such as taking attendance) that may be required by your specific program.

Instructor's Guide: Lesson Eight
Bravo ASL! Curriculum

©1996 Sign Enhancers, Inc.
ALL RIGHTS RESERVED.

Lesson Eight: *A School 'Daze' - The Sequel*

8.2 Homework Review

A Funny Thing Happened At School

Activity Goal: To provide feedback on previously assigned homework and to reinforce materials learned in earlier lessons.

Activity Instructions:

1. **Ask** students to read *A Funny Thing Happened At School* in their workbooks (activity 8.2).

2. **Divide** the class into groups of three or four students.

3. **Instruct** students in each group to take turns signing the story about a day at school (*Homework Assignment 7.27*). **Remind** students that their story should include at least six school-related signs and three directional verbs.

4. **Circulate** among the groups to **observe** their progress.

5. When students have finished practicing, **ask** for volunteers to demonstrate their stories for the class. If possible, **videotape** each student's performance of this activity.

6. **Close** this activity by **modeling** any signs or grammatical features the students may have had trouble producing.

Student Workbook: Activity 8.2

> 8.2 Homework Review
>
> *A Funny Thing Happened At School*
>
> **Activity Goal:** To show the results of your homework assignment.
>
> **Activity Instructions:** In small groups, take turns signing the story about a day at school that you practiced for your homework assignment.
>
> Remember to include at least six new school-related signs and three directional verbs. Be creative! Ask questions about each other's stories using ASL.

8.3 Pretest
What Do You Know?

Pretest Goal: To identify students' current level of knowledge pertaining to the lesson content.

Pretest Instructions:
1. **Ask** students to read and answer the questions in their workbooks (activity 8.3).

2. **Show** overhead (Appendix 8.3) and **ask** individual students to indicate the correct answers on the overhead while class members correct their own work.

3. **Inform** students that the contents of the pretest will be taught throughout the lesson.

Student Workbook: Activity 8.3

Overhead Master: Appendix 8.3

8.3 Pretest

What Do You Know?

Pretest Goal: To see how much you already know about what will be taught in this lesson.

Pretest Instructions: Read each question and circle the best answer.

1. One benefit of a residential school for the Deaf is that all of the students are Deaf.
   A. True
   B. False

2. The first school for the Deaf established in America was the _____.
   A. Model School for the Deaf
   B. United States School for the Deaf
   C. American School for the Deaf
   D. Hartford School for the Deaf

3. What year was the first school for the Deaf established?
   A. 1955
   B. 1857
   C. 1917
   D. 1817

4. Members of the Deaf community often view the local school for the Deaf as:
   A. A place that helps and supports Deaf people.
   B. Providing a strong sense of belonging.
   C. A place with warm childhood memories.
   D. All of the above

5. In ASL, a simple side-to-side headshake can turn a positive statement into a negative.
   A. True
   B. False

Lesson Eight: *A School 'Daze' - The Sequel*

8.4 Lesson Objectives

Planning for Success

Goal: To identify the learning outcomes associated with successful completion of this lesson.

Instructions:
1. **Ask** students to read the objectives in their workbooks (activity 8.4).

2. **Show** overhead (Appendix 8.4) and **read** through the objectives with the class.

Student Workbook: Activity 8.4

Overhead Master: Appendix 8.4

> 8.4 Lesson Objectives
>
> *Planning for Success*
>
> **Goal:** To see what you will learn by the end of this lesson.
>
> **Instructions:** Read the objectives below.
>
> Upon completing this VideoCourse lesson, you will be able to...
>
> 1. Recognize and accurately produce the vocabulary introduced in this and all previous lessons.
>
> 2. Summarize the benefits of attending a residential school for the Deaf.
>
> 3. Explain the history and importance of the American School for the Deaf.
>
> 4. Explain the Deaf community's view of residential schools for the Deaf.
>
> 5. When formulating signed sentences, choose conceptually accurate signs that are based on meaning.

8.5 Lesson Focus

Math Whiz Quiz

Activities Video

Activity Goal: To develop a need for the ASL vocabulary introduced in this lesson.

Activity Instructions:

1. **Ask** students to read *Math Whiz Quiz* in their workbooks (activity 8.5).

2. **Play** the segment from the Activities Video (segment 8.5). **Instruct** students to watch the ten signed math problems.

3. **Tell** students to circle the correct answer to each problem in their workbooks. If students do not understand the signed numbers, **encourage** them to guess.

4. **Ask** individual students to write the problems and answers on the board while class members correct their own quizzes.

5. When students have completed this activity, you may **choose**:

   Option A: **Lead** a discussion using the following Thought/Discussion Questions:

   1) What are some signed numbers that would have been useful to know during this activity?
   2) How did it feel to be limited in your ability to understand the problems?
   3) Do you think Deaf people ever feel that way?

   OR

   Option B: **Ask** students to complete the above Thought/Discussion Questions in their workbooks in class or for homework. **Collect** for grading or to provide students with written feedback.

6. **Inform** students that they will learn the numbers they needed to perform this activity by the end of the lesson.

Note: You may want to repeat this activity at the end of the lesson so students can see how much they've learned.

Lesson Eight: *A School 'Daze' - The Sequel*

Video Segment Content: The following are the signed math problems:
(4 Minutes)

1. 1 + 2   = ____   6. 20 - 10 = ____
2. 3 + 13 = ____   7. 12 + 8 = ____
3. 5 + 6   = ____   8. 11 - 6 = ____
4. 11 - 7 = ____   9. 1 + 18 = ____
5. 15 - 8 = ____   10. 2 + 16 = ____

Student Workbook:
Activity 8.5

8.5 Lesson Focus

Math Whiz Quiz

Activity Goal: To solve math problems presented in ASL.

Activity Instructions: You will see ten signed math problems. Solve each problem and circle the correct answer below. If you don't know the signed numbers, try your best guess!

Don't worry - after this lesson you will know the ASL numbers you need to solve these problems!

1. A. 2   6. **A. 10**
   B. 3   B. 11
   C. 5   C. 30
   D. 1   D. 9

2. A. 23   7. A. 19
   B. 13   B. 10
   C. 16   **C. 20**
   D. 3   D. 4

3. A. 0   8. A. 4
   B. 11   B. 17
   C. 16   C. 2
   D. 7   **D. 5**

4. **A. 4**   9. **A. 19**
   B. 10   B. 18
   C. 6   C. 17
   D. 1   D. 2

5. A. 23   10. A. 14
   B. 7   B. 8
   C. 5   C. 6
   D. 26   **D. 18**

Thought/Discussion Questions

1. What are some signed numbers that would have been useful to know during this activity?

2. How did it feel to be limited in your ability to understand the problems?

3. Do you think Deaf people ever feel that way?

Lesson Eight: *A School 'Daze' - The Sequel*

8.6 Video Learning Experience

Bravo Family Visit

Viewing Goal: To review what happened in Anna's dream at school (Lesson Seven).

Viewing Instructions:
1. **Ask** students to read *Bravo Family Visit* in their workbooks (activity 8.6).
2. **Play** the video (segment 8.6) in which Billy reminds students what occurred at the Oregon School for the Deaf. Because Billy's introduction is beyond the linguistic ability of beginning students, please **turn on** audio and/or captions to optimize its educational value.
3. **Instruct** students to watch for review and write a summary of the main points.

Video Segment Content: (3 Minutes)

The following is a summary of the Bravo family interaction:

Billy: Hello! Welcome back to the Oregon School for the Deaf and to Anna's dream. As you remember, Anna had been getting tired of everyone always telling her "No." Remember? Let's review what happened.

Family walking Scott and Anna to school: The family is walking down a path. Dad asks the kids if they are ready for school. Scott says "Yes" and Anna says "No." Anna throws a wrapper on the ground and both parents stop her and tell her "No."

Anna sees a flower and starts to pick it. The groundskeeper walks up and tells her not to pick the flower.

Anna goes into the library and finds a book she wants to borrow, but the librarian tells her it is only for teachers, not for students. She walks into the classroom and sits down. The teacher tells her she cannot sit in that chair, she must sit in another chair.

Anna is tired of people telling her "No" all the time. She decides that when she is an adult and in charge, she will tell children "Yes" instead of "No." Anna puts her head down and falls asleep.

Billy: See what happened? Anna was so tired of it all that she fell asleep in class. She began to dream of what it would be like to be the one in charge. Anna was sure things would be different. Do you think that is true? Let's see what happens now.

Lesson Eight: *A School 'Daze' - The Sequel*

Anna's Dream: The students in Anna's class are arguing and throwing paper. Anna flashes the lights and tells them to sit down. She tells them they cannot play around and goof off. They all start imitating her signing "No, no, no."

Student Workbook: Activity 8.6

8.6 Video Learning Experience

Bravo Family Visit

Viewing Goal: To help you remember Anna's dream at the School for the Deaf from Lesson Seven.

Viewing Instructions: Watch the review of what happened at the School for the Deaf. In the space below, write a summary of the main points.

Summary: _____
_____
_____
_____

8.7 Language Learning Instruction

Learning New Signs

Goal: To use ASL and visual aids to introduce this lesson's vocabulary.

Instructions:
1. **Ask** students to read *Learning New Signs* in their workbooks (activity 8.7).

2. **Show** the overhead (Appendix 8.7). **Introduce** the vocabulary by **pointing** to items presented in the pictures while **demonstrating** the signs.

3. **Reinforce** retention and **check** students' comprehension by **using** these signs to **ask** students questions.

Note: For a step-by-step review of this method, see Lesson One (activities 1.6 and 1.12).

4. **Continue** this process until all the ASL vocabulary items have been introduced.

Lesson Eight: *A School 'Daze' - The Sequel*

Overhead Content: Use the pictures in the overhead (Appendix 8.7) to introduce the signs representing the following concepts:

1. #11
2. #12
3. #13
4. #14
5. #15
6. #16
7. #17
8. #18
9. #19
10. #20

Overhead Master:
Appendix 8.7

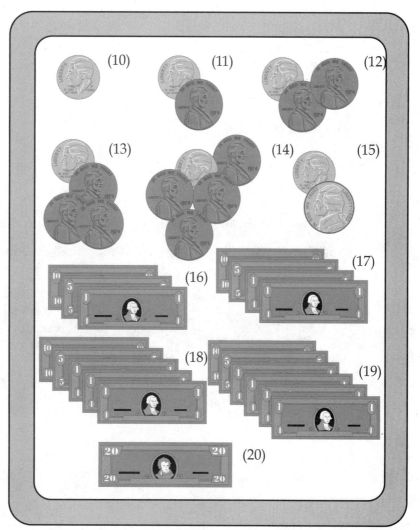

Lesson Eight: *A School 'Daze' - The Sequel*

Student Workbook:
Activity 8.7

8.7 Language Learning Instruction

Learning New Signs

Goal: To help you learn the numbers 11-20.

Instructions: Your instructor will teach you new signs! Watch closely to learn what these signs mean and how they are produced.

In the space below, record any notes to help you remember the signs.

Notes: _____
_____
_____
_____

8.8 Video Learning Experience

Practice Session: Numbers

Viewing Goal: To assist students in recognizing and producing numbers 1-20.

Viewing Instructions:
1. **Ask** students to read *Practice Session: Numbers* in their workbooks (activity 8.8).

2. **Play** the video segment entitled *Practice Session: Numbers* (segment 8.8). After a brief introduction, Billy reviews numbers 1-10 and introduces numbers 11-20.

3. **Instruct** students to watch how Billy produces the numbers.

4. **Suggest** that students copy the numbers as Billy signs each one.

Lesson Eight: *A School 'Daze' - The Sequel*

Video Segment Content: See the following Student Workbook excerpt for the content
(3 1/2 Minutes) of this video segment.

Student Workbook: Activity 8.8

8.8 Video Learning Experience

Practice Session: Numbers

Viewing Goal: To review numbers 1-10 and learn numbers 11-20.

Viewing Instructions: Watch how Billy produces the numbers.

In the space below, record any notes that will help you remember these numbers.

1. #1   6. #6   11. #11   16. #16
2. #2   7. #7   12. #12   17. #17
3. #3   8. #8   13. #13   18. #18
4. #4   9. #9   14. #14   19. #19
5. #5   10. #10   15. #15   20. #20

Notes: _____
_____
_____
_____

8.9 Language Learning Instruction

Learning New Signs

Goal: To use ASL and visual aids to introduce this lesson's vocabulary.

Instructions:
1. **Ask** students to read *Learning New Signs* in their workbooks (activity 8.9).

2. **Show** the overhead (Appendix 8.9). **Introduce** the vocabulary by **pointing** to items presented in the pictures while **demonstrating** the signs.

3. **Reinforce** retention and **check** students' comprehension by **using** these signs to **ask** students questions.

   Note: For a step-by-step review of this method, see Lesson One (activities 1.6 and 1.12).

4. **Continue** this process until all the ASL vocabulary items have been introduced.

Lesson Eight: *A School 'Daze' - The Sequel*

Overhead Content: Use the pictures in the overhead (Appendix 8.9) to introduce the signs representing the following concepts:

1. MATH
2. PLUS
3. MINUS/NEGATIVE
4. EQUAL
5. RIGHT/CORRECT
6. WRONG/INCORRECT
7. KNOW
8. CALCULATOR
9. COUNT
10. COME
11. ADD
12. TOGETHER
13. UNDERSTAND

Note: Some of the pictures can be used to represent several concepts. For verbs and more abstract concepts, you may need to supplement these pictures with mime, gestures, using actual objects, and acting out the concepts in class.

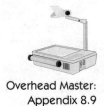

Overhead Master: Appendix 8.9

Student Workbook: Activity 8.9

8.9 Language Learning Instruction

Learning New Signs

Goal: To help you learn new ASL signs.

Instructions: Your instructor will teach you new signs! Watch closely to learn what these signs mean and how they are produced.

In the space below, record any notes that will help you remember the signs.

Notes: _____
_____
_____
_____

Lesson Eight: *A School 'Daze' - The Sequel*

8.10 Video Learning Experience

Introduction to New Vocabulary

Viewing Goal: To provide a signed demonstration of the accurate production of the new ASL vocabulary.

Viewing Instructions:
1. **Ask** students to read *Introduction to New Vocabulary* in their workbooks (activity 8.10).

2. **Play** the video segment entitled *Introduction to New Vocabulary* (segment 8.10). Billy introduces and signs each new vocabulary item twice. (If you wish to keep this a strictly visual presentation, **turn off** audio.)

3. **Instruct** students to watch how Billy produces the signs and the accompanying facial/body expressions.

4. **Ask** students to copy the signs and the facial/body expressions as Billy repeats each one.

Video Segment Content: See the following Student Workbook excerpt for the content
(2 Minutes) of this video segment.

Student Workbook: Activity 8.10

8.10 Video Learning Experience

Introduction to New Vocabulary

Viewing Goal: To help you learn new ASL vocabulary.

Viewing Instructions: Watch how Billy produces each sign. Be sure to notice the facial/body expressions. Copy the signs as Billy repeats each one.

Signs representing the following concepts are introduced:

1. MATH
2. PLUS
3. MINUS/NEGATIVE
4. EQUAL
5. RIGHT/CORRECT
6. WRONG/INCORRECT
7. KNOW
8. CALCULATOR
9. COUNT
10. COME
11. ADD
12. TOGETHER
13. UNDERSTAND

Lesson Eight: *A School 'Daze' - The Sequel*

8.11 Experiential Activity

Fish, Go You!

Activity Goal: To improve receptive and expressive skills using numbers.

Activity Instructions:

1. **Ask** students to read *Fish, Go You!* in their workbooks (activity 8.11).

2. **Divide** the class into groups of four or five students.

3. **Give** each group a deck of regular playing cards.

4. **Explain** the rules of the game as follows:

   A. Each player gets six cards dealt face down. The remaining cards are placed face down in the center of the group.

   B. The goal is for players to find a match for each card by asking another, in ASL, if s/he has the card the player is looking for.

   C. Students should use appropriate sentence structure to ask for cards. For example:
   $$\underline{\qquad t \qquad}\;\underline{\qquad q \qquad}$$
   EIGHT, HAVE YOU

   D. If the student asked does not have the card requested, s/he should sign,
   $$\underline{\qquad t \qquad}\qquad\underline{\qquad t \qquad}$$
   NO, EIGHT, HAVE NOT, FISH, GO YOU! This means that the first player will need to "fish" from the deck by drawing a card from the pile. If the player selects the card s/he needs, s/he gets another turn.

   E. If a player has a card requested by another player, s/he *must* hand it over and draw a card from the pile.

   F. The first player to match all the cards in his/her hand wins.

5. **Model** asking for a card as described above, then **tell** students to begin playing.

6. **Circulate** among groups to **observe** their performance.

Lesson Eight: *A School 'Daze' - The Sequel*

Student Workbook: Activity 8.11

8.11 Experiential Activity

Fish, Go You!

Activity Goal: To improve your expressive and receptive skills with numbers.

Activity Instructions: Your instructor will divide you into groups to play a version of the game "Go Fish." We call our game "FISH, GO YOU!" (following ASL topic/comment sentence structure).

The dealer gives each player six cards, face down. The remaining cards should be placed in a pile face down in the center of the group. The goal is to find a match for each card by asking another player, in ASL, if s/he has the card you need.

When it is your turn, ask for a card using ASL correct topic/comment structure. For example,

_____t _____q*
EIGHT, HAVE YOU.

Be sure you sign your numbers and the non-manual grammatical markers correctly.

When asked for a card that you do not have, tell the player: (repeat the number),

_____t   _____t
EIGHT, HAVE NOT... FISH, GO YOU!

S/he will need to "fish" for the card by drawing a card from the pile. If s/he picks the card, s/he gets another turn.

If you have a card that a player requests, you **must** give it to him/her and then replace it with a card from the deck.

The first person to match all the cards in his/her hand wins.

*****Note:** The "t" indicates the topic of the sentence. Remember that your eyebrows are raised, head tilted slightly, and the sign is held a little longer. The "q" means you are asking a yes/no question. Remember to raise your eyebrows, tilt your head, and maintain direct eye contact while you wait for the answer.

8.12 Video Learning Experience

Bravo Family Visit

Viewing Goal: To improve ASL comprehension skills by watching a Bravo family interaction.

Viewing Instructions:
1. **Ask** students to read *Bravo Family Visit* in their workbooks (activity 8.12).

2. **Play** the video of the continuation of Anna's dream (segment 8.12). Anna teaches a math lesson to her class.

Lesson Eight: *A School 'Daze' - The Sequel*

3. **Instruct** students to watch for comprehension and write a summary of the main points.

4. **Replay** any portion of this video segment that students experienced difficulty understanding.

Video Segment Content: (4 Minutes)

The following is a summary of the Bravo family interaction:

Anna tells the class that it is time for math. The class does not look happy. Anna writes a math problem on the board and asks for an answer. One student raises his hand, goes to the board and writes the wrong answer. Anna explains the answer and writes another problem: "15 + 5 = ?" Each student gives a different guess at the answer. One student finally gets the correct answer, but gets caught with a calculator.

The class counts from one to twenty along with Anna. As Anna writes another problem on the board, the students begin throwing paper again.

Billy: Wow! This dream of Anna's is really turning into a nightmare. But help is on the way! The principal is about to visit the class. Before we meet him and see what happens, let me teach you some new signs. I'll do that now.

Student Workbook: Activity 8.12

8.12 Video Learning Experience

Bravo Family Visit

Viewing Goal: To improve your ASL comprehension skills by watching a Bravo family interaction.

Viewing Instructions: Watch the signed interaction and write a summary of the main points.

Summary: _____
_____
_____
_____

Lesson Eight: *A School 'Daze' - The Sequel*

8.13 Comprehension Quiz

What Did You Understand?

Quiz Goal: To assess students' comprehension of the signed interaction.

Quiz Instructions:

1. **Instruct** students to complete the quiz in their workbooks (activity 8.13).

2. **Collect** for grading or **show** overhead (Appendix 8.13) and **ask** individual students to indicate the correct answers on the overhead while class members correct their own work.

3. **Ask** students to indicate which item(s) from the quiz they found difficult. **Review** by **modeling** or **replaying** that segment of the videotape.

Student Workbook: Activity 8.13

Overhead Master: Appendix 8.13

8.13 Comprehension Quiz

What Did You Understand?

Quiz Goal: To see how much of the Bravo family interaction you understood.

Quiz Instructions: Read and answer each question below.

1. Anna's class has a(n) _____ lesson during our visit.
   A. English
   B. Math
   C. Science
   D. German

2. Did the student have the right answer to the first math problem?
   A. Yes
   B. No

3. One student uses a(n) _____ to get the right answer.
   A. Dictionary
   B. Encyclopedia
   C. Computer
   D. Calculator

4. Anna's class practices counting from one to thirty.
   A. True
   B. False

5. The sign for the number 17 is made up of what two signs?
   A. ONE and SEVEN
   B. TEN and SEVEN
   C. NINE and EIGHT
   D. TWO and FIFTEEN

Instructor's Guide: Lesson Eight
Bravo ASL! Curriculum

©1996 Sign Enhancers, Inc.
ALL RIGHTS RESERVED.

Lesson Eight: *A School 'Daze' - The Sequel*

8.14 Language Learning Instruction

Learning New Signs

Goal: To use ASL and visual aids to introduce this lesson's vocabulary.

Instructions:
1. **Ask** students to read *Learning New Signs* in their workbooks (activity 8.14).

2. **Show** the overhead (Appendix 8.14). **Introduce** the vocabulary by **pointing** to items presented in the pictures while **demonstrating** the signs.

3. **Reinforce** retention and **check** students' comprehension by **using** these signs to **ask** students questions.

   Note: For a step-by-step review of this method, see Lesson One (activities 1.6 and 1.12).

4. **Continue** this process until all the ASL vocabulary items have been introduced.

Overhead Content: Use the pictures in the overhead (Appendix 8.14) to introduce the signs representing the following concepts:

1. CLASS
2. ROOM
3. PAY-ATTENTION
4. PRINCIPAL
5. DREAM
6. SLEEP
7. BOY
8. GIRL
9. GOOD
10. BAD
11. NAME
12. MAYBE

Note: Some pictures can be used to represent several concepts. For verbs and more abstract concepts, you may need to supplement these pictures with mime, gestures, using actual objects, and acting out the concepts in class.

Lesson Eight: *A School 'Daze' - The Sequel*

Overhead Master:
Appendix 8.14

Student Workbook:
Activity 8.14

8.14 Language Learning Instruction

Learning New Signs

Goal: To help you learn new ASL vocabulary.

Instructions: Your instructor will teach you new signs! Watch closely to learn what these signs mean and how they are produced.

In the space below, record any notes that will help you remember the signs.

Notes: _____
_____
_____
_____

Lesson Eight: *A School 'Daze' - The Sequel*

8.15 Video Learning Experience

Introduction to New Vocabulary

Viewing Goal: To provide a signed demonstration of the accurate production of the new ASL vocabulary.

Viewing Instructions:

1. **Ask** students to read *Introduction to New Vocabulary* in their workbooks (activity 8.15).

2. **Play** the video segment entitled *Introduction to New Vocabulary* (segment 8.15). Billy introduces and signs each new vocabulary item twice. (If you wish to keep this a strictly visual presentation, **turn off** audio.)

3. **Instruct** students to watch how Billy produces the signs and the accompanying facial/body expressions.

4. **Ask** students to copy the signs and the facial/body expressions as Billy repeats each one.

Video Segment Content: (2 Minutes) See the following Student Workbook excerpt for the content of this video segment.

Student Workbook: Activity 8.15

8.15 Video Learning Experience

Introduction to New Vocabulary

Viewing Goal: To help you learn new ASL vocabulary.

Viewing Instructions: Watch how Billy produces each sign. Be sure to notice the facial/body expressions. Copy the signs as Billy repeats each one.

Signs representing the following concepts are introduced:

1. CLASS
2. ROOM
3. PAY-ATTENTION
4. PRINCIPAL
5. DREAM
6. SLEEP
7. BOY
8. GIRL
9. GOOD
10. BAD
11. NAME
12. MAYBE

8.16 Video Learning Experience

Bravo Family Visit

Viewing Goal: To improve ASL comprehension skills by watching a signed interaction.

Viewing Instructions:
1. **Ask** students to read *Bravo Family Visit* in their workbooks (activity 8.16).
2. **Play** the video segment of Anna's dream (segment 8.16). The principal visits Anna's class.
3. **Instruct** students to watch for comprehension and write a summary of the main points.
4. **Replay** any portion of this video segment that students experienced difficulty understanding.

Video Segment Content: (4 1/2 Minutes)

The following is a summary of the Bravo family interaction:

The students in Anna's class are still throwing paper. The principal walks in and says good morning to everyone. He asks what is going on. Anna explains to the principal that there are bad boys and girls in her class, and they don't pay attention or do their work.

The principal asks the students if their teacher signs "No, no, no" a lot. And the students all nod their heads. He asks the students which of them were not paying attention or doing their work and they all look around at each other and shrug. He asks the class which of the boys and girls are being bad and none of them raise their hands.

The principal turns back to Anna and tells her that she has good students in her class. Then he asks them to all get their pencils out and they do it. Next he asks them to get out paper and they do. The principal asks the students to do different tasks such as read and write and they do it. Again, he tells Anna that her students are good. He tells her she must be dreaming and it is time for her to wake up.

Anna wakes up because her real teacher is tapping her arm. Anna tells her teacher about her bad dream. Anna tells the teacher she wants to be told "No." The confused teacher tells Anna she cannot sleep at school and Anna happily says OK.

Lesson Eight: *A School 'Daze' - The Sequel*

Billy: Oh! Well, Anna found out that it is not so fun or easy being a grown-up. It's true. It's not that easy. Hmmm... I wonder how would it be if I were twelve years old again. Oh, no! That was when I had my tonsils removed. No thanks!

Well, just as Anna is still learning, adults are still learning, too. You are still learning new signs, let's practice those signs now.

Student Workbook: Activity 8.16

8.16 Video Learning Experience

Bravo Family Visit

Viewing Goal: To improve your ASL comprehension skills by watching a Bravo family interaction.

Viewing Instructions: Watch the signed interaction and write a summary of the main points.

Summary: _____
_____
_____
_____

8.17 Comprehension Quiz

What Did You Understand?

Quiz Goal: To assess students' comprehension of the signed interaction.

Quiz Instructions:
1. **Instruct** students to complete the quiz in their workbooks (activity 8.17).

2. **Collect** for grading or **show** overhead (Appendix 8.17) and **ask** individual students to indicate the correct answers on the overhead while class members correct their own work.

3. **Ask** students to indicate which item(s) from the quiz they found difficult. **Review** by **modeling** or **replaying** that segment of the videotape.

Lesson Eight: *A School 'Daze' - The Sequel*

Student Workbook:
Activity 8.17

Overhead Master:
Appendix 8.17

8.17 Comprehension Quiz

What Did You Understand?

Quiz Goal: To see how much of the Bravo family interaction you understood.

Quiz Instructions: Read and answer each question below.

1. Who comes to visit Anna's classroom?
   The principal.

2. What did Anna tell the visitor was wrong in her class?
   There are bad boys and girls in her classroom who won't pay attention.

3. When the visitor asks the students to take out a piece of paper, what do the students do?
   A. Take out paper
   B. Throw paper at the teacher
   C. Throw paper at each other
   D. They all started signing "No, no, no."

4. What does the visitor tell Anna about her students?
   That they are all good students.

5. When she wakes up, what does Anna want her real teacher to do?
   Tell her "No."

8.18 Video Learning Experience

Review Session

Viewing Goal: To reinforce recognition and production of the signs introduced in this lesson.

Viewing Instructions:

1. **Ask** students to read *Review Session* in their workbooks (8.18).

2. **Play** the video segment entitled *Review Session* (segment 8.18). Billy reviews all the ASL vocabulary and provides visual cues and origin information. Because the presentation of this segment is beyond the linguistic ability of beginning students, please **turn on** the audio and/or captions to optimize its educational value.

3. **Ask** students to pay careful attention to the signed vocabulary items and take note of visual hints offered by Billy that might help them remember.

4. **Suggest** that students copy the signs to reinforce retention of sign production.

Lesson Eight: *A School 'Daze' - The Sequel*

Video Segment Content: See the following Student Workbook excerpt for the content
(9 Minutes) of this video segment.

Student Workbook:
Activity 8.18

8.18 Video Learning Experience

Review Session

Viewing Goal: To help you remember how to produce the signs introduced in this lesson.

Viewing Instructions: Watch this video segment carefully to see how each sign is made, and take note of any hints given that might help you remember. You may want to copy the signs as you watch Billy.

After Billy reviews numbers 1-20, the following vocabulary is explained:

MATH	The old sign developed long ago meant TO-FIGURE. It has since become an initialized sign.
PLUS	This sign looks like the addition (plus) symbol.
MINUS	This sign looks like the subtraction (minus) symbol.
EQUAL	This sign shows it is not higher or lower, but the same (equal).
ADD	The one hand has something, the other hand adds to it.
COUNT	This is like counting coins in your hand. One, two, and so on.
CALCULATOR	This sign shows how a CALCULATOR is used.
TOGETHER	One hand is alone, the other is, too. Now we put them TOGETHER.
RIGHT	This sign is a symbol meaning RIGHT.
WRONG	This is also a symbol representing the concept of WRONG.
GOOD	You have already learned this sign on another tape. The palm orientation is up, meaning GOOD.
BAD	The palm orientation is the opposite of GOOD. It turns down as if you want to keep something away from you.
UNDERSTAND	This is like a light bulb that is connected to your head. When it goes on, you UNDERSTAND.
KNOW	You already have the information in your mind.
NAME	This sign is a symbol meaning NAME.
CLASS	This sign represents several people in a group.
ROOM	This sign shows the four walls of a room.
PAY-ATTENTION	This sign comes from the blinders which are placed on horses. It prevents them from looking from side to side, therefore it forces them to PAY-ATTENTION.

Instructor's Guide: Lesson Eight
Bravo ASL! Curriculum

Lesson Eight: *A School 'Daze' - The Sequel*

COME	This is an action sign showing where to go.
PRINCIPAL	One hand can represent a school, business or institution. The boss on top of it all is the PRINCIPAL.
DREAM	This sign is like the little white cloud you see in cartoons representing a dream.
SLEEP	This sign shows the eyes closing.
BOY	This sign represents the bill of a boy's baseball cap.
GIRL	Long ago, when the pioneers moved west, girls always wore bonnets. This sign comes from the strap tied under the chin.
MAYBE	One hand is YES, the other hand is NO. It's as if you are weighing the choices... MAYBE.

8.19 Video Learning Experience

Cultural Notes

Viewing Goal: To assist students in learning about the cultural aspects of ASL.

Viewing Instructions:

1. **Ask** students to read *Cultural Notes* in their workbooks (activity 8.19).

2. **Play** the video segment entitled *Cultural Notes* (segment 8.19). Because the presentation of this segment is beyond the linguistic ability of beginning students, please **turn on** the audio and/or captions to optimize its educational value.

3. **Instruct** students to view the segment.

4. At completion of the video segment, **review** the content presented and **answer** any questions students may have.

Lesson Eight: *A School 'Daze' - The Sequel*

Video Segment Content: See the following Student Workbook excerpt for the content
(5 Minutes) of this video segment.

Student Workbook:
Activity 8.19

8.19 Video Learning Experience

Cultural Notes

Viewing Goal: To learn about the cultural aspects of ASL.

Viewing Instructions: View the *Cultural Notes* segment carefully for the following:

I. The *Cultural Notes* segment discusses some of the benefits and disadvantages of attending a school for the Deaf.
   A. Benefits
      1. All the students are Deaf.
      2. Some teachers are Deaf, providing role models.
      3. Everyone knows and uses Sign Language.
      4. Establishes strong ties and connections to Deaf culture.
      5. Promotes language development and growth.
      6. Provides a strong positive impact for Deaf children.
      7. Varied opportunities presented to all students equally:
         a. Sports
         b. Drama
         c. Field trips
         d. Social functions such as school dances
         e. Dormitories provide excellent opportunities for peer interaction
      8. Fosters Deaf leadership skills.
      9. Adult role models assist in development of self-esteem and language.
   B. A disadvantage of schools for the Deaf: families are often separated from the Deaf child because of distance.
      1. Some families move closer to schools for the Deaf.
      2. When children commute to school from home, they can still participate in social activities.

II. The first Deaf school in America was the American School for the Deaf. It is located in Hartford, Connecticut, and was established in 1817.

III. The Deaf community views schools for the Deaf with high regard:
   A. Place of help.
   B. Strong sense of belonging.
   C. Warm memories.
   D. Often considered "home."

IV. Deaf schools should not be viewed as a last educational option.
   A. They are an equal option.
   B. May be the best educational option for many children.
   C. Schools for the Deaf should be respected and supported.

8.20 Experiential Activity

Special Guests

Activity Goal: To provide students the opportunity to meet Deaf people and learn firsthand about their educational experiences.

Activity Instructions:

1. **Invite** several Deaf people to attend your ASL class. It is recommended that you **select** people with varying educational experiences (residential, day school, mainstreamed setting, etc.). You may **choose** to have an interpreter available for full communication access during this activity.

2. **Ask** students to read *Special Guests* in their workbooks (activity 8.20).

3. **Encourage** the speakers to share their educational experiences. You may choose to **ask**:

    A. Where did you attend school?

    B. What type of program was this?

    C. What was the communication method(s) used at your school?

    D. Did you experience any frustrations or barriers to receiving a good education?

    E. If your school used ASL, did you have formal classes for developing ASL skills? How did you learn to sign?

    F. If you could do it all again, what would you change about your educational experiences?

4. Following this panel discussion, you may **choose**:

    Option A: **Lead** a discussion **using** the following Thought/Discussion Questions:

    1) What did you learn from this panel?

    2) How did each of the panel members feel about their educational experiences?

    3) Did this panel change your opinion about any particular educational option(s)?

    OR

    Option B: **Ask** students to complete the Thought/Discussion Questions in their workbooks in class or for homework. **Collect** for grading or to provide written feedback.

Lesson Eight: *A School 'Daze' - The Sequel*

Student Workbook: Activity 8.20

8.20 Experiential Activity

Special Guests

Activity Goal: To give you the opportunity to meet Deaf people and learn firsthand about their personal educational experiences.

Activity Instructions: Use the space below to record any information you find to be valuable or interesting. You may also want to record questions for the speaker(s) or your teacher.

Notes: _____
_____
_____

Thought/Discussion Questions:

1. What did you learn from this panel?

2. How did each of the panel members feel about their educational experiences?

3. Did this panel change your opinion about any particular educational option(s)?

8.21 Video Learning Experience

Grammatical Notes

Viewing Goal: To assist students in learning about the grammatical aspects of ASL.

Viewing Instructions:
1. **Ask** students to read *Grammatical Notes* in their workbooks (activity 8.21).

2. **Play** the video segment entitled *Grammatical Notes* (segment 8.21). Because the presentation of this segment is beyond the linguistic ability of beginning students, please **turn on** the audio and/or captions to optimize its educational value.

3. **Instruct** students to view the segment.

4. At completion of segment, **review** the content presented and **answer** any questions students may have.

Lesson Eight: *A School 'Daze' - The Sequel*

Video Segment Content: See the following Student Workbook excerpt for the content
(3 Minutes) of this video segment.

Student Workbook:
Activity 8.21

8.21 Video Learning Experience

Grammatical Notes

Viewing Goal: To learn about the grammatical aspects of ASL.

Viewing Instructions: Conceptual accuracy is the topic of this *Grammatical Notes* segment. View it carefully for the following:

A. Your choice and use of a sign must fit the conceptual meaning of what you are expressing. The signs you choose need to be selected based on their meaning, **not** based on English words. The following are examples of English words that represent several different meanings. Billy demonstrates how these multiple meanings are expressed by using conceptually accurate sign choices:

1. The word "like" has several meanings. Each meaning would be represented by a different sign:
   a. Like (related to feelings)
   b. Like (used to compare)

2. The word "play" has several meanings. Each meaning would be represented by a different sign:
   a. Play (violin)
   b. Play (drums)
   c. Play (piano)
   d. Play (tennis)
   e. Play (drama)

3. The word "right" has several meanings. Each meaning would be represented by a different sign:
   a. Right (I am right)
   b. Right (turn right)
   c. Right (my rights)

B. Conceptual accuracy is <u>not</u> based on English spelling or pronunciation.
   Example: PAY-ATTENTION. The meaning is not related to paying money. The meaning is more closely related to focusing or concentrating, so the sign is produced as demonstrated on the video.

C. Conceptual accuracy is important! Correct conceptual meaning creates visual clarity and accuracy.

Instructor's Guide: Lesson Eight
Bravo ASL! Curriculum

Lesson Eight: *A School 'Daze' - The Sequel*

8.22 Experiential Activity

What Do You Mean?

Activity Goal: To provide students the opportunity to choose ASL signs based on meaning (conceptual accuracy).

Activity Instructions:

1. **Ask** students to read *What Do You Mean?* in their workbooks (activity 8.22).

2. **Tell** students to read the sentences and determine the sign that best matches the meaning of the word appearing in **bold**.

3. **Show** the overhead (Appendix 8.22) and **ask** individual students to demonstrate the appropriate sign(s) for the class.

4. **Model** correct answers as needed.

Student Workbook: Activity 8.22

Overhead Master: Appendix 8.22

8.22 Experiential Activity

What Do You Mean?

Activity Goal: To choose ASL signs based on meaning.

Activity Instructions: English words may have several different meanings. ASL signs do not relate to English words, but to the meaning of what is being expressed.

Read each of the sentences below. Decide what sign you would use for the meaning of the word/concept that is printed in **bold**. A space has been provided for you to record your answers.

1. I have **gone** to the store before.
2. The food is all **gone**.
3. The light is **on** the table.
4. Turn **on** the light.
5. The book is **there**.
6. The book is **theirs**.
7. That **dog** is mine.
8. I am **dog** tired.

Instructor's Guide: Lesson Eight
Bravo ASL! Curriculum

8.23 Video Learning Experience

Practice Session: Sentences

Viewing Goal: To improve comprehension skills by watching sentences presented in ASL.

Viewing Instructions:
1. **Ask** students to read *Practice Session: Sentences* in their workbooks (activity 8.23).

2. **Play** the video segment entitled *Practice Session: Sentences* (segment 8.23). Each sentence is signed twice and an English translation is provided.

3. **Remind** students to watch the face of each signer to see the facial/body expressions and non-manual grammatical markers as well as the signs.

Video Segment Content: (2 Minutes)

The following are English translations of the practice sentences:

1. 11 + 2 = 13
2. 16 + 4 = 20
3. Incorrect! 20 - 1 does not equal 14.
4. You must pay attention to the teacher!
5. My school has 20 teachers and 1 principal.
6. That's right! 20 - 1 = 19. You're right.

Student Workbook: Activity 8.23

> 8.23 Video Learning Experience
>
> *Practice Session: Sentences*
>
> **Viewing Goal:** To improve your comprehension skills by watching sentences presented in ASL.
>
> **Viewing Instructions:** Watch the signed sentences for comprehension. Remember to watch the face of each signer to see the facial/body expressions and the non-manual grammatical markers as well as the signs.
>
> It is recommended that you copy each signed sentence when it is repeated.
>
> In the space below, record any questions or notes you have regarding the sentences.
>
> Notes: _____
> _____
> _____
> _____

Lesson Eight: *A School 'Daze' - The Sequel*

8.24 Experiential Activity

Sign-A-Problem

Activity Goal: To improve receptive and expressive ASL skills when using numbers.

Activity Instructions:

1. **Ask** students to read *Sign-A-Problem* in their workbooks (activity 8.24).

2. **Divide** the class into pairs.

3. **Ask** each student to write down ten addition or subtraction math problems using the numbers 1-20 in the spaces provided in their workbooks. Students should also record the answers to their math problems.

4. **Instruct** students to take turns signing their math problems to their partners. Each partner should record the math problems signed to him/her in his/her workbook and sign the answers.

5. **Circulate** among the students and **observe** their performance. **Model** equations or numbers as needed.

Student Workbook: Activity 8.24

8.24 Experiential Activity

Sign-A-Problem

Activity Goal: To practice understanding numbers and mathematical problems in ASL.

Activity Instructions: Use the spaces below marked **My Problems** to create and write mathematical problems you will sign to your partner. The problems should be addition or subtraction, using the numbers 1-20. Solve each problem so you can check your partner's answers.

In the spaces below marked **My Partner's Problems**, write the math problems that your partner signs to you. Complete the math. Sign your answers to one another. If there are errors, sign those problems again.

My Problems:

1. _____   6. _____
2. _____   7. _____
3. _____   8. _____
4. _____   9. _____
5. _____   10. _____

Instructor's Guide: Lesson Eight
Bravo ASL! Curriculum

Lesson Eight: *A School 'Daze' - The Sequel*

My Partner's Problems:

1. _____ 6. _____
2. _____ 7. _____
3. _____ 8. _____
4. _____ 9. _____
5. _____ 10. _____

8.25 Video Learning Experience

Practice Session: Story

Viewing Goal: To improve comprehension skills by watching a story presented in ASL.

Viewing Instructions:
1. **Ask** students to read *Practice Session: Story* in their workbooks (activity 8.25).

2. **Show** the video segment entitled *Practice Session: Story* (segment 8.25). Billy signs a story using the vocabulary introduced in this lesson. **Turn off** audio and captions.

3. **Instruct** students to watch the signed story and write a summary of the main points.

Video Segment Content: (2 Minutes)

The following is an English translation of the story:

Once there was a Deaf boy. He went to school. The teacher was Deaf and signed very fluently. The boy liked the school. The other children in the school were Deaf. The boy learned reading, writing, and arithmetic.

The boy's family was hearing. He taught them Sign Language.

Lesson Eight: *A School 'Daze' - The Sequel*

At school, the boy was a student. At home the boy was a teacher. The boy was happy and proud.

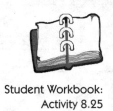

Student Workbook: Activity 8.25

8.25 Video Learning Experience

Practice Session: Story

Viewing Goal: To improve your comprehension skills by watching a story presented in ASL.

Viewing Instructions: Watch the signed story for comprehension and write a summary to help you remember.

Summary: _____
_____
_____
_____

8.26 Comprehension Quiz

What Did You Understand?

Quiz Goal: To assess students' comprehension of the signed story.

Quiz Instructions:
1. **Instruct** students to complete the quiz in their workbooks (activity 8.26).

2. **Collect** for grading or **show** overhead (Appendix 8.26) and **ask** individual students to indicate the correct answers on the overhead while class members correct their own work.

3. **Ask** students to indicate which item(s) from the quiz they found difficult. **Review** by **modeling** or **replaying** that segment of the videotape.

Lesson Eight: *A School 'Daze' - The Sequel*

Student Workbook:
Activity 8.26

Overhead Master:
Appendix 8.26

8.26 Comprehension Quiz

What Did You Understand?

Quiz Goal: To see how much of the signed story you understood.

Quiz Instructions: Read and answer each question below.

1. The character in the story was a _____.
   A. Hearing girl
   B. Hearing boy
   C. Deaf boy
   D. Deaf girl

2. The teacher was Deaf and signed fluently.
   A. True
   B. False

3. The student's family was Deaf.
   A. True
   B. False

4. The other children at school were _____.
   A. Deaf and hearing
   B. Hearing
   C. Older
   D. Deaf

5. According to the story, the student was also a _____.
   A. Cub scout
   B. Baseball player
   C. Teacher
   D. Swimmer

8.27 Homework Assignment

A Dramatic Day At School!

Homework Goal: To provide students with the opportunity to improve their ASL expressive and receptive skills.

Homework Instructions:

1. **Ask** students to read *A Dramatic Day At School!* in their workbooks (activity 8.27).

2. **Divide** class into groups of five or six to prepare and perform a role-play.

3. **Assign** students the task of creating a short skit involving a classroom scene. **Tell** students to be prepared to perform these skits during the next session (or inform them of the date this activity will be performed).

Instructor's Guide: Lesson Eight
Bravo ASL! Curriculum
©1996 Sign Enhancers, Inc.
ALL RIGHTS RESERVED.

Lesson Eight: *A School 'Daze' - The Sequel*

4. **Remind** students that they are to use as much of the vocabulary from Lessons Seven and Eight as possible.

5. **Ask** students to incorporate all of the grammatical principles taught in Lessons One through Eight, including: yes/no-questions; wh-questions; adjective placement, negation, topic/comment structure; parameters of sign production; directional verbs; and conceptual sign choices.

6. **Provide** the teams an opportunity to meet to plan their dramas.

Instructor Tip: *An opportunity for students to perform this assignment has been scheduled in the next lesson (Homework Review 9.2). If possible, it is recommended that you arrange to videotape each group's performance of this activity.*

Student Workbook: Activity 8.27

> 8.27 Homework Assignment
>
> *A Dramatic Day at School!*
>
> **Homework Goal:** To practice using the vocabulary learned in Lessons Seven and Eight and the grammatical principles taught in all previous lessons.
>
> **Homework Instructions:** Work with your group to prepare a short skit that shows a *Dramatic Day At School!*
>
> Use as many of the signs you learned in Lessons Seven and Eight as possible. Be sure to include: yes/no-questions; wh-questions, adjective placement; negation; topic/comment structure; parameters of sign production; directional verbs; and conceptual sign choices.
>
> Your instructor will let you know when this drama will be performed in class. All members of the group must have signing roles in the drama.
>
> This is your chance to be *creative* and *dramatic*!

8.28 Post-test
What Do You Know Now?

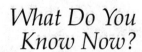

Assessment Video

Post-test Goal: To assess students' mastery of the lesson objectives.

Post-test Instructions:
1. **Ask** students to read the Post-test Introduction in their workbooks (activity 8.28).

2. **Copy** and **distribute** the Lesson Eight Post-test (Appendix 8.28).

Lesson Eight: *A School 'Daze' - The Sequel*

3. **Play** the Assessment Video (segment 8.28) and **allow** students to complete Section One (comprehension portion) of the test.

4. **Instruct** students to complete Section Two (culture and grammar portion) of the test individually and hand in their papers when they are finished.

5. **Assign** Section Three (expressive portion) of the test and **schedule** a time when students are to perform. If possible, it is strongly recommended that you **videotape** this portion of the Post-test.

6. **Determine** grading options based upon programmatic requirements. A recommended guideline for measuring successful mastery of objectives is 80% accuracy.

Video Segment Content: The following is an English translation of the comprehension
(1 Minute) story:

Rick is Deaf and goes to a Deaf school. All of his classmates know Sign Language and so does his teacher.

Rick likes math class. Today, in math class, Rick will learn how to use a calculator. He already understands how to add and subtract because he pays attention. Rick is a good student.

Student Workbook:
Activity 8.28

8.28 Post-test Introduction

What Do You Know Now?

Post-test Goal: To assess your mastery of the lesson objectives.

Post-test Introduction: This test has three sections:

   Section One: The Comprehension section tests your ability to understand ASL.

   Section Two: The Culture and Grammar section tests your knowledge of the material presented in the *Cultural* and *Grammatical Notes*.

   Section Three: The Expressive portion tests your ability to use ASL.

Simply follow the instructions for each section. **Good luck!**

Lesson Eight: *A School 'Daze' - The Sequel*

Post-test Master: Appendix 8.28

8.28 Post-test

Section One: Comprehension

Instructions: You will see a signed story. Watch carefully and answer each question below.

1. What is the student's name in the story?
   A. Mike
   B. Rick
   C. Billy
   D. Nick

2. He attends a hearing school.
   A. True
   B. False

3. Does his teacher know Sign Language?
   A. Yes
   B. No

4. Today, in class, what was he going to learn?
   A. How to subtract
   B. How to add
   C. How to use a calculator
   D. How to multiply

5. According to the story, he understands because _____.
   A. He has a tutor
   B. He pays attention in class
   C. His mother is a math teacher
   D. His Deaf friends help him

6. According to the story, he is a good student.
   A. True
   B. False

Instructor's Guide: Lesson Eight
Bravo ASL! Curriculum

Lesson Eight: *A School 'Daze' - The Sequel*

Post-test Master: Appendix 8.28

8.28 Post-test

Section Two: Culture and Grammar

Instructions: Read each statement carefully and write your answers in the space provided.

7. As you have learned, there are several educational options available to Deaf students. Discuss at least three benefits of attending a School for the Deaf.
All students are Deaf, Deaf role models, everyone uses Sign Language, ties to Deaf culture/community, promotes language development, equal access/opportunities, etc.

8. What might be considered an unfortunate aspect of attending a residential school for the Deaf?
Being separated from family.

9. What was the name of the first school for the Deaf in the United States? When and where was it established?
The American School for the Deaf, established in 1817 in Hartford, Connecticut.

10. Explain what is meant by "conceptual accuracy."
This means signs are selected based on the meaning of the ideas being expressed.

Lesson Eight: *A School 'Daze' - The Sequel*

Post-test Master:
Appendix 8.28

8.28 Post-test

Section Three: Expressive Portion

Instructions: Create a story about your favorite class using at least seven signs learned in this lesson. Be certain to use at least three conceptually accurate signs/choices and be prepared to identify them.

Your instructor will schedule a time for you to perform this section of the Post-test. You may prepare and practice prior to your scheduled time. Use the space below to prepare for your expressive presentation.

Include at least seven signs from Lesson Eight.

11. _____
12. _____
13. _____
14. _____
15. _____
16. _____
17. _____

Conceptually accurate signs:

18. _____
19. _____
20. _____

Congratulations!
You have completed
Lesson Eight!

Lesson 9
Dollar Signs

Materials Needed:

Equipment: VCR and TV monitor
Overhead projector and screen
Optional: video camera for activities 9.2 and 9.32

Materials: Instructor's Guide
Student Workbook: one per student
Overhead transparencies for activities 9.3, 9.4, 9.7, 9.10, 9.13, 9.16, 9.17, 9.21, 9.24, and 9.29 (see Appendix for masters)
Various board games with play money for activities 9.5 and 9.30, one game for every four or five students (or have students bring their own)
Tic-Tac-Dough cards for activities 9.5 and 9.19 (see Appendix for masters)
Optional: blank videotape (or have students bring their own) for activities 9.2 and 9.32
Post-test: Appendix 9.32

Videotapes: The Beginning ASL VideoCourse Lesson Nine
Activities Video for activity 9.24
Assessment Video for Post-test 9.32

9.1 Begin Class
Housekeeping

Goal: To prepare students for this lesson.

Instructions:
1. **Welcome** students to Lesson Nine of the VideoCourse.
2. **Perform** any necessary tasks (such as taking attendance) that may be required by your specific program.

Lesson Nine: *Dollar Signs*

9.2 Homework Review

A Dramatic Day at School!

Activity Goal: To provide feedback on previously assigned homework and to reinforce materials learned in earlier lessons.

Activity Instructions:

1. **Ask** students to read *A Dramatic Day at School!* in their workbooks (activity 9.2).

2. **Divide** the class into the same small groups that worked together in *Homework Assignment 8.27*. **Give** groups a few minutes to review and practice the skits they prepared for homework.

3. When students have finished practicing, **instruct** groups to take turns performing their skits (*Homework Assignment 8.27*) while the rest of the class practices comprehension. If possible, **videotape** each group's performance of this activity.

4. **Encourage** the class to use ASL to ask questions about each skit to indicate accurate comprehension.

5. **Observe** student performance and **model** corrections as needed.

Student Workbook: Activity 9.2

> 9.2 Homework Review
>
> *A Dramatic Day at School!*
>
> **Activity Goal:** To show the results of your homework assignment.
>
> **Activity Instructions:** Your group will perform its skit, *A Dramatic Day at School!*, as assigned in Lesson Eight. Remember to include the school-related vocabulary introduced in Lessons Seven and Eight as well as the grammatical features you learned in Lessons One through Eight.
>
> While other groups perform their skits, pay close attention and practice your ASL comprehension skills! Use ASL to ask questions about your classmates' *Dramatic Days at School!*

Lesson Nine: *Dollar Signs*

9.3 Pretest

What Do You Know?

Pretest Goal: To identify students' current level of knowledge pertaining to the lesson content.

Pretest Instructions:

1. **Ask** students to read and answer the questions in the pretest in their workbooks (activity 9.3).

2. **Show** overhead (Appendix 9.3) and **ask** individual students to indicate the correct answers on the overhead while class members correct their own work.

3. **Inform** students that the contents of the pretest will be taught throughout the lesson.

Student Workbook: Acitivity 9.3

Overhead Master: Appendix 9.3

9.3 Pretest

What Do You Know?

Pretest Goal: To see how much you already know about what will be taught in this lesson.

Pretest Instructions: Read and answer each question.

1. In the past, employment options for Deaf people have been limited to jobs involving menial labor.
   A. True
   B. False

2. The telephone has been and still is a complete communication barrier in the workplace for Deaf people.
   A. True
   B. False

3. What type of jobs are available to Deaf people today?

   Deaf people today hold jobs such as counselors, secretaries, teachers, lawyers, artists, administrators, dancers, etc.

4. Some Deaf people now own businesses.
   A. True
   B. False

5. The sign for ONE DOLLAR is made with a different movement than the sign for the number ONE.
   A. True
   B. False

6. Signs for dollar amounts of $10 or more are made differently than the signs for $9 or less.
   A. True
   B. False

7. The sign for "bank" is actually a fingerspelled loan sign.
   A. True
   B. False

Instructor's Guide: Lesson Nine
Bravo ASL! Curriculum

Lesson Nine: *Dollar Signs*

9.4 Lesson Objectives
Planning for Success

Goal: To identify the learning outcomes associated with successful completion of this lesson.

Instructions:
1. **Ask** students to read the objectives in their workbooks (activity 9.4).
2. **Show** overhead (Appendix 9.4) and **read** through the objectives with the class.

Student Workbook: Activity 9.4

Overhead Master: Appendix 9.4

> 9.4 Lesson Objectives
>
> *Planning for Success*
>
> **Goal:** To see what you will learn by the end of this lesson.
>
> **Instructions:** Read the objectives below.
>
> Upon completing this VideoCourse lesson, you will be able to...
>
> 1. Recognize and accurately produce the ASL vocabulary introduced in this and all previous lessons.
> 2. Compare the employment opportunities available to Deaf workers in the past with those opportunities available today.
> 3. Explain why the telephone is less of a barrier for Deaf workers today than it was in the past, particularly in regards to employment or owning a business.
> 4. Recognize and accurately produce number signs related to money.

Lesson Nine: *Dollar Signs*

9.5 Lesson Focus

The Silent Games

Activity Goal: To develop a need for the ASL vocabulary introduced in this lesson.

Activity Instructions:

1. **Ask** students to read *The Silent Games* in their workbooks (activity 9.5).

2. **Divide** class into groups of four or five students and **distribute** various board games with play money to each group (or **ask** the students to take out their own). Suggested games include Monopoly, Life, Payday, etc.

3. **Ask** students to play the games. **Tell** students they are not to use their voices. They should communicate in ASL whenever possible, trying to communicate the monetary and banking information the best they can.

4. **Remind** students that they can use other methods to communicate including gesturing, miming, pointing, etc.

5. **Circulate** among the groups to **observe** their progress.

6. At completion of the activity, you may **choose**:

   Option A: **Bring** the whole class together and **lead** a discussion using the following Thought/Discussion Questions:

   1) What are some signs related to money that would have been useful to know during this activity?

   2) How did it feel to be limited in your ability to communicate?

   3) What are some techniques Deaf people could use to communicate about money with people who do not sign?

   OR

   Option B: **Ask** students to complete the above Thought/Discussion Questions in their workbooks in class or for homework. **Collect** for grading or to provide students with written feedback.

7. **Inform** students that they will learn the signs needed to communicate about money and banking by the end of this lesson.

8. **Inform** students that they will have another opportunity to play the games, using the signs they will learn (activity 9.30).

Lesson Nine: *Dollar Signs*

Student Workbook:
Activity 9.5

9.5 Lesson Focus

The Silent Games

Activity Goal: To experience playing games with money using ASL.

Activity Instructions: Your group will play a game involving money. During the game, communicate using ASL, gestures, mime, and fingerspelling - but do not use your voice!

Follow the game rules supplied with each game. Have fun and good luck!

Thought/Discussion Questions

1. What are some signs related to money that would have been useful to know during this activity?

2. How did it feel to be limited in your ability to communicate?

3. What are some techniques Deaf people could use to communicate about money with people who don't sign?

9.6 Video Learning Experience

Bravo Family Visit

Viewing Goal: To introduce students to this lesson.

Viewing Instructions:
1. **Ask** students to read *Bravo Family Visit* in their workbooks (activity 9.6).

2. **Play** the video segment of Dad and Scott at the bank (segment 9.6). They will use the new ASL vocabulary within the context of banking. Billy will then introduce the lesson. Because Billy's introduction is beyond the linguistic ability of beginning students, please **turn on** the audio and/or captions to optimize its educational value.

3. **Instruct** students to watch for comprehension and write a summary of the main points.

4. **Replay** any portion of this video segment that students had difficulty understanding.

Video Segment Content: The following is a summary of the Bravo family interaction:
(1 1/2 Minutes)

Dad and Scott in front of the bank: Scott tells Dad that he wants ice cream. Dad tells him they will have to see, because it's getting late and he has to meet Mom at four o'clock. Scott asks what they're doing now and Dad tells him they're going in the bank. He hopes that it doesn't take long.

Lesson Nine: *Dollar Signs*

Billy: Oh! Hello again! Welcome to another Sign Enhancers, Inc. VideoCourse Lesson! Today's topic is something everybody likes: Money!

Dad wants to surprise Mom. As it happened, Dad received a bonus at work. He wants to open a new savings account and deposit his bonus. Mom knows nothing about it.

This is a good opportunity for you to learn some new signs related to money. I'll show them to you now.

Student Workbook: Activity 9.6

9.6 Video Learning Experience

Bravo Family Visit

Viewing Goal: To improve your ASL comprehension by watching a Bravo family interaction.

Viewing Instructions: Watch the interaction with Scott and Dad at the bank. Billy helps you understand what this lesson is about.

In the space below, write a summary of the main points to help you remember the interaction.

Summary: _____
_____
_____
_____

9.7 Language Learning Instruction

Learning New Signs

Goal: To use ASL and visual aids to introduce this lesson's vocabulary.

Instructions:
1. **Ask** students to read *Learning New Signs* in their workbooks (activity 9.7).

2. **Show** the overhead (Appendix 9.7). **Introduce** the vocabulary by **pointing** to items presented in the pictures while **demonstrating** the signs.

3. **Reinforce** retention and **check** students' comprehension by **using** these signs to **ask** students questions.

   Note: For a step-by-step review of this method, see Lesson One (activities 1.6 and 1.12).

4. **Continue** this process until all the ASL vocabulary items have been introduced.

Lesson Nine: *Dollar Signs*

Overhead Content: Use the pictures in the overhead (Appendix 9.7) to introduce the signs representing the following concepts:

1. BANK
2. MONEY
3. SAVE
4. SAVINGS
5. INTEREST
6. DEPOSIT
7. SLOW
8. HOW-MUCH
9. THOUSAND
10. THREE+THOUSAND

Note: Some pictures can be used to represent several concepts. For verbs and more abstract concepts, you may need to supplement these pictures with mime, gestures, using actual objects, and acting out the concepts in class.

Overhead Master: Appendix 9.7

Lesson Nine: *Dollar Signs*

Student Workbook: Activity 9.7

9.7 Language Learning Instruction

Learning New Signs

Goal: To help you learn new ASL vocabulary.

Instructions: Your instructor will teach you new signs! Watch closely to learn what these signs mean and how they are produced.

In the space below, record any notes to help you remember the signs.

Notes: _____
_____
_____
_____

9.8 Video Learning Experience

Introduction to New Vocabulary

Viewing Goal: To provide a signed demonstration of the accurate production of the new ASL vocabulary.

Viewing Instructions:
1. **Ask** students to read *Introduction to New Vocabulary* in their workbooks (activity 9.8).

2. **Play** the video segment entitled *Introduction to New Vocabulary* (segment 9.8). Billy introduces and signs each new vocabulary item twice. (If you wish to keep this a strictly visual presentation, **turn off** audio.)

3. **Instruct** students to watch how Billy produces the signs as well as the accompanying facial/body expressions.

4. **Ask** students to copy the signs and the facial/body expressions as Billy repeats each one.

Lesson Nine: *Dollar Signs*

Video Segment Content: See the following Student Workbook excerpt for the content
(1 1/2 Minutes) of this video segment.

Student Workbook:
Activity 9.8

9.8 Video Learning Experience

Introduction to New Vocabulary

Viewing Goal: To help you learn the new ASL vocabulary.

Viewing Instructions: Watch how Billy produces each sign. Be sure to notice the facial/body expressions. Copy the signs as Billy repeats each one.

Signs representing the following concepts are introduced in this video segment:

1. BANK
2. MONEY
3. SAVE
4. SAVINGS
5. INTEREST
6. DEPOSIT
7. SLOW
8. HOW-MUCH
9. THOUSAND
10. THREE+THOUSAND

9.9 Video Learning Experience

Bravo Family Visit

Viewing Goal: To improve ASL comprehension skills by watching a Bravo family interaction.

Viewing Instructions:
1. **Ask** students to read *Bravo Family Visit* in their workbooks (activity 9.9).

2. **Play** the video segment of Dad and Scott (segment 9.9) as they use the new ASL vocabulary within the context of a visit to the bank. Because this segment includes an interaction with a hearing person, **turn on** audio and/or captions to optimize its educational value.

3. **Instruct** students to watch for comprehension and write a summary of the main points.

4. **Replay** any portion of this video segment that students experienced difficulty understanding.

Lesson Nine: *Dollar Signs*

**Video Segment Content:
(5 Minutes)**

The following is a summary of the Bravo family interaction:

A bank teller welcomes Dad and Scott and invites them to sit down. Dad writes her a note explaining that he is Deaf and would like to open an account. She asks him which kind of account - checking or savings? Dad tells her he wants a savings account. She asks him how much money he wants to deposit, but he doesn't understand and he asks her to write her question. He tells her he wants to deposit $3,000.

Scott interrupts and tells Dad he wants to go get ice cream now!

The bank teller continues to ask Dad questions about his account while learning signs at the same time. She explains to Dad the difference between the regular savings account and the money market account.

Scott makes a joke to Dad about the woman not knowing anything and Dad sends him to another part of the bank to sit and wait.

Scott wishes that everybody knew signs so communication would go much faster.

Note: Stop the tape at this point in order for students to take *Comprehension Quiz 9.10*.

Student Workbook:
Activity 9.9

9.9 Video Learning Experience

Bravo Family Visit

Viewing Goal: To improve your ASL comprehension by watching a Bravo family interaction.

Viewing Instructions: Watch the signed interaction and write a summary of the main points.

Summary: _____
_____
_____
_____

Instructor's Guide: Lesson Nine
Bravo ASL! Curriculum

©1996 Sign Enhancers, Inc.
ALL RIGHTS RESERVED.

Lesson Nine: *Dollar Signs*

9.10 Comprehension Quiz

What Did You Understand?

Quiz Goal: To assess students' comprehension of the signed interaction.

Quiz Instructions:
1. **Instruct** students to complete the quiz in their workbooks (activity 9.10).

2. **Collect** for grading or **show** overhead (Appendix 9.10) and **ask** individual students to indicate the correct answers on the overhead while class members correct their own work.

3. **Ask** students to indicate which item(s) from the quiz they found difficult. **Review** by **modeling** or **replaying** that segment of the videotape.

Student Workbook:
Activity 9.10

Overhead Master:
Appendix 9.10

9.10 Comprehension Quiz

What Did You Understand?

Quiz Goal: To see how much of the Bravo family interaction you understood.

Quiz Instructions: Read and answer each question.

1. What does Dad want to do at the bank?
   A. He wants open a savings account.
   B. He wants to make a deposit to his checking account.
   C. He wants to apply for a job as a bank teller.
   D. He wants to open a checking account.

2. How much money is Dad depositing?
   Three thousand dollars ($3,000).

3. What does Scott want to do instead of wait for Dad at the bank?
   He wants to go get some ice cream.

4. Why is Scott sent to sit someplace else?
   He made a joke about the bank teller.

5. What does Scott wish?
   Scott wishes everyone knew Sign Language.

Instructor's Guide: Lesson Nine
Bravo ASL! Curriculum

Lesson Nine: *Dollar Signs*

9.11 Video Learning Experience

Communication Strategies

Viewing Goal: To expose students to effective communication strategies for interactions between signing and non-signing people.

Viewing Instructions:
1. **Ask** students to read *Communication Strategies* in their workbooks (activity 9.11).
2. **Play** the video segment in which Billy points out appropriate communication strategies (segment 9.11) as applied by the bank teller in segment 9.9.
3. **Instruct** students to attend carefully to this information.

Video Segment Content: See the following Student Workbook excerpt for the content
(1 1/2 Minutes) of this video segment.

Student Workbook: Activity 9.11

> 9.11 Video Learning Experience
>
> *Communication Strategies*
>
> **Viewing Goal:** To help you learn communication strategies for interactions between signing and non-signing people.
>
> **Viewing Instructions:** Watch the video carefully to learn important communication strategies.
>
> Billy mentions four communication strategies used by the bank teller when she was communicating with Dad:
>
> 1. Maintain direct and consistent eye contact.
> 2. Learn new signs as you are communicating.
> 3. Write things down to be sure communication is clear and to avoid misunderstandings.
> 4. Be patient, friendly, and respectful of the communication needs of other people.

Instructor's Guide: Lesson Nine
Bravo ASL! Curriculum

©1996 Sign Enhancers, Inc.
ALL RIGHTS RESERVED.

Lesson Nine: *Dollar Signs*

9.12 Experiential Activity

Crossing the Communication Barrier

Activity Goal: To help students apply effective communication strategies between signing and non-signing people.

Activity Instructions:

1. **Ask** students to read *Crossing the Communication Barrier* in their workbooks (activity 9.12).

2. **Divide** class into groups of three or four.

3. **Instruct** students to role-play a banking situation similar to the one shown on the video (segment 9.9). **Tell** students to have one member of each group role-play the bank teller while another assumes the role of a Deaf customer. **Ask** the remaining members of each group to observe carefully and provide feedback based on the critique sheet in their workbooks.

4. **Encourage** students to apply the techniques explained by Billy in the video segment.

5. **Circulate** among the groups and **assist** as needed.

Student Workbook: Activity 9.12

> 9.12 Experiential Activity
>
> *Crossing the Communication Barrier*
>
> **Activity Goal:** To help you apply the communication strategies taught in this lesson.
>
> **Activity Instructions:** In small groups, role-play a banking situation. One person in the group acts as the bank teller while another role-plays a Deaf customer.
>
> Remaining group members will observe and evaluate the role-players' communication strategies.
>
> The bank teller:
>
> 1. Maintained direct and consistent eye contact.
>   Yes ___ No ___
>
> 2. Learned new signs as s/he communicated.
>   Yes ___ No ___
>
> 3. Wrote things down to be sure communication was clear.
>   Yes ___ No ___
>
> 4. Was patient and friendly and respectful of the communication needs of the customer.
>   Yes ___ No ___

Lesson Nine: *Dollar Signs*

9.13 Language Learning Instruction

Learning New Signs

Goal: To use ASL and visual aids to introduce this lesson's vocabulary.

Instructions:
1. **Ask** students to read *Learning New Signs* in their workbooks (activity 9.13).

2. **Show** the overhead (Appendix 9.13). **Introduce** the vocabulary by **pointing** to items presented in the pictures while **demonstrating** the signs.

3. **Reinforce** retention and **check** students' comprehension by **using** these signs to **ask** students questions.

   Note: For a step-by-step review of this method, see Lesson One (activities 1.6 and 1.12).

4. **Continue** this process until all the ASL vocabulary items have been introduced.

Overhead Content: Use the pictures in the overhead (Appendix 9.13) to introduce the signs representing the following concepts:

1. ONE+HUNDRED
2. WITHDRAW
3. BALANCE
4. CHARGE/FEE
5. MORE
6. ALL
7. PEOPLE
8. FAST
9. SAME
10. PERCENT

Note: Some pictures can be used to represent several concepts. For verbs and more abstract concepts, you may need to supplement these pictures with mime, gestures, using actual objects, and acting out the concepts in class.

Lesson Nine: *Dollar Signs*

Overhead Master:
Appendix 9.13

Student Workbook:
Activity 9.13

9.13 Language Learning Instruction

Learning New Signs

Goal: To help you learn new ASL vocabulary.

Instructions: Your instructor will teach you new signs! Watch closely to learn what these signs mean and how they are produced.

In the space below, record any notes to help you remember the signs.

Notes: _____
_____
_____
_____

Instructor's Guide: Lesson Nine
Bravo ASL! Curriculum

Lesson Nine: *Dollar Signs*

9.14 Video Learning Experience

Introduction to New Vocabulary

Viewing Goal: To provide a signed demonstration of the accurate production of the new ASL vocabulary.

Viewing Instructions:
1. **Ask** students to read *Introduction to New Vocabulary* in their workbooks (activity 9.14).

2. **Play** the video segment entitled *Introduction to New Vocabulary* (segment 9.14). Billy introduces and signs each new vocabulary item twice. (If you wish to keep this a strictly visual presentation, **turn off** audio.)

3. **Instruct** students to watch how Billy produces the signs and the accompanying facial/body expressions.

4. **Ask** students to copy the signs and the facial/body expressions as Billy repeats each one.

Video Segment Content: See the following Student Workbook excerpt for the content
(1 1/2 Minutes) of this video segment.

Student Workbook:
Activity 9.14

9.14 Video Learning Experience

Introduction to New Vocabulary

Viewing Goal: To help you learn new ASL vocabulary.

Viewing Instructions: Watch how Billy produces each sign. Be sure to notice the facial/body expressions. Copy the signs as Billy repeats each one.

Signs representing the following concepts are introduced:

1. ONE+HUNDRED
2. WITHDRAW
3. BALANCE
4. CHARGE/FEE
5. MORE

6. ALL
7. PEOPLE
8. FAST
9. SAME
10. PERCENT

Instructor's Guide: Lesson Nine
Bravo ASL! Curriculum

©1996 Sign Enhancers, Inc.
ALL RIGHTS RESERVED.

Lesson Nine: *Dollar Signs*

9.15 Video Learning Experience

Bravo Family Visit

Viewing Goal: To improve ASL comprehension skills by watching a Bravo family interaction.

Viewing Instructions:

1. **Ask** students to read *Bravo Family Visit* in their workbooks (activity 9.15).

2. **Play** the video segment of the Bravos (segment 9.15). They will use the new ASL vocabulary within the context of opening a bank account. Because this segment includes an interaction with a hearing person, **turn on** audio and/or captions to optimize its educational value.

3. **Instruct** students to watch for comprehension and write a summary of the main points.

4. **Replay** any portion of this video segment that students experienced difficulty understanding.

Video Segment Content: (5 1/2 Minutes)

The following is a summary of the Bravo family interaction:

The bank teller continues to explain the difference between a money market account and a regular savings account to Dad. She explains the opening deposit limit, the limit on withdrawals per month, and the minimum balance to have no charge on each account. Dad decides to open a money market account.

Dad looks over at Scott and finds that he has fallen asleep. Dad smiles.

In Scott's dream: Dad and Scott are greeted by the same bank teller. This time, after Dad tells her that he is Deaf, she asks them to wait for just a second. Another woman walks up, reads Dad's note and begins signing. She tells them that she is Deaf also. She goes through the same process with Dad, asking which kind of account he wants, asking how much he wants to deposit, explaining the difference between a money market account and a regular savings account and the benefits of each. The interaction happens much faster this time, since the teller is Deaf and uses ASL.

Dad selects the money market account and the teller starts the paperwork.

Lesson Nine: *Dollar Signs*

Student Workbook: Activity 9.15

9.15 Video Learning Experience

Bravo Family Visit

Viewing Goal: To improve your ASL comprehension by watching a Bravo family interaction.

Viewing Instructions: Watch the signed interaction and write a summary of the main points.

Summary: _____

_____

_____

_____

9.16 Comprehension Quiz

What Did You Understand?

Quiz Goal: To assess students' comprehension of the signed interaction.

Quiz Instructions:
1. **Instruct** students to complete the quiz in their workbooks (activity 9.16).

2. **Collect** for grading or **show** overhead (Appendix 9.16) and **ask** individual students to indicate the correct answers on the overhead while class members correct their own work.

3. **Ask** students to indicate which item(s) from the quiz they found difficult. **Review** by **modeling** or **replaying** that segment of the videotape.

Lesson Nine: *Dollar Signs*

Student Workbook:
Activity 9.16

Overhead Master:
Appendix 9.16

9.16 Comprehension Quiz

What Did You Understand?

Quiz Goal: To see how much of the Bravo family interaction you understood.

Quiz Instructions: Read and answer each question below.

1. The teller explained the difference between which two types of accounts?
   A. Checking and savings
   B. Money market and checking
   C. Money market and regular savings
   D. Checking and CD

2. Which type of account does Dad decide to open?
   A. Money market
   B. Checking
   C. Regular savings
   D. CD

3. What is different between the real teller and the teller in Scott's dream?
   A. Scott's teller is nicer.
   B. Scott's teller is Deaf.
   C. Scott's teller is hearing.
   D. Scott's teller gives him ice cream.

4. In Scott's dream, the banking transaction was much slower because Dad and the teller used ASL.
   A. True
   B. False

9.17 Language Learning Instruction

Learning New Signs

Goal: To use ASL and visual aids to introduce this lesson's vocabulary.

Instructions:
1. **Ask** students to read *Learning New Signs* in their workbooks (activity 9.17).

2. **Show** the overhead (Appendix 9.17). **Introduce** the vocabulary by **pointing** to items presented in the pictures while **demonstrating** the signs.

3. **Reinforce** retention and **check** students' comprehension by **using** these signs to **ask** students questions.

Note: For a step-by-step review of this method, see Lesson One (activities 1.6 and 1.12).

Lesson Nine: *Dollar Signs*

4. **Continue** this process until all the ASL vocabulary items have been introduced.

Overhead Content: Use the pictures in the overhead (Appendix 9.17) to introduce the signs representing the following concepts:

1. ADDRESS
2. NUMBER
3. TELEPHONE
4. SOCIAL+SECURITY
5. BIRTHDAY
6. DRIVE
7. LICENSE
8. SIGNATURE
9. CHECK
10. DOLLAR
11. ONE-DOLLAR
12. FIVE-DOLLAR
13. TEN+DOLLAR
14. TWENTY+DOLLAR
15. FIFTY+DOLLAR
16. MILLION

Note: Some pictures can be used to represent several concepts. For verbs and more abstract concepts, you may need to supplement these pictures with mime, gestures, using actual objects, and acting out the concepts in class.

Overhead Master: Appendix 9.17

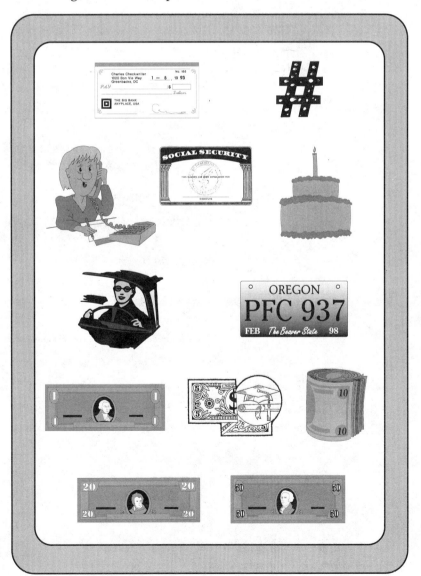

Lesson Nine: *Dollar Signs*

**Student Workbook:
Activity 9.17**

> 9.17 Language Learning Instruction
>
> *Learning New Signs*
>
> **Goal:** To help you learn new ASL vocabulary.
>
> **Instructions:** Your instructor will teach you new signs! Watch closely to learn what these signs mean and how they are produced.
>
> Notes: _____
> _____
> _____

9.18 Video Learning Experience

Introduction to New Vocabulary

Viewing Goal: To provide a signed demonstration of the accurate production of the new ASL vocabulary.

Viewing Instructions:
1. **Ask** students to read *Introduction to New Vocabulary* in their workbooks (activity 9.18).
2. **Play** the video segment entitled *Introduction to New Vocabulary* (segment 9.18). Billy introduces and signs each new vocabulary item twice. (If you wish to keep this a strictly visual presentation, **turn off** audio.)
3. **Instruct** students to watch how Billy produces the signs and the accompanying facial/body expressions.
4. **Ask** students to copy the signs and the facial/body expressions as Billy repeats each one.

**Video Segment Content:
(2 1/2 Minutes)** See the following Student Workbook excerpt for the content of this video segment.

**Student Workbook:
Activity 9.18**

> 9.18 Video Learning Experience
>
> *Introduction to New Vocabulary*
>
> **Viewing Goal:** To help you learn new ASL vocabulary.
>
> **Viewing Instructions:** Watch how Billy produces each sign. Signs representing the following concepts are introduced:
>
> 1. ADDRESS
> 2. NUMBER
> 3. TELEPHONE
> 4. SOCIAL-SECURITY
> 5. BIRTHDAY
> 6. DRIVE
> 7. LICENSE
> 8. SIGNATURE
> 9. CHECK
> 10. DOLLAR
> 11. ONE-DOLLAR
> 12. FIVE-DOLLAR
> 13. TEN+DOLLAR
> 14. TWENTY+DOLLAR
> 15. FIFTY+DOLLAR
> 16. MILLION

Lesson Nine: *Dollar Signs*

9.19 Experiential Activity

Tic-Tac-Dough

Activity Goal: To improve ASL receptive and expressive skills.

Activity Instructions:

1. **Make** a copy of the Tic-Tac-Dough master on the following page (page 9-24) and **cut** individual cards apart.

2. **Ask** students to read *Tic-Tac-Dough* in their workbooks (activity 9.19). **Draw** a large Tic-Tac-Toe grid on the board. **Tape** a Tic-Tac-Dough picture card in each of the nine squares.

3. **Divide** the class into two teams (Team X and Team O).

4. **Ask** two students from Team X to come to the front of the room.

5. **Instruct** the first player to produce a sign or signs that represent one of the pictures on the game grid. The second Team X player must correctly identify which picture the sign represents and repeat the sign. Both players must produce the sign accurately before drawing an X on the board in the correct square.

6. **Instruct** teams to take turns until one wins by getting three marks in a row. **Play** the game again by mixing up the pictures and taping them randomly in the squares of the game grid.

Student Workbook: Activity 9.19

> 9.19 Experiential Activity
>
> *Tic-Tac-Dough*
>
> **Activity Goal:** To help you recognize the new ASL vocabulary.
>
> **Activity Instructions:** Your instructor will divide the class into two teams (Team X and Team O).
>
> You will see a Tic-Tac-Dough (similar to Tic-Tac-Toe) grid on the board. Two players from Team X will go to the board. The first player will choose a picture and show the correct sign to the second player. The second player must point to the right picture and repeat the sign. If both players have produced the sign correctly, they can place an X on the correct square.
>
> The two teams will take turns until one team gets three marks in a row.
>
> Good luck and have fun!

Lesson Nine: *Dollar Signs*

9.19 Tic-Tac-Dough Cards Master

Instructor's Guide: Lesson Nine
Bravo ASL! Curriculum

©1996 Sign Enhancers, Inc.
ALL RIGHTS RESERVED.

Lesson Nine: *Dollar Signs*

9.20 Video Learning Experience

Bravo Family Visit

Viewing Goal: To improve ASL comprehension skills by watching a Bravo family interaction.

Viewing Instructions:

1. **Ask** students to read *Bravo Family Visit* in their workbooks (activity 9.20).

2. **Play** the video segment in which Scott's dream at the bank continues (segment 9.20).

3. **Instruct** students to watch for comprehension and write a summary of the main points.

4. **Replay** any portion of this video segment that students experienced difficulty understanding.

Video Segment Content:
(7 1/2 Minutes)

The following is a summary of the Bravo family interaction:

The Deaf bank teller is filling out the paperwork for Dad's account. She asks for Dad's name, his wife's name, his address, telephone number, social security number, and the amount of his deposit. She then asks Dad for his date of birth, driver's license number, and for his signature. Scott wants to sign the paper too, but she tells him that will not be necessary. Dad gives her his deposit and she gives him a deposit book.

Dad tells Scott they can go for ice cream now. Scott tells him that he wants to make a deposit also. He lays out a one-dollar bill, a five-dollar bill, a ten-dollar bill, a twenty-dollar bill, a fifty, a hundred-dollar bill, a check for a thousand dollars, and a check for a million dollars! Scott looks at the camera and says, "Well, it's my dream! I want ice cream now." The dream ends.

Dad walks over and wakes Scott up and tells him it's time for ice cream. As they are leaving, the hearing bank teller says good-bye and then Scott notices the Deaf bank teller (from his dream) at another desk. She tells him to enjoy his ice cream. Scott looks confused.

After Scott leaves, Billy appears and introduces the viewers to Cathy, the Deaf bank teller. She really works in a bank and she really is Deaf. She explains that her job includes a variety of banking tasks and that she is a good example of what Deaf workers can accomplish.

Lesson Nine: *Dollar Signs*

She informs Billy that she needs to get back to work. He doesn't leave right away, so she twitches her nose and makes him disappear!

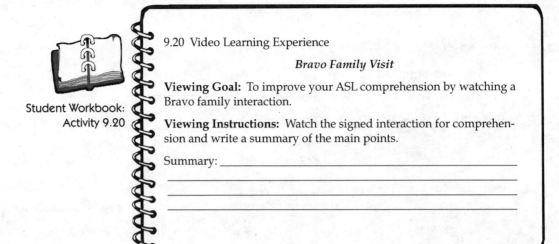

Student Workbook: Activity 9.20

9.20 Video Learning Experience

Bravo Family Visit

Viewing Goal: To improve your ASL comprehension by watching a Bravo family interaction.

Viewing Instructions: Watch the signed interaction for comprehension and write a summary of the main points.

Summary: _____
_____
_____
_____

9.21 Comprehension Quiz

What Did You Understand?

Quiz Goal: To assess students' comprehension of the signed interaction.

Quiz Instructions:

1. **Instruct** students to complete the quiz in their workbooks (activity 9.21).

2. **Collect** for grading or **show** overhead (Appendix 9.21) and **ask** individual students to indicate the correct answers on the overhead while class members correct their own work.

3. **Ask** students to indicate which item(s) from the quiz they found difficult. **Review** by **modeling** or **replaying** that segment of the videotape.

Instructor's Guide: Lesson Nine
Bravo ASL! Curriculum

©1996 Sign Enhancers, Inc.
ALL RIGHTS RESERVED.

Lesson Nine: *Dollar Signs*

Student Workbook:
Activity 9.21

Overhead Master:
Appendix 9.21

9.21 Comprehension Quiz

What Did You Understand?

Quiz Goal: To see how much of the Bravo family interaction you understood.

Quiz Instructions: Read and answer each question below.

1. The bank teller asks Dad for his address, telephone number, and the amount of his deposit.
   A. True
   B. False

2. The bank teller tells Scott he needs to sign the form.
   A. True
   B. False

3. Instead of going for ice cream, Scott tells his Dad that he wants to _____.
   A. Go home
   B. Go to the park
   C. Make a deposit
   D. Make a withdrawal

4. When Dad wakes Scott up, he tells him it's time _____.
   A. To wake up
   B. To go home
   C. To go to another bank
   D. To go get ice cream

5. As Scott and Dad leave the bank, the Deaf bank teller tells Scott to _____.
   A. Enjoy his ice cream
   B. Have a nice day
   C. Be careful
   D. Save his money

9.22 Video Learning Experience

Cultural Notes

Viewing Goal: To assist students in learning about the cultural aspects of ASL.

Viewing Instructions:
1. **Ask** students to read *Cultural Notes* in their workbooks (activity 9.22).

2. **Play** the video segment entitled *Cultural Notes* (segment 9.22). Because the presentation of this segment is beyond the linguistic ability of beginning students, please **turn on** the audio and/or captions to optimize its educational value.

3. **Instruct** students to view the segment.

4. At completion of the segment, **review** the content presented and **answer** any questions students may have.

Lesson Nine: *Dollar Signs*

Video Segment Content: See the following Student Workbook excerpt for the content
(2 Minutes) of this video segment.

Student Workbook:
Activity 9.23

> 9.22 Video Learning Experience
>
> *Cultural Notes*
>
> **Viewing Goal:** To learn about the cultural aspects of ASL.
>
> **Viewing Instructions:** View the *Cultural Notes* segment carefully for the following:
>
> I. Employment options for Deaf people:
>   A. Historically, Deaf people were limited to areas such as assembly, printing, post office jobs, sewing, other menial labor work.
>   B. Today, options have increased. Deaf people hold positions as: artists; directors; dancers; photographers; counselors; secretaries; teachers; lawyers; doctors; etc.
>   C. Access to the workplace has improved. Some Deaf people actually own their own businesses.
>
> II. The telephone is less of a barrier because of:
>   A. Relay services
>   B. Professional interpreters
>   C. TTYs

9.23 Video Learning Experience

Grammatical Notes

Viewing Goal: To assist students in learning about the grammatical aspects of ASL.

Viewing Instructions:
1. **Ask** students to read *Grammatical Notes* in their workbooks (activity 9.23).

2. **Play** the video segment entitled *Grammatical Notes* (segment 9.23). Because the presentation of this segment is beyond the linguistic ability of beginning students, please **turn on** the audio and/or captions to optimize its educational value.

3. **Instruct** students to view the segment.

4. At completion of the segment, **review** the content presented and **answer** any questions students may have.

Lesson Nine: *Dollar Signs*

Video Segment Content: See the following Student Workbook excerpt for the content
(2 Minutes) of this video segment.

Student Workbook:
Activity 9.23

> 9.23 Video Learning Experience
>
> *Grammatical Notes*
>
> **Viewing Goal:** To learn about the grammatical aspects of ASL.
>
> **Viewing Instructions:** View the *Grammatical Notes* segment carefully for the following:
>
> When the signs representing numbers are related to money, the movement of the sign changes.
>
> A. The signs for the numbers 1 - 9, when showing dollar amounts, move in a twisting motion from the wrist. This movement lets you know it is a dollar amount.
>
> B. Billy demonstrates the production of the signs, $1-$9 in this video segment.
>
> C. Dollar amounts for $10 and higher are signed the same way as regular number signs, but are followed by the sign for DOLLAR.

9.24 Experiential Activity

Is the Price Right?

Activities Video

Activity Goal: To improve students' ASL comprehension skills.

Activity Instructions:
1. **Ask** students to read *Is the Price Right?* in their workbooks (activity 9.24).

2. **Inform** students that signers on the video will describe several items and the correct price for each item in ASL.

3. **Play** the activities video (segment 9.24).

4. **Ask** students to find the picture of that item and write the correct price on the corresponding price tag.

5. At the completion of the activity, **show** the overhead (Appendix 9.24) and **ask** individual students to indicate correct answers on the overhead while class members correct their own work.

6. **Replay** video segment as needed.

Lesson Nine: *Dollar Signs*

Video Segment Content: The following are the items and prices:
(3 1/2 Minutes)

Item	Price	Item	Price
COFFEE	$1.00	COUCH	$100.00
DOG	$5.00	CHAIR	$10.00
SHOWER	$4.00	KNIFE	$9.00
SPIDER	$6.00	EGGS	$2.00
BOWL	$7.00	TELEPHONE	$18.00

Student Workbook:
Activity 9.24

Overhead Master:
Appendix 9.24

9.24 Experiential Activity

Is the Price Right?

Activity Goal: To improve your ASL comprehension skills.

Activity Instructions: You will see a signer describing the items below and their correct prices in ASL. Find the picture of each item and write the correct price on its price tag.

Lesson Nine: *Dollar Signs*

9.25 Experiential Activity

Dollar-to-Dollar

Activity Goal: To improve students' expressive and receptive skills with signs related to money.

Activity Instructions:
1. **Ask** students to read *Dollar-to-Dollar* in their workbooks (activity 9.25).

2. **Divide** class into pairs. **Ask** students to select ten of the dollar amounts from the list and record the amounts in the space provided in their workbooks. **Tell** them to take turns signing and recording each other's dollar amounts.

3. **Model** the signs for various dollar amounts as needed.

Student Workbook: Activity 9.25

9.25 Experiential Activity

Dollar-to-Dollar

Activity Goal: To help you recognize and produce dollar amounts.

Activity Instructions: You have just learned how to sign dollar amounts. In the spaces below, marked **My Dollars**, select ten of the dollar amounts listed below. Take turns signing the dollar amounts with a partner. Record the various amounts your partner signs to you in the column marked **My Partner's Dollars**. Check each other when you are finished to see how well you understood the signs.

Dollar amounts:
- $1.00 - $9.00
- $10.00 - $20.00
- $50.00
- $100.00
- $1,000
- $3,000
- $1,000,000 (ONE+MILLION)

My Dollars
1. _____
2. _____
3. _____
4. _____
5. _____
6. _____
7. _____
8. _____
9. _____
10. _____

My Partner's Dollars
1. _____
2. _____
3. _____
4. _____
5. _____
6. _____
7. _____
8. _____
9. _____
10. _____

Lesson Nine: *Dollar Signs*

9.26 Video Learning Experience

Review Session

Viewing Goal: To reinforce recognition and production of the signs introduced in this lesson.

Viewing Instructions:
1. **Ask** students to read *Review Session* in their workbooks activity 9.26).

2. **Play** the video segment entitled *Review Session* (segment 9.26). Billy reviews all the ASL vocabulary and provides visual cues and origin information. Because the presentation of this segment is beyond the linguistic ability of beginning students, please **turn on** the audio and/or captions to optimize its educational value.

3. **Ask** students to pay attention to the signed vocabulary items and take note of visual hints offered by Billy that might help them remember.

4. **Suggest** that students copy the signs to reinforce retention of sign production.

Video Segment Length: (8 1/2 Minutes) See the following Student Workbook excerpt for the content of this video segment.

Student Workbook: Activity 9.26

9.26 Video Learning Experience

Review Session

Viewing Goal: To help you remember how to produce the signs introduced in this lesson.

Viewing Instructions: Watch this video segment carefully to see how each sign is made. Take note of hints that will help you remember. You may want to copy the signs as you watch Billy.

The following are the vocabulary and explanations offered in this video segment:

B-A-N-K — This is a fingerspelled loan sign. This means that the fingerspelled sign is borrowed from the fingerspelled word. Due to the production and fast movement, it is actually considered a sign.

SAVINGS — Money is put into a place where it adds up and is not spent.

MONEY — This sign is like taking the money and placing it in your hand.

HOW-MUCH — This sign is like throwing money into the air and counting it to see HOW-MUCH.

Lesson Nine: *Dollar Signs*

DEPOSIT	You take the money to the bank and you put it in the account.
FIFTY	This is a compound sign using the signs FIVE+ZERO.
ONE+HUNDRED	The "C" handshape represents the Roman numeral symbol for 100.
ONE+THOUSAND	This sign follows the Roman numeral "M" for 1,000.
THREE+THOUSAND	This is a compound sign using the signs THREE+THOUSAND.
MILLION	This sign also follows the Roman numeral. It represents a thousand thousands.
INTEREST	One hand represents a savings account. As you earn money, it is added to the top of your account. The other hand represents the INTEREST.
MONEY+MARKET	The "M"+"M" represents the two words "money" and "market." It is abbreviated so it is not necessary to fingerspell it.
SLOW	This sign shows how a glacier moves - very slowly.
MORE	One hand represents what you have. The other hand is giving you more of it.
ALL	There are things in front of you and you take all of them.
PEOPLE	When there are many persons, it is shown with this sign for PEOPLE.
FAST	This sign shows how a bullet leaves a gun. It's very FAST.
WITHDRAW	One hand represents money in an account. The other hand shows you're removing it or taking it out.
BALANCE	Two signs are described. 1. BALANCE: meaning is there a positive or negative balance. 2. BALANCE: This represents the "money left in the bank."
PERCENT	This sign follows the way we actually write the symbol for percent (%).
SAME/ME-TOO	The movement of this sign between us means you and I are the SAME.
LIMIT	This sign shows the upper and lower limits.
ADDRESS	This comes from the sign TO-LIVE which is a verb. When we do the movement twice, it becomes the noun, ADDRESS.
NUMBER	This sign comes from the old symbol for number (#). Over time, the handshape and movement have evolved to the current sign.
TELEPHONE	This sign follows the shape and the use of a telephone.

Lesson Nine: *Dollar Signs*

SOCIAL+SECURITY	In order to avoid fingerspelling those long words over and over, we abbreviate them "S" + "S."
BIRTHDAY	This sign represents a child being born.
DRIVE	How do you drive a car? You use a steering wheel.
LICENSE	This sign follows the shape of a license.
SIGNATURE	You put your name down on a piece of paper. This sign represents that action.
CHECK	This sign follows the shape of a check.
DOLLAR	This sign follows the shape of an actual dollar.
SET-UP	You can SET-UP or OPEN an account. Either sign is fine.
REGULAR	If something happens on a regular basis, it occurs again and again, it is REGULAR.
FILL-OUT-FORM	One hand represents the piece of paper with all the lines on it. The other hand is filling in all those lines.
LEAVE	This sign shows that something is there that you don't touch or take... you LEAVE it.
MONTH	This sign comes from the grid of a calendar and represents four weeks.
MONTHLY	You have one month on a calendar. When you turn the page to the next month and the next... it is MONTHLY.

9.27 Video Learning Experience

Practice Session: Sentences

Viewing Goal: To improve comprehension skills by watching sentences presented in ASL.

Viewing Instructions:

1. **Ask** students to read *Practice Session: Sentences* in their workbooks (activity 9.27).

2. **Play** the video segment entitled *Practice Session: Sentences* (segment 9.27).

3. **Inform** students that each sentence is signed twice and an English translation is provided.

4. **Remind** students to watch the face of each signer to see the facial/body expressions and non-manual grammatical markers as well as the signs.

Video Segment Content: (2 Minutes)

The following are English translations of the practice sentences:

1. I have $3,000.
2. What is your social security number?
3. What am I going to do now? Go to the bank.
4. How much money do you have?
5. Give me your phone number.
6. Do you have an IRA? I do, too.
7. My address is on my driver's license.

Student Workbook: Activity 9.27

9.27 Video Learning Experience

Practice Session: Sentences

Viewing Goal: To improve your ASL comprehension skills by watching signed sentences.

Viewing Instructions: Watch the signed sentences for comprehension. Remember to watch the face of each signer to see the facial/body expressions and the non-manual grammatical markers as well as the signs.

It is recommended that you copy each signed sentence when it is repeated.

In the space below, record any questions or notes you have regarding the sentences.

Notes: _____
_____
_____
_____

Lesson Nine: *Dollar Signs*

9.28 Video Learning Experience

Practice Session: Story

Viewing Goal: To improve ASL comprehension skills by watching a signed story.

Viewing Instructions:
1. **Ask** students to read *Practice Session: Story* in their workbooks (activity 9.28).
2. **Show** the video segment entitled *Practice Session: Story* (segment 9.28). Billy signs a story using the vocabulary introduced in this lesson. **Turn off** audio and captions.
3. **Instruct** students to watch the signed story for comprehension and write a summary of the main points.

Video Segment Content: (2 1/2 Minutes)

The following is an English translation of the story:

This morning I woke up and realized it was my birthday.

My parents gave me a check for $100. Oh, boy! Now, what would I do with the money? I decided to go to the bank.

When I arrived, the teller asked me if I wanted to deposit the money. I said, "Yes, I want to deposit it."

The teller then asked if I wanted to deposit it in a savings or a checking account. I told him I wanted a savings account. He then gave me a form telling me I needed to fill it out so a savings account could be opened. I worked on the form.

It asked for my name, my address, my birth date (which made me smile), and my social security number.

Then I thought, "If I put my money into a savings account, the interest is five percent. If I left the money in for one month it would mean I would have $105. If I left it in for two months I would have $110. But if I left it in for three months...."

No, I didn't want the interest. I wanted my money right now. I didn't want to finish filling out the form. I didn't want to deposit the money. I wanted to sign the check and have the money in my hand. And that's what I did.

I happily received my cash and quickly left the bank to buy a new television set. I showed my parents the television and then I gave them a flower to say "Thank you."

Lesson Nine: *Dollar Signs*

Student Workbook:
Activity 9.28

9.28 Video Learning Experience

Practice Session: Story

Viewing Goal: To improve your ASL comprehension by watching a story presented in ASL.

Viewing Instructions: Watch the signed story for comprehension. In the space below, write a summary to help you remember the story.

Summary: _____
_____
_____
_____

9.29 Comprehension Quiz

What Did You Understand?

Quiz Goal: To assess students' comprehension of the signed story.

Quiz Instructions:
1. **Instruct** students to complete the quiz in their workbooks (activity 9.29).

2. **Collect** for grading or **show** overhead (Appendix 9.29) and **ask** individual students to indicate the correct answers on the overhead while class members correct their own work.

3. **Ask** students to indicate which item(s) from the quiz they found difficult. **Review** by **modeling** or **replaying** that segment of the videotape.

Instructor's Guide: Lesson Nine
Bravo ASL! Curriculum
©1996 Sign Enhancers, Inc.
ALL RIGHTS RESERVED.

Lesson Nine: *Dollar Signs*

Student Workbook:
Activity 9.29

Overhead Master:
Appendix 9.29

9.29 Comprehension Quiz

What Did You Understand?

Quiz Goal: To see how much of the signed story you understood.

Quiz Instructions: Read and answer each question below.

1. What was the special event that happened in the story?
   A birthday.

2. What did the signer get for the special event?
   $100

3. Who gave him the gift?
   His parents.

4. Where did he take his gift first? Why?
   To the bank. He wanted to open a savings account.

5. What did the signer finally do with his gift?
   Bought a new television set and a flower.

9.30 Experiential Activity

The Silent Games: Revisited

Activity Goal: To provide students with the opportunity to apply what they have learned in this lesson to the *Silent Games* activity they performed earlier (*Lesson Focus, 9.5*).

Activity Instructions:

1. **Ask** students to read *The Silent Games: Revisited* in their workbooks (activity 9.30).

2. **Distribute** the board games played earlier in the lesson (or **ask** students to take out their own).

3. **Divide** class into groups of four or five students. **Tell** groups to play the games again, this time using the ASL vocabulary learned in this lesson.

4. **Circulate** among the groups to **observe** their progress and **model** corrections as needed.

5. **Bring** the whole class together again and **ask** the students if their communication was improved the second time they played the games.

Lesson Nine: *Dollar Signs*

Student Workbook:
Activity 9.30

> 9.30 Experiential Activity
>
> *The Silent Games: Revisited*
>
> **Activity Goal:** To use your new ASL vocabulary for playing the *Silent Games*.
>
> **Activity Instructions:** Your group will play a game that involves play money again. During the game, use ASL (no voices needed!).
>
> Try to use as many of your new ASL vocabulary words as you can. You can also use gestures, fingerspelling, mime, pointing, etc.
>
> See if your communication skills have improved!
>
> Have fun!!

9.31 Homework Assignment
Silent Auction

Homework Goal: To improve students' expressive and receptive ASL skills.

Homework Instructions:
1. **Ask** students to read *Silent Auction* in their workbooks (9.31).

2. **Request** that students bring small, individually-wrapped items that can be sold to other students, such as: snack cakes; candy; canned soda; juice boxes; pencils; chips; crackers; notebooks or magazines.

3. **Inform** students when the auction will take place and **encourage** them to practice a sales pitch for their items using ASL.

4. **Explain** that during the auction, each student will demonstrate the sales pitch, while the rest of the students bid on the items. Each auction item will go to the highest bidder! **Tell** students they will all start with the same amount of play money (from the games used in activity 9.30). The student who is able to buy the most items with the money is the winner.

Instructor Tip:

An opportunity for students to perform this assignment has been scheduled in the next lesson (Homework Review 10.2). Be prepared to act as the auctioneer in order to encourage all students to actively participate.

Lesson Nine: *Dollar Signs*

Student Workbook:
Activity 9.31

9.31 Homework Assignment

Silent Auction

Homework Goal: To participate in an auction conducted in ASL.

Homework Instructions: Your class will have a *Silent Auction* where you can buy and sell items using play money.

Remember to bring some individually-wrapped items that your classmates might be interested in buying, such as snack cakes; candy; canned soda; juice boxes; pencils; chips; crackers; notebooks; or magazines.

Be prepared to use ASL to present an exciting sales pitch describing the items you have for sale.

Your classmates will bid on each item. The highest bidder will pay with play money from the board games in previous activities.

NOTE: You will all begin with the same amount of play money. See who can buy the most items with the money.

9.32 Post-test

What Do You Know Now?

Assessment Video

Post-test Goal: To assess students' mastery of the lesson objectives.

Post-test Instructions:
1. **Ask** students to read the Post-test Introduction in their workbooks (activity 9.32).

2. **Copy** and **distribute** the Lesson Nine Post-test (Appendix 9.32).

3. **Play** the Assessment Video (segment 9.32) and allow students to complete Section One (comprehension portion) of the test.

4. **Instruct** students to complete Section Two (culture and grammar portion) of the test individually and hand in their papers when they are finished.

5. **Assign** Section Three (expressive portion) of the test and **schedule** a time when students are to perform. It is strongly recommended that you **videotape** this portion of the Post-test.

6. **Determine** grading options based upon programmatic requirements. A recommended guideline for measuring successful mastery of objectives is 80% accuracy.

Lesson Nine: *Dollar Signs*

**Video Segment Content:
(2 Minutes)**

The following is an English translation of the comprehension story:

My new girlfriend is coming to my house to have coffee with me. My couch and coffee table need to be replaced. I went shopping. I found a green and yellow couch I love! It costs $100. I want to also buy a brown coffee table which costs $20.

I didn't have enough money in my wallet so I needed to go to the bank. I have savings and checking accounts. The balance in my checking account is $18. The balance in my savings account is $3,000.

I will deduct $200 from savings and deposit it in my checking account. I will sign my check with my address on it.

Do you think my new girlfriend will love my couch and coffee table? Oh no! I have to buy some coffee! Bye!

Student Workbook:
Activity 9.32

9.32 Post-test Introduction

What Do You Know Now?

Post-test Goal: To assess your mastery of the lesson objectives.

Post-test Introduction: This test has three sections.

Section One: The Comprehension section tests your ability to understand ASL.

Section Two: The Culture and Grammar section tests your knowledge of the material presented in the *Cultural* and *Grammatical Notes*.

Section Three: The Expressive portion tests your ability to use ASL.

Simply follow the instructions for each section. Good luck!

Lesson Nine: *Dollar Signs*

Post-test Master: Appendix 9.32

9.32 Post-test

Section One: Comprehension

Instructions: You will see a signed story. Watch carefully and answer each question below.

1. What does the signer want to buy?
   A. A coffee machine
   B. A couch and coffee table
   C. A yellow and green house

2. The signer has to go to:
   A. The bank
   B. The bathroom
   C. His girlfriend's house

3. What information was on the signer's check?
   A. Social security number
   B. Account balance
   C. **Address**

4. What was the savings account balance before this transaction?
   A. $ 18
   B. $ 300
   C. $ 3,000

5. What color is the couch that the signer bought?
   Green and yellow

6. How much did the couch cost?
   $100.00

7. What does the signer need to buy now?
   A. A TV
   B. Coffee
   C. A lamp

Post-test Master: Appendix 9.32

9.32 Post-test

Section Two: Culture and Grammar

Instructions: Read and answer each question.

8. What kind of jobs can Deaf people do?
   All kinds of jobs.

9. Explain why the telephone is less of a barrier than it used to be for Deaf people.
   TTY, relay services, and professional interpreters

10. Explain how money signs are produced.
    $1 - $9 are made with a twisting movement from the wrist.
    $10 or more add the sign DOLLAR to the numbers.

Lesson Nine: *Dollar Signs*

Post-test Master: Appendix 9.32

9.32 Post-test

Section Three: Expressive Portion

Instructions: Describe a trip to the bank, using at least ten signs learned in Lesson Nine.

Your instructor will schedule a specific time for you to perform this section of the Post-test. You may prepare and practice prior to your scheduled time.

Include at least ten signs from Lesson Nine.

11. _____
12. _____
13. _____
14. _____
15. _____
16. _____
17. _____
18. _____
19. _____
20. _____

Congratulations!
You have completed
Lesson Nine!

Lesson 10
REVIEW & PRACTICE SESSION

Materials Needed:

Equipment: VCR and TV monitor
Overhead projector and screen
Optional: video camera for activities 10.16, 10.22, 10.28, 10.30, 10.34 and 10.37

Materials: Instructor's Guide
Student Workbook: one per student
Overhead transparencies for activities 10.3 and 10.18
Silent Auction items for activity 10.2
Color markers/crayons (or have students bring their own) for activity 10.5
Handouts for activity 10.12 (see Appendix for master)
Optional: blank videotape (or have students bring their own) for activities 10.16, 10.22, 10.28, 10.30, 10.34 and 10.37
Post-test: Appendix 10.37

Videotapes: The Beginning ASL VideoCourse Lesson Ten
Activities Video for activity 10.12
Assessment Video for Post-test 10.37

10.1 Begin Class

Housekeeping

Goal: To prepare students for this lesson.

Instructions:
1. **Welcome** students to Lesson Ten of the VideoCourse.

2. **Perform** any necessary tasks (such as taking attendance) that may be required by your specific program.

Lesson Ten: *Review & Practice Session*

10.2 Homework Review

Silent Auction

Activity Goal: To provide feedback on previously assigned homework and to reinforce materials learned in earlier lessons.

Activity Instructions:

1. **Ask** students to read *Silent Auction* in their workbooks (activity 10.2).

2. **Hand out** equal amounts of play money to each student. **Explain** that the goal is for each student to purchase as many auction items as possible with the play money. Items will go to the highest bidders.

3. **Instruct** students to take turns presenting their ASL "sales pitches" for each of the items they brought, as assigned in *Homework Assignment 9.31*. **Serve** as the auctioneer and **encourage** all students to participate.

4. **Tell** students to use ASL to bid on each item and pay with their play money.

5. **Close** this activity by **allowing** students to consume the edible products they purchased!

Student Workbook: Activity 10.2

10.2 Homework Review

Silent Auction

Activity Goal: To show the results of your homework assignment.

Activity Instructions: It's time for the Silent Auction! Take turns signing the "sales pitch" you prepared for each of your auction items. Your instructor will serve as the auctioneer.

You will be given play money. Bid (in ASL) on the items you want... the items will go to the highest bidder! See who can buy the most with the play money.

Good luck, and remember this is a *Silent Auction!*

Lesson Ten: *Review & Practice Session*

10.3 Lesson Objectives

Planning for Success

Goal: To identify the learning outcomes associated with successful completion of this lesson.

Instructions:
1. **Ask** students to read the objectives in their workbooks (activity 10.3).

2. **Show** the overhead (Appendix 10.3) and **read** through the objectives with the class.

Student Workbook: Activity 10.3

Overhead Master: Appendix 10.3

10.3 Lesson Objectives

Planning for Success

Goal: To see what you will learn by the end of this lesson.

Instructions: Read the objectives below.

Upon completing this VideoCourse lesson, you will be able to...

1. Recognize and accurately produce the ASL vocabulary introduced in Lessons Six, Seven, Eight, and Nine.

2. Demonstrate knowledge of the cultural information presented in Lessons Six, Seven, Eight, and Nine.

3. Recognize and apply the grammatical features presented in Lessons Six, Seven, Eight, and Nine.

4. Accurately use the ASL vocabulary and grammatical features presented in Lessons Six, Seven, Eight, and Nine in sentences, dialogues, and stories.

Lesson Ten: *Review & Practice Session*

10.4 Video Learning Experience

Lesson Introduction

Viewing Goal: To assist students in understanding the format of this review lesson.

Viewing Instructions:
1. **Ask** students to read *Lesson Introduction* in their workbooks (activity 10.4).

2. **Play** the video segment in which Billy introduces the format of this review lesson (segment 10.4). Because the presentation of this segment is beyond the linguistic ability of beginning students, please **turn on** the audio and/or captions to optimize its educational value.

3. **Instruct** students to watch this segment to learn what to expect in this lesson.

Video Segment Content: The following is the English translation of Billy's introduction:
(1 Minute)

Hi! Welcome to Sign Enhancers, Inc. American Sign Language VideoCourse Lesson Ten.

In this tape, we will review Lessons Six through Nine. We will condense the information from those lessons by selecting several points from each tape for review. We'll do this through vocabulary review, practice with sentences, dialogues, and a story. We'll also present parts of the *Grammatical and Cultural Notes* for review.

I will also challenge you with some questions. Are you ready? Well, we'll see...

Student Workbook:
Activity 10.4

10.4 Video Learning Experience

Lesson Introduction

Viewing Goal: To help you prepare for this review session.

Viewing Instructions: Billy will explain what to expect from this *Review & Practice Session*.

Pay attention to what Billy is signing, but also notice *how* he expresses these ideas with facial/body expression, non-manual grammatical markers, and use of space. Perhaps you will learn a few more signs!

In the space below, write any notes or questions you may have.

Notes: _____
_____
_____
_____

Instructor's Guide: Lesson Ten
Bravo ASL! Curriculum

©1996 Sign Enhancers, Inc.
ALL RIGHTS RESERVED.

Lesson Ten: *Review & Practice Session*

10.5 Experiential Activity

Color Commands

Activity Goal: To reinforce students' skills with Lesson Six vocabulary.

Activity Instructions:
1. **Ask** students to read *Color Commands* in their workbooks (activity 10.5).

2. **Divide** the class into pairs.

3. **Distribute** color markers, crayons or pens (or **ask** students to take out their own).

4. **Instruct** each student to choose one of the pictures from their workbooks and take turns signing to their partner what color to make each of the objects in their picture. The partner follows the instructions by selecting and using the correct colors.

5. **Circulate** to **observe** students' performance, **modeling** corrections as needed.

Student Workbook:
Activity 10.5

10.5 Experiential Activity

Color Commands

Activity Goal: To help you remember the ASL vocabulary learned in Lesson Six.

Activity Instructions: Work with a partner and decide which of the two pictures below you will each use. Select an object or person from your partner's picture and use ASL to instruct your partner how to color the items in the picture s/he selected. When this is completed, switch roles.

You can choose from the following colors:

BLACK	ORANGE	RED	GOLD
WHITE	TEN	YELLOW	PINK
SILVER	BLUE	TAN	BROWN

Note: If you don't have the right color marker or crayon, write the name of the color on each item in the picture.

Partner A's Picture:

Instructor's Guide: Lesson Ten
Bravo ASL! Curriculum

Lesson Ten: *Review & Practice Session*

Partner B's Picture:

10.6 Video Learning Experience

Lesson Six Review: Vocabulary

Viewing Goal: To reinforce comprehension with the ASL vocabulary introduced in Lesson Six.

Viewing Instructions:
1. **Ask** students to read *Lesson Six Review: Vocabulary* in their workbooks (activity 10.6).

2. **Play** the video segment entitled *Lesson Six Review: Vocabulary* (segment 10.6). Billy reviews and signs each ASL vocabulary item twice. A review of fingerspelling is also provided.

   Note: For a more challenging review, **turn off** audio and **cover** the bottom right-hand corner of the TV monitor so students cannot see the glosses.

3. **Instruct** students to copy the signs as they watch the vocabulary review. **Encourage** students to raise their hands if they have difficulty remembering a particular sign.

Instructor Tip: *Use this review as needed. If individual students need an in-depth review, this video can be made available in a lab setting.*

Lesson Ten: *Review & Practice Session*

Video Segment Content: See the following Student Workbook excerpt for the content
(3 1/2 Minutes) of this video segment.

Student Workbook:
Activity 10.6

10.6 Video Learning Experience

Lesson Six Review: Vocabulary

Viewing Goal: To help you review the ASL vocabulary from Lesson Six.

Viewing Instructions: Watch the Lesson Six vocabulary review while you copy the signs. Raise your hand if there is a sign you do not remember, and your instructor will help you.

Signs representing the following concepts are reviewed in this video segment:

1. ORANGE
2. BLUE
3. GREEN
4. RED
5. YELLOW
6. PURPLE
7. WHITE

8. BROWN
9. SILVER
10. GOLD
11. PINK
12. BLACK
13. TAN

Note: A review of fingerspelling is also provided in this video segment. Billy fingerspells each letter of the alphabet. It is suggested that you copy Billy as he produces each letter.

10.7 Video Learning Experience

Lesson Six Review: Sentences

Viewing Goal: To improve students' comprehension skills by watching sentences presented in ASL.

Viewing Instructions:
1. **Ask** students to read *Lesson Six Review: Sentences* in their workbooks (activity 10.7).

2. **Play** the video segment entitled *Lesson Six Review: Sentences* (segment 10.7). Each sentence is signed twice and an English translation is provided.

3. **Remind** students to watch the face of each signer to see the facial/body expressions and non-manual grammatical markers as well as the signs.

Instructor's Guide: Lesson Ten
Bravo ASL! Curriculum

©1996 Sign Enhancers, Inc.
ALL RIGHTS RESERVED.

Lesson Ten: *Review & Practice Session*

Video Segment Content:
(1 Minute)

The following are English translations of the practice sentences:

1. The banana is yellow.
2. The girl's name is Barb.
3. The boy's name is Tom.
4. Which do you like? Blue or purple?

Student Workbook:
Activity 10.7

10.7 Video Learning Experience

Lesson Six Review: Sentences

Viewing Goal: To improve your comprehension skills by watching sentences presented in ASL.

Viewing Instructions: Watch the signed sentences for comprehension. Remember to watch the face of each signer to see the facial/body expressions and the non-manual grammatical markers as well as the signs.

It is recommended that you copy each signed sentence when it is repeated.

In the space below, record any questions or notes you have regarding the sentences.

Notes: _____
_____
_____
_____

10.8 Video Learning Experience

Lesson Six Review: Fingerspelling Practice

Viewing Goal: To reinforce students' comprehension skills with fingerspelling.

Viewing Instructions:

1. **Ask** students to read *Lesson Six Review: Fingerspelling Practice* in their workbooks (activity 10.8).

2. **Play** the video segment entitled *Lesson Six Review: Fingerspelling Practice* (segment 10.8). Dad, Mom, Scott, and Anna each fingerspell several words. English translations are provided and the fingerspelled words are repeated.

Lesson Ten: *Review & Practice Session*

3. **Remind** students to watch the face of each signer, instead of the hand, to see the facial/body expressions and non-manual grammatical markers as well as the fingerspelling.

4. **Encourage** students to watch for the fingerspelled word as a whole unit instead of individual letters.

Video Segment Content: The following are the fingerspelled words:
(2 Minutes)

Dad:	Mom:	Scott:	Anna:
G-I-N	C-A-T	N-O-T	B-O-Y
D-I-N	M-A-P	C-O-T	C-O-Y
W-I-N	N-A-P	D-O-T	T-O-Y
S-I-N	S-A-P	P-O-T	S-O-Y
T-I-N		T-O-T	
F-I-N			

Student Workbook: Activity 10.8

10.8 Video Learning Experience

Lesson Six Review: Fingerspelling Practice

Viewing Goal: To improve your fingerspelling comprehension skills.

Viewing Instructions: Watch the fingerspelled words for comprehension. Remember to watch the face of each signer to see the facial/body expressions and the non-manual grammatical markers as well as the fingerspelled words.

Sound out the letters the way you would if you were reading. Notice the patterns of letter combinations such as IN, AT, AP, OT and OY.

In the space below, record notes or questions you may have.

Notes: _____
_____
_____
_____

Lesson Ten: *Review & Practice Session*

10.9 Experiential Activity

Flying Fingers

Activity Goal: To improve students' fingerspelling skills.

Activity Instructions:

1. **Ask** students to read *Flying Fingers* in their workbooks (activity 10.9).

2. **Divide** the class into pairs.

3. **Instruct** students to take turns fingerspelling the words and letter combinations in their workbook while their partners repeat the fingerspelled words. **Encourage** students to continue practicing with the names of people and places.

4. **Circulate** among the groups to **observe** student performance.

Student Workbook: Activity 10.9

10.9 Experiential Activity

Flying Fingers

Activity Goal: To help improve your fingerspelling skills.

Activity Instructions: With a partner, take turns fingerspelling words from the list below. When it is your partner's turn to fingerspell, watch carefully and fingerspell the words back to him/her.

C-A-T	T-E-D	S-I-T	N-A-P	M-I-K-E	B-O-B	N-A-N-C-Y
B-A-T	N-E-D	B-I-T	C-A-P	L-I-K-E	C-O-B	F-A-N-C-Y
S-A-T	F-E-D	K-I-T	Z-A-P	P-I-K-E	C-O-N	C-L-A-N-C-Y
M-A-T	B-E-D	Z-I-T	L-A-P	T-I-K-E	D-O-N	D-A-N-C-Y

When you have practiced the above letter combinations, practice with names of places and people you know while your partner fingerspells them back to you.

Lesson Ten: *Review & Practice Session*

10.10 Video Learning Experience

Lesson Six Review: Practice Dialogue

Viewing Goal: To improve comprehension skills by watching a dialogue presented in ASL.

Viewing Instructions:
1. **Ask** students to read *Lesson Six Review: Practice Dialogue* in their workbooks (activity 10.10).
2. **Show** the video segment entitled *Lesson Six Review: Practice Dialogue* (segment 10.10).
3. **Instruct** students to watch the dialogue for comprehension.
4. When the dialogue on the video is finished, **divide** the class into pairs.
5. **Ask** pairs to create a similar dialogue, asking each other about the colors in their own homes.
6. When students are ready, **select** several pairs to demonstrate their dialogues to the class.
7. **Provide** feedback and corrections as needed.

Video Segment Content: (1/2 Minute)

The following is a summary of the dialogue presented in this segment:

Dad and Anna are talking about the colors of the kitchen and bedroom and whether they like them or not. Dad asks Anna the color of her book, bed, and dresser.

Student Workbook: Activity 10.10

10.10 Video Learning Experience

Lesson Six Review: Practice Dialogue

Viewing Goal: To improve your comprehension skills by watching a dialogue presented in ASL.

Viewing Instructions: Watch the signed dialogue for comprehension. With a partner, create a similar dialogue about the colors of your own home.

Notes: _____

Lesson Ten: *Review & Practice Session*

10.11 Video Learning Experience

Bravo Family Revisited

Viewing Goal: To reinforce ASL comprehension skills by reviewing a Bravo family interaction from Lesson Six.

Viewing Instructions:
1. **Ask** students to read *Bravo Family Revisited* in their workbooks (activity 10.11).

2. **Play** the video segment of the signed interaction (segment 10.11). The Bravos will use the ASL vocabulary as the children teach the art teacher signs related to color.

3. **Instruct** students to watch for review and take notes or write a summary of the main points.

4. **Replay** any portion of this video segment that students experienced difficulty understanding.

Video Segment Content: The following is a summary of the Bravo family interaction:
(2 1/2 Minutes)

The children take the art teacher through the vegetable department of the grocery store teaching her the signs for ORANGE; GREEN; BLUE; PURPLE; YELLOW; WHITE; RED; BROWN; SILVER; and GOLD. Then the kids tell her they have to leave.

Student Workbook:
Activity 10.11

10.11 Video Learning Experience

Bravo Family Revisited

Viewing Goal: To reinforce your ASL comprehension skills by reviewing a Bravo family interaction from Lesson Six.

Viewing Instructions: Watch the signed interaction for review and take notes or write a summary in the space below.

Notes/Summary: _____
_____
_____
_____

10.12 Experiential Activity

Crossword Puzzle

Activity Goal: To reinforce students' skills with the vocabulary from Lesson Seven.

Activity Instructions:
1. **Copy** the Crossword Puzzle Clues below.
2. **Ask** students to locate the *Crossword Puzzle* in their workbooks (activity 10.12).
3. **Divide** the class into small groups of four or five and **ask** that each group select a "puzzle leader."
4. **Hand out** one copy of the clues to each puzzle leader. (Do not let other students see it.)
5. **Tell** puzzle leaders to begin signing the clues to their group while group members fill in the puzzles. The first group to accurately fill in the entire puzzle earns the title "Puzzle Masters."

Crossword Clues

10.12 Experiential Activity

Crossword Puzzle Clues

Instructions: Sign the following clues to your classmates. First, sign the location on the puzzle (example: 1 across), then demonstrate the sign that best matches the meaning of each word.

Across	Down
1. FINISH	2. HERE
3. PAPER	3. PLEASE
4. STUDENT	5. TIRED
8. GIVE	6. TEACHER
10. WHO	7. FLOWER
12. LATE	8. GOOD
14. READ	9. STUDY
15. SORRY	11. PLAY
	13. NOT

Lesson Ten: *Review & Practice Session*

Student Workbook:
Activity 10.12

10.12 Experiential Activity

Crossword Puzzle

Activity Goal: To help you remember the ASL vocabulary learned in Lesson Seven.

Activity Instructions: In your group, select one person to be the "puzzle leader." That person will sign all the clues to the puzzle below. Watch carefully, and select the word which best matches the signer's meaning and fits in the correct boxes in the puzzle. See if your group can be the first to correctly complete the puzzle and earn the title of "Puzzle Masters."

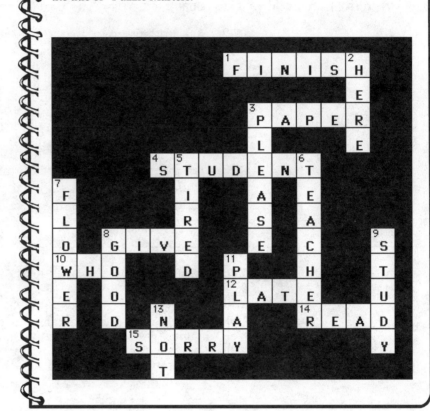

10.13 Video Learning Experience

Lesson Seven Review: Vocabulary

Viewing Goal: To reinforce comprehension of the ASL vocabulary introduced in Lesson Seven.

Viewing Instructions:

1. **Ask** students to read *Lesson Seven Review: Vocabulary* in their workbooks (activity 10.13).

2. **Play** the video segment entitled *Lesson Seven Review: Vocabulary* (segment 10.13). Billy reviews and signs each ASL vocabulary item twice.

    Note: **Use** this review as needed. **Place** in a lab setting for individual viewing or **increase** the level of difficulty by **turning off** audio and **covering** glosses on the monitor.

3. **Instruct** students to copy the signs as they watch the vocabulary review. **Encourage** students to raise their hands if they have difficulty remembering a particular sign.

Video Segment Content: See the following Student Workbook excerpt for the content
(3 1/2 Minutes) of this video segment.

Student Workbook: Activity 10.13

10.13 Video Learning Experience

Lesson Seven Review: Vocabulary

Viewing Goal: To help you review the ASL vocabulary from Lesson Seven.

Viewing Instructions: Watch the Lesson Seven vocabulary review while you copy the signs. Raise your hand if there is a sign you do not recognize, and your instructor will help you.

Signs representing the following concepts are reviewed in this video segment:

1. SCHOOL	11. THERE	21. WHO
2. TEACHER	12. GROW-UP	22. PENCIL
3. BOOK	13. TEACH	23. PAPER
4. READ	14. LEARN	24. GOOD
5. SIT	15. STUDENT	25. NEED
6. TIRED	16. STUDY	26. PLEASE
7. SORRY	17. GIVE	27. HAVE
8. FLOWER	18. PLAY	28. WANT
9. PICK+FLOWER	19. WHAT-WRONG	29. LATE
10. HERE	20. NOT	30. FINISH

Lesson Ten: *Review & Practice Session*

10.14 Video Learning Experience

Lesson Seven Review: Sentences

Viewing Goal: To improve students' comprehension skills by watching sentences presented in ASL.

Viewing Instructions:
1. **Ask** students to read *Lesson Seven Review: Sentences* in their workbooks (activity 10.14).

2. **Play** the video segment entitled *Lesson Seven Review: Sentences* (segment 10.14). Each sentence is signed twice and an English translation is provided.

3. **Remind** students to watch the face of each signer to see the facial/body expressions and non-manual grammatical markers as well as the signs.

Video Segment Content: (2 Minutes)

The following are English translations of the practice sentences:

1. Now I'm going to write. Do you have a pencil and paper?
2. The girl and boy go to school.
3. What do we learn at school? We learn to read and write.
4. I like to read. I don't like math.
5. In the future, do you want to be a teacher?
6. My class has eleven boys and twelve girls.

Student Workbook: Activity 10.14

10.14 Video Learning Experience

Lesson Seven Review: Sentences

Viewing Goal: To improve your comprehension skills by watching sentences presented in ASL.

Viewing Instructions: Watch the signed sentences for comprehension. Remember to watch the face of each signer to see the facial/body expressions and the non-manual grammatical markers as well as the signs.

It is recommended that you copy each signed sentence when it is repeated.

In the space below, record any questions or notes you have regarding the sentences.

Notes: _____
_____
_____
_____

10.15 Video Learning Experience

Lesson Seven Review: Practice Dialogue

Viewing Goal: To improve comprehension skills by watching a dialogue presented in ASL.

Viewing Instructions:
1. **Ask** students to read *Lesson Seven Review: Practice Dialogue* in their workbooks (activity 10.15).
2. **Show** the video segment entitled *Lesson Seven Review: Practice Dialogue* (segment 10.15).
3. **Instruct** students to watch the dialogue for comprehension and write a summary in the space provided.

Video Segment Content: (1 Minute)

The following is a summary of the dialogue presented in this segment:

Mom is telling Dad that because the children are starting school soon, they will have to buy them some supplies. They decide that the children will need paper, pencils, and books.

Mom says they will need to buy flowers, also. Dad looks confused and figures they are for the teacher, but Mom tells him that they are for her!

Student Workbook: Activity 10.15

10.15 Video Learning Experience

Lesson Seven Review: Practice Dialogue

Viewing Goal: To improve your comprehension skills by watching a dialogue presented in ASL.

Viewing Instructions: Watch the signed dialogue for comprehension and take notes or write a summary in the space provided.

Notes/Summary: _____
_____
_____
_____

Lesson Ten: *Review & Practice Session*

10.16 Experiential Activity

Dynamic-Duo Dialogue

Activity Goal: To improve students' expressive and receptive ASL skills.

Activity Instructions:
1. **Ask** students to read *Dynamic-Duo Dialogue* in their workbooks (activity 10.16).
2. **Divide** the class into pairs.
3. **Instruct** students to create dialogues using the vocabulary from Lesson Seven. Each student should take a minimum of five turns.
4. After students have practiced, **ask** for volunteers to share their dialogues with the class. If possible, **videotape** each of the dialogues.
5. **Correct** production by **modeling** as needed.

Student Workbook: Activity 10.16

10.16 Experiential Activity

Dynamic-Duo Dialogue

Activity Goal: To improve your expressive and receptive ASL skills.

Activity Instructions: Work with a partner to create a dialogue using the Lesson Seven vocabulary (see the Sign Illustration Section for Lesson Seven vocabulary). Use ASL (no voices needed!) and be sure each person takes at least five turns.

Be prepared to share your dialogue with the class!

In the space below, record ideas or notes regarding the dialogue.

Notes: _____
_____
_____
_____

Instructor's Guide: Lesson Ten
Bravo ASL! Curriculum

Lesson Ten: *Review & Practice Session*

10.17 Video Learning Experience

Bravo Family Revisited

Viewing Goal: To reinforce ASL expressive and receptive skills by reviewing a Bravo family interaction from Lesson Seven.

Viewing Instructions:

1. **Ask** students to read *Bravo Family Revisited* in their workbooks (activity 10.17).

2. **Play** the video segment of the signed interaction (segment 10.17). They will use the ASL vocabulary when Anna dreams that she is the teacher.

3. **Instruct** students to watch for review.

4. **Divie** the class into groups of three.

5. **Instruct** students to use ASL to recreate the scene of Mom and Dad fighting over the textbook with the "teacher" mediating. **Encourage** students to use directional verbs as demonstrated in the video segment.

Video Segment Content:
(2 Minutes)

The following is a summary of the Bravo family interaction:

We are back in Anna's dream where she is the teacher. Anna tells the students to get out pencils and papers. One student doesn't have a pencil, another doesn't have paper. Anna gives the items to them.

Two of the students begin arguing over a book. Anna stops them and asks to whom the book belongs. Finally, the owner is found and he loans the book to the other student to read.

Student Workbook:
Activity 10.17

10.17 Video Learning Experience

Bravo Family Revisited

Viewing Goal: To reinforce your ASL expressive and receptive skills by reviewing a Bravo family interaction from Lesson Seven.

Viewing Instructions: Watch the Bravo family interaction. Be prepared to work with your classmates to recreate the "fight" over the book. Be sure to use directional verbs as shown in the video.

Summary: _____
_____
_____
_____

Instructor's Guide: Lesson Ten
Bravo ASL! Curriculum

©1996 Sign Enhancers, Inc.
ALL RIGHTS RESERVED.

Lesson Ten: *Review & Practice Session*

10.18 Experiential Activity

Matchmaker

Activity Goal: To reinforce comprehension of Lesson Eight vocabulary.

Activity Instructions:

1. **Ask** students to read *Matchmaker* in their workbooks (activity 10.18).

2. **Instruct** students to draw a line from the sign illustration to the picture that best matches its meaning.

3. **Show** the overhead (Appendix 10.18) and **ask** individual students to indicate the correct answers on the overhead.

Student Workbook: Activity 10.18

Overhead Master: Appendix 10.18

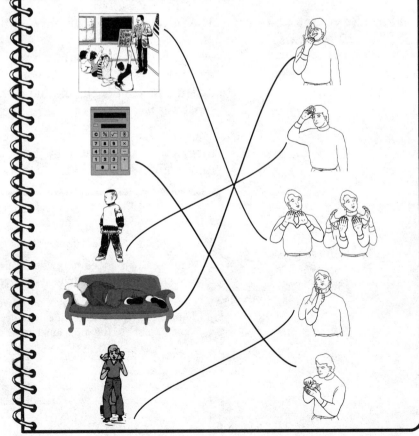

10.18 Experiential Activity

Matchmaker

Activity Goal: To help you remember some of the ASL vocabulary learned in Lesson Eight.

Activity Instructions: Look at the illustrations below. Draw a line from the sign illustration to the picture that best matches its meaning.

Instructor's Guide: Lesson Ten
Bravo ASL! Curriculum

©1996 Sign Enhancers, Inc.
ALL RIGHTS RESERVED.

Lesson Ten: *Review & Practice Session*

10.19 Video Learning Experience

Lesson Eight Review: Vocabulary

Viewing Goal: To reinforce comprehension of the ASL vocabulary introduced in Lesson Eight.

Viewing Instructions:
1. **Ask** students to read *Lesson Eight Review: Vocabulary* in their workbooks (activity 10.19).

2. **Play** the video segment entitled *Lesson Eight Review: Vocabulary* (segment 10.19). Billy reviews and signs each ASL vocabulary item twice.

   Note: **Use** this review as needed. **Place** in a lab setting for individual viewing or **increase** the level of difficulty by **turning off** audio and **covering** glosses on the monitor.

3. **Instruct** students to copy the signs as they watch the vocabulary review. **Encourage** students to raise their hands if they have difficulty remembering a particular sign.

Video Segment Content: (5 Minutes) See the following Student Workbook excerpt for the content of this video segment.

Student Workbook: Activity 10.19

10.19 Video Learning Experience

Lesson Eight Review: Vocabulary

Viewing Goal: To help you review the ASL vocabulary from Lesson Eight.

Viewing Instructions: Watch the Lesson Eight vocabulary review while you copy the signs. Raise your hand if there is a sign you do not recognize, and your instructor will help you.

Signs representing the following concepts are reviewed in this video segment:

1. #1	16. #16	31. ADD
2. #2	17. #17	32. TOGETHER
3. #3	18. #18	33. UNDERSTAND
4. #4	19. #19	34. CLASS
5. #5	20. #20	35. ROOM
6. #6	21. MATH	36. PAY-ATTENTION
7. #7	22. PLUS	37. PRINCIPAL
8. #8	23. MINUS/NEGATIVE	38. DREAM
9. #9	24. EQUAL/FAIR	39. SLEEP
10. #10	25. RIGHT/CORRECT	40. BOY
11. #11	26. WRONG/INCORRECT	41. GIRL
12. #12	27. KNOW	42. GOOD
13. #13	28. CALCULATOR	43. BAD
14. #14	29. COUNT	44. NAME
15. #15	30. COME	45. MAYBE

Lesson Ten: *Review & Practice Session*

10.20 Video Learning Experience

Lesson Eight Review: Sentences

Viewing Goal: To improve students' comprehension skills by watching sentences presented in ASL.

Viewing Instructions:
1. **Ask** students to read *Lesson Eight Review: Sentences* in their workbooks (activity 10.20).

2. **Play** the video segment entitled *Lesson Eight Review: Sentences* (segment 10.20). Each sentence is signed twice and an English translation is provided.

3. **Remind** students to watch the face of each signer to see the facial/body expressions and non-manual grammatical markers as well as the signs.

Video Segment Content: (2 Minutes)

The following are English translations of the practice sentences:

1. The boy paid attention to the girl instead of the teacher!
2. That woman is our principal. Do you know her?
3. The boy didn't pay attention to the teacher.
4. In math, are you good at adding and subtracting?
5. While sleeping, Anna dreamt she was a teacher.
6. Dad's tired. Are you tired?

Student Workbook: Activity 10.20

10.20 Video Learning Experience

Lesson Eight Review: Sentences

Viewing Goal: To improve your comprehension skills by watching sentences presented in ASL.

Viewing Instructions: Watch the signed sentences for comprehension. Remember to watch the face of each signer to see the facial/body expressions and the non-manual grammatical markers as well as the signs.

It is recommended that you copy each signed sentence when it is repeated.

In the space below, record any questions or notes you have regarding the sentences.

Notes: _____
_____
_____
_____

10.21 Video Learning Experience

Lesson Eight Review: Practice Dialogue

Viewing Goal: To improve students' comprehension skills by watching a dialogue presented in ASL.

Viewing Instructions:
1. **Ask** students to read *Lesson Eight Review: Dialogue* in their workbooks (activity 10.21).
2. **Show** the video segment entitled *Lesson Eight Review: Dialogue* (segment 10.21).
3. **Instruct** students to watch the dialogue for comprehension and write a summary in the space provided.

Video Segment Content: (1 Minute)

The following is a summary of the dialogue presented in this segment:

Scott tells Anna that he is good at math and she is not. She disagrees with him and they challenge each other with some math problems. They both answer correctly. Scott and Anna decide that they are both good at math.

Student Workbook: Activity 10.21

10.21 Video Learning Experience

Lesson Eight Review: Practice Dialogue

Viewing Goal: To improve your comprehension skills by watching a dialogue presented in ASL.

Viewing Instructions: Watch the signed dialogue for comprehension and write a summary in the space provided.

Summary: _____
_____
_____
_____

Instructor's Guide: Lesson Ten
Bravo ASL! Curriculum

©1996 Sign Enhancers, Inc.
ALL RIGHTS RESERVED.

Lesson Ten: *Review & Practice Session*

10.22 Experiential Activity

Dynamic-Duo Dialogue

Activity Goal: To improve students' expressive and receptive ASL skills.

Activity Instructions:

1. **Ask** students to read *Dynamic-Duo Dialogue* in their workbooks (activity 10.22).

2. **Divide** the class into pairs.

3. **Instruct** students to create dialogues using the vocabulary from Lesson Eight. Each student should take a minimum of four turns.

4. After students have practiced, **ask** for volunteers to share their dialogues with the class. If possible, **videotape** each dialogue.

5. **Correct** production by **modeling** as needed.

Student Workbook: Activity 10.22

10.22 Experiential Activity

Dynamic-Duo Dialogue

Activity Goal: To improve your expressive and receptive ASL skills.

Activity Instructions: Work with a partner to create a dialogue using the Lesson Eight vocabulary (see activity 10.19 for the vocabulary list). Use ASL (no voices needed!) and be sure each person takes at least four turns.

Be prepared to share your dialogue with the class!

In the space below, record any ideas or notes regarding the dialogue.

Notes: _____
_____
_____
_____

Instructor's Guide: Lesson Ten
Bravo ASL! Curriculum

©1996 Sign Enhancers, Inc.
ALL RIGHTS RESERVED.

Lesson Ten: *Review & Practice Session*

10.23 Video Learning Experience

Bravo Family Revisited

Viewing Goal: To reinforce ASL comprehension skills by reviewing a Bravo family interaction from Lesson Eight.

Viewing Instructions:
1. **Ask** students to read *Bravo Family Revisited* in their workbooks (activity 10.23).

2. **Play** the video segment of the signed interaction (segment 10.23). They will use the ASL vocabulary within the context of Anna's dream as the teacher.

3. **Instruct** students to watch for review and take notes of the main points.

4. When the video segment is over, **divide** the class into pairs.

5. **Instruct** pairs to use ASL to create a summary of Anna's dream.

6. When they have finished, **select** several students to demonstrate their signed summaries.

Video Segment Content: (2 Minutes)

The following is a summary of the Bravo family interaction:

We are back in Anna's dream where she is the teacher. The students in Anna's class are still throwing paper. The principal walks in and says good morning to everyone. He asks what is going on. Anna explains to the principal that there are bad boys and girls in her class. They don't pay attention or do their work.

The principal asks the students if their teacher signs, "No, no, no" a lot. The students all nod their heads. He asks the students who was not paying attention or doing their work and they look around at each other and shrug. He asks the class which of the boys and girls are being bad and none of them raise their hands.

The principal turns back to Anna and tells her that she has good students in her class. He asks them to get their pencils out and they do it. Next, he asks them to get out paper and they do. The principal asks the students to do different tasks such as read and write - and they do it.

Lesson Ten: *Review & Practice Session*

Student Workbook:
Activity 10.23

10.23 Video Learning Experience

Bravo Family Revisited

Viewing Goal: To reinforce your ASL comprehension skills by reviewing a Bravo family interaction from Lesson Eight.

Viewing Instructions: Watch the *Bravo Family Revisited* for review. Be prepared to use ASL to summarize what happened in this video segment!

Notes/Summary: _____
_____
_____
_____

10.24 Experiential Activity

Point and Sign

Activity Goal: To reinforce comprehension and expressive skills with Lesson Nine vocabulary.

Activity Instructions:
1. **Divide** the class into pairs.

2. **Instruct** students to read *Point and Sign* in their workbooks (activity 10.24).

3. **Instruct** pairs of students to take turns pointing to pictures in their workbooks while partners sign sentences using the sign(s) that best match the meaning of each picture.

4. **Inform** students that this activity is to be done entirely in ASL (no voice).

5. **Ask** students to begin the activity and **circulate** among the pairs to **observe** student performance, **assisting** as needed.

Instructor's Guide: Lesson Ten
Bravo ASL! Curriculum

©1996 Sign Enhancers, Inc.
ALL RIGHTS RESERVED.

Lesson Ten: *Review & Practice Session*

Student Workbook:
Activity 10.24

10.24 Experiential Activity

Point and Sign

Activity Goal: To improve your skills with the ASL vocabulary introduced in Lesson Nine.

Activity Instructions: Using the pictures below, follow your teacher's instructions to practice your signing skills.

Lesson Ten: *Review & Practice Session*

10.25 Video Learning Experience

Lesson Nine Review: Vocabulary

Viewing Goal: To reinforce comprehension skills of the ASL vocabulary introduced in Lesson Nine.

Viewing Instructions:

1. **Ask** students to read *Lesson Nine Review: Vocabulary* in their workbooks (activity 10.25).

2. **Play** the video segment entitled *Lesson Nine Review: Vocabulary* (segment 10.25). Billy reviews and signs each ASL vocabulary item twice.

   Note: **Use** this review as needed. **Place** in a lab setting for individual viewing or **increase** the level of difficulty by **turning off** audio and **covering** glosses on the monitor.

3. **Instruct** students to copy the signs as they watch the vocabulary review. **Encourage** students to raise their hands if they have difficulty remembering a particular sign.

Video Segment Content: (5 Minutes) See the following Student Workbook excerpt for the content of this video segment.

Student Workbook: Activity 10.25

10.25 Video Learning Experience

Lesson Nine Review: Vocabulary

Viewing Goal: To help you review the ASL vocabulary from Lesson Nine.

Viewing Instructions: Watch the Lesson Nine vocabulary review. Raise your hand if there is a sign you do not recognize, and your instructor will help you.

Signs representing the following concepts are reviewed in this video segment:

1. BANK	13. BALANCE	25. BIRTHDAY
2. MONEY	14. CHARGE/FEE	26. DRIVE
3. SAVE	15. MORE	27. LICENSE
4. SAVINGS	16. ALL	28. SIGNATURE
5. INTEREST	17. PEOPLE	29. CHECK
6. DEPOSIT	18. FAST	30. DOLLAR
7. SLOW	19. SAME	31. $1.00
8. HOW-MUCH	20. PERCENT	32. $5.00
9. THOUSAND	21. ADDRESS	33. $10.00
10. THREE+THOUSAND	22. NUMBER	34. $20.00
11. 100	23. TELEPHONE	35. $50.00
12. WITHDRAW	24. SOCIAL-SECURITY	36. MILLION

10.26 Video Learning Experience

Lesson Nine Review: Sentences

Viewing Goal: To improve students' comprehension skills by watching sentences presented in ASL.

Viewing Instructions:
1. **Ask** students to read *Lesson Nine Review: Sentences* in their workbooks (activity 10.26).
2. **Play** the video segment entitled *Lesson Nine Review: Sentences* (segment 10.26). Each sentence is signed twice and an English translation is provided.
3. **Remind** students to watch the face of each signer to see the facial/body expressions and non-manual grammatical markers as well as the signs.

Video Segment Content: (2 Minutes)

The following are English translations of the practice sentences:

1. I put my savings in the bank.
2. To withdraw $2,000, a signature is needed.
3. I have no money. Is it the same for you?
4. A money market has what percent interest?
5. I am going to the bank to deposit $50.
6. The driver's license has the address and birth date on it.

Student Workbook: Activity 10.26

10.26 Video Learning Experience

Lesson Nine Review: Sentences

Viewing Goal: To improve your comprehension skills by watching sentences presented in ASL.

Viewing Instructions: Watch the signed sentences for comprehension. Remember to watch the face of each signer to see the facial/body expressions and the non-manual grammatical markers as well as the signs.

It is recommended that you copy each signed sentence when it is repeated.

In the space below, record any questions or notes you have regarding the sentences.

Notes: _____
_____
_____
_____

Lesson Ten: *Review & Practice Session*

10.27 Video Learning Experience

Lesson Nine Review: Practice Dialogue

Viewing Goal: To improve students' comprehension skills by watching a dialogue presented in ASL.

Viewing Instructions:
1. **Ask** students to read *Lesson Nine Review: Practice Dialogue* in their workbooks (activity 10.27).
2. **Show** the video segment entitled *Lesson Nine Review: Practice Dialogue* (segment 10.27)
3. **Instruct** students to watch the dialogue for comprehension and write a summary in the space provided.

Video Segment Content: (1 Minute)

The following is a summary of the dialogue presented in this segment:

Mom is surprised at how much money Scott got from his birthday presents. Scott tells her that all together he got $50 and asks Mom if she wants to go shopping.

Mom explains that it is better to put the money into a savings account.

Scott asks Mom if the savings account earns interest and if he should deposit all of his money.

Mom tells him to go ahead and deposit it all. He will be able to withdraw some later if he wants.

Scott tells her he doesn't want to withdraw it, he wants to write checks.

Student Workbook: Activity 10.27

10.27 Video Learning Experience

Lesson Nine Review: Practice Dialogue

Viewing Goal: To improve your comprehension skills by watching a dialogue presented in ASL.

Viewing Instructions: Watch the signed dialogue for comprehension and write a summary in the space provided.

Notes/Summary: _____
_____
_____
_____

Instructor's Guide: Lesson Ten
Bravo ASL! Curriculum

©1996 Sign Enhancers, Inc.
ALL RIGHTS RESERVED.

Lesson Ten: *Review & Practice Session*

10.28 Experiential Activity

Dynamic-Duo Dialogue

Activity Goal: To improve students' expressive and receptive ASL skills.

Activity Instructions:

1. **Ask** students to read *Dynamic-Duo Dialogue* in their workbooks (activity 10.28).

2. **Divide** the class into pairs.

3. **Instruct** pairs of students to create dialogues using the vocabulary from Lesson Nine. Each student should take a minimum of four turns.

4. After students have practiced, **ask** for volunteers to share their dialogues with the class. If possible, **videotape** each dialogue.

5. **Correct** production by **modeling** as needed.

Student Workbook: Activity 10.28

10.28 Experiential Activity

Dynamic-Duo Dialogue

Activity Goal: To improve your expressive and receptive ASL skills.

Activity Instructions: Work with a partner to create a dialogue using the vocabulary from Lesson Nine (see the Sign Illustration Section for Lesson Nine vocabulary). Use ASL (no voices needed!) and be sure each person takes at least four turns.

Be prepared to share your dialogue with the class!

In the space below, record any ideas or notes you have regarding the dialogue.

Notes: _____
_____
_____
_____

Instructor's Guide: Lesson Ten
Bravo ASL! Curriculum

Lesson Ten: *Review & Practice Session*

10.29 Video Learning Experience

Bravo Family Revisited

Viewing Goal: To reinforce ASL comprehension skills by reviewing a Bravo family interaction from Lesson Nine.

Viewing Instructions:
1. **Ask** students to read *Bravo Family Revisited* in their workbooks (activity 10.29).

2. **Play** the video segment of the signed interaction (segment 10.29). Dad and Scott will use the ASL vocabulary within the context of opening a bank account. Because this segment includes an interaction with a hearing person, **turn on** audio and/or captions to optimize its educational value.

3. **Instruct** students to watch for review and write a summary of the main points.

4. **Replay** any portion of this video segment that students experienced difficulty understanding.

Video Segment Content: (2 Minutes)

The following is a summary of the Bravo family interaction:

Dad and Scott are in the bank opening an account. The bank teller is explaining the difference between a money market and a regular savings account. She continues to ask Dad questions about his account while learning signs at the same time. She asks for the sign for percent and Scott makes a joke to his Dad about the woman not knowing anything. Dad sends him to another part of the bank to sit and wait. Scott wishes everybody knew ASL because then things would be faster.

Student Workbook:
Activity 10.29

10.29 Video Learning Experience

Bravo Family Revisited

Viewing Goal: To reinforce your ASL comprehension skills by reviewing a Bravo family interaction from Lesson Nine.

Viewing Instructions: Watch the *Bravo Family Revisited* for review and write a summary of the main points.

Summary: _____
_____
_____
_____

Lesson Ten: *Review & Practice Session*

10.30 Experiential Activity

Pictures in the Air

Activity Goal: To improve students' expressive and comprehension skills.

Activity Instructions:
1. **Ask** students to read *Pictures in the Air* in their workbooks (activity 10.30).

2. **Divide** the class into four groups.

3. **Assign** each group one of the pictures provided in the Student Workbook. **Tell** each group to create a short skit about their picture using ASL (no voice).

4. **Instruct** students to begin the activity by planning and practicing their skit with their groups (no voice!).

5. **Circulate** among the groups to **observe** student performance, **assisting** as needed.

6. **Ask** each group to perform their skit for the class. If possible, it is recommended that you **videotape** each group's performance of this activity.

Student Workbook:
Activity 10.30

10.30 Experiential Activity

Pictures in the Air

Activity Goal: To improve your expressive and comprehension skills.

Activity Instructions: Your instructor will divide the class into four groups and assign each group one of the pictures below.

Based on your picture, work with your group to create a skit using ASL (no voice!). Your group will have time to prepare and practice your skit and then show it to the whole class.

A.  B.

C.   D.

Instructor's Guide: Lesson Ten
Bravo ASL! Curriculum

©1996 Sign Enhancers, Inc.
ALL RIGHTS RESERVED.

Lesson Ten: *Review & Practice Session*

10.31 Video Learning Experience

Lessons Six Thru Nine Review: Cultural Notes

Viewing Goal: To assist students in reviewing the cultural aspects of ASL presented in Lessons Six, Seven, Eight, and Nine.

Viewing Instructions:

1. **Ask** students to read *Lessons Six Thru Nine Review: Cultural Notes* in their workbooks (activity 10.31).

2. **Instruct** students to complete the questions in their workbooks before viewing the segment.

3. **Play** the video segment entitled *Lessons Six Thru Nine Review: Cultural Notes* (segment 10.31) while students correct their work. Because the presentation of this segment is beyond the linguistic ability of beginning students, please **turn on** the audio and/or captions to optimize its educational value.

4. At completion of the segment, **answer** any questions students may have.

Video Segment Content: See the following Student Workbook excerpt for the content
(3 Minutes) of this video segment.

Student Workbook: Activity 10.31

10.31 Video Learning Experience

Lessons Six Thru Nine Review: Cultural Notes

Viewing Goal: To help you review the cultural aspects of ASL presented in Lessons Six, Seven, Eight, and Nine.

Viewing Instructions: Answer the questions below to see how well you remember these cultural aspects of ASL. When you are finished, watch the video. Billy will provide you with the answers to correct your work.

1. Why is it so important to sign when a Deaf adult or child is around?
   A. To make her/him feel socially included
   B. To allow equal access
   C. To build self-esteem

2. When parents are considering educational options for their Deaf child, what two issues must be considered?
   1) Whether the educational option nurtures positive self-esteem
   2) Whether it provides full and equal access for the child

Instructor's Guide: Lesson Ten
Bravo ASL! Curriculum

©1996 Sign Enhancers, Inc.
ALL RIGHTS RESERVED.

Lesson Ten: *Review & Practice Session*

3. List four reasons why going to a school for the Deaf is beneficial to a Deaf child.
    1) **Communication**
    2) **Social interaction**
    3) **Cultural affiliation**
    4) **Deaf adult role models**

4. Can you think of three ways the telephone is accessible to a Deaf person?
    1) **TTY/TDD**
    2) **Relay services**
    3) **A professional interpreter**

5. When a Deaf person is considering employment possibilities, is there one specific job suited for Deaf workers
   No! Deaf people can work at any job!

10.32 Video Learning Experience

Lessons Six Thru Nine Review: Grammatical Notes

Viewing Goal: To review the grammatical aspects of ASL presented in Lessons Six through Nine.

Viewing Instructions:

1. **Ask** students to read *Lessons Six Thru Nine Review: Grammatical Notes* in their workbooks (activity 10.32).

2. **Instruct** students to complete the questions in their workbooks before viewing the segment.

3. **Play** the video segment entitled *Lessons Six Thru Nine Review: Grammatical Notes* (segment 10.32) while students correct their own work. Because the presentation of this segment is beyond the linguistic ability of beginning students, please **turn on** the audio and/or captions to optimize its educational value.

4. At completion of the segment, **review** the content presented, and **answer** any questions students may have.

Lesson Ten: *Review & Practice Session*

Video Segment Content: See the following Student Workbook excerpt for the content
(5 Minutes) of this video segment.

Student Workbook:
Activity 10.32

> 10.32 Video Learning Experience
>
> Lessons Six Thru Nine Review: Grammatical Notes
>
> **Viewing Goal:** To help you apply the grammatical aspects of ASL presented in Lessons Six through Nine.
>
> **Viewing Instructions:** Answer the questions below to see how well you remember these grammatical aspects of ASL. When you are finished, watch the video. Billy will provide the answers so you can see how well you did.
>
> 1. In American Sign Language, each sign has four main components or parameters. One is a distinct handshape. Can you name the other three?
>   1) Distinct handshape
>   2) **Specific movement**
>   3) **Specific location**
>   4) **Palm orientation**
>
> 2. In the video, Dad uses the sign GIVE. What information was added to the verb GIVE by the use of directionality?
>   **It told us who had the book, where it went, and who received it.**
>
> 3. You saw several examples of sign choices based on meaning (right/correct vs. right/direction). What do we call this principle?
>   **Conceptual accuracy.**
>
> 4. Practice signing the amounts $1-$9 with Billy!
>
> 5. Explain how you sign "ten dollars."

10.33 Video Learning Experience

Lessons Six Thru Nine Review: Practice Dialogue

Viewing Goal: To improve students' comprehension skills by watching a dialogue presented in ASL.

Viewing Instructions:
1. **Ask** students to read *Lessons Six Thru Nine Review: Practice Dialogue* in their workbooks (activity 10.33).

2. **Show** the video segment entitled *Lessons Six Thru Nine Review: Practice Dialogue* (segment 10.33).

Lesson Ten: *Review & Practice Session*

3. **Instruct** students to watch the dialogue for comprehension and write a summary in the space provided.

Video Segment Content: (2 Minutes)

The following is a summary of the dialogue presented in this segment:

Anna is telling Scott that she read a book about rainbows at school. She asks him if he wants her to teach him. He says yes, that he will pay attention. Scott asks Anna to teach slow. Anna tells him the different colors of the rainbow. Scott corrects her, telling her that she forgot gold. Anna realizes that he is talking about the pot of gold at the end of the rainbow.

Scott begins dreaming of counting the gold. $1, $2, $3...

Anna interrupts his dream and asks him how much gold there was and what he will do with it.

Scott tells her there is no limit to the amount of gold and that he will deposit it in the bank.

Anna tells him that if there is no limit to the gold, he will be there forever depositing it and the line will back up and people will get mad.

He tells her that he will give each of the people in line some gold so they will be happy.

Anna decides that she is going to the bank to wait in line.

Student Workbook: Activity 10.33

10.33 Video Learning Experience

Lessons Six Through Nine Review: Practice Dialogue

Viewing Goal: To improve your comprehension skills by watching a dialogue presented in ASL.

Viewing Instructions: Watch the signed dialogue for comprehension and write a summary of the main points.

Summary: _____
_____
_____
_____

Instructor's Guide: Lesson Ten
Bravo ASL! Curriculum

©1996 Sign Enhancers, Inc.
ALL RIGHTS RESERVED.

Lesson Ten: *Review & Practice Session*

10.34 Experiential Activity

Dynamic-Duo Dialogue

Activity Goal: To improve students' expressive and receptive ASL skills.

Activity Instructions:

1. **Ask** students to read *Dynamic-Duo Dialogue* in their workbooks (activity 10.34).

2. **Divide** the class into pairs.

3. **Instruct** students to create dialogues using the vocabulary from Lessons Six through Nine. Each student should take a minimum of four turns.

4. After students have practiced, **ask** for volunteers to share their dialogues with the class. If possible, **videotape** each dialogue.

5. **Correct** production by **modeling** as needed.

Student Workbook: Activity 10.34

10.34 Experiential Activity

Dynamic-Duo Dialogue

Activity Goal: To improve your expressive and receptive ASL skills.

Activity Instructions: Work with a partner to create a dialogue using the vocabulary from Lessons Six, Seven, Eight and Nine. Use ASL (no voices needed!) and be sure each person takes at least four turns.

Be prepared to share your dialogue with the class!

In the space below, record any ideas or notes you have regarding the dialogue.

Notes: _____
_____
_____
_____

Instructor's Guide: Lesson Ten
Bravo ASL! Curriculum

Lesson Ten: *Review & Practice Session*

10.35 Video Learning Experience

Lessons Six Thru Nine Review: Practice Story

Viewing Goal: To improve ASL comprehension skills by watching a signed story.

Viewing Instructions:

1. **Ask** students to read *Lessons Six Thru Nine Review: Practice Story* in their workbooks (activity 10.35).

2. **Show** the video segment entitled *Lessons Six Thru Nine Review: Practice Story* (segment 10.35). Billy signs a story using the vocabulary from Lessons Six, Seven, Eight, and Nine. **Turn off** audio and captions.

3. **Instruct** students to watch the story for comprehension and write a summary of the main points.

Video Segment Content: (3 Minutes)

The following is an English translation of the story:

Now I'm going to tell a story. You can practice reading signs, copying facial expressions, and the movement of the signs. OK?

I was not paying attention in school. I sat in class bored during reading, writing, and math lessons. The teacher gave me a book. I read it, but I was so tired that I put my head on the desk and fell fast asleep.

I began to have a good dream. It was a wonderful math lesson of one plus one equals two - what's wrong? You don't understand why I'm smiling? - Well, in my dream I met a girl. The girl and I equal two. Ha, ha, ha.

And you know what? I wrote a note to the girl that said, "I love you." Then I signed my name, folded it up, and handed it to her.

The girl read the note and wrote down her name, address, and telephone number, and then gave it back to me. When I read it, I got really excited!

I noticed some red, pink, and white flowers. I picked them and gave them to her. We went out and played. I have a driver's license, so we went to get a soda pop. As we were driving, I realized that I didn't have any money. I told the girl I was very sorry. The girl gave me seven dollars. Just then I woke up and realized I was having a bad dream.

Lesson Ten: *Review & Practice Session*

I looked around and all the students had gone home. I went home late because I had to quickly go to the bank and withdraw some money. I had learned my lesson. I would be ready with cash when the girl and I went out.

Student Workbook: Activity 10.35

10.35 Video Learning Experience

Lessons Six Thru Nine Review: Practice Story

Viewing Goal: To improve your ASL comprehension skills by watching a story presented in ASL.

Viewing Instructions: Watch the signed story for comprehension and write a summary of the main points.

Summary: _____
_____
_____
_____

10.36 Homework Assignment

Create-A-Story

Activity Goal: To improve students' expressive and receptive ASL skills.

Activity Instructions:
1. **Ask** students to read *Create-A-Story* in their workbooks (activity 10.36).

2. **Instruct** students to create stories using a topic they choose from the list provided in their workbooks. These topics are included in the following excerpt of the Student Workbook:

3. **Tell** students to be prepared to perform their stories for the class.

Instructor Tip: *An opportunity for students to perform this assignment has been scheduled in the next lesson (Homework Review 11.2). If possible, it is recommended that you arrange to videotape each student's performance of this activity.*

Lesson Ten: *Review & Practice Session*

Student Workbook:
Activity 10.36

10.36 Homework Assignment

Create-A-Story

Activity Goal: To improve your expressive ASL skills.

Activity Instructions: Create a story using one of the topics below. Be prepared to demonstrate your story for the class!

A. You'll never guess the color of my home!

B. I love school because...

C. Today, at school...

D. If I had a million dollars, I would...

E. I went to the bank, and...

10.37 Post-test

What Do You Know Now?

Assessment Video

Post-test Goal: To assess students' mastery of the lesson objectives.

Post-test Instructions:

1. **Ask** students to read the Post-test Introduction in their workbooks (activity 10.37).

2. **Copy** and **distribute** the Lesson Ten Post-test (Appendix 10.37).

3. **Play** the Assessment Video (segment 10.37) and allow students to complete Section One (comprehension portion) of the test.

4. **Instruct** students to complete Section Two (culture and grammar portion) of the test individually and hand in their papers when they are finished.

5. **Assign** Section Three (expressive portion) of the test and **schedule** a time when students are to perform. If possible, it is strongly recommended that you **videotape** this portion of the Post-test.

6. **Determine** grading options based upon programmatic requirements. A recommended guideline for measuring successful mastery of objectives is 80% accuracy.

Lesson Ten: *Review & Practice Session*

Video Segment Content:
(3 Minutes)

The following is an English translation of the comprehension story:

A student named Joan was reading a book. She wanted to learn math. She wanted to learn to add, subtract, and multiply.

A boy named Tom liked Joan. He gave her a purple and yellow flower and his phone number. Did she call him? Yes. She asked him to come to her house!

He was happy she liked him!

He went to her house. What did she want to do? Study math! She gave him a pencil and paper, but no calculator!

She asked him, "How much is seven plus eight?"

He worked out the problem with the pencil and paper and told her the answer was fifteen.

She then asked, "How much is twelve plus five?"

Again he worked out the problem on paper and told her the answer was seventeen.

She asked, "What is nineteen minus fourteen?"

Once again, he went to work and answered, "five."

Tom helped her learn math for a long time. He became tired. He went home to get some sleep.

The next day at school, Tom gave Joan a present... a calculator. They were both happy!

Student Workbook:
Activity 10.37

10.37 Post-test Introduction

What Do You Know Now?

Post-test Goal: To assess your mastery of the lesson objectives.

Post-test Introduction: This test has three sections:

- Section One: The Comprehension section tests your ability to understand ASL.
- Section Two: The Culture and Grammar section tests your knowledge of the material presented in the *Cultural* and *Grammatical Notes*.
- Section Three: The Expressive portion tests your ability to use ASL.

Simply follow the instructions for each section. **Good luck!**

Lesson Ten: *Review & Practice Session*

Post-test Master:
Appendix 10.37

10.37 Post-test

Section One: Comprehension

Instructions: You will see a signed story. Watch carefully and answer each question.

1. What was the girl's name?
   A. Jan
   B. Joan
   C. Tammy
   D. Cheri

2. What was the boy's name?
   A. Tag
   B. Tom
   C. Ted
   D. Thatcher

3. What did the girl want to do?
   A. Date the boy
   B. Meet with the teacher
   C. Eat lunch with the boy
   D. Learn more about math

4. What did the boy give the girl?
   A. A flower
   B. His phone number
   C. A calculator
   D. All of the above

5. Did the girl call him?
   A. Yes
   B. No

6. What did the girl want to talk about?
   A. English grammar
   B. Math problems
   C. Marriage and family
   D. The math teacher

Instructor's Guide: Lesson Ten
Bravo ASL! Curriculum

©1996 Sign Enhancers, Inc.
ALL RIGHTS RESERVED.

Post-test Master: Appendix 10.37

10.37 Post-test

Section Two: Culture and Grammar

Instructions: Read each statement carefully and determine if it is true or false (circle your answer).

7. Signing when there is a Deaf child present helps the child feel involved, equal, and valuable.
   A. True
   B. False

8. Full access to a school's educational activities is necessary.
   A. True
   B. False

9. Full access to a school's social activities is not necessary.
   A. True
   B. False

10. A school for the Deaf will have Deaf adult role models.
    A. True
    B. False

11. Employment opportunities for Deaf people are limited to those jobs not requiring any use of the telephone.
    A. True
    B. False

12. There are several ways Deaf people can access the phone system.
    A. True
    B. False

13. Each sign has four parts, called paralanguages.
    A. True
    B. False

14. The four parts of every sign are: handshape, movement, location, and palm orientation.
    A. True
    B. False

15. Directional verbs all move in a forward direction.
    A. True
    B. False

Lesson Ten: *Review & Practice Session*

Post-test Master:
Appendix 10.37

10.37 Post-test

Section Three: Expressive Portion

Instructions: Create a story based on one of the questions below.

Your instructor will schedule a time for you to perform this section of the Post-test. You may prepare and practice prior to your scheduled time.

1. What is the funniest thing that ever happened to you in a bank?
2. What is your favorite school story?
3. What's your favorite color and why?

Include at least eight signs from Lesson Six, Seven, Eight, and Nine. Be sure to demonstrate at least two directional verbs in your story.

16. _____
17. _____
18. _____
19. _____
20. _____
21. _____
22. _____
23. _____

Directional verbs:

24. _____
25. _____

Congratulations!
You have completed
Lesson Ten!

Instructor's Guide: Lesson Ten
Bravo ASL! Curriculum

©1996 Sign Enhancers, Inc.
ALL RIGHTS RESERVED.

Lesson 11
PLAYING IN THE PARK

Materials Needed

Equipment: VCR and TV monitor
Overhead projector and screen
Optional: video camera for activities 11.2 and 11.25

Materials: Instructor's Guide
Student Workbook: one per student
Overhead transparencies for activities 11.3, 11.4, 11.6, 11.10, 11.11, 11.18, and 11.22 (see Appendix for masters)
Optional: blank videotape (or have students bring their own) for activities 11.2 and 11.25
Post-test: Appendix 11.25

Videotapes: The Beginning ASL VideoCourse Lesson Eleven
Activities Video for activity 11.8
Assessment Video for Post-test 11.25

11.1 Begin Class

Housekeeping

Goal: To prepare students for this lesson.

Instructions:
1. **Welcome** students to Lesson Eleven of the VideoCourse.

2. **Perform** any necessary tasks (such as taking attendance) that may be required by your specific program.

Instructor's Guide: Lesson Eleven
Bravo ASL! Curriculum
©1996 Sign Enhancers, Inc.
ALL RIGHTS RESERVED.

Lesson Eleven: *Playing in the Park*

11.2 Homework Review

Create-A-Story

Activity Goal: To provide feedback on previously assigned homework and to reinforce materials learned in earlier lessons.

Activity Instructions:

1. **Ask** students to read *Create-A-Story* in their workbooks (activity 11.2).

2. **Instruct** students to find a partner and practice the stories they prepared for homework (*Homework Assignment 10.37*).

3. When students have finished practicing, **ask** individual students to take turns demonstrating their stories for the rest of the class. If possible, it is recommended that you **videotape** this activity.

4. **Encourage** the class to use ASL to ask questions about each of the stories to indicate accurate comprehension.

5. **Observe** student performance and **model** corrections as necessary.

6. **Continue** process until all students have performed their stories.

Student Workbook: Activity 11.2

11.2 Homework Review

Create-A-Story

Activity Goal: To show the results of your homework assignment.

Activity Instructions: You will be asked to share the story you created for homework using one of the topics below.

1. You'll never guess the color of my home!
2. I love school because…
3. Today, at school…
4. If I had a million dollars, I would…
5. I went to the bank, and…

While other students perform their stories, pay close attention and practice your comprehension skills! Use ASL to ask questions about the signed stories.

Lesson Eleven: *Playing in the Park*

11.3 Pretest

What Do You Know?

Pretest Goal: To identify students' current level of knowledge pertaining to the lesson content.

Pretest Instructions:
1. **Ask** students to read and answer the pretest questions in their workbooks (activity 11.3).

2. **Show** the overhead (Appendix 11.3) and **ask** individual students to indicate the correct answers on the overhead while class members correct their own work.

3. **Inform** students that the contents of the pretest will be taught throughout the lesson.

Student Workbook: Activity 11.3

Overhead Master: Appendix 11.3

11.3 Pretest

What Do You Know?

Pretest Goal: To see how much you already know about what will be taught in this lesson.

Pretest Instructions: Read and answer each question.

1. In ASL, the way signs are used in space often copies the movement of the people and objects involved in the actual events being described.
   A. True
   B. False

2. In an emergency situation, what can medical staff do to improve communication with a patient who is Deaf? Check all that apply:
   _X_ A. Look at and speak directly to the Deaf person
   _X_ B. Be willing to use gestures
   _X_ C. Maintain direct eye contact
   _X_ D. Be willing to write or draw pictures

3. During an emergency situation, what are some special concerns a Deaf person might have? Check all that apply:
   _X_ A. Will there be a communication problem at the hospital?
   _X_ B. Will anyone know Sign Language?
   _X_ C. Will there be an interpreter?
   ___ D. Will I have a TV in my room?

4. What issues do you think are important to Deaf people during a medical emergency? Check all that apply:
   _X_ A. Getting good medical care
   _X_ B. Having communication access
   _X_ C. Getting good interpreting services
   ___ D. Getting a color TV in their room

Lesson Eleven: *Playing in the Park*

11.4 Lesson Objectives

Planning for Success

Goal: To identify the learning outcomes associated with successful completion of this lesson.

Instructions:
1. **Ask** students to read the objectives in their workbooks (activity 11.4).

2. **Show** the overhead (Appendix 11.4) and **read** through the objectives with the class.

Student Workbook: Activity 11.4

Overhead Master: Appendix 11.4

> 11.4 Lesson Objectives
>
> *Planning for Success*
>
> Goal: To see what you will learn by the end of this lesson.
>
> Instructions: Read the objectives below. Your instructor will answer any questions you may have.
>
> Upon completing this VideoCourse lesson, you will be able to...
>
> 1. Recognize and accurately produce the ASL vocabulary introduced in this and all previous lessons.
>
> 2. Identify and explain some of the communication and access issues Deaf people face in a medical emergency.
>
> 3. Identify and describe several ways the use of space feature is used in ASL.

11.5 Lesson Focus

Summer Camp Fun!

Activity Goal: To develop a need for the ASL vocabulary introduced in this lesson.

Activity Instructions:

1. **Ask** students to read *Summer Camp Fun!* in their workbooks (activity 11.5).

2. **Instruct** students to consider how, as summer camp counselors, they would communicate the sports activities listed in their workbooks to a group of campers who are Deaf.

3. **Divide** the class into groups of four or five.

4. **Instruct** students to take turns role-playing a camp counselor who has to describe a sport using signs, mime, and gestures. The other students should try to guess what sport is being described.

5. When the group work is completed, **ask** several students to demonstrate the most effective communication strategies for the whole class.

6. When students have completed this activity, you may **choose**:

    Option A: **Lead** a discussion using the following Thought/Discussion Questions:

    1) What are some signs related to sports/games that would have been useful to know for this activity?

    2) How did it feel to be limited in your ability to communicate?

    3) How can Deaf people communicate about sports and games to people who don't sign?

    OR

    Option B: **Ask** students to complete the above Thought/Discussion Questions in their workbooks in class or for homework. **Collect** for grading or to provide students with written feedback.

7. **Inform** students that this VideoCourse lesson will teach them the signs related to nature and sports.

Lesson Eleven: *Playing in the Park*

Student Workbook:
Activity 11.5

11.5 Lesson Focus

Summer Camp Fun!

Activity Goal: To role-play communicating about sports to children who are Deaf.

Activity Instructions: Imagine that you are a camp counselor for a group of children who are Deaf. Your job is to teach the children about the sports and games listed below.

In your group, take turns role-playing a counselor and teaching your campers about the activities. Use signs, mime, and gestures (do not use your voice or write). See if your classmates can guess which activity you are describing.

You are a camp counselor. How would you visually describe…

1. Baseball
2. Tennis
3. Hiking
4. Running
5. Golf
6. Fishing
7. Basketball
8. Climbing
9. A picnic

During this lesson, you will learn the signs for these activities and more. If you ever become a camp counselor, you'll be ready!

Thought/Discussion Questions

1. What are some signs related to sports/games that would have been useful to know for this activity?

2. How did it feel to be limited in your ability to communicate?

3. How can Deaf people communicate about sports and games to people who don't sign?

Lesson Eleven: *Playing in the Park*

11.6 Language Learning Instruction

Learning New Signs

Goal: To use ASL and visual aids to introduce this lesson's vocabulary.

Instructions:

1. **Ask** students to read *Learning New Signs* in their workbooks (activity 11.6).

2. **Show** the overhead (Appendix 11.6). **Introduce** the vocabulary by **pointing** to items presented in the pictures while **demonstrating** the signs.

3. **Reinforce** retention and **check** students' comprehension by **using** these signs to **ask** students questions.

    Note: For a step-by-step review of this method, see Lesson One (activities 1.6 and 1.12).

4. **Continue** this process until all the ASL vocabulary items have been introduced.

Overhead Content: Use the pictures in the overhead (Appendix 11.6) to introduce the signs representing the following concepts:

1. TREE
2. CLIMB-TREE
3. TREES
4. FLOWER
5. SMELL
6. BLACK+BERRY
7. BRIDGE
8. WATER
9. RIVER
10. GRASS
11. SUN
12. HOT
13. LEAF
14. COOL
15. BUTTERFLY
16. BASKETBALL
17. BASEBALL
18. BALL
19. TENNIS
20. BEAT-ME
21. GOLF
22. FRISBEE
23. GAMES
24. PLAY
25. PICNIC
26. WALK
27. RUN
28. FALL-DOWN

Note: Some pictures can be used to represent several concepts. For verbs and more abstract concepts, you may need to supplement these pictures with mime, gestures, using actual objects, and acting out the concepts in class.

Instructor's Guide: Lesson Eleven
Bravo ASL! Curriculum

©1996 Sign Enhancers, Inc.
ALL RIGHTS RESERVED.

Lesson Eleven: *Playing in the Park*

Overhead Master:
Appendix 11.6

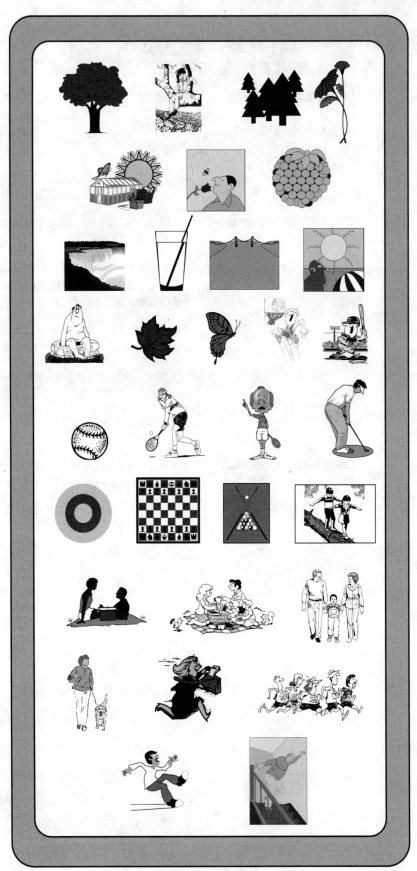

Instructor's Guide: Lesson Eleven
Bravo ASL! Curriculum

Lesson Eleven: *Playing in the Park*

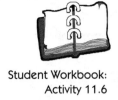

Student Workbook: Activity 11.6

11.6 Language Learning Instruction

Learning New Signs

Goal: To help you learn new ASL vocabulary.

Instructions: Your instructor will teach you new signs! Watch closely to learn what these signs mean and how they are produced.

In the space below, record any notes to help you remember the signs.

Notes: _____
_____
_____
_____

11.7 Video Learning Experience

Introduction to New Vocabulary

Viewing Goal: To provide a signed demonstration of the accurate production of the new ASL vocabulary.

Viewing Instructions:
1. **Ask** students to read *Introduction to New Vocabulary* in their workbooks (activity 11.7).

2. **Play** the video segment entitled *Introduction to New Vocabulary* (segment 11.7). Billy magically pops in and out around the park introducing ASL vocabulary related to nature and sports. Because the introduction at the beginning of this segment is beyond the linguistic ability of beginning students, please **turn on** audio and/or captions to optimize its educational value. Billy then signs each new vocabulary item twice. (If you wish to keep this introduction to the vocabulary strictly visual, **turn off** audio.)

3. **Instruct** students to watch how Billy produces the signs as well as the accompanying facial/body expressions.

4. **Ask** students to copy the signs and the facial/body expressions as Billy repeats each one.

Instructor's Guide: Lesson Eleven
Bravo ASL! Curriculum

©1996 Sign Enhancers, Inc.
ALL RIGHTS RESERVED.

Lesson Eleven: *Playing in the Park*

Video Segment Content: See the following Student Workbook excerpt for the content
(10 Minutes) of this video segment.

Student Workbook:
Activity 11.7

11.7 Video Learning Experience

Introduction to New Vocabulary

Viewing Goal: To help you learn new ASL vocabulary.

Viewing Instructions: Watch how Billy produces each sign. Be sure to notice the facial/body expressions. Copy the signs as Billy repeats each one.

Signs representing the following concepts are introduced:

1. TREE
2. CLIMB+TREE
3. TREES
4. FLOWER
5. SMELL
6. BLACK+BERRY
7. BRIDGE
8. WATER
9. RIVER
10. GRASS
11. SUN
12. HOT
13. LEAF
14. COOL
15. BUTTERFLY
16. BASKETBALL
17. BASEBALL
18. BALL
19. TENNIS
20. BEAT-ME
21. GOLF
22. FRISBEE
23. GAMES
24. PLAY
25. PICNIC
26. WALK
27. RUN
28. FALL-DOWN

In the space below, record any notes to help you remember the signs.

Notes: _____
_____
_____
_____

11.8 Experiential Activity

Spot the Sport

Activities Video

Activity Goal: To assist students in recognizing the new ASL vocabulary and use of space features.

Activity Instructions:
1. **Ask** students to read *Spot the Sport* in their workbooks (activity 11.8) and locate the pictures provided.

2. **Play** the Activities Video (segment 11.8) that describes several sports in ASL. Each description will be numbered.

Lesson Eleven: *Playing in the Park*

3. **Ask** students to write the correct number next to the picture that best represents the sport signed on the videotape.

4. When the video segment is over, ask individual students to indicate the answers on the overhead while class members correct their own work.

Video Segment Content: (5 1/2 Minutes)

The following are English translations of the signed descriptions presented in this segment:

1. A girl playing baseball
2. A boy playing baseball
3. A man playing baseball
4. A father teaches his son baseball
5. A woman playing basketball
6. A man playing basketball
7. A man fishing
8. People fishing
9. A woman playing golf
10. A man hiking
11. A woman playing tennis
12. A man playing tennis
13. Man walking with a baby
14. A man playing football
15. A ball

Student Workbook: Activity 11.8

Overhead Master: Appendix 11.8

11.8 Experiential Activity

Spot the Sport

Activity Goal: To assist you in recognizing the new ASL vocabulary.

Activity Instructions: You will see signed descriptions of the pictures below. Each of the signed samples will be numbered. Put the number next to the picture that best matches the meaning of each signed description.

13   11   14   12   5

6   9   1   7   8

3   15   2   4   10

Lesson Eleven: *Playing in the Park*

11.9 Video Learning Experience

Bravo Family Visit

Viewing Goal: To improve ASL comprehension skills by watching a Bravo family interaction.

Viewing Instructions:
1. **Ask** students to read *Bravo Family Visit* in their workbooks (activity 11.9).

2. **Play** the video segment of the Bravo family (segment 11.9). The Bravos will use the new ASL vocabulary within the context of their visit to the park.

3. **Instruct** students to watch for comprehension and write a summary of the main points.

4. **Replay** any portion of this video segment that students experienced difficulty understanding.

Video Segment Summary: (5 1/2 Minutes)

The following is a summary of the Bravo family interaction:

The Bravo family has just arrived at the park. Their dog, Lady, walks up with a Frisbee in her mouth. Anna and Dad discuss how much Lady loves to play Frisbee. Scott asks if he can play Frisbee with Lady. Mom tells him that he can, but that they are going to eat soon and when she calls him he needs to hurry back. Scott goes off to play with Lady.

Anna asks if Dad wants to play tennis. Dad explains that he and Mom are setting up the picnic and that after they eat they will play tennis. Anna decides that she will go practice her tennis so when they play later, she can beat Dad.

Mom talks about what a beautiful place and day it is, mentioning the trees, flowers, river, and sunshine. Dad gives her a strange look and she asks him what he means by it. He explains that the trees are beautiful, the flowers are beautiful, the river is beautiful, the sunshine is beautiful, and... Mom is beautiful. They kiss.

Mom doesn't know what she's going to do after lunch. Anna wants to play tennis. Scott wants to play baseball. Mom asks Dad what he is going to do. Dad doesn't know what he's going to do. He knows Anna really wants to play tennis, Scott really wants to play baseball, Lady really wants to play Frisbee, and that he wants to play golf.

Lesson Eleven: *Playing in the Park*

Dad asks Mom what she wants to play. Mom says she doesn't want to play anything, she just wants to sit by the river. Dad tells her that he is hungry and asks her to help him get everything set up for lunch.

Scott is still playing Frisbee with Lady when Mom calls him to come eat. Lady hears her calling and stops running to look at Mom. That lets Scott know Mom is calling. Scott tells Lady he will play with her again after they eat. He tells her just to leave the Frisbee where it is. He assures her it will be there when they get back.

Some children walk by and pick up the Frisbee and start playing with it. They are called by their mother and told to leave the Frisbee. They toss it back toward the park.

The Frisbee lands in a woman's bag. She looks around and doesn't see anyone, so she tosses it and it lands in the river. There is a man fishing in the river and the Frisbee gets caught on his line, he tosses it back onto the field where Scott left it. Scott and Lady come back and Scott tells Lady, "See, I told you it would stay here!"

He grabs the Frisbee and they run off to play.

Student Workbook: Activity 11.9

11.9 Video Learning Experience

Bravo Family Visit

Viewing Goal: To improve your ASL comprehension skills by watching a Bravo family interaction.

Viewing Instructions: Watch the signed interaction and write a summary of the main points.

Summary: _____
_____
_____
_____

Instructor's Guide: Lesson Eleven
Bravo ASL! Curriculum

©1996 Sign Enhancers, Inc.
ALL RIGHTS RESERVED.

Lesson Eleven: *Playing in the Park*

11.10 Comprehension Quiz

What Did You Understand?

Quiz Goal: To assess students' comprehension of the signed interaction.

Quiz Instructions:

1. **Instruct** students to complete the quiz in their workbooks (activity 11.10).

2. **Collect** for grading or **show** overhead (Appendix 11.10) and **ask** individual students to indicate the correct answers on the overhead while class members correct their own work.

3. **Ask** students to indicate which item(s) from the quiz they found difficult. **Review** by **modeling** or **replaying** that segment of the videotape.

Student Workbook: Activity 11.10

Overhead Master: Appendix 11.10

11.10 Comprehension Quiz

What Did You Understand?

Quiz Goal: To see how much of the Bravo family interaction you understood.

Quiz Instructions: Read and answer each question below.

1. Anna and Dad discuss how much Lady loves to _____.
   A. Swim
   B. Sleep
   C. Play Frisbee
   D. Play with the ball

2. Anna asks Dad if he wants to play _____.
   A. Frisbee
   B. Tennis
   C. Golf
   D. Football

3. Dad explains that _____ is/are beautiful.
   A. The trees
   B. The flowers
   C. Mom
   D. All of the above

4. After lunch, Dad says he wants to _____.
   A. Play golf
   B. Play tennis
   C. Swim
   D. All of the above

5. After lunch, Mom wants to _____.
   A. Play tennis
   B. Play golf
   C. Play Frisbee
   D. Sit by the river

Lesson Eleven: *Playing in the Park*

11.11 Language Learning Instruction

Learning New Signs

Goal: To use ASL and visual aids to introduce this lesson's vocabulary.

Instructions:
1. **Ask** students to read *Learning New Signs* in their workbooks (activity 11.11).

2. **Show** the overhead (Appendix 11.11). **Introduce** the vocabulary by **pointing** to items presented in the pictures while **demonstrating** the signs.

3. **Reinforce** retention and **check** students' comprehension by **using** these signs to **ask** students questions.

   Note: For a step-by-step review of this method, see Lesson One (activities 1.6 and 1.12).

4. **Continue** this process until all the ASL vocabulary items have been introduced.

Overhead Content: Use the pictures in the overhead (Appendix 11.11) to introduce the signs representing the following concepts:

1. MAN
2. WOMAN
3. FISHING
4. PURSE/BAG
5. FIND

Note: Some pictures can be used to represent several concepts. For verbs and more abstract concepts, you may need to supplement these pictures with mime, gestures, using actual objects, and acting out the concepts in class.

Lesson Eleven: *Playing in the Park*

Overhead Master:
Appendix 11.11

Student Workbook:
Activity 11.11

11.11 Language Learning Instruction

Learning New Signs

Goal: To help you learn new ASL vocabulary.

Instructions: Your instructor will teach you new signs! Watch closely to learn what these signs mean and how they are produced.

In the space below, record any notes to help you remember the signs.

Notes: _____
_____
_____
_____

Lesson Eleven: *Playing in the Park*

11.12 Video Learning Experience

Introduction to New Vocabulary

Viewing Goal: To provide a signed demonstration of the accurate production of the new ASL vocabulary.

Viewing Instructions:
1. **Ask** students to read *Introduction to New Vocabulary* in their workbooks (activity 11.12).

2. **Play** the video segment entitled *Introduction to New Vocabulary* (segment 11.12). Billy introduces and signs each new vocabulary item twice. (If you wish to keep this a strictly visual presentation, **turn off** audio.)

3. **Instruct** students to watch how Billy produces the signs and the accompanying facial/body expressions.

4. **Ask** students to copy the signs and the facial/body expressions as Billy repeats each one.

Video Segment Content: See the following Student Workbook excerpt for the content
(2 Minutes) of this video segment.

Student Workbook: Activity 11.12

11.12 Video Learning Experience

Introduction to New Vocabulary

Viewing Goal: To help you learn new ASL vocabulary.

Viewing Instructions: Watch how Billy produces each sign. Be sure to notice the facial/body expressions. Copy the signs as Billy repeats each one.

Signs representing the following concepts are introduced:

1. MAN
2. WOMAN
3. FISHING
4. PURSE/BAG
5. FIND

Instructor's Guide: Lesson Eleven
Bravo ASL! Curriculum

©1996 Sign Enhancers, Inc.
ALL RIGHTS RESERVED.

Lesson Eleven: *Playing in the Park*

11.13 Video Learning Experience

Bravo Family Visit

Viewing Goal: To improve ASL comprehension skills by watching a Bravo family interaction.

Viewing Instructions:
1. **Ask** students to read *Bravo Family Visit* in their workbooks (activity 11.13).

2. **Play** the video segment of Billy telling the students what happened to the Frisbee (segment 11.13).

3. **Instruct** students to watch carefully for comprehension and write a summary of the main points.

4. **Replay** this segment. **Ask** students to copy the signs, facial/body expressions and the use of space features.

Video Segment Content: (1 1/2 Minutes)

The following is a summary of the signed interaction:

Now I'm going to tell you what happened. Watch me, and if you'd like to copy my signs, you can.

The Frisbee was on the ground. Two girls came walking by, found the Frisbee, ran to pick it up, and tossed it back and forth. Their mom came, so the girls had to toss the Frisbee away.

Now, there was a woman walking by and the Frisbee accidentally landed in her bag. The woman took the Frisbee out of her bag and tossed it. The Frisbee flew through the air and landed in the river.

A man who was fishing thought he'd caught a fish. But it wasn't a fish, it was the Frisbee. He looked at it and tossed it in the air and the Frisbee landed in the same place it had started.

Scott and the dog thought the Frisbee had stayed in the same place, but it hadn't. Ha, ha, ha.

Lesson Eleven: *Playing in the Park*

Student Workbook: Activity 11.13

11.13 Video Learning Experience

The Frisbee Story

Viewing Goal: To improve your ASL receptive skills.

Viewing Instructions: Watch carefully as Billy signs the *Frisbee Story*. Watch for your new ASL vocabulary and see how the movement of the signs mimics what actually happened to the Frisbee.

Practice signing the following concepts with Billy:

1. The Frisbee was on the ground.

2. Two girls came walking by, found the Frisbee, picked it up, and tossed it back and forth.

3. Their mom came, so the girls had to toss the Frisbee away.

4. There was a woman walking by and the Frisbee landed right in her bag.

5. The woman took the Frisbee out of her bag and tossed it.

6. The Frisbee flew through the air and landed in the river.

7. A man who was fishing thought he'd caught a fish, but it wasn't a fish, it was the Frisbee. He tossed it away and it landed where Scott had left it.

8. Scott thought the Frisbee had stayed in the same place the entire time.

11.14 Video Learning Experience

Grammatical Notes

Viewing Goal: To assist students in learning about the grammatical aspects of ASL.

Viewing Instructions:

1. **Ask** students to read *Grammatical Notes* in their workbooks (activity 11.14).

2. **Play** the video segment entitled *Grammatical Notes* (segment 11.14). Because the presentation of this segment is beyond the linguistic ability of beginning students, please **turn on** the audio and/or captions to optimize its educational value.

3. **Instruct** students to view the segment.

4. At completion of the video segment, **review** the content presented and **answer** any questions students may have.

Lesson Eleven: *Playing in the Park*

Video Segment Content:
(4 1/2 Minutes)

See the following Student Workbook excerpt for the content of this video segment.

Student Workbook:
Activity 11.14

> 11.14 Video Learning Experience
>
> *Grammatical Notes*
>
> **Viewing Goal:** To learn about the grammatical aspects of ASL.
>
> **Viewing Instructions:** View the *Grammatical Notes* segment carefully for the following:
>
> The Frisbee story demonstrates the use of space grammatical feature of ASL:
>
> A. The movements of ASL signs mimic the actual events being described.
>
> B. Some examples from *The Frisbee Story*:
>
>   1. It was established that the Frisbee started its journey lying on the ground.
>
>   2. Two girls ran to the Frisbee.
>
>   3. The Frisbee was tossed in the direction of the river and it landed on the river. The movement of the signs imitated the movement of the river (bobbing up and down).
>
>   4. The Frisbee floated with the current, and the signs indicated the actual movement of the river.

11.15 Experiential Activity

Up, Up, and Away!

Activity Goal: To apply the content of the *Grammatical Notes* by creating a story about a Frisbee that incorporates use of space features.

Activity Instructions:

1. **Ask** students to read *Up, Up, and Away* in their workbooks (activity 11.15).

2. **Divide** the class into groups of four or five.

3. **Instruct** each group to make up a Frisbee Story. Each student in the group will sign one sentence telling what happened to the Frisbee. The next student will repeat what was signed and add a new incident to the story. As the Frisbee Story is passed from student to student, it will grow!

4. **Model** the following examples with the students:

   Student #1: WOMAN, THROW-FRISBEE... BATHROOM, IN

   Student #2: WOMAN, THROW-FRISBEE-BATHROOM, IN... MAN, BATHROOM, THROW-FRISBEE-TREE

   Student #3: WOMAN, THROW-FRISBEE-BATHROOM, IN... MAN, BATHROOM, THROW-FRISBEE-TREE BUTTERFLY, TREE, THROW-FRISBEE... PURSE-IN

5. **Ask** each group to share their story with the class. **Point out** the use of space features within each story.

Student Workbook: Activity 11.15

11.15 Experiential Activity

Up, Up, and Away!

Activity Goal: To improve your ASL expressive skills by practicing the use of space feature.

Activity Instructions: Your group is going to create its own Frisbee Story. One person in the group will sign a sentence that tells who or what threw the Frisbee and where it landed. The next person repeats the story and adds another sentence. Pay attention to your classmates so you don't lose the Frisbee!

In the space below, draw a map of your Frisbee's journey. Use arrows to indicate what direction the Frisbee moved.

Hint: You can have your Frisbee go into a tree, into the bathroom, the living room, the river, the school, etc.

Up, Up, and Away Map

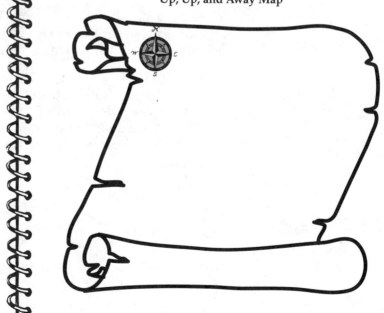

Lesson Eleven: *Playing in the Park*

11.16 Video Learning Experience

Bravo Family Visit

Viewing Goal: To improve ASL comprehension skills by watching a Bravo family interaction.

Viewing Instructions:

1. **Ask** students to read *Bravo Family Visit* in their workbooks (activity 11.16).

2. **Play** the video segment of the Bravo family (segment 11.16). The Bravos will use the new ASL vocabulary in the park. Because some of this presentation is beyond the linguistic ability of beginning students, **turn on** the audio and/or captions to optimize its educational value.

3. **Instruct** students to watch for comprehension and write a summary of the main points.

4. **Replay** any portion of this video segment that students experienced difficulty understanding.

Video Segment Content: (2 1/2 Minutes)

The following is a summary of the Bravo family interaction:

Scott throws the Frisbee and it gets caught in a tree. He knows that Mom and Dad told him not to climb trees, but he tries it anyway. Scott falls from the tree and can't get up.

He sends Lady to get Mom and Dad, but they don't understand and tell her to go play. Lady finds Anna. She follows Lady to Scott. Anna runs to get Mom and Dad.

Billy: You look worried. When Mom and Dad see Scott they will be worried, too. Suppose someone in your family got hurt. How would you feel? What would you think about? What do you do when an emergency happens? I'd like to discuss how Deaf people react in this type of emergency.

Student Workbook: Activity 11.16

11.16 Video Learning Experience

Bravo Family Visit

Viewing Goal: To improve ASL comprehension skills by watching a Bravo family interaction.

Viewing Instructions: Watch the Bravo family interaction for comprehension. In the space below, write a summary of the main points.

Summary: _____
_____
_____

Lesson Eleven: *Playing in the Park*

11.17 Video Learning Experience

Cultural Notes

Viewing Goal: To assist students in learning about the cultural aspects of ASL.

Viewing Instructions:
1. **Ask** students to read *Cultural Notes* in their workbooks (activity 11.17).

2. **Play** the video segment entitled *Cultural Notes* (segment 11.17). Because the presentation of this segment is beyond the linguistic ability of beginning students, please **turn on** audio and/or captions to optimize its educational value.

3. **Instruct** students to view the segment.

4. At completion of segment, **review** the content presented and **answer** any questions students may have.

Video Segment Content (4 1/2 Minutes)

See the following Student Workbook excerpt for the content of this video segment.

Student Workbook: Activity 11.17

11.17 Video Learning Experience

Cultural Notes

Viewing Goal: To learn about the cultural aspects of ASL.

Viewing Instructions: View the *Cultural Notes* segment carefully for the following:

I. Anyone who has a family member involved in a medical emergency would have many things to think about, including:
   A. Will the person be all right?
   B. Should I call an ambulance?
   C. Will a doctor be available?
   D. Will there be a painful wait?

II. Deaf people have additional concerns, including:
   A. Will I understand all that occurs at the hospital?
   B. Will any of the hospital staff know Sign Language?
   C. Will there be an interpreter available?
   D. In addition to dealing with the emergency, is it my responsibility to teach the hospital staff how to communicate effectively with Deaf people?
   E. Will the medical professionals be sensitive to communication needs?

III. What can medical staff do to facilitate good communication?
   A. Look at and speak directly to the Deaf person.
   B. Be willing to use gestures.
   C. Maintain direct eye contact.
   D. Be willing to write or draw pictures.

Instructor's Guide: Lesson Eleven
Bravo ASL! Curriculum

©1996 Sign Enhancers, Inc.
ALL RIGHTS RESERVED.

Lesson Eleven: *Playing in the Park*

11.18 Experiential Activity

It's an Emergency!

Activity Goal: To apply the cultural information presented in this lesson regarding medical emergencies involving Deaf people.

Activity Instructions:

1. **Ask** students to read *It's an Emergency!* in their workbooks (activity 11.18).

2. **Instruct** students to read each situation and write down some potential communication and access issues and suggest methods of dealing with each.

3. When students have completed recording their answers, you may **choose**:

   Option A: **Show** the overhead (Appendix 11.18) and **discuss** the situations while students correct their own work. You may choose to **ask** the following Thought/Discussion Questions for each of the situations:

   1) What are some potential problems for a Deaf person in this situation?

   2) In this situation, how can communication access be assured?

   3) What are some possible emotional reactions of a Deaf person in this situation?

   4) How might the hearing people in this situation respond?

   OR

   Option B: **Ask** students to complete the above Thought/Discussion Questions in their workbooks. **Collect** for grading or to provide students with written feedback.

Lesson Eleven: *Playing in the Park*

Student Workbook:
Activity 11.18

Overhead Master:
Appendix 11.18

11.18 Experiential Activity

It's an Emergency!

Activity Goal: To apply the cultural information you have learned about medical emergencies and Deaf people.

Activity Instructions: Read each situation below and write down potential communication and access issues and the solutions for each.

1. A Deaf four-year-old goes into the hospital for an emergency operation:
   _____
   _____
   _____

2. A Deaf woman goes into labor three weeks early and is admitted to the hospital:
   _____
   _____
   _____

3. A Deaf construction worker is in a work-related accident:
   _____
   _____
   _____

4. A hearing woman is involved in a car accident and wants her Deaf husband to be called:
   _____
   _____
   _____

Thought/Discussion Questions

1. In these situations, how can communication access be assured?
2. What are some possible emotional reactions of a Deaf person in each of these situations?
3. How might the hearing people in each of these situations respond?

Lesson Eleven: *Playing in the Park*

11.19 Video Learning Experience

Review Session

Viewing Goal: To reinforce recognition and production of the signs introduced in this lesson.

Viewing Instructions:

1. **Ask** students to read *Review Session* in their workbooks (activity 11.19).

2. **Play** the video segment entitled *Review Session* (segment 11.19). Billy reviews all the ASL vocabulary and provides visual cues and origin information. Because the presentation of this segment is beyond the linguistic ability of beginning students, please **turn on** the audio and/or captions to optimize its educational value.

3. **Ask** students to pay careful attention to the signed vocabulary items and take note of visual hints offered by Billy that might help them remember.

4. **Suggest** that students copy the signs to reinforce retention of sign production.

Video Segment Content: (8 Minutes) See the following Student Workbook excerpt for the content of this video segment.

Student Workbook: Activity 11.19

11.19 Video Learning Experience

Review Session

Viewing Goal: To help you remember how to produce the signs introduced in this lesson.

Viewing Instructions: Watch this video segment carefully to see how each sign is produced, and take note of any hints given that might help you remember. You may want to copy the signs as you watch Billy.

The following are the vocabulary and explanations offered in this video segment:

TREE This sign follows the shape of a tree, showing the trunk and all the branches on the top.

TREES The movement of this sign shows not just one tree, but many TREES.

TALL This sign follows the shape of a tree trunk. You have to look up because it is TALL!

CLIMB This sign looks like the action of climbing.

Lesson Eleven: *Playing in the Park*

FLOWER	When you pick a flower you might put it by your nose to smell it... so the sign for FLOWER is made near the nose.
BEAUTIFUL	This comes from the idea of a "beautiful face" so these signs are made around the face.
BLACK+BERRY	As you may remember, the sign for the color BLACK is made on the forehead. The sign for BERRY is made at the tip of your finger. BLACK+BERRY combines these two signs.
BAG/PURSE	This signs shows how you carry a bag or a purse on your arm.
WATER	This is based on the old sign DRINK as in milk, soda, or other beverages. For WATER we use the "W" handshape.
BRIDGE	This sign shows what a bridge looks like, with the support holding up the BRIDGE from underneath.
RIVER	The first part of the sign indicates it is WATER. This is followed by the demonstration of the current or movement of the water.
GRASS	This is an old sign that looks like lying on the ground with the grass in front of your face.
SUN	This sign is made to show the sun as a large circle in the sky. It's like the "eye in the sky."
SUN+SHINE	This shows the round shape of the sun, with the fingers as the sun's rays streaming down.
HOT	This sign is made from the mouth, coming from how the warmth of your breath is used to warm your hands.
LEAF	The index finger of one hand is a twig and the other hand is the leaf which falls off and floats to the ground.
COOL	This comes from how you might fan yourself to cool off, or how the wind feels when it is COOL.
BASEBALL	This sign shows how a person holds and uses a bat.
TENNIS	This sign copies how a person actually plays tennis.
GOLF	This sign looks like taking a swing when playing golf.
FRISBEE	This sign shows how you would toss a Frisbee.
GAME	Each hand represents a person. They challenge one another so the hands hit up against each other.
PICNIC	Two signs are demonstrated. One reflects the enthusiasm for going on the outing (rubbing hands together). The other sign depicts the sandwiches you eat on a PICNIC.
WALK	Each hand represents a foot and the movement shows WALKING.

Instructor's Guide: Lesson Eleven
Bravo ASL! Curriculum

©1996 Sign Enhancers, Inc.
ALL RIGHTS RESERVED.

Lesson Eleven: *Playing in the Park*

RUN Do you remember the sign for FAST? Connect your hands and move the index fingers as shown. This sign means to RUN.

FALL This sign looks like a person falling.

FIND You're looking for something and you find it.

STAY This sign tells you to remain. Don't move.

MOVE You take something from one area and move it to another.

MAN Remember the sign for BOY? Generally, signs referring to males are produced on or around the forehead.

WOMAN Generally, signs that indicate female gender are produced on or near the chin.

FISHING You're holding a long fishing pole... waiting for a bite.

11.20 Video Learning Experience

Practice Session: Sentences

Viewing Goal: To improve comprehension skills by watching sentences presented in ASL.

Viewing Instructions:

1. **Ask** students to read *Practice Session: Sentences* in their workbooks (activity 11.20).

2. **Play** the video segment entitled *Practice Session: Sentences* (segment 11.20). Each sentence is signed twice and an English translation is provided.

3. **Remind** students to watch the face of each signer to see the facial/body expressions and non-manual grammatical markers as well as the signs.

Video Segment Content: The following are English translations of the practice
(2 1/2 Minutes) sentences:

1. The grass is green.
2. That man, Tom, is good at golf!
3. Now the sun is shining hot!
4. The boy throws the Frisbee and the dog runs.
5. The girl ran fast and fell.
6. Which game do you like? Tennis or baseball?
7. Flowers are beautiful.

Lesson Eleven: *Playing in the Park*

Student Workbook:
Activity 11.20

11.20 Video Learning Experience

Practice Session: Sentences

Viewing Goal: To improve your comprehension skills by watching sentences presented in ASL.

Viewing Instructions: Watch the signed sentences for comprehension. Remember to watch the face of each signer to see the facial/body expressions and the non-manual grammatical markers as well as the signs.

It is recommended that you copy each signed sentence when it is repeated.

In the space below, record any questions or notes you have regarding the sentences.

Notes: _____
_____
_____
_____

11.21 Video Learning Experience

Practice Session: Story

Viewing Goal: To improve comprehension skills by watching a story presented in ASL.

Viewing Instructions:
1. **Ask** students to read *Practice Session: Story* in their workbooks (activity 11.21).

2. **Show** the video segment entitled *Practice Session: Story* (segment 11.21). Billy signs a story using the vocabulary introduced in this lesson. **Turn off** audio and captions.

3. **Instruct** students to watch the signed story and write a summary of the main points.

Instructor's Guide: Lesson Eleven
Bravo ASL! Curriculum

©1996 Sign Enhancers, Inc.
ALL RIGHTS RESERVED.

Lesson Eleven: *Playing in the Park*

Video Segment Content:
(3 Minutes)

The following is an English translation of the story:

A man and a woman liked playing games. Unfortunately for the man, the woman beat him all the time.

When they played tennis, the woman beat him. When they played golf, the woman beat him. When they played baseball, the woman beat him! When they went running, the woman beat him!!

The man thought about it and he got a great idea!

"I'll beat her in fishing," he said.

The man and the woman went to the river and cast their lines. Then they looked at each other. The man soon had a bite and pulled in his fish. With pride, he set the fish down and once again cast his line.

The woman fished more diligently. Again, the man caught a fish and put it down with even more pride. He baited his hook and cast his line. The woman continued fishing.

When they finished fishing, the man bragged, "I have six fish."

The woman said, "Wow! You are a good fisherman. Let me count how many fish I have in my basket."

She opened it up and began counting. Then she said, "I have eight fish... I beat you!"

The man once again experienced the agony of defeat.

Student Workbook:
Activity 11.21

11.21 Video Learning Experience

Practice Session: Story

Viewing Goal: To improve your comprehension by watching a story presented in ASL.

Viewing Instructions: Watch the signed story for comprehension. In the space below, write a summary of the main points.

Summary: _____
_____
_____
_____

Lesson Eleven: *Playing in the Park*

11.22 Comprehension Quiz

What Did You Understand?

Quiz Goal: To assess students' comprehension of the signed story.

Quiz Instructions:
1. **Instruct** students to complete the quiz in their workbooks (activity 11.22).

2. **Collect** for grading or **show** overhead (Appendix 11.22) and **ask** individual students to indicate the correct answers on the overhead while class members correct their own work.

3. **Ask** students to indicate which item(s) from the quiz they found difficult. **Review** by **modeling** or **replaying** that segment of the videotape.

Student Workbook:
Activity 11.22

Overhead Master:
Appendix 11.22

11.22 Comprehension Quiz

What Did You Understand?

Quiz Goal: To see how much of the signed story you understood.

Quiz Instructions: Read and answer each question below.

1. Who always won the games?
   A. The woman
   B. The man
   C. The children
   D. The dog

2. The last sport they competed in was _____.
   A. Golf
   B. Frisbee
   C. Running
   D. Fishing

3. The _____ caught the first fish.
   A. Boy
   B. Woman
   C. Man
   D. Girl

4. The man caught ____ fish.
   A. Four
   B. Nine
   C. Six
   D. Eight

5. The woman caught ____ fish.
   A. Eight
   B. Seven
   C. Six
   D. Nine

Instructor's Guide: Lesson Eleven
Bravo ASL! Curriculum

Lesson Eleven: *Playing in the Park*

11.23 Experiential Activity

Use of Space Exercise!

Practice Session: Story

Activity Goal: To improve students' ability to identify use of space features.

Activity Instructions:

1. **Ask** students to read *Use of Space Exercise!* in their workbooks (activity 11.21).

2. **Replay** video segment entitled, *Practice Session: Story* (segment 11.21). Be sure to **turn off** the audio and captions.

3. **Instruct** students to watch Billy's use of space in identifying each of the characters. **Tell** students to stand up when Billy characterizes the woman in the story and sit down when he characterizes the man.

4. When the story is over, **ask** students to draw a picture of the two people fishing.

Student Workbook: Activity 11.23

11.23 Experiential Activity

Use of Space Exercise!

Activity Goal: To help you recognize the use of space ASL grammatical feature.

Activity Instructions: Your teacher will replay the video segment *Practice Session: Story*. When you see Billy showing where the woman is or "becoming" the woman in the story, stand up! When you see Billy showing where the man is or "becoming" the man in the story, sit down!

When the story is over, draw a picture of the man and woman fishing. Don't worry about how good your drawing is, just be sure to locate the people in your picture in the same places Billy put them in his "signed picture."

Picture of the man and woman fishing:

Lesson Eleven: *Playing in the Park*

11.24 Homework Assignment

A Healthy Visit to the Doctor

Homework Goal: To provide students with the opportunity to see if local medical care facilities are prepared to meet the needs of Deaf patients.

Homework Instructions:

1. **Ask** students to read *A Healthy Visit to the Doctor* in their workbooks (activity 11.24).

2. **Instruct** students to visit a local hospital, walk-in clinic, doctor's office, or dentist's office. Once there, they should speak with someone about accessibility for individuals who are Deaf.

3. **Suggest** that students visit their own doctors or dentists or **provide** students with a list of possible local sites to visit. It is strongly recommended that you **contact** these sites in advance to **request** permission for your students to visit.

4. **Model** how students should identify themselves and explain that this interview is part of a class project. **Encourage** students to be courteous and non-judgmental as they conduct their interviews.

5. **Refer** students to the questions listed in their workbooks. Students can use these questions, as well as their own, to interview someone at the clinic.

6. **Ask** students to write a one- to three-page paper based on their interviews.

Instructor Tip: *An opportunity for students to share the results of this assignment has been scheduled in the next lesson (Homework Review 12.2).*

Instructor's Guide: Lesson Eleven
Bravo ASL! Curriculum

Lesson Eleven: *Playing in the Park*

Student Workbook:
Activity 11.24

11.24 Homework Assignment

A Healthy Visit to the Doctor

Homework Goal: To see how well a medical care facility may be prepared to assist Deaf patients.

Homework Instructions: Visit your own doctor or dentist, a local hospital, or clinic. Interview someone about accessibility for Deaf individuals.

You may use the following questions during your interview:

1. If a Deaf person came here looking for medical help, how would you communicate with him/her?
2. Has any type of training been provided to your staff to help them meet the needs of Deaf patients?
3. How often have you provided services to Deaf patients?
4. Do you maintain a list of certified/qualified interpreters to contact?
5. How would you obtain the services of Sign Language interpreters?
6. Who would pay for the interpreting services?
7. Do you have a TDD?
8. Have you ever received a relay call from a Deaf person?

Use the information from your interview to write a one- to three-page paper describing how prepared this medical care facility is to serve Deaf patients.

11.25 Post-test

What Do You Know Now?

Assessment Video

Post-test Goal: To assess students' mastery of the lesson objectives.

Post-test Instructions:
1. **Ask** students to read the Post-test Introduction in their workbooks (activity 11.25).
2. **Copy** and **distribute** the Lesson Eleven Post-test (11.25).
3. **Play** the Assessment Video (segment 11.25) and **allow** students to complete Section One (comprehension portion) of the test.
4. **Instruct** students to complete Section Two (culture and grammar portion) of the test individually and hand in their papers when they are finished.

Lesson Eleven: *Playing in the Park*

5. **Assign** Section Three (expressive portion) of the test and **schedule** a time when students are to perform. If possible, it is strongly recommended that you **videotape** this portion of the Post-test.

6. **Determine** grading options based upon programmatic requirements. A recommended guideline for measuring successful mastery of objectives is 80% accuracy.

Video Segment Content: (2 1/2 Minutes)

The following is an English translation of the comprehension story:

Tom and his brother Jake went to the park. Their father had packed a picnic lunch for them. He had put in two oranges, popcorn, but only one cookie!

Both of the boys wanted the cookie. Tom said, "Let's play baseball. If I beat you, I get to eat the cookie."

Jake said, "No. I have a better idea. Let's play basketball. If I beat you, I can eat the cookie."

Tom said, "No. See that tree over there? If I can climb all the way to the top, the cookie is mine!"

Jake agreed and said, "Okay, you climb the tree."

So Tom began climbing the tree. He made his way higher and higher until he finally reached the top. When he looked down, what did he see? Jake happily eating the cookie!

Tom hurried back down the tree. Jake was standing near the river. Tom gave him a big push and he went flying into the water. Jake laughed hard, as did his brother, Tom. Oh well!

Student Workbook: Activity 11.25

11.25 Post-test Introduction

What Do You Know Now?

Post-test Goal: To assess your mastery of the lesson objectives.

Post-test Introduction: This test has three sections.

Section One: The Comprehension section tests your ability to understand ASL.

Section Two: The Culture and Grammar section tests your knowledge of the material presented in the *Cultural* and *Grammatical Notes*.

Section Three: The Expressive portion tests your ability to use ASL.

Simply follow the instructions for each section. **Good luck!**

Lesson Eleven: *Playing in the Park*

Post-test Master:
Appendix: 11.25

11.25 Post-test

Section One: Comprehension

Instructions: You will see a signed story. Watch the video carefully and then answer each question below.

1. The two boys were named Tom and _____.
   A. Billy
   B. Jim
   C. Sammy
   D. Jake

2. The boys had brought _____.
   A. A football
   B. A picnic lunch
   C. A Frisbee
   D. A basketball

3. Who packed their picnic food?
   A. Their mom
   B. Their younger brother
   C. Their dad
   D. They packed the food themselves

4. What did they both want?
   A. The popcorn
   B. To play with the dog
   C. The orange
   D. The cookie

5. What did Jake do when Tom was in the tree?
   A. Ate the popcorn
   B. Played with the dog
   C. Ate the orange
   D. Ate the cookie

Post-test Master:
Appendix: 11.25

11.25 Post-test

Section Two: Culture and Grammar

Instructions: Read each statement carefully and write your response in the space provided.

6. What information is provided by the use of space feature?

   The relative location and movement of people, things, and events in space.

7. Discuss three concerns that Deaf people experience when faced with medical emergencies.

   Will I understand all that occurs at the hospital?
   Will any of the hospital staff know Sign Language?
   Will an interpreter be available?
   Will the medical staff be sensitive to communication needs?

8. What are three things the staff of a medical clinic could do to communicate with Deaf people in a medical emergency?

   Be willing to use gestures.
   Maintain direct eye contact.
   Look at and speak directly to the Deaf person.
   Be willing to write or draw pictures.

Lesson Eleven: *Playing in the Park*

Post-test Master:
Appendix: 11.25

11.25 Post-test

Section Three: Expressive Portion

Instructions: Create a story about *A Day at the Park*, using at least six signs learned in this lesson. Also sign at least one sentence in which you utilize use of space as taught in this lesson.

Your instructor will schedule a time for you to perform this section of the Post-test. You may prepare and practice prior to your scheduled time. Use the space below to prepare for your expressive performance.

Include at least six signs from Lesson Eleven.

9. _____
10. _____
11. _____
12. _____
13. _____
14. _____

Use of space feature used:

15. _____

Congratulations! You have completed Lesson Eleven!

Lesson 12
THE DOCTOR IS IN!

Materials Needed:

Equipment: VCR and TV monitor
Overhead projector and screen
Optional: video camera for activities 12.19 and 12.32

Materials: Instructor's Guide
Student Workbook: one per student
Overhead Transparencies for activities 12.3, 12.4, 12.5, 12.7, 12.11 12.15, 12.17, 12.21 and 12.29 (see Appendix for masters)
Optional: blank videotape (or have students bring their own) for activities 12.19 and 12.32
Post-test: Appendix 12.32

Videotapes: The Beginning ASL VideoCourse Lesson Twelve
Activities Video for activity 12.15
Assessment Video for Post-test 12.32

12.1 Begin Class

Housekeeping

Goal: To prepare students for this lesson.

Instructions:
1. **Welcome** students to Lesson Twelve of the VideoCourse.
2. **Perform** any necessary tasks (such as taking attendance) that may be required by your specific program.

Lesson Twelve: *The Doctor Is IN!*

12.2 Homework Review

A Healthy Visit to The Doctor

Activity Goal: To provide feedback on previously assigned homework and to reinforce materials learned in earlier lessons.

Activity Instructions:

1. **Ask** students to read *A Healthy Visit to the Doctor* in their workbooks (activity 12.2).

2. You may **choose**:

   Option A: **Lead** a class discussion and **ask** students to share the main points of their homework experience (*Homework Assignment 11.24*). You may want to **use** the following Thought/Discussion Questions:

   1) Where did you go?
   2) Who did you interview?
   3) How did these people react to your questions?
   4) Is there anything you learned that surprised you?
   5) If you were Deaf, would you want to go there in an emergency?
   6) What could be done to improve access at the facility you visited?

   Collect the homework assignment for grading or to provide written feedback.

   OR

   Option B: **Ask** students to read and answer the Thought/Discussion Questions in their workbooks in class or for homework. **Collect** the homework and/or Thought/Discussion Questions for grading or to **provide** students with written feedback.

Lesson Twelve: *The Doctor Is IN!*

Student Workbook: Activity 12.2

12.2 Homework Review

A Healthy Visit to the Doctor

Activity Goal: To help you learn from your homework experience.

Activity Instructions: Read and answer the Thought/Discussion Questions below.

Thought/Discussion Questions

1. Where did you go?
2. Who did you interview?
3. How did people react to your questions?
4. Is there anything you learned that surprised you? If so, what?
5. If you were Deaf, would you want to go to this facility during an emergency?
6. What could be done to improve access to the facility you visited?

12.3 Pretest

What Do You Know?

Pretest Goal: To identify students' current level of knowledge pertaining to the lesson content.

Pretest Instructions:

1. **Ask** students to read and answer the questions in the pretest in their workbooks (activity 12.3).

2. **Show** overhead (Appendix 12.3) and **ask** individual students to indicate the correct answers on the overhead while class members correct their own work.

3. **Inform** students that the contents of the pretest will be taught throughout the lesson.

Lesson Twelve: *The Doctor Is IN!*

Student Workbook:
Activity 12.3

Overhead Master:
Appendix 12.3

12.3 Pretest

What Do You Know?

Pretest Goal: To see how much you already know about what will be taught in this lesson.

Pretest Instructions: Read each question below and circle the best answer.

1. In ASL, a lot of information is given through facial expression.
   A. True
   B. False

2. Each ASL sign has only one meaning and one English word to describe it.
   A. True
   B. False

3. ASL uses facial expression the same way English uses adjectives.
   A. True
   B. False

4. All medical facilities are fully accessible to Deaf people.
   A. True
   B. False

5. Medical facilities and personnel are becoming more sensitive to accessibility issues as they relate to the Deaf community.
   A. True
   B. False

12.4 Lesson Objectives

Planning for Success

Goal: To identify the learning outcomes associated with successful completion of this lesson.

Instructions:
1. **Ask** students to read the lesson objectives in their workbooks (activity 12.4).

2. **Show** overhead (Appendix 12.4) and **read** through the objectives with the class.

Lesson Twelve: *The Doctor Is IN!*

Student Workbook:
Activity 12.4

Overhead Master:
Appendix 12.4

12.4 Lesson Objectives

Planning For Success

Goal: To see what you will learn by the end of this lesson.

Instructions: Read the objectives below.

Upon completing this VideoCourse lesson, you will be able to...

1. Recognize and accurately produce the ASL vocabulary introduced in this and all previous lessons.
2. Identify and explain some of the accessibility issues for Deaf people involved in medical emergencies.
3. Explain the role of facial expression in ASL.
4. Accurately recognize and use facial expression within signed communication.

12.5 Lesson Focus

Help! We Need Help!

Activity Goal: To develop a need for the ASL vocabulary introduced in this lesson.

Activity Instructions:
1. **Ask** students to read *Help! We Need Help!* in their workbooks (activity 12.5).

2. **Tell** students to take a few minutes to consider the situation given in their workbooks (a traveling companion falls and gets hurt in a non-English-speaking setting). **Instruct** students to record their ideas in the space provided.

3. **Divide** the class into groups of four or five for role-playing this situation.

4. **Remind** students that they can use a variety of methods to communicate, such as gesturing, miming, pointing, etc.

5. **Circulate** among the groups to **observe** their progress.

6. **Bring** the whole class together again. **Show** overhead (Appendix 12.5) and **ask** the students to demonstrate the communication strategies they found most effective.

7. **Inform** students that they will learn the signs for these and other medical-related concepts throughout this lesson.

Instructor's Guide: Lesson Twelve
Bravo ASL! Curriculum

©1996 Sign Enhancers, Inc.
ALL RIGHTS RESERVED.

Lesson Twelve: *The Doctor Is IN!*

Student Workbook:
Activity 12.5

Overhead Master:
Appendix 12.5

12.5 Lesson Focus

Help! We Need Help!

Activity Goal: To experience a role-play related to medical emergencies when communication is limited.

Activity Instructions: Imagine that you are traveling in a foreign country. The people do not understand English. Your traveling companion falls on the train and hurts her ankle.

How would you communicate the questions or information below without the use of spoken or written communication?

Remember, you can use a variety of methods to communicate, such as gesturing, miming, pointing, etc.

You may make notes of your ideas below:

1. Where is the hospital? _____
2. My friend fell on a train. _____
3. Her ankle hurts very badly. _____
4. Her ankle is swollen. _____
5. Will she need a shot? _____
6. Will you give her medicine? _____
7. Does she need crutches? _____

12.6 Video Learning Experience

Bravo Family Visit

Welcome to the Lesson

Viewing Goal: To prepare students for the lesson by reviewing the incidents leading to the medical emergency in Lesson Eleven.

Viewing Instructions:

1. **Ask** students to read *Welcome to the Lesson* in their workbooks (activity 12.6).

2. **Play** the video segment of the Bravo family (segment 12.6). Billy reviews the accident that happened in Lesson Eleven.

3. **Instruct** students to watch the segment and take notes to help them remember.

Lesson Twelve: *The Doctor Is IN!*

**Video Segment Content:
(4 Minutes)**

The following is a summary of the Bravo family interaction:

The Bravo family is rushing into the hospital. Dad is carrying Scott, who is injured. They all look worried. Anna hands Scott his shoe and he says, "Thank you."

Billy: Hello! Welcome to another Sign Enhancers, Inc. American Sign Language VideoCourse Lesson.

Wow! I am impressed! In spite of all the pain Scott is having, he is still polite, saying thank you. If I were in his place, I would be complaining and very grouchy.

Remember, the Bravo family went to the park to have fun. Scott was playing with the dog and tossing a Frisbee, which the dog retrieved.

The Frisbee got stuck in a tree. Remember what happened? Well, to help you, we will show it again. Watch.

At the park with Scott and Lady: Scott and Lady were playing Frisbee. Scott threw the Frisbee and it got caught in the tree. Scott knew that Mom and Dad told him not to climb trees, but he tries it anyway.

Scott falls down and tries to get up, but he can't. He sends Lady to get Mom and Dad.

Billy: We're at the hospital. Scott was brought here because of an injury to his ankle. We don't know if it was twisted, sprained, or broken; but we will know after the doctor examines the ankle.

In today's video lesson, we will be focusing on signs related to medicine. You will be learning medical signs. I have a few I want to show you right now.

Student Workbook:
Activity 12.6

12.6 Video Learning Experience

Welcome to the Lesson

Viewing Goal: To review how Scott got hurt in the park.

Viewing Instructions: Watch the signed interaction and take notes to help you remember.

Notes: _____
_____
_____
_____

Instructor's Guide: Lesson Twelve
Bravo ASL! Curriculum

Lesson Twelve: *The Doctor Is IN!*

12.7 Language Learning Instruction

Learning New Signs

Goal: To use ASL and visual aids to introduce this lesson's vocabulary.

Instructions:
1. **Ask** students to read *Learning New Signs* in their workbooks (activity 12.7).

2. **Show** the overhead (Appendix 12.7). **Introduce** the vocabulary by **pointing** to items presented in the pictures while **demonstrating** the signs.

3. **Reinforce** retention and **check** students' comprehension by **using** these signs to **ask** students questions.

   Note: For a step-by-step review of this method, see Lesson One (activities 1.6 and 1.12).

4. **Continue** this process until all the ASL vocabulary items have been introduced.

Overhead Content: Use the pictures in the overhead (Appendix 12.7) to introduce the signs representing the following concepts:

1. HOSPITAL
2. DOCTOR
3. NURSE
4. EMERGENCY
5. TAKE-CARE-OF
6. HURT/PAIN
7. ALL-RIGHT/RIGHTS
8. COMMUNICATE
9. WAIT
10. INTERPRET
11. INTERPRETER
12. HOLD/HUG

Note: Some pictures can be used to represent several concepts. For verbs and more abstract concepts, you may need to supplement these pictures with mime, gestures, using actual objects, and acting out the concepts in class.

Lesson Twelve: *The Doctor Is IN!*

Overhead Master:
Appendix 12.7

Student Workbook:
Activity 12.7

12.7 Language Learning Instruction

Learning New Signs

Goal: To help you learn new ASL vocabulary.

Instructions: Your instructor will teach you new signs! Watch closely to learn what these signs mean and how they are produced.

In the space below, record any notes to help you remember the signs.

Notes: _____
_____
_____

Lesson Twelve: *The Doctor Is IN!*

12.8 Video Learning Experience

Introduction to New Vocabulary

Viewing Goal: To provide a signed demonstration of the accurate production of the new ASL vocabulary.

Viewing Instructions:
1. **Ask** students to read *Introduction to New Vocabulary* in their workbooks (activity 12.8).

2. **Play** the video segment entitled *Introduction to New Vocabulary* (segment 12.8). Billy introduces and signs each new vocabulary item twice. (If you wish to keep this a strictly visual presentation, **turn off** audio.)

3. **Instruct** students to watch how Billy produces the signs as well as the accompanying facial/body expressions.

4. **Ask** students to copy the signs and the facial/body expressions as Billy repeats each one.

Video Segment Content: See the following Student Workbook excerpt for the content
(2 1/2 Minutes) of this video segment.

Student Workbook: Activity 12.8

12.8 Video Learning Experience

Introduction to New Vocabulary

Viewing Goal: To help you learn new ASL vocabulary.

Viewing Instructions: Watch how Billy produces each sign. Be sure to notice the facial/body expressions. Copy the signs as Billy repeats each one.

Signs representing the following concepts are introduced:

1. HOSPITAL
2. DOCTOR
3. NURSE
4. EMERGENCY
5. TAKE-CARE
6. HURT/PAIN
7. ALL-RIGHT/RIGHTS
8. COMMUNICATE
9. WAIT
10. INTERPRET
11. INTERPRETER
12. HOLD/HUG

Instructor's Guide: Lesson Twelve
Bravo ASL! Curriculum

©1996 Sign Enhancers, Inc.
ALL RIGHTS RESERVED.

Lesson Twelve: *The Doctor Is IN!*

12.9 Experiential Activity

Point and Sign

Activity Goal: To improve students' receptive and expressive ASL skills.

Activity Instructions:

1. **Ask** students to read *Point and Sign* in their workbooks (activity 12.9).

2. **Divide** the class into pairs.

3. **Select** and **model** the variation of the *Point and Sign* activity you would like your students to perform.

    Variation A:
    1) **Ask** students to take turns pointing to an object or action in the picture and producing a signed sentence that best matches its meaning.
    2) **Instruct** partners to provide feedback on the correct choice and production of the signs.

    Variation B:
    1) **Ask** pairs to have one student point to an object or action in the picture.
    2) **Instruct** the partners to produce a signed sentence that best matches its meaning.

    Variation C:
    1) **Ask** pairs to have one student produce a sign or sentence that corresponds to one of the objects or actions in the picture.
    2) **Instruct** the partners to point to the object or action in the picture that best matches the meaning of the sign or sentence.

    Variation D:
    1) **Ask** pairs to have one student use ASL to ask a question about one of the items in the pictures.
    2) Instruct the partners to respond to the question using ASL and point to the item in the picture.

4. **Inform** students that this activity is to be done using ASL (no voices needed!).

5. **Circulate** among the pairs to **observe** student performance and **assist** as needed.

Lesson Twelve: *The Doctor Is IN!*

Student Workbook: Activity 12.9

12.9 Experiential Activity

Point and Sign

Activity Goal: To improve your ASL receptive and expressive skills.

Activity Instructions: Using the pictures below, follow your teacher's instructions and practice using your new sign vocabulary, such as: HOSPITAL; DOCTOR; NURSE; EMERGENCY; HURT; COMMUNICATE; INTERPRET; INTERPRETER; and HOLD.

12.10 Video Learning Experience

Bravo Family Visit

Viewing Goal: To improve ASL comprehension skills by watching a Bravo family interaction.

Viewing Instructions:
1. **Ask** students to read *Bravo Family Visit* in their workbooks (activity 12.10).

2. **Play** the video segment of the Bravo family (segment 12.10). The Bravos will use the new ASL vocabulary within the context of a trip to the hospital. Because this segment includes an interaction with a hearing person, **turn on** audio and/or captions to optimize its educational value.

Lesson Twelve: *The Doctor Is IN!*

3. **Instruct** students to watch for comprehension and write a summary of the main points.

4. **Replay** any portion of this video segment that students experienced difficulty understanding.

Video Segment Content:
(2 1/2 Minutes)

The following is a summary of the Bravo family interaction:

Mom goes to the receptionist and explains that Scott hurt himself. (She is signing and using her voice at the same time.) The receptionist asks if Scott is Deaf. Mom tells her that he and the rest of her family are Deaf. The nurse gives her some paperwork to fill out.

Dad puts Scott down in the waiting room and goes to speak to the receptionist. Mom interprets for him. Dad explains that he and Scott need to be involved in all communication and tells the receptionist that the hospital is required by law to hire an interpreter. He asks her if she has a list of certified interpreters. She tells him to have a seat and she will make some calls.

Billy: Good for them! The Bravos know their rights. Even though Scott is suffering, they are able to require that their rights be fulfilled. That's good! And they are educating others about those rights. It is very difficult for injured Deaf people to act as advocates for themselves in times of crisis. Many hospitals have no knowledge of their responsibility as dictated by federal law.

In the past, Deaf people were frustrated trying to fulfill their medical needs because clear communication was not established with the doctor. The doctors were frustrated, as they could not explain the diagnosis and treatment. Today, this has improved. But we still have a long way to go.

By studying these tapes and learning about American Sign Language and Deaf culture, you are helping to bridge the communication gap between the Deaf and hearing communities. Now, let's go back and see what is happening to the Bravo family. Let's watch, OK?

Lesson Twelve: *The Doctor Is IN!*

Student Workbook:
Activity 12.10

12.10 Video Learning Experience

Bravo Family Visit

Viewing Goal: To learn about Deaf people's right to access in the medical setting by watching a Bravo family interaction.

Viewing Instructions: Watch the video and take note of new information.

Summary: _____
_____
_____
_____

12.11 Cultural Quiz

What Did You Learn?

Quiz Goal: To assess students' comprehension of the cultural aspects regarding access which are depicted in the Bravo family interaction.

Quiz Instructions:
1. **Instruct** students to complete the quiz in their workbooks (activity 12.11).

2. **Collect** for grading or **show** overhead (Appendix 12.11) and **ask** individual students to indicate the correct answers on the overhead while class members correct their own work.

Lesson Twelve: *The Doctor Is IN!*

Student Workbook:
Activity 12.11

Overhead Master:
Appendix 12.11

12.11 Cultural Quiz

What Did You Learn?

Quiz Goal: To see what cultural aspects of the Bravo family interaction you understood.

Quiz Instructions: Read and answer each question below.

1. Why is Mom signing and talking at the same time when she is at the hospital?
   She is communicating with the hearing receptionist who doesn't sign and she wants to be sure her family understands what is happening.

2. Why is it important for hospitals to know about the rights of the Deaf community *before* a Deaf person visits?
   It is very difficult for injured Deaf people to act as advocates for themselves in times of crisis.

3. Why are Deaf people frustrated as they try to fulfill their medical needs?
   Clear communication is not always established with the doctor.

4. Dad served as an advocate for the rights of Deaf people. How did he do this?
   He informed the receptionist of the hospital's legal obligation to hire an interpreter.

12.12 Video Learning Experience

Bravo Family Visit

Viewing Goal: To improve ASL comprehension skills by watching a Bravo family interaction.

Viewing Instructions:

1. **Ask** students to read *Bravo Family Visit* in their workbooks (activity 12.12).

2. **Play** the video segment of the Bravo family (segment 12.12). The Bravos will use the new ASL vocabulary within the context of a trip to the hospital. Included in this interaction is "Doctor" Billy's examination of a sick Deaf patient. Because this segment includes an interaction with a hearing person, **turn on** audio and/or captions to optimize its educational value.

3. **Instruct** students to watch for comprehension and write a summary of the main points.

4. **Replay** any portion of this video segment that students experienced difficulty understanding.

Instructor's Guide: Lesson Twelve
Bravo ASL! Curriculum

©1996 Sign Enhancers, Inc.
ALL RIGHTS RESERVED.

Lesson Twelve: *The Doctor Is IN!*

**Video Segment Content:
(4 1/2 Minutes)**

The following is a summary of the signed interactions:

In the waiting room: The receptionist tells the family that she has requested an interpreter. The agency will be sending someone as soon as possible. The receptionist asks the Bravos if they would like to wait for the interpreter or see the doctor immediately.

Anna suggests that Mom interpret so Scott doesn't have to wait in pain. Scott wants the doctor to help him right away.

Dad tells the woman (with Mom interpreting) that they want to go ahead and see the doctor right away. They hope the interpreter shows up soon, because Mom can't hold Scott and interpret at the same time.

Dad tells the woman he will start filling out the forms.

Billy: Hi again! While the Bravo family is waiting for the doctor, let's go ahead and learn some more new signs related to the medical experience. We will learn these signs by observing a doctor who is very handsome and brilliant. As he meets with his patients, watch carefully and you will learn more new signs. Here's the doctor.

("Doctor" Billy walks out in a doctor's uniform.) As I told you, the doctor is very handsome and brilliant. Watch him and you will learn more new signs.

Doctor Billy: Now, there is a long line of sick and injured people. I need to get to work and begin my examinations. I'll see you later. Good-bye!

Billy: Good luck!

Doctor Billy helping patients: The doctor walks in to greet his first patient. The patient explains that he has a stomachache. The doctor asks him about his symptoms. He explains that he's been nauseous and throwing up.

Doctor Billy: Did you see that? This is the sign for NAUSEA. This sign (VOMIT) is pretty obvious. It requires no explanation. This patient could have the flu, or maybe it was something he ate. I think I should check his temperature. Wouldn't you agree?

The doctor puts a thermometer in the patient's mouth. The patient explains that he was nauseous and vomited that morning.

Doctor Billy: Did you see that? It's pretty cool. One of the advantages of Sign Language is that you can talk with a thermometer in your mouth!

Lesson Twelve: *The Doctor Is IN!*

The patient goes on to explain that on the day before he ate a hamburger. After taking a few bites, he looked at the hamburger and saw that it was green! Now the doctor understands why the patient is sick.

Doctor Billy: Why don't you check up on the Bravo family and I will take care of my patient. Green hamburger! Now I am nauseated!

Student Workbook: Activity 12.12

12.12 Video Learning Experience

Bravo Family Visit

Viewing Goal: To improve ASL comprehension skills by watching a signed interaction.

Viewing Instructions: Watch the signed interaction and write a summary of the main points.

Summary: _____
_____
_____
_____

12.13 Video Learning Experience

Bravo Family Visit

Viewing Goal: To improve ASL comprehension skills by watching a Bravo family interaction.

Viewing Instructions:
1. **Ask** students to read *Bravo Family Visit* in their workbooks (activity 12.13).

2. **Play** the video segment of the Bravo family (segment 12.13). The Bravos will use the new ASL vocabulary while in the waiting room at the hospital.

3. **Instruct** students to watch for comprehension and write a summary of the main points.

4. **Replay** any portion of this video segment that students experienced difficulty understanding.

Instructor's Guide: Lesson Twelve
Bravo ASL! Curriculum

©1996 Sign Enhancers, Inc.
ALL RIGHTS RESERVED.

Lesson Twelve: *The Doctor Is IN!*

Video Segment Content:
(1 1/2 Minutes)

The following is a summary of the Bravo family interaction:

Back in the waiting room: Mom is holding Scott and Dad is filling out paperwork. Dad asks Mom if she has the insurance card. She doesn't, so Dad checks his wallet and finds it.

Anna is surprised at all the information the hospital requests: name, address, place of work, insurance company, and insurance number! Dad agrees with her. He doesn't like paperwork.

Billy: Wow! Dad's face is really animated. Now I would like to give you a quick *Grammatical Note*.

Student Workbook:
Activity 12.13

12.13 Video Learning Experience

Bravo Family Visit

Viewing Goal: To improve ASL comprehension skills by watching a Bravo family interaction.

Viewing Instructions: Watch the signed interaction and write a summary of the main points.

Summary: _____
_____
_____
_____

12.14 Video Learning Experience

Grammatical Notes

Viewing Goal: To assist students in learning about the grammatical aspects of ASL.

Viewing Instructions:
1. **Ask** students to read *Grammatical Notes* in their workbooks (activity 12.14).

2. **Play** the video segment entitled *Grammatical Notes* (segment 12.14). Because the presentation of this segment is beyond the linguistic ability of beginning students, please **turn on** the audio and/or captions to optimize its educational value.

Lesson Twelve: *The Doctor Is IN!*

3. **Instruct** students to view the segment.

4. At completion of segment, **review** the content presented and **answer** any questions students may have.

Video Segment Content: See the following Student Workbook excerpt for the content
(2 1/2 Minutes) of this video segment.

Student Workbook: Activity 12.14

12.14 Video Learning Experience

Grammatical Notes

Viewing Goal: To learn about the grammatical aspects of ASL.

Viewing Instructions: View the *Grammatical Notes* carefully for the following:

I. ASL uses facial expression to complete and enhance the meaning of the signed message:

 A. Dad didn't like filling out the forms so a negative expression was used with the signs:

 eyes rolling and negative expression on face
 PAPER+PAPER+WRITE+WRITE

 B. Billy demonstrates how you can adjust the expression that goes with these same signs to indicate, "happily filling out forms,"

 happy expression on face
 PAPER+PAPER+WRITE+WRITE

II. Expression can change the meaning of signs through degree. Facial expressions serve as the adjectives of the message or sentence. For example, Billy demonstrates how the sign HEADACHE can have three different meanings, depending on the accompanying facial expression:

 A. SMALL HEADACHE

 B. MILD HEADACHE

 C. TERRIBLE HEADACHE

III. Facial expression is a natural part of ASL. A lack of expression can make the signer look like a robot.

Lesson Twelve: *The Doctor Is IN!*

12.15 Experiential Activity

What Kind of Face Is That?

Activities Video

Activity Goal: To apply the grammatical information by identifying the meaning of facial expressions within the context of sentences presented in ASL.

Activity Instructions:

1. **Ask** students to read *What Kind of Face is That?* in their workbooks (activity 12.15).

2. **Inform** students that they will see several sentences presented in ASL. **Instruct** them to select the adjective that best describes the emotion expressed in each sentence and circle each answer in their workbooks.

3. **Play** the Activities Video (segment 12.15).

4. When the activity is finished, **show** overhead (Appendix 12.15) and **ask** individual students to indicate the correct answers on the overhead while class members correct their own work.

Video Segment Content: (4 Minutes)

The following are English translations of the signed sentences:

1. I'm going to school tomorrow. (sad)
2. I'm going to school tomorrow. (happy)
3. I am working. (bored)
4. I am working. (happy)
5. I'm going to the park to play baseball. (happy)
6. There's a spider in my bed.. (scared)
7. My mom gave me a dog. (happy)
8. I got a shot that really hurt. (sad)
9. I want to go shopping. (happy)
10. My computer broke. (sad)

Lesson Twelve: *The Doctor Is IN!*

Student Workbook:
Activity 12.15

Overhead Master:
Appendix 12.15

12.15 Experiential Activity

What Kind of Face is That?

Activity Goal: To help you recognize the emotions expressed with facial expressions in ASL.

Activity Instructions: You will see ten sentences signed in ASL. Watch the facial/body expressions of each signer and circle the adjective that best describes the emotion shown in each signed sentence.

1.	Happy	**Sad**	Bored	Scared
2.	**Happy**	Sad	Bored	Scared
3.	Happy	Sad	**Bored**	Scared
4.	**Happy**	Sad	Bored	Scared
5.	**Happy**	Sad	Bored	Scared
6.	Happy	Sad	Bored	**Scared**
7.	**Happy**	Sad	Bored	Scared
8.	Happy	**Sad**	Bored	Scared
9.	**Happy**	Sad	Bored	Scared
10.	Happy	**Sad**	Bored	Scared

12.16 Video Learning Experience

Bravo Family Visit

Viewing Goal: To improve ASL comprehension skills by watching a Bravo family interaction.

Viewing Instructions:
1. **Ask** students to read *Bravo Family Visit* in their workbooks (activity 12.16).

2. **Play** the video segment of the Bravo family (segment 12.16). The Bravos will use the new ASL vocabulary while Scott is being examined by the doctor. Because the segment includes an interaction with a hearing person, **turn on** audio and/or captions to optimize its educational value.

3. **Instruct** students to watch the interaction and write a summary of the main points.

4. **Replay** any portion of this video segment that students experienced difficulty understanding.

Lesson Twelve: *The Doctor Is IN!*

Video Segment Content: (2 1/2 Minutes)

The following is a summary of the Bravo family interaction:

Back in the waiting room: Mom is still holding Scott. Dad asks him how he is doing. Scott describes his pain. A nurse comes with a wheelchair and gestures for Scott to sit in it.

Mom and Scott are in the examining room and the doctor comes in and introduces himself. The doctor asks Mom if she will be interpreting. Mom explains that she will until the arrival of the interpreter that the hospital called.

The doctor asks Scott what happened and Scott describes his accident. The doctor jokes with Scott about his doing some experiments with gravity. Scott asks what gravity means and the doctor explains it. The doctor begins the examination.

Scott asks the doctor if his ankle is broken. The doctor tells him he thinks that it is only sprained, but that they will do some X-rays to make sure.

The nurse comes in and informs Mom that the interpreter has arrived.

Student Workbook: Activity 12.16

12.16 Video Learning Experience

Bravo Family Visit

Viewing Goal: To learn more about how Deaf people are treated in a medical setting.

Viewing Instructions: Watch the signed interaction and write a summary of the main points.

Summary: _____
_____
_____
_____

Lesson Twelve: *The Doctor Is IN!*

12.17 Language Learning Instruction

Learning New Signs

Goal: To use ASL and visual aids to introduce this lesson's vocabulary.

Instructions:
1. **Ask** students to read *Learning New Signs* in their workbooks (activity 12.17).

2. **Show** the overhead (Appendix 12.17). **Introduce** the vocabulary by **pointing** to items presented in the pictures while **demonstrating** the signs.

3. **Reinforce** retention and **check** students' comprehension by **using** these signs to **ask** students questions.

    Note: For a step-by-step review of this method, see Lesson One (activities 1.6 and 1.12).

4. **Continue** this process until all the ASL vocabulary items have been introduced.

Overhead Content: Use the pictures in overhead (Appendix 12.17) to introduce the signs representing the following concepts:

1. SICK
2. FEEL
3. HOW
4. MEDICINE
5. SNEEZE
6. COLD
7. COUGH
8. SORE-THROAT
9. PILL
10. TEMPERATURE

Note: Some pictures can be used to represent several concepts. For verbs and more abstract concepts, you may need to supplement these pictures with mime, gestures, using actual objects, and acting out the concepts in class.

Lesson Twelve: *The Doctor Is IN!*

Overhead Master: Appendix 12.17

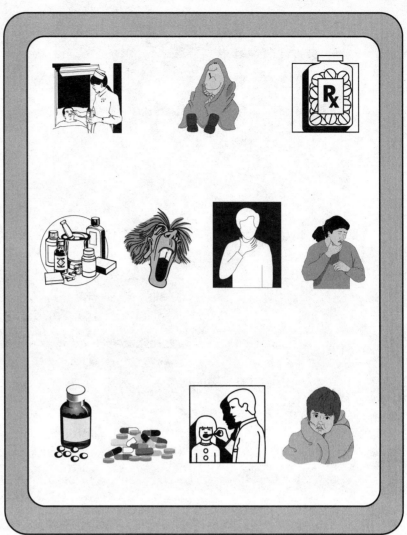

Student Workbook: Activity 12.17

12.17 Language Learning Instruction

Learning New Signs

Goal: To help you learn new ASL vocabulary.

Instructions: Your instructor will teach you new signs! Watch closely to learn what these signs mean and how they are produced.

In the space below, record any notes to help you remember the signs.

Notes: _____
_____
_____
_____

Lesson Twelve: *The Doctor Is IN!*

12.18 Video Learning Experience

Introduction to New Vocabulary

Viewing Goal: To provide a signed demonstration of the accurate production of the new ASL vocabulary.

Viewing Instructions:
1. **Ask** students to read *Introduction to New Vocabulary* in their workbooks (activity 12.18).

2. **Play** the video segment entitled *Introduction to New Vocabulary* (segment 12.18). Billy introduces and signs each new vocabulary item twice. (If you wish to keep this a strictly visual presentation, **turn off** audio.)

3. **Instruct** students to watch how Billy produces the signs and the accompanying facial/body expressions.

4. **Ask** students to copy the signs and the facial/body expressions as Billy repeats each one.

Video Segment Content: See the following Student Workbook excerpt for the content
(1 1/2 Minutes) of this video segment.

Student Workbook: Activity 12.18

12.18 Video Learning Experience

Introduction to New Vocabulary

Viewing Goal: To help you learn new ASL vocabulary.

Viewing Instructions: Watch how Billy produces each sign. Be sure to notice the facial/body expressions. Copy the signs as Billy repeats each one.

Signs representing the following concepts are introduced:

1. SICK
2. FEEL
3. HOW
4. MEDICINE
5. SNEEZE
6. COLD
7. COUGH
8. SORE-THROAT
9. PILL
10. TEMPERATURE

Instructor's Guide: Lesson Twelve
Bravo ASL! Curriculum

©1996 Sign Enhancers, Inc.
ALL RIGHTS RESERVED.

Lesson Twelve: *The Doctor Is IN!*

12.19 Experiential Activity

Diagnosis Dialogue

Activity Goal: To improve students' ASL expressive and receptive skills.

Activity Instructions:

1. **Ask** students to read *Diagnosis Dialogue* in their workbooks (activity 12.19).

2. **Divide** the class into pairs.

3. **Instruct** students to create a dialogue in which one student role-plays a doctor and the other a patient. **Ask** the patient to use the new vocabulary to describe his/her symptoms to the doctor. **Tell** the doctor to make a diagnosis and recommendation for treatment using the new vocabulary.

4. After the dialogues have been developed, **ask** students to share their dialogues with the class. If possible, **videotape** each student's performance of this activity.

5. **Correct** production by **modeling** as needed.

Student Workbook: Activity 12.19

12.19 Experiential Activity

Diagnosis Dialogue

Activity Goal: To improve your expressive and receptive ASL skills.

Activity Instructions: Work with a partner. Decide who will role-play the doctor and who will role-play the patient.

Using ASL (no voices needed!), create a dialogue in which the patient tells the doctor what is wrong and the doctor makes a diagnosis and treatment recommendation.

Be sure to use your new vocabulary including: SICK; FEEL; HOW; MEDICINE; SNEEZE; COLD; COUGH; SORE-THROAT; PILL; and TEMPERATURE.

Be prepared to share this dialogue with the class!

Lesson Twelve: *The Doctor Is IN!*

12.20 Video Learning Experience

Bravo Family Visit

Viewing Goal: To improve ASL comprehension skills by watching a signed interaction.

Viewing Instructions:
1. **Ask** students to read *Bravo Family Visit* in their workbooks (activity 12.20).
2. **Play** the video segment of "Doctor" Billy examining another patient (segment 12.20).
3. **Instruct** students to watch for comprehension and write a summary of the main points.
4. **Replay** any portion of this video segment that students experienced difficulty understanding.

Video Segment Content:
(2 1/2 Minutes)

The following is a summary of the Bravo family interaction:

A little boy (Billy in disguise) walks into the room sneezing. The doctor hands him a tissue. The patient explains that he has been sneezing a lot. The doctor asks him how he is feeling and if he has been coughing. The patient tells the doctor he feels okay and that he has not been coughing. Then he coughs! He tells the doctor he has been coughing a little. The doctor asks him if he has a sore throat and he says yes.

The doctor tells him that he probably has a cold. The patient looks frightened and asks if he is going to have to get a shot. The doctor tells him he doesn't need a shot or medicine. He also tells him that he can't go to school. The patient is happy. The doctor then informs him that he cannot play, either.

The patient looks sad. The doctor asks the patient to go get his mother and bring her back with him. The patient leaves.

Lesson Twelve: *The Doctor Is IN!*

Student Workbook:
Activity 12.20

12.20 Video Learning Experience

Bravo Family Visit

Viewing Goal: To improve your ASL comprehension skills by watching a signed interaction.

Viewing Instructions: Watch the signed interaction and write a summary of the main points.

Summary: _____
_____
_____
_____

12.21 Comprehension Quiz

What Did You Understand?

Quiz Goal: To assess students' comprehension of the signed interaction.

Quiz Instructions:
1. **Instruct** students to complete the quiz in their workbooks (activity 12.21).

2. **Collect** for grading or **show** overhead (Appendix 12.21) and **ask** individual students to indicate the correct answers on the overhead while class members correct their own work.

3. **Ask** students to indicate which item(s) from the quiz they found difficult. **Review** by **modeling** or **replaying** that segment of the videotape.

Lesson Twelve: *The Doctor Is IN!*

Student Workbook:
Activity 12.21

Overhead Master:
Appendix 12.21

12.21 Comprehension Quiz

What Did You Understand?

Quiz Goal: To see how much of the doctor/patient interaction you understood.

Quiz Instructions: Read the questions and circle the best answer.

1. According to Dr. Billy's patient, what is the problem?
   A. He has a fever.
   B. He's nauseated.
   C. He's been sneezing a lot.
   D. He broke his leg.

2. Dr. Billy asks the patient if he's been coughing.
   A. True
   B. False

3. The patient told the doctor he has a sore throat.
   A. True
   B. False

4. The patient is afraid of _____.
   A. The doctor
   B. Getting a shot
   C. Missing school
   D. Losing his teddy bear

5. The patient was happy because he would miss school, but sad because_____.
   A. He has to stay in the hospital.
   B. He has to take medicine.
   C. He has to get a shot.
   D. He has to rest and can't play.

12.22 Video Learning Experience

Bravo Family Visit

Viewing Goal: To improve ASL comprehension skills by watching a Bravo family interaction.

Viewing Instructions:
1. **Ask** students to read *Bravo Family Visit* in their workbooks (activity 12.22).

2. **Play** the video segment of Scott being treated by the doctor (segment 12.22). The Bravos will use the new ASL vocabulary within the context of Scott's examination. Because this segment includes an interaction with a hearing person, **turn on** audio and/or captions to optimize its educational value.

Lesson Twelve: *The Doctor Is IN!*

3. **Instruct** students to watch for comprehension.

4. When the segment is over, **divide** the class into pairs.

5. **Tell** pairs to take turns using ASL to sign a summary of this interaction.

6. When the signed summaries have been developed, **ask** individuals to share their signed summary with the whole class.

Video Segment Content: The following is a summary of the Bravo family interaction:
(3 Minutes)

Scott in the examining room: The doctor is looking at Scott's X-rays. Scott asks if his ankle is broken. The doctor tells him it is only sprained. An interpreter is there to assist with communication. Mom informs everyone that she is going back to the waiting room to tell Dad and Anna what is happening.

The doctor then tells Scott that sprains are treated with "rice." Scott looks confused and asks what he means. The doctor explains: "R" stands for rest, "I" for ice, "C" for compression, and "E" for elevation.

The doctor jokingly tells Scott not to experiment with gravity. The interpreter checks to see if Scott knows what "gravity" means and he tells her he does. She interprets the joke and Scott laughs.

The doctor brings Scott crutches and he heads out the door.

Back in the waiting room Dad and Anna are playing "Thumbs" while they wait. Mom comes in and tells them that Scott's foot is only sprained. Anna asks if the doctor took an X-ray of Scott's foot. Dad asks if Scott needs a shot or medicine. Mom doesn't know. She tells them that the doctor is wrapping Scott's foot and also that Scott can't walk for ten days; he has to use crutches.

Student Workbook:
Activity 12.22

12.22 Video Learning Experience

Bravo Family Visit

Viewing Goal: To improve ASL comprehension skills by watching a Bravo family interaction.

Viewing Instructions: Watch the signed interaction and be prepared to use ASL to produce a summary of the main points.

Summary: _____
_____
_____
_____

Lesson Twelve: *The Doctor Is IN!*

12.23 Video Learning Experience

Cultural Notes

Viewing Goal: To assist students in learning about the cultural aspects of ASL.

Viewing Instructions:
1. **Ask** students to read *Cultural Notes* in their workbooks (activity 12.23).

2. **Play** the video segment entitled *Cultural Notes* (segment 12.23). Because the presentation of this segment is beyond the linguistic ability of beginning students, please **turn on** the audio and/or captions to optimize its educational value.

3. **Instruct** students to view the segment.

4. At the completion of the video segment, **review** the content presented and **answer** any questions students may have.

Video Segment Content: (1 Minute) See the following Student Workbook excerpt for the content of this video segment.

Student Workbook: Activity 12.23

12.23 Video Learning Experience

Cultural Notes

Viewing Goal: To help you learn about the cultural aspects of ASL.

Viewing Instructions: View the *Cultural Notes* segment carefully for the following:

I. Awareness and sensitivity about Deaf patients' needs are growing in the medical community.

II. Medical services are becoming more accessible because of:
   A. Deaf people's activism.
   B. State and federal legislation.
   C. People like you learning to interact with the Deaf community.

Instructor's Guide: Lesson Twelve
Bravo ASL! Curriculum
©1996 Sign Enhancers, Inc.
ALL RIGHTS RESERVED.

Lesson Twelve: *The Doctor Is IN!*

12.24 Video Learning Experience

Bravo Family Visit

Viewing Goal: To improve ASL comprehension skills by watching a Bravo family interaction.

Viewing Instructions:
1. **Ask** students to read *Bravo Family Visit* in their workbooks (activity 12.24).
2. **Play** the video segment of the Bravo family leaving the hospital (segment 12.24). The Bravos will use the new ASL vocabulary as they leave the hospital.
3. **Instruct** students to watch for comprehension.
4. When the video segment is over, **divide** the class into pairs.
5. **Tell** each pair to re-enact the scene between Scott and Anna. **Inform** students the role-play need not be exactly the same, but they should try to include the main points.
6. After the role-plays are developed, **ask** pairs to demonstrate their re-enactment for the class.

Video Segment Content: The following is a summary of the Bravo family interaction:
(1 1/2 Minutes)

The Bravo family outside the hospital: The family walks out of the hospital together. Scott is on crutches. Mom and Dad go to get the car. Anna offers to help Scott while he is on crutches. Scott thanks her and tells her that he will be sitting around while she is working and working. Anna looks sad. Scott tells her to smile; he is only teasing. Anna tells him that she was only teasing when she said she would help him!

Student Workbook:
Activity 12.24

12.24 Video Learning Experience

Bravo Family Visit

Viewing Goal: To improve ASL comprehension skills by watching a Bravo family interaction.

Viewing Instructions: Watch the signed interaction and be prepared to role-play the "discussion" between Scott and Anna.

Note: Your role-play does not have to be exactly the same as the video, but try to include the main points.

Instructor's Guide: Lesson Twelve
Bravo ASL! Curriculum

©1996 Sign Enhancers, Inc.
ALL RIGHTS RESERVED.

Lesson Twelve: *The Doctor Is IN!*

12.25 Video Learning Experience

Review Session

Viewing Goal: To reinforce recognition and production of the signs introduced in this lesson.

Viewing Instructions:

1. **Ask** students to read *Review Session* in their workbooks (activity 12.25).

2. **Play** the video segment entitled *Review Session* (segment 12.25). Billy reviews all the ASL vocabulary and provides visual cues and origin information. Because the presentation of this segment is beyond the linguistic ability of beginning students, please **turn on** the audio and/or captions to optimize its educational value.

3. **Ask** students to pay careful attention to the signed vocabulary items and take note of visual hints offered by Billy that might help them remember.

4. **Suggest** that students copy the signs to reinforce retention of sign production.

Video Segment Content: (9 Minutes)

See the following Student Workbook excerpt for the content of this video segment.

Student Workbook: Activity 12.25

12.25 Video Learning Experience

Review Session

Viewing Goal: To help you remember how to produce the signs introduced in this lesson.

Viewing Instructions: Watch this video segment carefully to see how each sign is produced, and take note of any hints given that might help you remember. You may want to copy the signs as you watch Billy.

The following are the vocabulary and explanations:

HOSPITAL	This sign follows the shape of a medical (Red Cross) symbol on the shoulder.
DOCTOR	This sign shows how a doctor takes a patient's pulse.
NURSE	It's the same idea as DOCTOR, but we use the "N" handshape.
EMERGENCY	This sign shows the flashing lights of an ambulance carrying an injured person.
TAKE-CARE	This sign actually comes from the sign meaning CAREFUL. You are directing that care to another person.

Instructor's Guide: Lesson Twelve
Bravo ASL! Curriculum

©1996 Sign Enhancers, Inc.
ALL RIGHTS RESERVED.

Lesson Twelve: *The Doctor Is IN!*

HURT/PAIN	This is like wringing something out, a painful twist in opposite directions. It hurts!
RIGHTS	This is a symbol for the concept RIGHTS. Your facial expression is very important to this sign.
COMMUNICATION	This shows communication going between two people.
INTERPRET	There is a message and you need to express the same meaning in a different language.
INTERPRETER	The AGENT sign is added to the sign for INTERPRET to mean a person who interprets, or an INTERPRETER.
HUG/HOLD	When you hug or hold a person, you do it like this.
UNDERSTAND	It's like a light bulb switches on when you UNDERSTAND.
WAIT	This sign mimics the body's posture and behavior when you are waiting.
FEEL	This is like touching something to see how it feels. You are touching the heart to show your FEELINGS.
SICK	This is like the recent explanation for FEEL. When you are sick, how do you feel in your stomach and your head? Your facial expression must reflect the feeling SICK.
STOMACH	This sign shows where the stomach is.
NAUSEA	Your stomach doesn't feel so good. It is churning and very uncomfortable.
THROW-UP	This sign needs no explanation. It looks like a person THROWING-UP.
TEMPERATURE	This sign reflects the mercury in a thermometer rising when it is hot and falling when it is cold.
INSURANCE	This is a symbol meaning INSURANCE.
SWOLLEN	You hurt yourself and the injury swells. Produce this sign on the body part that was injured.
THROB	This sign's placement, movement, and the accompanying facial expressions should reflect the THROBBING.
AWKWARD/CLUMSY	This shows the clumsy way a duck walks.
BROKE	Something has been broken.
SPRAIN	If a part of the body, for example the joint in your knee, turns the wrong way, it can be SPRAINED.
TWISTED	A joint in the body is TWISTED.

Lesson Twelve: *The Doctor Is IN!*

MEDICINE	This sign refers to the action of using a mortar and pestle to grind medication into powder.
SNEEZE	This looks like what most people do when they SNEEZE.
COLD	When you have a cold, you blow your nose again and again.
COUGH	This sign reflects how you look when you COUGH.
PILL	I've already shown you medicine. This shows how you take a PILL.
THROAT	This sign indicates where the throat is located.
SORE-THROAT	The facial expression with this sign conveys that is hurts!
SHOT	This shows how we get shots. There is another sign that shows the plunger pushing medication through the needle.
X-RAY	This sign is often fingerspelled, X-R-A-Y.
BANDAGE	This sign depicts wrapping an injury with a BANDAGE.
PREGNANT	This is what a pregnant woman looks like with a baby inside.
TEASE	It's like an insult. Ouch! When the index finger is bent (hooked), the insult is softer, funny (TEASE). Your facial expression is important to show the intensity of the teasing.

12.26 Experiential Activity

Signs and Origins

Activity Goal: To assist students in remembering how to produce a sign by applying the visual cues and origin information introduced in the *Review Session*.

Activity Instructions:

1. **Ask** students to read *Signs and Origins* in their workbooks (activity 12.26).

2. **Divide** the class into pairs.

3. **Encourage** students to use ASL to discuss and record the hints and origin information provided by Billy for the concepts given in their workbooks.

4. **Remind** students to use ASL (no voices!).

Lesson Twelve: *The Doctor Is IN!*

Student Workbook:
Activity 12.26

12.26 Experiential Activity

Signs and Origins

Activity Goal: To help you remember how to produce some of the new ASL vocabulary.

Activity Instructions: With a partner, use ASL to discuss the hints and origin information that Billy gave you in the video review session for each of the signs below. These will help you to remember how to make each sign.

Record your notes below.

Sign	Origin/visual hint
1. DOCTOR	
2. HURT	
3. HUG	
4. UNDERSTAND	
5. FEEL	
6. SICK	
7. BROKE	
8. SNEEZE	
9. PILL	
10. PREGNANT	

12.27 Video Learning Experience

Practice Session: Sentences

Viewing Goal: To improve comprehension skills by watching sentences presented in ASL.

Viewing Instructions:
1. **Ask** students to read *Practice Session: Sentences* in their workbooks (activity 12.27).

2. **Play** the video segment entitled *Practice Session: Sentences* (segment 12.27).

3. **Inform** students that each sentence is signed twice and an English translation is provided.

4. **Remind** students to watch the face of each signer to see the facial/body expressions and non-manual grammatical markers as well as the signs.

Lesson Twelve: *The Doctor Is IN!*

Video Segment Content:
(2 Minutes)

The following are English translations of the practice sentences:

1. I fell out of a tree and hurt my ankle.
2. I have a headache from reading so much.
3. There are many doctors and nurses at the hospital.
4. In the past, I was sick. I coughed and sneezed.
5. When Deaf people go to the hospital, interpreters are hired for communication.

Student Workbook: Activity 12.27

12.27 Video Learning Experience

Practice Session: Sentences

Viewing Goal: To improve your comprehension skills by watching sentences presented in ASL.

Viewing Instructions: Watch the signed sentences for comprehension. Remember to watch the face of each signer to see the facial/body expressions and the non-manual grammatical markers as well as the signs.

It is recommended that you copy each signed sentence when it is repeated.

In the space below, record any questions or notes you have regarding the sentences.

Notes: _____
_____
_____
_____

12.28 Video Learning Experience

Practice Session: Story

Viewing Goal: To improve comprehension skills by watching a story presented in ASL.

Viewing Instructions:
1. **Ask** students to read *Practice Session: Story* in their workbooks (activity 12.28).

2. **Show** the video segment entitled *Practice Session: Story* (segment 12.28). Billy signs a story using the vocabulary introduced in this lesson. **Turn off** audio and captions.

3. **Instruct** students to watch the signed story and write a summary of the main points.

Lesson Twelve: *The Doctor Is IN!*

Video Segment Content: (2 Minutes)

The following is an English translation of the comprehension story:

Once a man named Dave (his name sign is demonstrated) did not feel good. He did not sleep well. His head hurt. He took a pill and went to sleep.

He woke up feeling nauseous. He ran to the bathroom to throw up. He was coughing and feeling bad. He had a sore throat and knew he needed to see a doctor.

He went to the hospital and sat there waiting, filling out forms, putting down his insurance card number, waiting, coughing, and sneezing.

After a long wait, the doctor arrived. The doctor asked, "Where does it hurt?"

Dave said, "I have a headache, a sore throat, and my stomach hurts. Can you give me some medicine?"

The doctor said, "I'm not going to give you any medicine. You need water, juice, and plenty of sleep."

Dave said, "My mother told me the same thing. She's a better doctor than you!"

Student Workbook: Activity 12.28

12.28 Video Learning Experience

Practice Session: Story

Viewing Goal: To improve your comprehension by watching a story presented in ASL.

Viewing Instructions: Watch the signed story for comprehension. In the space below, write summary of the main points.

Summary: _____
_____
_____
_____

Lesson Twelve: *The Doctor Is IN!*

12.29 Comprehension Quiz

What Did You Understand?

Quiz Goal: To assess students' comprehension of the signed story.

Quiz Instructions:

1. **Instruct** students to complete the quiz in their workbooks (activity 12.29).

2. **Collect** for grading or **show** overhead (Appendix 12.29) and **ask** individual students to indicate the correct answers on the overhead while class members correct their own work.

3. **Ask** students to indicate which item(s) from the quiz they found difficult. **Review** by **modeling** or **replaying** that segment of the videotape.

Student Workbook: Activity 12.29

Overhead Master: Appendix 12.29

12.29 Comprehension Quiz

What Did You Understand?

Quiz Goal: To see how much of the signed story you understood.

Quiz Instructions: Read and answer each question below.

1. What is the man's name in the story?
   The man's name is Dave.

2. How did he get to sleep?
   He took a pill to help him sleep.

3. What did he do when he got up?
   He ran to the bathroom to throw up.

4. When he left the house, where did he go?
   Dave went to the hospital to see a doctor.

5. What did he do while waiting?
   Filled out forms, coughed, and sneezed.

6. What were the doctor's instructions?
   The doctor told him to drink water and juice and to get plenty of sleep.

Lesson Twelve: *The Doctor Is IN!*

12.30 Experiential Activity

Help! We Need Help Again!

Activity Goal: To improve ASL expressive and receptive skills and show students how much they have learned in this lesson.

Activity Instructions:

1. **Ask** students to read *Help! We Need Help Again!* in their workbooks (activity 12.30).

2. **Divide** class into groups of four or five. **Tell** them that they're going to role-play a situation in which a Deaf friend gets hurt.

3. **Instruct** students to begin the activity, following the instructions in their workbooks.

4. **Circulate** among the groups to **observe** their progress.

5. **Bring** the class together again. **Ask** students to demonstrate how to use ASL to communicate these ideas to the class.

6. **Remind** students this is a repeat of the Lesson Focus (activity 12.5). **Ask** students to compare their earlier performances to how they communicate now.

Student Workbook: Activity 12.30

12.30 Experiential Activity

Help! We Need Help Again!

Activity Goal: To experience a role-play related to medical emergencies and apply new communication skills.

Activity Instructions: Imagine that you are traveling with a Deaf friend. Your friend falls on the train and hurts her ankle. Everyone uses ASL.

How would you try to communicate the questions and information below using American Sign Language? Take turns communicating the following information.

1. Where is the hospital?
2. My friend fell on a train.
3. Her ankle hurts very badly.
4. Her ankle is swollen.
5. Will she need a shot?
6. Will you give her medicine?
7. Does she need crutches?

Lesson Twelve: *The Doctor Is IN!*

12.31 Homework Assignment

Accessibility Analysis

Activity Goal: To assist students in identifying accessibility issues when Deaf people are involved in medical emergencies.

Activity Instructions:
1. **Ask** students to read *Accessibility Analysis* in their workbooks (activity 12.31).

2. **Request** that students watch an episode of a medically-oriented television drama or movie.

3. **Tell** students to watch the program/movie and take notes on accessibility issues that might arise if a Deaf person were introduced into that medical setting.

4. **Instruct** students to list the issues in their workbooks. **Ask** students to also record their recommendations for helping medical personnel become more sensitive to the needs of the Deaf community and making the medical facilities more accessible to Deaf people.

Instructor Tip: *An opportunity for students to share this assignment has been scheduled in the next lesson (Homework Review 13.2).*

Lesson Twelve: *The Doctor Is IN!*

Student Workbook:
Activity 12.31

12.31 Homework Assignment

Accessibility Analysis

Homework Goal: To identify accessibility issues when Deaf people are involved in medical emergencies.

Homework Instructions: Watch a TV drama or movie involving a medical setting.

If a Deaf person needed medical care in the situation presented in your TV drama or movie, consider what communication and access problems might exist.

Use the space below to list those problems and recommend what could be done to help medical personnel become more sensitive to the needs of Deaf patients. How could the facilities involved be more accessible to Deaf people?

Accessibility issues: Recommendations:
1. _____ _____
2. _____ _____
3. _____ _____
4. _____ _____
5. _____ _____

12.32 Post-test

What Do You Know Now?

Assessment Video

Post-test Goal: To assess students' mastery of the lesson objectives.

Post-test Instructions:
1. **Ask** students to read the Post-test Introduction in their workbooks (activity 12.32).

2. **Copy** and **distribute** the Lesson Twelve Post-test (Appendix 12.32).

3. **Play** the Assessment Video (segment 12.32) and **allow** students to complete Section One (comprehension portion) of the test.

4. **Instruct** students to complete Section Two (culture and grammar portion) of the test individually and hand in their papers when they are finished.

5. **Assign** Section Three (expressive portion) of the test and **schedule** when students are to perform. It is strongly recommended that you **videotape** this portion of the Post-test.

Lesson Twelve: *The Doctor Is IN!*

6. **Determine** grading options based upon programmatic requirements. A recommended guideline for measuring successful mastery of objectives is 80% accuracy.

Video Segment Content:
(1 1/2 Minutes)

The following is an English translation of the comprehension story:

My name is Jesse. I feel sick! My head hurts, I have a sore throat, and I feel like throwing up. My mother told me I didn't have to go to school, but I couldn't go play. I feel sad.

The doctor gave me some medicine to take. I have big, blue pills. I got a shot, too. Now my arm hurts. The nurse took my temperature. It was 100. My mother and I had an interpreter at the hospital. I was good. I wasn't even afraid!

Student Workbook:
Activity 12.32

12.32 Post-test Introduction

What Do You Know Now?

Post-test Goal: To assess your mastery of the lesson objectives.

Post-test Introduction: This test has three sections:

Section One: The Comprehension section tests your ability to understand ASL.

Section Two: The Culture and Grammar section tests your knowledge of the material presented in the *Cultural* and *Grammatical Notes*.

Section Three: The Expressive portion tests your ability to use ASL.

Simply follow the instructions for each section. **Good luck!**

Lesson Twelve: *The Doctor Is IN!*

Post-test Master:
Appendix 12.32

12.32 Post-test

Section One: Comprehension

Instructions: You will see a signed story. Watch carefully and answer each question below.

1. What is the signer's name?
   A. Jan
   B. Jesse
   C. Justin

2. The signer is sick. What is wrong with him?
   A. A fall
   B. A sore throat
   C. A sprained ankle

3. What did Mom say the signer could **not** do?
   A. See a doctor
   B. Go to sleep
   C. Go to school or play

4. What did the doctor give the signer?
   A. Crutches
   B. Cough syrup
   C. A shot and some pills

5. What was the signer's temperature?
   A. 104
   B. 100
   C. 98

Post-test Master:
Appendix 12.32

12.32 Post-test

Section Two: Culture and Grammar

Instructions: Read and answer each question below.

6. What information does facial expression add to a sign?
   Facial expressions show the emotion of the communication.

7. Explain what is meant by "facial expressions are often the adjectives of the message."
   Facial expressions function the same in ASL as adjectives do in English. They can change the meaning of a message by adding valuable information.

8. If a hospital receives federal funding, it is required to provide access to:
   A. Color TVs
   B. Private rooms for Deaf patients
   C. Sign Language classes
   D. Sign Language interpreters

Lesson Twelve: *The Doctor Is IN!*

Post-test Master:
Appendix 12.32

12.32 Post-test

Section Three: Expressive Portion

Instructions: Create a story in which you describe a time when you were sick. Use at least ten signs learned in Lesson Twelve and clearly demonstrate at least two emotions with facial expressions.

Your instructor will schedule a time for you to perform this section of the Post-test. You may prepare and practice prior to your scheduled time. Use the space below to prepare for your expressive performance.

Include at least ten signs from Lesson Twelve.

9. _____
10. _____
11. _____
12. _____
13. _____
14. _____
15. _____
16. _____
17. _____
18. _____

Emotions shown with facial expression:

19. _____
20. _____

Congratulations!
You have completed
Lesson Twelve!

Instructor's Guide: Lesson Twelve
Bravo ASL! Curriculum

©1996 Sign Enhancers, Inc.
ALL RIGHTS RESERVED.

Lesson 13
BUSINESS AS UNUSUAL

Materials Needed

Equipment: VCR and TV monitor
Overhead projector and screen
Optional: video camera for activities 13.16 and 13.32

Materials: Instructor's Guide
Student Workbook: one per student
Overhead transparencies for activities 13.3, 13.4, 13.5, 13.6, 13.9, 13.10, 13.13, 13.14, 13.18, 13.19, 13.22, 13.28, and 13.30 (see Appendix for masters)
Optional: blank videotape (or have students bring their own) for activities 13.16 and 13.32
Post-test: Appendix 13.32

Videotapes: The Beginning ASL VideoCourse Lesson Thirteen
Activities Video for activity 13.28
Assessment Video for Post-test 13.32

13.1 Begin Class

Housekeeping

Goal: To prepare students for this lesson.

Instructions: 1. **Welcome** students to Lesson Thirteen of the VideoCourse.

2. **Perform** any necessary tasks (such as taking attendance) that may be required by your specific program.

Lesson Thirteen: *Business as UNusual*

13.2 Homework Review

Accessibility Analysis

Activity Goal: To provide feedback on previously assigned homework and to reinforce materials learned in earlier lessons.

Activity Instructions:

1. **Ask** students to read *Accessibility Analysis* in their workbooks (activity 13.2).

2. **Divide** the class into groups of three.

3. **Remind** students that they were to view a medically-oriented TV program or movie and consider the communication/access problems that might exist if a Deaf person were introduced into the setting (*Homework Assignment 12.31*).

4. **Instruct** students to use ASL (no voice) to discuss the results of this activity with their partners. **Encourage** students to ask each other questions about their findings.

5. **Inform** the students that each group should choose a particular issue to share with the class (using ASL).

6. At the completion of the activity, **collect** homework for grading or to provide written feedback.

Student Workbook: Activity 13.2

13.2 Homework Review

Accessibility Analysis

Activity Goal: To show the results of your homework assignment.

Activity Instructions: Use ASL to discuss with your group the communication/access issues you thought might impact a Deaf patient in the medically-oriented television drama or movie you watched. Be sure to share with your group members (using ASL) some of your recommendations for solving these problems.

You can review your notes from *Homework Assignment 12.31*.

Your group should prepare to share its findings with the class.

13.3 Pretest

What Do You Know?

Pretest Goal: To identify students' current level of knowledge pertaining to the lesson content.

Pretest Instructions:
1. **Ask** students to read and answer the pretest questions in their workbooks (activity 13.3).

2. **Show** overhead (Appendix 13.3) and **ask** individual students to indicate the correct answers on the overhead while class members correct their own work.

3. **Inform** students that the contents of the Pretest will be taught throughout the lesson.

Student Workbook: Activity 13.3

Overhead Master: Appendix 13.3

13.3 Pretest

What Do You Know?

Pretest Goal: To see how much you already know about what will be taught in this lesson.

Pretest Instructions: Read and answer each question.

1. Since a Deaf person can't use the telephone, s/he can't work as a secretary.
   A. True
   B. False

2. Deaf people can't be successful in business because of communication barriers.
   A. True
   B. False

3. Companies that become accessible to Deaf workers are also accessible to Deaf consumers.
   A. True
   B. False

4. What is a relay service?
   A. It is an interpreter referral service.
   B. It is a special TTY that helps a Deaf person to use the phone.
   C. It is a service that relays calls between voice and TTYs.
   D. It is an operator who is Deaf who relays calls to other Deaf people.

5. What type of jobs are available to Deaf people today?
   A. Sign Language teachers and printers.
   B. Photographers, artists, directors, and dancers.
   C. Counselors, secretaries, teachers, lawyers, and doctors.
   D. All of the above.

Lesson Thirteen: *Business as UNusual*

13.4 Lesson Objectives

Planning for Success

Goal: To identify the learning outcomes associated with successful completion of this lesson.

Instructions:
1. **Ask** students to read the objectives in their workbooks (activity 13.4).

2. **Show** overhead (Appendix 13.4) and **read** through the objectives with the class.

Student Workbook: Activity 13.4

Overhead Master: Appendix 13.4

13.4 Lesson Objectives

Planning for Success

Goal: To see what you will learn by the end of this lesson.

Instructions: Read the objectives below.

Upon completing this VideoCourse lesson, you will be able to...

1. Recognize and accurately produce the vocabulary introduced in this and all previous lessons.

2. Describe equipment commonly used by Deaf people for gaining access to telecommunication.

3. Describe what a telephone relay service is and how it functions.

4. Identify ways in which the workplace is becoming more accessible to Deaf employees.

5. Accurately produce signs that incorporate numbers.

13.5 Lesson Focus

Help Wanted

Activity Goal: To allow students the opportunity to explore the possibilities and challenges for Deaf people in the workplace.

Activity Instructions:

1. **Ask** students to read *Help Wanted* in their workbooks (activity 13.5).

2. **Ask** students to read each of the job descriptions and take some time to consider potential communication issues and solutions for each. **Tell** students to record the answers in their workbooks.

3. When individual work is completed, **divide** the class into groups of four or five.

4. **Instruct** students to use ASL to share their answers with their group.

5. **Circulate** among the groups to **observe** their progress and **offer** assistance where needed.

6. **Show** the overhead (Appendix 13.5) and **ask** volunteers from each group to record the challenges and solutions on the overhead for everyone to see.

7. **Inform** the students that they will learn more about the workplace and its accessibility to Deaf workers later in this lesson.

Student Workbook:
Activity 13.5

Overhead Master:
Appendix 13.5

13.5 Lesson Focus

Help Wanted

Activity Goal: To explore the possibilities and challenges for Deaf people in the workplace.

Activity Instructions: Imagine that you are an employer looking for employees for the jobs described below. You recently interviewed several Deaf people and you were impressed with each person's abilities. You're considering hiring them. You've never had Deaf employees.

Consider modifications to job descriptions or the work environment that might be necessary. How might you make the workplace more accessible to a Deaf employee? Write your ideas below:

Lesson Thirteen: *Business as UNusual*

13.5 Lesson Focus

JOB TITLE: Computer Programmer

MAIN RESPONSIBILITIES:

1) Meet with clients to determine the specifics of their project.

2) Work with team of programmers to design a computer program to meet the client's needs.

3) Check with client(s) throughout process to obtain client feedback.

4) At completion of project, present program and training to client to maximize effective use of program.

Potential communication challenge:	Potential solution:
1. _____	_____
2. _____	_____
3. _____	_____
4. _____	_____

JOB TITLE: Administrative Secretary

MAIN RESPONSIBILITIES:

1) Greet customers as they enter the office.

2) Provide support (such as typing and filing) for staff.

3) Record financial deposits and payables, make bank deposits.

4) At the end of each quarter, write a report regarding the financial status of the company, and present it to the staff.

5) Coordinate company meetings, arranging for food and beverages.

Potential communication challenge:	Potential solution:
1. _____	_____
2. _____	_____
3. _____	_____
4. _____	_____
5. _____	_____

Lesson Thirteen: *Business as UNusual*

> 13.5 Lesson Focus
>
> JOB TITLE: Research Librarian
>
> MAIN RESPONSIBILITIES:
>
> 1) Meet with students to help them find appropriate research material.
>
> 2) Work with teachers and staff members researching information for various school projects.
>
> 3) Supervise all research assistants employed by the library.
>
> 4) Train students and teachers to use the computerized database.
>
> Potential communication challenge: Potential solution:
>
> 1. _____   _____
> 2. _____   _____
> 3. _____   _____
> 4. _____   _____

13.6 Language Learning Instruction

Learning New Signs

Goal: To use ASL and visual aids to introduce this lesson's vocabulary.

Instructions:
1. **Ask** students to read *Learning New Signs* in their workbooks (13.6).

2. **Show** overhead (Appendix 13.6). **Introduce** the vocabulary by **pointing** to items presented in the pictures while **demonstrating** the signs.

3. **Reinforce** retention and **check** students' comprehension by **using** these signs to **ask** students questions.

   Note: For a step-by-step review of this method, see Lesson One (activities 1.6 and 1.12).

4. **Continue** this process until all the ASL vocabulary items have been introduced.

Lesson Thirteen: *Business as UNusual*

Overhead Content: Use the pictures in the overhead (Appendix 13.6) to introduce the signs representing the following concepts:

1. BUSINESS
2. COMPANY
3. PAY
4. HIRE
5. FIRE
6. FIRST
7. IDEA
8. EXPLAIN
9. BORING

Note: Some pictures can be used to represent several concepts. For verbs and more abstract concepts, you may need to supplement these pictures with mime, gestures, using actual objects, and acting out the concepts in class.

Overhead Master: Appendix 13.6

Lesson Thirteen: *Business as UNusual*

Student Workbook:
Activity 13.6

13.6 Language Learning Instruction

Learning New Signs

Goal: To help you learn new ASL vocabulary.

Instructions: Your instructor will teach you new signs! Watch closely to learn what these signs mean and how they are produced.

In the space below, record any notes to help you remember the signs.

Notes: _____
_____
_____
_____

13.7 Video Learning Experience

Introduction to New Vocabulary

Viewing Goal: To provide a signed demonstration of the accurate production of the new ASL vocabulary.

Viewing Instructions:
1. **Ask** students to read *Introduction to New Vocabulary* in their workbooks (activity 13.7).

2. **Play** the video segment entitled *Introduction to New Vocabulary* (segment 13.7). Billy introduces and signs each new vocabulary item twice. (If you wish to keep this a strictly visual presentation, **turn off** audio.)

3. **Instruct** students to watch how Billy produces the signs as well as the accompanying facial/body expressions.

4. **Ask** students to copy the signs and the facial/body expressions as Billy repeats each one.

Instructor's Guide: Lesson Thirteen
Bravo ASL! Curriculum

©1996 Sign Enhancers, Inc.
ALL RIGHTS RESERVED.

Lesson Thirteen: *Business as UNusual*

Video Segment Content: See the following Student Workbook excerpt for the content
(2 Minutes) of this video segment.

Student Workbook:
Activity 13.7

13.7 Video Learning Experience

Introduction to New Vocabulary

Viewing Goal: To help you learn new ASL vocabulary.

Viewing Instructions: Watch how Billy produces each sign. Be sure to notice the facial/body expressions. Copy the signs as Billy repeats each one.

Signs representing the following concepts are introduced in this video segment.

1. BUSINESS   4. HIRE   7. IDEA
2. COMPANY   5. FIRE   8. EXPLAIN
3. PAY   6. FIRST   9. BORING

13.8 Video Learning Experience

Bravo Family Visit

Viewing Goal: To improve ASL comprehension skills by watching a Bravo family interaction.

Viewing Instructions:
1. **Ask** students to read *Bravo Family Visit* in their workbooks (activity 13.8).

2. **Play** the video segment of the Bravo Family (segment 13.8). The Bravos will use the new ASL vocabulary while discussing Mom's job.

3. **Instruct** students to watch for comprehension and write a summary of the main points.

4. **Replay** any portion of this video segment that students experienced difficulty understanding.

Video Segment Content: The following is a summary of the Bravo family interaction:
(1 1/2 Minutes)

The family is sitting on a bench having lunch. Anna asks Mom what she does for work. Mom explains about her business. Anna asks for more details about what Mom does. Mom would rather show Anna than explain. She asks Anna if she wants to help her at her office for a day. Anna excitedly says yes and wonders if she will be paid.

Lesson Thirteen: *Business as UNusual*

Scott teases Anna by telling Mom to pay her nothing. Anna tells Scott that her first job will be to fire him!

Billy (at Mom's office): You guessed it! Anna's curiosity takes us here, to the workplace. That's great, because there are many signs related to the workplace that I can teach you. I have some that I'll show you right now.

Student Workbook: Activity 13.8

13.8 Video Learning Experience

Bravo Family Visit

Viewing Goal: To improve your ASL comprehension skills by watching a Bravo family interaction.

Viewing Instructions: Watch the signed interaction and write a summary of the main points.

Summary: _____
_____
_____
_____

13.9 Comprehension Quiz

What Did You Understand?

Quiz Goal: To assess students' comprehension of the signed interaction.

Quiz Instructions:
1. **Instruct** students to complete the quiz in their workbooks (activity 13.9).

2. **Collect** for grading or **show** the overhead (Appendix 13.9) and **ask** individual students to indicate the correct answers on the overhead while class members correct their own work.

3. **Ask** students to indicate which item(s) from the quiz they found difficult. **Review** by **modeling** or **replaying** that segment of the videotape.

Instructor's Guide: Lesson Thirteen
Bravo ASL! Curriculum

©1996 Sign Enhancers, Inc.
ALL RIGHTS RESERVED.

Lesson Thirteen: *Business as UNusual*

Student Workbook:
Activity 13.9

Overhead Master:
Appendix 13.9

13.9 Comprehension Quiz

What Did You Understand?

Quiz Goal: To see how much of the Bravo family interaction you understood.

Quiz Instructions: Read and answer each question.

1. What does Anna ask her mother?
   What she does for work.

2. What does Mom invite Anna to do?
   Visit her office.

3. Does Anna want to do this?
   Yes!

4. What does Scott tell Mom NOT to do?
   Scott tells Mom not to pay Anna.

5. What does Anna plan to do for her first task?
   Fire Scott.

13.10 Language Learning Instruction

Learning New Signs

Goal: To use ASL and visual aids to introduce this lesson's vocabulary.

Instructions:
1. **Ask** students to read *Learning New Signs* in their workbooks (activity 13.10).

2. **Show** the overhead (Appendix 13.10). **Introduce** the vocabulary by **pointing** to items presented in the pictures while **demonstrating** the signs.

3. **Reinforce** retention and **check** students' comprehension by **using** these signs to **ask** students questions.

   Note: For a step-by-step review of this method, see Lesson One (activities 1.6 and 1.12).

4. **Continue** this process until all the ASL vocabulary items have been introduced.

Instructor's Guide: Lesson Thirteen
Bravo ASL! Curriculum

Lesson Thirteen: *Business as UNusual*

Overhead Content: Use the pictures in the overhead (Appendix 13.10) to introduce the signs representing the following concepts:

1. WORK
2. OFFICE
3. DESK/TABLE
4. TYPE
5. TYPEWRITER
6. COMPUTER
7. ADVERTISE
8. SECRETARY
9. INTERVIEW
10. SKILL
11. NEED
12. OH-I-SEE
13. ASK-QUESTION

Note: Some pictures can be used to represent several concepts. For verbs and more abstract concepts, you may need to supplement these pictures with mime, gestures, using actual objects, and acting out the concepts in class.

Overhead Master:
Appendix 13.10

Lesson Thirteen: *Business as UNusual*

Student Workbook:
Activity 13.10

13.10 Language Learning Instruction

Learning New Signs

Goal: To help you learn new ASL vocabulary.

Instructions: Your instructor will teach you new signs! Watch closely to learn what these signs mean and how they are produced.

In the space below, record any notes to help you remember the signs.

Notes: _____
_____
_____
_____

13.11 Video Learning Experience

Introduction to New Vocabulary

Viewing Goal: To provide a signed demonstration of the accurate production of the new ASL vocabulary.

Viewing Instructions:
1. **Ask** students to read *Introduction to New Vocabulary* in their workbooks (activity 13.11).

2. **Play** the video segment entitled *Introduction to New Vocabulary* (segment 13.11). Billy introduces and signs each new vocabulary item twice. (If you wish to keep this a strictly visual presentation, **turn off** audio.)

3. **Instruct** students to watch how Billy produces the signs and the accompanying facial/body expressions.

4. **Ask** students to copy the signs and the facial/body expressions as Billy repeats each one.

Lesson Thirteen: *Business as UNusual*

Video Segment Content: See the following Student Workbook excerpt for the content
(3 Minutes) of this video segment.

Student Workbook:
Activity 13.11

13.11 Video Learning Experience

Introduction to New Vocabulary

Viewing Goal: To help you learn new ASL vocabulary.

Viewing Instructions: Watch how Billy produces each sign. Be sure to notice the facial/body expressions. Copy the signs as Billy repeats each one.

Signs representing the following concepts are introduced in this video segment:

1. WORK
2. OFFICE
3. DESK/TABLE
4. TYPE
5. TYPEWRITER
6. COMPUTER
7. ADVERTISE
8. SECRETARY
9. INTERVIEW
10. SKILL
11. NEED
12. OH-I-SEE
13. ASK-QUESTION

13.12 Video Learning Experience

Bravo Family Visit

Viewing Goal: To improve ASL comprehension skills by watching a Bravo family interaction.

Viewing Instructions:
1. **Ask** students to read *Bravo Family Visit* in their workbooks (activity 13.12).

2. **Play** the video segment of the Bravo family (segment 13.12). The Bravos will use the new ASL vocabulary within the context of visiting Mom's office.

3. **Instruct** students to watch for comprehension and write a summary of the main points.

4. **Replay** any portion of this video segment that students experienced difficulty understanding.

Lesson Thirteen: *Business as UNusual*

Video Segment Content:
(3 Minutes)

The following is a summary of the Bravo family interaction:

Mom and Anna walk into Mom's office. Anna runs and sits in Mom's chair and puts her feet on the desk.

Mom shows Anna where she will sit in front of the computer. Anna asks Mom if there are games on the computer. Mom tells her no, that the computer is used for work and shows Anna a flyer for a secretarial opening that she has printed. Anna thinks about what is required of a secretary and decides she can handle the job. She asks Mom if she can be her secretary for the day.

Mom tells her that she will have to interview Anna first to ask about her skills. Anna tells her that she has TTY skills. Just then the phone rings. It's a TTY call. Mom starts to answer it, but then lets Anna take over. Anna is excited and types her message. She then looks disappointed and tells Mom it's only Scott.

Billy: Anna's first business call was a disappointment. Let's see how she handles her other job responsibilities. First, I have more signs I want to show you.

Student Workbook:
Activity 13.12

13.12 Video Learning Experience

Bravo Family Visit

Viewing Goal: To improve your ASL comprehension skills by watching a Bravo family interaction.

Viewing Instructions: Watch the signed interaction and write a summary of the main points.

Summary: _____
_____
_____
_____

Lesson Thirteen: *Business as UNusual*

13.13 Comprehension Quiz

What Did You Understand?

Quiz Goal: To assess students' comprehension of the signed interaction.

Quiz Instructions:
1. **Instruct** students to complete the quiz in their workbooks (activity 13.13).

2. **Collect** for grading or **show** the overhead (Appendix 13.13) and **ask** individual students to indicate the correct answers on the overhead while class members correct their own work.

3. **Ask** students to indicate which item(s) from the quiz they found difficult. **Review** by **modeling** or **replaying** that segment of the videotape.

Student Workbook: Activity 13.13

Overhead Master: Appendix 13.13

13.13 Comprehension Quiz

What Did You Understand?

Quiz Goal: To see how much of the Bravo family interaction you understood.

Quiz Instructions: Read and answer each question.

1. What does Anna want to know about the computer?
   If there are any games on the computer.

2. What is Mom's computer used for?
   It is used for work.

3. What does Anna want to do to help Mom?
   She wants to be the secretary.

4. What does Mom do before "hiring" Anna?
   Mom firsts interviews Anna about her skills.

5. When Anna answers the phone, who is the caller?
   The TTY call is from Scott.

Lesson Thirteen: *Business as UNusual*

13.14 Language Learning Instruction

Learning New Signs

Goal: To use ASL and visual aids to introduce this lesson's vocabulary.

Instructions:
1. **Ask** students to read *Learning New Signs* in their workbooks (activity 13.14).

2. **Show** overhead (Appendix 13.14). **Introduce** the vocabulary by **pointing** to items presented in the pictures while **demonstrating** the signs.

3. **Reinforce** retention and **check** students' comprehension by **using** these signs to **ask** students questions.

    Note: For a step-by-step review of this method, see Lesson One (activities 1.6 and 1.12).

4. **Continue** this process until all the ASL vocabulary items have been introduced.

Overhead Content: Use the pictures in the overhead (Appendix 13.14) to introduce the signs representing the following concepts:

1. BOSS
2. LETTER
3. COPY
4. LAZY
5. FILE
6. FILES
7. STAMP
8. ENVELOPE
9. SIGNATURE/SIGN
10. SHELF
11. COMPUTER+PRINTER

Note: Some pictures can be used to represent several concepts. For verbs and more abstract concepts, you may need to supplement these pictures with mime, gestures, using actual objects, and acting out the concepts in class.

Lesson Thirteen: *Business as UNusual*

Overhead Master:
Appendix 13.14

Student Workbook:
Activity 13.14

13.14 Language Learning Instruction

Learning New Signs

Goal: To help you learn new ASL vocabulary.

Instructions: Your instructor will teach you new signs! Watch closely to learn what these signs mean and how they are produced.

In the space below, record any notes to help you remember the signs.

Notes: _____
_____
_____

Lesson Thirteen: *Business as UNusual*

13.15 Video Learning Experience

Introduction to New Vocabulary

Viewing Goal: To provide a signed demonstration of the accurate production of the new ASL vocabulary.

Viewing Instructions:
1. **Ask** students to read *Introduction to New Vocabulary* in their workbooks (activity 13.15).

2. **Play** the video segment entitled *Introduction to New Vocabulary* (segment 13.15). Billy introduces and signs each new vocabulary item twice. (If you wish to keep this a strictly visual presentation, **turn off** audio.)

3. **Instruct** students to watch how Billy produces the signs and the accompanying facial/body expressions.

4. **Ask** students to copy the signs and the facial/body expressions as Billy repeats each one.

Video Segment Content: (1 Minute) See the following Student Workbook excerpt for the content of this video segment.

Student Workbook: Activity 13.15

13.15 Video Learning Experience

Introduction to New Vocabulary

Viewing Goal: To help you learn new ASL vocabulary.

Viewing Instructions: Watch how Billy produces each sign. Be sure to notice the facial/body expressions. Copy the signs as Billy repeats each one.

Signs representing the following concepts are introduced in this video segment:

1. BOSS
2. LETTER
3. COPY
4. LAZY
5. FILE
6. FILES
7. STAMP
8. ENVELOPE
9. SIGNATURE/SIGN
10. SHELF
11. COMPUTER+PRINTER

Lesson Thirteen: *Business as UNusual*

13.16 Experiential Activity

Point and Sign

Activity Goal: To improve students' receptive and expressive ASL skills.

Activity Instructions:
1. **Ask** students to read *Point and Sign* in their workbooks (activity 13.16).

2. **Divide** the class into pairs.

3. **Select** and **model** the variation of the *Point and Sign* activity you would like your students to perform. You may **choose** to have students perform all three variations.

4. **Inform** students that this activity is to be done using ASL (no voices needed!).

    Variation A: **Ask** students to take turns having one partner point to an object or action in the picture and having the other partner sign a sentence representing its meaning.

    Variation B: **Ask** students to take turns having one partner sign a sentence or short story and having the other partner point to the object or action in the picture that best matches its meaning.

    Variation C: **Ask** each pair of students to create an ASL dialogue using as many of the pictures as possible. **Encourage** students take at least four turns during the dialogue.

5. **Circulate** among the pairs to **observe** student performance. **Encourage** students to use vocabulary items such as: BOSS; LETTER; COPY; FILE; ENVELOPE; SIGNATURE; SHELF; COMPUTER; and PRINTER.

6. **Model** the signs as needed.

Instructor's Guide: Lesson Thirteen
Bravo ASL! Curriculum

Lesson Thirteen: *Business as UNusual*

Student Workbook: Activity 13.16

13.16 Experiential Activity

Point and Sign

Activity Goal: To improve your ASL receptive and expressive skills.

Activity Instructions: Using the pictures below, follow your teacher's instructions and use your new sign vocabulary, such as: BOSS; LETTER; COPY; FILE; ENVELOPE; SIGNATURE; SHELF; COMPUTER; and PRINTER.

13.17 Video Learning Experience

Bravo Family Visit

Viewing Goal: To improve ASL comprehension skills by watching a Bravo family interaction.

Viewing Instructions:
1. **Ask** students to read *Bravo Family Visit* in their workbooks (activity 13.17).

2. **Play** the video segment of the Bravo family (segment 13.17). Mom and Anna will use ASL in the context of working in Mom's office.

3. **Instruct** students to watch for comprehension and write a summary of the main points.

4. **Replay** any portion of this video segment that students experienced difficulty understanding.

Instructor's Guide: Lesson Thirteen
Bravo ASL! Curriculum

©1996 Sign Enhancers, Inc.
ALL RIGHTS RESERVED.

Lesson Thirteen: *Business as UNusual*

**Video Segment Content:
(4 Minutes)**

The following is a summary of the Bravo family interaction:

Mom is explaining to Anna that she is Anna's boss. When she tells Anna what to do, Anna has to do it. The first thing that she wants her to do is type a letter. She hands the letter to Anna. Anna starts typing.

When Anna is done with the letter, she takes it to Mom. She tells Mom that she is a good secretary. Mom agrees with her and tells her that she typed the letter fast.

Mom goes to make a copy of the letter. Mom tells Anna that next she needs to file the letter. Anna asks her where. Mom shows her which file to put it in. Anna asks what Mom is going to do with the letter. Mom tells her they will mail it... after the president signs it. Mom signs the letter.

Anna asks Mom where the envelopes and stamps are kept. Mom tells Anna she is going to the post office. She also gives Anna a promotion from secretary to vice president.

Billy: Whoa! Wow! Promoted to vice president on her first day at work! That is fast work. Can Anna handle the responsibilities of her new executive status? Can you handle the responsibility of learning new signs? We'll see. Because I am going to show you some right now.

Student Workbook:
Activity 13.17

13.17 Video Learning Experience

Bravo Family Visit

Viewing Goal: To improve your ASL comprehension skills by watching a Bravo family interaction.

Viewing Instructions: Watch the signed interaction and write a summary of the main points.

Summary: _____
_____
_____
_____

Lesson Thirteen: *Business as UNusual*

13.18 Comprehension Quiz

What Did You Understand?

Quiz Goal: To assess students' comprehension of the signed interaction.

Quiz Instructions:
1. **Instruct** students to complete the quiz in their workbooks (activity 13.18).

2. **Collect** for grading or **show** overhead (Appendix 13.18) and **ask** individual students to indicate the correct answers on the overhead while class members correct their own work.

3. **Ask** students to indicate which item(s) from the quiz they found difficult. **Review** by **modeling** or **replaying** that segment of the videotape.

Student Workbook: Activity 13.18

Overhead Master: Appendix 13.18

13.18 Comprehension Quiz

What Did You Understand?

Quiz Goal: To see how much of the Bravo family interaction you understood.

Quiz Instructions: Read and answer each question.

1. Mom explains that she is Anna's boss.
   A. True
   B. False

2. What is the first job Mom gives Anna?
   A. Filing
   B. Computer work
   C. Typing a letter
   D. Going to the post office

3. Who has to sign the letter?
   A. The vice president
   B. The secretary
   C. The president
   D. Anna

4. Mom goes to the post office.
   A. True
   B. False

5. Anna is promoted to what position?
   A. President
   B. Vice president
   C. Secretary
   D. Owner

Lesson Thirteen: *Business as UNusual*

13.19 Language Learning Instruction

Learning New Signs

Goal: To use ASL and visual aids to introduce this lesson's vocabulary.

Instructions:
1. **Ask** students to read *Learning New Signs* in their workbooks (activity 13.19).

2. **Show** the overhead (Appendix 13.19). **Introduce** the vocabulary by **pointing** to items presented in the pictures while **demonstrating** the signs.

3. **Reinforce** retention and **check** students' comprehension by **using** these signs to **ask** students questions.

   Note: For a step-by-step review of this method, see Lesson One (activities 1.6 and 1.12).

4. **Continue** this process until all the ASL vocabulary items have been introduced.

Overhead Content: Use the pictures in the overhead (Appendix 13.19) to introduce the signs representing the following concepts:

1. PAPER
2. SCISSORS
3. TAPE
4. PAPER+CLIP
5. STAPLER
6. RUBBER-BAND

Note: Some pictures can be used to represent several concepts. For verbs and more abstract concepts, you may need to supplement these pictures with mime, gestures, using actual objects, and acting out the concepts in class.

Lesson Thirteen: *Business as UNusual*

Overhead Master:
Appendix 13.19

Student Workbook:
Activity 13.19

13.19 Language Learning Instruction

Learning New Signs

Goal: To help you learn new ASL vocabulary.

Instructions: Your instructor will teach you new signs! Watch closely to learn what these signs mean and how they are produced.

In the space below, record any notes to help you remember the signs.

Notes: _____
_____
_____
_____

Lesson Thirteen: *Business as UNusual*

13.20 Video Learning Experience

Introduction to New Vocabulary

Viewing Goal: To provide a signed demonstration of the accurate production of the new ASL vocabulary.

Viewing Instructions:
1. **Ask** students to read *Introduction to New Vocabulary* in their workbooks (activity 13.20).

2. **Play** the video segment entitled *Introduction to New Vocabulary* (segment 13.20). Billy introduces and signs each new vocabulary item twice. (If you wish to keep this a strictly visual presentation, **turn off** audio.)

3. **Instruct** students to watch how Billy produces the signs and the accompanying facial/body expressions.

4. **Ask** students to copy the signs and the facial/body expressions as Billy repeats each one.

Video Segment Content: (2 Minutes) See the following Student Workbook excerpt for the content of this video segment.

Student Workbook: Activity 13.20

13.20 Video Learning Experience

Introduction to New Vocabulary

Viewing Goal: To help you learn new ASL vocabulary.

Viewing Instructions: Watch how Billy produces each sign. Be sure to notice the facial/body expressions. Copy the signs as Billy signs each one.

Signs representing the following concepts are introduced:

1. PAPER
2. SCISSORS
3. TAPE
4. PAPER+CLIP
5. STAPLER
6. RUBBER-BAND

Instructor's Guide: Lesson Thirteen
Bravo ASL! Curriculum

©1996 Sign Enhancers, Inc.
ALL RIGHTS RESERVED

Lesson Thirteen: *Business as UNusual*

13.21 Video Learning Experience

Bravo Family Visit

Viewing Goal: To improve ASL comprehension skills by watching a Bravo family interaction.

Viewing Instructions:

1. **Ask** students to read *Bravo Family Visit* in their workbooks (activity 13.21).

2. **Play** the video segment of the Bravo family (segment 13.21). They will use the new ASL vocabulary in the context of a visit to Mom's office.

3. **Instruct** students to watch for comprehension and write a summary of the main points.

4. **Replay** any portion of this video segment that students experienced difficulty understanding.

Video Segment Content: (3 1/2 Minutes)

The following is a summary of the Bravo family interaction:

Dad and Scott walk in as Anna is finishing up her "art project." Anna asks if she can help them and Dad tells her he wants to buy her art work and asks her how much it costs. He gives her money and she gives him the art.

Dad asks where the president, Jennifer, is. Anna checks the schedule and asks Dad and Scott if they have an appointment. She explains that you must have an appointment to see the president.

Just then, Mom walks in. Scott tells her it was a good thing she showed up because the secretary was being crabby. Dad tells Mom that the secretary was telling them they needed an appointment. Anna corrected them, telling them she was the vice president, not the secretary.

Scott tells Anna to let him know if she needs an assistant. Dad says that they will leave to let the women work. He tells them they will have to get together for dinner to celebrate Anna's promotion. Dad and Scott leave.

At five o'clock, Mom informs Anna that work is finished, they can leave now to go meet Dad and Scott to celebrate. Anna tells Mom that she earned money today. Mom asks her who paid her. Anna tells her that Dad did and shows Mom the money. Mom looks sad. She tells Anna she wanted to pay her. Anna tells Mom that she can still pay her. Mom gives Anna a check made out for a "big hug."

Lesson Thirteen: *Business as UNusual*

Billy: Hello. Coffee break is over, right? OK. We have got to get back to work now. Let's focus on those new signs that we recently learned.

Student Workbook: Activity 13.21

13.21 Video Learning Experience

Bravo Family Visit

Viewing Goal: To improve ASL comprehension skills by watching a Bravo family interaction.

Viewing Instructions: Watch the signed interaction and write a summary of the main points.

Summary: _____
_____
_____
_____

13.22 Comprehension Quiz

What Did You Understand?

Quiz Goal: To assess students' comprehension of the signed interaction.

Quiz Instructions:
1. **Instruct** students to complete the quiz in their workbooks (activity 13.22).

2. **Collect** for grading or **show** the overhead (Appendix 13.22) and **ask** individual students to indicate the correct answers on the overhead while class members correct their own work.

3. **Ask** students to indicate which item(s) from the quiz they found difficult. **Review** by **modeling** or **replaying** that segment of the videotape.

Lesson Thirteen: *Business as UNusual*

Student Workbook:
Activity 13.22

Overhead Master:
Appendix 13.22

13.22 Comprehension Quiz

What Did You Understand?

Quiz Goal: To see how much of the Bravo family interaction you understood.

Quiz Instructions: Read and answer each question.

1. What does Dad tell Anna he would like to do?
   Buy her art work.

2. When Dad wants to see Mom, what does Anna ask him?
   If he and Scott have an appointment.

3. What does Dad want to do after the women finish working?
   Go out to dinner to celebrate Anna's promotion.

4. What time is it when Mom says work is finished?
   Five o'clock.

5. How is Anna paid by Mom for her hard work?
   With a check for a "big hug."

13.23 Video Learning Experience

Review Session

Viewing Goal: To reinforce recognition and production of the signs introduced in this lesson.

Viewing Instructions:

1. **Ask** students to read *Review Session* in their workbooks (activity 13.23).

2. **Play** the video segment entitled *Review Session* (segment 13.23). Billy reviews all the ASL vocabulary and provides visual cues and origin information. Because the presentation of this segment is beyond the linguistic ability of beginning students, please **turn on** the audio and/or captions to optimize its educational value.

3. **Ask** students to pay careful attention to the signed vocabulary items and take note of visual hints offered by Billy that might help them remember.

4. **Suggest** that students copy the signs to reinforce retention of sign production.

Lesson Thirteen: *Business as UNusual*

Video Segment Content: (11 Minutes)

See the following Student Workbook excerpt for the content of this video segment.

Student Workbook: Activity 13.23

13.23 Video Learning Experience

Review Session

Viewing Goal: To help you remember how to produce the signs introduced in this lesson.

Viewing Instructions: Watch this video segment carefully to see how each sign is produced, and take note of any hints that might help you remember. You may want to copy the signs as you watch Billy.

The following are the vocabulary and explanations:

BUSY	Originally based on the sign for WORK, the sign has become BUSY.
BUSINESS	This sign is based on the sign for BUSY, but it is a little more formal.
COMPANY	Words that are required to be fingerspelled are often abbreviated, because it is faster. We abbreviate company as C-O.
BOSS	This sign is like the epaulets that the commanders wear on the shoulders in the military.
PAY	I am giving money to another person.
HIRE	I am inviting another person to come to work.
FIRE	The fist is a person's body. The head is on top and we cut it off.
FIRST	You have a list of things and this sign represents the first on the list.
EXPLAIN	You have many things and you pull one thing out at a time and define it.
BORING	This is based on the old English phrase, "Put your nose to the grindstone."
OFFICE	This is a compound sign using the signs WORK+ ROOM. The other way is to fingerspell the word, O-F-F-I-C-E.
PROFESSION	There are different fields of work and you concentrate on one area.
CONSULT	This sign shows sending you some of my knowledge.
TYPE	This sign follows the action of how one uses a typewriter.
TYPEWRITER	This is similar to the sign TYPE, but now we are referring to the machine itself.
COMPUTER	This is the same idea as a typewriter but we show the monitor. An older sign depicts the reel-to-reel tape movement.

Lesson Thirteen: *Business as UNusual*

COMPUTER+PRINTER	This is the sign for PRINT. We add this to the sign for COMPUTER.
LETTER	You write it, fold it, put it in an envelope, and then you put a stamp on it.
SIGNATURE/SIGN	You have a piece of paper that you put (SIGN) your name on.
ENVELOPE	This shows the shape of the envelope and how you seal it.
STAMP	This sign represents putting the stamp on an envelope.
SEND	You have just finished the letter, you put a stamp on it then you mail it.
DESK	This sign reflects the flat surface of the DESK.
DRAWER	This sign shows how you open a DRAWER.
SHELF	This sign shows what a shelf, or shelves, look like.
COPY	This sign shows how an image is copied from a page.
FILE	There is a folder and documents are put in or stored in the folder.
FILES	The sign for FILE is repeated several times.
LAZY	When you're lazy your body slumps. We use the "L" handshape.
PRESIDENT	This is like the bull who is the leader of the herd. We show the horns of the bull to make the sign for PRESIDENT.
VICE-PRESIDENT	This is an abbreviation instead of finger-spelling VICE PRESIDENT (V-P). Also, the signing space is a little lower than that for PRESIDENT.
POST-OFFICE	An abbreviation for P-O-S-T O-F-F-I-C-E is P-O.
SCISSORS	This sign mirrors how scissors are used.
STAPLE/STAPLER	This sign shows how you use a STAPLER.
CHECK	This sign shows the shape of a CHECK.
TAPE	This is based on how one uses TAPE.
PAPER+CLIP	You have already learned the sign for PAPER, the other hand shows the CLIP on the paper.
RUBBER-BAND	A rubber band is circular and very elastic.
MEETING	This sign represents a group of people together discussing something.

Lesson Thirteen: *Business as UNusual*

EARN	There is a pile of money here and I collect it.
SCHEDULE	This is like the grid of days and weeks shown on a calendar.
APPOINTMENT	You are holding or reserving a time. It is like having a calendar and holding on to one day.
ASSISTANT	The one hand represents the boss, the other hand is below, supporting the boss.
ASK	This sign often expresses a request. Another way is with the index finger making the shape of a question mark.
INTERVIEW	This sign reflects a dialogue between two people. We use the "I" handshape.
SKILL	This sign is based on the old sign for GREASE. A professional knows what to do in their field. They are "smooth as oil."
NEED	This is a symbolic representation. There are several meanings to this sign but the facial expression tells you this is NEED.
OH-I-SEE	Hearing people have vocal responses like hmmm, oh, really, and ahhh. Deaf people use the "Y" handshape and the specific feeling is added through facial expression. OH-I-SEE.

13.24 Video Learning Experience

Practice Session: Sentences

Viewing Goal: To improve comprehension skills by watching sentences presented in ASL.

Viewing Instructions:
1. **Ask** students to read *Practice Session: Sentences* in their workbooks (activity 13.24).

2. **Play** the video segment entitled *Practice Session: Sentences* (segment 13.24). Each sentence is signed twice and an English translation is provided.

3. **Remind** students to watch the face of each signer to see the facial/body expressions and non-manual grammatical markers as well as the signs.

Lesson Thirteen: *Business as UNusual*

Video Segment Content:
(2 Minutes)

The following are English translations of the practice sentences:

1. Are you skilled at typing?
2. If you work hard you will get promoted!
3. Which do you want? The tape or the stapler?
4. My office has a computer.
5. I made a copy of the letter.
6. Today I have an appointment for a job interview.
7. I will be a company president.

Student Workbook:
Activity 13.24

13.24 Video Learning Experience

Practice Session: Sentences

Viewing Goal: To improve your comprehension skills by watching sentences presented in ASL.

Viewing Instructions: Watch the signed sentences for comprehension. Remember to watch the face of each signer to see the facial/body expressions and the non-manual grammatical markers as well as the signs.

It is recommended that you copy each signed sentence when it is repeated.

In the space below, record any questions or notes you have regarding the sentences.

Notes: _____
_____
_____
_____

Lesson Thirteen: *Business as UNusual*

13.25 Experiential Activity

Create-A-Sentence

Activity Goal: To improve expressive and comprehension skills using sentences presented in ASL.

Activity Instructions:
1. **Ask** students to read *Create-A-Sentence* in their workbooks (activity 13.25).
2. **Divide** class into pairs.
3. **Instruct** students to take turns creating sentences in ASL using at least one vocabulary item provided in Column A and at least one vocabulary item in Column B.
4. **Circulate** among pairs, **observing** student performance and **modeling** corrections as needed.

Student Workbook: Activity 13.25

13.25 Experiential Activity

Create-A-Sentence

Activity Goal: To improve your expressive and comprehension skills by creating ASL sentences.

Activity Instructions: With a partner, take turns creating sentences in ASL. Choose at least one vocabulary item from Column A and at least one from Column B to form each sentence.

Column A	Column B
JOB	SIGNATURE
INTERVIEW	BOSS
SKILL	NEED
LAZY	SEND
TYPEWRITER	ASK-QUESTION
LETTER	FIRE
FILE	DRAWER
CHECK	COMPUTER

Instructor's Guide: Lesson Thirteen
Bravo ASL! Curriculum

©1996 Sign Enhancers, Inc.
ALL RIGHTS RESERVED.

Lesson Thirteen: *Business as UNusual*

13.26 Video Learning Experience

Cultural Notes

Viewing Goal: To assist students in learning about the cultural aspects of ASL.

Viewing Instructions:
1. **Ask** students to read *Cultural Notes* in their workbooks (activity 13.26).

2. **Play** the video segment entitled *Cultural Notes* (segment 13.26). Because the presentation of this segment is beyond the linguistic ability of beginning students, please **turn on** the captions and/or audio to optimize its educational value.

3. **Instruct** students to view the segment.

4. At completion of the video segment, **review** the content presented and **answer** any questions students may have.

Instructor Tip:

Because Cultural Notes includes information about relay services, an optional activity students may complete is to use a telephone relay service to communicate with a Deaf student. Or - you may contact Deaf adults in your community in advance and verify that they would be willing to take a relay call from your students.

Video Segment Content:
(4 Minutes)

See the following Student Workbook excerpt for the content of this video segment.

Student Workbook:
Activity 13.26

13.26 Video Learning Experience

Cultural Notes

Viewing Goal: To learn about the cultural aspects of ASL.

Viewing Instructions: View the *Cultural Notes* segment carefully for the following:

I. Telephones and their impact on employment for Deaf people:
   A. Deaf people have been denied jobs or discriminated against because the job required the use of a telephone.
   B. Modern technologies, including those listed below, have improved this situation.
      1. TTYs
      2. Relay services
      3. Computer networks

Lesson Thirteen: *Business as UNusual*

II. Telephone relay service:

    A. Facilitates communication between a person with a TTY and a person using a voice-only telephone.

        1. A relay operator translates the spoken message of a hearing person to a typed message for the Deaf person and vice versa.

        2. The relay service can be used by both hearing and Deaf people.

    B. Relay services help make more jobs accessible to Deaf people.

III. As technology continues to develop, the barriers to communication are decreasing.

13.27 Video Learning Experience

Grammatical Notes

Viewing Goal: To assist students in learning about the grammatical aspects of ASL.

Viewing Instructions:

1. **Ask** students to read *Grammatical Notes* in their workbooks (activity 13.27).

2. **Play** the video segment entitled *Grammatical Notes* (segment 13.27). Because the presentation of this segment is beyond the linguistic ability of beginning students, please **turn on** the audio and/or captions to optimize its educational value.

3. **Instruct** students to view the segment.

4. At completion of segment, **review** the content presented and **answer** any questions students may have.

Instructor's Guide: Lesson Thirteen
Bravo ASL! Curriculum

©1996 Sign Enhancers, Inc.
ALL RIGHTS RESERVED.

Lesson Thirteen: *Business as UNusual*

Video Segment Content: See the following Student Workbook excerpt for the content
(3 1/2 Minutes) of this video segment.

Student Workbook:
Activity 13.27

13.27 Video Learning Experience

Grammatical Notes

Viewing Goal: To learn about the grammatical aspects of ASL.

Viewing Instructions: View the *Grammatical Notes* for the following:

Combining numbers and signs:

A. Numbers can be incorporated with pronouns:
   1. TWO-OF-US uses the number TWO sign.
   2. FOUR-OF-US uses the number FOUR sign.

B. Numbers can be incorporated with time:
   1. ONE-MONTH, TWO-MONTH, etc.
   2. ONE-WEEK, TWO-WEEK, etc.

13.28 Experiential Activity

Name the Number

Activities Video

Activity Goal: To apply the grammatical information regarding the use of numbers incorporated with pronouns.

Activity Instructions:
1. **Ask** students to read *Name the Number* in their workbooks (activity 13.28).

2. **Show** students the segment entitled *Name the Number* of the Activities Video (segment 13.28). Each signed sentence will be presented twice.

3. **Instruct** students to view the sentences carefully and select the picture that best illustrates the sentence. **Ask** students to record the answers in their workbooks.

4. **Upon** completing this activity, **show** the overhead (Appendix 13.28) and **review** the answers.

Lesson Thirteen: *Business as UNusual*

Video Segment Content:
(2 Minutes)

The following are translations of the sentences presented in the Activities Video (segment 13.28)

1. The two of us will go to the office tomorrow.
2. The check is for the three of you.
3. The family, the four of us, will go to eat now.
4. The two men will buy a new computer.
5. Tomorrow, you, the interpreter, and the boss will interview.

LESSON THIRTEEN

Student Workbook: Activity 13.28

Overhead Master: Appendix 13.28

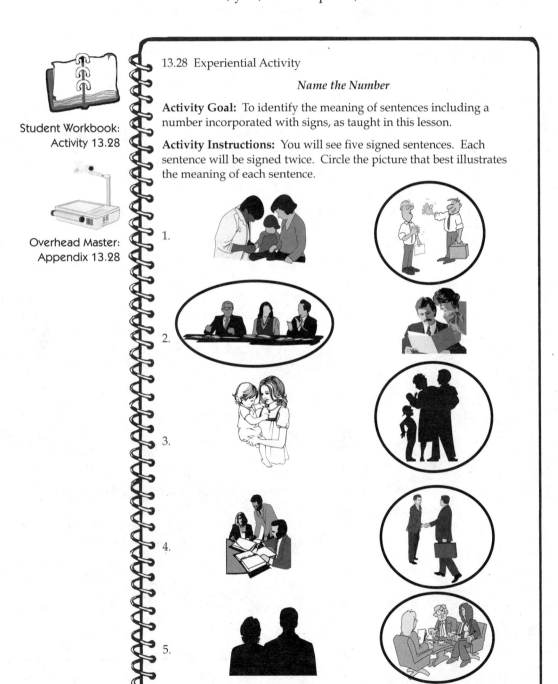

13.28 Experiential Activity

Name the Number

Activity Goal: To identify the meaning of sentences including a number incorporated with signs, as taught in this lesson.

Activity Instructions: You will see five signed sentences. Each sentence will be signed twice. Circle the picture that best illustrates the meaning of each sentence.

Instructor's Guide: Lesson Thirteen
Bravo ASL! Curriculum

©1996 Sign Enhancers, Inc.
ALL RIGHTS RESERVED.

Lesson Thirteen: *Business as UNusual*

13.29 Video Learning Experience

Practice Session: Story

Viewing Goal: To improve ASL comprehension skills by watching a signed story.

Viewing Instructions:
1. **Ask** students to read *Practice Session: Story* in their workbooks (activity 13.29).

2. **Show** the video segment entitled *Practice Session: Story* (segment 13.29). Billy signs a story using the vocabulary introduced in this lesson. **Turn off** audio and captions.

3. **Instruct** students to watch the signed story and write a summary of the main points.

Video Segment Content: (1 1/2 Minutes)

The following is a translation of the story:

Anna works at her mother's company. Anna helps her Mother. Scott wants to help. As the boss, Anna interviews Scott. She hires Scott. Scott is not a good worker. He does not concentrate on his work. He concentrates on his computer games. He plays, and plays, and plays. He wads up papers and throws them across the room. As Anna walks by, Scott takes a rubber band and shoots her. Scott says, "I want my pay! I want a promotion!" What does Anna do? She fires him!

Student Workbook: Activity 13.29

13.29 Video Learning Experience

Practice Session: Story

Viewing Goal: To improve your comprehension by watching a story presented in ASL.

Viewing Instructions: Watch the signed story for comprehension. In the space below, write a summary of the main points.

Summary: _____
_____
_____
_____

13.30 Comprehension Quiz

What Did You Understand?

Quiz Goal: To assess students' comprehension of the signed story.

Quiz Instructions:
1. **Instruct** students to complete the quiz in their workbooks (activity 13.30).

2. **Collect** for grading or **show** the overhead (Appendix 13.30) and **ask** individual students to indicate the correct answers on the overhead while class members correct their own work.

3. **Ask** students to indicate which item(s) from the quiz they found difficult. **Review** by **modeling** or **replaying** that segment of the videotape.

Student Workbook: Activity 13.30

Overhead Master: Appendix 13.30

> 13.30 Comprehension Quiz
>
> *What Did You Understand?*
>
> **Quiz Goal:** To see how much of the signed story you understood.
>
> **Quiz Instructions:** Read and answer each question.
>
> 1. Where does Anna work?
>   **At her mother's company.**
>
> 2. Who does Anna interview?
>   **She interviews Scott.**
>
> 3. What kind of worker is the new employee?
>   **He is not a good worker. He does not concentrate on his work.**
>
> 4. What does the new employee do instead of work?
>   **He spends time playing computer games.**
>
> 5. What does the new employee do to Anna?
>   **He shoots her with a rubber band.**
>
> 6. What does the new employee demand of Anna?
>   **His pay and a promotion.**
>
> 7. What does Anna do instead?
>   **She fires him!**

Lesson Thirteen: *Business as UNusual*

13.31 Homework Assignment

A Day at the Office

Homework Goal: To provide students with the opportunity to improve ASL expressive skills.

Homework Instructions:
1. **Ask** students to read *A Day at the Office* in their workbooks (activity 13.31).

2. **Ask** students to create a story about a day at the office using the illustrations provided in their workbook. **Inform** students that the story should include:

   A) At least eight of the vocabulary items introduced in this lesson, and

   B) At least three numbers incorporated into signs as presented in the *Grammatical Notes* segment.

Instructor Tip: *An opportunity for students to perform this assignment has been scheduled in the next lesson (Homework Review 14.2). If possible, it is recommended that you arrange to videotape each student's performance of this activity.*

Student Workbook: Activity 13.31

13.31 Homework Assignment

A Day at the Office

Homework Goal: To help you improve your ASL expressive skills.

Homework Instructions: Create a story about a day at the office using the pictures below. The story must include at least eight of the ASL vocabulary introduced in this lesson and use at least three numbers incorporated into signs as presented in the *Grammatical Notes* segment. Be prepared to share your story with the class.

Lesson Thirteen: *Business as UNusual*

13.32 Post-test

What Do You Know Now?

Assessment Video

Post-test Goal: To assess students' mastery of the lesson objectives.

Post-test Instructions:

1. **Ask** students to read the Post-test Introduction in their workbooks (activity 13.32).

2. **Copy** and **distribute** the Lesson Thirteen Post-test (Appendix 13.32).

3. **Play** the Assessment Video (segment 13.32) and allow students to complete Section One (comprehension portion) of the test.

4. **Instruct** students to complete Section Two (culture and grammar portion) of the test individually and hand in their papers when they are finished.

5. **Assign** Section Three (expressive portion) of the test and **schedule** a time when students are to perform. **Inform** students they are to select a partner for the role-play described in the expressive portion instructions. If possible, it is strongly recommended that you **videotape** this portion of the Post-test.

6. **Determine** grading options based upon programmatic requirements. A recommended guideline for measuring successful mastery of objectives is 80% accuracy.

Video Segment Content:
(2 Minutes)

The following is an English translation of the comprehension story:

I am the president of a company. I need a secretary. The secretary must be skilled at typing. Two people wanted to interview for the job. Their names were Billy and Liza.

After I interviewed both of them, I asked them to type a letter on the computer. Liza typed very fast without one mistake. Billy typed very slow and had many mistakes. I hired Liza as my new secretary. Her first job was to file all my papers.

Instructor's Guide: Lesson Thirteen
Bravo ASL! Curriculum

©1996 Sign Enhancers, Inc.
ALL RIGHTS RESERVED.

Lesson Thirteen: *Business as UNusual*

Student Workbook:
Activity 13.32

13.32 Post-test Introduction

What Do You Know Now?

Post-test Goal: To assess your mastery of the lesson objectives.

Post-test Introduction: This test has three sections:

Section One: The Comprehension section tests your ability to understand ASL.

Section Two: The Culture and Grammar section tests your knowledge of the material presented in the *Cultural* and *Grammatical Notes*.

Section Three: The Expressive portion tests your ability to use ASL.

Simply follow the instructions for each section. **Good luck!**

Post-test Master:
Appendix 13.32

13.32 Post-test

Section One: Comprehension

Instructions: Watch the signed sample carefully and answer each question below.

1. The president needed to hire someone for the job of _____.
   A. Boss
   B. Secretary
   C. Assistant

2. Who applied for the position?
   A. Liza and Billy
   B. Kathy and Bob
   C. John and Jenna

3. After the interview, what did the president ask each person to do?
   A. Clean the office
   B. File papers
   C. Type a letter

4. The president hired _____ for the job.
   A. Liza
   B. Billy
   C. Tom

5. The secretary's first job was to _____.
   A. Buy a computer
   B. Type a letter
   C. File papers

Post-test Master:
Appendix 13.32

13.32 Post-test

Section Two: Culture and Grammar

Instructions: Read each statement carefully and determine if it is true or false (circle your answer).

6. Telephones have never been an obstacle to Deaf people getting jobs.
   A. True
   B. False

7. Today, TTYs allow Deaf people to communicate on the telephone.
   A. True
   B. False

8. Relay services are only beneficial to Deaf people.
   A. True
   B. False

9. Numbers can be combined with some time signs.
   A. True
   B. False

10. Numbers, when combined with classifiers, can give even more information about how many people are involved.
    A. True
    B. False

Lesson Thirteen: *Business as UNusual*

Post-test Master:
Appendix 13.32

13.32 Post-test

Section Three: Expressive Portion

Instructions: For this portion of your test, you and a partner will role-play being employees, an employee and a boss, or two bosses of a large company.

Each of you must use at least seven signs learned in Lesson Thirteen during your role-play. Each person must also include three pronoun signs incorporating numbers.

Your individual grade depends on your expressive ability and not your partner's. Both participants must follow the guidelines above to receive full credit.

Your instructor will schedule a time for you to perform this section of the Post-test. You may prepare and practice prior to your scheduled time. Use the space below to prepare for your expressive performance.

Include at least seven signs from Lesson Thirteen.

11. _____
12. _____
13. _____
14. _____
15. _____
16. _____
17. _____

Include three pronoun signs incorporating numbers (for example, TWO-OF-US):

18. _____
19. _____
20. _____

Congratulations! You have completed Lesson Thirteen!

Lesson 14
LET'S GO CLOTHES SHOPPING!

Materials Needed:

Equipment: VCR and TV monitor
Overhead projector and screen
Optional: video camera for activities 14.2 and 14.27

Materials: Instructor's Guide
Student Workbook: one per student
Overhead transparencies for activities 14.3, 14.4, 14.5, 14.6, 14.10, 14.11, 14.17, and 14.25 (see Appendix for masters)
Clothing articles (old hats, shoes, shirts, tie, sweaters, etc) for activity 14.23
Optional: blank videotape (or have students bring their own) for activities 14.2 and 14.27
Post-test: Appendix 14.27

Videotapes: The Beginning ASL VideoCourse Lesson Fourteen
Activities Video for activities 14.5 and 14.21
Assessment Video for Post-test 14.27

14.1 Begin Class

Housekeeping

Goal: To prepare students for this lesson.

Instructions:
1. **Welcome** students to Lesson Fourteen of the VideoCourse.
2. **Perform** any necessary tasks (such as taking attendance) that may be required by your specific program.

Instructor's Guide: Lesson Fourteen
Bravo ASL! Curriculum

©1996 Sign Enhancers, Inc.
ALL RIGHTS RESERVED.

Lesson Fourteen: *Let's Go Clothes Shopping!*

14.2 Homework Review

A Day at the Office

Activity Goal: To provide feedback on previously assigned homework and to reinforce materials learned in earlier lessons.

Activity Instructions:

1. **Ask** students to read *A Day at the Office* in their workbooks (activity 14.2).

2. **Divide** the class into groups of three or four.

3. **Instruct** groups to take turns signing the stories they were asked to prepare (*Homework Assignment 13.31*) while group members practice comprehension.

4. **Encourage** students to use ASL to ask each other questions about the stories.

5. **Circulate** to **observe** student performances and **model** corrections as necessary.

6. When students have finished practicing the stories with their groups, **ask** individual students to demonstrate their stories for the class. It is recommended that you **videotape** this activity.

Student Workbook:
Activity 14.2

14.2 Homework Review

A Day at the Office

Activity Goal: To show the results of your homework assignment.

Activity Instructions: Take turns in your group signing the story *A Day at the Office* assigned for homework in Lesson Thirteen. You may look at the pictures in activity 13.31 to help you.

When it is your turn to sign your story, remember to include at least eight of the work-related signs you learned in Lesson Thirteen, and at least three examples of incorporating numbers with signs, as instructed in the *Grammatical Notes*.

When your classmates are signing, pay close attention and practice your ASL comprehension skills. Use ASL to ask questions about their stories.

Be prepared to sign your story to the class.

Lesson Fourteen: *Let's Go Clothes Shopping!*

14.3 Pretest

What Do You Know?

Pretest Goal: To identify students' current level of knowledge pertaining to the lesson content.

Pretest Instructions:

1. **Ask** students to read and answer the pretest questions in their workbooks (activity 14.3).

2. **Show the overhead** (Appendix 14.3) and **ask** individual students to indicate the correct answers on the overhead while class members correct their own work.

3. **Inform** students that the contents of the pretest will be taught throughout the lesson.

Student Workbook: Activity 14.3

Overhead Master: Appendix 14.3

14.3 Pretest

What Do You Know?

Pretest Goal: To see how much you already know about what will be taught in this lesson.

Pretest Instructions: Read and answer each question.

1. Most Deaf children are born to hearing parents.
   A. True
   B. False
2. Many hearing parents with Deaf children never learn to sign.
   A. True
   B. False
3. Parents must consider the individual needs of their child before making important decisions about communication.
   A. True
   B. False
4. If a child learns to sign, that means s/he will never learn to talk.
   A. True
   B. False
5. The term "classifiers" refers to:
   A. A class of people who use ASL.
   B. A class of Deaf children who misbehave.
   C. A class of objects represented by a certain handshape.
   D. A class of students that urgently want to learn ASL.
6. Which of these vehicles cannot be signed with the "3" handshape?
   A. Car
   B. Motorcycle
   C. Boat
   D. Airplane
7. What numbers can be incorporated into classifiers?
   X A. 1
   X B. 2
   X C. 3
   X D. 4

Lesson Fourteen: *Let's Go Clothes Shopping!*

14.4 Lesson Objectives

Planning for Success

Goal: To identify the learning outcomes associated with successful completion of this lesson.

Instructions:
1. **Ask** students to read the objectives in their workbooks (activity 14.4).
2. **Show** the overhead (Appendix 14.4) and **read** through the objectives with the class.

Student Workbook: Activity 14.4

Overhead Master: Appendix 14.4

14.4 Lesson Objectives

Planning for Success

Goal: To see what you will learn by the end of this lesson.

Instructions: Read the objectives below.

Upon completing this VideoCourse lesson, you will be able to...

1. Recognize and accurately produce the ASL vocabulary introduced in this and all previous lessons.
2. Identify some of the key issues parents face in making decisions regarding communication when raising a Deaf child.
3. Identify some of the communication options available to Deaf children.
4. Define "classifiers" and recognize their use in signed communication.
5. Accurately produce and use classifiers within the context of signed communication.

Lesson Fourteen: *Let's Go Clothes Shopping!*

14.5 Lesson Focus

What Are They Wearing?

Activities Video

Activity Goal: To develop a need for the ASL vocabulary introduced in this lesson.

Activity Instructions:

1. **Ask** students to read *What Are They Wearing?* in their workbooks (activity 14.5).

2. **Play** Activities Video segment (segment 14.5). **Instruct** students to watch each signed description and circle the picture in their workbooks that best matches its meaning. **Encourage** students to guess if they do not understand the signs.

3. **Show** the overhead (Appendix 14.5) and **ask** individual students to indicate the correct answers on the overhead while class members correct their own work.

4. At the completion of the activity, you may **choose**:

   Option A: **Lead** a discussion using the following Thought/Discussion Questions:

   1) What are some signs related to clothing that would have been useful to know during this activity?

   2) How did it feel to be limited in your ability to understand the signed descriptions?

   3) What are some techniques that Deaf people could use in describing people and their clothes to people who do not sign?

   OR

   Option B: **Ask** students to complete the Thought/Discussion Questions in their workbooks in class or for homework. **Collect** for grading or to provide students with written feedback.

5. **Inform** students that they will learn the signs needed to communicate about clothing throughout this lesson.

   Note: You may want to repeat this activity at the end of the lesson to reinforce material and show students how much they've learned.

Lesson Fourteen: *Let's Go Clothes Shopping!*

Video Segment Content:
(2 1/2 Minutes)

The following are English translations for this video segment:

1. The girl wearing a hat, skirt, and backpack.
2. The boy wearing no hat, a coat and tie, nice pants and black shoes.
3. The man wearing comfortable pants and a horizontally-striped sweater.
4. The woman wearing a fancy, expensive dress, black hat, long gloves, and fancy shoes.

Student Workbook: Activity 14.5

Overhead Master: Appendix 14.5

14.5 Lesson Focus

What Are They Wearing?

Activity Goal: To find out what clothing signs you know (and which you need to learn).

Activity Instructions: You will see several signed descriptions of people and what they are wearing. Watch carefully, and for each description, circle the correct picture below.

1. A.   B.   C.

2. A.   B.   C.

3. A.   B. 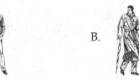 C.

4. A.  B.   C.

Thought/Discussion Questions

1. What are some signs related to clothing that would have been useful to know during this activity?
2. How did it feel to be limited in your ability to understand the signed descriptions?
3. What are some techniques that Deaf people could use in describing people and their clothes to people who do not sign?

14.6 Language Learning Instruction

Learning New Signs

Goal: To use ASL and visual aids to introduce this lesson's vocabulary.

Instructions:

1. **Ask** students to read *Learning New Signs* in their workbooks (activity 14.6).

2. **Show** the overhead (Appendix 14.6). **Introduce** the vocabulary by **pointing** to items presented in the pictures while **demonstrating** the signs.

3. **Reinforce** retention and **check** students' comprehension by **using** these signs to **ask** students questions.

   Note: For a step-by-step review of this method, see Lesson One (activities 1.6 and 1.12).

4. **Continue** this process until all the ASL vocabulary items have been introduced.

Overhead Content: Use the pictures in the overhead (Appendix 14.6) to introduce the signs representing the following concepts:

1. CLOTHES
2. STORE
3. SHOPPING/BUYING
4. TOWEL
5. LIKE
6. DON'T-LIKE
7. TALL
8. TWO-OF-US
9. THREE-OF-US
10. PANTS
11. SHIRT/SWEATER
12. TIE
13. HAT

Note: Some pictures can be used to represent several concepts. For verbs and more abstract concepts, you may need to supplement these pictures with mime, gestures, using actual objects, and acting out the concepts in class.

Lesson Fourteen: *Let's Go Clothes Shopping!*

Overhead Master:
Appendix 14.6

Lesson Fourteen: *Let's Go Clothes Shopping!*

Student Workbook:
Activity 14.6

14.6 Language Learning Instruction

Learning New Signs

Goal: To help you learn new ASL vocabulary.

Instructions: Your instructor will teach you new signs! Watch closely to learn what these signs mean and how they are produced.

In the space below, record any notes to help you remember the signs.

Notes: _____
_____
_____
_____

14.7 Video Learning Experience

Introduction to New Vocabulary

Viewing Goal: To provide a signed demonstration of the accurate production of the new ASL vocabulary.

Viewing Instructions:
1. **Ask** students to read *Introduction to New Vocabulary* in their workbooks (activity 14.7).

2. **Play** the video segment entitled *Introduction to New Vocabulary* (segment 14.7). Billy introduces and signs each new vocabulary item twice. (If you wish to keep this a strictly visual presentation, **turn off** audio.)

3. **Instruct** students to watch how Billy produces the signs as well as the accompanying facial/body expressions.

4. **Ask** students to copy the signs and the facial/body expressions as Billy repeats each one.

Video Segment Content:
(3 Minutes)

The Bravo family enters Sears. The children hide by posing as mannequins in the store. Mom and Dad are searching for them. They stop right in front of the kids and pretend to not see them. Dad signs that because they can't find the children, it won't be necessary to buy them new clothes. Mom and Dad walk away. The kids look at each other, then run after their parents.

Lesson Fourteen: *Let's Go Clothes Shopping!*

Billy: Hello again! Welcome to Sign Enhancers, Inc. American Sign Language VideoCourse, Lesson Fourteen

Do you like shopping? Shopping is a great way for you to learn new signs. As the Bravos do their shopping, we will have fun watching, and you will learn new signs. But first I want to get you started by teaching you several new signs...

See the following Student Workbook excerpt for the ASL signs taught in this video segment.

Student Workbook: Activity 14.7

14.7 Video Learning Experience

Introduction to New Vocabulary

Viewing Goal: To help you learn the new ASL vocabulary.

Viewing Instructions: Watch how Billy produces each sign. Be sure to notice the facial/body expressions. Copy the signs as Billy repeats each one.

Signs representing the following concepts are introduced in this video segment:

1. CLOTHES
2. STORE
3. SHOPPING/BUYING
4. TOWEL
5. LIKE
6. DON'T-LIKE
7. TALL
8. TWO-OF-US
9. THREE-OF-US
10. PANTS
11. SHIRT/SWEATHER
12. TIE
13. HAT

14.8 Experiential Activity

Point and Sign

Activity Goal: To improve students' receptive and expressive ASL skills.

Activity Instructions:
1. **Instruct** students to read *Point and Sign* in their workbooks (activity 14.8).

2. **Divide** the class into groups of four or five.

3. **Ask** groups to look at the pictures in their workbooks and use ASL to have a group discussion (using as many of the new signs as possible).

Lesson Fourteen: *Let's Go Clothes Shopping!*

4. **Circulate** among the groups to **observe** student performance. **Encourage** students to use the following vocabulary:

   1. CLOTHES
   2. STORE
   3. SHOPPING/BUYING
   4. TOWEL
   5. LIKE
   6. DON'T-LIKE
   7. TALL
   8. TWO-OF-US
   9. THREE-OF-US
   10. PANTS
   11. SHIRT/SWEATER
   12. TIE
   13. HAT

5. **Model** the signs and grammatically correct ASL sentence structure as needed.

Student Workbook: Activity 14.8

14.8 Experiential Activity

Point and Sign

Activity Goal: To help you recognize and produce the new ASL vocabulary.

Activity Instructions: Using ASL, discuss the pictures below with your group. Use your new ASL vocabulary such as: CLOTHES; TWO-OF-US; STORE; THREE-OF-US; SHOPPING/BUYING; PANTS; TOWEL; SHIRT/SWEATER; LIKE; TIE; DON'T-LIKE; HAT; and TALL.

Instructor's Guide: Lesson Fourteen
Bravo ASL! Curriculum

Lesson Fourteen: *Let's Go Clothes Shopping!*

14.9 Video Learning Experience

Bravo Family Visit

Viewing Goal: To improve ASL comprehension skills by watching a Bravo family interaction.

Viewing Instructions:

1. **Ask** students to read *Bravo Family Visit* in their workbooks (activity 14.9).

2. **Play** the video segment of the Bravo family (segment 14.9). They will use the new ASL vocabulary within the context of a trip to the store. Because this segment includes an interaction with a hearing person, **turn on** audio and/or captions to optimize its educational value.

3. **Instruct** students to watch for comprehension and write a summary of the main points.

4. **Replay** any portion of this video segment that students experienced difficulty understanding.

Video Segment Content:
(7 1/2 Minutes)

The following is a summary of the Bravo family interaction:

The Bravo family at the store: Mom and Dad are discussing which towel they'd prefer to buy. Anna starts mimicking them. Mom tells her to stop.

Scott begins watching another family looking at towels nearby. The woman picks out a towel and asks her husband if he likes it. The husband takes the towel, taps his son on the shoulder, and asks if he likes the color.

The son misunderstands and takes the towel and places it under his arm. His father talks slowly and uses gestures while trying to ask the question again. The son turns away and his father is frustrated.

Scott continues watching. The boy starts to touch a strange-looking scale. His mother tells the boy not to touch the scale. The son gestures, asking what it is used for. His mother mouths the word "scale," but he does not understand what she is trying to say. She digs into her purse for paper and a pen, but can't find it. She is frustrated and angrily says, "Just don't touch it!"

Scott gets the boy's attention. Scott signs that he is Deaf and asks if the boy is Deaf, too. The boy gestures to indicate that he is. Scott introduces himself and asks the boy's name. The boy awkwardly fingerspells T-O-M-M-Y. Scott gives Tommy a name sign ("T" with the movement of the sign TALL).

Scott asks Tommy if he wants to walk around the store together. Tommy doesn't understand. Scott explains. Anna joins them. The parents are amazed as they watch the kids sign and laugh together.

Mom and Dad approach Tommy's parents. Mom introduces herself and Dad. Tommy's father starts talking to Dad. Dad asks Mom to interpret what the man said. The man apologizes for not realizing Dad is Deaf. They talk about their children briefly. They turn to see the children playing and laughing.

Tommy's father tells the Bravos that he didn't think Tommy knew Sign Language and that he is surprised at how much fun Tommy's having with Anna and Scott.

The children join their parents. Scott asks if he, Tommy, and Anna can walk around the store together. Tommy's mother says OK (thumb up) and the kids take off.

Tommy's father is amazed at how fast Tommy is learning Sign Language. They thought it would be hard to learn. Dad asks if Tommy's parents would like to learn a few signs to surprise their son. They agree.

Meanwhile, Scott is teaching Tommy the signs for pants, shirt, etc. Scott and Tommy play a joke on Anna.

Dad teaches Tommy's father the signs for tie, gloves, and hat. Dad sees something strange in the mirror. It seems one of the mannequins is signing to him. But when he turns around, it is only a mannequin. The two fathers head off.

Billy (the mannequin): Well, you are not the only ones learning new signs. Dennis is helping the other father to learn signs also. That means I had better teach you some new signs. Let's do that now.

Student Workbook:
Activity 14.9

14.9 Video Learning Experience

Bravo Family Visit

Viewing Goal: To improve your ASL comprehension by watching a Bravo family interaction.

Viewing Instructions: Watch the signed interaction and write a summary of the main points.

Summary: _____
_____
_____
_____

Lesson Fourteen: *Let's Go Clothes Shopping!*

14.10 Comprehension Quiz

What Did You Understand?

Quiz Goal: To assess students' comprehension of the signed interaction.

Quiz Instructions:
1. **Instruct** students to complete the quiz in their workbooks (activity 14.10).

2. **Collect** for grading or **show** the overhead (Appendix 14.10) and **ask** individual students to indicate the correct answers on the overhead while class members correct their own work.

3. **Ask** students to indicate which item(s) from the quiz they found difficult. **Review** by **modeling** or **replaying** that segment of the videotape.

Student Workbook:
Activity 14.10

Overhead Master:
Appendix 14.10

14.10 Comprehension Quiz

What Did You Understand?

Quiz Goal: To see how much of the Bravo family interaction you understood.

Quiz Instructions: Read and answer each question.

1. When Scott first meets Tommy, what does he ask?
   A. "How old are you?"
   B. "Do you have a sister?"
   C. "Where is your father?"
   D. "Are you Deaf?"

2. After Tommy fingerspelled his name, what did Scott do?
   A. Gave him a new name.
   B. Gave him a name sign.
   C. Told him his fingerspelling was too slow.
   D. Told him he was too tall.

3. What does Scott ask Tommy?
   A. If he wants to buy pants.
   B. If he wants to buy a mask.
   C. If he wants to walk around the store together.
   D. If he wants Anna as a girlfriend.

4. What are some of the signs Scott taught Tommy?
   A. MASK, PANTS, and SISTER
   B. PANTS, SHIRT, SOCKS and SHOES
   C. DEAF, HEARING, SISTER, and BROTHER
   D. SCARE, PETER PAN, CLOTHES, and COAT

5. What are some of the signs Dad taught Tommy's father?
   A. HAT, TIE, and GLOVES
   B. MIRROR, OVERALLS, and HAT
   C. EXPENSIVE, BUY, and DRESS
   D. MONEY, SON, and FAMILY

Instructor's Guide: Lesson Fourteen
Bravo ASL! Curriculum

Lesson Fourteen: *Let's Go Clothes Shopping!*

14.11 Language Learning Instruction

Learning New Signs

Goal: To use ASL and visual aids to introduce this lesson's vocabulary.

Instructions:
1. **Ask** students to read *Learning New Signs* in their workbooks (activity 14.11).

2. **Show** the overhead (Appendix 14.11). **Introduce** the vocabulary by **pointing** to the pictures while **demonstrating** the signs.

3. **Reinforce** retention and **check** students' comprehension by **using** these signs to **ask** students questions.

    Note: For a step-by-step review of this method, see Lesson One (activities 1.6 and 1.12).

4. **Continue** this process until all the ASL vocabulary items have been introduced.

Overhead Content: Use the pictures in the overhead (Appendix 14.11) to introduce the signs representing the following concepts:

1. DRESS	6. BACKPACK	11. FANCY
2. SKIRT	7. PURSE	12. COMFORTABLE
3. COAT	8. PRICE/COST	13. LUCKY
4. SOCKS	9. BIG/LARGE	14. DINNER
5. SHOES	10. CUTE	15. LOVE-IT

Note: Some pictures can be used to represent several concepts. For verbs and more abstract concepts, you may need to supplement these pictures with mime, gestures, using actual objects, and acting out the concepts in class.

Instructor's Guide: Lesson Fourteen
Bravo ASL! Curriculum

©1996 Sign Enhancers, Inc.
ALL RIGHTS RESERVED.

Lesson Fourteen: *Let's Go Clothes Shopping!*

Overhead Master:
Appendix 14.11

Lesson Fourteen: *Let's Go Clothes Shopping!*

Student Workbook:
Activity 14.11

14.11 Language Learning Instruction

Learning New Signs

Goal: To help you learn new ASL vocabulary.

Instructions: Your instructor will teach you new signs! Watch closely to learn what these signs mean and how they are produced.

In the space below, record any notes to help you remember the signs.

Notes: _____
_____
_____
_____

14.12 Video Learning Experience

Introduction to New Vocabulary

Viewing Goal: To provide a signed demonstration of the accurate production of the new ASL vocabulary.

Viewing Instructions:
1. **Ask** students to read *Introduction to New Vocabulary* in their workbooks (activity 14.12).

2. **Play** the video segment entitled *Introduction to New Vocabulary* (segment 14.12). Billy introduces and signs each new vocabulary item twice. (If you wish to keep this a strictly visual presentation, **turn off** audio.)

3. **Instruct** students to watch how Billy produces the signs and the accompanying facial/body expressions.

4. **Ask** students to copy the signs and the facial/body expressions as Billy repeats each one.

Instructor's Guide: Lesson Fourteen
Bravo ASL! Curriculum

14–17

©1996 Sign Enhancers, Inc.
ALL RIGHTS RESERVED.

Lesson Fourteen: *Let's Go Clothes Shopping!*

Video Segment Content: See the following Student Workbook excerpt for the content
(2 Minutes) of this video segment.

Student Workbook:
Acticity 14.12

14.12 Video Learning Experience

Introduction to New Vocabulary

Viewing Goal: To help you learn new ASL vocabulary.

Viewing Instructions: Watch how Billy produces each sign. Be sure to notice the facial/body expressions. Copy the signs as Billy repeats each one.

Signs representing the following concepts are introduced in this video segment:

1. DRESS
2. SKIRT
3. COAT
4. SOCKS
5. SHOES
6. BACKPACK
7. PURSE
8. PRICE/COST
9. BIG/LARGE
10. CUTE
11. FANCY
12. COMFORTABLE
13. LUCKY
14. DINNER
15. LOVE-IT

14.13 Video Learning Experience

Bravo Family Visit

Viewing Goal: To improve ASL comprehension skills by watching a Bravo family interaction.

Viewing Instructions:
1. **Ask** students to read *Bravo Family Visit* in their workbooks (activity 14.13).

2. **Play** the video segment of the Bravo family (segment 14.13). The Bravos will use the new ASL vocabulary within the context of their continued clothes shopping trip. Because this segment includes an interaction with hearing people, **turn on** audio and/or captions to optimize its educational value.

3. **Instruct** students to watch for comprehension and write a summary of the main points.

4. **Replay** any portion of this video segment that students experienced difficulty understanding.

Lesson Fourteen: *Let's Go Clothes Shopping!*

Video Segment Content: The following is a summary of the Bravo family interaction:
(2 Minutes)

Back in the store: The two women are looking at a dress. They think it is very fancy. When they look at the price tag, they discover it is also very expensive. They agree that neither of them dresses that fancy and they laugh together.

The men join them. Tommy's mother asks her husband (using ASL) if he is going to buy the fancy dress. He tells her - using signs - that he is going to buy a tie and hat.

Mom is surprised at how fast this couple has learned the signs. The couple regret that they didn't start learning sooner.

Billy: You know, parents have a difficult job. Our *Cultural Note* for today will focus on hearing parents raising a Deaf child.

Student Workbook:
Activity 14.13

14.13 Video Learning Experience

Bravo Family Visit

Viewing Goal: To improve your ASL comprehension skills by watching a Bravo family interaction.

Viewing Instructions: Watch the signed interaction and write a summary of the main points.

Summary: _____
_____
_____
_____

14.14 Video Learning Experience

Cultural Notes

Viewing Goal: To assist students in learning about the cultural aspects of ASL.

Viewing Instructions:
1. **Ask** students to read *Cultural Notes* in their workbooks (activity 14.14).

2. **Play** the video segment entitled *Cultural Notes* (segment 14.14). Because the presentation of this segment is beyond the linguistic ability of beginning students, please **turn on** the audio and/or captions to optimize its educational value.

3. **Instruct** students to view the segment.

Lesson Fourteen: *Let's Go Clothes Shopping!*

4. At completion of the video segment, **review** the content presented and **answer** any questions students may have.

Video Segment Content: See the following Student Workbook excerpt for the content
(4 Minutes) of this video segment.

Student Workbook:
Activity 14.14

14.14 Video Learning Experience

Cultural Notes

Viewing Goal: To learn about the cultural aspects of ASL.

Viewing Instructions: View the *Cultural Notes* carefully for the following:

I. Most Deaf children are born to hearing parents.
   A. Many hearing parents know little or no Sign Language.
   B. They have had little, if any, contact with other Deaf people.
   C. It is hard for parents to know what to do, in deciding the best way to raise their Deaf child.
   D. Many professionals like doctors, counselors, teachers, disagree on which communication method is best.
      1. For example, some doctors tell parents that if their child learns Sign Language they will never learn to speak.
      2. Some doctors advocate strongly that hearing aids and speech training must be used.
      3. Some doctors advise the use of Sign Language and natural language development through visual means.

II. Sign Enhancers believes that there is not one right way to raise all Deaf children.
   A. Each child's individual needs must be identified and addressed.
   B. Parents have the responsibility to research the various methods and options.
   C. Parents should weigh the positive and negative aspects of each option before a decision can be reached.

III. Another important point is that parents must keep a close watch on their child as the child grows.
   A. Parents need to monitor the child's response.
   B. Parents must remain flexible, making changes that best suit their child. Billy shares, "For me personally, as a Deaf person, I greatly value American Sign Language. It has helped me connect to the world in ways which helped me find out more about who I am and how I fit in.
   "My parents are hearing and they do not use Sign Language. I attended an oral, mainstream program where Sign Language wasn't used.
   "If I could live my life over and change anything I wanted, I would make it so American Sign Language was introduced to me at a very young age. I know I would have been happier."

IV. The most important thing is communication.
   A. Tommy and his parents discovered the excitement of learning American Sign Language.
   B. By expanding communication options, it could change their lives.
   C. You are never too old - nor is it ever too late - to learn a new language.

Lesson Fourteen: *Let's Go Clothes Shopping!*

14.15 Experiential Activity

Panel Discussion

Activity Goal: To provide students the opportunity to meet Deaf people and learn firsthand about their communication preferences.

Activity Instructions:

1. **Invite** several Deaf visitors to your ASL class. It is recommended that you **select** people with various backgrounds and communication styles (Deaf and hearing parents, ASL users, PSE users, etc.). You may **choose** to have an interpreter available during this activity.

2. **Ask** students to read *Panel Discussion* in their workbooks (activity 14.15).

3. **Encourage** the speakers to share about their family backgrounds and communication preferences. You may **choose** to **ask**:

   A. Were you the only Deaf person in your family?

   B. What communication methods were used in your home? How did you feel about this?

   C. What communication methods were used at your school? How did you feel about this?

   D. When and how did you learn to sign?

   E. If you could live your life over, what would you change about how you communicated?

4. Following this panel discussion, you may **choose**:

   Option A: **Lead** a discussion **using** the following Thought/Discussion Questions:

   1) What did you learn from this panel?

   2) How did each of the panel members feel about their communication options?

   3) Did this panel change your opinion about any particular communication option(s)?

   OR

   Option B: **Ask** students to complete the Thought/Discussion Questions in their workbooks in class or for homework. **Collect** for grading or to provide students with written feedback.

Instructor's Guide: Lesson Fourteen
Bravo ASL! Curriculum

Lesson Fourteen: *Let's Go Clothes Shopping!*

Student Workbook: Activity 14.15

14.15 Experiential Activity

Panel Discussion

Activity Goal: To give you the opportunity to meet Deaf people and learn firsthand about their personal communication options and preferences.

Activity Instructions: Your instructor will invite some Deaf people to have a panel discussion. Use the space below for notes. You may also want to write down questions you have for the speakers or for your instructor.

Notes: _____
_____
_____
_____

Thought/Discussion Questions

1. What did you learn from this panel?

2. How did each of the panel members feel about their communication options?

3. Did this panel change your opinion about any particular communication option(s)?

14.16 Video Learning Experience

Bravo Family Visit

Viewing Goal: To improve ASL comprehension skills by watching a Bravo family interaction.

Viewing Instructions:
1. **Ask** students to read *Bravo Family Visit* in their workbooks (activity 14.16).

2. **Play** the video segment of the Bravo family (segment 14.16). The Bravos will use the new ASL vocabulary as they continue to shop. Because this segment includes an interaction with hearing people, **turn on** audio and/or captions to optimize its educational value.

3. **Instruct** students to watch for comprehension and write a summary of the main points.

4. **Replay** any portion of this video segment that students experienced difficulty understanding.

Instructor's Guide: Lesson Fourteen
Bravo ASL! Curriculum

©1996 Sign Enhancers, Inc.
ALL RIGHTS RESERVED

Video Segment Content:
(4 Minutes)

The following is a summary of the signed interaction:

Back at the store: Anna tells Scott and Tommy that she needs new school clothes. They offer to help her shop. Scott picks up a dress. Anna tells him she doesn't like it. Tommy tells her he likes the dress. He then learns the signs for pants, skirt, and coat.

Scott tells Anna the coat she tried on looks good on her and asks her if she plans to buy it. Anna tells him it is too big. Anna decides she needs socks. Scott demonstrates the sign to Tommy and teaches him the sign for shoes. Anna picks out socks, but then decides that she's not going to buy them because they are too expensive.

Tommy comes up with a backpack on, miming hiking. Tommy asks Anna if she likes the backpack. She tells him she likes purses. Scott takes the purse and both boys tease Anna. Anna grabs a Superman costume and makes fun of boys' muscles that flop under the arm instead of bulging above the arm.

The three kids notice Mom and run to her. Scott tells Mom that they are teaching Tommy signs. Mom tells Scott she is proud of them. She tells them she is a lucky Mom. Scott tells her that he and Anna are lucky that their Mom and Dad are fluent in Sign Language. They hug.

Tommy's parents approach. His father tells Tommy that he and his mom are learning Sign Language. He asks Tommy if he likes Sign Language. Tommy tells him that he loves it. His father doesn't understand that sign, so Mom explains it to him. Tommy's dad tells Tommy he loves him.

They thank the Bravos for introducing them to sign. The family gives Mom and Dad their phone number and tells them to call and come over for dinner sometime soon.

Anna asks Tommy if he wants her phone number. Scott makes fun of Anna and she chases him off. The families say goodbye.

As Tommy and his parents walk away, Tommy stops his parents and signs that he loves them. They hug.

Lesson Fourteen: *Let's Go Clothes Shopping!*

Student Workbook: Activity 14.16

14.16 Video Learning Experience

Bravo Family Visit

Viewing Goal: To improve your ASL comprehension by watching a Bravo family interaction.

Viewing Instructions: Watch the signed interaction and write a summary of the main points.

Summary: _____
_____
_____
_____

14.17 Comprehension Quiz

What Did You Understand?

Quiz Goal: To assess students' comprehension of the signed interaction.

Quiz Instructions:
1. **Instruct** students to complete the quiz in their workbooks (activity 14.17).

2. **Collect** for grading or **show** the overhead (Appendix 14.17) and **ask** individual students to indicate the correct answers on the overhead while class members correct their own work.

3. **Ask** students to indicate which item(s) from the quiz they found difficult. **Review** by **modeling** or **replaying** that segment of the videotape.

Student Workbook:
Activity 14.17

Overhead Master:
Appendix 14.17

14.17 Comprehension Quiz

What Did You Understand?

Quiz Goal: To see how much of the Bravo family interaction you understood.

Quiz Instructions: Read and answer each question.

1. Anna likes the dress because Tommy said he liked it.
   A. True
   B. False

2. What does Scott tell Anna about the coat she tried on?
   A. "It looks too big on you."
   B. "You look warm."
   C. "It looks good on you."
   D. "You look cold."

3. What does Tommy ask Anna?
   A. "Do you like backpacks?"
   B. "Do you like purses?"
   C. "Why don't you carry a purse?"
   D. "Do you want to go hiking?"

4. What does Scott tell Mom when they meet again?
   A. "Tommy is my new friend."
   B. "Tommy doesn't know how to sign."
   C. "We've been teaching Tommy signs!"
   D. "Anna likes Tommy!"

5. Why does Scott say he and Anna are lucky?
   A. Because they bought socks and a coat for Anna.
   B. Because they have a new friend
   C. Because they know how to sign.
   D. Because their parents sign.

6. What does Tommy's father tell him when he says he loves Sign Language?
   A. "It's too late to learn now."
   B. "I love you."
   C. "I love Sign Language, too."
   D. "I love this store."

Lesson Fourteen: *Let's Go Clothes Shopping!*

14.18 Video Learning Experience

Review Session

Viewing Goal: To reinforce recognition and production of the signs introduced in this lesson.

Viewing Instructions:
1. **Ask** students to read *Review Session* in their workbooks (activity 14.18).

2. **Play** the video segment entitled *Review Session* (segment 14.18). Billy reviews all the ASL vocabulary and provides visual cues and origin information. Because the presentation of this segment is beyond the linguistic ability of beginning students, please **turn on** the audio and/or captions to optimize its educational value.

3. **Ask** students to pay careful attention to the signed vocabulary items and take note of visual hints offered by Billy that might help them remember.

4. **Suggest** students copy the signs to reinforce retention of sign production.

Video Segment Content: See the following Student Workbook excerpt for the content
(7 Minutes) of this video segment.

Student Workbook:
Activity 14.18

14.18 Video Learning Experience

Review Session

Viewing Goal: To help you remember how to produce the signs introduced in this lesson.

Viewing Instructions: Watch this video segment carefully to see how each sign is made, and take note of any hints given to help you remember. You may want to copy the signs as you watch Billy.

The following are the vocabulary and explanations offered in this video segment:

CLOTHES	This sign represents the clothes covering the body.
STORE	The sign for SELL moves once. For a place that has many things to sell, the sign moves twice. It is a STORE.
SHOPPING/BUYING	The sign for BUY moves once. When you buy a number of things, moving the sign several times, you are SHOPPING.

Instructor's Guide: Lesson Fourteen
Bravo ASL! Curriculum

©1996 Sign Enhancers, Inc.
ALL RIGHTS RESERVED.

TOWEL	You take a towel and dry your back. This sign shows that action.
LIKE	Your body is drawn to something you see, it attracts you.
DON'T-LIKE	This is the opposite of LIKE. You don't want it near you, so you turn it away.
TALL	Billy demonstrates two signs. One sign represents the concept TALL. The other sign specifically shows the top of a person's head.
TWO-OF-US	This sign points to a person and the signer.
THREE-OF-US	This indicates the signer and two others.
PANTS	Billy shows two ways to sign PANTS. The first clearly shows putting pants on. The other sign shows the shape and design.
SHIRT	This shows how a shirt is worn on the body.
TIE	This sign shows what a tie looks like and how it is worn.
HAT	This shows something on the top of the head.
DRESS	This shows the shape and location of a DRESS.
SKIRT	This sign shows the skirt starting from the waist and indicates the shape and location of a SKIRT.
COAT	The movement of this sign indicates the action of putting on a coat with thick, heavy material.
SOCKS	Billy demonstrates two signs for SOCKS. In the first sign, the fingers are the legs. The second sign shows one hand as the foot and the other hand as putting the sock over the foot.
SHOES	This sign represents the hard covering on your feet.
BACKPACK	This sign shows how the straps attach the BACKPACK.
PURSE	How do you use a purse? You carry it by the handle or you can hang it from your arm.
PRICE/COST	This is like the old hand-held machine used to place labels and tags on items, indicating the price of an item.
LARGE/BIG	This shows that something is LARGE.
CUTE	What does an adult will do to a cute child? Pinch the child's chin.
FANCY	When something is really fine, it is FANCY.

Lesson Fourteen: *Let's Go Clothes Shopping!*

EXPENSIVE	Make the sign for MONEY and then show that there is a pile of it.
COMFORTABLE	This represents what your hands do when sitting back comfortably.
LUCKY	This is a symbolic representation.
DINNER	This is a compound sign indicating when you eat dinner, EAT+NIGHT
LOVE-IT	You kiss the back of your hand, meaning you really like or cherish something.

14.19 Experiential Activity

The Wacky Wardrobe Stories

Viewing Goal: To improve ASL skills with signs related to clothing.

Viewing Instructions:

1. **Ask** students to read *The Wacky Wardrobe Stories* in their workbooks (activity 14.19).

2. **Divide** class into pairs.

3. **Instruct** students to look at the pictures provided in their workbooks and create stories using as many signs representing those pictures as possible. **Tell** students to circle the pictures they plan to include in their stories.

4. **Ask** one student in each pair (Partner A) to sign the story for his/her partner (Partner B).

5. **Instruct** Partner B to watch the story and put an "X" by the pictures which were used in the story. When the story is over, Partner B is to sign the number of each picture used in A's story.

6. **Tell** Partner A to provide feedback as to whether his/her partner indicated the correct pictures.

7. **Repeat** the above steps with the partners switching roles.

Instructor's Guide: Lesson Fourteen
Bravo ASL! Curriculum

Lesson Fourteen: *Let's Go Clothes Shopping!*

Student Workbook:
Activity 14.19

14.19 Experiential Activity

Wacky Wardrobe Stories

Viewing Goal: To improve your ASL skills with signs related to clothing.

Viewing Instructions: Your teacher will divide your class into pairs. Take a few minutes to study the pictures below. Each partner will sign a *Wacky Wardrobe Story*, using as many of the pictures below as possible. Circle the pictures you plan to use when you sign your story.

When you and your partner are ready, Partner A will sign your story while Partner B watches and places an X by each picture s/he recognizes in the story.

When the story is over, Partner B should sign to Partner A the numbers of all the pictures used in the story. Partner A will check to see if Partner B got them all!

Repeat this activity, switching roles.

Lesson Fourteen: *Let's Go Clothes Shopping!*

14.20 Video Learning Experience

Grammatical Notes

Viewing Goal: To assist students in learning about the grammatical aspects of ASL.

Viewing Instructions:
1. **Ask** students to read *Grammatical Notes* in their workbooks (activity 14.20).

2. **Play** the video segment entitled *Grammatical Notes* (segment 14.20). Because the presentation of this segment is beyond the linguistic ability of beginning students, please **turn on** the audio and/or captions to optimize its educational value.

3. **Instruct** students to view the segment.

4. At completion of the segment, **review** the content presented and **answer** any questions students may have.

Video Segment Content: See the following Student Workbook excerpt for the content
(4 Minutes) of this video segment.

Student Workbook:
Activity 14.20

14.20 Video Learning Experience

Grammatical Notes

Viewing Goal: To learn about the grammatical aspects of ASL.

Viewing Instructions: View the *Grammatical Notes* segment carefully for the following:

I. Classifiers (abbreviated as CL):
   A. There are many classifiers, which show a *class* of objects/people. For example, the 1-handshape can represent or become a number of cylinder-like objects, such as a person, pole, tree, pencil, etc.
   B. It is possible - with the addition of facial expressions and body language - to express different ideas. For example, PERSON-WALKING can be modified to be a casual walk, a determined walk, a hurried walk, or even a sad walk.
   C. We can use the other hand (with 1-handshape) to show two people greeting each other and walking on (or perhaps, intentionally avoiding each other).

II. Classifiers with the 2-handshape:
   A. When upright, it can mean TWO-PEOPLE-WALKING.
   B. Turned upside down, it can represent the legs of a person or animal:
      JUMPING
      FALLING
      WALKING-QUIETLY

Instructor's Guide: Lesson Fourteen
Bravo ASL! Curriculum

Lesson Fourteen: *Let's Go Clothes Shopping!*

> III. Classifiers with the 3- handshape can represent THREE-PEOPLE-WALKING. In the video, Billy shows the children using this classifier.
>
> IV. Classifiers with the 4-handshape can be used to represent a number of people standing and waiting in a line.
>
> V. Classifiers with V-handshapes can represent the four legs of an animal:
> RUNNING (galloping)
> KICKING (front legs)
> KICKING (back legs)
> LYING-DOWN
>
> VI. Classifiers with the 3-handshape (thumb facing up) can be used to refer to vehicles such as:
> CAR   TRAIN
> TRUCK   MOTORCYCLE
> BUS   BICYCLE
> BOAT
>
> **Note**: Because of its location and movement, AIRPLANE's classifier is different. It is demonstrated on the video.

14.21 Experiential Activity

Classy Classifiers

Activities Video

Viewing Goal: To improve students' comprehension skills with ASL classifiers.

Viewing Instructions:

1. **Ask** students to read *Classy Classifier* in their workbooks (activity 14.21).

2. **Play** the Activities Video (segment 14.21).

3. **Instruct** students to view the signed sentences and select the answer that best matches the meaning of each.

4. **Ask** individual students to use ASL to demonstrate the correct answers while class members correct their own work.

Instructor's Guide: Lesson Fourteen
Bravo ASL! Curriculum

Lesson Fourteen: *Let's Go Clothes Shopping!*

Video Segment Content: The following are English translations of the signed
(4 1/2 Minutes) sentences:

1. The man walked to the store.
2. The mother hurried to the house.
3. The man drove up the hill.
4. The dog ran fast!
5. The mother and father strolled through the store.
6. The airplane landed safely.
7. The four of us took a walk together.
8. Dad tiptoed through the bedroom.
9. The students waited in line for the food.
10. Sally was so happy, she jumped up and down!

Student Workbook:
Activity 14.21

14.21 Experiential Activity

Classy Classifiers

Viewing Goal: To improve your comprehension skills with ASL classifiers.

Viewing Instructions: View the signed sentences and select the answer that best matches the meaning of each.

1. **A The man walked to the store.**
   B. The woman walked to the store.
   C. The man drove to the store.
   D. The man walked fast to the store.

2. A. The father hurried home.
   B. The mother drove fast.
   C. The mother hurried to the house.
   D. The mother asked where the house was.

3. A. The man took a train.
   B. The man drove up the hill.
   C. The boy rode his bike up a hill.
   D. The man drove down the hill.

4. A. The car went fast!
   B. The man ran fast!
   C. The horse ran fast!
   D. The dog ran fast!

5. A. The children ran through the store.
   B. The mother and father strolled through the store.
   C. The children walked slowly through the school.
   D. The mother and father hurried through the store.

6. A. The car drove on the street.
   B. The airplane took off.
   C. The airplane landed safely.
   D. The boat rode on the water.

Instructor's Guide: Lesson Fourteen
Bravo ASL! Curriculum

Lesson Fourteen: *Let's Go Clothes Shopping!*

7. A. The two of us took a walk together.
   B. The three of us took a walk together.
   C. The four of us took a walk together.
   D. The five of us took a walk together.

8. A. Dad hurried to the bathroom.
   B. Dad carefully walked to the kitchen.
   C. Dad jumped up and down on the bed.
   D. Dad tiptoed through the bedroom.

9. **A. The students waited in line for the food.**
   B. The eight of us walked together.
   C. The line moved fast.
   D. The students went to class.

10. A. Sara fell.
    B. Sara was so happy, she jumped up and down!
    C. Sally was so happy, she jumped up and down!
    D. Sally skipped around the house.

14.22 Video Learning Experience

Practice Session: Sentences

Viewing Goal: To improve comprehension skills by watching sentences presented in ASL.

Viewing Instructions:

1. **Ask** students to read *Practice Session: Sentences* in their workbooks (activity 14.22).

2. **Play** the video segment entitled *Practice Session: Sentences* (segment 14.22).

3. **Inform** students that each sentence is signed twice and an English translation is provided.

4. **Remind** students to watch the face of each signer to see the facial/body expressions and non-manual grammatical markers as well as the signs.

Instructor's Guide: Lesson Fourteen
Bravo ASL! Curriculum
©1996 Sign Enhancers, Inc.
ALL RIGHTS RESERVED.

Lesson Fourteen: *Let's Go Clothes Shopping!*

Video Segment Content: (2 Minutes)

The following are English translations of the practice sentences:

1. The store is very big! Wow!
2. I don't like dresses. I like pants.
3. The clothes I need for work are a shirt, pants, and a tie.
4. I'm going shopping. Do you want to go?
5. The price of the shoes is $100! That's expensive!

Student Workbook: Activity 14.22

14.22 Video Learning Experience

Practice Session: Sentences

Viewing Goal: To improve your ASL comprehension skills by watching signed sentences.

Viewing Instructions: Watch the signed sentences for comprehension. Remember to watch the face of each signer to see the facial/body expressions and the non-manual grammatical markers as well as the signs.

It is recommended that you copy each signed sentence when it is repeated.

In the space below, record any questions or notes you have regarding the sentences.

Notes: _____
_____
_____
_____

14.23 Experiential Activity

You're Going To Wear That!?!

Activity Goal: To improve students' expressive and receptive ASL skills related to clothing signs.

Activity Instructions:

1. **Ask** students to read *You're Going To Wear That!?!* in their workbooks (activity 14.23).

2. **Bring** (or ask students to bring) clothing items such as old hats, shoes, shirts, sweaters, coats, etc. **Place** all the items in a pile at the front of the room.

Lesson Fourteen: *Let's Go Clothes Shopping!*

3. **Ask** for a volunteer to come to the front of the room. **Tell** the student at the front to select another student and use ASL to explain what clothes from the pile the second student should put on. After that student is "dressed," s/he selects another student to "dress," and so on. **Request** all the "dressed" students to remain at the front of the room.

4. **Encourage** students to be "wildly" creative! **Challenge** students to have the person they dress look the most outrageous. **Ask** the remaining students to vote on who was the most creative.

Student Workbook: Activity 14.23

14.23 Experiential Activity

You're Going to Wear That!?!

Activity Goal: To improve your expressive and receptive ASL skills with clothing signs.

Activity Instructions: A volunteer will go to the front of the room, where there will be a pile of clothing and accessories. The volunteer will select a classmate and use ASL to tell that person what to wear from the pile. When the classmate is "dressed," s/he will select another student to "dress," and so on.

Be creative! Choose the wildest combination of colors and styles you can find! Try to make the person you dress look outrageous.

The class will vote to see who was dressed the wildest.

14.24 Video Learning Experience

Practice Session: Story

Viewing Goal: To improve ASL receptive skills by watching a signed story.

Viewing Instructions:
1. **Ask** students to read *Practice Session: Story* in their workbooks (activity 14.24).

2. **Show** the video segment entitled *Practice Session: Story* (segment 14.24). Billy signs a story using the vocabulary introduced in this lesson. **Turn off** audio and captions.

3. **Instruct** students to watch the story for comprehension and write a summary of the main points.

Lesson Fourteen: *Let's Go Clothes Shopping!*

Video Segment Content:
(2 Minutes)

The following is an English translation of the story:

A girl named Anna and her mother went shopping. They were shopping for clothes. Mom wanted to buy Anna a beautiful dress, a pink skirt, shoes, and a purse. Mom thought they were all beautiful.

Anna didn't like that. Anna wanted to buy blue pants, a shirt, socks, and a backpack. Mom told her she could buy the pants but she would have to use her own money. If she wanted a dress, Mom would pay. Anna bought the blue pants. Mom, well... she paid for them anyway. Anna smiled happily.

Billy: Wow! Good job! You have worked diligently through fourteen lessons. Congratulations! You have learned a lot. Now, the next tape will be a review and practice lesson. I hope to see you then. Watching the next tape, you'll be amazed at how much you have learned. OK, I hope to see you soon. Goodbye and good luck.

Student Workbook:
Activity 14.24

14.24 Video Learning Experience

Practice Session: Story

Viewing Goal: To improve your ASL comprehension by watching a story presented in ASL.

Viewing Instructions: Watch the signed story for comprehension. In the space below, write a summary of the main points.

Summary: _____
_____
_____
_____

Lesson Fourteen: *Let's Go Clothes Shopping!*

14.25 Comprehension Quiz

What Did You Understand?

Quiz Goal: To assess students' comprehension of the signed story.

Quiz Instructions:

1. **Instruct** students to complete the quiz in their workbooks (activity 14.25).

2. **Collect** for grading or **show** the overhead (Appendix 14.25) and **ask** individual students to indicate the correct answers on the overhead while class members correct their own work.

3. **Ask** students to indicate which item(s) from the quiz they found difficult. **Review** by **modeling** or **replaying** that segment of the videotape.

Student Workbook: Activity 14.25

Overhead Master: Appendix 14.25

14.25 Comprehension Quiz

What Did You Understand?

Quiz Goal: To see how much of the signed story you understood.

Quiz Instructions: Read and answer each question below.

1. What was the girl's name in the story?
   A. Amy
   B. Angie
   C. Anna
   D. Alice

2. What did the girl's mother want to buy?
   A. A purple skirt with a pink blouse.
   B. A blue skirt with a purple blouse.
   C. Blue pants, a shirt, and a backpack.
   D. A pink skirt, blouse, and purse.

3. What did the girl want to buy
   A. A purple skirt with a pink blouse.
   B. A blue skirt with a purple blouse.
   C. Blue pants, a shirt, and a backpack.
   D. All of the above.

4. What choice did the girl's mother give her?
   If she bought the dress, the mother would pay for it. If she bought the pants, the girl would have to use her own money.

5. What did the girl decide to buy?
   The blue pants.

Instructor's Guide: Lesson Fourteen
Bravo ASL! Curriculum

©1996 Sign Enhancers, Inc.
ALL RIGHTS RESERVED.

Lesson Fourteen: *Let's Go Clothes Shopping!*

14.26 Homework Assignment

ASL SitCom!

Homework Goal: To provide students with the opportunity to perform a short skit in ASL related to clothes shopping.

Homework Instructions:

1. **Ask** students to read *ASL SitCom* in their workbooks (activity 14.26).

2. **Divide** the class into groups of five or six.

3. **Instruct** the groups to prepare a short situation comedy, *The Hilarious Clothing Store Adventure*, to be performed in class. **Tell** students that their skits and all the preparation work is to be done using ASL.

4. **Require** all students to have a part and actively participate in the creation and performance of the skit.

5. **Instruct** students to use at least ten new ASL vocabulary from this lesson as well as at least five classifiers in their sitcom.

6. If possible, **arrange** to **videotape** the skits (it is also recommended that you have popcorn on hand).

Instructor Tip: An opportunity for students to perform this assignment has been scheduled in the next lesson (Homework Review 15.2).

Student Workbook: Activity 14.26

14.26 Homework Assignment

ASL SitCom

Homework Goal: To provide you with the opportunity to create and perform a short situation comedy using the ASL vocabulary related to clothes shopping.

Homework Instructions: Work with your group to create and perform a skit entitled, *The Hilarious Clothing Store Adventure!*

Your group's skit and all preparation work is to be done using ASL (no voices needed!). Every student in the group must have a part and actively participate in the creation and performance of the skit.

Be sure to use at least ten new ASL vocabulary from this lesson and at least five classifiers in your skit. Be prepared to perform your skit for the rest of the class. Who knows - it might even end up on television!

Have fun... and please pass the popcorn!

Lesson Fourteen: *Let's Go Clothes Shopping!*

14.27 Post-test

What Do You Know Now?

Assessment Video

Post-test Goal: To assess students' mastery of the lesson objectives.

Post-test Instructions:

1. **Ask** students to read the Post-test Introduction in their workbooks (activity 14.27).

2. **Copy** and **distribute** the Lesson Fourteen Post-test (Appendix 14.27).

3. **Play** the Assessment Video (segment 14.27) and allow students to complete Section One (comprehension portion) of the test.

4. **Instruct** students to complete Section Two (culture and grammar portion) of the test individually and hand in their papers when they are finished.

5. **Assign** Section Three (expressive portion) of the test and **schedule** a time when students are to perform. If possible, it is strongly recommended that you **videotape** this portion of the Post-test.

6. **Determine** grading options based upon programmatic requirements. A recommended guideline for measuring successful mastery of objectives is 80% accuracy.

Video Segment Content: The following is an English translation of the comprehension
(3 1/2 Minutes) story:

Kyle is cooking dinner. Kyle likes a woman named Susan. As he cooks, he thinks that he'd like to have Susan come to his house so they could eat together. He calls her on the TTY to invite her.

She says that she would like to come and asks what time Kyle wants her to arrive. He tells her to come at 7:00 and she agrees.

She doesn't know what to wear! She runs into her bedroom and frantically searches through her closet. She finds a blouse, but it is orange! The pants she has are yellow! She digs out a pair of shoes, but they are red! She finds a hat, but it is green. She looks for a purse, but there is only a backpack! What will she do?

Instructor's Guide: Lesson Fourteen
Bravo ASL! Curriculum

©1996 Sign Enhancers, Inc.
ALL RIGHTS RESERVED.

Lesson Fourteen: *Let's Go Clothes Shopping!*

She decides she has to go clothes shopping! She runs to her car and drives quickly to a clothing store. She shops quickly and finds a nice, black dress. She finds matching black shoes and a black purse. She buys all three and gets dressed in her new clothes.

She puts her orange, yellow, red, and green clothes in her car and drives to Kyle's house. Susan knocks on the door and is surprised when Kyle opens the door, because he is wearing a green shirt, yellow pants, a pink tie, red shoes, a white backpack, and a purple hat!

Susan tells Kyle to wait just a moment. She runs back to her car and changes into her orange blouse, yellow pants, red shoes, and green hat. She then joins Kyle and they happily enjoy a nice dinner together.

Student Workbook: Activity 14.27

14.27 Post-test Introduction

What Do You Know Now?

Post-test Goal: To assess your mastery of the lesson objectives.

Post-test Introduction: This test has three sections:

- Section One: The Comprehension section tests your ability to understand ASL.
- Section Two: The Culture and Grammar section tests your knowledge of the material presented in the *Cultural* and *Grammatical Notes*.
- Section Three: The Expressive portion tests your ability to use ASL.

Simply follow the instructions for each section. **Good luck!**

Lesson Fourteen: *Let's Go Clothes Shopping!*

Post-test Master:
Appendix 14.27

14.27 Post-test

Section One: Comprehension

Instructions: You will see a signed story. Watch carefully and answer each question below.

1. What was the man's name in the story?
   A. Kyle
   B. Kevin
   C. Kid
   D. Ken

2. Who did the man like?
   A. Sally
   B. Susan
   C. Shelly
   D. Shawna

3. Who is going to cook dinner?
   A. The woman
   B. The man

4. The woman has a problem. What is it?
   A. She doesn't like him and doesn't want to go.
   B. She already has another date.
   C. She doesn't have a car.
   D. She can't find anything she wants to wear.

5. What does she do about this problem?
   A. She tells him no and doesn't go.
   B. She cancels her other date.
   C. She goes to the store and buys a car.
   D. She goes clothes shopping.

6. What was the man wearing?
   A. All black clothes.
   B. His pajamas.
   C. Very colorful clothes.
   D. A backpack and hiking boots.

Lesson Fourteen: *Let's Go Clothes Shopping!*

Post-test Master:
Appendix 14.27

14.27 Post-test

Section Two: Culture and Grammar

Instructions: Read each statement carefully and determine if it is true or false (circle your answer).

7. Some parents with Deaf children never learn to sign.
   A. True
   B. False

8. Professionals such as doctors, counselors, and teachers often disagree about what would be best for a Deaf child.
   A. True
   B. False

9. It is never too late to learn a new language.
   A. True
   B. False

10. Classifiers identify a "class" of objects.
    A. True
    B. False

11. There are many classifiers used in ASL.
    A. True
    B. False

12. Classifiers are another way to produce fingerspelled names.
    A. True
    B. False

13. Using a 3-handshape moving forward can represent a train.
    A. True
    B. False

14. Using a 3-handshape moving forward can represent a boat.
    A. True
    B. False

15. Using a 3-handshape moving forward can represent a plane.
    A. True
    B. False

Lesson Fourteen: *Let's Go Clothes Shopping!*

Post-test Master:
Appendix 14.27

14.27 Post-test

Section Three: Expressive Portion

Instructions: Create a story about the picture below. Be sure to use at least four of your new clothing signs and at least one classifier.

Your instructor will schedule a time for you to perform this section of the Post-test. You may prepare and practice prior to your scheduled time. Use the space below to prepare for your expressive performance.

Include at least four signs from Lesson Fourteen.

16. _____
17. _____
18. _____
19. _____

Include at least one classifier:

20. _____

Congratulations!
You have completed
Lesson Fourteen!

Instructor's Guide: Lesson Fourteen
Bravo ASL! Curriculum

Lesson 15
REVIEW & PRACTICE SESSION

Materials Needed:

Equipment: VCR and TV monitor
Overhead projector
Optional: video camera for activities 15.2, 15.5, 15.9, 15.11, 15.15, 15.21, 15.27, and 15.32

Materials: Instructor's Guide
Student Workbook: one per student
Overhead transparencies for activities: 15.3, 15.14, and 15.17 (see Appendix for masters).
Optional: blank videotape (or have students bring their own) for activities 15.2, 15.5, 15.9, 15.11, 15.15, 15.21, 15.27, and 15.32
Post-test: Appendix 15.32

Videotapes: The Beginning ASL VideoCourse Lesson Fifteen
Assessment Video for Post-test 15.32

15.1 Begin Class

Housekeeping

Goal: To prepare students for this lesson.

Instructions:
1. **Welcome** students to Lesson Fifteen of the VideoCourse.
2. **Perform** any necessary tasks (such as taking attendance) that may be required by your specific program.

Lesson Fifteen: *Review & Practice Session*

15.2 Homework Review

ASL SitCom!

Activity Goal: To provide feedback on previously assigned homework and to reinforce materials learned in earlier lessons.

Activity Instructions:

1. **Ask** students to read *ASL SitCom!* in their workbooks (activity 15.2).

2. **Divide** the class into the same student groups as in activity 14.26 and **tell** them to practice their skits for a few minutes.

3. When students are finished practicing, **instruct** groups to take turns signing the skits they prepared (*Homework Assignment 14.26*) while the rest of the class practices comprehension. If possible, **videotape** each group's performance of this activity.

4. **Close** this activity by **modeling** any signs or grammatical features the students may have had trouble producing.

Student Workbook: Activity 15.2

15.2 Homework Review

ASL SitCom!

Activity Goal: To perform the skits you prepared for homework.

Activity Instructions: Your group will have the chance to perform your skit, *The Hilarious Clothing Store Adventure!*

Remember, every student in each group must have a part and actively participate in the performance.

Be sure to use at least ten of the ASL vocabulary learned in Lesson Fourteen and at least five classifiers.

Smile... you might be on camera!

Lesson Fifteen: *Review & Practice Session*

15.3 Lesson Objectives

Planning for Success

Goal: To identify the learning outcomes associated with successful completion of this lesson.

Instructions:
1. **Ask** students to read the objectives in their workbooks (activity 15.3).
2. **Show** overhead (Appendix 15.3) and **read** through the objectives with the class.

Student Workbook: Activity 15.3

Overhead Master: Appendix 15.3

15.3 Lesson Objectives

Planning for Success

Goal: To see what you will learn by the end of this lesson.

Instructions: Read the objectives below.

Upon completing this VideoCourse lesson, you will be able to...

1. Recognize and accurately produce the ASL vocabulary introduced in Lessons Eleven, Twelve, Thirteen, and Fourteen.

2. Demonstrate knowledge of the cultural information presented in Lessons Eleven, Twelve, Thirteen, and Fourteen.

3. Recognize and apply the grammatical features presented in Lessons Eleven, Twelve, Thirteen, and Fourteen.

4. Accurately use the ASL vocabulary and grammatical features presented in Lessons Eleven, Twelve, Thirteen, and Fourteen in sentences, dialogues, and stories.

Lesson Fifteen: *Review & Practice Session*

15.4 Video Learning Experience

Lesson Introduction

Viewing Goal: To assist students in understanding the format of this review lesson.

Viewing Instructions:
1. **Ask** students to read the *Lesson Introduction* in their workbooks (activity 15.4).

2. **Play** the video segment in which Billy introduces the format of this review lesson (segment 15.4). Because the presentation of this segment is beyond the linguistic ability of beginning students, please **turn on** the audio and/or captions to optimize its educational value.

3. **Instruct** students to watch this segment to learn what to expect in this lesson.

Video Segment Content: (1 Minute)

The following is an English translation of Billy's introduction:

Hello! Welcome to another Sign Enhancers, Inc. American Sign Language VideoCourse, Lesson Fifteen.

This lesson is a review. We will be watching segments of Lessons Eleven through Fifteen practicing vocabulary and the many things you have learned.

This tape will include a number of things: vocabulary review, practice with sentences, dialogues and a story. We'll also look at different aspects of the *Grammatical* and *Cultural Notes*. Okay? So enjoy yourself!

Student Workbook: Activity 15.4

15.4 Video Learning Experience

Lesson Introduction

Viewing Goal: To help you prepare for this review session.

Viewing Instructions: Billy will explain what you can expect from this *Review & Practice Session*.

Pay attention to what he is signing, but also notice *how* he expresses these ideas with facial/body expression, non-manual grammatical markers, and use of space. Perhaps you will learn a few more signs!

In the space below, write any notes or questions you may have.

Notes: _____
_____
_____

Lesson Fifteen: *Review & Practice Session*

15.5 Experiential Activity

Sports Stories

Activity Goal: To reinforce students' skills with the vocabulary introduced in Lesson Eleven.

Activity Instructions:

1. **Ask** students to read *Sports Stories* in their workbooks (activity 15.5).

2. **Divide** the class into groups of four or five students.

3. **Instruct** groups to select one of the topics provided in their workbooks and create a story using the ASL vocabulary from Lesson Eleven.

4. When the group activity is finished, **ask** each group to demonstrate their story to the class. It is recommended that you **videotape** this activity.

5. **Assist** students by **modeling** as needed.

Student Workbook: Activity 15.5

15.5 Experiential Activity

Sport Stories

Activity Goal: To help you remember the ASL vocabulary learned in Lesson Eleven.

Activity Instructions: In your group, choose one of the topics below and create an ASL story. Everyone must sign part of the story! Use as many of the ASL vocabulary that you learned in Lesson Eleven as possible (see the Illustration Section for Lesson Eleven vocabulary).

Have fun... and be prepared to sign your story for the class!

Sport Story Topics:

1. The day we played basketball in the park...
2. How the golfer fell in the river...
3. Fishing from the bridge...
4. The basketball game that was interrupted by a butterfly...

In the space below, write notes to help you develop and remember the story.

Notes: _____
_____
_____
_____

Instructor's Guide: Lesson Fifteen
Bravo ASL! Curriculum

©1996 Sign Enhancers, Inc.
ALL RIGHTS RESERVED.

Lesson Fifteen: *Review & Practice Session*

15.6 Video Learning Experience

Lesson Eleven Review: Vocabulary

Viewing Goal: To reinforce comprehension skills of the ASL vocabulary introduced in Lesson Eleven.

Viewing Instructions:
1. **Ask** students to read *Lesson Eleven Review: Vocabulary* in their workbooks (activity 15.6).

2. **Play** the video segment entitled *Lesson Eleven Review: Vocabulary* (segment 15.6). Billy reviews all the ASL vocabulary. Please **turn on** the audio and/or captions to optimize this segment's educational value.

3. **Instruct** students to copy the signs and **encourage** students to raise their hands if they have difficulty remembering a particular sign.

Video Segment Content: See the following Student Workbook excerpt for the content
(8 Minutes) of this video segment.

Student Workbook:
Activity 15.6

15.6 Video Learning Experience

Lesson Eleven Review: Vocabulary

Viewing Goal: To help you review the ASL vocabulary from Lesson Eleven.

Viewing Instructions: Watch the Lesson Eleven vocabulary review. Raise your hand if there is a sign you do not remember.

Signs representing the following concepts are reviewed:

1. TREE
2. TREES
3. TALL
4. CLIMB
5. FLOWER
6. PRETTY / BEAUTIFUL
7. BLACK+BERRY
8. BAG/PURSE
9. WATER
10. BRIDGE
11. RIVER
12. GRASS
13. SUN
14. SUN+SHINE
15. HOT
16. LEAF
17. COOL
18. BASEBALL
19. TENNIS
20. GOLF
21. FRISBEE
22. GAME
23. PICNIC
24. WALK
25. RUN
26. FALL
27. FIND
28. STAY
29. MOVE
30. MAN
31. WOMAN
32. FISHING

15.7 Video Learning Experience

Lesson Eleven Review: Sentences

Viewing Goal: To improve students' comprehension skills by watching sentences presented in ASL.

Viewing Instructions:
1. **Ask** students to read *Lesson Eleven Review: Sentences* in their workbooks (activity 15.7).

2. **Play** the video segment entitled *Lesson Eleven Review: Sentences* (segment 15.7). Each sentence is signed twice and an English translation is provided.

3. **Remind** students to watch the face of each signer to see the facial/body expressions and non-manual grammatical markers as well as the signs.

Video Segment Content: The following are English translations of the practice
(2 1/2 Minutes) sentences:

1. I climbed a very tall tree!
2. I walked across the bridge.
3. Do you want to play Frisbee with me?
4. The man and his daughter fished at the river.
5. The sun is hot! Phew!
6. The trees, flowers, and sun are beautiful!
7. Which game do you like? Tennis or golf?

Student Workbook:
Activity 15.7

> 15.7 Video Learning Experience
>
> *Lesson Eleven Review: Sentences*
>
> **Viewing Goal:** To improve your comprehension skills by watching sentences presented in ASL.
>
> **Viewing Instructions:** Watch the signed sentences for comprehension. Remember to watch the face of each signer to see the facial/body expressions and the non-manual grammatical markers as well as the signs.
>
> It is recommended that you copy each signed sentence when it is repeated.
>
> In the space below, record questions or notes regarding the sentences.
>
> Notes: _____
> _____
> _____
> _____

15.8 Video Learning Experience

Lesson Eleven Review: Practice Dialogue

Viewing Goal: To improve comprehension skills by watching a dialogue presented in ASL.

Viewing Instructions:
1. **Ask** students to read *Lesson Eleven Review: Practice Dialogue* in their workbooks (activity 15.8).
2. **Show** the video segment entitled *Lesson Eleven Review: Practice Dialogue* (segment 15.8).
3. **Instruct** students to watch the dialogue for comprehension and write a summary in the space provided.

Video Segment Content: (1 1/2 Minutes)

The following is a summary of the dialogue presented in this segment:

Dad tells Mom that he is good at basketball, baseball, tennis, and golf. Mom tells him that he is not good at golf. She says he would miss the ball.

Dad disagrees and explains that the sun would be shining, the ball would be on the green, he would swing and the ball would sail off into the distance.

Mom tells him that he's right. It would sail through the air right into a river and Dad would fall in looking for it.

Dad explains that he would be getting into the water to cool off.

Mom tells him if he likes to get into the water he should go fishing, not golfing.

Dad pouts.

Student Workbook: Activity 15.8

15.8 Video Learning Experience

Lesson Eleven Review: Practice Dialogue

Viewing Goal: To improve your comprehension skills by watching a dialogue presented in ASL.

Viewing Instructions: Watch the signed dialogue for comprehension and write a summary in the space provided.

Summary: _____
_____
_____
_____

Lesson Fifteen: *Review & Practice Session*

15.9 Experiential Activity

Dynamic-Duo Dialogue

Activity Goal: To improve students' expressive and receptive ASL skills.

Activity Instructions:

1. **Ask** students to read *Dynamic-Duo Dialogue* in their workbooks (activity 15.9).

2. **Divide** the class into pairs.

3. **Instruct** students to create dialogues using the vocabulary from Lesson Eleven. Each student should take a minimum of five turns.

4. After students have practiced, **ask** for volunteers to share their dialogues with the class. If possible, **videotape** each dialogue.

5. **Correct** production by **modeling** as needed.

Student Workbook: Activity 15.9

15.9 Experiential Activity

Dynamic-Duo Dialogue

Activity Goal: To improve your expressive and receptive ASL skills.

Activity Instructions: Work with a partner to create a dialogue using the Lesson Eleven vocabulary (see activity 15.6 for the vocabulary list). Use ASL (no voices needed!) and be sure each person takes at least five turns signing.

Be prepared to share your dialogue with the class!

In the space below, record ideas or notes you have regarding the dialogue.

Notes: _____
_____
_____
_____

Instructor's Guide: Lesson Fifteen
Bravo ASL! Curriculum

©1996 Sign Enhancers, Inc.
ALL RIGHTS RESERVED.

Lesson Fifteen: *Review & Practice Session*

15.10 Video Learning Experience

Bravo Family Revisited

Viewing Goal: To reinforce ASL comprehension skills by reviewing a Bravo family interaction from Lesson Eleven.

Viewing Instructions:

1. **Ask** students to read *Bravo Family Revisited* in their workbooks (activity 15.10).

2. **Play** the video segment of the Bravo family (segment 15.10). They'll use the vocabulary during their picnic in the park.

3. **Instruct** students to watch for review.

4. When the video segment is over, **divide** the class into pairs.

5. **Instruct** pairs to use ASL to create a summary of the Bravo visit.

6. When they have finished, **ask** pairs to demonstrate their signed summaries for the class.

Video Segment Content: (2 Minutes)

The following is a summary of the Bravo family interaction:

The Bravo family has just arrived at the park. Their dog, Lady, walks up with a Frisbee in her mouth. Anna and Dad discuss how much Lady loves to play Frisbee. Scott asks if he can play Frisbee with Lady. Mom tells him that he can, but that they are going to eat soon, and when she calls him he needs to hurry back. Scott goes off to play with Lady.

Anna asks if Dad wants to play tennis. Dad explains that he and Mom are setting up the picnic, and that after they eat, they will play tennis. Anna decides that she will go practice her tennis so when they play later, she can beat Dad.

Student Workbook: Activity 15.10

15.10 Video Learning Experience

Bravo Family Revisited

Viewing Goal: To reinforce your ASL comprehension skills by reviewing a Bravo family interaction from Lesson Eleven.

Viewing Instructions: Watch the *Bravo Family Revisited* for review. Be prepared to use ASL to summarize what happened in this video segment.

Notes/Summary: _____
_____
_____
_____

Lesson Fifteen: *Review & Practice Session*

15.11 Experiential Activity

Medical Drama

Activity Goal: To reinforce student's skills with Lesson Twelve vocabulary.

Activity Instructions:

1. **Ask** students to read *Medical Drama* in their workbooks (activity 15.11).

2. **Divide** the class into small groups of five or six.

3. **Instruct** students to create a skit that takes place in a medical setting, using as many of the Lesson Twelve vocabulary items as possible.

4. When the group work is finished, **ask** each group to perform their "medical drama" for the class. It is recommended that you **videotape** this activity.

5. **Model** corrections as needed.

Student Workbook: Activity 15.11

15.11 Experiential Activity

Medical Drama

Activity Goal: To help you improve your skills with the ASL vocabulary learned in Lesson Twelve.

Activity Instructions: Work with your group to create and perform a skit involving the medical setting. Use as many of the ASL signs you learned in Lesson Twelve as possible (see the Illustration Section for Lesson Twelve vocabulary). Everyone in the group needs to have an active role in the drama!

Be prepared to perform your *Medical Drama* for the class!

Lesson Fifteen: *Review & Practice Session*

15.12 Video Learning Experience

Lesson Twelve Review: Vocabulary

Viewing Goal: To reinforce comprehension skills of the ASL vocabulary introduced in Lesson Twelve.

Viewing Instructions:

1. **Ask** students to read *Lesson Twelve Review: Vocabulary* in their workbooks (activity 15.12).

2. **Play** the video segment entitled *Lesson Twelve Review: Vocabulary* (segment 15.12). Billy reviews and signs each ASL vocabulary item twice.

   Note: **Use** this review as needed. **Place** in a lab setting for individual viewing or **increase** the level of difficulty by **turning off** audio and **covering** glosses on the monitor.

3. **Instruct** students to copy the signs as they watch the vocabulary review. **Encourage** students to raise their hands if they have difficulty remembering a particular sign.

Video Segment Content: See the following Student Workbook excerpt for the content of this video segment.
(3 Minutes)

Student Workbook: Activity 15.12

15.12 Video Learning Experience

Lesson Twelve Review: Vocabulary

Viewing Goal: To help you review the ASL vocabulary from Lesson Twelve.

Viewing Instructions: Watch the Lesson Twelve vocabulary review. Raise your hand if there is a sign you do not remember, and your instructor will help you.

Signs representing the following concepts are reviewed in this video segment:

1. HOSPITAL
2. DOCTOR
3. NURSE
4. EMERGENCY
5. TAKE-CARE
6. HURT/PAIN
7. ALL-RIGHT/RIGHTS
8. COMMUNICATE
9. WAIT
10. INTERPRET
11. INTERPRETER
12. HOLD/HUG
13. SICK
14. FEEL
15. HOW
16. MEDICINE
17. SNEEZE
18. COLD
19. COUGH
20. SORE-THROAT
21. PILL
22. TEMPERATURE

Instructor's Guide: Lesson Fifteen
Bravo ASL! Curriculum

Lesson Fifteen: *Review & Practice Session*

15.13 Video Learning Experience

Lesson Twelve Review: Sentences

Viewing Goal: To improve students' comprehension skills by watching sentences presented in ASL.

Viewing Instructions:
1. **Ask** students to read *Lesson Twelve Review: Sentences* in their workbooks (activity 15.13).
2. **Play** the video segment entitled *Lesson Twelve Review: Sentences* (segment 15.13). Each sentence is signed twice and an English translation is provided.
3. **Remind** students to watch the face of each signer to see the facial/body expressions and non-manual grammatical markers as well as the signs.

Video Segment Content:
(2 1/2 Minutes)

The following are English translations of the practice sentences:

1. The girl fell and broke her arm.
2. You are sneezing and coughing. You have a cold.
3. That woman, Carol, is pregnant. Her baby is due soon.
4. What's wrong? Oh, your stomach hurts.
5. My daughter really studies well. She will become a doctor.
6. I don't want to take a pill!

Student Workbook: Activity 15.13

15.13 Video Learning Experience

Lesson Twelve Review: Sentences

Viewing Goal: To improve your comprehension skills by watching sentences presented in ASL.

Viewing Instructions: Watch the signed sentences for comprehension. Remember to watch the face of each signer to see the facial/body expressions and the non-manual grammatical markers as well as the signs.

It is recommended that you copy each signed sentence when it is repeated.

In the space below, record any questions or notes you have regarding the sentences.

Notes: _____
_____
_____
_____

15.14 Video Learning Experience

Lesson Twelve Review: Practice Dialogue

Viewing Goal: To improve comprehension skills by watching a dialogue presented in ASL.

Viewing Instructions:
1. **Ask** students to read *Lesson Twelve Review: Practice Dialogue* in their workbooks (activity 15.14).
2. **Show** the video segment entitled *Lesson Twelve Review: Practice Dialogue* (segment 15.14).
3. **Instruct** students to watch dialogue for comprehension and answer the questions provided in their workbooks.
4. **Show** overhead (Appendix 15.14) and **ask** individual students to indicate the correct answers on the overhead while class members correct their own work.

Video Segment Content: (1 Minute)

The following is a summary of the dialogue presented in this segment:

Scott tells Anna she must leave soon for school. Anna tells him she is not going to school, she is sick. She tells him that she is sneezing and coughing.

He laughs and tells her she doesn't have a cold. He says Mom will take her temperature, find it is normal, and send her to school.

Anna says okay, but then is struck by a stomachache. Scott tells her Mom will watch her vomit and then she can go to school.

Anna decides that she has a headache. Scott tells her to take some medicine and head for school.

Anna looks defeated and says okay, she'll go to school.

Lesson Fifteen: *Review & Practice Session*

Student Workbook:
Activity 15.14

Overhead Master:
Appendix 15.14

15.14 Video Learning Experience

Lesson Twelve Review: Practice Dialogue

Viewing Goal: To improve your comprehension skills by watching a dialogue presented in ASL.

Viewing Instructions: Watch the signed dialogue for comprehension and answer the questions below.

1. What does Scott tell Anna at the beginning of the dialogue?
   Scott tells Anna she is going to be late for school.

2. Anna tells Scott that she is not going to school. What is the first reason she gives him?
   She has a cold (sneezing and coughing).

3. According to Scott, how will Mom know she is faking?
   Mom will take her temperature and see she doesn't have a fever.

4. What is the second symptom Anna tells Scott about?
   She has a stomachache.

5. When Anna tells Scott that she has a headache, how does he respond?
   He laughs and says that she will take aspirin, then have to go to school.

6. In the end, does Anna decide to go to school or stay home?
   She decides to go to school.

15.15 Experiential Activity

Dynamic-Duo Dialogue

Activity Goal: To improve students' expressive and receptive ASL skills.

Activity Instructions:

1. **Ask** students to read *Dynamic-Duo Dialogue* in their workbooks (15.15).

2. **Divide** the class into pairs.

3. **Instruct** students to create a dialogue using the vocabulary from Lesson Twelve. Each student should take a minimum of five turns.

4. After students have practiced, **ask** for volunteers to share their dialogues with the class. If possible, **videotape** each dialogue.

5. **Correct** production by **modeling** as needed.

Instructor's Guide: Lesson Fifteen
Bravo ASL! Curriculum

Lesson Fifteen: *Review & Practice Session*

Student Workbook:
Activity 15.15

15.15 Experiential Activity

Dynamic-Duo Dialogue

Activity Goal: To improve your expressive and receptive ASL skills.

Activity Instructions: Work with a partner to create a dialogue using the Lesson Twelve vocabulary (see the Illustration Section for Lesson Twelve vocabulary). Use ASL (no voices needed!) and be sure each person takes at least five turns signing.

Be prepared to share your dialogue with the class!

In the space below, record ideas or notes you have regarding the dialogue.

Notes: _____
_____
_____
_____

15.16 Video Learning Experience

Bravo Family Revisited

Viewing Goal: To reinforce ASL comprehension skills by watching a Bravo family interaction from Lesson Twelve.

Viewing Instructions:
1. **Ask** students to read *Bravo Family Revisited* in their workbooks (activity 15.16).

2. **Play** the video segment of the Bravo family (segment 15.16). The Bravos use the ASL vocabulary during Scott's visit to the Doctor.

3. **Instruct** students to watch for review and take notes or write a summary of the main points.

4. **Replay** any portion of this video segment that students experienced difficulty understanding.

Lesson Fifteen: *Review & Practice Session*

Video Segment Content: (2 1/2 Minutes)

The following is a summary of the Bravo family interaction:

The receptionist tells the family that she has requested an interpreter. The agency will be sending someone as soon as possible. The receptionist asks if the Bravos would like to wait for the interpreter or see the doctor immediately.

Anna suggests that Mom interpret so that Scott doesn't have to wait in pain. Scott wants the doctor to help him right away.

Dad tells the woman (with Mom interpreting) that they want to go see the doctor right away. They hope the interpreter shows up soon, because Mom can't hold Scott and interpret at the same time.

Dad tells the woman he will start filling out the forms.

Billy: Hi again! While the Bravo family is waiting for the doctor, let's go ahead and learn some more new signs related to the medical experience. We will learn these signs by observing a doctor who is very handsome and brilliant. As he meets with his patients, watch carefully and you will learn more new signs. Here's the doctor.

("Doctor" Billy walks out in a doctor's uniform): As I told you, the doctor is very handsome and brilliant. Watch him and you will learn more new signs.

Doctor Billy: Now, there is a long line of sick and injured people. I need to get to work and begin my examinations. I'll see you later. Goodbye!

Billy: Good luck!

Student Workbook: Activity 15.16

15.16 Video Learning Experience

Bravo Family Revisited

Viewing Goal: To improve your ASL comprehension skills by reviewing a Bravo family interaction.

Viewing Instructions: Watch the *Bravo Family Revisited* for review and write a summary in the space below.

Summary: _____
_____
_____
_____

Lesson Fifteen: *Review & Practice Session*

15.17 Experiential Activity

Matchmaker

Activity Goal: To reinforce students' comprehension of Lesson Thirteen vocabulary.

Activity Instructions:

1. **Ask** students to read *Matchmaker* in their workbooks (activity 15.17).

2. **Instruct** students to draw a line from each sign illustration to the picture that best matches its meaning.

3. **Show** the overhead (Appendix 15.17) and **ask** individual students to indicate the correct answers on the overhead while class members correct their own work.

Student Workbook: Activity 15.17

Overhead Master: Appendix 15.17

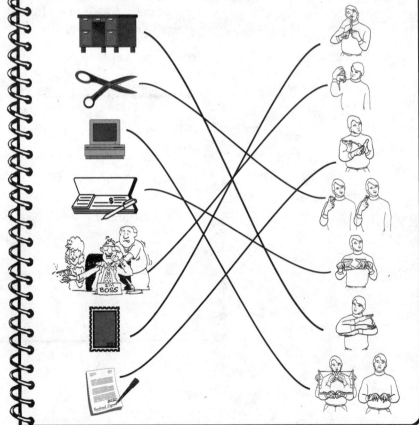

Instructor's Guide: Lesson Fifteen
Bravo ASL! Curriculum

Lesson Fifteen: *Review & Practice Session*

15.18 Video Learning Experience

Lesson Thirteen Review: Vocabulary

Viewing Goal: To reinforce comprehension skills of the ASL vocabulary introduced in Lesson Thirteen.

Viewing Instructions:

1. **Ask** students to read *Lesson Thirteen Review: Vocabulary* in their workbooks (activity 15.18).

2. **Play** the video segment entitled *Lesson Thirteen Review: Vocabulary* (segment 15.18). Billy reviews and signs each ASL vocabulary item twice.

    Note: **Use** this review as needed. **Place** in a lab setting for individual viewing or **increase** the level of difficulty by **turning off** audio and **covering** glosses on the monitor.

3. **Instruct** students to copy the signs as they watch the vocabulary review. **Encourage** students to raise their hands if they have difficulty remembering a particular sign.

Video Segment Content:
(6 Minutes)

See the following Student Workbook excerpt for the content of this video segment.

Student Workbook: Activity 15.18

15.18 Video Learning Experience

Lesson Thirteen Review: Vocabulary

Viewing Goal: To help you review the ASL vocabulary from Lesson Thirteen.

Viewing Instructions: Watch the Lesson Thirteen vocabulary review while you copy the signs.

Signs representing the following concepts are reviewed:

1. BUSINESS
2. COMPANY
3. PAY
4. HIRE
5. FIRE
6. FIRST
7. IDEA
8. EXPLAIN
9. BORING
10. WORK
11. OFFICE
12. DESK/TABLE
13. TYPE
14. TYPEWRITER
15. COMPUTER
16. ADVERTISE
17. SECRETARY
18. INTERVIEW
19. SKILL
20. NEED
21. OH-I-SEE
22. ASK-QUESTION
23. BOSS
24. LETTER
25. COPY
26. LAZY
27. FILE
28. FILES
29. STAMP
30. ENVELOPE
31. SIGNATURE/SIGN
32. SHELF
33. COMPUTER+PRINTER
34. PAPER
35. SCISSORS
36. TAPE
37. PAPER+CLIP
38. STAPLER
39. RUBBER-BAND

Instructor's Guide: Lesson Fifteen
Bravo ASL! Curriculum

©1996 Sign Enhancers, Inc.
ALL RIGHTS RESERVED.

Lesson Fifteen: *Review & Practice Session*

15.19 Video Learning Experience

Lesson Thirteen Review: Sentences

Viewing Goal: To improve students' comprehension skills by watching sentences presented in ASL.

Viewing Instructions:
1. **Ask** students to read *Lesson Thirteen Review: Sentences* in their workbooks (activity 15.19).

2. **Play** the video segment entitled *Lesson Thirteen Review: Sentences* (segment 15.19). Each sentence is signed twice and an English translation is provided.

3. **Remind** students to watch the face of each signer to see the facial/body expressions and non-manual grammatical markers as well as the signs.

Video Segment Content: (2 Minutes)

The following are English translations of the practice sentences:

1. What work do you do?
2. I need scissors and a paper clip.
3. Deaf people work good.
4. My company wants to hire you!
5. Dan's boss fired him.
6. Do you have an appointment to meet with the president?

Student Workbook: Activity 15.19

15.19 Video Learning Experience

Lesson Thirteen Review: Sentences

Viewing Goal: To improve your comprehension skills by watching sentences presented in ASL.

Viewing Instructions: Watch the signed sentences for comprehension. Remember to watch the face of each signer to see the facial/body expressions and the non-manual grammatical markers as well as the signs.

It is recommended that you copy each signed sentence when it is repeated.

In the space below, record any questions or notes you have regarding the sentences.

Notes: _____
_____
_____

Lesson Fifteen: *Review & Practice Session*

15.20 Video Learning Experience

Lesson Thirteen Review: Practice Dialogue

Viewing Goal: To improve students' comprehension skills by watching a dialogue presented in ASL.

Viewing Instructions:

1. **Ask** students to read *Lesson Thirteen Review: Practice Dialogue* in their workbooks (activity 15.20).

2. **Show** the video segment entitled *Lesson Thirteen Review: Practice Dialogue* (segment 15.20).

3. **Instruct** students to watch the dialogue for comprehension and write a summary in the space provided.

Video Segment Content: (1 Minute)

The following is a summary of the dialogue presented in this segment:

Scott tells Dad that he loves him and that he is a wonderful father. Dad asks him what he wants.

Scott tells him that he wants a computer. Dad asks him if he wants a computer to play video games on. Scott says no, that he wants the computer for school work, such as book reports.

Dad asks him if he would play games after he was done with his school work. Scott answers no and tells Dad that once he is done, that Dad can type a letter on the computer.

Dad tells him that means they would need a printer. Scott reminds Dad that he loves him.

Dad tells Scott that he is not going to buy him a computer, but he loves Scott, too.

Student Workbook: Activity 15.20

15.20 Video Learning Experience

Lesson Thirteen Review: Practice Dialogue

Viewing Goal: To improve your comprehension skills by watching a dialogue presented in ASL.

Viewing Instructions: Watch the signed dialogue for comprehension and write a summary in the space provided.

Notes/Summary: _____
_____
_____
_____

Instructor's Guide: Lesson Fifteen
Bravo ASL! Curriculum

©1996 Sign Enhancers, Inc.
ALL RIGHTS RESERVED.

Lesson Fifteen: *Review & Practice Session*

15.21 Experiential Activity

Dynamic-Duo Dialogue

Activity Goal: To improve students' expressive and receptive ASL skills.

Activity Instructions:

1. **Ask** students to read *Dynamic-Duo Dialogue* in their workbooks (activity 15.21).

2. **Divide** the class into pairs.

3. **Instruct** students to create dialogues using the vocabulary from Lesson Thirteen. Each student should take a minimum of five turns.

4. After students have practiced, **ask** for volunteers to share their dialogues with the class. If possible, **videotape** each dialogue.

5. **Correct** production by **modeling** as needed.

Student Workbook: Activity 15.21

15.21 Experiential Activity

Dynamic-Duo Dialogue

Activity Goal: To improve your expressive and receptive ASL skills.

Activity Instructions: Work with a partner to create a dialogue using the Lesson Thirteen vocabulary (see the Illustration Section for Lesson Thirteen vocabulary). Use ASL (no voices needed!) and be sure each person takes at least five turns.

Be prepared to share your dialogue with the class!

In the space below, record ideas or notes you have regarding the dialogue.

Notes: _____
_____
_____
_____

Instructor's Guide: Lesson Fifteen
Bravo ASL! Curriculum

©1996 Sign Enhancers, Inc.
ALL RIGHTS RESERVED.

15.22 Video Learning Experience

Bravo Family Revisited

Viewing Goal: To reinforce ASL comprehension skills by reviewing a Bravo family interaction from Lesson Thirteen.

Viewing Instructions:
1. **Ask** students to read *Bravo Family Revisited* in their workbooks (activity 15.22).

2. **Play** the video segment of the Bravo family (segment 15.22). They will use the ASL vocabulary while visiting Mom's office.

3. **Instruct** students to watch for review and take note of the main points.

4. When the video segment is over, **divide** the class into groups of four.

5. **Instruct** students to use ASL to role-play the Bravo family interaction. Each student should assume the role of one of the Bravo family members and re-enact the scene as much as possible.

Video Segment Content: (2 Minutes)

The following is a summary of the Bravo family interaction:

Dad and Scott walk in as Anna is finishing up her "art project." Anna asks if she can help them and Dad tells her he wants to buy her art work and asks her how much it costs. He gives her money and she gives him the art.

Dad asks where the president, Jennifer, is. Anna checks the schedule and asks Dad and Scott if they have an appointment. She explains that you must have an appointment to see the president.

Just then Mom walks in. Scott tells her it was a good thing she showed up because the secretary was being crabby. Dad tells Mom that the secretary was telling them they needed an appointment. Anna corrected them, telling them she was the vice president, not the secretary.

Scott tells Anna to let him know if she needs an assistant. Dad says that they will leave to let the women work. He tells them they will have to get together for dinner to celebrate Anna's promotion. Dad and Scott leave.

Lesson Fifteen: *Review & Practice Session*

Student Workbook:
Activity 15.22

15.22 Video Learning Experience

Bravo Family Revisited

Viewing Goal: To reinforce your ASL comprehension skills by reviewing a Bravo family interaction from Lesson Thirteen.

Viewing Instructions: Watch the signed interaction carefully for review. Be prepared to role-play this interaction with your classmates. Each person in your group will take on the character of one of the Bravo family members.

Notes: _____
_____
_____
_____

15.23 Experiential Activity

Point and Sign

Activity Goal: To improve your skills with the ASL vocabulary learned in Lesson Fourteen.

Activity Instructions:

1. **Divide** the class into pairs.

2. **Instruct** students to read *Point and Sign* in their workbooks (activity 15.23).

3. **Instruct** students to look at the pictures and take turns pointing to items while partners sign sentences using sign(s) that best match the meaning of each picture.

4. **Inform** students that this activity is to be done entirely in ASL (no voice).

5. **Circulate** among the pairs to **observe** student performance. **Correct** production by **modeling** as needed.

Lesson Fifteen: *Review & Practice Session*

Student Workbook:
Activity 15.23

15.23 Experiential Activity

Point and Sign

Activity Goal: To help you review the ASL vocabulary learned in Lesson Fourteen.

Activity Instructions: Using the pictures below, follow your teacher's instructions and practice using the Lesson Fourteen sign vocabulary.

15.24 Video Learning Experience

Lesson Fourteen Review: Vocabulary

Viewing Goal: To reinforce comprehension skills of the ASL vocabulary introduced in Lesson Fourteen.

Viewing Instructions:
1. **Ask** students to read *Lesson Fourteen Review: Vocabulary* in their workbooks (activity 15.24).

2. **Play** the video segment entitled *Lesson Fourteen Review: Vocabulary* (segment 15.24). Billy reviews and signs each ASL vocabulary item twice.

Instructor's Guide: Lesson Fifteen
Bravo ASL! Curriculum
©1996 Sign Enhancers, Inc.
ALL RIGHTS RESERVED.

Lesson Fifteen: *Review & Practice Session*

Note: Use this review as needed. **Place** in a lab setting for individual viewing or **increase** the level of difficulty by **turning off** audio and **covering** glosses on the monitor.

3. **Instruct** students to copy the signs as they watch the vocabulary review. **Encourage** students to raise their hands if they have difficulty remembering a particular sign.

Video Segment Content: See the following Student Workbook excerpt for the content
(3 Minutes) of this video segment.

Student Workbook:
Activity 15.24

15.24 Video Learning Experience

Lesson Fourteen Review: Vocabulary

Viewing Goal: To help you review the ASL vocabulary from Lesson Fourteen.

Viewing Instructions: Watch the Lesson Fourteen vocabulary review while you copy the signs. Raise your hand if there is a sign you do not recognize, and your instructor will help you.

Signs representing the following concepts are reviewed in this video segment:

1. CLOTHES
2. STORE
3. SHOPPING/BUYING
4. TOWEL
5. LIKE
6. DON'T-LIKE
7. TALL
8. TWO-OF-US
9. THREE-OF-US
10. PANTS
11. SHIRT/SWEATER
12. TIE
13. HAT
14. DRESS
15. SKIRT
16. COAT
17. SOCKS
18. SHOES
19. BACKPACK
20. PURSE
21. PRICE/COST
22. BIG/LARGE
23. CUTE
24. FANCY
25. COMFORTABLE
26. LUCKY
27. DINNER
28. LOVE-IT

Lesson Fifteen: *Review & Practice Session*

15.25 Video Learning Experience

Lesson Fourteen Review: Sentences

Viewing Goal: To improve students' comprehension skills by watching sentences presented in ASL.

Viewing Instructions:
1. **Ask** students to read *Lesson Fourteen Review: Sentences* in their workbooks (activity 15.25).

2. **Play** the video segment entitled *Lesson Fourteen Review: Sentences* (segment 15.25). Each sentence is signed twice and an English translation is provided.

3. **Remind** students to watch the face of each signer to see the facial/body expressions and non-manual grammatical markers as well as the signs.

Video Segment Content:
(1 1/2 Minutes)

The following are English translations of the practice sentences:

1. Where are my shoes?
2. I really love to shop!
3. Clothes are expensive. A shirt costs $50. Wow!
4. My daughter doesn't want a purse. She wants a backpack.
5. I want to buy a hat.

Student Workbook:
Activity 15.25

15.25 Video Learning Experience

Lesson Fourteen Review: Sentences

Viewing Goal: To improve your comprehension skills by watching sentences presented in ASL.

Viewing Instructions: Watch the signed sentences for comprehension. Remember to watch the face of each signer to see the facial/body expressions and the non-manual grammatical markers as well as the signs.

It is recommended that you copy each signed sentence when it is repeated.

In the space below, record any questions or notes you have regarding the sentences.

Notes: _____
_____
_____

Instructor's Guide: Lesson Fifteen
Bravo ASL! Curriculum

©1996 Sign Enhancers, Inc.
ALL RIGHTS RESERVED

Lesson Fifteen: *Review & Practice Session*

15.26 Video Learning Experience

Bravo Family Revisited

Viewing Goal: To reinforce ASL comprehension skills by reviewing a Bravo family interaction from Lesson Fourteen.

Viewing Instructions:
1. **Ask** students to read *Bravo Family Revisited* in their workbooks (activity 15.26).
2. **Play** the video segment of the Bravo family (segment 15.26). They will use the ASL vocabulary within the context of going clothes shopping.
3. **Instruct** students to watch for review and write a summary of the main points.
4. **Replay** any portion of this video segment that students experienced difficulty understanding.

Video Segment Content: (2 1/2 Minutes)

The following is a summary of the Bravo family interaction:

Scott is teaching Tommy signs for items in the store. Scott and Tommy play a joke on Anna.

Dad teaches Tommy's father the signs for tie, gloves, and hat. Dad sees something strange in the mirror. It seems one of the mannequins is signing to him. But when he turns around, it is only a mannequin.

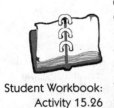

Student Workbook: Activity 15.26

15.26 Video Learning Experience

Bravo Family Revisited

Viewing Goal: To improve your ASL comprehension skills by reviewing a Bravo family interaction.

Viewing Instructions: Watch the *Bravo Family Revisited* for review and write a summary in the space below.

Summary: _____
_____
_____
_____

Lesson Fifteen: *Review & Practice Session*

15.27 Experiential Activity

Pictures in the Air

Activity Goal: To improve students' expressive and comprehension skills.

Activity Instructions:

1. **Ask** students to read *Pictures in the Air* in their workbooks (activity 15.27).

2. **Divide** the class into groups of four or five.

3. **Assign** each group one of the pictures provided in their Student Workbooks. **Tell** each group to create a short skit about their picture using ASL (no voice).

4. **Instruct** students to begin the activity by planning and practicing their skits with their small groups.

5. **Circulate** among the groups to **observe** student performance.

6. **Ask** each group to perform their skit for the class. If possible, it is recommended that you **videotape** each group's performance of this activity. **Correct** production errors by **modeling** the accurate production of the signs.

Student Workbook: Activity 15.27

Instructor's Guide: Lesson Fifteen
Bravo ASL! Curriculum

Lesson Fifteen: *Review & Practice Session*

15.28 Video Learning Experience

Lessons Eleven Thru Fourteen Review: Grammatical Notes

Viewing Goal: To review the grammatical aspects of ASL presented in Lessons Eleven through Fourteen.

Viewing Instructions:
1. **Ask** students to read *Lessons Eleven Thru Fourteen Review: Grammatical Notes* in their workbooks (activity 15.28).

2. **Instruct** students to complete the questions in their workbooks before watching the review segment.

3. **Play** the video segment entitled *Lessons Eleven Thru Fourteen Review: Grammatical Notes* (segment 15.28) while students correct their work. Because the presentation of this segment is beyond the linguistic ability of beginning students, please **turn on** the audio and/or captions to optimize its educational value.

4. At completion of the segment, **answer** any questions students may have.

Video Segment Content: See the following Student Workbook excerpt for the content
(7 1/2 Minutes) of this video segment.

Student Workbook: Activity 15.28

15.28 Video Learning Experience

Lessons Eleven Thru Fourteen Review: Grammatical Notes

Viewing Goal: To help you apply the ASL grammatical aspects presented in Lessons Eleven, Twelve, Thirteen, and Fourteen.

Viewing Instructions: Answer the questions below to see how well you remember these grammatical aspects. When you are finished, watch the video. Billy will provide the answers so you can see how well you did.

1. What is the grammatical feature of ASL that allows the signs to mirror actual events, following the same direction of movement, location, and relative size of objects?
   A. Use of signs
   B. Use of space
   C. Use of adjectives
   D. Use of facial expression

Instructor's Guide: Lesson Fifteen
Bravo ASL! Curriculum

©1996 Sign Enhancers, Inc.
ALL RIGHTS RESERVED.

Lesson Fifteen: *Review & Practice Session*

2. Signs and numbers are sometimes combined and used together. Can you think of two examples showing a number incorporated within a sign?

   A. _____
   B. _____

3. What is the grammatical feature which prevents signing from looking boring?

   Facial expression.

4. How would you explain what a classifier is?

   Classifiers are handshapes which are used to illustrate a "class" of objects.

15.29 Video Learning Experience

Lessons Eleven Thru Fourteen Review: Cultural Notes

Viewing Goal: To assist students in reviewing the cultural aspects of ASL presented in Lessons Eleven, Twelve, Thirteen, and Fourteen.

Viewing Instructions:

1. **Ask** students to read *Lessons Eleven Thru Fourteen Review: Cultural Notes* in their workbooks (activity 15.29).

2. **Instruct** students to complete the questions in their workbooks before viewing the segment.

3. **Play** the video segment entitled *Lessons Eleven Thru Fourteen Review: Cultural Notes* (segment 15.29) while students correct their work. Because the presentation of this segment is beyond the linguistic ability of beginning students, please **turn on** the audio and/or captions to optimize its educational value.

4. At completion of the segment, **answer** any questions students may have.

Instructor's Guide: Lesson Fifteen
Bravo ASL! Curriculum
©1996 Sign Enhancers, Inc.
ALL RIGHTS RESERVED

Lesson Fifteen: *Review & Practice Session*

Video Segment Content: See the following Student Workbook excerpt for the content
(5 Minutes) of this video segment.

Student Workbook:
Activity 15.29

15.29 Video Learning Experience

Lessons Eleven Thru Fourteen Review:
Cultural Notes

Viewing Goal: To review the cultural aspects presented in Lessons Eleven, Twelve, Thirteen, and Fourteen.

Viewing Instructions: Answer the questions below to see how well you remember these cultural aspects of ASL. When you are finished, watch the video. Billy will provide you with the answers to correct your work.

1. What are some issues and concerns a Deaf person faces in a medical emergency? (Check all that apply.)
   _X_ **A. Will the medical services be accessible?**
   _X_ **B. Can the hospital staff sign?**
   _X_ **C. Will there be an interpreter available?**
   _X_ **D. Will I be able to get my medical needs met?**

2. There are actually federal laws requiring equal accessibility and communication at hospitals receiving federal funding.
   A. True
   B. False

3. Unfortunately, the laws are not always followed.
   A. True
   B. False

4. Today however, the world is changing. More people are learning ASL, and learning about Deaf culture.
   A. True
   B. False

5. What are two benefits of making businesses accessible to Deaf people?
   A. Deaf employees are an asset.
   B. The business also gains access to Deaf customers.

6. The majority of Deaf children have hearing parents.
   A. True
   B. False

7. Parents need to focus on their child's unique needs when making choices regarding communication options.
   A. True
   B. False

8. When communicating with a Deaf person, what can you do to be sensitive to that person's needs? (Check all that apply):
   A. Address the person directly.
   B. Maintain eye contact.
   C. Write or draw if needed.
   D. Speak loudly and slowly.

15.30 Video Learning Experience

Lessons Eleven Thru Fourteen Review: Practice Story

Viewing Goal: To improve students' comprehension skills by watching a signed story.

Viewing Instructions:

1. **Ask** students to read *Lessons Eleven Thru Fourteen Review: Practice Story* in their workbooks (activity 15.30).

2. **Show** the video segment entitled *Lessons Eleven Thru Fourteen Review: Practice Story*. Billy signs a story using the vocabulary from Lessons Eleven, Twelve, Thirteen, and Fourteen. **Turn off** audio and captions.

3. **Instruct** students to watch the story for comprehension.

4. When the segment is over, **divide** class into pairs.

5. **Instruct** pairs to take turns practicing using ASL to retell the story.

6. **Replay** video (segment 15.30) and tell students to copy Billy's version.

Video Segment Content: (3 Minutes)

The following is an English translation of the story:

A man walked to work. It was a beautiful day. The man wore a hat, coat, and gloves. The man was happy to walk under the sun's rays. But soon he became hot. He didn't need his coat, gloves, or hat. He took them off and continued walking.

He was admiring a very tall tree when he tripped and fell, hurting his foot. He limped along very slowly.

When he arrived at work, he called the hospital, saying he needed a doctor's appointment. When the man saw his foot, it was blue and purple, bruised, swollen, and throbbing.

Because the man was not a doctor, he felt a little nauseous looking at his injury. He knew he needed help, so he called his secretary. His secretary came in and he explained that he had fallen and broken his foot.

"I need to go to the hospital," he said, "I can't walk there. I need my foot wrapped. Can you help me?" The secretary said

Lesson Fifteen: *Review & Practice Session*

yes, and cut his pant leg with her scissors.

She could see that he was hurt badly. She cut off the man's tie and used it to wrap his foot. She taped it up until it was just right. The secretary was a skilled worker and just like a doctor, she had good medical skills.

The man was in pain. His stomach hurt, his head hurt, he was dizzy, he felt like he would throw-up. He needed some medication to make him feel better.

What? Are you worried about the man? Would you like to send him a flower?

The man went to the hospital and sat there. A doctor looked at his foot and said that it was not broken. The man said he was in great pain. The doctor gave him a shot which took away the pain. The man could now walk again.

Oh, his secretary? She quit her job and now works as a nurse.

Student Workbook: Activity 15.30

15.30 Video Learning Experience

Lessons Eleven Thru Fourteen Review: Practice Story

Viewing Goal: To improve your ASL comprehension skills by watching a story presented in ASL.

Viewing Instructions: Watch the signed story for comprehension. Be prepared to use ASL to retell the story.

15.31 Video Learning Experience

Congratulations, You Did It!

Viewing Goal: To congratulate students and encourage them to continue improving their ASL skills.

Viewing Instructions:
1. **Ask** students to read *Congratulations, You Did It!* in their workbooks (activity 15.31).

2. **Show** the video segment in which Jenna Cassell, founder and president of Sign Enhancers, Inc., congratulates the students who have completed all fifteen lessons.

Instructor's Guide: Lesson Fifteen
Bravo ASL! Curriculum
©1996 Sign Enhancers, Inc.
ALL RIGHTS RESERVED.

Lesson Fifteen: *Review & Practice Session*

3. Because the presentation of this segment is beyond the linguistic ability of beginning students, please **turn on** the audio and/or captions to optimize its educational value.

4. **Instruct** students to watch the segment for reinforcement and encouragement.

Video Segment Content: (3 Minutes)

The following is an English translation of the message presented by Jenna Cassell:

Hello. I'm Jenna Cassell. I am the producer of this fifteen-lesson ASL VideoCourse and the founder of Sign Enhancers, Inc.

I wanted to personally meet and congratulate you. If you have completed all fifteen lessons, you have worked really hard and learned a lot. We are proud of you.

We strongly encourage you to continue improving your signing skills by associating with Deaf people and becoming involved with the Deaf community. You will learn more and improve greatly.

If you are a professional working with Deaf people, we strongly encourage you to continue learning and improving your skills on an ongoing basis. If you are a parent with a Deaf child, congratulations on beginning to learn how to communicate all the love you have for your child. If you are Deaf, you can be very proud to have such a wonderful culture and beautiful language.

Whatever your reasons for learning Sign Language, we would like to continue to be of assistance. Please call us free at the number shown on the screen if we can be of service to you, or if you are curious to learn of other Sign Enhancers materials that are available.

You may be interested to know, after all these lessons of watching the Bravo family, we thought maybe you'd be curious about who the people behind the Bravo characters are in real life. We now have a video available entitled, "The People Behind the Bravo Family." Billy interviews each member of the family and you can watch and learn more about the private lives of the actors that played the Bravo family.

Well, that is it for now. We at Sign Enhancers have a dream. We want to enhance communication between Deaf and hearing people. I want to thank you for helping us to accomplish this.

Well, as Billy would say - and now it is my turn - Goodbye and good luck!

Lesson Fifteen: *Review & Practice Session*

Student Workbook:
Activity 15.31

15.31 Video Learning Experience

Congratulations, You Did It!

Viewing Goal: To receive well-deserved congratulations!

Viewing Instructions: Sign Enhancers wants to congratulate you on a job well done! Watch the signed message for encouragement to continue improving your skills.

15.32 Post-test

What Do You Know Now?

Assessment Video

Post-test Goal: To assess students' mastery of the lesson objectives.

Post-test Instructions:

1. **Ask** students to read the Post-test Introduction in their workbooks (activity 15.32).

2. **Copy** and **distribute** the Lesson Fifteen Post-test (Appendix 15.32).

3. **Play** the Assessment Video (segment 15.32) and allow students to complete Section One (comprehension portion) of the test.

4. **Instruct** students to complete Section Two (culture and grammar portion) of the test individually and hand in their papers when they are finished.

5. **Assign** Section Three (expressive portion) of the test and **schedule** a time when students are to perform. If possible, it is strongly recommended that you **videotape** this portion of the Post-test.

6. **Determine** grading options based upon programmatic requirements. A recommended guideline for measuring successful mastery of objectives is 80% accuracy.

Lesson Fifteen: *Review & Practice Session*

Video Segment Content: (3 Minutes)

The following is an English translation of the comprehension story:

There was a woman, named Karen (name sign, K on shoulder). Karen was a Sign Language interpreter. She loved her work.

John, a Deaf man, went shopping with his hearing son Tommy, who is four.

John's boss had just promoted him to vice president, so John wanted to buy a new tie for work.

John and Tommy went shopping together. John was looking at the shirts and ties when he noticed Tommy was gone.

He turned and looked, but couldn't find Tommy. He looked around the pants, but Tommy wasn't there. John looked around the shoes, but he couldn't find his son.

John was getting scared. Tommy likes to run. Maybe he fell and hurt himself. Maybe he'd have to go to the hospital! John started to feel sick.

Just then, John felt a tap on his shoulder. It was Karen. She signed, "Are you Deaf?" He signed, "Yes." Karen signed, "I think your son is playing a game with you. He is behind the coats."

John said, "Thanks. Do you want to help me teach him? Walk with me." They walked away from Tommy. Tommy got scared and ran after them. They both laughed.

John said to Karen, "Thank you for your help." Karen answered, "My daughter tries to fool me, too! It was nice to meet you. Bye."

John found a tie he liked, bought it, and he and Tommy went home.

Student Workbook: Activity 15.32

15.32 Post-test Introduction

What Do You Know Now?

Post-test Goal: To assess your mastery of the lesson objectives.

Post-test Introduction: This test has three sections:

Section One: The Comprehension section tests your ability to understand ASL.

Section Two: The Culture and Grammar section tests your knowledge of the material presented in the *Cultural* and *Grammatical Notes*.

Section Three: The Expressive portion tests your ability to use ASL.

Simply follow the instructions for each section. **Good luck!**

Post-Test Master: Appendix 15.32

15.32 Post-test

Section One: Comprehension

Instructions: You will see a signed story. Watch carefully and answer each question below.

1. What was the man's name in the story?
   A. Jack
   B. Joseph
   C. Jasper
   D. John

2. Was the man Deaf or hearing?
   A. Deaf
   B. Hearing

3. Who did the man have with him?
   A. His five-year-old daughter
   B. His four-year-old son
   C. His wife, who was an interpreter
   D. His girlfriend, who had a daughter

4. Why did the man go to the store?
   A. To find a new job
   B. To buy some pants
   C To buy a new tie
   D. To find his family

5. What happened that made him so scared?
   He couldn't find his son, Tommy.

6. Who did he meet at the store?
   A. Kathy
   B. Karen
   C. Kendra
   D. Kelly

7. What did this woman do for a living?
   She was a Sign Language interpreter.

8. What did the man do to teach the child a lesson?
   Walked away from him.

Post-Test Master:
Appendix 15.32

15.32 Post-test

Section Two: *Culture and Grammar*

Instructions: Read each statement carefully and determine if it is True or False (circle your answer).

9. Communication access is less important in a medical emergency.
   A. True
   B. False

10. Deaf employees can be a great asset to a company.
    A. True
    B. False

11. The majority of Deaf children have Deaf parents.
    A. True
    B. False

12. When communicating with a Deaf person, it is considered rude to draw or write.
    A. True
    B. False

13. Deaf customers are more likely to spend money at businesses that are accessible.
    A. True
    B. False

14. A "classifier" that can be used for a car is made with a 1 handshape.
    A. True
    B. False

15. Facial expression is an important grammatical feature of ASL.
    A. True
    B. False

Lesson Fifteen: *Review & Practice Session*

Post-Test Master:
Appendix 15.32

15.32 Post-test

Section Three: Expressive Portion

Instructions: Create a story about one of the topics listed below.

1. The best picnic I ever went to…
2. The medical emergency I lived through…
3. When I went clothes shopping…
4. The job I really want is…

Please use at least two classifiers, demonstrate at least one example of the use of space feature, use appropriate facial expressions, and use at least one example of a number within a sign.

Your instructor will schedule a time for you to perform this section of the Post-test. You may prepare and practice prior to your scheduled time.

Include at least two classifiers.

16. _____

17. _____

Demonstrate at least one example of the use of space feature.

18. _____

Use appropriate facial expressions.

19. _____

And at least one number incorporated within a sign.

20. _____

*Congratulations!
You have completed
Lesson Fifteen!*

Sign Illustration Index

Gloss	Lesson #	Page #
A	6	S-16
ADD	8	S-24
ADDRESS	9	S-27
ADVERTISE	13	S-39
ALL	9	S-27
ALL-GONE	4	S-11
ALMOST	1	S-1
APPOINTMENT	13	S-39
ASK (a)	13	S-39
ASK (b)	13	S-39
ASSISTANT	13	S-39
AWKWARD	12	S-35
B	6	S-16
B-A-N-K	9	S-27
BABY	1	S-1
BACKPACK	14	S-45
BAD	8	S-24
BALANCE	9	S-27
BANANA	2	S-5
BANANA	4	S-11
BANDAGE	12	S-35
BASEBALL	11	S-31
BATH	3	S-8
BED	1	S-1
BED	3	S-8
BED+ROOM	3	S-8
BEHIND	3	S-8
BIRTHDAY	9	S-27
BLACK	6	S-15
BLACK+BERRY	11	S-31
BLUE	6	S-15
BOOK	7	S-19
BORING	13	S-39
BOSS	13	S-39
BOY	8	S-24
BREAD	4	S-11
BREAKFAST	1	S-1
BRIDGE	11	S-31
BROKEN	12	S-35
BROWN	6	S-15
BRUSH-TEETH	1	S-1
BUSINESS	13	S-39
BUSY	13	S-39
C	6	S-16
CALCULATOR	8	S-24
CANDY	4	S-11
CARROT (a)	4	S-11
CARROT (b)	4	S-11
CEREAL	2	S-5
CHAIR	3	S-8
CHARGE/FEE	9	S-27
CHECK	13	S-39
CHECK	9	S-27
CHEESE	4	S-11
CHICKEN	4	S-11
CHILDREN	1	S-1
CLASS	8	S-24
CLIMB+TREE	11	S-31
CLOTHES	14	S-45
COAT	14	S-45
COFFEE	1	S-1
COLD	12	S-35
COME	8	S-24
COMFORTABLE	14	S-45
COMMUNICATION	12	S-35
COMPANY	13	S-39
COMPUTER (a)	13	S-39
COMPUTER (b)	13	S-40
COMPUTER+PRINTER	13	S-40
CONSULT	13	S-40
COOK	2	S-5
COOKIES	4	S-11
COOL	11	S-31
COPY	13	S-40
COUCH	3	S-8
COUGH	12	S-35
COUNT	8	S-24
COW	4	S-11
CUTE	14	S-45
D	6	S-16
DAUGHTER	1	S-1
DEAF	1	S-1
DEPOSIT	9	S-27
DESK	13	S-40
DINNER	14	S-45
DO-WHAT	2	S-5
DOCTOR	12	S-35
DOG	1	S-1
DOG+FOOD	4	S-12
DOLLAR	9	S-27
DON'T-LIKE	14	S-45
DRAWER	13	S-40
DREAM	8	S-24
DRESS	14	S-45
DRESSER	3	S-8
DRIVE	9	S-27
E	6	S-16
EARN	13	S-40
EAT	2	S-5
EGG	2	S-5
EGG+PLANT	4	S-12
EIGHT	4	S-14
EIGHT	8	S-22
EIGHTEEN	8	S-23
ELEVEN	8	S-22
EMERGENCY	12	S-35
ENVELOPE	13	S-41
EQUAL	8	S-24
EXPENSIVE	14	S-45
EXPLAIN	13	S-41
F	6	S-16
FALL-DOWN	11	S-31

Instructor's Guide: Sign Illustration Index
Bravo ASL! Curriculum

©1996 Sign Enhancers, Inc.
ALL RIGHTS RESERVED.

Sign Illustration Index

Gloss	Lesson #	Page #
FANCY	14	S-45
FAST	9	S-27
FEEL	12	S-35
FIFTEEN	8	S-23
FIFTY+DOLLAR	9	S-30
FILE	13	S-41
FILES	13	S-41
FIND	11	S-31
FINISH	7	S-19
FIRED	13	S-41
FIRST	13	S-41
FISH	4	S-12
FISHING	11	S-31
FIVE	4	S-14
FIVE	8	S-22
FIVE-DOLLAR	9	S-29
FLASHING-LIGHT	3	S-8
FLOWER	11	S-31
FLOWER	7	S-19
FOOD	4	S-12
FOOL-YOU	1	S-2
FORK	2	S-5
FOUR	4	S-14
FOUR	8	S-22
FOURTEEN	8	S-23
FRISBEE	11	S-31
G	6	S-16
GAME	11	S-32
GET-DRESSED	1	S-2
GIRL	8	S-24
GIVE	2	S-5
GIVE	7	S-19
GLASS	2	S-5
GO	1	S-2
GOLD	6	S-15
GOLF	11	S-32
GONE	2	S-5
GOOD	1	S-2
GOOD	7	S-19
GOOD	8	S-24
GRASS	11	S-32
GREEN	6	S-15
GROW-UP	7	S-19
H	6	S-16
HAMBURGER	4	S-12
HAT	14	S-46
HAVE	7	S-19
HEARING	1	S-2
HELP	2	S-6
HERE	7	S-19
HIRE	13	S-41
HOSPITAL	12	S-35
HOT	11	S-32
HOT-DOG	4	S-12
HOW	12	S-35
HOW-MUCH	9	S-28
HUG/HOLD	12	S-35
HUNGRY	1	S-2
HURT/PAIN	12	S-36
I	6	S-16
ICE-CREAM	4	S-12
IDEA	13	S-41
IN	3	S-8
INSURANCE	12	S-36
INTEREST	9	S-28
INTERPRET	12	S-36
INTERPRETER	12	S-36
INTERVIEW	13	S-41
J	6	S-17
K	6	S-17
KETCHUP	4	S-12
KITCHEN	1	S-2
KNIFE	2	S-6
KNOW	8	S-25
L	6	S-17
LARGE/BIG	14	S-46
LATE	7	S-19
LAZY	13	S-41
LEAF	11	S-32
LEARN	7	S-19
LETTER	13	S-41
LETTUCE	4	S-12
LICENSE	9	S-28
LIGHT	3	S-8
LIKE	14	S-46
LIVING+ROOM	3	S-9
LOBSTER	4	S-13
LOVE	1	S-2
LOVE-IT	14	S-46
LUCKY	14	S-46
M	6	S-17
MAN	11	S-32
MATH	8	S-25
MAYBE	8	S-25
MEDICINE	12	S-36
MEETING	13	S-41
MELON	4	S-13
MILK	2	S-6
MILK	4	S-13
MILLION	9	S-28
MINUS/NEGATIVE	8	S-25
MOM/MOTHER	1	S-2
MONEY	9	S-28
MORE	9	S-28
MORNING	1	S-2
MOVE	11	S-32
MY-TURN	2	S-6
N	6	S-17
NAME	8	S-25
NAPKIN	2	S-6
NAUSEA	12	S-36
NEED	13	S-42

Sign Illustration Index

Gloss	Lesson #	Page #
NEED	7	S-19
NINE	4	S-14
NINE	8	S-22
NINETEEN	8	S-23
NO	1	S-2
NOT	7	S-19
NUMBER	9	S-28
NURSE	12	S-36
O	6	S-17
OFFICE	13	S-42
OH-I-SEE	13	S-42
ON	3	S-9
ONE	2	S-6
ONE	4	S-14
ONE	8	S-22
ONE-DOLLAR	9	S-29
ONE-HUNDRED	9	S-30
ONION	4	S-13
ORANGE	6	S-15
ORANGE-JUICE	2	S-6
OVEN	3	S-9
P	6	S-17
PANTS	14	S-46
PAPER	7	S-20
PAPER+CLIP	13	S-42
PAST/BEFORE	1	S-3
PAY	13	S-42
PAY-ATTENTION	8	S-25
PENCIL	7	S-20
PEOPLE	9	S-28
PERCENT	9	S-28
PICK+FLOWER	7	S-20
PICNIC	11	S-32
PILL	12	S-36
PINK	6	S-15
PLANT	4	S-13
PLATE	2	S-6
PLAY	7	S-20
PLEASE	7	S-20
PLUS	8	S-25
POPCORN	4	S-13
POST-OFFICE	13	S-42
PREGNANT	12	S-36
PRESIDENT	13	S-42
PRETTY/BEAUTIFUL	11	S-32
PRICE/COST	14	S-46
PRINCIPAL	8	S-25
PROFESSION	13	S-42
PURPLE	6	S-15
PURSE	14	S-46
PURSE/BAG	11	S-32
Q	6	S-17
R	6	S-17
READ	7	S-20
RED	6	S-15
REFRIGERATOR	3	S-9
REMOTE-CONTROL	3	S-9
RIGHT/CORRECT	8	S-25
RIGHTS	12	S-36
RIVER	11	S-33
ROOM	8	S-25
RUBBER-BAND	13	S-42
RUN	11	S-33
S	6	S-17
S	6	S-17
SAME	9	S-28
SAVE	9	S-28
SAVINGS	9	S-29
SCARED/AFRAID	1	S-3
SCHEDULE	13	S-43
SCHOOL	1	S-3
SCHOOL	7	S-20
SCISSORS	13	S-43
SECRETARY	13	S-43
SEND	13	S-43
SET-TABLE	2	S-6
SEVEN	4	S-14
SEVEN	8	S-22
SEVENTEEN	8	S-23
SHELF	13	S-43
SHIRT	14	S-46
SHOES	14	S-46
SHOPPING	4	S-13
SHOPPING/BUYING	14	S-46
SHOT (a)	12	S-37
SHOT (b)	12	S-37
SHOWER	1	S-3
SICK	12	S-37
SIGNATURE	9	S-29
SIGNATURE/SIGN	13	S-43
SILVER	6	S-15
SINK	3	S-9
SIT	7	S-20
SIX	4	S-14
SIX	8	S-22
SIXTEEN	8	S-23
SKILL	13	S-43
SKIRT	14	S-47
SLEEP	8	S-25
SLOW	9	S-29
SNEEZE	12	S-37
SOCIAL-SECURITY	9	S-29
SOCKS	14	S-47
SODA/POP	4	S-13
SON	1	S-3
SORE-THROAT	12	S-37
SORRY	7	S-20
SOUP	4	S-13
SPIDER	1	S-3
SPOON	2	S-7
SPRAIN	12	S-37
STAMP	13	S-43

Sign Illustration Index

Gloss	Lesson #	Page #
STAPLE/STAPLER	13	S-43
STAY	11	S-33
STOMACH	12	S-37
STORE	14	S-47
STUDENT	7	S-21
STUDY	7	S-21
SUN	11	S-33
SUN+SHINE	11	S-33
SWOLLEN	12	S-37
T	6	S-17
T.V.	3	S-10
TAKE-CARE	12	S-37
TALL	11	S-33
TALL	14	S-47
TAN	6	S-16
TAPE	13	S-43
TEACH	7	S-21
TEACHER	7	S-21
TEASE	12	S-37
TELEPHONE	3	S-9
TELEPHONE	9	S-29
TELL	2	S-7
TEMPERATURE	12	S-37
TEN	4	S-14
TEN	8	S-22
TEN+DOLLAR	9	S-29
TENNIS	11	S-33
THANK-YOU	1	S-3
THERE	7	S-21
THIRTEEN	8	S-23
THOUSAND	9	S-29
THREE	4	S-14
THREE	8	S-22
THREE-OF-US	14	S-47
THREE-THOUSAND	9	S-29
THROAT	12	S-38
THROB	12	S-38
THROW-UP	12	S-38
TIE	14	S-47
TIME	1	S-3
TIRED	7	S-21
TOAST	2	S-7
TOGETHER	8	S-26
TOILET/BATHROOM	1	S-3
TOMATO	4	S-14
TOWEL	14	S-47
TREE	11	S-33
TREES/FOREST	11	S-33
TTY/TDD	3	S-9
TURKEY	4	S-14
TWELVE	8	S-23
TWENTY	8	S-23
TWENTY+DOLLAR	9	S-30
TWIST	12	S-38
TWO	2	S-7
TWO	4	S-14
TWO	8	S-22
TWO-OF-US	14	S-47
TYPE	13	S-43
TYPEWRITER	13	S-44
U	6	S-17
UNDER	3	S-10
UNDERSTAND	12	S-38
UNDERSTAND	8	S-26
UPSTAIRS	3	S-10
V	6	S-18
VICE-PRESIDENT	13	S-44
W	6	S-18
WAIT	12	S-38
WAITER	2	S-7
WAKE-UP	1	S-3
WALK	11	S-33
WANT	1	S-3
WANT	7	S-21
WASH	2	S-7
WATER	11	S-34
WHAT-WRONG	7	S-21
WHERE	1	S-4
WHICH	1	S-4
WHITE	6	S-16
WHO	7	S-21
WITHDRAW	9	S-29
WOMAN	11	S-34
WORK	13	S-44
WORK	2	S-7
WRONG/INCORRECT	8	S-26
X	6	S-18
X-R-A-Y	12	S-38
X-RAY	12	S-38
Y	6	S-18
YELLOW	6	S-16
YES	1	S-4
YESTERDAY	2	S-7
YOUR-TURN	2	S-7
Z	6	S-18

Instructor's Guide: Sign Illustration Index
Bravo ASL! Curriculum

©1996 Sign Enhancers, Inc.
ALL RIGHTS RESERVED.

LESSON ONE: ASL VOCABULARY

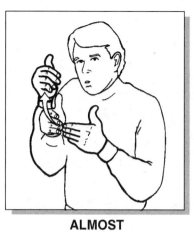
ALMOST

BABY

BED

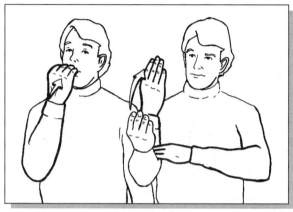
BREAKFAST

BRUSH-TEETH

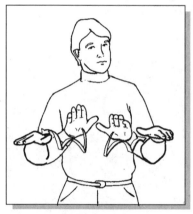
CHILDREN

COFFEE

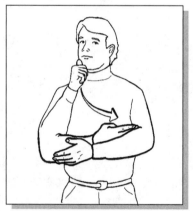
DAUGHTER

DEAF

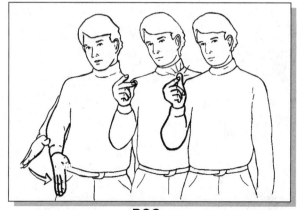
DOG

LESSON ONE: ASL VOCABULARY

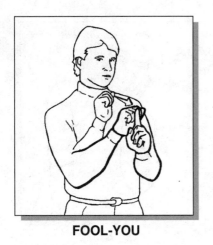
FOOL-YOU

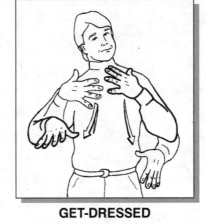
GET-DRESSED

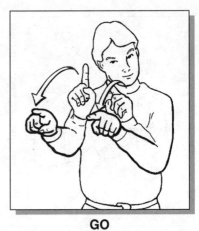
GO

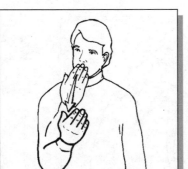
GOOD

HEARING

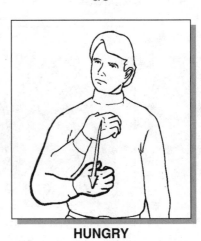
HUNGRY

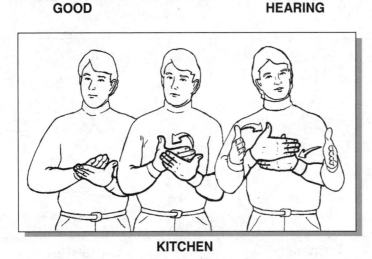
KITCHEN

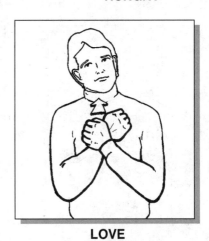
LOVE

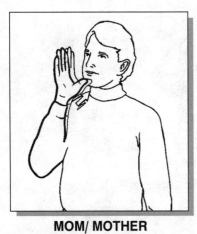
MOM/ MOTHER

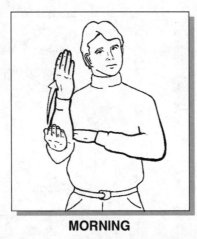
MORNING

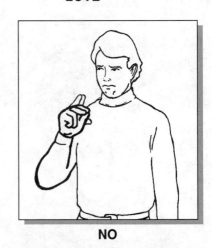
NO

Instructor's Guide: Sign Illustrations
Bravo ASL! Curriculum

©1996 Sign Enhancers, Inc.
ALL RIGHTS RESERVED.

LESSON ONE: ASL VOCABULARY

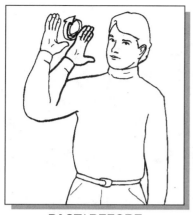
PAST/ BEFORE

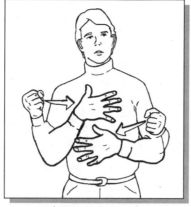
SCARED/ AFRAID

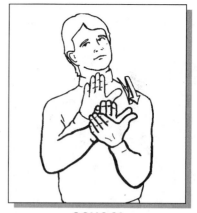
SCHOOL

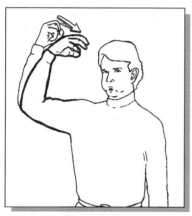
SHOWER

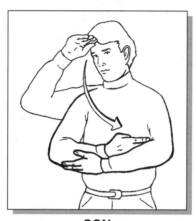
SON

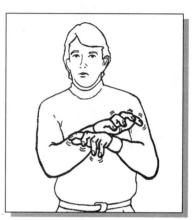
SPIDER

THANK-YOU

TIME

TOILET/ BATHROOM

WAKE-UP

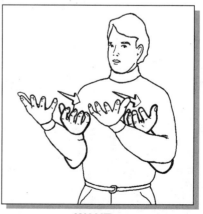
WANT

Instructor's Guide: Sign Illustrations
Bravo ASL! Curriculum

©1996 Sign Enhancers, Inc.
ALL RIGHTS RESERVED.

LESSON ONE: ASL VOCABULARY

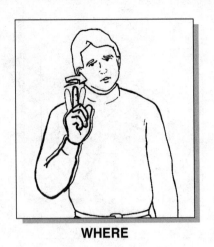 WHERE

 WHICH

 YES

LESSON TWO: ASL VOCABULARY

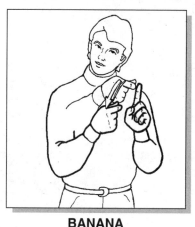
BANANA

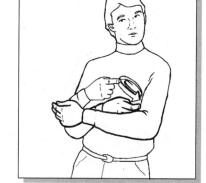
CEREAL

COOK

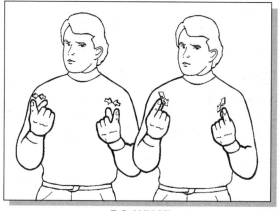
DO-WHAT

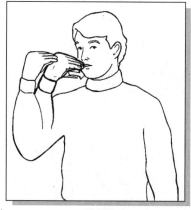
EAT

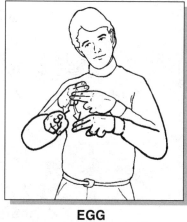
EGG

FORK

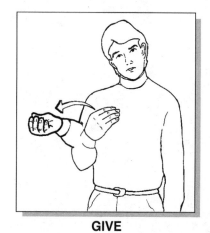
GIVE

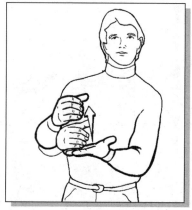
GLASS

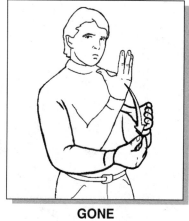
GONE

LESSON TWO: ASL VOCABULARY

HELP

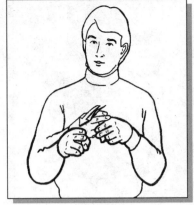
KNIFE

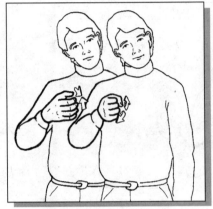
MILK

MY-TURN

NAPKIN

ONE

ORANGE-JUICE

PLATE

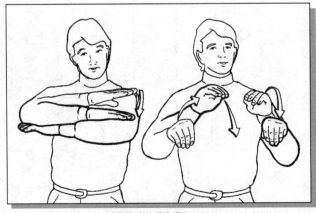
SET-TABLE

LESSON TWO: ASL VOCABULARY

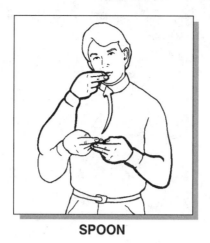
SPOON

TELL

TOAST

TWO

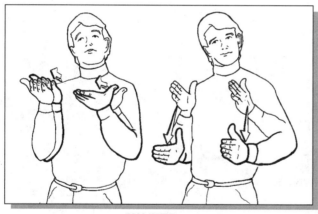
WAITER

WASH

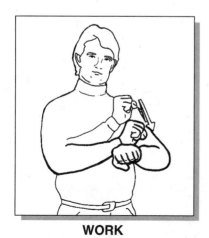
WORK

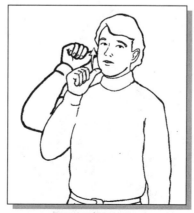
YESTERDAY

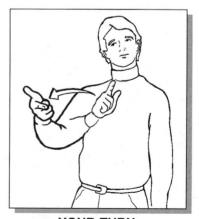
YOUR-TURN

LESSON THREE: ASL VOCABULARY

BATH

BED

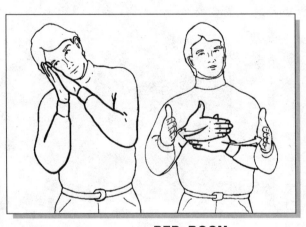
BED+ROOM

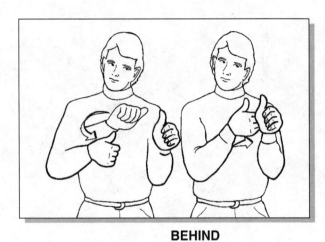
BEHIND

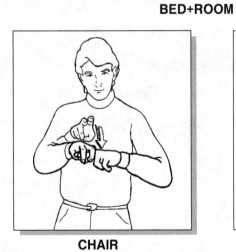
CHAIR

COUCH

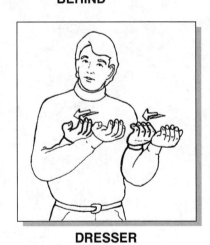
DRESSER

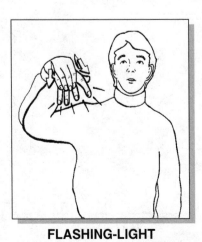
FLASHING-LIGHT

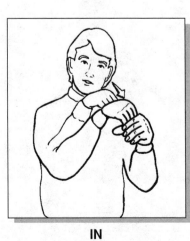
IN

LIGHT

LESSON THREE: ASL VOCABULARY

LIVING+ROOM

ON

OVEN

REFRIGERATOR

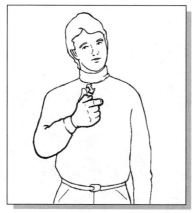
REMOTE-CONTROL

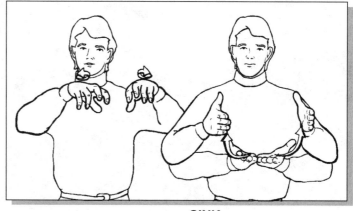
SINK

TELEPHONE

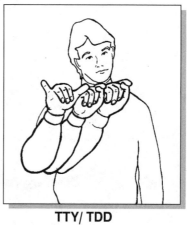
TTY/ TDD

LESSON THREE: ASL VOCABULARY

T.V.

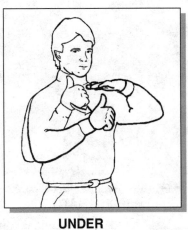
UNDER

UPSTAIRS

LESSON FOUR: ASL VOCABULARY

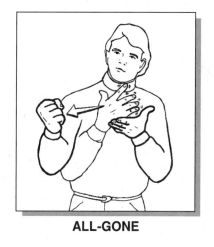
ALL-GONE

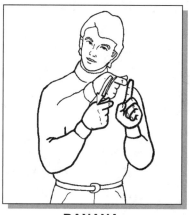
BANANA

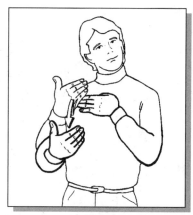
BREAD

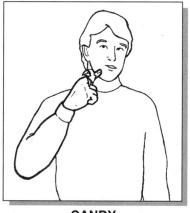
CANDY

CARROT (a)

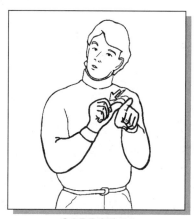
CARROT (b)

CHEESE

CHICKEN

COOKIES

COW

LESSON FOUR: ASL VOCABULARY

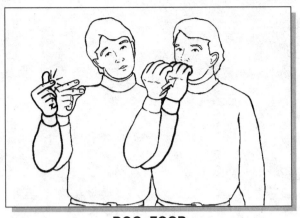
DOG+FOOD

EGG+PLANT

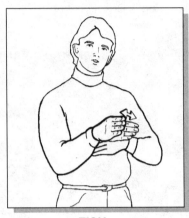
FISH

FOOD

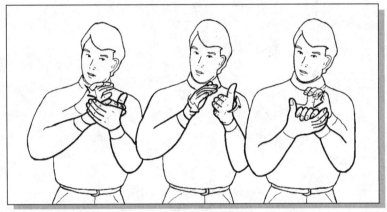
HAMBURGER

HOT-DOG

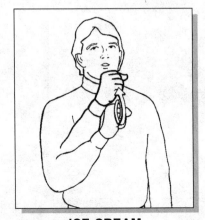
ICE-CREAM

KETCHUP

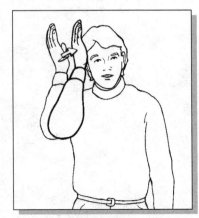
LETTUCE

LESSON FOUR: ASL VOCABULARY

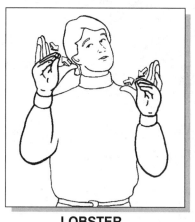
LOBSTER

MELON

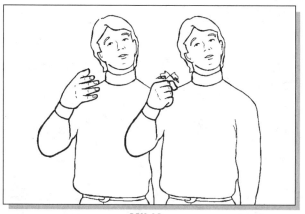
MILK

ONION

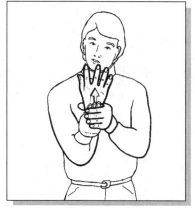
PLANT

POPCORN

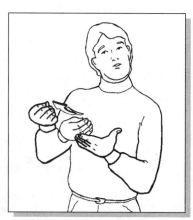
SHOPPING

SODA/POP

SOUP

LESSON FOUR: ASL VOCABULARY

TOMATO

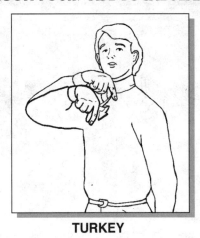
TURKEY

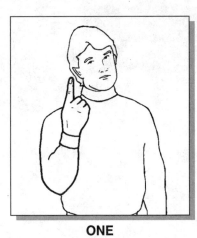
ONE

TWO

THREE

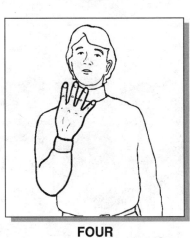
FOUR

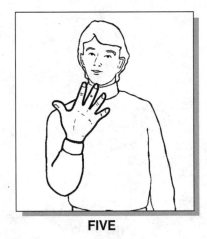
FIVE

SIX

SEVEN

EIGHT

NINE

TEN

Instructor's Guide: Sign Illustrations
Bravo ASL! Curriculum

©1996 Sign Enhancers, Inc.
ALL RIGHTS RESERVED.

LESSON SIX: ASL VOCABULARY

BLACK

BLUE

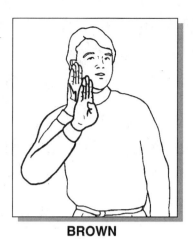
BROWN

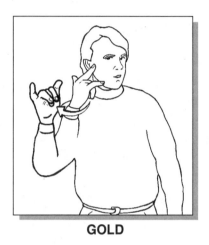
GOLD

GREEN

ORANGE

PINK

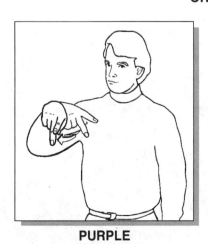
PURPLE

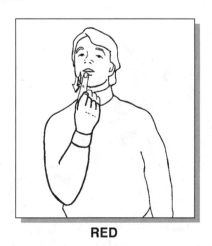
RED

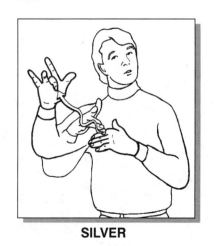
SILVER

LESSON SIX: ASL VOCABULARY

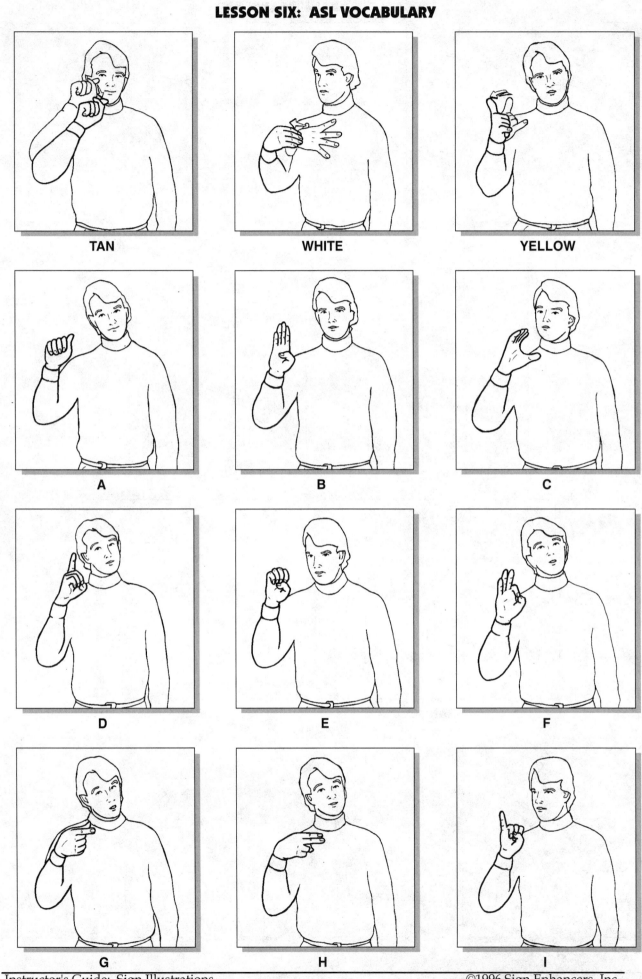

LESSON SIX: ASL VOCABULARY

LESSON SIX: ASL VOCABULARY

V

W

X

Y

Z

LESSON SEVEN: ASL VOCABULARY

 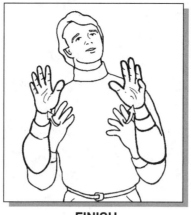 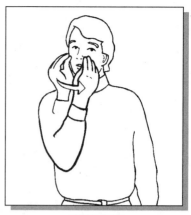

BOOK　　　　　FINISH　　　　　FLOWER

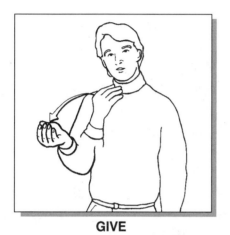  

GIVE　　　　　GOOD　　　　　GROW-UP

  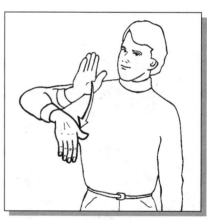

HAVE　　　　　HERE　　　　　LATE

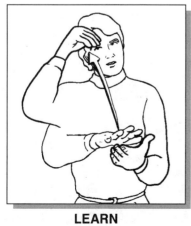 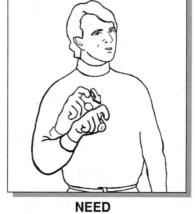 

LEARN　　　　　NEED　　　　　NOT

LESSON SEVEN: ASL VOCABULARY

PAPER

PENCIL

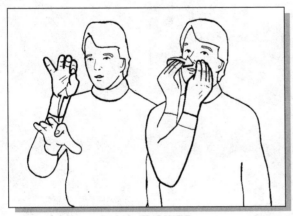

PICK+FLOWER

PLAY

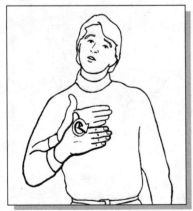

PLEASE

READ

SCHOOL

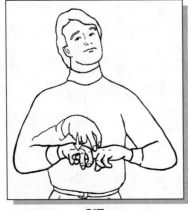

SIT

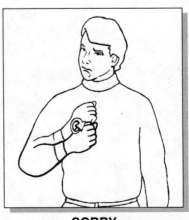

SORRY

LESSON SEVEN: ASL VOCABULARY

 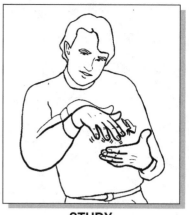

STUDENT STUDY

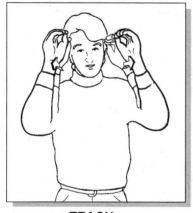 

TEACH TEACHER

 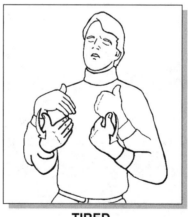 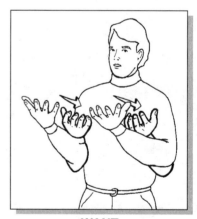

THERE TIRED WANT

WHAT-WRONG WHO

LESSON EIGHT: ASL VOCABULARY

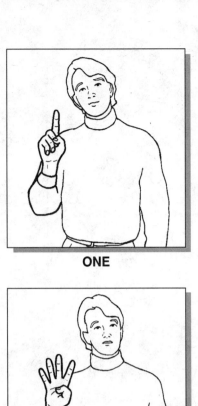
ONE

TWO

THREE

FOUR

FIVE

SIX

SEVEN

EIGHT

NINE

TEN

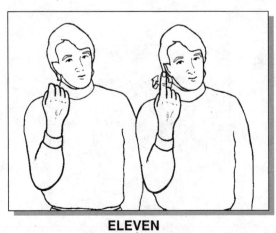
ELEVEN

LESSON EIGHT: ASL VOCABULARY

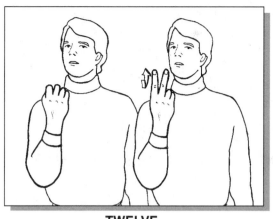
TWELVE

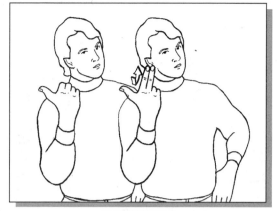
THIRTEEN

FOURTEEN

FIFTEEN

SIXTEEN

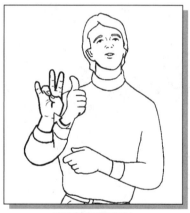
SEVENTEEN

EIGHTEEN

NINETEEN

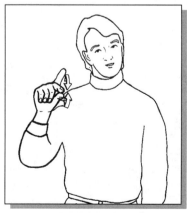
TWENTY

LESSON EIGHT: ASL VOCABULARY

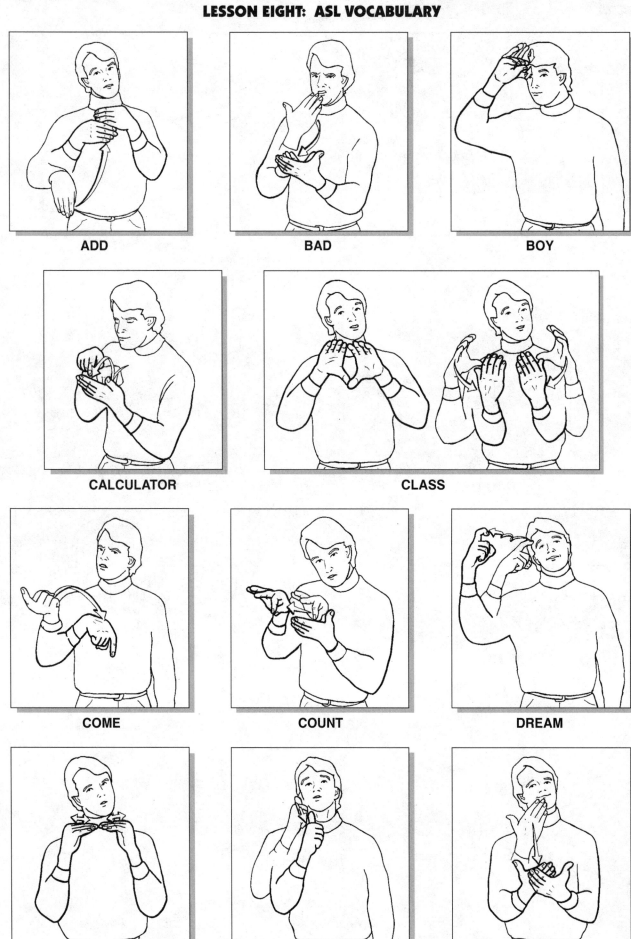

LESSON EIGHT: ASL VOCABULARY

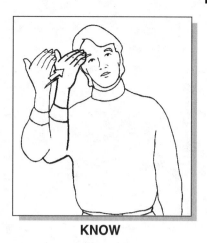
KNOW

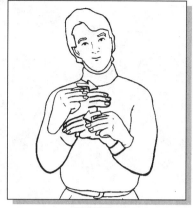
MATH

MAYBE

MINUS/ NEGATIVE

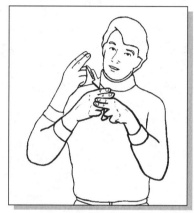
NAME

PAY-ATTENTION

PLUS

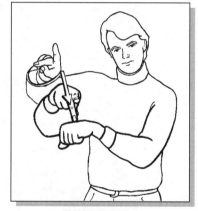
PRINCIPAL

RIGHT/ CORRECT

ROOM

SLEEP

LESSON EIGHT: ASL VOCABULARY

TOGETHER

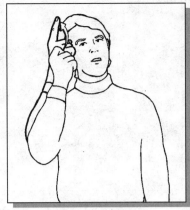
UNDERSTAND

WRONG/ INCORRECT

LESSON NINE: ASL VOCABULARY

ADDRESS

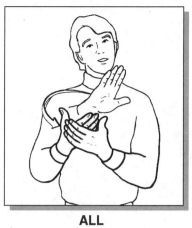
ALL

BALANCE

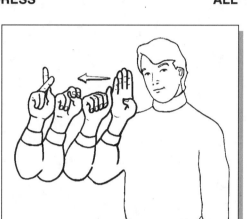
B-A-N-K

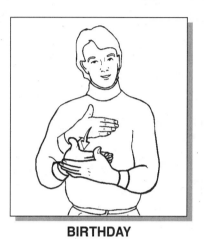
BIRTHDAY

CHARGE/ FEE

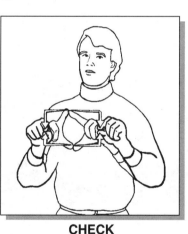
CHECK

DEPOSIT

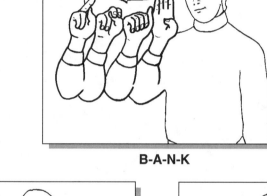
DOLLAR

DRIVE

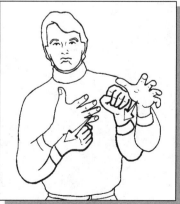
FAST

LESSON NINE: ASL VOCABULARY

HOW-MUCH

INTEREST

LICENSE

MILLION

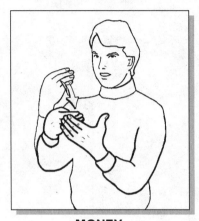
MONEY

MORE

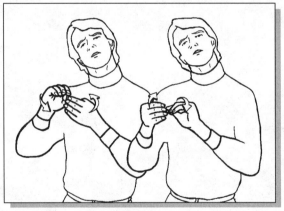
NUMBER

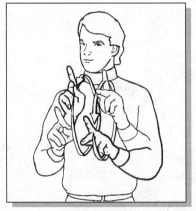
PEOPLE

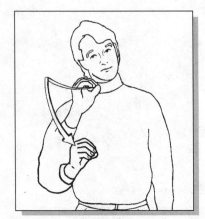
PERCENT

SAME

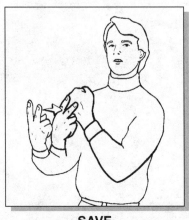
SAVE

LESSON NINE: ASL VOCABULARY

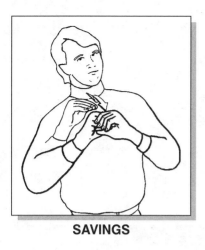
SAVINGS

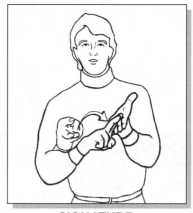
SIGNATURE

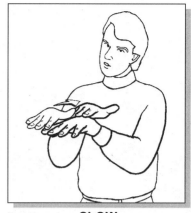
SLOW

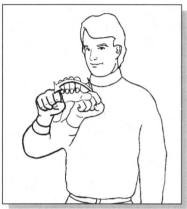
SOCIAL-SECURITY

TELEPHONE

THOUSAND

THREE-THOUSAND

WITHDRAW

ONE-DOLLAR

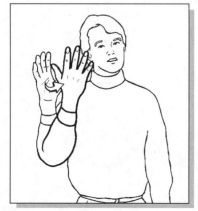
FIVE-DOLLAR

TEN+DOLLAR

Instructor's Guide: Sign Illustrations
Bravo ASL! Curriculum

©1996 Sign Enhancers, Inc.
ALL RIGHTS RESERVED.

LESSON NINE: ASL VOCABULARY

TWENTY+DOLLAR

FIFTY+DOLLAR

100

LESSON ELEVEN: ASL VOCABULARY

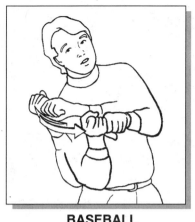
BASEBALL

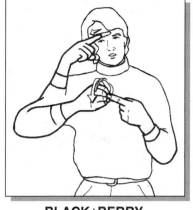
BLACK+BERRY

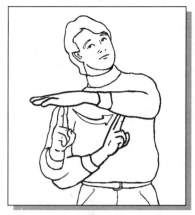
BRIDGE

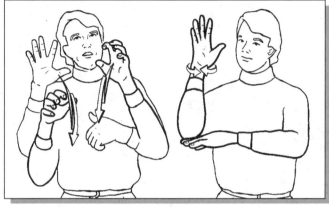
CLIMB+TREE

COOL

FALL-DOWN

FIND

FISHING

FLOWER

FRISBEE

LESSON ELEVEN: ASL VOCABULARY

 GAME

 GOLF

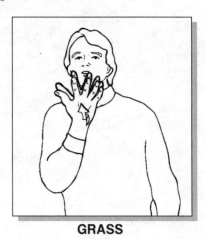 GRASS

 HOT

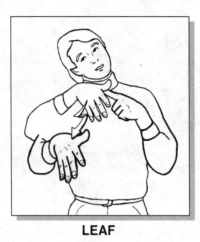 LEAF

 MAN

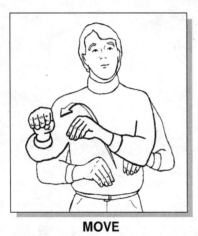 MOVE

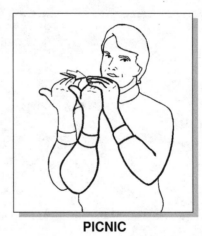 PICNIC

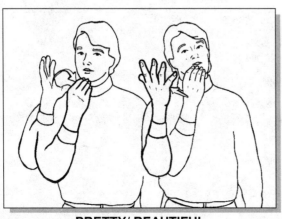 PRETTY/ BEAUTIFUL

 PURSE/ BAG

LESSON ELEVEN: ASL VOCABULARY

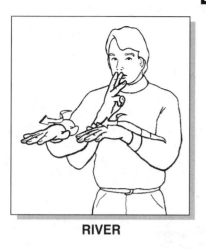
RIVER

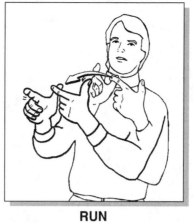
RUN

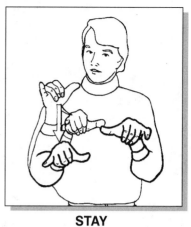
STAY

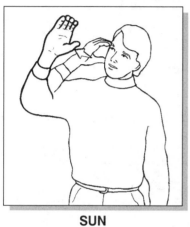
SUN

SUN+SHINE

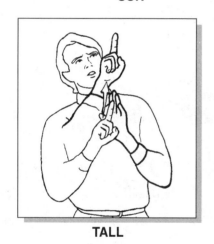
TALL

TENNIS

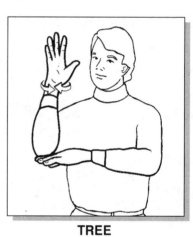
TREE

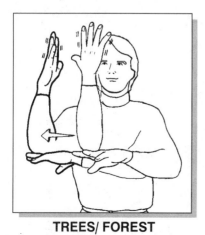
TREES/ FOREST

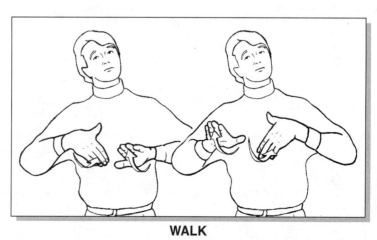
WALK

LESSON ELEVEN: ASL VOCABULARY

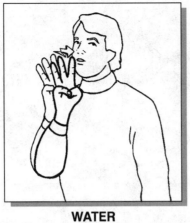
WATER

WOMAN

LESSON TWELVE: ASL VOCABULARY

 AWKWARD

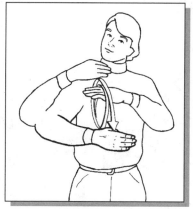 BANDAGE

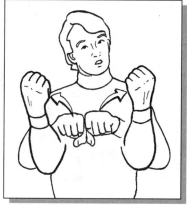 BROKEN

 COLD

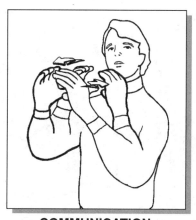 COMMUNICATION

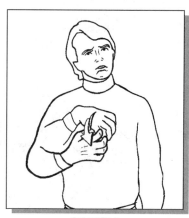 COUGH

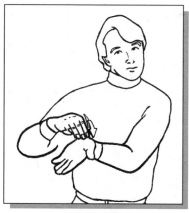 DOCTOR

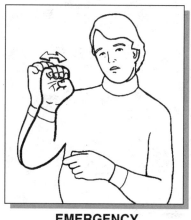 EMERGENCY

 FEEL

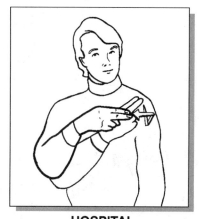 HOSPITAL

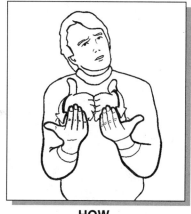 HOW

 HUG/ HOLD

LESSON TWELVE: ASL VOCABULARY

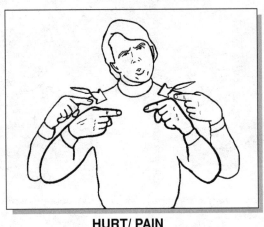
HURT/ PAIN

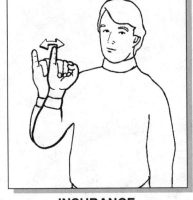
INSURANCE

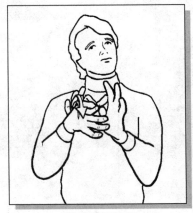
INTERPRET

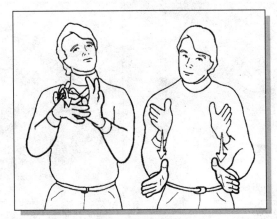
INTERPRETER

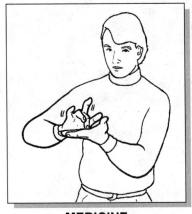
MEDICINE

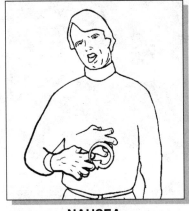
NAUSEA

NURSE

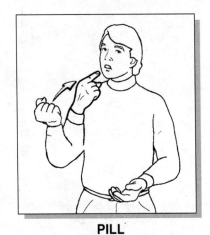
PILL

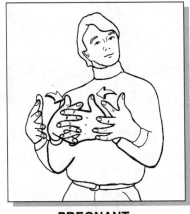
PREGNANT

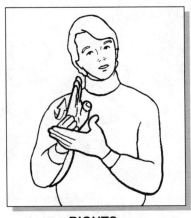
RIGHTS

LESSON TWELVE: ASL VOCABULARY

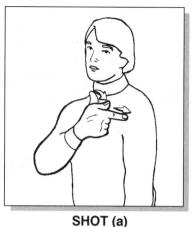
SHOT (a)

SHOT (b)

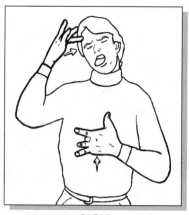
SICK

SNEEZE

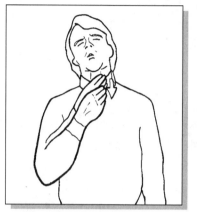
SORE-THROAT

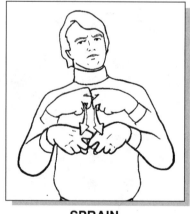
SPRAIN

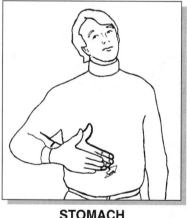
STOMACH

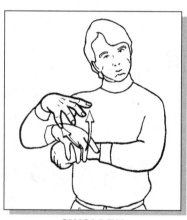
SWOLLEN

TAKE-CARE

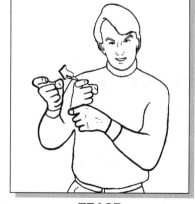
TEASE

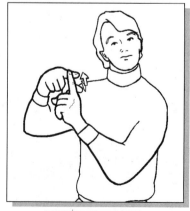
TEMPERATURE

LESSON TWELVE: ASL VOCABULARY

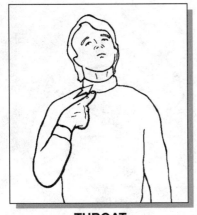
THROAT

THROB

THROW-UP

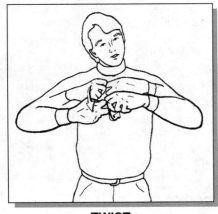
TWIST

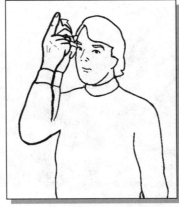
UNDERSTAND

WAIT

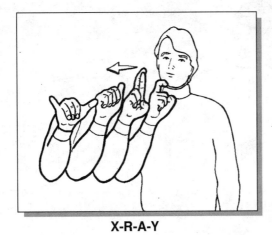
X-R-A-Y

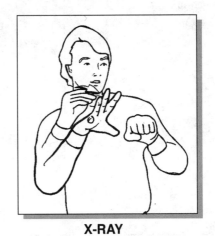
X-RAY

LESSON THIRTEEN: ASL VOCABULARY

ADVERTISE

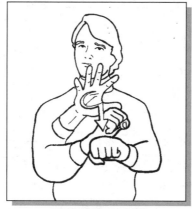
APPOINTMENT

ASK (a)

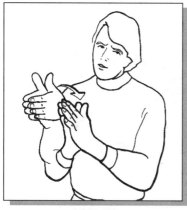
ASK (b)

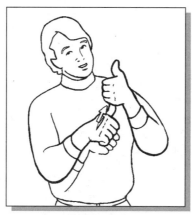
ASSISTANT

BORING

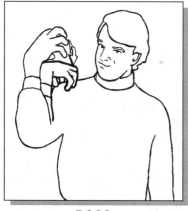
BOSS

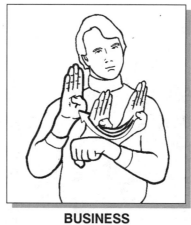
BUSINESS

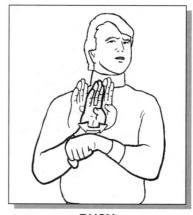
BUSY

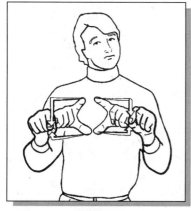
CHECK

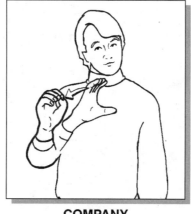
COMPANY

COMPUTER (a)

LESSON THIRTEEN: ASL VOCABULARY

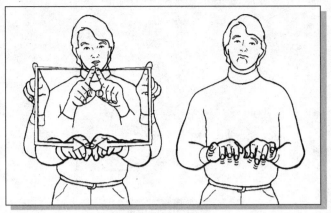

COMPUTER (b)

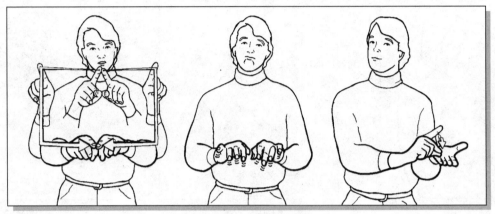

COMPUTER+PRINTER

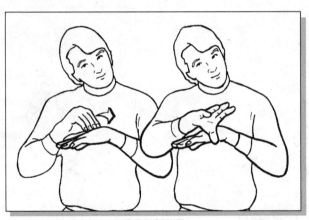

CONSULT

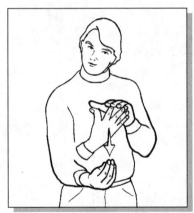

COPY

DESK

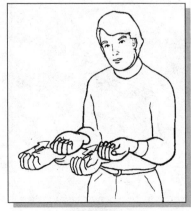

DRAWER

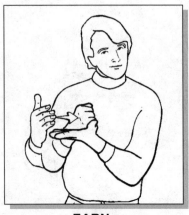

EARN

LESSON THIRTEEN: ASL VOCABULARY

ENVELOPE

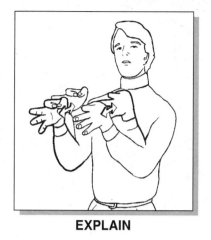
EXPLAIN

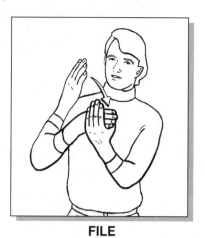
FILE

FILES

FIRED

FIRST

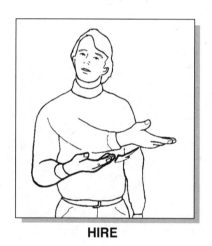
HIRE

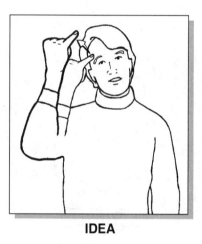
IDEA

INTERVIEW

LAZY

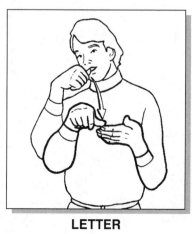
LETTER

MEETING

LESSON THIRTEEN: ASL VOCABULARY

NEED

OFFICE

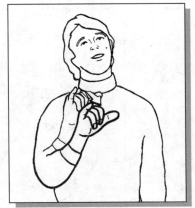
OH-I-SEE

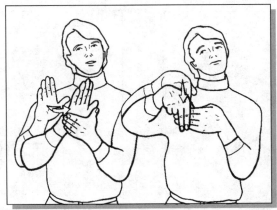
PAPER+CLIP

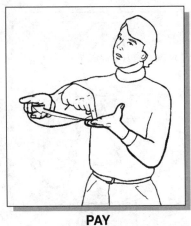
PAY

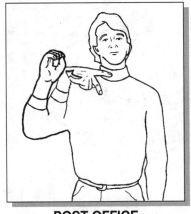
POST-OFFICE

PRESIDENT

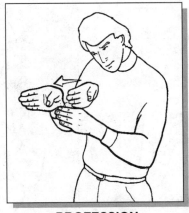
PROFESSION

RUBBER-BAND

LESSON THIRTEEN: ASL VOCABULARY

SCHEDULE　　　　　SCISSORS

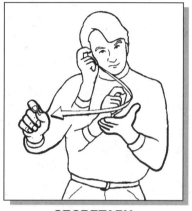  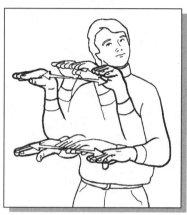

SECRETARY　　　　SEND　　　　SHELF

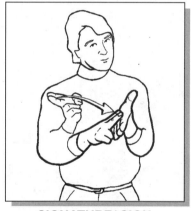 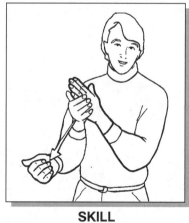 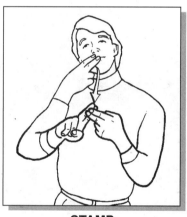

SIGNATURE/ SIGN　　　SKILL　　　　STAMP

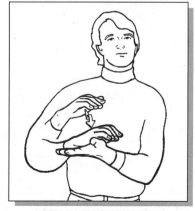  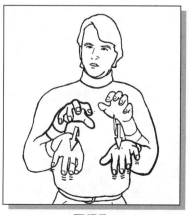

STAPLE/ STAPLER　　　TAPE　　　　TYPE

LESSON THIRTEEN: ASL VOCABULARY

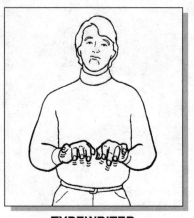
TYPEWRITER

VICE-PRESIDENT

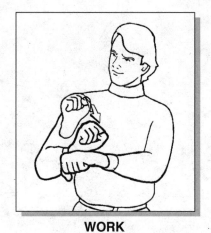
WORK

LESSON FOURTEEN: ASL VOCABULARY

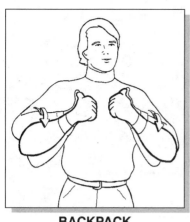
BACKPACK

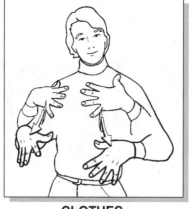
CLOTHES

COAT

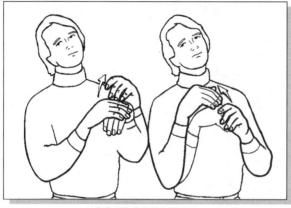
COMFORTABLE

CUTE

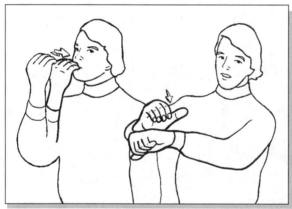
DINNER

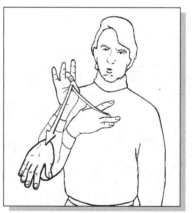
DON'T-LIKE

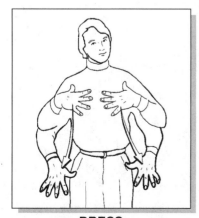
DRESS

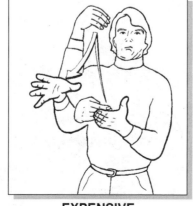
EXPENSIVE

FANCY

LESSON FOURTEEN: ASL VOCABULARY

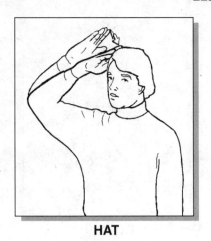
HAT

LARGE/ BIG

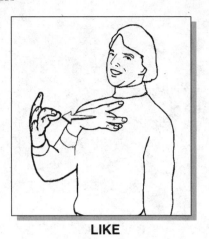
LIKE

LOVE-IT

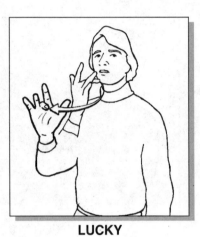
LUCKY

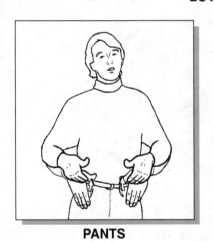
PANTS

PRICE/ COST

PURSE

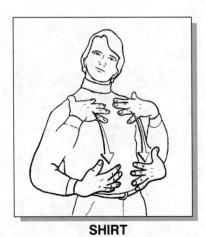
SHIRT

SHOES

SHOPPING/ BUYING

LESSON FOURTEEN: ASL VOCABULARY

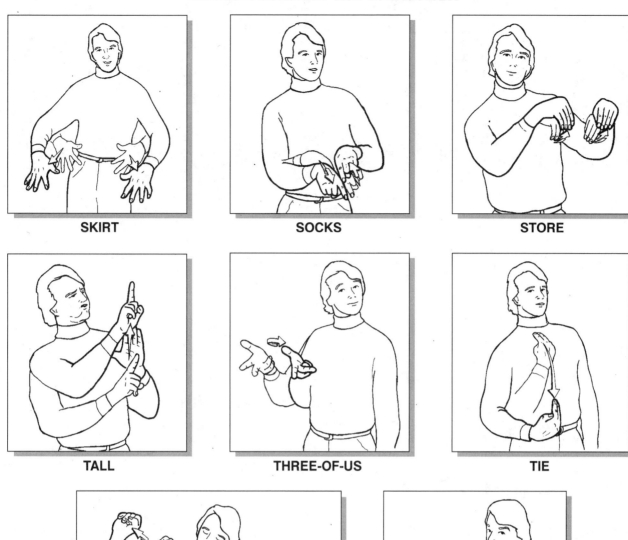

SKIRT   SOCKS   STORE

TALL   THREE-OF-US   TIE

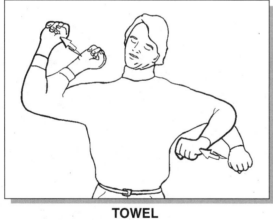

TOWEL

TWO-OF-US

1.1 Overhead Master

1.2 Pretest

What Do You Know?

Pretest Goal: To see how much you already know about what will be taught in this lesson.

Pretest Instructions: Read each question and circle the best answer.

1. Deaf people actually have their own culture.
   A. True
   B. False

2. American Sign Language is not a real language, it is a shortened form of English.
   A. True
   B. False

3. In ASL, a statement can become a question by simply raising the eyebrows and tilting the head slightly.
   A. True
   B. False

4. The sign for LOVE looks like you are hugging someone.
   A. True
   B. False

5. If you want to get a Deaf person's attention, it would be appropriate to flash the lights.
   A. True
   B. False

6. If you want to get a Deaf person's attention, it would be appropriate to throw a light object at him/her.
   A. True
   B. False

7. ASL grammar is the same as English grammar except that ASL is visual.
   A. True
   B. False

1.3 Lesson Objectives

Planning for Success

Goal: To see what you will learn by the end of this lesson.

Instructions: Read the objectives below.

Upon completing this VideoCourse lesson, you will be able to...

1. Identify the four members of the Bravo family (including their names, name signs, who is Deaf, who is hearing and the children's ages).

2. Recognize and accurately produce the ASL vocabulary introduced in this lesson.

3. Identify Deaf people as a cultural group with their own language, customs and values.

4. Describe culturally appropriate ways to get a Deaf person's attention.

5. Describe culturally appropriate ways to wake a Deaf person.

6. Identify ASL as a distinct language with its own grammatical rules.

7. Recognize and identify yes/no and wh-question types.

8. Accurately produce these two question types including the non-manual grammatical markers associated with each.

1.6 Overhead Master

1.8 Overhead Master

1.10 Comprehension Quiz

What Did You Understand?

Quiz Goal: To see how much of the Bravo family interaction you understood.

Quiz Instructions: Read and answer each question below.

1. Dad offers Mom coffee. Does she want any?
   A. Yes
   B. No

2. Mom asks Dad where the children are. What does he tell her?
   A. "At school."
   B. "Eating breakfast."
   C. "Sleeping upstairs."
   D. "Playing with the dog."

3. What does Anna ask Mom?
   A. "A long time ago, did you want a hearing or Deaf baby?"
   B. "A long time ago, did you have a hearing baby?"
   C. "Did you want all your babies to be Deaf?"
   D. "Did you want all your babies to be hearing?"

4. How does Mom answer this question?
   A. "I want you to shower."
   B. "I wanted a hearing child."
   C. "I wanted a Deaf child."
   D. "I wanted you."

5. When Mom asks Anna if she wanted a Deaf or hearing mom, Anna said she would have preferred a Deaf mom, but she loves her mom anyway.
   A. True
   B. False

1.12 Overhead Master

Instructor's Guide: Appendix
Bravo ASL! Curriculum

A-7

©1996 Sign Enhancers, Inc.
ALL RIGHTS RESERVED.

1.14 Overhead Master

1.16 Comprehension Quiz

What Did You Understand?

Quiz Goal: To see how much of the Bravo family interaction you understood.

Quiz Instructions: Read and answer each question below.

1. When Mom went into Scott's room, what did she find in his bed?

    A. There was a spider on Scott's head.
    B. A spider was in the dog's mouth.
    C. The dog was in the bed with Scott.
    D. The dog was in bed instead of Scott.

2. Did Scott fool Mom?

    A. Yes, she almost sent the dog to school.
    B. No, she knew the spider was there the whole time.
    C. No, she knew the dog was there the whole time.
    D. Yes, she thought the spider was the dog.

3. How does Mom feel about spiders?

    A. She eats them for breakfast.
    B. She is scared of them.
    C. She likes them better than dogs.
    D. She didn't want to talk about it because it was time for breakfast.

4. Scott wanted to go straight to school since he was not very hungry.

    A. True
    B. False

1.20 Experiential Activity

What Kind of Question is That?!

Activity Goal: To apply the grammatical information you learned.

Activity Instructions: You will see several signed questions. Watch each sample closely and decide whether the question is a yes/no-question or a wh-question.

Don't worry if you do not understand the meaning of the question, just watch the non-manual grammatical markers to determine your answer.

Circle your answer:

1. yes/no   wh   6. yes/no   wh

2. yes/no   wh   7. yes/no   wh

3. yes/no   wh   8. yes/no   wh

4. yes/no   wh   9. yes/no   wh

5. yes/no   wh   10. yes/no   wh

1.22 Cultural and Grammatical Quiz

What Did You Learn?

Quiz Goal: To see how much of this lesson's cultural and grammatical information you learned.

Quiz Instructions: Read and answer each question below.

1. Deaf people do not have their own culture because they belong to the American culture.
   A. True
   B. False

2. Cultural information must be included within any language learning experience.
   A. True
   B. False

3. The French, German and American people have distinct cultures, but Deaf people only belong to a community.
   A. True
   B. False

4. All cultures, including that of Deaf people, include customs and values.
   A. True
   B. False

5. Culturally appropriate ways for getting a Deaf person's attention include (check all that apply):
   __ A gentle tap on the shoulder
   __ Wave one's hand toward the Deaf person
   __ Call out in a low tone
   __ Stomp a foot causing a vibration
   __ Gently spray water at the Deaf person

1.22 Cultural and Grammatical Quiz - 2

6. Culturally appropriate ways for waking a Deaf person include (check all that apply):
   __ A light flashed briefly
   __ A gentle tap
   __ Gently spray water at the Deaf person

7. The non-manual markers associated with a yes/no question are (check all that apply):
   __ Eyebrows raised   __ Slight head tilt
   __ Eyebrows furrowed   __ Lean back
   __ Direct eye contact   __ Last sign held for response

8. The non-manual markers associated with a wh-question are (check all that apply):
   __ Eyebrows raised   __ Slight head tilt
   __ Eyebrows furrowed   __ Lean back
   __ Direct eye contact   __ Last sign held for response

9. A yes/no question can be responded to with a "yes" or "no" answer.
   A. True
   B. False

10. A wh-question can ask (check all that apply):
    __ Which?   __ How?
    __ When?   __ Why?

1.25 Experiential Activity

What's the Sentence About?

Activity Goal: To improve your comprehension skills using sentences presented in ASL.

Activity Instructions: You will see five signed sentences. Each sentence will be signed twice. Determine what each sentence is about and circle the correct answer below:

1. A. Going to school
   B. A morning greeting
   C. Taking a shower

2. A. Looking for Dad
   B. Looking for Daughter
   C. Looking for Mom

3. A. Needing a bathroom
   B. Needing a drink
   C. Needing a shower

4. A. Time to eat
   B. Time to brush your teeth
   C. Time to have coffee

5. A. Asking about school
   B. Asking about work
   C. Asking about breakfast

1.28 Comprehension Quiz

What Did You Understand?

Quiz Goal: To see how much of the signed story you understood.

Quiz Instructions: Read and answer each question below.

1. When did this story take place?
   _____

2. Where did the story take place?
   _____

3. Who was there?
   _____

4. What did the children want?
   _____

5. What did Mom want the children to do?
   _____
   _____

6. How did the son respond?
   _____

7. How did the daughter respond?
   _____

8. What did the mother suggest?
   _____

9. Did Anna want to do that?
   _____

10. What did Anna decide to do?
    _____
    _____

1.30 Post-test

Section One: Comprehension

Instructions: You will see five signed sentences. Watch carefully and answer each question below.

1. The signer is _____.
    - A. Hearing
    - B. Deaf
    - C. A father

2. The daughter needs to go to _____.
    - A. The bathroom
    - B. The kitchen
    - C. School

3. Who wants coffee?
    - A. Father
    - B. Mother
    - C. The son

4. Where do the children go?
    - A. To the bathroom
    - B. To the kitchen
    - C. To school

5. Who loves the dog?
    - A. Father
    - B. Daughter
    - C. The son

1.30 Post-test

Section Two: Culture and Grammar

Instructions: Read each statement carefully and determine if it is True or False (circle your answer).

6. Deaf culture has its own language, customs, and values.
   A. True
   B. False

7. A gentle tap on the shoulder is an appropriate technique for getting a Deaf person's attention.
   A. True
   B. False

8. The non-manual markers associated with yes/no questions include raised eyebrows and the head slightly tilted.
   A. True
   B. False

9. The non-manual markers associated with wh-questions include raised eyebrows and the head slightly tilted.
   A. True
   B. False

10. ASL grammar is the same as English grammar except that ASL is visual.
    A. True
    B. False

1.30 Post-test

Section Three: Expressive Portion

Instructions: Describe your family's morning routine, using at least seven signs learned in Lesson One. Also include three questions: two yes/no questions and one wh-question. Be sure to use appropriate non-manual markers.

Your instructor will schedule a specific time for you to perform this section of the post-test. You may prepare and practice prior to your scheduled time. Use the space below to prepare for your expressive performance.

Include at least seven signs from Lesson One.

11. _____
12. _____
13. _____
14. _____
15. _____
16. _____
17. _____

Include two yes/no questions:

18. _____
19. _____

Include one wh-question:

20. _____

Congratulations! You have completed Lesson One!

2.3 Pretest

What Do You Know?

Pretest Goal: To see how much you already know about what will be taught in this lesson.

Pretest Instructions: Read each question and circle the best answer.

1. Deaf people should be viewed with pity.
   A. True
   B. False

2. Families with Deaf members can be closely connected.
   A. True
   B. False

3. Like English, adjectives in ASL are usually placed before the noun.
   A. True
   B. False

4. Signs can be modified by changing the movement of the sign.
   A. True
   B. False

5. Adjectives can be modified simply by changing facial expressions.
   A. True
   B. False

2.4 Lesson Objectives

Planning for Success

Goal: To see what you will learn by the end of this lesson.
Instructions: Read the objectives below.

Upon completing this VideoCourse lesson, you will be able to...

1. Recognize and accurately produce the ASL vocabulary introduced in this and the previous lesson.

2. Describe two distinct perspectives generally held regarding members of the Deaf community.

3. Use noun/adjective combinations appropriately in ASL.

4. Demonstrate how signs can be modified in ASL.

2.6 Overhead Master

2.8 Overhead Master

2.10 Comprehension Quiz

What Did You Understand?

Quiz Goal: To see how much of the Bravo family interaction you understood.

Quiz Instructions: Read and answer each question below.

1. Mom wants a(n) _____ for breakfast.
   A. Orange
   B. Banana
   C. Piece of toast
   D. Bowl of cereal

2. Scott orders ____ egg(s).
   A. One
   B. Two
   C. Three
   D. Four

3. Scott also orders a _____ glass of orange juice.
   A. Small
   B. Large

4. Anna orders _____ to drink.
   A. Milk
   B. Water
   C. Orange juice
   D. Coffee

5. Who will be washing the dishes after breakfast?
   A. Mom
   B. Dad
   C. Anna
   D. Scott

2.13 Experiential Activity

Instructions: Copy and separate each of the boxes below. Distribute the appropriate cultural description to the corresponding group of students.

Student Handout 2.13A

Grokker Culture: Orientation Training

You are now a proud member of the Grokker Culture!

Ours is a beautiful culture. We value loving connections with others above all else! We therefore choose only to communicate when physically touching one another. It is considered very rude and anti-loving to communicate unless you are touching the other person either shoulder-to-shoulder, foot-to-foot, or arm-to-arm.

The activity we most value is gathering in a loving group, shoulder-to-shoulder. We lovingly invite everyone to get "connected." Anyone NOT connected in a group is always invited. To invite someone to join in a group, we scratch our noses. To answer "Yes, I want to join!" we stomp our feet on the floor. To answer "No, I'd rather not join!" we nod our heads up and down.

The language we use is ASL. We mostly spend our time appreciating each other shoulder-to-shoulder, but when we do communicate, it is usually to discuss our favorite topic... FOOD! A very common greeting would include a question about what a person ate for breakfast.

We will visit another culture today - the Artifs. We know little about who they are or what they value. We must ask to "join" with others, Grokkers and Artifs alike, by nose scratching.

Good luck! May the loving connection be with you!

Student Handout 2.13B

Artif Culture: Orientation Training

You are a proud member of the Artif Culture!

Ours is a very intelligent and practical culture based on the productive goals of trade.

Ours is a mathematical and scientific world. We communicate in numerical values. For example, "3" means "yes" and "2" means "no" in our culture. We simply hold up the correct number of fingers to show the numbers.

Our goal is to trade and gather as many pens and pencils of like colors as we can from all people we meet. In our language, "1" means "pen" and "4" means "pencil."

We ask for a pen or pencil by holding up one or four fingers and then holding up fingers for the number of pens/pencils we want (1, 2, 3, etc.). To indicate desired color, we point to something with that color. For example, to ask for five red pens you would hold up one finger (pen), then five fingers, and then point to something red. Because we always keep our trading goals in mind, we are a people of few words!

We will visit another culture today - the Grokkers. We know little about who they are or what they value. We must trade with others - Grokkers and Artifs alike - in order to collect pens and pencils.

Good luck! May the numbers be with you!

2.16 Culture and Grammar Quiz

What Did You Learn?

Quiz Goal: To see how much of this lesson's cultural and grammatical information you learned.

Quiz Instructions: Read and answer each question below.

1. Families with Deaf members can be closely connected.
   A. True   B. False

2. The handicapped perspective views Deaf people in a positive manner.
   A. True   B. False

3. The culture of Deaf people is equal to all other cultures.
   A. True   B. False

4. The cultural perspective views Deaf people as having full lives.
   A. True   B. False

5. Adjective placement in ASL follows the same rules as adjective placement in English.
   A. True   B. False

6. In ASL, adjectives tend to be placed _____.
   A. Before the noun
   B. At the end of the sentence
   C. After the noun
   D. At the beginning of the sentence

7. Adjectives are modified in the following ways:
   __ Changing the movement of the sign
   __ Changing facial expression
   __ Changing body language
   __ Changing dominant/non-dominant hands

8. Signs can be modified by (check all that apply):
   __ Inflection
   __ Repetition
   __ Slight head tilt
   __ Changing location/placement

2.19 Experiential Activity

What's the Sentence About?

Activity Goal: To improve your comprehension skills using sentences presented in ASL.

Activity Instructions: You will see five signed sentences. Each sentence will be signed twice. Determine what each sentence is about, and circle the correct answer below:

1. A. Asking who wants milk
   B. Asking who wants to cook
   C. Asking who wants a banana

2. A. Cooking
   B. Washing the plate
   C. Washing the glass

3. A. A food the signer loves
   B. A person the signer loves
   C. A person who loves the signer

4. A. There is no time left
   B. There are no spoons left
   C. There is no food left

5. A. Looking for food
   B. Looking for a napkin
   C. Looking for a spoon

2.22 Comprehension Quiz

What Did You Understand?

Quiz Goal: To see how much of the signed story you understood.

Quiz Instructions: Read and answer each question below.

1. The family in the story consisted of...
    A. A mom, dad and a son
    B. A mom and a daughter
    C. A dad, son and a daughter
    D. A mom, dad, son, and a daughter

2. _____ family member(s) were Deaf.
    A. One
    B. Two
    C. Three
    D. Five

3. The family had a _____ for a pet.
    A. Spider
    B. Cow
    C. Dog
    D. Chicken

4. In the story, who cooked breakfast?
    A. Dad
    B. Mom
    C. Anna
    D. Mom and Anna

2.22 Comprehension Quiz - 2

5. Why didn't Anna eat?
    A. She doesn't like Dad's cooking.
    B. The dog had taken a bite out of her food.
    C. She wasn't hungry yet.
    D. She was late for school.

6. What did Anna do with her breakfast food?
   _____

7. Later on, what happened to Anna at school?
   _____

2.24 Post-test

Section One: Comprehension

Instructions: You will see a signed story. Watch carefully and answer each question below.

1. _____ was cooking breakfast for the family.
   A. The father
   B. The mother
   C. The son
   D. The daughter

2. _____ set the table for breakfast.
   A. The father
   B. The mother
   C. The son
   D. The daughter

3. Who poured the orange juice for breakfast?
   A. The father
   B. The mother
   C. The son
   D. The daughter

4. The daughter gave food to her _____.
   A. Brother
   B. Mother
   C. Sister
   D. Dog

5. What did Father eat for breakfast?
   A. Two eggs, two pieces of toast, an apple, and coffee
   B. Two eggs, two pieces of toast, an apple, and orange juice
   C. Three eggs, two pieces of toast, a banana, and coffee
   D. One egg, two pieces of toast, a banana, and coffee

2.24 Post-test

Section Two: Culture and Grammar

Instructions: Read and answer each question.

6. In the *Cultural Notes* section, two perspectives commonly held about Deaf people are described as...
   A. Disabled and handicapped
   B. Cultural and subcultural
   C. Monocultural and bicultural
   D. Handicapped and cultural

7. The cultural perspective perceives being Deaf as a problem that needs to be fixed.
   A. True
   B. False

8. According to our *Cultural Notes*, which is **NOT** true:
   A. The Deaf culture is made up of people who share a common language and enjoy loving support of one another.
   B. All cultures deserve equal respect.
   C. To learn ASL correctly, one must fly halfway around the world to experience the true culture.
   D. A non-signing, hearing person entering a room filled with Deaf people might experience a "communication handicap."

9. The way you can modify the meaning of a sign is by:
   A. Repeating the sign to indicate "for a long time."
   B. By changing the movement of the sign to show intensity.
   C. By using your facial expression and body language.
   D. All of the above are correct ways of modifying the meaning of a sign.

10. ASL often places the noun first, followed by the adjective.
    A. True
    B. False

2.24 Post-test

Section Three: Expressive Portion

Instructions: Create a story about your favorite breakfast, using at least eight signs learned in Lesson Two. Also, use at least two adjectives or signs you modify as demonstrated in the *Grammatical Notes*.

Your instructor will schedule a specific time for you to perform this section of the Post-test. You may prepare and practice prior to your scheduled time.

Include at least eight signs from Lesson Two:

11. _____
12. _____
13. _____
14. _____
15. _____
16. _____
17. _____
18. _____

Include at least two adjectives or sign modifications:

19. _____
20. _____

Congratulations!
You have completed
Lesson Two!

3.3 Pretest

What Do You Know?

Pretest Goal: To see how much you already know about what will be taught in this lesson.

Pretest Instructions: Read each question and circle the best answers.

1. What do Deaf people use in order to communicate on the telephone? (Circle all that apply.)
   A. Caption decoder
   B. TTY
   C. Specially trained hearing dogs
   D. TTY/TDD relay service

2. What does "GA" mean?
   A. Good Attempt
   B. Great Aunt
   C. Go Ahead
   D. Get Advice

3. What does "SK" mean?
   A. Spatial Kinetics
   B. Serial Kinetics
   C. Stop Kidding
   D. Stop Key

4. What are some ways that Deaf people gain access to the sounds in their homes? (Circle that all apply.)
   A. Flashing lights
   B. Caption decoders
   C. Specially trained hearing dogs
   D. TTY/TDD

5. In ASL, a simple side-to-side headshake can turn a positive statement into a negative.
   A. True
   B. False

6. In ASL, negation is always indicated at the beginning of the sentence for clarity.
   A. True
   B. False

3.4 Lesson Objectives

Planning for Success

Goal: To see what you will learn by the end of this lesson.
Instructions: Read the objectives below.

Upon completing this VideoCourse lesson, you will be able to...

1. Recognize and accurately produce the ASL vocabulary introduced in this and all previous lessons.

2. Name and describe several ways in which Deaf people make the sounds in their homes visible to gain more access and independence.

3. Explain the use of "GA" and "SK" within a TTY/TDD phone conversation.

4. Recognize how negation is demonstrated in ASL.

5. Recognize the "use of space" features of ASL addressed in this lesson.

3.6 Overhead Master

3.8 Experiential Activity

Matchmaker

Activity Goal: To help you recognize the new ASL vocabulary.

Activity Instructions: Look at the illustrations of your new ASL vocabulary below. Draw a line from the illustration of the sign to the picture that best matches its meaning.

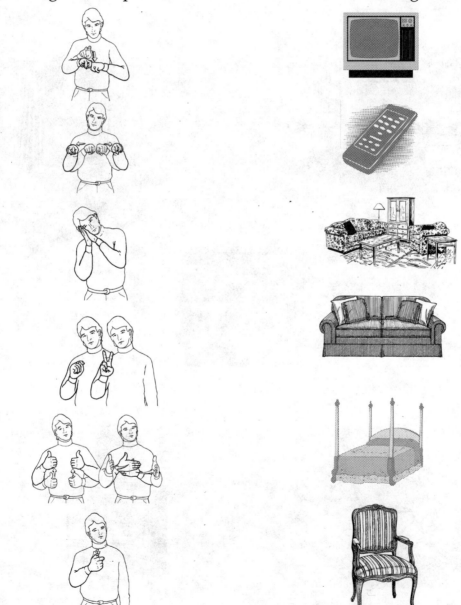

Instructor's Guide: Appendix
Bravo ASL! Curriculum

©1996 Sign Enhancers, Inc.
ALL RIGHTS RESERVED.

3.10 Comprehension Quiz

What Did You Understand?

Quiz Goal: To see how much of the Bravo family interaction you understood.

Quiz Instructions: Read each question and circle the best answer.

1. Where does Mom ask Scott to look for the TV remote control?
    - A. Next to the couch.
    - B. Under the couch.
    - C. In the bed.
    - D. All of the above.

2. Where does Anna look for the remote control?
    - A. In the closet.
    - B. In the dresser.
    - C. Behind the door.
    - D. In the bed.

3. Where does Anna find the remote control?
    - A. Under the bed.
    - B. Inside the bed.
    - C. On the dresser.
    - D. She doesn't find it.

4. Where does Scott find the remote?
    - A. Under the couch.
    - B. Behind the chair.
    - C. In the kitchen.
    - D. He doesn't find it.

3.11 Overhead Master

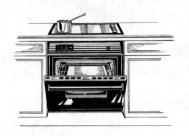
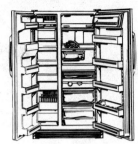

3.13 Experiential Activity

Put it There, Pal!

Activity Goal: To help you recognize the new ASL vocabulary and the spatial features of ASL.

Activity Instructions: Watch the video and put an "X" where the signer tells you to on each of the pictures below.

1.

2.

3.

4.

5.

6.

7.

8.

3.15 Comprehension Quiz

What Did You Understand?

Quiz Goal: To see how much of the Bravo family interaction you understood.

Quiz Instructions: Read and answer each question below.

1. Why did Mom think the TV remote control might be in the bathroom?
   _____

2. What did it mean when the light flashed?
   _____

3. When Anna came into the room after the light flashed, what did she ask Mom?
   _____

4. When Mom found Dad in the bathroom, what was he doing?
   _____

5. Anna is still on the phone when Mom passes her. What does Mom tell her?
   A. "Say hello to your friend for me."
   B. "Let me talk to your friend's mother."
   C. "Time to take the dog for a walk."
   D. "Time to end your phone conversation."

6. Where did the Bravo family find the remote control?
   _____

7. What did Scott say when the family looked at him accusingly?
   A. "It's not my fault, you didn't tell me to look there!"
   B. "I fooled you! I hid it there!"
   C. "I didn't want to watch TV anyway!"
   D. "Anna told me to put it there!"

3.17 Experiential Activity

Home Improvement

Activity Goal: To apply the cultural information you have learned about accessibility for Deaf people.

Activity Instructions: Read each situation below and consider what steps could be taken to ensure accessibility within each. For each situation, decide what visual modifications could be applied. Write your ideas and suggestions below.

Situation 1: A Deaf woman wants to start a business taking care of infants/children in her home.

Situation 2: A Deaf man needs to make a telephone call to his Deaf friend.

Situation 3: Your Deaf sister isn't waking up in time for school.

Situation 4: A Deaf girl needs to make a telephone call to her hearing friend.

Situation 5: A Deaf person is expecting a visit from a friend.

Situation 6: A Deaf college student needs to remain up-to-date with current world events.

3.19 Experiential Activity

To Be, or NOT To Be

Activity Goal: To practice identifying whether an ASL sentence is affirmative (positive) or negative.

Activity Instructions: You will see ten sentences signed in ASL. The sentences are either affirmative or negative. After viewing each sentence, circle the appropriate response below.

1. AFFIRMATIVE   NEGATIVE

2. AFFIRMATIVE   NEGATIVE

3. AFFIRMATIVE   NEGATIVE

4. AFFIRMATIVE   NEGATIVE

5. AFFIRMATIVE   NEGATIVE

6. AFFIRMATIVE   NEGATIVE

7. AFFIRMATIVE   NEGATIVE

8. AFFIRMATIVE   NEGATIVE

9. AFFIRMATIVE   NEGATIVE

10. AFFIRMATIVE   NEGATIVE

3.22 Experiential Activity

Now, Where Did I Put That...?

Activity Goal: To improve your comprehension skills with the spatial features of ASL.

Activity Instructions: You will see signed directions that tell you where in the house (see picture below) the ten items belong. Place the number corresponding to the item in the correct location in the house.

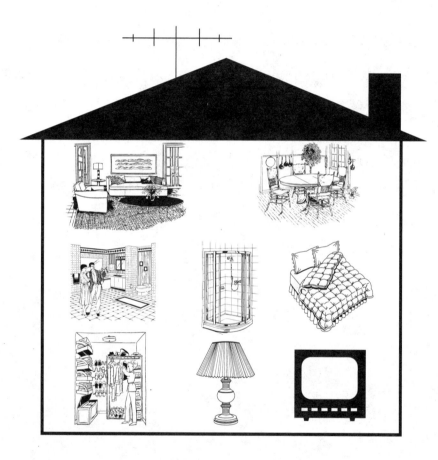

1. GLASS
2. REMOTE-CONTROL
3. COFFEE
4. BANANA
5. EGG
6. DOG
7. SPIDER
8. TELEPHONE
9. TTY
10. MILK

Instructor's Guide: Appendix
Bravo ASL! Curriculum

©1996 Sign Enhancers, Inc.
ALL RIGHTS RESERVED.

3.25 Comprehension Quiz

What Did You Understand?

Quiz Goal: To see how much of the signed story you understood.

Quiz Instructions: Read each question below and choose the best answer.

1. How many bedrooms does the house in the story have?
    A. One
    B. Two
    C. Three
    D. Four

2. The house in the story was unusual because it did not have a kitchen.
    A. True
    B. False

3. According to the story, where should you go if you are hungry?
    A. Since there is no kitchen, to a restaurant
    B. To a neighbor's house
    C. To the kitchen
    D. To a friend's house

4. According to this story, if a light is flashing, where should you go?
    A. To the bathroom
    B. To the bedroom
    C. To the front door
    D. To the phone

5. In this story, if you want to watch TV, where should you go?
    A. The bedroom
    B. The TV room
    C. The living room
    D. A hardware store to buy a new remote control

3.27 Post-test

Section One: Comprehension

Instructions: You will see a signed story. Watch carefully and answer each question below.

1. When Dad is watching TV, what is the problem?
   A. He can't find the TV remote.
   B. He is tired and can't find his bed.
   C. He hears someone crying, but can't find them.
   D. He smells something funny, but can't find what it is.

2. Where is the first place he looks?
   A. Bathroom
   B. Kitchen
   C. Garage
   D. Living Room

3. Does he find what he is looking for in the bathroom?
   A. Yes
   B. No

4. When he went into the kitchen, where did he look?
   A. On top of the refrigerator and in the sink
   B. Inside the sink, in the refrigerator and in the oven
   C. Inside the refrigerator and in the sink
   D. On and under the table

5. Where did Dad find what he was looking for?
   A. In the kitchen
   B. In the bathroom
   C. Under the couch
   D. On the TV

6. What was it that Dad found?
   A. An eggplant
   B. An apple
   C. A melon
   D. A banana

3.27 Post-test

Section Two: Culture and Grammar

Instructions: Read each statement carefully and determine if it is True or False (circle your answer).

7. A caption decoder can be used by a Deaf person to communicate on the telephone.
   A. True
   B. False

8. With simple modifications, a Deaf person is able to know when someone is at the door.
   A. True
   B. False

9. According to the video, a TTY can be used to wake a Deaf person.
   A. True
   B. False

10. In ASL, negatives usually appear at the end of a sentence.
    A. True
    B. False

11. When using a TTY, GA means "go ahead."
    A. True
    B. False

12. A TDD helps make the audio on a television visible.
    A. True
    B. False

13. A relay service can assist a hearing person who does not have a TDD to call a Deaf person.
    A. True
    B. False

14. It is very important to use a negative headshake when signing a negative statement in ASL.
    A. True
    B. False

15. When using ASL to express a sentence meaning, "I am not Deaf," it would be appropriate to sign DEAF first and then the sign NOT.
    A. True
    B. False

3.27 Post-test

Section Three: Expressive Portion

Instructions: Create a story about losing something and searching for it in your house, using at least four signs learned in this lesson. Also sign at least one sentence in which you apply negation as taught in this lesson.

Your instructor will schedule a time for you to perform this section of the Post-test. You may prepare and practice prior to your scheduled time.

Include at least four signs from Lesson Three.

16. _____

17. _____

18. _____

19. _____

Include negation:

20. _____

*Congratulations!
You have completed
Lesson Three!*

4.3 Pretest

What Do You Know?

Pretest Goal: To see how much you already know about what will be taught in this lesson.

Pretest Instructions: Read each question and circle the best answer.

1. ASL is often creative and imaginative.
   A. True
   B. False

2. ASL can make a "play on signs" like English can make a "play on words."
   A. True
   B. False

3. ASL and English have the same word order.
   A. True
   B. False

4. In ASL, the topic of a sentence is often signed first.
   A. True
   B. False

5. ASL has rules of grammar just like spoken languages.
   A. True
   B. False

6. A Number Story is always limited to two minutes.
   A. True
   B. False

4.4 Lesson Objectives

Planning For Success

Goal: To see what you will learn by the end of this lesson.
Instructions: Read the objectives below.

Upon completing this VideoCourse lesson, you will be able to...

1. Recognize and accurately produce the ASL vocabulary introduced in this and all previous lessons.

2. Describe a Number Story as a form of Deaf folklore and contribute to the creation of an original Number Story.

3. Name and describe several ways in which Deaf people share the folklore of Deaf culture.

4. Recognize and apply topic/comment grammatical structure.

4.6 Overhead Master

Instructor's Guide: Appendix
Bravo ASL! Curriculum

©1996 Sign Enhancers, Inc.
ALL RIGHTS RESERVED.

4.9 Con-SIGN-tration Cards Master

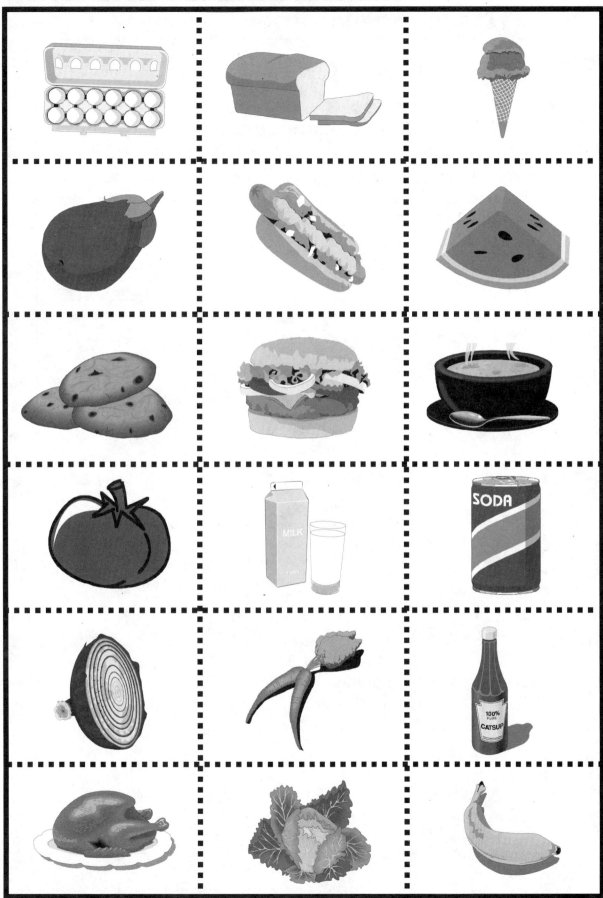

Instructor's Guide: Appendix
Bravo ASL! Curriculum

4.10 Experiential Activity

Don't Forget to Buy the...!

Activity Goal: To help you recognize the new ASL vocabulary.

Activity Instructions: You are going food shopping for three of your friends. Watch the video carefully as each one tells you what s/he wants you to buy at the grocery store. Circle the pictures of each of the items they sign so you don't forget!

Friend #1 wants you to buy...

Friend #2 wants you to buy...

Friend #3 wants you to buy...

4.12 Experiential Activity

What's the Sentence About?

Activity Goal: To improve your comprehension skills using sentences presented in ASL.

Activity Instructions: You will see five signed sentences. Each sentence will be signed twice. Determine what each sentence is about, and circle the correct answer below:

1. A. Watching fireworks
   B. Wanting lobster
   C. Wanting popcorn

2. A. Buying carrots
   B. Buying onions
   C. Eating cheese

3. A. Making soup
   B. Cooking onions
   C. Eating onions

4. A. Watching TV
   B. Watching me
   C. Eating TV dinners

5. A. Being good
   B. Being tired
   C. Being hungry

4.17 Experiential Activity

Topic Search

Activity Goal: To identify the topic within sentences presented in ASL.

Activity Instructions: You will see five sentences signed in ASL. For each sentence, circle the topic.

1. I love mother.

2. There are four hotdogs.

3. I love popcorn.

4. I want some milk.

5. The children are hungry.

4.19 Comprehension Quiz

What Did You Understand?

Quiz Goal: To see how much of the signed story you understood.

Quiz Instructions: Read and answer each question below.

1. What did the family in the story do?
    A. Go grocery shopping
    B. Go to the movies
    C. Cook breakfast
    D. Clean the house

2. _____ wanted to go alone, but everyone wanted to help.
    A. Scott
    B. Mom
    C. Dad
    D. Anna

3. Scott likes to go food shopping.
    A. True
    B. False

4. Name at least three things the family bought.
    _____
    _____
    _____

5. What did Scott buy?
    _____
    _____

4.21 Post-test

Section One: Comprehension

Instructions: You will see a signed story. Watch carefully and answer each question below.

1. _____ wanted to cook dinner for the family.
   A. Father
   B. Mother
   C. Son
   D. Daughter

2. Who went shopping?
   A. Father
   B. Mother
   C. Father and the children
   D. Mother and the children

3. What did the father find under the bread?
   A. Soda
   B. Ice cream
   C. Cookies
   D. Candy

4. What did the father find under the chicken?
   A. Ice cream
   B. Soda
   C. Candy
   D. Popcorn

5. What did Dad buy for dinner?
   A. Hot dogs
   B. Turkey
   C. Chicken
   D. Hamburgers

4.21 Post-test

Section Two: Culture and Grammar

Instructions: Read and answer each of the questions below.

6. The sentence structure for ASL is always the same as the sentence structure for English.
   A. True
   B. False

7. Because ASL is a visual language, it doesn't have any grammatical rules.
   A. True
   B. False

8. When signing a sentence, ASL tends to put the ____ first.
   A. Adjective
   B. Negative
   C. Topic
   D. Comment

9. Briefly describe what a Number Story is.
   _____
   _____
   _____

10. Because ASL has strict grammatical rules, you can't make a "play on signs" like English can make a "play on words."
    A. True
    B. False

4.21 Post-test

Section Three: Expressive Portion

Instructions: Create five sentences about food that you will sign using topic/comment structure. Use any of the ASL vocabulary you have learned from Lessons One through Four. You can write the topic and comment of your sentences in the space below to help you prepare.

Your instructor will schedule a time for you to perform this section of the Post-test. You may prepare and practice prior to your scheduled time.

Topic	Comment
11. _____	_____
12. _____	_____
13. _____	_____
14. _____	_____
15. _____	_____

Congratulations!
You have completed
Lesson Four!

5.3 Lesson Objectives

Planning for Success

Goal: To see what you will learn by the end of this lesson.
Instructions: Read the objectives below.

Upon completing this VideoCourse lesson, you will be able to...

1. Recognize and accurately produce the ASL vocabulary introduced in Lessons One, Two, Three, and Four.

2. Demonstrate knowledge of the cultural information presented in Lessons One, Two, Three, and Four.

3. Recognize and apply the grammatical rules presented in Lessons One, Two, Three, and Four.

4. Accurately use the ASL vocabulary and grammatical features presented in Lessons One, Two, Three, and Four in sentences, dialogues, and stories.

5.5 Experiential Activity

Crossword Puzzle

Activity Goal: To help you remember the ASL vocabulary learned in Lesson One.

Activity Instructions: You will see several ASL vocabulary items from Lesson One signed on the video, as well as each answer's location on the puzzle, for example: 1 Across - MOTHER.

Decide what English word describes what is being signed and fits in the puzzle. Write it in the correct boxes. Each sign will be presented twice.

Instructor's Guide: Appendix
Bravo ASL! Curriculum

©1996 Sign Enhancers, Inc.
ALL RIGHTS RESERVED.

5.17 Experiential Activity

Matchmaker

Activity Goal: To help you remember some of the ASL vocabulary learned in Lesson Three.

Activity Instructions: Look at the illustrations of the Lesson Three vocabulary below. Draw a line from the illustration of the sign to the picture that best matches its meaning.

5.35 Post-test

Section One: Comprehension

Instructions: You will see a signed story. Watch carefully and answer each question below.

1. What was the little girl doing?
    A. Looking for bugs
    B. Helping her mom cook in the kitchen
    C. Setting the table
    D. Trying to fool her mother

2. Name three things the girl put on the table:

    _____

3. How does the girl feel about the spider?
    A. She likes it.
    B. She's afraid of it.
    C. She wants to capture it.
    D. She wants to give it to her mother.

4. When she first sees the spider, where is it?
    A. On a fork
    B. On a spoon
    C. On a knife
    D. On a plate

5. What does she do when she sees the spider?
    A. Hits it with napkin
    B. Takes it outside
    C. Takes it to her mother
    D. Tells her mother about it

6. What happens when Mom comes to the table?
    A. She takes the spider outside.
    B. She gets mad at the spider.
    C. She can't find the spider.
    D. She fools the daughter about the spider.

5.35 Post-test

Section Two: Culture and Grammar

Instructions: Read each statement carefully and determine if it is true or false (circle your answer).

7. Since Deaf people are part of American culture, they don't have their own culture.
    A. True
    B. False

8. The non-manual markers associated with yes/no questions include a furrowed (down) brow.
    A. True
    B. False

9. ASL often places the noun first, followed by the adjective.
    A. True
    B. False

10. In ASL, negatives usually appear at the end of a sentence.
    A. True
    B. False

11. When using a TTY, GA means "go ask."
    A. True
    B. False

12. A TDD helps make the audio on a television visible.
    A. True
    B. False

13. A relay service can assist a hearing person who does not have a TDD to call a Deaf person.
    A. True
    B. False

14. Since ASL is a visual language, it doesn't have any grammatical rules.
    A. True
    B. False

15. A Number Story is an example of Deaf folklore.
    A. True
    B. False

5.35 Post-test

Section Three: Expressive Portion

Instructions: Create a story about one of the following topics:

1. Breakfast in My House
2. The Day Dad Broke the Chair
3. Food Shopping With My Family
4. My Morning Routine

Be sure to include:
One sentence that is a yes/no question.
One sentence with topic/comment structure.
One sentence that asks a wh-question.
One sentence that includes negation.
Appropriate facial expression and non-manual markers.

Your instructor will schedule a time for you to perform this section of the Post-test. You may prepare and practice prior to your scheduled time.

16. ____ One sentence that is a yes/no question
17. ____ One sentence with topic/comment structure
18. ____ One sentence that asks a wh-question
19. ____ One sentence that includes negation
20. ____ Appropriate facial expression and non-manual markers

Congratulations!
You have completed
Lesson Five!

6.3 Pretest

What Do You Know?

Pretest Goal: To see how much you already know about what will be taught in this lesson.

Pretest Instructions: Read each question and circle the best answer.

1. Since Deaf people have complete mobility (they can walk), "access" is never a problem.
    A. True
    B. False

2. If you do not sign when a Deaf person is present, that person is likely to feel excluded.
    A. True
    B. False

3. When there are Deaf children in a family, it is especially important for the entire family to sign at all times.
    A. True
    B. False

4. Every sign has four parts. These parts are called:
    A. Hand-parts
    B. Sign-parts
    C. Parameters
    D. Paragrammars

5. Every sign is made of what four parts?
    A. Slow, medium, intermediate, and fast movements
    B. Fingers, waving, flipping, and flashing movements
    C. Circular, perpendicular, horizontal, and vertical movements
    D. Handshape, movement, location, and palm orientation

6.3 Pretest – 2

6. A sign produced accurately, but with the wrong movement, can change the meaning completely.
   A. True
   B. False

7. The manual alphabet is also referred to as "fingerspelling."
   A. True
   B. False

8. There are two sets of manual alphabets, one for capital letters and one for lower case letters.
   A. True
   B. False

9. Fingerspelling is used for proper names that don't have established signs.
   A. True
   B. False

10. If you are with a hearing friend and you see a Deaf person enter the room, you should start to sign even if your hearing friend doesn't understand Sign Language.
    A. True
    B. False

6.4 Lesson Objectives

Planning for Success

Goal: To see what you will learn by the end of this lesson.

Instructions: Read the objectives below.

Upon completing this VideoCourse lesson, you will be able to...

1. Recognize and accurately produce the ASL vocabulary introduced in this and all previous lessons.

2. Explain the importance of equal access and inclusion of Deaf people in all communication events.

3. Define and demonstrate the four parameters of sign production.

4. Correctly identify and accurately produce all 26 handshapes that represent the letters of the American manual alphabet.

5. Understand when and how fingerspelling is used within the context of signed communication.

6.5 and 6.11 Overhead Master

Color Time

Activity Goal: To experience an activity with "colorful" signs!

Activity Instructions: Watch the signed instructions to see what colors to use for the objects in the pictures below. If you do not understand the signs, try to guess which colors to use.

Instructor's Guide: Appendix
Bravo ASL! Curriculum

6.7 Experiential Activity

Read My Lips

Activity Goal: To show you a lecture to help you learn.

Activity Instructions: Watch the video very carefully. There will be a quiz immediately following this segment.

Quiz:

1. What was the main topic of this talk?
   _____

2. The term speech-reading is also called_____.

3. The ability to lip-read is directly linked to a how smart a person is.
   A. True
   B. False

4. A person who lip-reads also gets a lot of information from _____.

5. According to the speaker, what percentage of the English language can be seen on the lips?
   _____

6.8 Overhead Master

6.16 Video Learning Experience

Practice Session: Fingerspelling Usage

Viewing Goal: To learn when to use fingerspelling and practice forming words.

Viewing Instructions: There are specific times when you should fingerspell words. There are also specific rules for fingerspelling. The following is an outline of what Billy teaches about the use of fingerspelling. Please review the information below.

I. When is fingerspelling used?
   - A. For a person's name.
   - B. For the name of a place.
   - C. For things for which there is no established sign.

II. Rules regarding fingerspelling:
   - A. Fingerspell smoothly (go from one letter to the next without extra movements).
   - B. Keep the movement going (avoid stopping after each letter).
   - C. Keep hand steady (do not bounce your hand with each letter).
   - D. When you are reading fingerspelling, sound the word out the way you do when you are reading a book (do not say each letter as it is signed).
   - E. When fingerspelling, look at the person to whom you are signing (rather than looking at your hand).

6.17A Experiential Activity

Fingercise #1

Activity Goal: To learn how to read fingerspelling by watching for the shape of words that are fingerspelled instead of trying to see each individual letter.

Activity Instructions: Fill in the blank boxes below with the correct letters. Think about the shape of the whole word as well as the category to which the word belongs.

Names: Animals: Fruits:

        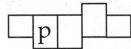

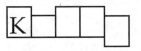   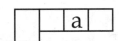

    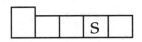   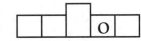

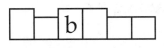   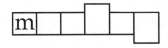   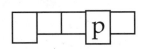

6.17B Experiential Activity

Fingercise #2

Activity Goal: To improve receptive fingerspelling skills.

Activity Instructions: Fill in the blanks below with the correct letters. This activity will help you see that you can miss several letters in a fingerspelled word and still be able to figure out what is being fingerspelled.

I w_n_ to g_ _o th_ s_ _ _ _.

Wh_ a_e y_ _ l_ _k_ _g at _e?

D_ y_ _ l_v_ S_ _ _ L_ _ _ _ _ _e?

H_ _ o_ _ ar_ y_ _?

F_ng_ _ _ _ _l_ _ _g c_ _ be f_ _!!

Instructor's Guide: Appendix
Bravo ASL! Curriculum

A-71

©1996 Sign Enhancers, Inc.
ALL RIGHTS RESERVED.

6.26 Comprehension Quiz

What Did You Understand?

Quiz Goal: To see how much of the signed story you understood.

Quiz Instructions: Your instructor will play the practice story again. Watch carefully and color the items in the picture below with the colors Billy describes in the story. If you don't have colored crayons or markers, write the name of the correct color on each item.

Instructor's Guide: Appendix
Bravo ASL! Curriculum

©1996 Sign Enhancers, Inc.
ALL RIGHTS RESERVED

6.28 Post-test

Section One: Comprehension

Instructions: You will see a short signed story. Watch carefully and answer each question below.

1. My mother's name is _____.
    A. Kay
    B. Pam
    C. Patty
    D. Kim

2. My father's name is _____.
    A. Ben
    B. Dan
    C. Bob
    D. Dave

3. The color of my bedroom is _____.
    A. Yellow
    B. Blue
    C. Purple
    D. Green

4. The color of my son's room is _____.
    A. Brown
    B. Silver
    C. Pink
    D. Red

5. My son's name is _____.
    A. Zack
    B. Bob
    C. Sam
    D. Steven

6.28 Post-test

Section Two: Culture and Grammar

Instructions: Read each statement carefully and circle the best answer.

6. There are two sets of manual alphabets, one for spelling the names of people and one for spelling the names of places.
   A. True
   B. False

7. When there are Deaf children in a family it is especially important for the entire family to sign at all times.
   A. True
   B. False

8. Every sign has four parts. These parts are called:
   A. Hand-parts
   B. Sign-parts
   C. Parameters
   D. Paragrammars

9. Every sign is made of four things: handshape, movement, location, and...
   A. Palm orientation
   B. Fingerspelling
   C. Two hands
   D. Fast movements

10. A sign can be produced accurately, but if the handshape is wrong, the meaning can be changed completely.
    A. True
    B. False

6.28 Post-test

Section Three: Expressive Portion

Instructions: Describe a friend's house and the people who live there, using at least five signs learned in Lesson Six. Also include at least three fingerspelled names.

Your instructor will schedule a time for you to perform this section of the Post-test. You may prepare and practice prior to your scheduled time. Use the space below to prepare for your expressive performance.

Include at least five signs from Lesson Six.

11. _____
12. _____
13. _____
14. _____
15. _____

Include three fingerspelled names:

16. _____
17. _____
18. _____

*Congratulations!
You have completed
Lesson Six!*

7.3 Pretest

What Do You Know?

Pretest Goal: To see how much you already know about what will be taught in this lesson.

Pretest Instructions: Read each question and circle the best answer.

1. All Deaf children attend schools for the Deaf.
   A. True
   B. False

2. In order for a Deaf child to attend a school for the Deaf, s/he must live away from home.
   A. True
   B. False

3. The self-esteem and self-identity of a Deaf child is an important factor when making educational decisions.
   A. True
   B. False

4. In ASL, the movement of a sign often gives vital information.
   A. True
   B. False

5. In ASL, the meaning of a sign can be changed by simply changing the movement of the sign.
   A. True
   B. False

7.4 Lesson Objectives

Planning For Success

Goal: To see what you will learn by the end of this lesson.
Instructions: Read the objectives below.

Upon completing this VideoCourse lesson, you will be able to...

1. Recognize and accurately produce the ASL vocabulary introduced in this and all previous lessons.

2. Explain what directional verbs are and how they are used.

3. Demonstrate at least three verbs that are directional.

4. Explain the importance of schools for the Deaf.

5. Explain the importance of fostering strong self-esteem and self-identity in Deaf children.

6. Identify some of the basic educational options available to Deaf children.

7. Identify the criteria that must be considered when choosing the best educational option for each Deaf child.

7.6 Overhead Master

7.9 Comprehension Quiz

What Did You Understand?

Quiz Goal: To see how much of the Bravo family interaction you understood.

Quiz Instructions: Read and answer each question below.

1. Scott and Anna are both ready to go to school.
   A. True
   B. False

2. The gardener invites Anna to pick a beautiful flower at her school.
   A. True
   B. False

3. The book Anna wants is only for _____.
   A. Students
   B. Mothers
   C. Teachers
   D. Children

4. Once in class, Anna is told by the teacher that she is in the wrong chair.
   A. True
   B. False

5. Anna decides to leave school for the day so nobody will tell her "No!"
   A. True
   B. False

7.10 Overhead Master

7.13 Experiential Activity

Crossword Puzzle

Activity Goal: To help you recognize the ASL vocabulary learned in this lesson.

Activity Instructions: You will see several of your new ASL vocabulary items signed with a reference as to where you should write them on the puzzle. For example, the signer might tell you, "One Across - SCHOOL."

Write the English word that fits in the puzzle and describes what is being signed in the correct boxes. Each item will be presented twice.

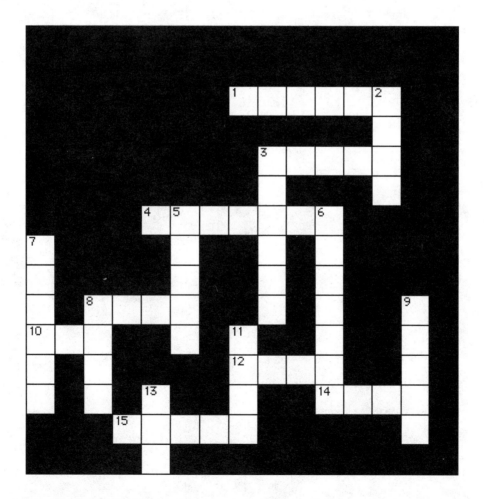

Instructor's Guide: Appendix
Bravo ASL! Curriculum

©1996 Sign Enhancers, Inc.
ALL RIGHTS RESERVED.

7.15 Comprehension Quiz

What Did You Understand?

Quiz Goal: To see how much of the Bravo family interaction you understood.

Quiz Instructions: Read and answer each question below.

1. The first student in Anna's class comes in feeling _____.
   A. Sick
   B. Tired
   C. Happy
   D. Hungry

2. The student who was late doesn't like school.
   A. True
   B. False

3. The student who was late told Anna that she was _____.
   A. Tired
   B. Sorry
   C. Good
   D. Playing

4. Anna asks her students to get their _____ ready.
   A. Books
   B. Flowers
   C. Paper and pencils
   D. Paper and crayons

5. Two students argue over a book. This book belongs to _____.
   A. Mom
   B. Dad
   C. The teacher
   D. The library

7.22 Cultural and Grammatical Quiz

What Did You Learn?

Quiz Goal: To see how much of this lesson's cultural and grammatical information you learned.

Quiz Instructions: Read and answer each question.

1. Self-esteem and self-identity are important factors in choosing a school for a Deaf child.
    A. True
    B. False

2. In order to get an education, Deaf children must live away from their families.
    A. True
    B. False

3. Having Deaf adult role models is one benefit of residential schools for the Deaf.
    A. True
    B. False

4. How can movement change an ASL sign? (Select all that apply.)
    A. Gives additional information
    B. Changes the meaning of the sign
    C. Changes the facial expression
    D. Changes who is doing the signing

5. Give two examples of ASL signs that are considered directional verbs.
    _____
    _____

6. If a Deaf student were to attend your school, what modifications (changes) would be needed so that student would gain full access to all educational activities? (Check all that apply.)
    A. Interpreters for classes
    B. Lights flashing for bells
    C. TTY for phone calls
    D. TV decoders for captioned videotapes

7.26 Comprehension Quiz

What Did You Understand?

Quiz Goal: To see how much of the signed story you understood.

Quiz Instructions: Read and answer each question below.

1. The teacher in the story signed fluently.
   A. True
   B. False

2. The other children in the class were also Deaf.
   A. True
   B. False

3. How many members of the boy's family were Deaf?
   A. 1
   B. 2
   C. 3
   D. 5

4. The boy taught his family _____.
   A. Math
   B. Sign Language
   C. Baseball plays
   D. English

5. The boy was not happy.
   A. True
   B. False

7.28 Post-test

Section One: Comprehension

Instructions: You will be presented with nine descriptions signed in ASL. Each sample will be numbered.

Below, you will find nine pictures. Choose the picture that best matches the signed description and write the correct number by each picture.

Instructor's Guide: Appendix
Bravo ASL! Curriculum

7.28 Post-test

Section Two: Culture and Grammar

Instructions: Read each statement carefully and choose the best answer.

6. Deaf children should have the following options for education (select all that apply):

    A. School for the Deaf (residential)
    B. School for the Deaf (day school)
    C. Mainstreamed classroom (with interpreter)
    D. Mainstreamed classroom (without interpreter)

7. Self-esteem and self-identity should always be considered when educational placement decisions are made concerning Deaf children.

    A. True
    B. False

8. Schools for the Deaf can be residential or day programs.

    A. True
    B. False

9. Changing the movement or direction of a sign does not change its meaning.

    A. True
    B. False

10. Which of the following are examples of directional verbs? (Circle all that apply):

    A. GIVE
    B. HELP
    C. FOOD
    D. WATCH

7.28 Post-test

Section Three: Expressive Portion

Instructions: Describe a room in your school, using at least seven signs learned in Lesson Seven. Include at least three directional verbs.

Your instructor will schedule a time for you to perform this section of the Post-test. You may prepare and practice prior to your scheduled time. Use the space below to prepare for your expressive performance.

Include at least seven signs from Lesson Seven.

11. _____
12. _____
13. _____
14. _____
15. _____
16. _____
17. _____

Include three directional verbs:

18. _____
19. _____
20. _____

Congratulations!
You have completed
Lesson Seven!

8.3 Pretest

What Do You Know?

Pretest Goal: To see how much you already know about what will be taught in this lesson.

Pretest Instructions: Read each question and circle the best answer.

1. One benefit of a residential school for the Deaf is that all of the students are Deaf.
    A. True
    B. False

2. The first school for the Deaf established in America was the _____.
    A. Model School for the Deaf
    B. United States School for the Deaf
    C. American School for the Deaf
    D. Hartford School for the Deaf

3. What year was the first school for the Deaf established?
    A. 1955
    B. 1857
    C. 1917
    D. 1817

4. Members of the Deaf community often view the local school for the Deaf as:
    A. A place that helps and supports Deaf people.
    B. Providing a strong sense of belonging.
    C. A place with warm childhood memories.
    D. All of the above

5. In ASL, a simple side-to-side headshake can turn a positive statement into a negative.
    A. True
    B. False

8.4 Lesson Objectives

Planning for Success

Goal: To see what you will learn by the end of this lesson.
Instructions: Read the objectives below.

Upon completing this VideoCourse lesson, you will be able to...

1. Recognize and accurately produce the vocabulary introduced in this and all previous lessons.

2. Summarize the benefits of attending a residential school for the Deaf.

3. Explain the history and importance of the American School for the Deaf.

4. Explain the Deaf community's view of residential schools for the Deaf.

5. When formulating signed sentences, choose conceptually accurate signs that are based on meaning.

8.7 Overhead Master

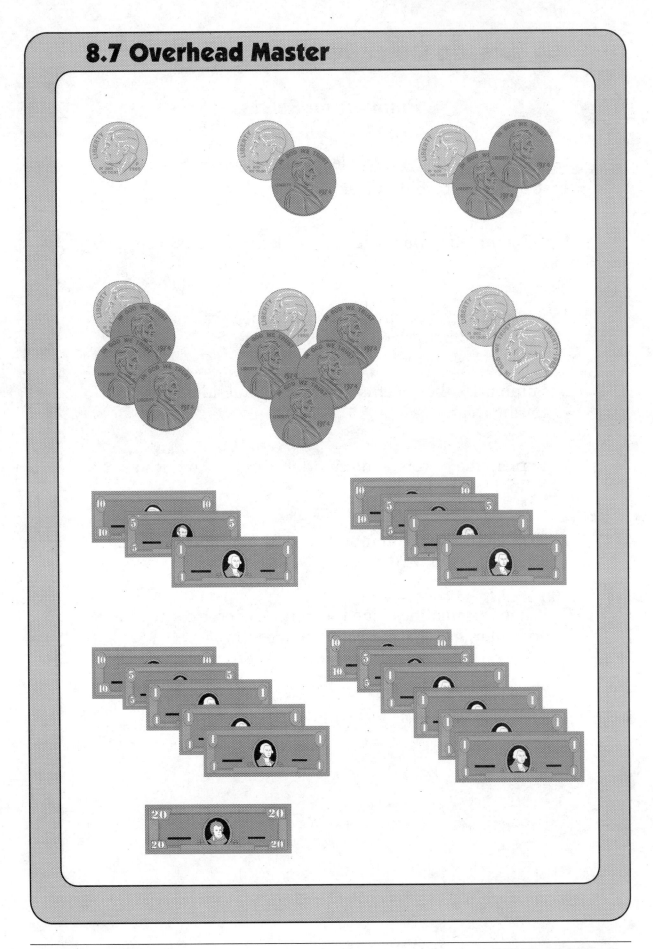

8.9 Overhead Master

8.13 Comprehension Quiz

What Did You Understand?

Quiz Goal: To see how much of the Bravo family interaction you understood.

Quiz Instructions: Read and answer each question below.

1. Anna's class has a(n) _____ lesson during our visit.
    A. English
    B. Math
    C. Science
    D. German

2. Did the student have the right answer to the first math problem?
    A. Yes
    B. No

3. One student uses a(n) _____ to get the right answer.
    A. Dictionary
    B. Encyclopedia
    C. Computer
    D. Calculator

4. Anna's class practices counting from one to thirty.
    A. True
    B. False

5. The sign for the number 17 is made up of what two signs?
    A. ONE and SEVEN
    B. TEN and SEVEN
    C. NINE and EIGHT
    D. TWO and FIFTEEN

8.14 Experiential Activity

8.17 Comprehension Quiz

What Did You Understand?

Quiz Goal: To see how much of the Bravo family interaction you understood.

Quiz Instructions: Read and answer each question below.

1. Who comes to visit Anna's classroom?
   _____

2. What did Anna tell the visitor was wrong in her class?
   _____
   _____

3. When the visitor asks the students to take out a piece of paper, what do the students do?
   A. Take out paper
   B. Throw paper at the teacher
   C. Throw paper at each other
   D. They all started signing "No, no, no."

4. What does the visitor tell Anna about her students?
   _____

5. When she wakes up, what does Anna want her real teacher to do?
   _____

8.22 Experiential Activity

What Do You Mean?

Activity Goal: To choose ASL signs based on meaning.

Activity Instructions: English words may have several different meanings. ASL signs do not relate to English words, but to the meaning of what is being expressed.

Read each of the sentences below. Decide what sign you would use for the meaning of the word/concept that is printed in **bold**. A space has been provided for you to record your answers.

_____ 1. I have **gone** to the store before.

_____ 2. The food is all **gone**.

_____ 3. The light is **on** the table.

_____ 4. Turn **on** the light.

_____ 5. The book is **there**.

_____ 6. The book is **theirs**.

_____ 7. That **dog** is mine.

_____ 8. I am **dog** tired.

8.26 Comprehension Quiz

What Did You Understand?

Quiz Goal: To see how much of the signed story you understood.

Quiz Instructions: Read and answer each question below.

1. The character in the story was a _____.
    A. Hearing girl
    B. Hearing boy
    C. Deaf boy
    D. Deaf girl

2. The teacher was Deaf and signed fluently.
    A. True
    B. False

3. The student's family was Deaf.
    A. True
    B. False

4. The other children at school were _____.
    A. Deaf and hearing
    B. Hearing
    C. Older
    D. Deaf

5. According to the story, the student was also a _____.
    A. Cub scout
    B. Baseball player
    C. Teacher
    D. Swimmer

8.28 Post-test

Section One: Comprehension

Instructions: You will see a signed story. Watch carefully and answer each question below.

1. What is the student's name in the story?
    A. Mike
    B. Rick
    C. Billy
    D. Nick

2. He attends a hearing school.
    A. True
    B. False

3. Does his teacher know Sign Language?
    A. Yes
    B. No

4. Today, in class, what was he going to learn?
    A. How to subtract
    B. How to add
    C. How to use a calculator
    D. How to multiply

5. According to the story, he understands because _____.
    A. He has a tutor
    B. He pays attention in class
    C. His mother is a math teacher
    D. His Deaf friends help him

6. According to the story, he is a good student.
    A. True
    B. False

8.28 Post-test

Section Two: Culture and Grammar

Instructions: Read each statement carefully and write your answers in the space provided.

7. As you have learned, there are several educational options available to Deaf students. Discuss at least three benefits of attending a School for the Deaf.
   _____
   _____
   _____

8. What might be considered an unfortunate aspect of attending a residential school for the Deaf?
   _____

9. What was the name of the first school for the Deaf in the United States? When and where was it established?
   _____
   _____

10. Explain what is meant by "conceptual accuracy."
    _____
    _____

8.28 Post-test

Section Three: Expressive Portion

Instructions: Create a story about your favorite class using at least seven signs learned in this lesson. Be certain to use at least three conceptually accurate signs/choices and be prepared to identify them.

Your instructor will schedule a time for you to perform this section of the Post-test. You may prepare and practice prior to your scheduled time. Use the space below to prepare for your expressive presentation.

Include at least seven signs from Lesson Eight.

11. _____
12. _____
13. _____
14. _____
15. _____
16. _____
17. _____

Conceptually accurate signs:

18. _____
19. _____
20. _____

Congratulations! You have completed Lesson Eight!

9.3 Pretest

What Do You Know?

Pretest Goal: To see how much you already know about what will be taught in this lesson.

Pretest Instructions: Read and answer each question.

1. In the past, employment options for Deaf people have been limited to jobs involving menial labor.
   A. True
   B. False

2. The telephone has been and still is a complete communication barrier in the workplace for Deaf people.
   A. True
   B. False

3. What type of jobs are available to Deaf people today?
   _____

4. Some Deaf people now own businesses.
   A. True
   B. False

5. The sign for ONE DOLLAR is made with a different movement than the sign for the number ONE.
   A. True
   B. False

6. Signs for dollar amounts of $10 or more are made differently than the signs for $9 or less.
   A. True
   B. False

7. The sign for "bank" is actually a fingerspelled loan sign.
   A. True
   B. False

9.4 Lesson Objectives

Planning for Success

Goal: To see what you will learn by the end of this lesson.
Instructions: Read the objectives below.

Upon completing this VideoCourse lesson, you will be able to...

1. Recognize and accurately produce the ASL vocabulary introduced in this and all previous lessons.

2. Compare the employment opportunities available to Deaf workers in the past with those opportunities available today.

3. Explain why the telephone is less of a barrier for Deaf workers today than it was in the past, particularly in regards to employment or owning a business.

4. Recognize and accurately produce number signs related to money.

9.7 Overhead Master

9.10 Comprehension Quiz

What Did You Understand?

Quiz Goal: To see how much of the Bravo family interaction you understood.

Quiz Instructions: Read and answer each question.

1. What does Dad want to do at the bank?
    A. He wants open a savings account.
    B. He wants to make a deposit to his checking account.
    C. He wants to apply for a job as a bank teller.
    D. He wants to open a checking account.

2. How much money is Dad depositing?
    _____

3. What does Scott want to do instead of wait for Dad at the bank?
    _____

4. Why is Scott sent to sit someplace else?
    _____
    _____

5. What does Scott wish?
    _____
    _____

9.13 Overhead Master

9.16 Comprehension Quiz

What Did You Understand?

Quiz Goal: To see how much of the Bravo family interaction you understood.

Quiz Instructions: Read and answer each question below.

1. The teller explained the difference between which two types of accounts?
   A. Checking and savings
   B. Money market and checking
   C. Money market and regular savings
   D. Checking and CD

2. Which type of account does Dad decide to open?
   A. Money market
   B. Checking
   C. Regular savings
   D. CD

3. What is different between the real teller and the teller in Scott's dream?
   A. Scott's teller is nicer.
   B. Scott's teller is Deaf.
   C. Scott's teller is hearing.
   D. Scott's teller gives him ice cream.

4. In Scott's dream, the banking transaction was much slower because Dad and the teller used ASL.
   A. True
   B. False

9.17 Overhead Master

Instructor's Guide: Appendix
Bravo ASL! Curriculum

©1996 Sign Enhancers, Inc.
ALL RIGHTS RESERVED.

9.21 Comprehension Quiz

What Did You Understand?

Quiz Goal: To see how much of the Bravo family interaction you understood.

Quiz Instructions: Read and answer each question below.

1. The bank teller asks Dad for his address, telephone number, and the amount of his deposit.
   A. True
   B. False

2. The bank teller tells Scott he needs to sign the form.
   A. True
   B. False

3. Instead of going for ice cream, Scott tells his Dad that he wants to _____.
   A. Go home
   B. Go to the park
   C. Make a deposit
   D. Make a withdrawal

4. When Dad wakes Scott up, he tells him it's time _____.
   A. To wake up
   B. To go home
   C. To go to another bank
   D. To go get ice cream

5. As Scott and Dad leave the bank, the Deaf bank teller tells Scott to _____.
   A. Enjoy his ice cream
   B. Have a nice day
   C. Be careful
   D. Save his money

9.24 Experiential Activity

Is the Price Right?

Activity Goal: To improve your ASL comprehension skills.

Activity Instructions: You will see a signer describing the items below and their correct prices in ASL. Find the picture of each item and write the correct price on its price tag.

9.29 Comprehension Quiz

What Did You Understand?

Quiz Goal: To see how much of the signed story you understood.

Quiz Instructions: Read and answer each question below.

1. What was the special event that happened in the story?
   _____

2. What did the signer get for the special event?
   _____

3. Who gave him the gift?
   _____

4. Where did he take his gift first? Why?
   _____
   _____

5. What did the signer finally do with his gift?
   _____
   _____

9.32 Post-test

Section One: Comprehension

Instructions: You will see a signed story. Watch carefully and answer each question below.

1. What does the signer want to buy?
   A. A coffee machine
   B. A couch and coffee table
   C. A yellow and green house

2. The signer has to go to:
   A. The bank
   B. The bathroom
   C. His girlfriend's house

3. What information was on the signer's check?
   A. Social security number
   B. Account balance
   C. Address

4. What was the savings account balance before this transaction?
   A. $ 18
   B. $ 300
   C. $ 3,000

5. What color is the couch that the signer bought?
   _____

6. How much did the couch cost?
   _____

7. What does the signer need to buy now?
   A. A TV
   B. Coffee
   C. A lamp

9.32 Post-test

Section Two: Culture and Grammar

Instructions: Read and answer each question.

8. What kind of jobs can Deaf people do?
   _____
   _____
   _____

9. Explain why the telephone is less of a barrier than it used to be for Deaf people.
   _____
   _____
   _____

10. Explain how money signs are produced.
    _____
    _____
    _____

9.32 Post-test

Section Three: Expressive Portion

Instructions: Describe a trip to the bank, using at least ten signs learned in Lesson Nine.

Your instructor will schedule a specific time for you to perform this section of the Post-test. You may prepare and practice prior to your scheduled time.

Include at least ten signs from Lesson Nine.

11. _____
12. _____
13. _____
14. _____
15. _____
16. _____
17. _____
18. _____
19. _____
20. _____

Congratulations!
You have completed
Lesson Nine!

10.3 Lesson Objectives

Planning for Success

Goal: To see what you will learn by the end of this lesson.
Instructions: Read the objectives below.

Upon completing this VideoCourse lesson, you will be able to...

1. Recognize and accurately produce the ASL vocabulary introduced in Lessons Six, Seven, Eight, and Nine.

2. Demonstrate knowledge of the cultural information presented in Lessons Six, Seven, Eight, and Nine.

3. Recognize and apply the grammatical features presented in Lessons Six, Seven, Eight, and Nine.

4. Accurately use the ASL vocabulary and grammatical features presented in Lessons Six, Seven, Eight, and Nine in sentences, dialogues, and stories.

10.18 Experiential Activity

Matchmaker

Activity Goal: To help you remember some of the ASL vocabulary learned in Lesson Eight.

Activity Instructions: Look at the illustrations below. Draw a line from the sign illustration to the picture that best matches its meaning.

10.37 Post-test

Section One: Comprehension

Instructions: You will see a signed story. Watch carefully and answer each question.

1. What was the girl's name?

    A. Jan
    B. Joan
    C. Tammy
    D. Cheri

2. What was the boy's name?

    A. Tag
    B. Tom
    C. Ted
    D. Thatcher

3. What did the girl want to do?

    A. Date the boy
    B. Meet with the teacher
    C. Eat lunch with the boy
    D. Learn more about math

4. What did the boy give the girl?

    A. A flower
    B. His phone number
    C. A calculator
    D. All of the above

5. Did the girl call him?

    A. Yes
    B. No

6. What did the girl want to talk about?

    A. English grammar
    B. Math problems
    C. Marriage and family
    D. The math teacher

10.37 Post-test
Section Two: Culture and Grammar

Instructions: Read each statement carefully and determine if it is true or false (circle your answer).

7. Signing when there is a Deaf child present helps the child feel involved, equal, and valuable.
   A. True
   B. False

8. Full access to a school's educational activities is necessary.
   A. True
   B. False

9. Full access to a school's social activities is not necessary.
   A. True
   B. False

10. A school for the Deaf will have Deaf adult role models.
    A. True
    B. False

11. Employment opportunities for Deaf people are limited to those jobs not requiring any use of the telephone.
    A. True
    B. False

12. There are several ways Deaf people can access the phone system.
    A. True
    B. False

13. Each sign has four parts, called paralanguages.
    A. True
    B. False

14. The four parts of every sign are: handshape, movement, location, and palm orientation.
    A. True
    B. False

15. Directional verbs all move in a forward direction.
    A. True
    B. False

10.37 Post-test

Section Three: Expressive Portion

Instructions: Create a story based on one of the questions below.

Your instructor will schedule a time for you to perform this section of the Post-test. You may prepare and practice prior to your scheduled time.

1. What is the funniest thing that ever happened to you in a bank?
2. What is your favorite school story?
3. What's your favorite color and why?

Include at least eight signs from Lesson Six, Seven, Eight, and Nine. Be sure to demonstrate at least two directional verbs in your story.

16. _____
17. _____
18. _____
19. _____
20. _____
21. _____
22. _____
23. _____

Directional verbs:

24. _____
25. _____

*Congratulations!
You have completed
Lesson Ten!*

11.3 Pretest

What Do You Know?

Pretest Goal: To see how much you already know about what will be taught in this lesson.

Pretest Instructions: Read and answer each question.

1. In ASL, the way signs are used in space often copies the movement of the people and objects involved in the actual events being described.

    A. True
    B. False

2. In an emergency situation, what can medical staff do to improve communication with a patient who is Deaf? Check all that apply:

    __A. Look at and speak directly to the Deaf person.
    __B. Be willing to use gestures.
    __C. Maintain direct eye contact.
    __D. Be willing to write or draw pictures.

3. During an emergency situation, what are some special concerns a Deaf person might have? Check all that apply:

    __A. Will there be a communication problem at the hospital?
    __B. Will anyone know Sign Language?
    __C. Will there be an interpreter?
    __D. Will I have a TV in my room?

4. What issues do you think are important to Deaf people during a medical emergency? Check all that apply:

    __A. Getting good medical care
    __B. Having communication access
    __C. Getting good interpreting services
    __D. Getting a color TV in their room

11.4 Lesson Objectives

Planning for Success

Goal: To see what you will learn by the end of this lesson.

Instructions: Read the objectives below. Your instructor will answer any questions you may have.

Upon completing this VideoCourse lesson, you will be able to...

1. Recognize and accurately produce the ASL vocabulary introduced in this and all previous lessons.

2. Identify and explain some of the communication and access issues Deaf people face in a medical emergency.

3. Identify and describe several ways the use of space feature is used in ASL.

11.6 Overhead Master

Instructor's Guide: Appendix
Bravo ASL! Curriculum

11.8 Experiential Activity

Spot the Sport

Activity Goal: To assist you in recognizing the new ASL vocabulary.

Activity Instructions: You will see signed descriptions of the pictures below. Each of the signed samples will be numbered. Put the number next to the picture that best matches the meaning of each signed description.

11.10 Comprehension Quiz

What Did You Understand?

Quiz Goal: To see how much of the Bravo family interaction you understood.

Quiz Instructions: Read and answer each question below.

1. Anna and Dad discuss how much Lady loves to _____.
   - A. Swim
   - B. Sleep
   - C. Play Frisbee
   - D. Play with the ball

2. Anna asks Dad if he wants to play _____.
   - A. Frisbee
   - B. Tennis
   - C. Golf
   - D. Football

3. Dad explains that _____ is/are beautiful.
   - A. The trees
   - B. The flowers
   - C. Mom
   - D. All of the above

4. After lunch, Dad says he wants to _____.
   - A. Play golf
   - B. Play tennis
   - C. Swim
   - D. All of the above

5. After lunch, Mom wants to _____.
   - A. Play tennis
   - B. Play golf
   - C. Play Frisbee
   - D. Sit by the river

Instructor's Guide: Appendix
Bravo ASL! Curriculum

©1996 Sign Enhancers, Inc.
ALL RIGHTS RESERVED.

11.11 Overhead Master

11.18 Experiential Activity

It's An Emergency!

Activity Goal: To apply the cultural information you have learned about medical emergencies and Deaf people.

Activity Instructions: Read each situation below and write down potential communication and access issues and the solutions for each.

1. A Deaf four-year-old goes into the hospital for an emergency operation:
   _____
   _____
   _____

2. A Deaf woman goes into labor three weeks early and is admitted to the hospital:
   _____
   _____
   _____

3. A Deaf construction worker is in a work-related accident:
   _____
   _____
   _____

4. A hearing woman is involved in a car accident and wants her Deaf husband to be called:
   _____
   _____
   _____

11.22 Comprehension Quiz

What Did You Understand?

Quiz Goal: To see how much of the signed story you understood.

Quiz Instructions: Read and answer each question below.

1. Who always won the games?
   A. The woman
   B. The man
   C. The children
   D. The dog

2. The last sport they competed in was _____.
   A. Golf
   B. Frisbee
   C. Running
   D. Fishing

3. The ____ caught the first fish.
   A. Boy
   B. Woman
   C. Man
   D. Girl

4. The man caught ____ fish.
   A. Four
   B. Nine
   C. Six
   D. Eight

5. The woman caught ____ fish.
   A. Eight
   B. Seven
   C. Six
   D. Nine

11.25 Post-test

Section One: Comprehension

Instructions: You will see a signed story. Watch the video carefully and then answer each question below.

1. The two boys were named Tom and _____.
   A. Billy
   B. Jim
   C. Sammy
   D. Jake

2. The boys had brought _____.
   A. A football
   B. A picnic lunch
   C. A Frisbee
   D. A basketball

3. Who packed their picnic food?
   A. Their mom
   B. Their younger brother
   C. Their dad
   D. They packed the food themselves

4. What did they both want?
   A. The popcorn
   B. To play with the dog
   C. The orange
   D. The cookie

5. What did Jake do when Tom was in the tree?
   A. Ate the popcorn
   B. Played with the dog
   C. Ate the orange
   D. Ate the cookie

11.25 Post-test

Section Two: Culture and Grammar

Instructions: Read each statement carefully and write your response in the space provided.

6. What information is provided by the use of space feature?

   _____
   _____
   _____
   _____

7. Discuss three concerns that Deaf people experience when faced with medical emergencies.

   _____
   _____
   _____
   _____

8. What are three things the staff of a medical clinic could do to communicate with Deaf people in a medical emergency?

   _____
   _____
   _____
   _____

11.25 Post-test

Section Three: Expressive Portion

Instructions: Create a story about *A Day at the Park*, using at least six signs learned in this lesson. Also sign at least one sentence in which you utilize use of space as taught in this lesson.

Your instructor will schedule a time for you to perform this section of the Post-test. You may prepare and practice prior to your scheduled time. Use the space below to prepare for your expressive performance.

Include at least six signs from Lesson Eleven.

9. _____
10. _____
11. _____
12. _____
13. _____
14. _____

Use of space feature used:

15. _____

Congratulations! You have completed Lesson Eleven!

12.3 Pretest

What Do You Know?

Pretest Goal: To see how much you already know about what will be taught in this lesson.

Pretest Instructions: Read each statement below and determine if it is true or false.

1. In ASL, a lot of information is given through facial expression.
   A. True
   B. False

2. Each ASL sign has only one meaning and one English word to describe it.
   A. True
   B. False

3. ASL uses facial expression the same way English uses adjectives.
   A. True
   B. False

4. All medical facilities are fully accessible to Deaf people.
   A. True
   B. False

5. Medical facilities and personnel are becoming more sensitive to accessibility issues as they relate to the Deaf community.
   A. True
   B. False

12.4 Lesson Objectives

Planning For Success

Goal: To see what you will learn by the end of this lesson.
Instructions: Read the objectives below.

Upon completing this VideoCourse lesson, you will be able to...

1. Recognize and accurately produce the ASL vocabulary introduced in this and all previous lessons.

2. Identify and explain some of the accessibility issues for Deaf people involved in medical emergencies.

3. Explain the role of facial expression in ASL.

4. Accurately recognize and use facial expression within signed communication.

12.5 Lesson Focus

Help! We Need Help!

Activity Goal: To experience a role-play related to medical emergencies when communication is limited.

Activity Instructions: Imagine that you are traveling in a foreign country. The people do not understand English. Your traveling companion falls on the train and hurts her ankle.

How would you communicate the questions or information below without the use of spoken or written communication?

Remember, you can use a variety of methods to communicate, such as gesturing, miming, pointing, etc.

You may make notes of your ideas below:

1. Where is the hospital? _____

2. My friend fell on a train. _____

3. Her ankle hurts very badly. _____

4. Her ankle is swollen. _____

5. Will she need a shot? _____

6. Will you give her medicine? _____

7. Does she need crutches? _____

12.7 Overhead Master

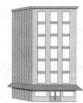

12.11 Cultural Quiz

What Did You Learn?

Quiz Goal: To see what cultural aspects of the Bravo family interaction you understood.

Quiz Instructions: Read and answer each question below.

1. Why is Mom signing and talking at the same time when she is at the hospital?

   _____
   _____

2. Why is it important for hospitals to know about the rights of the Deaf community *before* a Deaf person visits?

   _____
   _____

3. Why are Deaf people frustrated as they try to fulfill their medical needs?

   _____
   _____

4. Dad served as an advocate for the rights of Deaf people. How did he do this?

   _____
   _____

12.15 Experiential Activity

What Kind of Face is That?

Activity Goal: To help you recognize the emotions expressed with facial expressions in ASL.

Activity Instructions: You will see ten sentences signed in ASL. Watch the facial/body expressions of each signer and circle the adjective that best describes the emotion shown in each signed sentence.

Circle your answers:

1.	Happy	Sad	Bored	Scared
2.	Happy	Sad	Bored	Scared
3.	Happy	Sad	Bored	Scared
4.	Happy	Sad	Bored	Scared
5.	Happy	Sad	Bored	Scared
6.	Happy	Sad	Bored	Scared
7.	Happy	Sad	Bored	Scared
8.	Happy	Sad	Bored	Scared
9.	Happy	Sad	Bored	Scared
10.	Happy	Sad	Bored	Scared

12.17 Overhead Master

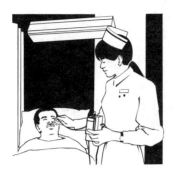

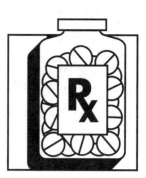

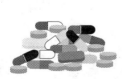
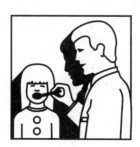

12.21 Comprehension Quiz

What Did You Understand?

Quiz Goal: To see how much of the doctor/patient interaction you understood.

Quiz Instructions: Read the questions and circle the best answer.

1. According to Dr. Billy's patient, what is the problem?
    A. He has a fever.
    B. He's nauseated.
    C. He's been sneezing a lot.
    D. He broke his leg.

2. Dr. Billy asks the patient if he's been coughing.
    A. True
    B. False

3. The patient told the doctor he has a sore throat.
    A. True
    B. False

4. The patient is afraid of _____.
    A. The doctor
    B. Getting a shot
    C. Missing school
    D. Losing his teddy bear

5. The patient was happy because he would miss school, but sad because _____.
    A. He has to stay in the hospital.
    B. He has to take medicine.
    C. He has to get a shot.
    D. He has to rest and can't play.

12.29 Comprehension Quiz

What Did You Understand?

Quiz Goal: To see how much of the signed story you understood.

Quiz Instructions: Read and answer each question below.

1. What is the man's name in the story?
   _____
   _____

2. How did he get to sleep?
   _____
   _____

3. What did he do when he got up?
   _____
   _____

4. When he left the house, where did he go?
   _____
   _____

5. What did he do while waiting?
   _____
   _____

6. What were the doctor's instructions?
   _____
   _____

12.32 Post-test

Section One: Comprehension

Instructions: You will see a signed story. Watch carefully and answer each question below.

1. What is the signer's name?
   A. Jan
   B. Jesse
   C. Justin

2. The signer is sick. What is wrong with him?
   A. A fall
   B. A sore throat
   C. A sprained ankle

3. What did Mom say the signer could not do?
   A. See a doctor
   B. Go to sleep
   C. Go to school or play

4. What did the doctor give the signer?
   A. Crutches
   B. Cough syrup
   C. A shot and some pills

5. What was the signer's temperature?
   A. 104
   B. 100
   C. 98

12.32 Post-test

Section Two: Culture and Grammar

Instructions: Read and answer each question below.

6. What information does facial expressions add to a sign?
   _____
   _____

7. Explain what is meant by "facial expressions are often the adjectives of the message."
   _____
   _____

8. If a hospital receives federal funding, it is required to provide access to:
   A. Color TVs
   B. Private rooms for Deaf patients
   C. Sign Language classes
   D. Sign Language Interpreters

12.32 Post-test

Section Three: Expressive Portion

Instructions: Create a story in which you describe a time when you were sick. Use at least ten signs learned in Lesson Twelve and clearly demonstrate at least two emotions with facial expressions.

Your instructor will schedule a time for you to perform this section of the Post-test. You may prepare and practice prior to your scheduled time. Use the space below to prepare for your expressive performance.

Include at least ten signs from Lesson Twelve.

9. _____
10. _____
11. _____
12. _____
13. _____
14. _____
15. _____
16. _____
17. _____
18. _____

Emotions shown with facial expression:

19. _____
20. _____

Congratulations!
You have completed
Lesson Twelve!

13.3 Pretest

What Do You Know?

Pretest Goal: To see how much you already know about what will be taught in this lesson.

Pretest Instructions: Read and answer each question.

1. Since a Deaf person can't use the telephone, s/he can't work as a secretary.
    A. True
    B. False

2. Deaf people can't be successful in business because of communication barriers.
    A. True
    B. False

3. Companies that become accessible to Deaf workers are also accessible to Deaf consumers.
    A. True
    B. False

4. What is a relay service?
    A. It is an interpreter referral service.
    B. It is a special TTY that helps a Deaf person to use the phone.
    C. It is a service that relays calls between voice and TTYs.
    D. It is an operator who is Deaf who relays calls to other Deaf people.

5. What type of jobs are available to Deaf people today?
    A. Sign Language teachers and printers.
    B. Photographers, artists, directors and dancers.
    C. Counselors, secretaries, teachers, lawyers and doctors.
    D. All of the above.

Instructor's Guide: Appendix
Bravo ASL! Curriculum

©1996 Sign Enhancers, Inc.
ALL RIGHTS RESERVED.

13.4 Lesson Objectives

Planning for Success

Goal: To see what you will learn by the end of this lesson.
Instructions: Read the objectives below.

Upon completing this VideoCourse lesson, you will be able to...

1. Recognize and accurately produce the vocabulary introduced in this and all previous lessons.

2. Describe equipment commonly used by Deaf people for gaining access to telecommunication.

3. Describe what a telephone relay service is and how it functions.

4. Identify ways in which the workplace is becoming more accessible to Deaf employees.

5. Accurately produce signs that incorporate numbers.

13.5 Lesson Focus-1

Help Wanted

Activity Goal: To explore the possibilities and challenges for Deaf people in the workplace.

Activity Instructions: Imagine that you are an employer looking for employees for the jobs described below. You recently interviewed several Deaf people and you were impressed with each person's abilities. You're considering hiring them. You've never had Deaf employees.

Consider modifications to job descriptions or the work environment that might be necessary. How might you make the workplace more accessible to a Deaf employee? Write your ideas below:

JOB TITLE: Computer Programmer

MAIN RESPONSIBILITIES:

1) Meet with clients to determine the specifics of their project.

2) Work with team of programmers to design a computer program to meet the client's needs.

3) Check with client(s) throughout process to obtain client feedback.

4) At completion of project, present program and training to client to maximize effective use of program.

Potential communication challenge:	Potential solution:
1. _____	_____
2. _____	_____
3. _____	_____
4. _____	_____

13.5 Lesson Focus – 2

JOB TITLE: Administrative Secretary

MAIN RESPONSIBILITIES:

1) Greet customers as they enter the office.

2) Provide support (such as typing and filing) for staff.

3) Record financial deposits and payables, make bank deposits.

4) At the end of each quarter, write a report regarding the financial status of the company, and present it to the staff.

5) Coordinate company meetings, arranging for food and beverages.

Potential communication challenge:	Potential solution:
1. _____	_____
2. _____	_____
3. _____	_____
4. _____	_____
5. _____	_____

13.5 Lesson Focus – 3

JOB TITLE: Research Librarian

MAIN RESPONSIBILITIES:

1) Meet with students to help them find appropriate research material.

2) Work with teachers and staff members researching information for various school projects.

3) Supervise all research assistants employed by the library.

4) Train students and teachers to use the computerized database.

Potential communication challenge:	Potential solution:
1. _____	_____
2. _____	_____
3. _____	_____
4. _____	_____
5. _____	_____

13.6 Overhead Master

13.9 Comprehension Quiz

What Did You Understand?

Quiz Goal: To see how much of the Bravo family interaction you understood.

Quiz Instructions: Read and answer each question.

1. What does Anna ask her mother?
   _____
   _____

2. What does Mom invite Anna to do?
   _____
   _____

3. Does Anna want to do this?
   _____
   _____

4. What does Scott tell Mom NOT to do?
   _____
   _____

5. What does Anna plan to do for her first task?
   _____
   _____

13.10 Overhead Master

13.13 Comprehension Quiz

What Did You Understand?

Quiz Goal: To see how much of the Bravo family interaction you understood.

Quiz Instructions: Read and answer each question.

1. What does Anna want to know about the computer?
   _____
   _____

2. What is Mom's computer used for?
   _____
   _____

3. What does Anna want to do to help Mom?
   _____
   _____

4. What does Mom do before "hiring" Anna?
   _____
   _____

5. When Anna answers the phone, who is the caller?
   _____
   _____

13.14 Overhead Master

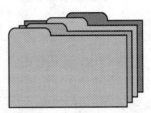

13.18 Comprehension Quiz

What Did You Understand?

Quiz Goal: To see how much of the Bravo family interaction you understood.

Quiz Instructions: Read and answer each question.

1. Mom explains that she is Anna's boss.
   A. True
   B. False

2. What is the first job Mom gives Anna?
   A. Filing
   B. Computer work
   C. Typing a letter
   D. Going to the post-office

3. Who has to sign the letter?
   A. The vice president
   B. The secretary
   C. The president
   D. Anna

4. Mom goes to the post office.
   A. True
   B. False

5. Anna is promoted to what position?
   A. President
   B. Vice president
   C. Secretary
   D. Owner

13.19 Overhead Master

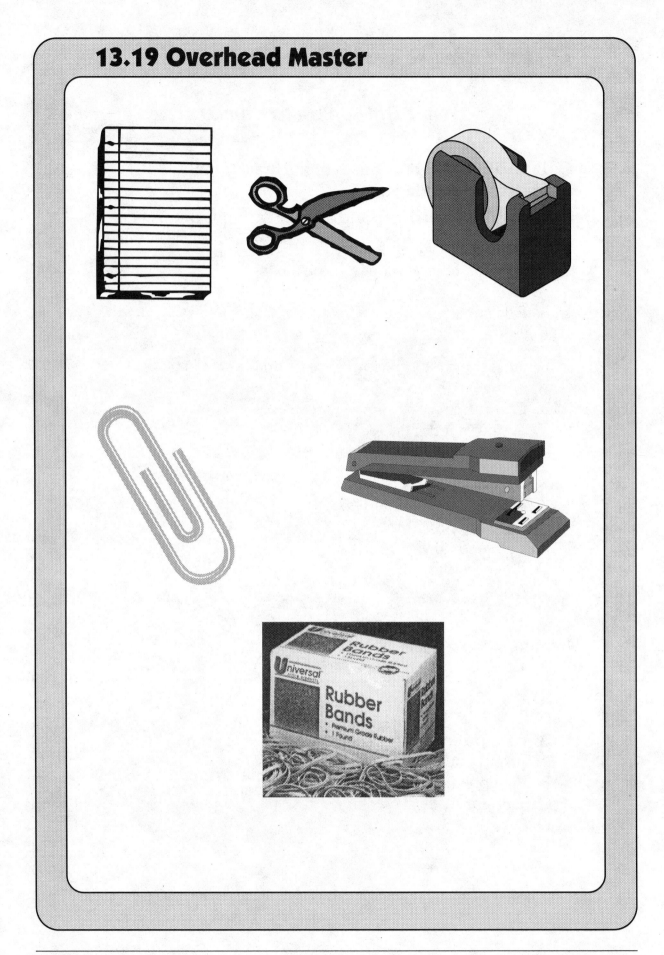

13.22 Comprehension Quiz

What Did You Understand?

Quiz Goal: To see how much of the Bravo family interaction you understood.

Quiz Instructions: Read and answer each question.

1. What does Dad tell Anna he would like to do?
   _____
   _____

2. When Dad wants to see Mom, what does Anna ask him?
   _____
   _____

3. What does Dad want to do after the women finish working?
   _____
   _____

4. What time is it when Mom says work is finished?
   _____
   _____

5. How is Anna paid by Mom for her hard work?
   _____
   _____

13.28 Experiential Activity

Name the Number

Activity Goal: To identify the number sign used in sentences presented in ASL.

Activity Instructions: You will see five signed sentences. Each sentence will be signed twice. Circle the picture that best illustrates the meaning of each sentence.

1.

2.

3.

4.

5.

13.30 Comprehension Quiz

What Did You Understand?

Quiz Goal: To see how much of the signed story you understood.

Quiz Instructions: Read and answer each question.

1. Where does Anna work?
   _____
   _____

2. Who does Anna interview?
   _____
   _____

3. What kind of worker is the new employee?
   _____
   _____

4. What does the new employee do instead of work?
   _____
   _____

5. What does the new employee do to Anna?
   _____
   _____

6. What does the new employee demand of Anna?
   _____
   _____

7. What does Anna do instead?
   _____
   _____

13.32 Post-test

Section One: Comprehension

Instructions: Watch the signed sample carefully and answer each question below.

1. The president needed to hire someone for the job of _____.

    A. Boss
    B. Secretary
    C. Assistant

2. Who applied for the position?

    A. Liza and Billy
    B. Kathy and Bob
    C. John and Jenna

3. After the interview, what did the president ask each person to do?

    A. Clean the office
    B. File papers
    C. Type a letter

4. The president hired _____ for the job.

    A. Liza
    B. Billy
    C. Tom

5. The secretary's first job was to _____.

    A. Buy a computer
    B. Type a letter
    C. File papers

13.32 Post-test

Section Two: Culture and Grammar

Instructions: Read each statement carefully and determine if it is true or false (circle your answer).

6. Telephones have never been an obstacle to Deaf people getting jobs.
   A. True
   B. False

7. Today, TTYs allow Deaf people to communicate on the telephone.
   A. True
   B. False

8. Relay services are only beneficial to Deaf people.
   A. True
   B. False

9. Numbers can be combined with some time signs.
   A. True
   B. False

10. Numbers, when combined with classifiers, can give even more information about how many people are involved.
    A. True
    B. False

13.32 Post-test

Section Three: Expressive Portion

Instructions: For this portion of your test, you and a partner will role-play being employees, an employee and a boss, or two bosses of a large company.

Each of you must use at least seven signs learned in Lesson Thirteen during your role-play. Each person must also include three pronoun signs incorporating numbers.

Your individual grade depends on your expressive ability and not your partner's. Both participants must follow the guidelines above to receive full credit.

Your instructor will schedule a time for you to perform this section of the Post-test. You may prepare and practice prior to your scheduled time. Use the space below to prepare for your expressive performance.

Include at least seven signs from Lesson Thirteen.

11. _____
12. _____
13. _____
14. _____
15. _____
16. _____
17. _____

Include three pronoun signs incorporating numbers (for example, TWO-OF-US):

18. _____
19. _____
20. _____

Congratulations!
You have completed
Lesson Thirteen!

14.3 Pretest

What Do You Know?

Pretest Goal: To see how much you already know about what will be taught in this lesson.

Pretest Instructions: Read and answer each question.

1. Most Deaf children are born to hearing parents.
    A. True
    B. False

2. Many hearing parents with Deaf children never learn to sign.
    A. True
    B. False

3. Parents must consider the individual needs of their child before making important decisions about communication.
    A. True
    B. False

4. If a child learns to sign, that means s/he will never learn to talk.
    A. True
    B. False

5. The term "classifiers" refers to:
    A. A class of people who use ASL.
    B. A class of Deaf children who misbehave.
    C. A class of objects represented by a certain handshape.
    D. A class of students that urgently want to learn ASL.

6. Which of these vehicles cannot be signed with the "3" handshape?
    A. Car
    B. Motorcycle
    C. Boat
    D. Airplane

7. What numbers can be incorporated into classifiers? (Check all that apply)
    ___ A. 1
    ___ B. 2
    ___ C. 3
    ___ D. 4

14.4 Lesson Objectives

Planning for Success

Goal: To see what you will learn by the end of this lesson.
Instructions: Read the objectives below.

Upon completing this VideoCourse lesson, you will be able to...

1. Recognize and accurately produce the ASL vocabulary introduced in this and all previous lessons.

2. Identify some of the key issues parents face in making decisions regarding communication when raising a Deaf child.

3. Identify some of the communication options available to Deaf children.

4. Define "classifiers" and recognize their use in signed communication.

5. Accurately produce and use classifiers within the context of signed communication.

14.5 Lesson Focus

What Are They Wearing?

Activity Goal: To find out what clothing signs you know (and which you need to learn).

Activity Instructions: You will see several signed descriptions of people and what they are wearing. Watch carefully, and for each description, circle the correct picture below.

1. A.  B.  C.

2. A.  B.  C.

3. A.  B.  C.

4. A.  B.  C.

14.6 Overhead Master

14.10 Comprehension Quiz

What Did You Understand?

Quiz Goal: To see how much of the Bravo family interaction you understood.

Quiz Instructions: Read and answer each question.

1. When Scott first meets Tommy, what does he ask?
   A. "How old are you?"
   B. "Do you have a sister?"
   C. "Where is your father?"
   D. "Are you Deaf?"

2. After Tommy fingerspelled his name, what did Scott do?
   A. Gave him a new name.
   B. Gave him a name sign.
   C. Told him his fingerspelling was too slow.
   D. Told him he was too tall.

3. What does Scott ask Tommy?
   A. If he wants to buy pants.
   B. If he wants to buy a mask.
   C. If he wants to walk around the store together.
   D. If he wants Anna as a girlfriend.

4. What are some of the signs Scott taught Tommy?
   A. MASK, PANTS, and SISTER
   B. PANTS, SHIRT, SOCKS, and SHOES
   C. DEAF, HEARING, SISTER, and BROTHER
   D. SCARE, PETER PAN, CLOTHES, and COAT

5. What are some of the signs Dad taught Tommy's father?
   A. HAT, TIE, and GLOVES
   B. MIRROR, OVERALLS, and HAT
   C. EXPENSIVE, BUY, and DRESS
   D. MONEY, SON, and FAMILY

14.11 Overhead Master

Instructor's Guide: Appendix
Bravo ASL! Curriculum

A-164

©1996 Sign Enhancers, Inc.
ALL RIGHTS RESERVED.

14.17 Comprehension Quiz

What Did You Understand?

Quiz Goal: To see how much of the Bravo family interaction you understood.

Quiz Instructions: Read and answer each question.

1. Anna likes the dress because Tommy said he liked it.
    A. True
    B. False

2. What does Scott tell Anna about the coat she tried on?
    A. "It looks too big on you."
    B. "You look warm."
    C. "It looks good on you."
    D. "You look cold."

3. What does Tommy ask Anna?
    A. "Do you like backpacks?"
    B. "Do you like purses?"
    C. "Why don't you carry a purse?"
    D. "Do you want to go hiking?"

4. What does Scott tell Mom when they meet again?
    A. "Tommy is my new friend."
    B. "Tommy doesn't know how to sign."
    C. "We've been teaching Tommy signs!"
    D. "Anna likes Tommy!"

5. Why does Scott say he and Anna are lucky?
    A. Because they bought socks and a coat for Anna.
    B. Because they have a new friend
    C. Because they know how to sign.
    D. Because their parents sign.

6. What does Tommy's father tell him when he says he loves Sign Language?
    A. "It's too late to learn now."
    B. "I love you."
    C. "I love Sign Language, too."
    D. "I love this store."

14.25 Comprehension Quiz

What Did You Understand?

Quiz Goal: To see how much of the signed story you understood.

Quiz Instructions: Read each question below and choose the best answer.

1. What was the girl's name in the story?
   A. Amy
   B. Angie
   C. Anna
   D. Alice

2. What did the girl's mother want to buy?
   A. A purple skirt with a pink blouse.
   B. A blue skirt with a purple blouse.
   C. Blue pants, a shirt, and a backpack.
   D. A pink skirt, blouse, and purse.

3. What did the girl want to buy?
   A. A purple skirt with a pink blouse.
   B. A blue skirt with a purple blouse.
   C. Blue pants, a shirt, and a backpack.
   D. A pink skirt, blouse, and purse.

4. What choice did the girl's mother give her?
   _____
   _____

5. What did the girl decide to buy?
   _____
   _____

Instructor's Guide: Appendix
Bravo ASL! Curriculum

14.27 Post-test

Section One: Comprehension

Instructions: You will see a signed story. Watch carefully and answer each question below.

1. What was the man's name in the story?
   A. Kyle
   B. Kevin
   C. Kid
   D. Ken

2. Who did the man like?
   A. Sally
   B. Susan
   C. Shelly
   D. Shawna

3. Who is going to cook dinner?
   A. The woman
   B. The man

4. The woman has a problem. What is it?
   A. She doesn't like him and doesn't want to go.
   B. She already has another date.
   C. She doesn't have a car.
   D. She can't find anything she wants to wear.

5. What does she do about this problem?
   A. She tells him no and doesn't go.
   B. She cancels her other date.
   C. She goes to the store and buys a car.
   D. She goes clothes shopping.

6. What was the man wearing?
   A. All black clothes.
   B. His pajamas.
   C. Very colorful clothes.
   D. A backpack and hiking boots.

14.27 Post-test

Section Two: Culture and Grammar

Instructions: Read each statement carefully and determine if it is true or false (circle your answer).

7. Some parents with Deaf children never learn to sign.
   A. True
   B. False

8. Professionals such as doctors, counselors, and teachers often disagree about what would be best for a Deaf child.
   A. True
   B. False

9. It is never too late to learn a new language.
   A. True
   B. False

10. Classifiers identify a "class" of objects.
    A. True
    B. False

11. There are many classifiers used in ASL.
    A. True
    B. False

12. Classifiers are another way to produce fingerspelled names.
    A. True
    B. False

13. Using a 3-handshape moving forward can represent a train.
    A. True
    B. False

14. Using a 3-handshape moving forward can represent a boat.
    A. True
    B. False

15. Using a 3-handshape moving forward can represent a plane.
    A. True
    B. False

14.27 Post-test

Section Three: Expressive Portion

Instructions: Create a story about the picture below. Be sure to use at least four of your new clothing signs and at least one classifier.

Your instructor will schedule a time for you to perform this section of the Post-test. You may prepare and practice prior to your scheduled time. Use the space below to prepare for your expressive performance.

Include at least four signs from Lesson Fourteen.

16. _____
17. _____
18. _____
19. _____

Include at least one classifier:

20. _____

Congratulations!
You have completed
Lesson Fourteen!

15.3 Lesson Objectives

Planning for Success

Goal: To see what you will learn by the end of this lesson.
Instructions: Read the objectives below.

Upon completing this VideoCourse lesson, you will be able to...

1. Recognize and accurately produce the ASL vocabulary introduced in Lessons Eleven, Twelve, Thirteen, and Fourteen.

2. Demonstrate knowledge of the cultural information presented in Lessons Eleven, Twelve, Thirteen, and Fourteen.

3. Recognize and apply the grammatical features presented in Lessons Eleven, Twelve, Thirteen, and Fourteen.

4. Accurately use the ASL vocabulary and grammatical features presented in Lessons Eleven, Twelve, Thirteen, and Fourteen in sentences, dialogues, and stories.

15.14 Video Learning Experience

Lesson Twelve Review: Practice Dialogue

Viewing Goal: To improve your comprehension skills by watching a dialogue presented in ASL.

Viewing Instructions: Watch the signed dialogue for comprehension and answer the questions below.

1. What does Scott tell Anna at the beginning of the dialogue?
   _____
   _____

2. Anna tells Scott that she is not going to school. What is the first reason she gives him?
   _____
   _____

3. According to Scott, how will Mom know she is faking?
   _____
   _____

4. What is the second symptom Anna tells Scott about?
   _____
   _____

5. When Anna tells Scott that she has a headache, how does he respond?
   _____
   _____

6. In the end, does Anna decide to go to school or stay home?
   _____
   _____

Instructor's Guide: Appendix
Bravo ASL! Curriculum

©1996 Sign Enhancers, Inc.
ALL RIGHTS RESERVED.

15.17 Experiential Activity

Matchmaker

Activity Goal: To help you remember some of the ASL vocabulary learned in Lesson Thirteen.

Activity Instructions: Look at the illustrations below. Draw a line from the illustration of the sign to the picture that best matches its meaning.

Instructor's Guide: Appendix
Bravo ASL! Curriculum

©1996 Sign Enhancers, Inc.
ALL RIGHTS RESERVED.

15.32 Post-test

Section One: Comprehension

Instructions: You will see a signed story. Watch carefully and answer each question below.

1. What was the man's name in the story?
   A. Jack
   B. Joseph
   C. Jasper
   D. John

2. Was the man Deaf or hearing?
   A. Deaf
   B. Hearing

3. Who did the man have with him?
   A. His five-year-old daughter
   B. His four-year-old son
   C. His wife, who was an interpreter
   D. His girlfriend, who had a daughter

4. Why did the man go to the store?
   A. To find a new job
   B. To buy some pants
   C To buy a new tie
   D. To find his family

5. What happened that made him so scared?
   _____

6. Who did he meet at the store?
   A. Kathy
   B. Karen
   C. Kendra
   D. Kelly

7. What did this woman do for a living?
   _____

8. What did the man do to teach the child a lesson?
   _____

15.32 Post-test

Section Two: Culture and Grammar

Instructions: Read each statement carefully and determine if it is True or False (circle your answer).

9. Communication access is less important in a medical emergency.
    A. True
    B. False

10. Deaf employees can be a great asset to a company.
    A. True
    B. False

11. The majority of Deaf children have Deaf parents.
    A. True
    B. False

12. When communicating with a Deaf person, it is considered rude to draw or write.
    A. True
    B. False

13. Deaf customers are more likely to spend money at businesses that are accessible.
    A. True
    B. False

14. A "classifier" that can be used for a car is made with a "1" handshape.
    A. True
    B. False

15. Facial expression is an important grammatical feature of ASL.
    A. True
    B. False

15.32 Post-test

Section Three: Expressive Portion

Instructions: Create a story about one of the topics listed below.

1. The best picnic I ever went to…
2. The medical emergency I lived through…
3. When I went clothes shopping…
4. The job I really want is…

Please use at least two classifiers, demonstrate at least one example of the use of space feature, use appropriate facial expressions, and use at least one example of a number within a sign.

Your instructor will schedule a time for you to perform this section of the Post-test. You may prepare and practice prior to your scheduled time.

Include at least two classifiers.

16. _____
17. _____

Demonstrate at least one example of the use of space feature.

18. _____

Use appropriate facial expressions.

19. _____

And at least one number incorporated within a sign.

20. _____

Congratulations! You have completed Lesson Fifteen!